Man and His Physical Environment
Readings in Environmental Geology

Man and His Physical Environment

Readings in Environmental Geology

Edited by

Garry D. McKenzie
Russell O. Utgard

Department of Geology
The Ohio State University

BURGESS PUBLISHING COMPANY • Minneapolis, Minnesota 55415

Printed in the United States of America

Library of Congress Catalog Card Number 79-187012

SBN 8087-1348-5

1 2 3 4 5 6 7 8 9 0

PREFACE

Man and His Physical Environment: Readings in Environmental Geology, brings together papers that are particularly suited to introductory studies relating to the geologic aspects of the environment. The readings are intended as an introduction to Environmental Geology for students who have had one or more courses in geology, although they could be used as supplementary reading for students in an introductory geology course, as well as in courses in several related fields.

This collection of readings is an outgrowth of the editors' need to produce materials for a course in Environmental Geology. As our reading list and mountainous accumulation of copies grew with our intensified search, we decided to assemble into a book readings that might not be conveniently available. We have included materials from scientific journals and reports, news magazines, and news releases. The result, we hope, is a book which treats the problems and facts of man's impact on the geologic environment at a level suitable for lower division college students.

We have attempted to select articles that deal with many different aspects of man's impact on the geologic environment, such as the geologic aspects of health and disease, waste disposal, mineral resources and conservation, land reclamation, land-use planning, and geologic hazards. Regrettably, many excellent papers could not be included for various reasons and some areas that deserve coverage may have been slighted.

The readings presented are written at different levels, with some articles providing a challenge to even the well-informed reader. In addition to providing valuable reading, the articles can be the basis for informed discussion and may provide a point of departure for further independent study and research. References cited in the original papers are included, and this should increase the book's usefulness for research and reference. Minor modifications have been made in some articles for the purpose of uniformity of style and clarity. Many illustrations, as well as portions of the text of lengthy articles, have been deleted, hopefully without distorting the original publication.

The authors recognize that environmental problems are generally highly complex and are not confined by academic boundary lines. The environment cannot be studied from a narrow viewpoint; therefore, several articles are included which in the opinion of the editors do have sufficient geologic interest and impact, even though the casual observer may regard them as nongeologic.

We wish to express our sincere appreciation to the many authors and publishers who have permitted inclusion of their material. We are also indebted to the many individuals whose efforts have influenced our views and selections, even though their own works have not been included. The support received from the office staff of the Department of Geology and from several of our colleagues at The Ohio State University is gratefully acknowledged.

January 1972

G.D.M.
R.O.U.

CONTENTS

Part One
INTRODUCTION
AND VIEWPOINTS

Photographs of the earth taken from space have revealed the finite nature of the planet. Many scientists, environmentalists, and others have come to recognize that, with the present population trend, the earth will reach its capacity to support people at some time in the near future. Both the physical and biological environments limit the earth's capacity. The physical environment, which is the realm of geology, presents limitations on space, mineral resources, nonrenewable energy sources, water, and other factors. It is the use and abuse of the physical environment which is the concern of Environmental Geology.

Selections in this introductory part contain the substance, the history of development, and the definition of Environmental Geology. In addition, the perspective from which the geologist views the environment and the role that he should play in developing guidelines for management of the environment, now and in the future, are presented. The interdisciplinary nature of environmental problems and the role of population in environmental problems, both of which must be constantly recognized, are also dealt with in this section.

1. CONTROLLING THE GEOLOGIC ENVIRONMENT FOR HUMAN WELFARE

GORDON B. OAKESHOTT

"Environmental geology" is a ridiculous term!

All geology is environmental, and the most basic element in every man's environment is the geologic factor. We all live on the surface of the earth, and we are all profoundly affected by geologic processes.

In spite of its shortcomings, the term "environmental geology" sprang into immediate popularity and has already become so firmly entrenched that it can hardly be dislodged. So, if we can't abolish it, let's define it to suit your own ends. I like Texas geologist Peter Flawn's definition:

"Environmental geology deals with the entire spectrum of man's use of the earth, both in cities and in rural and primitive regions—it includes the location and exploitation of natural resources, the disposal of wastes, the effects of both mass movements and tectonic movements on structures, and the effects of subtle variations in the composition of earth materials on health . . . It is the application of geology to problems arising out of the interaction of the human colony on earth."

Two decades ago the California Division of Mines began to tangibly react to the need for application of geologic principles for the public welfare by initiating interdisciplinary investigations of earthquakes. About ten years ago the Division enhanced the *relevance* of its work to geologic protection of the public by entering into an intensive program of large-scale urban mapping with cooperative funding from Los Angeles County. Greatly intensified use of the environment in that metropolitan area has turned ordinary geologic processes into "geologic hazards." Thus was born the "Geologic Hazards" program of the Division of Mines and Geology. There are no geologic hazards without people; the "hazards" arise from man's unwise, inept, and careless occupation and use or abuse of the geologic environment.

The next decade will be one of ramifying applications of geology toward the solution of environmental problems. Man will be employing the environment to meet the needs and desires of an increasing population.

Reprinted with permission of the author and publisher from the *Journal of Geological Education,* v. 18, no. 5, p. 193. Copyright 1970 by the National Association of Geology Teachers, Inc.

2. THE FUTURE OF MAN'S ENVIRONMENT

ROBERT W. LAMSON

In thinking about and acting to influence man's future environment, we must consider many factors—the physical, biological, and social; the "man-made" as well as the "natural." Man's future environment will include the human populations, the cities and institutions which man has created, as well as the physical, chemical, and nonhuman biological systems—the oceans, continents, river basins, and the populations of various species of plants, fish, insects, birds, and animals upon which man depends for his survival and well-being.

If we wish to protect and improve the social, physical, and biological aspects of our environment, we must attempt to answer and act upon the answers to the following three critical questions:

• What are the trends which are helping to modify or create the natural and man-made environments which man will inhabit during the next half century?

• What is the possible range of these alternative future environments?

• What might be done to influence these trends so as to shape the future in desired directions?

This article discusses these questions, specifically as they concern the United States.

CONFRONTING THE UNITED STATES TRENDS AND CONDITIONS

Important trends which will affect man's future environment include population growth and distribution, resource supply and use, output of wastes, and growth and use of technological and organizational power.

Population growth and distribution. The current world population of about 3.5 billion could double and reach 7 billion or more by the year 2000 if current trends continue. Projected United States population for the year 2015

Reprinted with the publisher's permission from *The Science Teacher,* v. 36, no. 1, p. 25-30, January 1969. Copyright 1968 by the National Science Teachers Association, Inc., Washington, D. C.

ranges between 325 and 483 million. In just 50 years, the nation's population could grow by 125 to 280 million over today's population of about 200 million.

Throughout the world, people have been moving from rural areas to more densely populated urban areas, and in the United States, a very large percentage of the growing population lives and is projected to live on a very small percentage of the land.

Supply and use of resources. The United States contains a supply of renewable and non-renewable natural resources which is not unlimited, which can be depleted, but which can also be expanded and upgraded through application of scientific research, and used more efficiently through better management.

Use of many resources in the United States is projected to increase even more rapidly than population, due to increased per capita demand for resources caused by increased industrialization and use of technology, urbanization, rising levels of income and individual expectations, increased leisure, and outdoor recreation. Increasing demand for resources sometimes involves a requirement for higher quality resources, for instance, water.

Output of wastes. Output of wastes—solid, liquid, and gaseous—is increasing for the nation and per capita, thereby intensifying the threat of pollution to our air, land, and water. Sources of pollution include cities, industries, farms, heat from power generation, automobiles, recreation, mining, boating, and commercial shipping. The types, sources, and amounts of wastes will tend to increase with the growth of population, industry, and use of technology and resources. Many types of wastes are also projected to increase more rapidly than will population.

The factors which help to increase demands for resources, for clean water, pure air, and unlittered land, also help to increase the output of wastes, thereby making demands more difficult to satisfy. While we have placed increasing demands upon the environment, we have also increased our dumping of wastes into it.

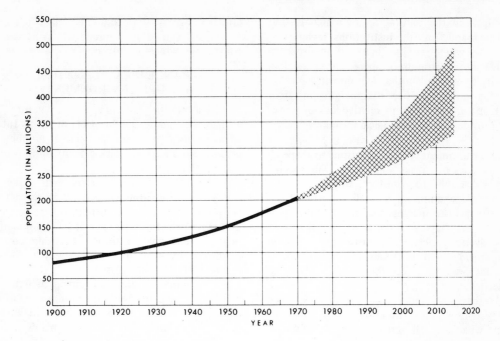

Although we may not be in immediate danger of exhausting our supply of many types of resources, we are in danger, because of declining quality, of jeopardizing our usable supply.

Growth of technological and organizational power. By applying our knowledge and experience to solve practical problems, we are increasing our technological and organizational ability to:

1. Push back many of the constraints of nature, of distance, time, and disease, and of our formerly low capacity to manipulate the environment;
2. Shape and create widespread, intense, and long-lasting changes in the natural environment; some of these changes could be irreversible and adverse to man's long-term survival, health, and well-being;
3. Create "artificial" or man-made environments (for instance, cities and manned satellites), and to live in new environments (under the ocean and on the moon);
4. Perceive, predict, and monitor as well as to control, influence, or manage environmental changes, for example, via new techniques (systems analysis), tools (microscopes, telescopes, satellites, and computers), laws (domestic rules as well as international agreements concerning conservation, use of

Estimates and projections of the population of the United States, 1900 to 2015. The figures relate to 50 states in all years and to armed forces overseas. (Source: Population Estimates, Series P-25, No. 381, December 18, 1967, Bureau of the Census.)

resources, and technology), and institutions (river basin commissions);

5. Increase rapidly the production of food and energy, transform raw materials into finished products through industrial processes, and transport people, goods, energy, and information.

Changing proportion of "natural" and "man-made" aspects of the environment. As a result of population growth and of using our increased technological and organizational power, more and more of man's environment is becoming man-affected or man-made, except where special provision has been made to keep the influence of man and his machines at a minimum (for example, in wilderness areas and natural areas created to provide a base line for ecological studies).

The primary threats to man's physical and psychic survival, to his health and well-being, now increasingly stem from his own creations, from the environments which he has created or altered, from the natural forces which he has harnessed, and from the institutions, techniques, and tools which he has invented in order to remove the constraints of space, time, and low capacity to manipulate the environment.

Man no longer has the margin for error which space, time, and his relative lack of power once provided for his ecological mistakes.

He must, therefore, take care, in his relation to the environment and in his actions to shape it, that he does not make himself and his society more vulnerable to sabotage, disruption, and disaster—for example, if a small element of the system which he designs does not perform perfectly, if his shaping of the environment should have adverse effects, or if disturbances in the environment, such as floods, earthquakes, and hurricanes, should affect the areas in which he has settled.

We have had some sharp, recent experience with systems which created potentially disastrous effects when a small part of the system failed— for instance, the Northeast power failure and the Torrey Canyon tanker disaster.

In attempting to use our power to influence the environment, we should design for a range of contingencies—for the optimist when all works well and for the pessimist when much goes wrong. The test of our technical creations is not how well they perform when all parts work as designed, but how well the system runs and how widespread the damage is when a part of the system fails.

Since the environment influences man himself, and since man has increased power to influence his environment, man is, in many ways, through intent as well as inadvertence, and perhaps in ways he does not understand, increasingly influencing his own genetic, physical, and psychological nature—and that of his children— through the environments which he creates.

Because man's increased power to manipulate the environment has created a total environment which is increasingly man-made and in which man's margin for error is reduced, his only protection now is knowledge and wisdom in using his technological and organizational power. Man's ability to create adverse effects may be greater than his ability to perceive, judge, prevent, and control them. As a result of his inability to control wisely the purposes to which he puts his power, man may find that he is creating

effects in his "natural" and "man-made" environments, as well as in himself, which he cannot control and which are adverse and irreversible.

RANGE OF ALTERNATIVE FUTURE ENVIRONMENTS

In attempting to look at the "natural" as well as the "man-made" aspects of man's future environment, one can project a number of possible alternatives, ranging from optimistic to pessimistic.

The many elements which will make up man's future environment vary with respect to: (1) probability of occurrence; from impossible to inevitable or zero to 100 percent; (2) popularity, or the extent to which the event is desired by the public or by specific groups, today or in the future; and (3) desirability.

The actual future environment which man will inhabit depends upon the nature and unfolding of the various trends which are helping to shape the environment and upon man's actions to influence these trends.

The crucial problem in looking at the future is to decide what is desirable among the range of possible future events and then to work for it, taking into consideration the probability that the future event will occur, the difficulty and costs of bringing it about, and the consequences of not doing so.

Within the range of possible future social and ecological environments, many pessimistic possibilities could be realized in the absence of adequate policies to prevent their occurrence.

For example, problems of external defense, international order, and war could become worse, with general nuclear war one pessimistic possibility for rapidly decimating our population, and, at the same time severely damaging our natural environment and our cities.

Large-scale loss of life due to ecological and technological disasters is not impossible, particularly if large and densely concentrated populations depend upon an ecology and large-scale systems of technology and organization which are highly vulnerable to disruption, breakdown, and misuse.

In the absence of adequate policies to protect against such natural hazards as storms, earthquakes, and floods, larger numbers of people could become vulnerable to disaster.

Other possible adverse effects of misusing

our technological power have been mentioned, for example, global ecological imbalances and more intense and widespread disasters caused by:

1. Environmental pollution which upsets the chemical-thermal balance of the earth's atmosphere because of increased burning of fossil fuels, pollution of the upper atmosphere, and impairment of the cycle by which the carbon-oxygen balance in the atmosphere is maintained, through photosynthesis, by plants on land and in the ocean;

2. Soil depletion and increased salinity of the soil;

3. Poorly planned, large-scale, environmental engineering projects which trigger worldwide ecological effects—rapid or slow—which are adverse to man and irreversible.

Increasing pressures to mass produce and construct, in a short time, large numbers of new buildings and housing units could cause a decline in diversity, quality, and choice in our cities. Without proper protection, the quality of the countryside, also, could continue to deteriorate because of junkyards, billboards, power lines, overenriched lakes ruined by algae growth fed by wastes from cities and farms, polluted streams, and erosion of hillsides and of the many new inadequately protected construction sites.

The cumulative and mutually reinforcing effects of many environmental changes on the ecology and on man's physical and psychic health are potentially dangerous but not well known.

For example, we do not know enough about the long-term ecological, somatic, and genetic effects of various chemicals used in fertilizers, pesticides, and herbicides; of such environmental contaminants as radioactive wastes and lead; of the concentration of various poisons through the food chain, or of their cumulative and interactive effects. Nevertheless, the outpouring of toxic materials into the environment is already great and increasing.

Even though the nation's economy, our gross national product, and our per capita income will continue to grow, individual standards of living could decline because of inadequate policies and programs to protect the environment. Since the social, physical, and biological aspects of man's environment interact, deterioration of the nonhuman environment could help to create economic and social decline.

Moreover, failure on the social and political level could, in turn, contribute to deterioration of our physical and biological surroundings. For example, the educational system could fail to transmit to succeeding generations the cultural values which underlie the nation's political system as well as the attitudes and skills essential to maintaining environmental quality.

Internal order as well as ecological balance and environmental quality could break down or become more difficult to maintain. Or, their maintenance could be based more and more on "external controls" and repressive measures, on the threat of punishment and constriction of freedom.

Man's actions to avert the various environmental threats which now confront him will help to determine whether or not his future environment will be one in which he can thrive as well as exist.

Depending on his actions to prevent the occurrence of future pessimistic possibilities, and to realize optimistic ones, man could enjoy more widespread and heightened values of, for example: natural beauty, clean air, water, and unlittered land; cities which are beautiful, exciting, and a joy to live in; rising levels of living; tranquillity and silence; privacy as well as sociability; diversity, individuality, and choice; justice and security; political freedom, the opportunity to influence and participate in the decisions which affect his welfare and that of his children; democratic, representative government; and the opportunity to develop his personality to the maximum extent.

We must remember that the optimistic projections will not automatically come about without human effort. Nor will we prevent the pessimistic projections from coming true if we do not work at it. In fact, projections can become self-denying or self-fulfilling prophecies, depending upon their effect on human attitudes, effort, and will.

When people view any particular future alternative as necessarily inevitable, such an attitude tends to generate self-fulfilling or self-denying prophecies, depending on whether we see the inevitable as optimistic or pessimistic. For example, a pessimistic projection which is viewed as inevitable can become a self-confirming prophecy through reducing any effort to prevent its occurrence, thereby increasing the probability that it will come true. An optimistic projection which is viewed as inevitable can become a self-denying prophecy through reducing the effort devoted to bringing it about, thereby reducing the probability of its coming true.

On the other hand, if the future is regarded as open and subject, to some extent, to human manipulation, then this will tend to leave room for the creative exercise of human wisdon, will, and effort.

CONTROL OR INFLUENCE OF TRENDS

Having outlined some of the important trends confronting the United States, and a range of alternative environmental outcomes associated with these trends, the question arises: Should we attempt to "adjust" to the trends, or to "influence" and "control" them, or both?

Assuming that "adjustment," by itself, is not an adequate guide if we wish to promote economic growth, individual well-being, and environmental quality, we then need to consider what can be done to "control"—or at least to "influence" the various trends which will affect man's future environment. What can be done to make more probable the optimistic rather than the pessimistic projections?

Technological and organizational power. It is crucial that we control the uses of our increasing technological and organizational power to affect our environment since to date, we have used this growing power in an unbalanced way:

• To limit deaths, but not, at the same time and in the same degree, to limit births. As a result, no matter how efficient the technology, skill, and organization devoted to producing, expanding, and making more efficient use of resources, population now outpaces production in many parts of the world, with tragic results.

• To use, destroy, and deplete resources for immediate benefit, without sufficient regard for the resource needs of future generations and without providing adequate knowledge and skills to compensate for the depletion.

• To pollute our land, air, and water, but not to prevent pollution, clean it up where it occurs, and restore the damaged environment.

• To promote economic and population growth, but not to protect and promote environmental quality.

• To create and apply new knowledge and powerful technologies without, at the same time, acting to prevent and limit the damaging side effects of using this knowledge and technology.

There is a need now to restore the balance in our use of science and technology—in our attitudes, laws, and institutions—for science and engineering, by themselves, cannot save us from our lack of wisdom and vision in using science and in managing our technological power.

Additional technological power and efficiency, applied in the same manner that we have applied them in the past to our environment and to the forces of nature, will not necessarily save us from our lack of balance and wisdom in using that power.

We need, therefore, to perceive, predict, evaluate, influence, and control the effects of using our technological and organizational power so that the optimistic rather than the pessimistic possibilities will come to pass.

To carry out the research, planning, and operational programs to perform these activities, we need to create the necessary laws and institutions, in government, at the federal, state, and local levels, as well as in the private sector, in universities and industry.

We need to use our technological power in such a way as to affect the trends which, if unchecked, would realize the pessimistic possibilities. In other words, we need to influence population growth and distribution, the supply of and demand for resources and services, and the output of wastes.

Population growth and distribution. Problems of population increase as well as density could seriously jeopardize the ability of this and other nations to meet, concomitantly, their national goals for security, economic growth, welfare and well-being, resources, conservation, and environmental quality.

There is, therefore, a need to develop a population policy based on analysis to determine:

1. What, if various alternative projections for future population growth and distribution were to come true, the effects would be on the success and costs of our policies:

   A. *To supply and conserve resources* (land, water, air, food, minerals, energy, timber, wildlife, wilderness, outdoor recreation and park areas, open spaces, natural beauty, silence, etc.)

   B. *To provide services* (transportation, health, welfare, housing, sanitation, education, etc.); and

   C. At the same time, *to protect and pro-*

mote environmental quality; that is, to prevent further pollution of our land, air, and water, to clean up what pollution remains, to restore the damaged environment, to rebuild our deteriorated cities and to create new ones;

D. To solve these problems within the existing framework of government and political and personal values (to protect and strengthen freedom of choice and representative, popular government and to limit the extent of intrusion of government into the personal lives of citizens).

2. Which, if any, of the various alternative projections for future population growth and distribution we should regard as goals for population policy, and the costs and benefits of achieving each; and

3. How, by what methods, we could achieve each goal. Programs for action to influence population growth rates and distribution could be based on such analyses.

Alternative goals for population growth might include, for example: (1) to insure that all American families will have access to information and services that will enable them to plan the number and spacing of their children and thereby, to insure that any future American child will be a "wanted child"; (2) to achieve population growth in the United States which would increase more rapidly or more slowly than is projected; and (3) to stabilize United States (and world) population at less than its present size, or double its present size, or greater by a factor of 2.5, 3, or 4. Here, the question arises: At what level and when should this stabilization occur—in 40, 60, 75, 100, or 200 years?

Supply and use of resources and services. To help satisfy the increasing demands for resources, there is a need to increase the available supply, through research and exploration programs, and to make more efficient use of the existing supply through improved conservation, management, and pricing.

Moreover, if our aim is to increase individual well-being and standards of living, access to resources and services, as well as to promote overall economic growth, then the question arises whether we should attempt to limit the rate at which demand grows as well as to "satisfy" increasing demands for resources and services. This would require us to limit the rate at which population grows and puts pressure on our not unlimited ability to provide resources and services.

Control of waste output. If we are to protect the environment adequately, we must bring under control and manage the wastes of our society which threaten to poison and bury us and to destroy the ecological systems upon which we depend. We must, therefore, prevent, limit, manage, and control waste and pollution at each step in the process by which our economy and industry transform energy and materials, from raw materials through to finished products, to ultimate use and disposal.

This requires us to create more efficient and less wasteful industrial and economic processes, and to provide for use, reuse, recovery, and recycling of the waste products—solid, liquid, and gaseous—which are generated at each stage in our economic system.

PERSONAL AND POLITICAL VALUES AND CONTROL OF TRENDS

To control and influence the trends outlined above requires "management" and control of people and institutions as well as of the environment. What is the relation between: (1) "management" of the environment and of the "trends" which will affect the environment, and (2) personal and political values?

"Environmental management" involves the monitoring and manipulation of physical, chemical, and nonhuman biological systems—the oceans, river basins, watersheds, airsheds, industrial, agricultural, and municipal wastes, and populations of various species of fish, birds, animals, insects, and plants.

But such objects are only part of the environmental quality problem. Human persons, their attitudes, ideologies, practices, social systems, and institutions are also part of the problem of maintaining environmental quality. They must also be part of the cure.

If more "efficient environmental management" involves human persons, attitudes, and institutions, then what are the implications of "efficient environmental management" for such values as freedom, privacy, autonomy of personality, dispersal of power and pluralism (particularly under conditions of rapidly increasing population), industrialization, urbanization, and use of technological power to manipulate the environment?

How can the United States promote environmental quality, and, at the same time, protect and promote various important personal and political values under conditions in which an additional 100 million people are projected to be added to the United States population in a short 30 years?

If the United States is to control the effects of its citizens' actions on the environment, and at the same time, to protect their personal and political values, there will be a need to rely, to a large extent, on internal psychological controls—rather than on the external threat of law or punishment. And, if such internal controls are to be used with a rapidly expanding population, then great reliance must be placed on education for conservation and environmental quality—at each stage of a person's life—in the home, through school, and in other areas of activity.

The need to promote and to reconcile "environmental quality" and "environmental management" with such values as freedom, privacy, and autonomy of personality, dispersal of power, and pluralism is one which places a critical responsibility on the educational system in general, and on the teachers of science in particular.

CONCLUSION

Our current environmental crisis is due to man's misuse of power—to one-sided use of his capacity to control the forces of nature and to his lack of understanding of himself and his lack of wisdom in using his power.

Much remains to be done for environmental quality—in many areas—in terms of attitudes and education, laws and institutions, research, planning, and operational programs.

Science teachers who convey the attitudes and skills needed to protect and promote environmental quality are on the forefront of man's effort to restore balance and harmony—within himself, within nature, and between himself and nature.

We must restore wisdom and balance in our actions, in the use of our power, and in nature. Time is short. Much of our damage to the environment is irreversible; what we destroy cannot be restored and is lost forever.

The accelerating damage which we do to nature and to ourselves will not wait for us to catch up, nor will it wait while we refine our understanding of this damage.

We must learn, and science teachers must help future generations to learn, to restore the balance:

- Between our power and our wisdom in using that power
- Between our power to create and our power to destroy and disrupt
- Between our efforts to prevent injury and our efforts to heal the damaged environment
- Between our efforts to understand environmental problems and our actions to prevent and correct these problems.

Our power has exceeded our wisdom.

Our power to destroy the environment has surpassed our power to correct the damage, to conserve and create.

Our efforts to prevent have lagged behind our efforts to cure.

Our cures have been too little and too late.

And, we have often allowed the quest for more perfect knowledge to deflect us from acting now with what knowledge we have.

3. A GEOLOGIST VIEWS THE ENVIRONMENT

JOHN C. FRYE

When the geologist considers the environment, and particularly when he is concerned with the diversified relations of man to his total physical environment, he takes an exceptionally broad and long-term view. It is broad because all of the physical features of the earth are the subject matter of the geologist. It is long term because the geologist views the environment of the moment as a mere point on a very long time-continuum that has witnessed a succession of physical and biological changes—and that at present is dynamically undergoing natural change.

Let us first consider the time perspective of the geologist, then consider the many physical factors that are important to man's activity on the face of the earth, and, third, turn our attention to specific uses of geologic data for the maintenance or development of an environment that is compatible with human needs.

THE LONG VIEW

The earth is known to be several billion years old, and the geologic record of physical events and life-forms on the earth is reasonably good for more than the most recent 500 million years. Throughout this span of known time the environment has been constantly changing—sometimes very slowly, but at other times quite rapidly. Perhaps a few dramatic examples will serve as illustrations. Less than 20,000 years ago the area occupied by such North American cities as Chicago, Cleveland, Detroit, and Toronto were deeply buried under glacial ice. The land on which New York City is now built was many miles inland from the seashore. And part of the area now occupied by Salt Lake City lay beneath a fresh-water lake. Twelve thousand years ago glacial ice covered the northern shores and formed the northern wall of what was then the

Reprinted from *Environmental Geology Notes,* No. 42, February 1971, Illinois State Geological Survey, Urbana, Illinois. Originally prepared for "Voice of America," Earth Science Series, Dr. Charles F. Park, Jr., Coordinator.

Great Lakes, and much of the outflow from those lakes was to the Gulf of Mexico rather than to the Atlantic Ocean through the St. Lawrence River, as it is now. Although firm scientific information is not available to permit equally positive statements about atmospheric changes during the past few tens of thousands of years, deductions from the known positions of glaciers and from the fossil record make it clear that the atmospheric circulation patterns were quite different from those of the present, and studies of radiocarbon show that the isotopic content of the atmosphere changed measurably through time.

The purpose of listing these examples is to emphasize that the environment is a dynamic system that must be understood and accommodated by man's activities, rather than a static, unchanging system that can be "preserved." The living, or biological systems of the earth are generally understood to be progressively changing, but much less well understood by the public is that the nonliving, physical aspects of the earth also undergo change at an equal or greater rate.

Clearly, a dynamic system is more difficult to understand fully, and it is more difficult to adapt man's activities to a constantly changing situation than to an unchanging or static system. On the other hand, the very fact of constant change opens many avenues of modification and accommodation that would not be available in a forever constant and unchanging system.

THE PROBLEM

Although it is important that we have in mind the long-term facts concerning earth history, modern man has become such an effective agent of physical and chemical change that he has been able to produce major modifications, some of which run counter to the normal evolution of our earthly environment, and to compress millennia of normal evolutionary changes into days. These rapid modifications are, almost without exception, made by man with the intention of producing improvements and advantages for people. Problems result from the fact that by-products and side effects do occur that are neither desirable nor pleasing, and at some times and places may be hazardous or even calamitous. In some cases the undesirable side effects are unknown or are unpredictable; in other cases they are tolerated as a supposed "necessary price" to pay for the desirable end result. It is our intent to examine the role of the earth scientist in defining some of these problems and in devising ways of minimizing or eliminating them.

The ways in which man treats his physical surroundings, produces and uses the available nonliving resources, and plans for his future needs are, of course, social determinations. However, in order that social decisions can be made in such a way that we, and our children, will not find reason to regret them, they should be made in the light of all the factual information that it is possible to obtain. If we, collectively, decide to use the available supply of a nonrenewable resource—for example, petroleum—at a particular rate, we should know how long it will last and what substitute materials are available to replace it when the supply is exhausted; if we decide to dam a river, we should know what the side effects will be in all directions, how long the facility will last, and what the replacement facility might be; if we develop huge piles of discarded trash, we should know whether or not they will cause pollution of water supplies or the atmosphere, and whether or not the terrane is sufficiently stable to retain them; if we substitute one fuel for another with the desire to abate air pollution, we should know if it will make a net overall improvement in the pollution problem, and if it will be available in the quantity required so that man's needs can be met; and if we plan expanding metropolitan areas we should have full information on the terrane conditions at depth and on the raw material resources that will be rendered unusable by urbanization.

ROLE OF EARTH SCIENCE IN SOLVING PROBLEMS

When we consider the role of earth science in solving problems, we see that the earth sciences can and should develop answers to all of the questions we have asked. Many of the problem areas overlap one another, but it will be easier to discuss them if we class the contributions of the earth scientist to environmental problem solving in five general categories. The

first of these is collecting data for planning the proper use of the terrane, or perhaps we should say the most efficient adjustment of man's use of the earth's surface to all of the physical features and characteristics at and below the surface—particularly in expanding urban areas. Second is determination of the factors that influence the safety and permanence of disposal of waste materials and trash of all kinds—both in the rocks near the surface and at great depth in mines and wells. Third is providing information for the planning and development of safe, adequate, and continuing water supplies in locations that will serve populated areas. Fourth is the identification of rock and mineral resources to provide for future availability of needed raw materials, or of appropriate substitute materials. And, fifth is the recognition of man as a major geologic agent by monitoring the changes he has caused in his environment and by providing remedies where these changes are, or may become, harmful.

PROPER USE OF LAND

The first of these general categories—procuring data for physical planning of the proper use of the land surface and of the rocks below the surface—covers data provided by topographic and geologic maps, by engineering geology and soil mechanics investigations, by predictions of potential landslides and other geologic hazards, and by a complete inventory of available mineral resources and future potential water supplies. Much of the geologic data needed in this category can be produced by conventional methods of research, but, to be effective, the research program must be oriented toward environmental applications. Furthermore, the results must be presented in a form that is readily understandable to, and usable by, planners and administrators who often are unfamiliar with science and, particularly, do not have a working knowledge of the geological sciences. Perhaps the best way to explain what I mean by environmental orientation is to cite a few examples.

The first example of the use of geologic research oriented for planning is a laboratory study involving clay mineralogy, petrography, and chemistry. It was prompted by numerous incidences of structural failure of earth materials. In rapidly expanding suburban residential areas there has been a great increase in the use of septic tanks and, simultaneously, a rapid increase in the household use of detergents and water softeners. A laboratory research program was initiated to study the changes induced in the clay minerals by these chemical substances when they were introduced into the near-surface deposits by discharge from septic tanks. Preliminary results showed that the materials in septic tank effluent did, indeed, produce significant and undesirable changes in the properties of some earth materials. The data made it possible to predict changes that could occur in the structural characteristics of common surficial deposits and, thus, to prevent structural failure. Therefore, the conclusions were presented to planners, health officials, architects, and other groups that might have need of the information.

In strong contrast to such a sharply focused and specific research project is a second example provided by a study of a county at the northwest fringe of the Chicago metropolitan area, into which urbanization is spreading from that metropolis. Because of impending problems, the county government organized a regional planning commission, which called upon the State Geological Survey and other agencies to collect data on the physical environment that were essential to wise, long-range planning. Where some of the fields of activity of the agencies overlapped, they cooperated informally so that they could most effectively work with the planning commission. Essential to the project were modern topographic maps of the county, and, even though much of the county had been geologically mapped previously, several man-years of geologist time were devoted to the project.

This project to characterize the physical environment involved many types of geological study. These included (1) analysis of the physical character of the major land forms within the county; (2) interpretation of the relation between geologic units near the surface and the agricultural soil units; (3) establishment of the character of the many layers of rocks and glacial deposits penetrated at depth by drilling below the surface; (4) definition of the occurrence and character of water-bearing strata in the near-surface glacial deposits and the deeper bedrock layers; (5) determination of the geologic feasibility of water-resource management programs; (6) determination of the geologic feasibility of waste management programs; (7) delineation of the geographic occurrence and description of the characteristics of construction material resources; (8) location of commercial mineral resources and assessment of their economic value; (9) determination of the engineering characteristics of the

geologic units near the surface; and (10) geologic evaluation of surface reservoir conditions and proposed reservoir sites.

The approach to such development of data includes field work by surficial geologists, engineering geologists, ground-water geologists, stratigraphers, and economic geologists. In the laboratory, chemists, mineralogists, and stratigraphers conduct studies of the subsurface by use of cores and cuttings of the deposits at all depths; make chemical, mineralogical, and textural analyses of all deposits and rocks; determine physical properties; compile statistics; and make economic analyses of the many mineral resource situations. The results of these studies are compiled on interpretative maps, which the planning commission combines with the results of studies by specialists of other agencies and by the commission itself for preparation of maps that show the recommendations for land use. These maps, together with explanatory, nontechnical text, serve as a basis for county zoning and long-range development planning.

DEVELOPMENT OF WASTE DISPOSAL FACILITIES

Our second category of environmental geologic information includes those geologic data needed for proper and safe development of waste disposal facilities. Man has the propensity to produce toxic and noxious waste materials in progressively increasing quantity and in an ever-increasing variety and degree. Waste products result from manufacturing, processing, and mining—but of even greater concern is the concentrated production of waste by the inhabitants of our large cities. Traditionally, man has used fresh water to dilute liquid waste and the atmosphere to dilute the gaseous waste products of combustion. He has often indiscriminately used the land or large bodies of water for disposal of solid waste. However, even the general public is now aware of the fact that we are exhausting the capacity of fresh waters and the atmosphere to absorb our waste products. Along the sea coasts there is still the ocean—although even the ocean is being restricted as a waste disposal medium—but in the vast region of the continental interior we have no ocean in which to dump our wastes. Instead, our choices are limited to (1) selective recycling, accompanied by essentially complete purification of the residue of waste materials; (2) selective recycling accompanied by land disposal of non-recyclable residues; or (3) the use of the rocks of the earth's crust for the total future expansion of waste disposal capacity. Geologists, who traditionally have been concerned with the discovery of valuable deposits of minerals and their extraction from the crust, now also must concern themselves with the study of the rocks of the earth's crust as a possibly safe place for the disposal and containment of potentially harmful waste products.

Petroleum geologists were introduced to one aspect of the problem of large quantity underground disposal of waste material more than a quarter century ago when it became necessary to find methods for injecting into deep wells the increasing quantities of brines produced with petroleum in oil fields. However, it was not until population densities approached their present levels that we became genuinely concerned with the most critical problems of the future—that is, the safe disposal of industrial and human waste materials in large quantity, other than by dilution. As some of these undesirable materials are destined to increase at an exponential rate in the future, it is obvious that we must devote our best geologic effort to solution of the problems of disposal. The problem of disposal of high-level and intermediate-level radioactive wastes has already attracted a major research effort, probably because these radioactive materials are obviously so highly dangerous for such a long period of time, and a body of scientific data now exists concerning their safe management.

In my own state of Illinois, solid waste disposal is generally accomplished by sanitary landfill, and frequently the State Geological Survey is asked by state and local departments of health to make geologic evaluations of proposed sites. However, precise and universally accepted criteria for this type of evaluation are only now being developed. Several disposal sites of differing geologic character are being intensively studied by coring and instrumentation of test holes, and analyses are being made of the liquids leached from the wastes and the containing deposits. In addition to laboratory study of the obvious characteristics of the containing deposits—such as texture, permeability, strength, clay mineralogy, and thickness of the units that do not transmit water (and thus protect the aquifers)—studies must be made of the less obvious effects of the seepage of liquids on the structural character of the deposit, the removal of objectionable chemicals from water solutions

by the clay minerals of the containing deposits, and the microflow patterns of water in earth materials surrounding the wastes. For some of these determinations it is necessary to know the chemical composition of the liquids that pass through the wastes, as well as the chemistry and mineralogy of the deposits that contain them.

Disposal near the surface by landfill or lagooning methods requires detailed studies of the earth deposits at and immediately below the surface, with only minor data required on the deeper bedrock. On the other hand, disposal of industrial wastes in deep wells requires studies of the character and continuity of all rock layers down to the crystalline basement. Geologic data needed for deep disposal involve a combination of the types of information needed for the exploration for both oil and water, plus a knowledge of the confining beds of shale or clay. It should also enable us to predict possible changes that might be produced by the injected wastes.

A different type of pollution problem is represented by sulfur compounds and other undesirable materials released by the burning of coal, oil, and gas and discharged into the atmosphere. The earth scientist contributes to the solution of this problem by studies of the mineral matter in the coal, studies of methods of processing the coal before it is burned, studies of means of removing the harmful materials from the effluent gases produced by combustion, and research on the conversion of coal into gaseous or liquid fuels from which much of the objectionable material can be extracted.

PLANNING WATER SUPPLIES

The third category of concern for the earth scientist is water, its occurrence, quality, continuing availability, and pollution; its use as a resource, as a diluent for waste materials, as a facility for recreation, and as an aesthetic attribute. Many of the problems and areas of data collection for water resources fall mainly in the province of the engineer, the chemist, the biologist, or the geographer. But, it would be unrealistic to exclude water from the subjects requiring significant and major data input by the geologist, because to a greater or lesser degree geologic data is needed for the proper development and management of each of the above aspects. The occurrence, quality, availability, development, and replenishment of ground water require major attention by the geological scientist because all of these aspects are directly controlled by the character of the rocks at and to considerable distances below the surface.

Of the categories of environmental data we are discussing, water resources and water pollution are the most widely discussed in the news media and most generally recognized by the public and by municipal planners and administrators. Furthermore, an extensive cadre of earth scientists specializing in water-related problems has developed within governmental agencies and industry. There are many examples of the application of geologic data to management of water resources, ranging from dam site evaluations to the mapping of aquifers and determination of areas suitable for artificial recharge. Before we leave this category, however, I should point out that, in contrast to the rock and mineral resources of the earth's crust, water is a dynamic and renewable resource and, therefore, is subject to management. Even the long-range correction of the effects of unwise practices in the past may be possible in some cases.

FUTURE AVAILABILITY OF ROCK AND MINERAL MATERIALS

Our fourth category is, perhaps, the most complicated aspect of environmental geology. It is the problem of assuring adequate supplies of mineral and rock raw materials for the future, and especially of assuring their availability near densely populated areas where they are most needed. We have an increasing shortage of raw material resources to meet the needs of the increasing world population, and also a mounting conflict of interest for land use in and adjacent to our urbanizing regions. Conflict exists in populated regions because buildings and pavements commonly remove the possibility of extracting the rock or mineral raw materials underneath them. While the producer of rock or mineral products is exploring for the best deposit available from both a physical and economic standpoint, the urban developer may be planning surface installations without regard for the presence or absence of rock and mineral deposits, which he may be rendering unavailable. These unavailable resources may be urgently needed for community developments in the future, and it is important that the attitudes of the planner and mineral producer be brought into harmony, and that compatible working relations be evolved so that mineral resource development can move forward as an integral part of the urban plan. The

geological sciences can supply an accurate and detailed description and maps of all of the rock and mineral resources, not only in but also surrounding urbanizing areas for a distance reasonable for transporting bulk commodities to the metropolitan centers. Grades of deposits that might have utility in the coming 25 to 50 years as well as grades currently being developed should be included in the study.

An equally important role of the earth scientists now, and more particularly in the future, lies in regions remote from the cities where exploration is needed for the raw materials and fuels required by modern society. Although this topic has been discussed in detail in other talks in this series, it is mentioned here because it is a vital element of environmental application. Furthermore, research by the earth scientist, directed toward the identification of substitute materials and toward meeting more exacting and different specifications for future needs, is called for if we are to keep pace with expanding human needs. Information about natural resources is just as essential a part of needed environmental data as are flood hazard maps, physical data maps for engineering projects, and aquifer maps indicating the occurrence of ground-water supplies.

MAN AS A GEOLOGIC AGENT

Our fifth area is the recognition of man as a geologic agent, and here we have the culmination of the problems of Environmental Geology. Man's changes in his physical surroundings are made in order to obtain some real or imagined advantage for people. Some of these changes are designed to prevent natural events from happening and include levees and detention reservoirs to prevent flooding of land, revetments and terracing to prevent erosion, and irrigation to prevent the effects of droughts. But many other changes are intended to produce effects that are not in the natural sequence of things. In both cases, nature is liable to provide unplanned and undesirable side effects. It is the role of the earth scientist to determine the effects of man-made physical changes on all aspects of the physical environment before structural changes are made so that provision can be made to negate undesirable by-product effects—or, if the side effects are too severe, so that a decision against the environmental changes can be made.

A special facet of man-made changes is in the area of mineral and fuel resources. The public need and demand for energy, and for products based on mineral raw materials, is constantly increasing at the same time that increasing populations require that land resources be maintained at maximum utility. Here again, the earth scientist must add to his traditional role of finding and developing sources of energy and mineral resources the equal or more difficult role of devising methods of producing these resources in such a way that land resources have a maximum potential for other human uses. This has led to the concept of planning for multiple sequential use—that is, designing a mineral extraction operation in advance so that the land area will first have a beneficial use before the minerals need to be extracted, then be turned over to mineral extraction, and, finally, be returned to a beneficial use, perhaps quite different from the original use.

CONCLUSIONS

The earth scientist is concerned with the physical framework of the environment wherever it may be, with the supply of raw materials essential to modern civilization, and with the management of the earth's surface so that it will all have maximum utility for its living inhabitants. It is this last item that is a relatively new role for the earth scientist, and one in which he must work cooperatively with the engineer, the biologist, and the social scientist. The earth scientist must become the interpreter of the physical environment, and he must do it in the long-term context of a dynamically changing earth so that "architectural" designs will be in harmony with natural forces 50, 100, or 500 years from now, as well as with the conditions of the moment.

4. MAN'S USE OF THE ENVIRONMENT:
THE NEED FOR ECOLOGICAL GUIDELINES

R. O. SLATYER

Man is an animal, and is part of the so-called "web of life." There is, however, an important difference between man and all other organisms. To an unprecedented degree, man has been able to manipulate other species and the environment itself. In the process his numbers and needs have increased dramatically, and are still increasing. Yet the capacity of the environment to supply these needs is limited, and man's exploitation of the environment tends to reduce that capacity. Clearly, this constitutes a collision course, vividly reflected in the axiom that man's future existence on earth is not threatened by any species other than himself.

The thesis I wish to expound is that failure to observe some ecological ground rules has put man into this position. Ecology is the study of organisms in relation to their environment; it deals with the environmental requirements of single species and with whole populations or communities, with the way in which organisms influence, and are influenced by, their environment; and with the way in which organisms interact with one another. If man is to persist on this planet indefinitely, I believe he must adopt a new ethic, based on ecological premises, to guide his future activity.

I would like to consider first aspects of the evolution of the global environment itself, and of the way in which organisms live together, finally looking at the effect of man's past activities, and pointers to the future.

EVOLUTION OF THE GLOBAL ENVIRONMENT

The history of the earth as a planet still contains many secrets and considerable controversy surrounds aspects of its formation and early development. As far as man is concerned, it is the evolution of the atmosphere and the

Reprinted with permission of the publisher from *The Australian Journal of Science*, v. 32, no. 4, p. 146-153. This paper is an abridged form of a lecture entitled "Man's Place in Nature," given by Professor Slatyer in the Australian National University's Lecture Series for 1969.

hydrosphere which is of particular interest, since both are quite essential to life as we know it. Without these thin surface films, the earth would be exposed to wide temperature extremes, the land would be bombarded by lethal radiation, and it would not contain the water and gases necessary for biological activity.

As a crude analogy, the barren surface of the moon provides a useful illustration of their role in creating a favourable environment for life on earth.

The atmosphere and hydrosphere only represent a tiny fraction—about 0.024 per cent—of the earth's mass. The atmosphere itself represents only 0.37 per cent of the hydrosphere (Mason, 1958). As we all learn in high school physics, its mass would be equivalent to a layer of water covering the earth to a depth of about 33 ft. Even so, the actual quantities involved are very large. The atmosphere, converted to the density of water and heaped on the continent of Australia, would form a layer almost half a mile deep. The oceans would form a layer about 150 miles deep.

It now seems to be generally accepted that the primitive earth had virtually no atmosphere or hydrosphere (at least in the context of their present characteristics), and that both have accumulated gradually during geological time as a result of the escape of water vapour, carbon dioxide, nitrogen and other substances, from intrusive and extrusive rocks within the earth's interior (Rubey, 1963).

Before the evolution of life much of the water vapour so evolved had condensed to form the oceans, many of the other gases dissolved in the water so formed. Carbon dioxide and nitrogen, after water probably the main constituents of the internal emissions, followed different paths. Carbon dioxide, as well as dissolving in water, was continuously removed by reaction with silicate rocks to form, in a series of geochemical reactions, carbonates and silica, the former becoming the first of the great sedimentary rocks of today, the latter the ubiquitous mineral of the contemporary earth's surface.

Largely in consequence, only trace amounts of CO_2 remain in the atmosphere although these amounts are of great significance to man. By comparison, nitrogen, relatively insoluble in water, was also relatively inert chemically and tended to accumulate in the free atmosphere.

By comparison with today's atmosphere, this pre-life atmosphere was probably almost oxygen-free, and its carbon dioxide concentration may have been significantly higher. The general temperature range was probably not much different from today, although mean temperatures may have been higher than now because higher concentrations of carbon dioxide would have tended to accentuate the "glasshouse" effect of the atmosphere. (Like glass, CO_2 permits short-wave solar radiation to reach the earth's surface, but impedes the escape of long-wave thermal radiation.)

Another important difference, linked closely with the relative absence of oxygen, was the absence of ozone. Ozone is a remarkably effective filter of U-V (ultra-violet) radiation; its absence meant that radiation of this wavelength reached the earth. U-V radiation has a substantially higher energy content than visible radiation, so much so that it can photochemically dissociate many molecules. This meant that the atmosphere and surface layers of the hydrosphere became a vast chemical factory in which this energy enabled many types of organic compounds to be synthesized, including the chemical building blocks required for organic metabolism and self-replication. In consequence, in the period between the earth's formation and the appearance of life, the oceans became what Cole (1966) has termed a "dilute soup" of organic molecules.

From these building blocks, and in this reducing environment, the first life processes appear to have emerged 3.0 to 3.5 billion years ago (Cloud, 1968), and the first tremendous step towards the evolution of man occurred. It seems likely that the first self-replicating entities appeared in deep and protected waters. Since U-V radiation destroys biologically active molecules and is in fact lethal to life as we know it, life must have emerged in water at depths below the zone of penetration of ultra-violet radiation (about 30 ft.). The waters were almost certainly protected ones, since active stirring of the water by wave or tidal movements would have brought these first life-forms closer to the surface and into the zone of influence of disintegrating U-V.

It is not appropriate now to detail what is known of the exciting story of organic evolution—the development of the cell membrane, of the single cell and of multicellular organisms, of the various refinements and adaptations, that led to man. Many books have been written, and will probably be rewritten, on this subject. There are, however, some highlights of the evolutionary record which I do wish to mention because of their environmental as well as their biological significance.

The chief one of these concerns photosynthesis, the process by which green plants convert a flow of solar energy into stored chemical energy. This is the process on which all of us, directly or indirectly, are still dependent for our food supplies, our clothing, almost all of our fuel and power, and much of our shelter.

The first forms of life were heterotrophic, dependent on outside food sources—of chemical nutrients—for their survival. Although, when life first appeared, the "dilute soup" was so abundant that ample chemical energy, in the form of nutrients, was available for nutrition, it is clear that life could not persist indefinitely unless it became autotrophic—able to be self-sufficient for its basic energy needs.

The evolution of photosynthesis provided the key for this autotrophism. Photosynthesis utilizes carbon dioxide and water, as raw materials, producing carbohydrates and oxygen, while storing solar energy in the intramolecular structure of the carbohydrate molecules. In the presence of adequate carbon dioxide the rate of photosynthesis is closely dependent on light intensity.

The building blocks for photosynthesis were also formed in the "dilute soup," the first photosynthetic organisms are thought to have appeared about 2.7 billion years ago (Hoering and Abelson, 1961). Like their non-photosynthetic cousins, they were restricted to deep water by the need to avoid U-V damage; at these depths light intensity was also much reduced; so that the rate of photosynthesis was initially very slow.

Until photosynthesis began, it seems that the only oxygen in the atmosphere was that formed by the photodissociation of water molecules by U-V radiation (Berker and Marshall, 1965). While significant quantities of oxygen were made available by this process, although at a slow rate, and also some ozone, by the photodissociation of the oxygen molecules themselves, it seems likely that both oxygen and ozone were maintained at near zero levels by their rapid involvement in oxidation reactions.

The oxygen and energy produced by photosynthesis is consumed by the metabolism of the chains of organisms which feed on the photosynthetic products. This respiratory metabolism represents, in chemical terms, a net reserve of the overall photosynthetic reaction, energy being released as oxygen is consumed and carbon dioxide is produced. A net yield of oxygen is therefore only obtained, and a net store of energy conserved, when the photosynthetic products themselves, or fossil remnants from other organisms, accumulate at protected sites, such as in the ocean depths.

When photosynthesis first appeared, the oxygen evolved was also rapidly utilized in oxidative reactions both in the water itself, in the atmosphere, and in weathering processes on land. Very slowly, however, the oxygen concentration began to rise. When it reached a level sufficient to maintain a permanent concentration of ozone in the atmosphere, a major step forward in the evolution of life began, because the ozone began to filter out U-V radiation and reduce its intensity at the surface. In consequence its depth of penetration in the oceans began to decline and organisms began to occupy shallower waters, in which visible radiation was higher and photosynthesis could be much more rapid.

Gradually this trend accelerated, oxygen and ozone increasing until ozone levels were high enough to shield the land surfaces of the earth from lethal U-V. This provided tremendous opportunities for biological diversity, the scope for colonization on land can be appreciated when it is realized that the land surfaces were bare at this time. It is not surprising that in the relatively brief span of 30 million years, between the late Silurian period, 420 million years ago, and the early Devonian, virtually all the land surfaces were vegetated.

Since that time continued evolution has brought us the global environment we know today. Without an ozone screen to protect us from U-V, without oxygen for respiratory metabolism, without CO_2 for photosynthesis, life as we know it could not exist.

Many other features of the environment are also vital for our existence. Almost without exception all are in a dynamic state of balance, in which biological and geological factors interact to provide the attributes that now prevail. Thus our present global environment is not a relic from a bygone age, nor is it a resource which can be exploited by man as though it were limitless, or as though change can be made in one aspect without regard to the repercussions of that change to the whole.

In this overall environment biological evolution has led, through genetic innovation and natural selection, to the colonization of almost every environmental niche on earth, with a range of plant and animal species, each competing with, yet often dependent on, others for space and nourishment. In this way a range of biological environments has been developed; collectively they are termed the biosphere.

Man, although he frequently attempts to pretend otherwise, is a creature of his heredity and his environment. He has evolved through the mainstream of biological evolution and the biochemical building blocks which constitute his structure and regulate his function reflect the restraints and demands of the environments in which they evolved and to which they became adapted. Man cannot live in a range of climates much different from those on terrestrial earth (I do not regard planetary or deep ocean existences for man as living!); he cannot exist without a range of foodstuffs that contain the chemical nutrients essential for his metabolism. He undoubtedly has other requirements associated with his inherited behavioural patterns. Yet man is capable of changing his environment to such a degree that some of these primary requirements could be destroyed.

Before we turn to examine aspects of man's impact on his environment, let us look a little further at some of the main attributes of life itself.

ECOLOGY AND ENVIRONMENT

A primary feature of life on earth is that organisms do not exist in isolation; instead the entire biosphere is composed of a range of ecosystems, each of which contains a number of species and a number of microenvironments, with each species tending to utilize and occupy an environmental niche more effectively than its competitors; the whole assemblage of species tending to cohabit in a manner that provides a high degree of internal self-regulation. A forest, or a lake, provides examples of typical ecosystems, but the scale can vary widely; the entire biosphere constitutes the earth's ecosystem.

A primary feature of an ecosystem is that it tends towards self-regulation. Solar energy is absorbed by the green plants of an ecosystem, to provide, through photosynthesis, the basic energy input. Plants also absorb water and mineral elements from the soil. The plant components thus produced are then passed through a food chain, in which the initial products are eaten by herbivores, herbivores by carnivores, carnivores by other carnivores, and so on until decomposer organisms return the organic wastes and the remnants of the organisms in the food chain to the soil, in a form that enables their re-absorption by the green plants.

In most natural ecosystems, therefore, there tends to be no net production—in the human context of a net harvest of materials. The solar energy absorbed and stored by the green plants is gradually consumed by metabolism through the food chain and dissipated as heat. Thus there is a flow of energy through an ecosystem, starting from solar energy, passing through successive forms of chemical energy—at each stage, some energy being lost as heat—until it is all dissipated. Associated with this flow of energy is a cycling of nutrients through food chains so that the ecosystem as a whole tends to be balanced and self-contained.

Within an ecosystem the numbers of any one species change in response to opportunities afforded to it in the way of nutrients and space. An environmental catastrophe, such as fire or drought, generally affects some species more than others; the more successful species increase in number until other restraints develop to prevent their further increase. Similarly, invasion of an ecosystem by a new species better able to compete than some existing ones will be associated with an increase in the number of the better adapted species and a reduction in the number of the less well adapted ones. The weeds in your garden provide examples of this.

An important phenomenon associated with such a disturbance is that, when a new species enters an ecosystem, it first encounters competition from existing species. If it is successful in gaining entry, its numbers increase until, in the absence of other competition, its own increasing numbers and demands for space and nutrients prevent further increase—*i.e.,* it encounters competition from within its own species. A moral for man's explosive population increase can be seen here.

The stability of an ecosystem, its ability to adapt to invasion or catastrophe without major change, is largely a matter of its diversity. In turn this is largely a matter of the rate of nutrient cycling, or the rate of energy flow. An ecosystem with little diversity is vulnerable to invasion, and, especially if energy flow is slow, is often unable to adapt to the change, at least without a period of marked instability. The successful invasion of Australia by rabbits is a good example of limited species diversity in Australian ecosystems. The ability of rabbits to compete favourably with other animals for forage, and the absence of effective predators, meant that rabbit numbers increased dramatically until in many areas competition for food, between rabbits themselves, was the main factor limiting their numbers. The successful invasion of Queensland pastures by prickly pear is another example of ineffective competition and the absence of suitable animals in the food chain to consume it. Fortunately, the absence of predators for the insect *Cactoblastis,* introduced to control prickly pear, meant that this animal could control it effectively and the existing ecosystems, perhaps enlarged by these two species alone, forming another loop in the food chain, returned to a degree of stability.

The most impressive examples of potentially unstable communities, ripe for invasion by other species, are agricultural crops, where a single species may be grown over thousands of square miles. The opportunities for invasion by "weed," "pest" and "disease" species—all words of modern man's vocabulary—are tremendous.

Management of an ecosystem, in the sense of increasing the numbers of one, or a group of species within it, and perhaps in removing them from the ecosystem so that there is a net yield, need not disturb internal self-regulation. The primary need is to ensure that nutrients continue to be recycled, that other important organisms are not adversely affected, and that there is sufficient diversity in species composition to prevent the community from becoming unstable.

So we see that nature obtains stability by allowing energy to flow smoothly through ecosystems, by retaining and recycling nutrients and by encouraging species diversity. We should not think that natural ecosystems do not change; geological processes and climatic change bring slow changes in the composition and structure of ecosystems, as does the constant geographic movement of species and continued genetic evolution. Abnormal weather, fire and similar phenomena bring rapid changes.

Furthermore, the species themselves change. Apart from the evolution of distinct new species, existing species change in character as environmental change induces natural selection. The degree to which a species can change in a given period of time depends on its intrinsic capacity to change—its inbuilt genetic diversity—and on its generation time. The most resilient and adaptable species tend to be those with short generation times. It goes without saying that these include many of our pest and disease species. The rapid development of immunity of insects to DDT, of disease organisms to penicillin and of rabbits to myxomatosis reflect this property.

Let us now look at man's impact on the environment to see how he has adjusted ecologically to the biosphere in which he evolved. To my mind it is easiest to do this by looking at man in three stages of his cultural evolution—Man the hunter-gatherer, Man the herder-farmer and Man the technologist.

MAN'S IMPACT ON THE ENVIRONMENT

When man first appeared, of the order of a million or so years ago—a very brief period in geological time—the earth contained many of the species of plants and animals which exist today, most of the climates which exist today and many of today's topographic features. Although the distribution of climates and the location of shorelines have changed, the range of ecological situations available for life has not changed to a pronounced degree. In many regions the first men enjoyed the same type of weather, breathed the same kind of air, ate the same kinds of animals as did Neanderthal man only a few tens of thousands of years ago, or today's huntsmen-campers in areas remote from industrial centres.

Just why man appeared when he did, and rapidly demonstrated his mastery over his environment and over other species, is still a subject of some speculation. However, even if it is not surprising that man's superiority rapidly ensured his survival, man's place in nature, until his first deliberate activities in cultivation and animal herding, was virtually the same as that of any other creature. Man the hunter-gatherer preyed on, and was preyed on by, other animals. He gathered plant foods when and where they were available. He was, in all respects, part of the food chain of the ecosystems he lived in; the changes he was able to make to his immediate ecosystems, apart from reduction in the numbers of the animals he consumed, were probably less than those of rabbits. Clearly, he made no changes to the biosphere as a whole.

The Australian aboriginal, in many respects, lived this way prior to European colonization of Australia. If aborigines could not be seen, evidence of their previous presence at any location was meagre and short-lived. In most respects they were as well adjusted to the natural environment as the animals and plants they consumed.

These men really lived their ecological role. Admirable though this was in the sense of permitting nature's overall fulfilment, it clearly left man vulnerable as a species. So it was that man the farmer emerged.

Those of us who admire the noble savage must conclude that life since the emergence of agriculture has been one long downhill slide—from fun to work. Whether or not one agrees with this view, the fact is that when man became a farmer he began a commitment from which there was no escape.

As I mentioned previously, the numbers of any species in an ecosystem will tend to rise if it is protected from its competitors. Man the farmer sought to ensure his own survival by protecting his food supplies—the plants and animals he wished to consume—from competition and predation, and by deliberately cultivating them. In ecological terms he sought to maximize the energy flow passing through himself by maximizing the energy flow passing through the species directly ahead of him in the food chain.

Because he was also able to protect himself against predation, his numbers increased, and immediately his dependence on the "managed" ecosystems increased further. There was no going back. Not only did he become dependent on agriculture, but his increasing numbers started a demand-supply spiral which meant that continually he had to attempt to increase both the area under cultivation and the yield of any one area.

Furthermore, the more specialized his agriculture became—the more, if you like, he attempted to reduce the number of species in his managed ecosystem, the more unstable they tended to become. The tendency for undesirable species to invade his farms increased, the removal of existing vegetation exposed his lands to erosion, and this factor combined with the removal of nutrients from his ecosystems without replacement, began to reduce their productive potential.

Thus many of the early agricultural efforts tended to be highly exploitative, and a shifting agriculture arose. When productivity dropped, new farms were developed, and the old farmlands were left to revert to a natural ecosystem. The shifting agriculture still evident in parts of New Guinea is a good example of this.

With time, man learnt to replace nutrients on his fields by using crop residues and human and animal manure; he learnt to prevent erosion by maintaining ground cover and cultivating only level land. He learnt to give his domesticated species an edge over their competitors and predators by farming practice. Crop rotation, sanitation practices, and other procedures all helped in this regard. In consequence his ecological management practices improved, nutrient cycling was restored, and levels of stability were achieved.

Although some specific ecosystems were badly damaged (for example, those on the fringes of the Sahara where herding of goats caused almost completely new and much less productive ecosystems to be established), man's activities, in most cases, were still of little consequence to the biosphere as a whole. Not only was his capacity for major change limited by his muscle-power and that of his domesticated animals, but his numbers were still so small that there was always more land over the next hill or in the next valley.

Man the farmer was therefore able, if not to live an ecological role as fully as man the hunter, at least to avoid large-scale environmental change, although his low numbers were the main factor here. Even so, he barely managed to match food production against numbers—as periodic famine in peasant agricultural systems, even today, testifies. Thus in ecological terms he was stretching capacity.

The first signs of a new problem in ecological management were also evident whenever man congregated into villages and towns. In these centres there developed great accumulations of organic debris—body wastes, food scraps, the detritus of the range of human activities. At this stage the word "pollution" could well have been introduced to man's vocabulary. Pollution, in ecological terms, generally means the addition of materials to an ecosystem which accumulate because they overload the existing food chain pathways or because, in the modern idiom, they are "non-biodegradable," that is, they cannot be recycled at all, or fast enough to keep their levels low. In the former case the opportunities for species capable of capitalizing on the extra nutrients are increased considerably; in human terms these species are frequently pathogens or

carry pathogens, and epidemic disease is the logical result. In both cases, however, the materials may affect species other than man in quite different ways from those in which man is affected, and pronounced changes in ecosystem characteristics can follow.

The story of man the technologist is, in most respects, simply an extension of man the farmer. However, with the industrial revolution, man's ability to harness power to his needs meant that the impact of his activities on the environment increased tremendously.

To my mind this impact has two main, closely linked, aspects. The first has been the dramatic, and continuing, increase in man's numbers as his capacity to manipulate agricultural ecosystems for food production, and his control over human disease, have increased. The second has been the development of a great diversity of human activities, human demands, and human products. Thus not only has population itself increased rapidly, but the demands of each human being for factors other than basic food needs, have also increased. Man the technologist expects, not merely to survive, but to enjoy a socioeconomic infrastructure which provides transportation, education, housing, recreational space and many other cultural facets.

To satisfy these desires and needs, man has affected the environment both directly and indirectly. In a direct sense his mechanical activity—in constructing cities, highways, dams and in soil cultivation and mining—is the most striking and obvious. Indirectly, though, the other products of modern technology are also of great importance as agents of change.

These products, in the main, are those of chemical and engineering technology. They include the wide variety of products needed by modern industry, agriculture and commerce—agricultural and industrial chemicals, for example; as well as the by-products of these industries—manufacturing residues, exhaust fumes, hot water. They also include the debris of the modern consumer society — packaging materials, sewage and food wastes, detergents, worn-out and useless "durable" consumer goods, and so on.

In these activities, man the technologist has attempted to ignore the capacities and characteristics of his ecosystems. The agricultural ecosystems in which he produces his food have been still further removed from stability. He has loaded them with the products of chemical technology thinking only of maximizing food yield from a few species. In the process the nutrient and non-nutrient chemicals (fertilizers, pesticides, weedicides) which he has added have had repercussions far beyond the ecosystems to which they were applied.

Excess nutrition of agricultural fields can cause the enrichment of inland waters into which the nutrients drain. In time this can cause such an increase in aquatic photosynthesis that the aquatic ecosystems can be completely changed. In some cases lakes can fill in with photosynthetic products (Sperry, 1967). With regard to pesticides, there are many examples of target organisms developing immunity to the substances used to kill them, yet of other species remaining susceptible. Furthermore, not only are vulnerable species directly damaged or destroyed, but many of these substances remain biologically active for lengthy periods of time, and may accumulate, particularly in food chains involving sequences of carnivorous animals, until they kill species originally unaffected. Fish and birds are often affected in this way. In consequence agricultural practices have, in some cases, endangered the ecological stability of extensive regions.

In the ecosystems in which man has built his cities, he has also added vast quantities of nutrient and non-nutrient compounds—both domestic and industrial wastes. These too have affected regions far greater than the areas where these materials have been dumped (Beeton, 1965).

The results of these activities are all around us, and I do not need to recount them. A week seldom goes by without the Press providing examples. The stark realism of the situation is that, in the case of agriculture, I believe we are now dependent in large measure on these practices; and, in the case of our population centres, I think we have almost come to accept them as a fact of life.

The impact of these changes on the environment as a whole is now just beginning to be appreciated. Ever since his appearance on earth, man has attempted to exploit his local environment for his own ends. In a sense, all organisms have done this, whether deliberately or not. As long as man used natural methods for this exploitation, and the power of his own metabolism, and as long as his numbers were low, there was little likelihood of the changes he induced affecting more than his immediate environment—and

his early attempts at exploitation were still essentially conservative, in the sense that they preserved the basic diversity and character of the environment. Now, however, the situation has gone full circle; man is so abundant and so powerful that he is changing the properties of the entire biosphere. The rate of change is far greater than occurred even during the great transitions from one geological epoch to another. This is the collision course referred to before; clearly the trend must be reversed.

MAN AND THE FUTURE

The motivation for many of man's actions has been what Hardin (1968) has termed the philosophy of the Commons. He illustrates this philosophy by the following example: "Visualize a pasture open to all, on which a number of herdsmen are free to graze their stock." Each, as an independent entrepreneur, will attempt to keep as many stock as possible on this common ground.

Few problems arise until the total number of stock reaches the carrying capacity of the pasture. Then any one herdsman asks, "What is the value to me of adding one more animal to my herd?"

His profit is related to the number and condition of his stock. He knows that the addition of one animal to the total herd on the commons will reduce the nourishment available to each by a very small fraction indeed. By comparison that animal represents a relatively large increase in the size of his own herd.

As Hardin points out, "the rational herdsman concludes that the only sensible course for him to pursue is to add another animal to his herd. And another, and another ... But this is the conclusion reached by each and every rational herdsman sharing a commons. Therein lies the tragedy."

In how many cases can we see aspects of this philosophy being acted out. The chemical manufacturer who decides that rather than clean up the effluent from his factory it is cheaper for him to pollute a stream and pay only a share of the taxes levied by the city council to clean up the pollution so induced; or the farmer who keeps adding agricultural chemicals to increase his yield, without thought to the effect elsewhere; or even the family, in countries with pressing population problems, that adds more and more children to the load society as a whole largely bears.

Clearly, the freedom of the individual in

matters affecting other people cannot continue without restraint. The last great "commons" are the air and the sea, yet already changes are occurring there.

Let us look, for example, at changes which are occurring in atmospheric CO_2. The energy that man has used to power his industrial society has come primarily from the combustion and fossil fuels. You will recall that these have been laid down during geological time, and that it was largely their laying down that caused oxygen levels to rise to values which permitted man's evolution. Fortunately, consumption of these fuels is not likely to directly affect oxygen levels, at least to a significant degree, but already it has affected the level of CO_2 in the atmosphere as a whole.

The rate of combustion of these fuels is staggering. Last year the amount which was burnt was equivalent to a bush-fire which would destroy the entire vegetation of Australia. Small wonder that, if present trends continue, the amount of CO_2 added to the atmosphere is likely to be equivalent to the present concentration within 50 years (Revelle and Suess, 1957). So far it has not been possible to calculate the likely climatic effects of this change; suffice it to say that some estimations predict an increase of mean world temperature of several degrees (Plass, 1956). Should this occur, dramatic changes in, amongst other things, cloudiness, rainfall and agricultural productivity may take place.

What are the solutions to this collision course between man's numbers and demands on the one hand, and his environment on the other?

It is clear that the goal of the "greatest good for the greatest number" is impossible to achieve. Despite the bliss that this phrase may conjure up in some people's minds, man cannot maximize for both of these factors at once. Ecologically, it is probable he cannot maximize for either, unless the goal "of the greatest good" is identified with conservation of his own species. But our present numbers, our present technology, and our present attitudes are not consistent with this goal. What are the requirements if man is to maximize for conservation of his own species?

First, he must regulate his numbers. Unless population stability is achieved, everything else must ultimately fail.

Secondly, he must conserve and recycle the basic materials he uses to the greatest possible degree.

Thirdly, he must ensure that his food supply is adequate for his regulated numbers, and that the means of its production are not in themselves leading to environmental deterioration.

I believe the principle of conservation and recycling should be applied not only to renewable, but also to non-renewable materials. For example, the nutrients in domestic sewage (including food scraps as well as body wastes) at present move resources such as rock phosphate, or atmospheric nitrogen, to factories, to farms, to human mouths, and then through sewage systems to inland waters or to the sea. There is no effective link to recycle these nutrients to the agricultural ecosystems where they could be used again. In consequence, the sewage tends to pollute the ecosystems into which it is discharged, by overenrichment even if not in a pathological sense.

In much the same way metals for industry are largely obtained by digging fresh ore out of the ground, rather than by reusing it from worn-out commodities. These non-renewable resources are not inexhaustible. Furthermore, their extraction, processing and accumulation frequently pose problems in ecosystem stability. Although short-term "commons" type economics may indicate that present practices are cheaper than those which would involve resource conservation and recycling, I contend that serious attempts to reduce the cost of re-separation of primary substances from manufactured products—minerals from sewage, metals from durable consumer goods, etc.—may well make such procedures competitive with ore processing.

Similar remarks apply to energy. At present it is cheaper for us to use fossil fuel energy than energy in nature in the form of solar or tidal power. Only hydroelectric power appears to be competitive. Perhaps nuclear energy can be regarded separately, but it is clearly undesirable to continue to exploit fossil fuels purely as a source of energy. Apart from atmospheric contamination, these fuels represent chemical energy which could play an important role in recyclable human food supplies. In energy terms, the fossil fuels being burnt each year would feed the present world population for 20 years. Clearly, intensive research should be directed to the harnessing of natural energy sources.

The challenge to agriculture, as I see it, is to use, as far as possible, ecological principles to nourish crops, to control pests and diseases, and to prevent erosion. Agricultural chemicals should be used with much greater care and should preferably be of a type which can be rapidly utilized in food chains. As far as possible these chemicals should be retained on each farm. In this way agricultural ecosystems would not only gain more internal stability, but the reduced degree of erosion and chemical pollution would help to minimize the risk of contaminating other areas.

Clearly, there are limits to the degree to which ecological principles can be applied, for the reasons given before. To me this suggests that consideration should be given to isolating at least some agricultural ecosystems from natural ecosystems. Already there is a trend in this direction, reflected in the increasing use of greenhouses for horticultural crops, and in the methods used for chicken and egg production. In many cases these practices are more economic than conventional agriculture, and it would seem that much of our vegetable and meat production could take place in this way, thereby separating part of man's basic food chain from natural ecosystems and enabling foodstuffs to be produced in environments where pests and diseases could be safely and easily controlled without threat to other species.

However, the main use to which agricultural land is now put is to produce food grains—our primary energy foods. The areas used for such production are so vast that controlled environment culture would appear to be impossible, at least with present or foreseeable technology. In such areas agricultural scientists must devise ways of ensuring productivity while maintaining stability. This task should not be too great as long as the pressure to maximize productivity is relaxed and the pressure to maintain ecological stability is increased.

The only alternative to broad-acre agriculture for producing our main energy foods is to produce them synthetically. Instead of solar energy being captured by photosynthesis in field crops and converted into carbohydrates, is it conceivable to manufacture them in chemical factories? To date, chemical synthesis of only a few food compounds has been achieved, but present knowledge and technology would appear to be capable of developing procedures for producing the simple carbohydrates which are the basic energy foods for human and animal nutrition.

If such a development could occur, it would raise many problems associated with the energy needed for synthesis; associated with waste disposal; associated with cost or the integration of such forms of production with existing agriculture. However, it would be a logical extension of present trends in agriculture. We have seen food production change from a way of life to a highly technical business—perhaps we must recognize that the difficulties of conducting such a business out of doors, exposed to the vagaries of nature, must lead us to more and more control and, finally, at least for foods where energy rather than flavour is the main product, to chemical synthesis. Such a development would also have the long-term attribute of enabling much of man's food to be produced without a direct impact on the biosphere and on other species, and would enable much crop land to revert to other, or multiple, forms of land use. Again, it seems that much more research should be conducted on this subject.

Regardless of whether chemical food factories are practicable or not, these three main ground rules I have suggested—control of our numbers, control of our food supply in a way that minimizes the degree to which we jeopardize other species, and the recycling and conservation, as far as possible, of the materials which constitute our basic needs—all add up to living ecologically. There is no doubt in my mind that this is possible, but I realize that, in the short term, it probably makes economic nonsense.

What is required is a change in our basic philosophy—from an attitude to our environment which regards it as a resource to be exploited for short-term personal, regional or national gain— the attitude of the "commons"—to an attitude of living ecologically in a way that is essentially conservative of the environment. Perhaps one must ask where is the basic economy of economics if it is not consistent with this latter objective.

I think the biologist has an important role to play in pointing out the ecological rules for these changes, but the task is one for all mankind. If men of all nations can be made to see themselves, not engaged in battle against each other for a share of a "commons" which no longer exists, but rather as fellow members of a species which has passed from the stage of competition against other species to the infinitely more dangerous stage of competition within itself, perhaps we can really set ourselves on a new path of human progress in partnership.

References

Beeton, A. M. (1965): Limnol. Oceanog., 10, 240.

Berkner, L. V., and Marshall, L. C. (1965): J. Atmos. Sci., 22, 225.

Cloud, P. E., Jr. (1968): Science, 160, 729.

Cole, L. C. (1966): BioScience, 16, 243.

Hardin, G. (1968): Science, 162, 1243.

Hoering, T. C., and Abelson, P. H. (1961): Proc. Natl. Acad. Sci. U.S., 47, 623.

Mason, B. (1958): Principles of Geochemistry, 2nd ed. (New York: John Wiley & Sons.)

Plass, G. N. (1956): Tellus, 8, 140.

Revelle, R., and Suess, H. E. (1957): Tellus, 9, 18.

Rubey, W. W. (1963): In The Origin and Evolution of Atmospheres and Oceans, P. J. Brancazio and A. G. W. Cameron, eds. (New York: John Wiley & Sons.)

Sperry, K. (1967): Science, 158, 351.

5. NOBODY EVER DIES OF OVERPOPULATION

GARRETT HARDIN

Those of us who are deeply concerned about population and the environment—"econuts," we're called—are accused of seeing herbicides in trees, pollution in running brooks, radiation in rocks, and overpopulation everywhere. There is merit in the accusation.

I was in Calcutta when the cyclone struck East Bengal in November 1970. Early dispatches spoke of 15,000 dead, but the estimates rapidly escalated to 2,000,000 and then dropped back to 500,000. A nice round number: it will do as well as any, for we will never know. The nameless ones who died, "unimportant" people far beyond the fringes of the social power structure, left no trace of their existence. Pakistani parents repaired the population loss in just 40 days, and the world turned its attention to other matters.

What killed those unfortunate people? The cyclone, newspapers said. But one can just as logically say that overpopulation killed them. The Gangetic delta is barely above sea level. Every year several thousand people are killed in quite ordinary storms. If Pakistan were not overcrowded, no sane man would bring his family to such a place. Ecologically speaking, a delta belongs to the river and the sea; man obtrudes there at his peril.

In the web of life every event has many antecedents. Only by an arbitrary decision can we designate a single antecedent as "cause." Our choice is biased—biased to protect our egos against the onslaught of unwelcome truths. As T. S. Eliot put it in *Burnt Norton:*
Go, go, go, said the bird: human kind
Cannot bear very much reality.

Were we to identify overpopulation as the cause of a half-million deaths, we would threaten ourselves with a question to which we do not know the answer: *How can we control population without recourse to repugnant measures?* Fearfully we close our minds to an inventory of possibilities. Instead, we say that a cyclone caused the deaths, thus relieving ourselves of responsibility for this and future catastrophes. "Fate" is *so* comforting.

Every year we list tuberculosis, leprosy, enteric diseases, or animal parasites as the "cause of death" of millions of people. It is well known that malnutrition is an important antecedent of death in all these categories; and that malnutrition is connected with overpopulation. But overpopulation is not called the cause of death. We cannot bear the thought.

People are dying now of respiratory diseases in Tokyo, Birmingham, and Gary, because of the "need" for more industry. The "need" for more food justifies overfertilization of the land, leading to eutrophication of the waters, and lessened fish production—which leads to more "need" for food.

What will we say when the power shuts down some fine summer on our eastern seaboard and several thousand people die of heat prostration? Will we blame the weather? Or the power companies for not building enough generators? Or the econuts for insisting on pollution controls?

One thing is certain: we won't blame the deaths on overpopulation. No one ever dies of overpopulation. It is unthinkable.

Reprinted with permission of the author and publisher from *Science,* v. 171, no. 3971, p. 527, February 12, 1971. Copyright 1971 by the American Association for the Advancement of Science.

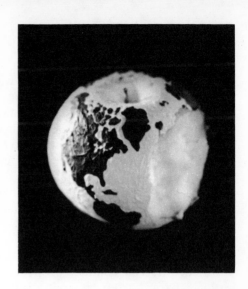

Part Two
GEOLOGIC HAZARDS

Geologic hazards are those geologic features and events that are hazardous or harmful to the extent that they frequently result in injuries or loss of life and property. Natural geologic processes which have been going on for millions of years may become geologic hazards when people get in the way. They include such diverse geologic phenomena as earthquakes, volcanic eruptions, floods, landslides, subsidence, tsunamis, soil creep, and glacier bursts. If not recognized, clearly understood, and accounted for in the activities of man, almost any geologic process or feature can become a geologic hazard. As so appropriately stated by Oakeshott (Selection 1), "There are no geologic hazards without people; the 'hazards' arise from man's unwise, inept, and careless occupation and use or abuse of the geologic environment."

Throughout history, there are many examples of geologic hazards which have resulted in disaster and have greatly affected the activities of man. Volcanic eruptions such as those of Vesuvius, which destroyed Pompeii nearly 1900 years ago, Krakatoa in 1883, and Mt. Pelée, which destroyed a city of 30,000 in 1902, are just a few examples. Ten great earthquakes in China between the eleventh and twentieth centuries, resulting in landslides and collapse of loessial cliffs, killed 1½ million people. We can cite numerous well-known earthquakes experienced by North Americans in this century; among them are the 1906 San Francisco earthquake, the 1964 Alaskan earthquake, and the 1971 San Fernando earthquake. The list of disasters caused by "naturally occurring geologic hazards," or those hazards over which man has no apparent control would indeed be lengthy.

Another category of geologic hazards is that of "man-induced hazards." Man's activity has helped to change the rate and place of occurrence of certain natural phenomena, resulting in hazard to himself. Some examples of man-induced hazards include: land subsidence caused by withdrawal of ground water and petroleum resulting in damage to foundations and other structures, and landslides and slumping resulting from highway construction which modifies stable slopes. The building of a reservoir in Vaiont Canyon near Milan, Italy, triggered a rock slide in 1963 which resulted in loss of 3,000 lives. Waste water injected into a 10,000 foot deep-well at Rocky Mountain Arsenal triggered several earthquakes in the Denver area during the 1960s.

Both naturally occurring and man-induced geologic hazards are merely normal geologic processes or events until man gets in the way; then these processes or events become hazards. Earthquakes are hazards when man lives too close to the active fault area, volcanic eruptions become so when man lives in close proximity to the volcano, and floods become hazards when man inhabits the floodplain.

What can the geologist do about geologic hazards? Working with adequate geologic knowledge he can conduct proper geologic investigations that can be used to prevent a geologic hazard from becoming a disaster. Recognition or identification of a geologic hazard at a certain locality must first be made. Once clearly identified and defined, there are several approaches to solving the problem, depending on the type of hazard. One solution is to avoid the problem by changing the proposed location of a structure such as a reservoir, nuclear power plant, or highway. This solution is often necessary in the case of naturally occurring hazards. Other alternatives are to eliminate the hazard or engineer the structure to withstand the hazard. Normally, the latter approaches are more costly than avoiding the problem. The urgency to avoid or prevent geologic hazards is a necessary outgrowth of a society characterized by increasing population and urbanization.

What hope do we have for eliminating disasters caused by geologic hazards? There is little hope that they can be eliminated completely, but they could be greatly reduced with an understanding of the geologic aspects of the environment. However, with time current solutions may not be so effective in reducing disasters if the present population trends continue. There will be greater competition for the "choice" space on the floodplain or the attractive building sites in rugged hillside areas and above seashore cliffs.

In the past several years, there has been much concern over the possibility of a devastating earthquake in the populated area of western United States. There is little doubt that sometime in the future a devastating earthquake, which could conceivably eliminate 50,000 to 100,000 people, will occur. Although we are not able to predict the time of such an earthquake, the knowledge that an earthquake will occur is all that is necessary for adequate planning. The important thing is to recognize that it will happen and to plan development to avoid the catastrophic effects. Hopefully, prediction and control of many geologic hazards will become a reality in the near future.

Earthquakes

6. EARTHQUAKE "BRIEFS"

U. S. GEOLOGICAL SURVEY

The scientific study of earthquakes is comparatively new. Until the 18th century, few factual descriptions of earthquakes were recorded, and the natural cause of earthquakes was little understood. Many people believed that an earthquake was a massive punishment and a warning to the unrepentant. An Italian scholar in the 16th century, for example, suggested that statues of Mercury and Saturn be placed on building walls to protect against earthquakes. Those who sought natural causes often reached fanciful conclusions; one popular theory was that earthquakes were caused by air rushing out of caverns deep in the earth's interior.

The first earthquake for which there is detailed descriptive information occurred on November 1, 1755 in the vicinity of Lisbon, Portugal. An estimated 30,000 people were killed, most of them crushed to death under the ruins of buildings in Lisbon. Shocks from the quake were felt in many parts of the world, including the American Colonies, where "chandeliers rattled." After the quake, Portugese priests documented their observations, and their records—still preserved—represent the first systematic attempt to investigate an earthquake and its effects. Since then, detailed records have been made of almost every major earthquake that has occurred.

The most widely felt earthquake in the recorded history of North America occurred in 1812 near New Madrid, Missouri. This quake was felt over an area of 2 million square miles—from Canada to the Gulf of Mexico, and from the Rocky Mountains to the Atlantic Ocean. Because the most intense effects were in a sparsely populated region, the destruction to human life and property was slight. If this earthquake occurred in the same area today, it probably would cause severe damage in many cities of the central Mississippi Valley.

The San Francisco earthquake of 1906 was one of the most destructive in the recorded history of North America—the earthquake and

the fires that followed killed nearly 700 people, and left the city in ruins. The Alaska earthquake of March 27, 1964, however, was of greater magnitude than the San Francisco earthquake. Releasing perhaps twice as much energy, it was felt over an area of almost 500,000 square miles. Loss of life and property would have been far greater had Alaska been more densely populated.

Most of the world's earthquakes occur in near-continuous seismically active "belts" that coincide with zones in which mountain-building processes are still taking place. About 80 percent of all earthquakes—as well as most of the world's active volcanoes—occur in areas bordering the Pacific Ocean. This circum-Pacific belt, called the "ring of fire," includes the Pacific coasts of North and South America, the Aleutians, Japan, Southeast Asia, and Australasia.

It is estimated that 3 to 5 million lives have been lost in the past 1,000 years from earthquakes and volcanoes. Records of past events suggest that a major destructive earthquake will strike the earth at least once a year. With the world's population expected to double in another 40 years, many major cities are becoming increasingly vulnerable to earthquake hazards.

An earthquake is the oscillatory and sometimes violent movement of the earth's surface that follows a release of energy in the earth's crust. This energy can be generated by a sudden dislocation of segments of the crust or by a volcanic eruption. Most of the destructive earthquakes are caused by dislocation of the crust.

When subjected to deep-seated forces (whose origins and natures are largely unknown) the earth's crust may first bend and then, when the stress exceeds the strength of the rocks, the crust breaks and "snaps" to a new position. In the process of breaking, vibrations called "seismic waves" are generated. These waves travel from the source of the earthquake to more distant places along the surface and through the earth at varying speeds depending on the medium through which they move. Some of the vibrations are of high enough frequency to be audible, while others are of low frequency—

From U. S. Department of the Interior "news release" of November 24, 1968.

actually many seconds or minutes between swings. These vibrations cause the entire planet to quiver or ring like a bell or tuning fork.

Geologists have found that earthquakes tend to reoccur along *faults*—fractures in the earth's crust along which two blocks of the crust have slipped with respect to each other. One crustal block may move horizontally in one direction while the block facing it moves in the opposite direction. Or, one block may move upward while the other moves downward. Along many faults, movement is both horizontal and vertical. Faults represent zones of weakness in the earth's crust, but the fact that a fault zone has recently experienced an earthquake offers no assurance that enough stress has been relieved to prevent another quake.

The location of an earthquake is commonly described by the geographic position of its *epicenter,* and by its *focal depth.* The epicenter of an earthquake is the point on the earth's surface directly above the point (focus) where an earthquake's energy originates. The focal depth is the depth from the epicenter to the focus. Focal depths for shallow earthquakes range from the surface to about 60 kilometers (38 miles). Intermediate earthquakes range from 60 to 300 kilometers (38 to 188 miles). The focus of deep earthquakes may reach depths of 700 kilometers (440 miles).

The focuses of most earthquakes are concentrated in the crust and in the upper mantle of the earth. Compared to a depth of about 4,000 miles to the center of the earth's core, earthquakes thus originate in relatively shallow parts of the earth's interior. Earthquakes in California along the San Andreas and associated faults have shallow focal depths; for most the depth is less than 10 miles. During the past 100 years, earth movements have occurred along more than half the entire length of the San Andreas fault, and the rupture itself is visible at the land surface in many places.

Very shallow earthquakes are probably caused by fracturing of the brittle rock in the crust, or by internal stresses that overcome the frictional resistance locking opposite sides of a fault.

Earthquakes beneath the ocean floor commonly generate immense sea waves or "tsunamis" (Japan's dread "hugh wave"). These waves travel across the ocean at speeds as great as 600 miles an hour, and may be 50 feet high or higher by the time they reach the shore. During the 1964 Alaska earthquake, tsunamis engulfing coastal areas caused much of the destruction at Kodiak, Seward, and other Alaskan communities. They also caused severe damage elsewhere along the west coast of North America, particularly at Crescent City, California. Some waves raced across the ocean to the coasts of Japan.

Water levels in artesian wells fluctuate as seismic waves travel through the rock layers that hold the water. During passage of seismic waves from a large earthquake, water levels in some wells fluctuate wildly, not only in the immediate vicinity of the earthquake, but also at great distances from it. In some wells, the water level change may be long-lasting or even permanent. The Alaskan quake appears to have caused water changes in wells in many areas both local and remote. For example, hydrologists of the U.S. Geological Survey noted that water levels at New Orleans, Louisiana, rose and fell as a result of the Alaska earthquake of 1964.

Landslides triggered by earthquakes often cause more destruction than the earthquake shocks themselves. During the 1964 Alaska quake, shock-induced landslides devastated the Turnagain Heights residential development and many downtown areas in Anchorage. The cause of the landslides and slumps that hit the Anchorage area can be traced to an unstable material called "Bootlegger Cove Clay" that underlies much of the city. During the 1964 earthquake, failure in the "Bootlegger Cove Clay" led to the landslides that caused most of the severe damage in the Anchorage area.

The vibrations produced by earthquakes are detected, recorded, and measured by instruments called *seismographs.* The zig-zag line made by a seismograph, called a "seismogram," reflects the varying amplitude of the vibrations by responding to the motion of the ground surface beneath the instrument. From the data expressed in seismograms, the time, the epicenter, and focal depth of an earthquake can be determined, and estimates can be made of the amount of energy that was released.

The two general types of vibrations produced by earthquakes are *surface waves,* which travel along the earth's surface, and *body waves,* which travel through the earth. Surface waves usually have the strongest vibrations and probably cause most of the damage done by earthquakes.

The severity of an earthquake can be expressed in several ways. The *magnitude* of an earthquake as expressed by the *Richter Scale* is a measure of the amplitude of the seismic waves and is related to the amount of energy released—an amount that can be estimated from seismograph recordings. The *intensity,* as expressed by the *Modified Mercalli Scale,* is a partly subjective measure which depends on the effects of a shock at a particular location. Damage or loss of life and property is another—and ultimately the most important measure—of an earthquake's severity.

The Richter Scale, named after Charles F. Richter of the California Institute of Technology, is the best known scale for measuring the magnitude of earthquakes. The scale is logarithmic, so that a magnitude of 7, for example, signifies a disturbance 10 times as large as a magnitude of 6. A quake of magnitude 2 is the smallest quake normally felt by humans. Earthquakes with a Richter value of 6 or more are commonly considered major in magnitude.

The Modified Mercalli Scale measures the intensity of an earthquake's effects in a given locality in values ranging from 1 to 12. The most commonly used adaptation covers the range of intensity from the condition of "1—Not felt except by very few, favorably situated," to "12—Damage total, lines of sight disturbed, objects thrown into air."

Earthquakes of large magnitude do not necessarily cause the most intense surface effects. The effect in a given region depends to a large degree on local surface and subsurface geologic conditions. An area underlain by unstable ground (sand, clay, or other unconsolidated materials), for example, is likely to experience much more noticeable effects than an area equally distant from the earthquake's epicenter, but underlain by firm ground such as granite.

The United States has experienced less destruction than other countries located in the "ring of fire," but millions of Americans live in potential quake areas, particularly in the western part of the United States. Increasing amounts of construction in many places where the danger of major earthquakes is ever present has created an urgent need for more information on the nature, causes, and effects of earthquakes.

The prediction of earthquakes is one of the objectives of current studies by the U.S. Geological Survey and other scientific groups. At present, it is not possible to predict the time, place, and size of a specific earthquake in advance, but considerable progress has been made in formulating the statistical probability that an earthquake of given magnitude will occur in a region within a specific span of time.

For the present, the best protection against earthquakes is to avoid construction in high-risk areas. For example, the Port of Valdez, Alaska, destroyed by the 1964 earthquake, was found to have been built on incipient landslide blocks. These blocks did not provide stable building sites. Because little property of value remained standing after the earthquake, and because the town was not heavily populated, the people of Valdez chose to rebuild their town at a new site—one recommended on the basis of geologic study. In large metropolitan areas, on the other hand, the emphasis in earthquake protection will inevitably have to be on land use, planning, and improved construction methods.

Earthquakes on the Island of Hawaii, site of the active volcanoes Kilauea and Mauna Loa, appear to be associated with volcanic activity. Abrupt increases in quake activity, at times, herald an eruption, and the location swarms of tremors can indicate where lava may break out. Also, prior to an eruption, the volcano "swells" measurably in response to the upward movement of molten rock. Continuous seismic and tiltmeter (a device that measures earth movements) records are maintained at the Geological Survey's Hawaiian Volcano Observatory, located on the rim of Kilauea Volcano where study of these records enables specialists to make short-range prediction of volcanic eruptions.

Scientific understanding of earthquakes is of vital importance to the nation. As the population increases, expanding urban development and construction works encroach upon areas susceptible to earthquakes. Earthquake research efforts have been intensified, and special studies of such earthquake-prone zones as the San Andreas fault in California by geologists, geophysicists, and seismologists of the U.S. Geological Survey's National Center for Earthquake Research, are yielding new insights into the nature and mechanisms of earthquakes, which, hopefully, may make earthquake predictions possible and which certainly will increase man's ability to live safely in earthquake zones.

7. FIFTH ANNIVERSARY OF ALASKA EARTHQUAKE

U. S. GEOLOGICAL SURVEY

Five years ago, on Good Friday, March 27, 1964, at 5:36 p.m., Alaska Standard Time, an earthquake with a Richter magnitude of 8.5 dealt a massive blow to south-central Alaska. Seismic energy, radiating from the focus of the earthquake miles beneath Prince William Sound triggered an almost incredible variety of geologic events.

Scientists of the U.S. Geological Survey, Department of the Interior, quickly reached the scene to determine and appraise the effects of the quake. Their studies and conclusions have helped make the earthquake the best documented and most thoroughly studied in history.

The magnitude, duration, and geographic extent of damage of the 1964 Alaska earthquake rank it among the major earthquakes in history. In Alaska, 114 persons were killed, $300 million worth of property was destroyed, and the state's economy suffered a crippling blow. That the death toll was not higher was due to a number of fortuitous circumstances: the affected area was sparsely populated; the earthquake occurred on the evening of a holiday when schools and most offices were empty; the sea was at low tide; the weather was generally mild and, at the time, it was the off-season for fishing. Had an earthquake of this magnitude and duration occurred in a densely populated region in the middle of a summer day it might easily have caused thousands of deaths and perhaps billions of dollars in damages.

On land and beneath the sea, large masses of earth were jarred into motion by the shock. Submarine slides generated seawaves which smashed back at Alaska coastal communities on the heels of the quake. On the land, slides and slumps destroyed or damaged residential and business areas, cut railroads, highways, and communication lines, and disrupted water, gas, and sewer services. Ground motion, resulting from the passage of seismic waves through relatively unconsolidated sediments, literally shook man's works into ruins. Highways were transformed into broken slabs of pavement. Bridges were destroyed, and modern buildings were fractured as a result of ground waves.

Less spectacular perhaps, but of exceptional interest to earth scientists, were the regional changes in land level created by the earthquake. These changes are closely related to a northeast-trending zone of seismic activity which contains the epicenter of the Good Friday earthquake and thousands of aftershocks. Along the western edge of this zone and farther to the west an area of about 30,000 square miles was lowered as much as 6 feet. To the east, an area of as much as 50,000 square miles was elevated, locally more than 33 feet. These vertical changes in the land and seafloor necessitated remapping and recharting vast areas in south-central Alaska.

The Alaska earthquake spurred a series of coordinated federal-state plans to cope with earthquake hazards. In both California and Alaska, geologic studies have been underway to evaluate geologic hazards and to help guide planning for urban development. The California studies are concentrated on the San Andreas fault zone, a fracture some 600 or more miles in length along which earthquakes and ground movements have repeatedly occurred.

Detailed studies of the San Andreas fault by scientists of the U.S. Geological Survey's National Center for Earthquake Research (NCER), established in 1966, are yielding a better understanding of the mechanism of major earthquakes. Earthquakes and crustal movements are being monitored and a variety of geophysical techniques are being used to probe deep beneath the surface and to learn the structure of the earth's crust and the forces that effect it. With increased knowledge, techniques may be developed that will provide the basis for an earthquake prediction system.

From U. S. Department of the Interior "news release" of March 27, 1969.

8. BENEFICIAL EFFECTS OF ALASKA EARTHQUAKE

EDWIN B. ECKEL

SOCIOECONOMIC BENEFITS

Devastating as was the Alaska earthquake of March 27, 1964, it had many long-term beneficial effects. Most of these benefits were in the fields of socioeconomics and engineering and are only mentioned briefly here.

Economically, the federal monies and other funds spent for reconstruction exceeded the total damage cost of the earthquake, largely because of decisions to upgrade or enlarge facilities beyond their preearthquake condition.

Many improvements resulted from the aid poured into reconstruction. One whole town, Valdez, was razed and rebuilt on a more stable site; the area of one of the most disastrous landslides in the business heart of Anchorage was permanently stabilized by a gigantic earth buttress; new and better port facilities were provided in all the affected seacoast towns; the fishing fleet acquired, under ·very favorable financial terms, new boats and modern floating or land-based canneries. The pattern of rail-sea transport was drastically changed, partly because of the discovery that the port of Anchorage could actually be used year-round, despite the ice in Knik Arm that had hitherto closed it in winter. (This change of pattern, of course, was hardly a benefit to Seward and Valdez.) Forced by pressures of reconstruction, builders learned that plastic tents over their buildings permitted construction work to continue during the sub-Arctic winter. These and many other direct benefits from the earthquake are summarized by George and Lyle and by Chance (in Hansen and others, 1966).

One of the more important social-political-economic developments was use by the federal government of a new device to channel and control reconstruction and rehabilitation aid: The Federal Reconstruction and Development Commission for Alaska represented both the

Extracted, with the author's permission, from "The Alaska Earthquake March 27, 1964: Lessons and Conclusions" by Edwin B. Eckel, *U. S. Geological Survey Professional Paper 546*, 57 p., 1970.

legislative and the executive arms of Government and included the heads of all federal agencies that had a part to play in the reconstruction effort. One of the Commission's offspring, the Scientific and Engineering Task Force, brought soils and structural engineers, geologists and seismologists together in an effort to apply their combined skills to guide decisions as to land use (Eckel and Schaem, in Hansen and others, 1966). The many opportunities that were provided by the reconstruction effort for team work and mutual understanding between engineers and earth scientists were themselves among the more valuable by-product benefits of the earthquake. In addition, scientists learned much that helps toward a better understanding of earthquake mechanisms and effects and how to investigate them. They also learned many new basic facts about the structural and historical geology and the hydrology of a large part of south-central Alaska. Some of these scientific benefits from the earthquake and its investigation are worthy of brief mention.

DIRECT GEOLOGIC BENEFITS

Truly beneficial direct geologic effects of the earthquake were few. Navigation conditions and harbor facilities were improved in a few places by tectonic uplift or subsidence, and tidewater and beach lands were improved or extended. For example, the subsidence that led to tidal flooding of Homer Spit also exposed new deposits of material to erosion, with the result that the spit began at once to heal itself and to build new storm berms (Stanley, in Waller, 1966; Stanley, 1968). Landslide hazards were averted, at least for some years to come, by uplift of Hinchinbrook Island; elsewhere imminent landslides and avalanches that might well have harmed people or property later were harmlessly triggered by the earthquake. Though the direct physical benefits of the earthquake were few, the earth sciences benefitted greatly from the intensive investigations of it. The knowledge thus gained added not only to the general fund of human knowledge; more importantly, it created an awareness of many potential hazards, previously unrecognized or ignored, both in Alaska and in other earthquake-prone areas, and of how to apply earth-science knowledge to reduce such hazards.

SCIENTIFIC BENEFITS

New and Corroborative Geologic and Hydrologic Information

One of the richest rewards of the earthquake study lay in the additions to geological and hydrologic knowledge and in corroborations of existing theory. The myriad observations essential to understanding the effects of the Alaska earthquake threw much new light on earthquake processes and earthquake effects in general. In addition, the investigations added greatly to our scientific knowledge of a large part of Alaska. Some of the knowledge so produced might never have come to light under ordinary circumstances. Other discoveries were advanced by many years under the earthquake-generated acceleration of basic investigations.

The earthquake investigations led to better understanding of the regional tectonics of south-central Alaska. The regional gravity field was better defined than it had been before, and it was reevaluated in terms of its relation to the underlying geology and to changes caused by the earthquake. Data, hitherto unavailable, were provided on the seismicity of the region. Knowledge of the structure and age of the rocks was greatly expanded. Thanks to the need to understand the vertical tectonic displacements caused by the earthquake, new knowledge was obtained on the history of submergence and emergence throughout Holocene time. Field evidence was augmented by many new radiocarbon datings. Reconnaissance marine geological and geophysical studies were undertaken over much of the Continental Shelf, slope, and contiguous deep-sea floor. These studies have materially increased our understanding of the submarine areas.

Detailed geologic maps became available for most of the affected cities and towns. Strip geologic maps along the ramifying rail and highway net provided a skeleton control of geologic knowledge of a wide area, particularly as to the distribution and nature of the unconsolidated deposits on which man does most of his building.

Accurate and abundant geodetic control, on stable ground, is essential for evaluating tectonic movements in the mobile belts of the world; the earthquake of 1964 gave impetus to establishment of such control. For a significant part of Alaska itself, better geodetic control resulted from the earthquake-caused need for accurate triangulation and leveling and for establishment of tidal bench marks and tide gages. These data will be invaluable in any studies of future tectonic dislocations of the land surface.

Support for the hypothesis that some great landslides and avalanches travel on cushions of compressed air came from the earthquake studies. Conversely, evidence was brought to light that tends to discount a widely held theory of glacial advance as a result of earthquakes (Tarr and Martin, 1912).

One kind of landslide that has received little attention in the past from geologists and engineers—the translatory slide that was so disastrous in Anchorage—is now well understood, although extrapolation of the knowledge gained to future earthquakes will still be extremely difficult. Extensive studies led to the beginning of an explosion of new knowledge on the behavior of sensitive clays and sands under dynamic conditions. A minor by-product of the Anchorage landslide studies was the discovery of microfossils that shed new light on the environmental conditions under which the Boot-legger Cove Clay was laid down, hitherto a puzzling point for geologists. Other by-products of these studies were (1) production of detailed topographic maps of highly complex landslide areas and (2) development of the "graben rule" (Hansen, 1965) by which the depth to the sliding plan of a translatory slide can be easily and rather accurately estimated.

Too little study was made of the response of shore processes to sudden changes in relative sea levels, but many bits of useful information were discovered nevertheless.

The shape, character, and stability of fiord deltas built to deep water is now better known than before as a result of intensive geologic, soils, hydrographic, and hydrologic studies both on land and under water. Such studies were essential to an understanding of the destructive subaqueous slides that had been almost unknown as important effects of great earthquakes.

Knowledge of the water resources of south-central Alaska was increased by earthquake-prompted studies of ground and surface waters; much new information also came to light as to the relations between earthquake-caused ground fissures and local water tables. The study of hydroseisms, or seiches and surges in surface-water bodies and wells, throughout the world produced greater understanding of the relation of hydrology to seismology.

Seismic sea waves, or tsunamis, have been studied intensively for many years because of the dangers they hold for coastal communities. The Alaska earthquake of 1964, however, presented an unparalleled opportunity to relate the source, generation, and propagation of a sea-wave train to measurable tectonic dislocations of the crust.

New and Improved Investigative Techniques

Virtually all investigative techniques known to earth scientists were applied in studies of the Alaska earthquake. Some, such as scuba diving, bathymetric surveys, and use of helicopters and fixed-wing aircraft were, of course, not new, but their widespread application to specific earthquake-connected problems was either new or little-used in the past. Many unorthodox photogrammetric, engineering, biological, and geodetic techniques and data were applied in the attempts to appraise preearthquake conditions in areas of poor horizontal and vertical control.

Some of these techniques, discussed briefly below, were new to Alaska or to individual investigators assigned there. A secondary result of the earthquake investigations of no mean significance, therefore, was the development of a large cadre of experienced and technologically well-equipped scientists who will be available for knowledgeable investigations of future great earthquakes.

Of utmost importance for the future is the fact that the knowledge gained from the Alaskan experience can be adapted by the scientific community to underline possible hazards in other earthquake-prone areas. Thus, it should be possible to relate ground conditions to urban planning, zoning regulations, and building codes in such a manner to forestall or minimize future earthquake disasters.

Uses of Recording Gages. The records from continuously recording gages served purposes not originally intended. A water-level gage at the power station on Kenai Lake, for example, enabled McCulloch (1966) to make a precise study of seiche action in a closed basin and to draw conclusions of far-reaching importance.

Again, fluctuations in the recording of an automatic outside-air temperature recorder at Whittier gave a rough measure of the duration of earthquake vibrations there (Kachadoorian, 1965). Stream gages on Kodiak Island, designed to measure the levels of flowing streams, suddenly became excellent recorders of wave runup and even served as tide gages when the mouths of streams on which they were installed were brought within the reach of tides by local and regional subsidence (Plafker and Kachadoorian, 1966; Waller, 1966b). By far the most significant extension of knowledge of the usefulness of recording gages came from the study of hydroseisms in wells and on surface waters on continent-wide or even larger bases. Investigations showed that, among other results, a network of recording water-level gages can act as a valuable adjunct to the worldwide seismograph network. It was also shown that any earthquake near a coast that is capable of causing as great fluctuations as that recorded by the Nunn-Bush well in Minnesota is also capable of generating a seismic sea wave (Vorhis, 1967; McGarr and Vorhis, 1968).

Television for Underground Observations. A novel application of television to the mapping of cracks in buried utilities—and incidentally of fractures of fault displacements in the surrounding soil—is described by Burton (in Logan, 1967). To avoid costly excavation of buried utility systems, a small-diameter borehole television camera was drawn through the ducts. Cracks were clearly visible and easily measured; their location and the amount and direction of offset of the ducts added materially to the general knowledge gained from other sources as to the character of ground movements in the Anchorage landslide areas.

Lakes as Tiltmeters. Kenai Lake was the only long lake that happened to have bench marks at both ends; hence McCulloch (1966) was able to use it as a unique giant tiltmeter. It gave a permanent record of landwarping caused by the earthquake. McCulloch's method of comparing the preearthquake height of the lake surface with preearthquake bench marks at the two ends of the lake necessarily left some ambiguity in the measurements because of difficulty in locating the preearthquake bench marks accurately, but it left no doubt whatever that the Kenai Lake basin was tilted westward about 3 feet. As a direct outgrowth of the earthquake investigations, and in order to monitor future crustal changes in south-central Alaska, a network of permanent bench marks has now been established on the shores of 17 large lakes within a 500-mile radius of Anchorage. These bench marks were referenced to the water levels of the lakes so that the direction and amount of any tilting can be obtained from periodic monitoring (Hansen and Eckel, 1966). A systematic study of these lake levels was started by D. S. McCulloch and Arthur Grantz in the summer of 1966 (written commun., 1968).

Measurement of Land-Level Changes. Measurement of the displacement of intertidal sessile marine organisms emerged as one of the most useful techniques for determining vertical tectonic movements along coasts. The technique had been used elsewhere, by Tarr and Martin (1912), for example, who studied the effects of the Yakutat Bay earthquake of 1899. With the aid of Dr. G. Dallas Hanna, a marine biologist of the California Academy of Sciences, however, the method was greatly refined and was applied by Plafker and his associates after the Alaska earthquake of March 27, 1964, to a far larger area than ever before (Plafker, 1969).

The deeply indented rocky coast of the area affected by the 1964 earthquake was ideal for application of the method. The common acorn barnacle (*Balanus balanoides* (Linnaeus), which is widely distributed and forms a prominent band with a sharply defined upper limit relative to tide level, was used in hundreds of "barnacle-line" measurements; in its absence the common olive-green rockweed (*Fucus distichus*) was almost equally useful. The normal preearthquake upper growth limit of barnacles and rockweed relative to mean lower low water was determined empirically for the range of tidal conditions in the area at 17 localities where the amount of vertical displacement was known from pre- and post-earthquake tide-gage readings. Departures of the post-earthquake barnacle line from its normal altitude above mean lower low water was taken as the amount of vertical displacement at any given place along the shore. By this method, absolute land-level changes could generally be measured to an accuracy within 1 foot; even under unfavorable circumstances, the error is probably less than 2 feet.

Other methods of determining land-level changes along the coasts and elsewhere were also employed. Changes in gravity, as determined before and after the earthquake with the same instrument, were used by Barnes (1966) in computing elevation changes. In subsided areas, it was noted that wells became brackish, vegetation was killed by invasion of salt water, beach berms and stream deltas were shifted landward and built up to higher levels, and roads or other installations along the shores were inundated by the tides. In tectonically uplifted areas, indications of uplift include new reefs and islands, raised sea cliffs, and surf-cut platforms. Wherever feasible, the method used was the most accurate known—comparison of pre- and post-earthquake tide-gage readings at accurately placed tidal bench marks of the U.S. Coast and Geodetic Survey. Even where gages were destroyed, some bench marks were recoverable and new series of readings could be made to determine land-level changes. Unfortunately, there were only a few permanent automatic recording gages in south-central Alaska, and also many tidal bench marks were on unconsolidated deposits where ties to bedrock were difficult or impossible to reestablish.

Distinction Between Local and Regional Subsidence. Clear distinctions between local subsidence caused by compaction of sediments and more widespread subsidence caused by tectonic downdrop of the region are not always easy to make. One technique used by Plafker and Kachadoorian (1966) on Kodiak and the nearby islands was to note the difference in amount of inundation of unconsolidated shoreline features as compared with nearby rock outcrops. The lowering of the rock cliffs, as measured by barnacle lines or other means, represents tectonic subsidence, whereas the lowering of beaches and delta surfaces represents a combination of tectonic subsidence and local compaction. By using a similar technique—measuring differences in the heights of piles whose tops were originally level—Plafker and Kachadoorian were able to distinguish between local compaction-subsidence of beach deposits and tectonic downdrop.

Casings of deep wells may also be helpful in distinguishing local and regional subsidence. Near the end of Homer Spit, for example, the top of a well casing that had previously been a known height above the ground stood several feet higher after the earthquake. Such protrusion could only have been caused by compaction and subsidence of the unconsolidated materials around the casing, for regional subsidence would have carried the casing down along with the land surface (Grantz and others, 1964, Fig. 6).

Evidence of Wave Action and Runup. As part of their studies of wave-damaged shorelines, various investigators made extensive use of natural materials that indicated the relative intensity and movement direction of waves (McCulloch, 1966; Plafker and others, 1969; Plafker and Kachadoorian, 1966). Runup heights were determined from strandlines of wave-deposited debris, abraded bark or broken branches in vegetation along the shore, and water stains on snow or structures. Movement directions of the waves could be inferred from the gross distribution of damage along shores, the directions in which limbs and trunks of trees and brush were scarred, bent, and broken off, and the directions in which objects such as buoys, structures, and shoreline deposits were displaced. To aid in comparative studies of wave-damaged shorelines along the coast, Plafker and Mayo devised a scale of relative magnitude of wave damage (Plafker and others, 1969)—a scale which was also used by McCulloch and Mayo (McCulloch, 1966) in modified form for plotting wave damage along the shore of Kenai Lake. The magnitude scale evolved is summarized below in order of increasing damage.

Wave-magnitude scale
[After Plafker and others, 1969, pl. 2]
1. Brush combed and scoured in direction of wave travel. Small limbs broken and minor scarring of trees. Runup heights only a few feet above extreme high-water level. Some wooden structures floated from foundations.
2. Trees and limbs less than 2 inches in diameter broken. Small trees uprooted. Driftwood and finer beach deposits thrown up above extreme high-water level. Piling swept from beneath some structures and wooden structures floated off their foundations. Runup reached about 25 feet on steep shores.
3. Trees and limbs as much as 8 inches in diameter broken; some large trees overturned. Rocks to cobble size eroded from intertidal zones and deposited above extreme high-water level. Soil stripped from bedrock areas. All inundated structures except those of reinforced concrete destroyed or floated away. Heavy machinery moved about. Maximum runup height 55 feet.
4. Trees larger than 8 inches in diameter broken, uprooted, and overturned. Boulders thrown above extreme high-water line. Loose rocks on cliffs moved. All structures and equipment damaged or destroyed in inundated areas. Maximum runup height 70 feet.
5. Extensive areas of total destruction of vegetation. Boulders deposited 50 feet or more above normal extreme high-water level. Maximum runup height 170 feet.

Using a wave-magnitude numbering system modified from an early version of Plafker and Mayo, to allow for the additional damage caused by ice, McCulloch (1966) mapped the distribution of intensity and maximum runup of waves on the shores of Kenai Lake. The highest runup measured there was 72 feet, where a wave struck a steep bank. By measuring the upper limit of wave damage to trees in the direction of wave travel, McCulloch also was able to show the history of the wave crests that overran several deltas.

REFERENCES

Barnes, D. F., 1966, Gravity changes during the Alaska earthquake: Jour. Geophys. Research, v. 71, no. 2, p. 451-456.

Grantz, Arthur, Plafker, George, and Kachadoorian, Reuben, 1964, Alaska's Good Friday earthquake, March 27, 1964—a preliminary geologic evaluation: U.S. Geol. Survey Circ. 491, 35 p.

Hansen, W. R., 1965, Effects of the earthquake of March 27, 1964, at Anchorage, Alaska: U.S. Geol. Survey Prof. Paper 542-A, p. A1-A68.

Hansen, W. R., and Eckel, E. B., 1966, A summary description of the Alaska earthquake—its setting and effects, *in* Hansen, W. R., and others, The Alaska earthquake March 27, 1964—Field investigations and reconstruction effort: U.S. Geol. Survey Prof. Paper 541, p. 1-37.

Hansen, W. R., and others, 1966, The Alaska earthquake March 27, 1964—Field investigations and reconstruction effort: U.S. Geol. Survey Prof. Paper 541, 111 p.

Kachadoorian, Reuben, 1965, Effects of the earthquake of March 27, 1964, at Whittier, Alaska: U.S. Geol. Survey Prof. Paper 542-B, p. B1-B21.

Logan, M. H., 1967, Effect of the earthquake of March 27, 1964, on the Eklutna Hydroelectric Project, Anchorage, Alaska, *with a section on* Television examination of earthquake damage to underground communication and electrical systems in Anchorage, by Lynn R. Burton: U.S. Geol. Survey Prof. Paper 545-A, p. A1-A30.

McCulloch, D. S., 1966, Slide-induced waves, seiching, and ground fracturing caused by the earthquake of March 27, 1964, at Kenai Lake Alaska: U.S. Geol. Survey Prof. Paper 543-A, p. A1-A41.

McGarr, Arthur, and Vorhis, R. C., 1968, Seismic seiches from the March 1964 Alaska earthquake: U.S. Geol. Survey Prof. Paper 544-E, p. E1-E43.

Plafker, George, 1969, Tectronics of the March 27, 1964, Alaska earthquake U.S. Geol. Survey Prof. Paper 543-I, p. I1-I74.

Plafker, rge, and Kachadoorian, Reuben, 1966, Geologic effects of the March 1964 earthquake and associated seismic sea waves on Kodiak and nearby islands, Alaska: U.S. Geol. Survey Prof. Paper 543-D, p. D1-D46.

Plafker, George, Kachadoorian, Reuben, Eckel, E. B., and Mayo, L. P., 1969, Effects of the earthquake of March 27, 1964, at various communities: U.S. Geol. Survey Prof. Paper 542-G, p. G1-G50.

Stanley, K. W., 1968, Effects of the Alaska earthquake of March 27, 1964 on shore processes and beach morphology: U.S. Geol. Survey Prof. Paper 543-J, p. J1-J21.

Tarr, R. S., and Martin, Lawrence, 1912, The earthquakes at Yakutat Bay, Alaska, in September, 1899: U.S. Geol. Survey Prof. Paper 69, p. 135.

Vorhis, R. C., 1967, Hydrologic effects of the earthquake of March 27, 1964, outside Alaska, *with sections on* Hydroseismograms from the Nunn-Bush Shoe Co. well, Wisconsin, by E. E. Rexin and R. C. Vorhis, *and* Alaska earthquake effects on ground water in Iowa, by R. W. Coble: U.S. Geol. Survey Prof. Paper 544-C, p. C1-C54.

Waller, R. M., 1966a, Effects of the earthquake of March 27, 1964, in the Homer area, Alaska *with a section on* Beach changes on Homer Spit, by K. W. Stanley: U.S. Geol. Survey Prof. Paper 542-D, p. D1-D28.

_____ , 1966b, Effects of the earthquake of March 27, 1964, on the hydrology of south-central Alaska: U.S. Geol. Survey Prof. Paper 544-A, p. A1-A28.

9. EARTHQUAKE PREDICTION AND CONTROL MAY BE POSSIBLE

U. S. GEOLOGICAL SURVEY

There is increasing optimism about the possibilities of developing a capability for short-range earthquake prediction and methods for earthquake control, according to scientists of the U.S. Geological Survey, Department of the Interior.

In the December 19, 1969, issue of *Science,* L. C. Pakiser, J. P. Eaton, J. H. Healy, and C. B. Raleigh, scientists affiliated with the U.S. Geological Survey's National Center for Earthquake Research (NCER), Menlo Park, California, say that "it seems reasonable to hope that short-range prediction of earthquakes (on the order of hours or days) may be achieved through continuous monitoring of ground tilt, strain, seismic activity, and possibly fluctuations in the earth's magnetic field."

On the subject of earthquake control, the scientists note that "it has been demonstrated that earthquakes can be artificially triggered by fluid injection, impounding of reservoirs, and explosions of nuclear devices underground, and also that many earthquakes in California and Nevada occur at depths accessible to the drill. From these observations we can soberly conclude that it may be possible to develop a practical method for artificially dislodging 'locked' sections of a major fault, and to induce steady creep or periodic release of accumulating elastic strain energy along the fault to inhibit the natural accumulation of sufficient energy to produce a disastrous earthquake."

The NCER scientists emphasized, however, that "it is clear that our current knowledge of the processes involved in the generation of earthquakes is insufficient to guide an engineering program for earthquake control." They suggest that "an intensified program of field, laboratory, and theoretical studies aimed at improving our understanding of earthquakes will not only advance the prospects for earthquake prediction, but also provide an adequate basis for planning and implementing earthquake control."

From U. S. Department of the Interior "news release" of December 19, 1969.

The scientists say that "the great Alaska earthquake of March 27, 1964, awakened public officials to the need for intensified research on earthquakes, their effects on man and his works, and possible means of reducing their hazards." Although the loss of life in Alaska and property damage were small for such a great earthquake, the realization that an earthquake of similar magnitude could occur in densely populated California, where loss of life would almost certainly be in the thousands, and property damage in the billions of dollars, dramatized the urgent need for remedial action.

Research programs fall far short of providing the information needed for safe development of coastal California and other earthquake-prone areas of the United States. The USGS authorities stress that "the magnitude of the problem can be seen by recalling that the Urban Land Institute has estimated that the population of California will increase from one-tenth to one-seventh of the national total by the year 2,000, or about 40 million in the national population of 300 million."

The USGS scientists said that a number of significant advances in basic research and instrumentation permits a growing optimism about earthquake prediction and the possibility that earthquake hazards can be reduced by the controlled release of stored strain energy in active fault zones. They emphasize, however, that such optimism must be coupled with the awareness of the need for intensified research efforts, and an understanding of the costs of such efforts. They discuss a number of significant events that have an important bearing on hopes for earthquake prediction and modification, including:

1. Revolutionary new concepts that provide a global tectonic framework in which can be envisioned, for the first time, the kinematic processes that operate to generate earthquakes at depths ranging from the shallow crust to depths of 700 kilometers;
2. Enormous advances in geophysical instrumentation, geophysical application of high-speed digital computers, and seismology that

could be adapted directly to earthquake problems;

3. Greatly intensified geologic, geophysical and geodetic research on the San Andreas fault system in California by federal and state government agencies and universities. Locations and the nature of movements on various active segments of the fault system have been accurately determined in some places, and the locations and mechanisms of microearthquakes in relation to fault structures have been determined with unprecedented precision;

4. The evidence that links earthquakes with man's activities such as the construction of dams, the injection of fluids into the rocks of the earth's crust, and the explosions of nuclear devices underground. These discoveries suggest the possibility of using fluid injection and perhaps explosions beneficially to control the release of stored tectonic stress and reduce earthquake hazards.

"Several developments of the 1960s lead us to conclude that the prospects for success during the next 10 years in the quest for earthquake prediction are good," Pakiser, Eaton, Healy and Raleigh write, and that "experiments in the controlled release of accumulated strain energy in fault zones or, conversely, in strengthening fault zones, should be conducted in the near future."

Floods

10. HYDROLOGY FOR URBAN LAND PLANNING
LUNA B. LEOPOLD

This circular attempts to summarize existing knowledge of the effects of urbanization on hydrologic factors. It also attempts to express this knowledge in terms that the planner can use to test alternatives during the planning process.

Of particular concern to the planner are those alternatives that affect the hydrologic functioning of the basins. To be interpreted hydrologically, the details of the land-use pattern must be expressed in terms of hydrologic parameters which are affected by land use. These parameters in turn become hydrologic variables by which the effects of alternative planning patterns can be evaluated in hydrologic terms.

There are four interrelated but separable effects of land-use changes on the hydrology of an area: changes in peak flow characteristics, changes in total runoff, changes in quality of water, and changes in the hydrologic amenities. The hydrologic amenities are what might be called the appearance or the impression which the river, its channel and its valleys, leaves with the observer. Of all land-use changes affecting the hydrology of an area, urbanization is by far the most forceful.

Runoff, which spans the entire regimen of flow, can be measured by number and by characteristics of rise in streamflow. The many rises in flow, along with concomitant sediment loads, control the stability of the stream channel. The two principal factors governing flow regimen are the percentage of area made impervious and the rate at which water is transmitted across the land to stream channels. The former is governed by the type of land use; the latter is governed by the density, size, and characteristics of tributary channels and thus by the provision of storm sewerage. Stream channels form in response to the regimen of flow of the stream. Changes in the regimen of flow, whether through land use or other changes, cause adjustments in the stream channels to accommodate the flows.

Extracted from "Hydrology for Urban Land Planning— A Guidebook on the Hydrologic Effects of Urban Land Use" by Luna B. Leopold, *U. S. Geological Survey Circular 554*, 18 p., 1968.

The volume of runoff is governed primarily by infiltration characteristics and is related to land slope and soil type as well as to the type of vegetative cover. It is thus directly related to the percentage of the area covered by roofs, streets, and other impervious surfaces at times of hydrograph rise during storms.

A summary of some data on the percentage of land rendered impervious by different degrees of urbanization is presented by Lull and Sopper (1966). Antoine (1964) presents the following data on the percentage of impervious surface area in residential properties:

Lot size of residential area (sq. ft.)	Impervious surface area (percent)
6,000	80
6,000–15,000	40
15,000	25

The percentage decreases markedly as size of lot increases. Felton and Lull (1963) estimate in the Philadelphia area that 32 percent of the surface area is impervious on lots averaging 0.2 acre in size, whereas only 8 percent of the surface area is impervious on lots averaging 1.8 acres.

As volume of runoff from a storm increases, the size of flood peak also increases. Runoff volume also affects low flows because in any series of storms the larger the percentage of direct runoff, the smaller the amount of water available for soil moisture replenishment and for ground-water storage. An increase in total runoff from a given series of storms as a result of imperviousness results in decreased ground-water recharge and decreased low flows. Thus, increased imperviousness has the effect of increasing flood peaks during storm periods and decreasing low flows between storms.

The principal effect of land use on sediment comes from the exposure of the soil to storm runoff. This occurs mainly when bare ground is exposed during construction. It is well known that sediment production is sensitive to land slope. Sediment yield from urban areas tends to be larger than in unurbanized areas even if there are only small and widely scattered units of unprotected soil in the urban area. In aggregate, these scattered bare areas are sufficient to yield considerable sediment.

A major effect of urbanization is the introduction of effluent from sewage disposal plants, and often the introduction of raw sewage, into channels. Raw sewage obviously degrades water quality, but even treated effluent contains dissolved minerals not extracted by sewage treatment. These minerals act as nutrients and promote algae and plankton growth in a stream. This growth in turn alters the balance in the stream biota.

Land use in all forms affects water quality. Agricultural use results in an increase of nutrients in stream water both from the excretion products of farm animals and from commercial fertilizers. A change from agricultural use to residential use, as in urbanization, tends to reduce these types of nutrients, but this tendency is counteracted by the widely scattered pollutants of the city, such as oil and gasoline products, which are carried through the storm sewers to the streams. The net result is generally an adverse effect on water quality. This effect can be measured by the balance and variety of organic life in the stream, by the quantities of dissolved material, and by the bacterial level. Unfortunately data describing quality factors in streams from urban versus unurbanized areas are particularly lacking.

Finally, the amenity value of the hydrologic environment is especially affected by three factors. The first factor is the stability of the stream channel itself. A channel, which is gradually enlarged owing to increased floods caused by urbanization, tends to have unstable and unvegetated banks, scoured or muddy channel beds, and unusual debris accumulations. These all tend to decrease the amenity value of a stream.

The second factor is the accumulation of artifacts of civilization in the channel and on the flood plain: beer cans, oil drums, bits of lumber, concrete, wire—the whole gamut of rubbish of an urban area. Though this may not importantly affect the hydrologic function of the channel, it becomes a detriment of what is here called the hydrologic amenity.

The third factor is the change brought on by the disruption of balance in the stream biota. The addition of nutrients promotes the growth

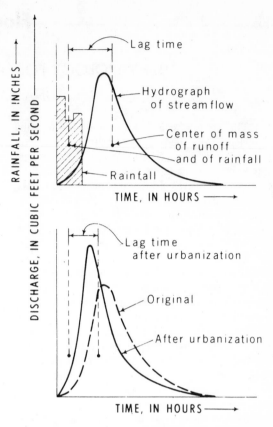

Figure 1. Hypothetical unit hydrographs relating runoff to rainfall, with definitions of significant parameters.

of plankton and algae. A clear stream, then, may change to one in which rocks are covered with slime; turbidity usually increases, and odors may develop. As a result of increased turbidity and reduced oxygen content desirable game fish give way to less desirable species. Although lack of quantitative objective data on the balance of stream biota is often a handicap to any meaningful and complete evaluation of the effects of urbanization, qualitative observations tend to confirm these conclusions.

AVAILABILITY OF DATA AND THE TECHNIQUE OF ANALYSIS

Basic hydrologic data on both peak flow and volume of runoff may be expressed in terms of the characteristics of the unit hydrograph, that is, the average time distribution graph of flow from a unit or standard storm. The unit hydrograph shows the percentage of the total storm runoff occurring in each successive unit of time.

The standard storm may be, for example, a typical storm which produced 1 inch of runoff (Fig. 1). Such data are derived from the study of individual storms and the associated runoff graphs measured at gaging stations.

One factor stating the relation between the storm and the runoff is lag time. This is defined as the time interval between the center of mass of the storm precipitation and the center of mass of the resultant hydrograph. Lag time is a function of two basin parameters—the mean basin slope and the basin length. These factors empirically correlate with lag time if expressed in the form of the basin ratio (basin length L divided by the square root of the mean basin gradient, s). This basin ratio is also related to drainage area. As drainage area increases, the basin length increases and the average value of slope generally decreases. Thus, natural basin characteristics can be translated into flood-flow characteristics.

Lag time may be materially altered by the effects of urbanization on the basin surface. Water runs off faster from streets and roofs than from natural vegetated areas. This tends to decrease the lag time. The construction of artificial channels, especially storm sewers, also decreases lag time. As the time required for a given amount of water to run off shortens, the peak rate of runoff (flood peak) increases.

In addition to the basin ratio and lag time, the regimen of a stream, however, can be described in many other ways, including flood frequency, flow duration, mean annual flood, discharge at bankfull stage, and frequency of bankfull stage. This is evidenced in past studies of the effect of urbanization on the hydrology of an area. Many different techniques of relating rainfall to runoff have been used, along with various parameters to measure the degree of urbanization. In order to evaluate our present knowledge, it is necessary to express the results of these studies in some common denominator.

Table 1 is an interpretation and summary of the effects of urbanization on peak discharges based on previous studies. Results of the studies were interpreted and extrapolated to a common denominator of 1 sq mi (square mile), a practical unit of size for planning.

As an indication of the change in impervious area resulting from urbanization, Harris and Rantz (1964) showed that an area near Palto Alto, Calif., changed from 5.7 percent to 19.1 percent impervious in a 10-year period.

TABLE 1. INCREASE IN DISCHARGE AS A RESULT OF URBANIZATION IN A 1-SQUARE-MILE AREA

[Discharge is mean annual flood; recurrence interval is 2.3 years. Data are expressed as ratio of discharge after urbanization to discharge under previous conditions. Data from James (1965) have no superscript]

Percentage of area served by storm sewerage	Percentage of area made impervious			
	0	20	50	80
0	1.0	[1]1.2	[1]1.8	[1]2.2
		[2]1.3	[2]1.7	[2]2.2
		1.3	1.6	2.0
20	1.1	[3]1.9	1.8	2.2
		1.4	—	—
50	1.3	[4]2.1	[1]3.2	[1]4.7
		[1]2.8	2.0	2.5
		[5]3.7	—	—
		[6]2.0	2.5	[3]4.2
		1.6	—	—
80	1.6	1.9	—	3.2
100	1.7	[1]3.6	[1]4.7	[4]5.6
		2.0	2.8	[1]6.0
		—	—	3.6

[1]Anderson (1968).
[2]Martens (1966).
[3]Wilson (1966).
[4]Carter (1961).
[5]Wiitala (1961).
[6]Espey, Morgan, and Masch (1966).

Data from Table 1 have been transposed into the graph shown in Figure 2. The ratios of peak discharge of urbanized to rural areas are presented for different percentages of sewerage and impervious area; lines of equal values of the ratio are drawn through the data. Briefly, these data show that for unsewered areas the differences between 0 and 100 percent impervious will increase peak discharge on the average 2.5 times. For areas that are 100 percent sewered, peak discharge for 0 percent impervious will be about 1.7 times the mean annual flood and the ratio increases to about eight for 100 percent impervious areas. Figure 2, then, reduces the basic data to the same units applicable to a 1-sq-mi drainage basin and to the mean annual flood.

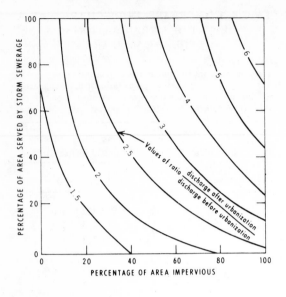

Figure 2. Effect of urbanization on mean annual flood for a 1-square-mile drainage area. (Based on data from table 1.)

A basin produces big flows from large and intense storms and smaller flows from less intense but more frequent storms. The great or catastrophic event is rare, and the storm of ordinary magnitude is frequent. These events can be arranged in order of magnitude and counted. For example, all discharge events exceeding 400 cfs (cubic feet per second) can be tabulated from the record at a stream-gaging station and arranged in order of magnitude; the values in the array can be plotted as a discharge-frequency curve. This has been done for the gaging station on West Branch Brandywine Creek at Coatesville, Pa., for 9 years of record (Fig. 3). The theory and practice of constructing such flow-frequency curves is well known. The plotting position or frequency often used is defined as

$$R = \frac{n+1}{m}$$

where R is the recurrence interval in years, n is number of years of record, and m is the rank of the individual event in the array.

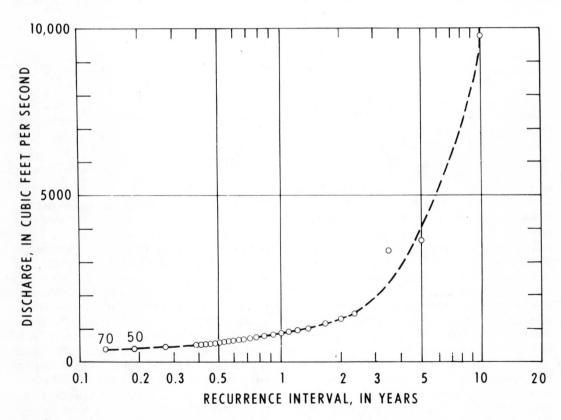

Figure 3. Flood-frequency curve for partial-duration series, West Branch Brandywine Creek at Coatesville, Pa., based on data for 1942, 1944-51.

Note in Figure 3 that the largest flow in the 9-year record was nearly 10,000 cfs. The number 50 printed on the graph means that there were 50 flows equal to or exceeding 500 cfs. Once a year, on the average, a discharge value of about 900 cfs will be equalled or exceeded.

A slightly different result would be obtained if, instead of using the peak flow for each storm, only the largest flow in each year were included in the array. The principle involved is similar. The arithmetic mean of the peak flows for the nine annual events is the "average annual flood." The statistics of this array are such that the recurrence interval of this average annual flood is the same regardless of the length of record, which specifically is 2.3 years. That is to say, a flood of that magnitude can be expected to be equalled or exceeded on an average of once in 2.3 years, or 10 times in 23 years.

Studies of river channels have shown that rivers construct and maintain channels which will carry without overflow a discharge somewhat smaller than the average annual flood. In fact the recurrence interval of the bankfull stage in most rivers is a flow having a recurrence interval of about 1.5 to 2 years.

Urbanization tends to increase the flood potential from a given basin. The channel then will receive flows which exceed its capacity not just once in 1.5 to 2 years on the average but more often. It is now proposed to estimate how much more often and to indicate the effect of this increased frequency on the channel itself.

EFFECT OF URBANIZATION ON INCREASING FREQUENCY OF OVERBANK FLOW

Taking the East Branch of Brandywine Creek as an example, the flow-frequency curve can be constructed for a typical subbasin having a 1-sq-mi drainage area. Figure 4A shows the relation of average annual flood to drainage area, and Figure 4B shows the flood-frequency curve for annual peaks for basins in the Brandywine area. The diagrams shown in Figure 4 are similar to those published in the nationwide series of flood reports, U.S. Geological Survey Water-Supply Papers 1671-1689.

From these curves a discharge-frequency relationship is developed for a drainage area of 1 sq mi. The average annual flood is read from the upper graph of Figure 4 as 75 cfs, and the lower graph is used to construct the frequency curve in

Figure 5 pertaining to a 1-sq-mi basin marked "unurbanized."

The arithmetic for the construction of the curve is as follows:

Recurrence interval of annual flood[1] (years)	Ratio to mean annual flood[2]	Discharge[3] (cfs)	Recurrence interval duration series[4] (years)
1.1	0.55	41	0.4
1.5	.75	56	.92
2.0	.90	68	1.45
2.3	1.0	75	1.78
5	1.45	110	4.5
10	1.9	145	9.5

[1]Only the highest flood each year.
[2]From figure 4B.
[3]Obtained by multiplying ratios by 75 cfs from figure 4A for a drainage area of 1 sq mi.
[4]All peaks during the year. The values in this column are mathematically related to those in the first.

The graph marked "unurbanized" in Figure 5 is constructed on semilogarithmic paper from the data listed in the third and fourth columns of the preceding table. The ordinate is the discharge, and the lower abscissa is the recurrence interval in the duration series. An auxiliary scale gives the average number of floods in a 10-year period (calculated as 10 years divided by the recurrence interval). Thus, the flow expected to occur once in 10 years would be about 145 cfs and the fifth largest would be 75 cfs. The latter would also be the average value of the largest flows each year during the 10-year record and thus would be the "average annual flood." It would plot, therefore, at an abscissa position approximately at 2.3-year recurrence interval. . .

The average annual flood of 75 cfs was then multiplied by the ratios in Figure 2 and plotted as shown in Figure 5 at the 2.3-year interval. These values form the basis of a series of frequency curves for combinations of sewered area and impervious area. The shapes of the curves are guided by the principle that the most infrequent floods occur under conditions that are not appreciably affected by imperviousness of the basin.

The most frequent flows are therefore increased by smaller ratios than would be the

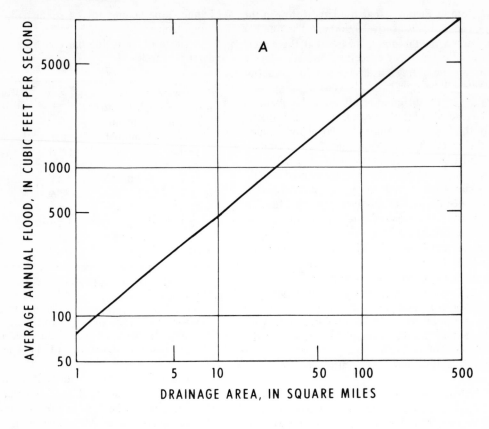

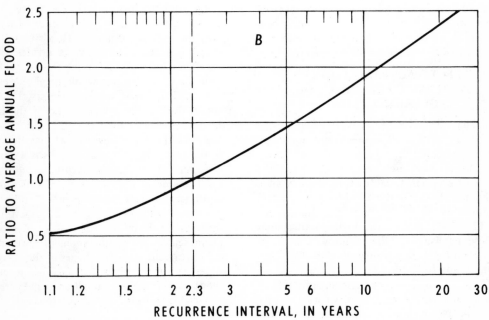

Figure 4. Regional flood-frequency data for the Brandywine Creek basin, Pennsylvania. *A*, Relation of average annual flood to drainage area. *B*, Flood-frequency curve for annual peaks.

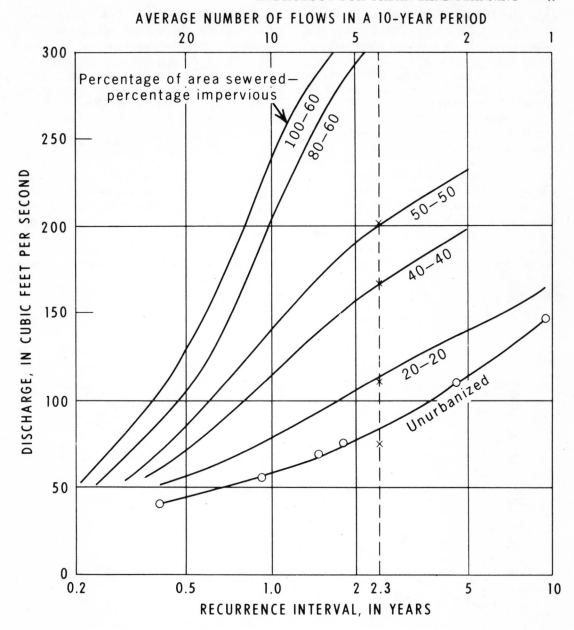

Figure 5. Flood-frequency curves for a 1-square-mile basin in various states of urbanization. (Derived from figures 2 and 4.)

average annual flood. Also, the most frequent flows are decreased in number because low flows from an urbanized area are not sustained by ground water as in a natural basin. The curves representing urbanized conditions therefore converge at low flow values.

Obviously the frequency curves in Figure 5 are extrapolations based on minimal data and require corroboration or revision as additional field data become available.

The flood-frequency curve under original (unurbanized) condition passes through a value of 67 cfs at a recurrence interval of 1.5 years. At bankfull condition natural channels generally can carry the flow having that recurrence interval. If one assumes that this flow approximates the capacity of the natural channels, the intersection of the estimated curves for different degrees of urbanization with the discharge value of 67 cfs can be used to estimate the increase in number of flows equal to or exceeding natural channel capacity. An auxiliary scale is shown at the top of Figure 5 to facilitate this.

For example, under natural conditions it is expected that a 10-year record would show about seven flows equal to or exceeding 67 cfs, or channel capacity. But if the average annual flood were increased 1.5 times (from 75 to 112 cfs) corresponding to 20 percent sewered and 20 percent impervious, the new frequency curve indicates that 14 flows of 67 cfs or greater would occur in a 10-year period, or a twofold increase in number of flows. Similarly, the ratio of number of flows exceeding bankfull capacity was

read from the intersection of the other curves in Figure 5 with the ordinate value of 67 cfs to obtain the ratios plotted in Figure 6.

Figure 6 shows that with an area 50 percent sewered and 50 percent impervious, for example, the number of flows equal to or exceeding bankfull channel capacity would, over a period of years, be increased nearly fourfold.

SEDIMENT PRODUCTION

The basic data available for analyzing the effect of urbanization on sediment yield, though sparse, have been summarized to some extent in the literature. Especially valuable is the report by Wolman (1964) who summarized not only the data obtained from sediment sampling stations in streams in Eastern United States but also studied the sediment yield from building construction

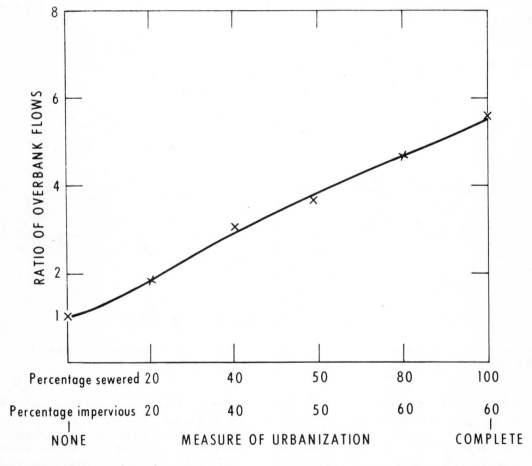

Figure 6. Increase in number of flows per year equal to or exceeding original channel capacity (1-square-mile drainage area), as ratio to number of overbank flows before urbanization, for different degrees of urbanization. (Derived from figure 5.)

activities. Sediment yields from urbanized or developing areas ranged from 1000 to more than 100,000 tons per square mile per year.

It should be recognized that sediment yield per square mile decreases with increasing drainage area, but nevertheless it is apparent that unurbanized drainage basins yield 200 to 500 tons per square mile per year, on the average. These figures are slightly higher for the farmed Piedmont lands, which may be expected to produce sediment yield of 500 tons per square mile per year, such as the Watts Branch basin near Rockville, Md.

The data on urbanized areas studied by Wolman are plotted in Figure 7 together with data from suspended load sampling stations of the U.S. Geological Survey as summarized by Wark and Keller (1963).

In the graph (Fig. 7) three bands or zones are labeled *A, C,* and *UC.* Wolman and Schick (1967) differentiated the following types of

activity: *A,* agricultural or natural; *C,* undergoing building construction, but highly diluted before reaching channels; and *UC,* undiluted sediment yields delivered to stream channels from construction sites.

They found that when building sites are denuded for construction, excavations are made, and dirt is piled without cover or protection near the site, the sediment movement in a rill or stream channel is very large in terms of tons per year immediately downhill from the construction site. If the channel contains little water except during storms (an ephemeral stream), there is no chance for dilution; during storm flow the sediment movement is great. If the construction debris gets into perennial channels, or for other reasons is distributed along a channel or dispersed over a wide area, the dilution lowers the yield per square mile per year. Thus, Wolman and Schick drew the distinction between agricultural, construction, and construction-undiluted.

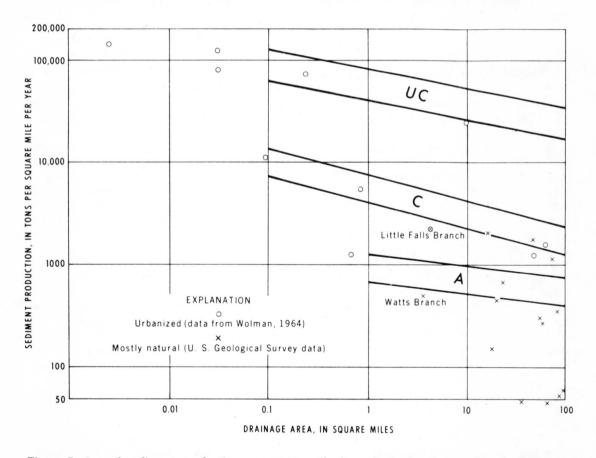

Figure 7. Annual sediment production per square mile for urbanized and natural areas. Zones: *A.* agricultural; *C,* under construction; *UC,* under construction and undiluted.

For very small areas, Wolman (1964) said, "Because construction denudes the natural cover and exposes the soil beneath, the tonnage of sediment derived by erosion from an acre of ground under construction in developments and highways may exceed 20,000 to 40,000 times the amount eroded from farms and woodlands in an equivalent period of time."

Figure 7 shows the data as a relation between annual sediment yield per square mile and drainage basin size. The usual suspended load station is on a basin of more than 10 sq mi in area. Seldom is urbanization complete for basins of this size.

The data measured or estimated by Wolman (1964) in small urbanizing, developed or industrial areas show clearly that the sediment yield is larger by 10 to 100 times that of rural areas. Guy and Ferguson (1962) observed an increase of 250 times in an area near Kensington, Md.

Most sediment carried by a stream is moved by high flows. In Brandywine Creek, for example, about 54 percent of the total sediment transported annually by the river (drainage area 312 sq mi) is carried by flows that occur, on the average, about 3 days each year.

Sediment production is importantly related to land slope. Using multiple correlation techniques for a large variety of data from experimental watersheds, Musgrave (1947) developed a multiple correlation in which the rate of erosion is found to be proportional to the 1.35 power of land slope and to the 0.35 power of the slope length. The same conclusion had been derived theoretically by Horton (1945) and verified by comparison with the percentage of area eroded in the Boise River basin, Idaho. Sediment yield, therefore, is more highly sensitive to land slope than to length of slope but is postively correlated with both.

Some idea, however, can be obtained of the difficulty in keeping steep slopes stable after the original vegetation has been disturbed, particularly during construction. If, for example, land slopes of 5 and 10 percent are compared, the doubling of the slope would increase the erosion rate by 2.3 times.

Increased slope length does not have such a large effect on erosion rate. Doubling slope length would increase the erosion rate by only 22 percent.

Because a slope of 10 percent drops 10 feet in a 100-foot horizontal, temporary storage in the form of depressions which might hold silt would be nearly absent. For land slopes above 10 percent, stream channels also would tend to be nearly devoid of areas or depressions which could hold up sediment during its passage downhill. From a practical standpoint, therefore, a figure of about 10 percent probably would be a physical and economic limit beyond which construction would be especially harmful insofar as sediment production is concerned. Any such limiting slope, however, would have to be determined by detailed economic studies.

Wark and Keller (1963) related the average annual sediment discharge in the Potomac River basin to percentage of forest cover and, separately, to the percentage of land in crops. Average annual sediment yield increased from 50 to 400 tons per square mile per year, or eightfold, as forest cover in the basin declined from 80 percent to 20 percent. Sediment yield increased from 70 to 300 tons per square mile per year, or fourfold, as land in crops increased from 10 to 50 percent.

EFFECT OF INCREASED PEAK FLOWS ON SEDIMENT YIELD

It has been pointed out in the comparison of sediment rating curves for urban versus rural areas that the rating curves do not appear to be as much different as the values of sediment yield on an annual yield basis. It has been mentioned that a slight increase of sediment concentration can make a large difference in total annual sediment yield owing to the fact that urban areas produce a larger number of high flows. If the number of flows above bankfull stage is increased by urbanization, the banks and bed of a channel in erodible material will not remain stable, but the channel will enlarge through erosion. Computation indicates the seriousness of this factor.

For example, assume that a channel is capable of carrying 55 cfs at bankfull stage. In the Brandywine area this represents a channel draining a basin slightly less than 1 sq mi in area. The channel necessary to carry 55 cfs at bankfull stage would probably have a velocity of slightly less than 2.5 feet per second and would be about 2 feet deep and 11 feet wide. In Figure 2, urbanization might cause a flow of this frequency to increase 2.7 times, or 150 cfs. If this channel had to adjust itself to carry a flood of 150 cfs at bankfull stage, it is estimated that the new velocity would be about 2.5 feet per second, and the necessary depth and width would have changed respectively to about 3 feet and 20 feet. In other words, this stream would deepen about 50 percent and increase in width a little less than twice its original size. If such erosion takes place through at least one-fourth mile of channel length in a drainage basin of 1 sq mi, the amount of sediment produced by this erosion would be 50,000 cubic feet. At 100 pounds per cubic foot, this amounts to 2,500 tons.

This amount can be compared with the mean annual sediment yield for Watts Branch, an unurbanized area near Rockville, Md. Annual sediment yield of Watts Branch is 516 tons per square mile. Thus, the channel erosion alone under the assumptions made would produce as much sediment as 5 years' usual production from an unurbanized area of the same size. Therefore, one can visualize that as urbanization proceeds, not only does construction activity have the potential of increasing sediment loads many thousands of times while construction is in progress, but also the result of the urbanization through its increase in peak flow would produce large amounts of sediment from channel enlargement as well. This emphasizes the need to provide temporary storage far upstream to counteract the tendency of urbanization to increase the number and size of high flows.

WATER QUALITY

There is little doubt that as urbanization increases, particularly from industrial use of land and water, the quality of water decreases. However, quantitative data to support this observation are sparse. There are two principal effects of urbanization on water quality. First, the influx of waste materials tends to increase the dissolved-solids content and decrease the dissolved-oxygen content. Second, as flood peaks increase as a result of the increased area of imperviousness and decreased lag time, less water is available for ground-water recharge. The stream becomes flashier in that flood peaks are higher and flows during nonstorm periods are lower.

A recent study on the Passaic River at Little Falls, N.J., by Anderson and Faust (1965) provides quantitative data on the effect of urbanization and industrialization on water quality. Seventeen years of data for the flow and chemical quality of the 760-sq-mi drainage basin were analyzed. During these 17 years, diversions of water for domestic and industrial supplies increased more than 30 percent between 1950 and 1963. Returns of waste waters into the basin became as much as 10 percent of the water withdrawn. Analysis of the data showed that at relatively low discharge the dissolved-solids content increased about 10 ppm (parts per million) between 1948 and 1955 but increased 75 ppm between 1955 and 1963. That is, during the period of greatest population growth the dissolved-solids content increased nearly 40 percent in a period of 8 years.

A long-term change in the average content of dissolved oxygen was also noted. Between 1950 and 1964 the dissolved-oxygen content dropped from an average of 78 percent of saturation to 62 percent of saturation. Further, the analysis demonstrated that these average changes in water quality occurred in all seasons of the year.

An aspect of population growth not generally appreciated is the large segment of population using septic tanks for disposal of sewage. In a given area this segment often becomes large before community water and sewerage systems are built. For the planner it should be important to know how septic-tank installations can affect water quality in streams and in the ground. In the upper East Branch of Brandywine Creek, a basin of 37 sq mi, the population in 1967 was 4,200. As of that date, there were no community water or sewerage systems; all the population was served by individual wells and septic tanks. Population projections indicate that the basin will have 14,000 persons by the year 1990. During the initial part of this projected growth at least, the number of wells and septic tanks can be expected to increase materially.

The soil, containing as it does a flourishing fauna of microorganisms, tends to destroy or adsorb pathogenic bacteria. Effluent draining from the seepage field of a septic tank tends therefore to be cleansed of its pathogens. McGauhey and Krone (1954) showed that the coliform count was reduced by three orders of magnitude in moving from an injection well a distance of 50 feet through sand and gravel. In 100 feet the count was reduced to a small number. As for rate of movement, Mallmann and Mack (1961) showed that bacteria introduced into a permeable soil by a septic-tank seepage field moved 10 feet in 2 days and 20 feet in 3 days and appeared in a well 30 feet away after 10 days.

Both the rate and effectiveness of the

process of pathogen reduction depend on the type of soil as has been summarized by Olson (1964), who emphasized that position of the ground-water table is a critical factor in the transmission of pollutants.

Studies by Wayman, Page, and Robertson (1965) of the changes in primary sewage effluent through natural materials in conditions of saturated flow showed that "most soils removed over 90 percent of the bacteria from sewage within a few feet of travel . . . [but there was] severe clogging in the finer-grained soils." They found, however, that "dissolved solids moved through the columns [of soil] virtually unaffected . . ."

The same authors report on infiltration of polluted river water through sandy loam. "ABS [synthetic detergent] and coliform bacteria are significantly reduced by infiltration through the unsaturated zone; dissolved solids do not seem to be removed . . . Once a pollutant gets into the ground water (saturated flow) little additional change in removal of ABS or dissolved solids, even for movement over extensive horizontal distances, is to be expected. This result is in agreement with the data . . . for flow of sewage effluent through various soil columns (saturated flow)."

The data are not definitive regarding the minimum distance a septic-tank seepage field should be separated from a stream channel, but the application of data cited above with general principles does indicate some tentative rules of thumb which might be useful to the planner. A perennial stream represents the intersection of the saturated zone (water table) with the earth's surface. The observations indicate that, for soil cleansing to be effective, contaminated water must move through unsaturated soil at least 100 feet. Owing to the gentle gradient of the water table near the perennial stream and the fact that seepage water moves vertically as well as toward a nearby channel, it would seem prudent that no septic tank should be as close to a channel as about 300 feet, if protection of the stream water quality is to be achieved. The distance should probably be greater from a perennial than from an ephemeral channel. (An ephemeral stream is one which contains flowing water only in storm periods.) In general, it might be advisable to have no source of pollution such as a seepage field closer than 300 feet to a channel or watercourse.

Even this minimum setback does not prevent the dissolved materials (nitrates, phosphates, chlorides) from enriching the stream water and thus potentially encouraging the proliferation of algae and otherwise creating a biotic imbalance.

The only detailed study of the effect of urbanization on water temperature is that of E. J. Pluhowski (1968), some of whose results are summarized here. He chose five streams on Long Island for detailed analysis and found that streams most affected by man's activities exhibit temperatures in summer from $10°$ to $15°$ above those in an unurbanized control. Connetquot River, the control stream, flows through one of the few remaining undeveloped areas of central Long Island. Temperatures in reaches most affected by ponding, realinement, or clear cutting of trees are significantly higher in summer, but winter temperatures are $5°$ to $10°F$ colder than those observed in reaches unaffected by man.

Solar radiation is the predominant factor in the energy balance determining a stream's thermal pattern. The more solar energy a stream absorbs, the greater its temperature variation diurnally as well as seasonally. By greatly increasing the surface area exposed to the sun's radiation, the construction of ponds and lakes has profoundly affected stream temperature regimen. On Long Island, Pluhowski found that ponds having mean depth of about 2 feet or less substantially increase downstream diurnal temperature fluctuations whereas ponds deeper than 2 feet exhibit a dampening effect on daily temperatures. For example, during the period October 31 to November 2, 1967, the mean daily range of temperatures at Swan River, in south-central Long Island, varied from $9°F$ in a reach immediately below a shallow pond (mean depth, 0.5 foot) to $3°F$ below Swan Lake (mean depth, 3 feet). In reaches unaffected by man's activities, the mean daily temperature fluctuation was about $4°F$.

Under natural conditions, less than 5 percent of the streamflow on Long Island originates as direct surface runoff. With the conversion of large areas of western Long Island from farmland to suburban use during the last 20 years, the proportion of streamflow originating as surface runoff has increased sharply. As a direct consequence, streams most affected by street runoff may exhibit temperature patterns that are markedly different from those observed in streams flowing through natural settings. During the period August 25 to 27, 1967, a series of heavy rainstorms overspread Long Island. Throughout this period, temperatures at each of the five observation sites on Connetquot River showed little day-to-day change. In contrast, temperatures in the upper reaches of East Meadow Brook, which drains highly urbanized central Nassau County, increased steadily in response to the relatively warm street runoff. Pluhowski found that by August 27, water temperatures had risen 10° to 12°F above prestorm levels and were 15°F higher than concurrent temperatures in the control stream.

REFERENCES

Anderson, D. G., 1968, Effects of urban development on floods in northern Virginia: U.S. Geol. Survey open-file rept., 39 p., 5 figs.

Anderson, Peter W., and Faust, Samuel D., 1965, Changes in quality of water in the Passaic River at Little Falls, New Jersey, as shown by long-term data, in Geological Survey research 1965: U.S. Geol. Survey Prof. Paper 525-D, p. D214-D218.

Antoine, L. H., 1964, Drainage and best use of urban land: Public Works [New York], v. 95, p. 88-90.

Carter, R. W., 1961, Magnitude and frequency of floods in suburban areas, in Short papers in the geologic and hydrologic sciences: U.S. Geol. Survey Prof. Paper 424-B, p. B9-B11.

Espey, W. H., Morgan, C. W., and Masch, F. D., 1966, Study of some effects of urbanization on storm runoff from a small watershed: Texas Water Devel. Board Rept. 23, 109 p.

Felton, P. N., and Lull, H. W., 1963, Suburban hydrology can improve watershed conditions: Public Works, v. 94, p. 93-94.

Guy, H. P., and Ferguson, G. E., 1962, Sediment in small reservoirs due to urbanization: Am. Soc. Civil Engineers Proc., HY 2, p. 27-37.

Harris, E. E., and Rantz, S. E., 1964, Effect of urban growth on streamflow regimen of Permanente Creek, Santa Clara County, California: U.S. Geol. Survey Water-Supply Paper 1591-B, 18 p.

Horton, R. E., 1945, Erosional development of streams and their drainage basins, hydrophysical approach to quantitative morphology: Geol. Soc. America Bull., v. 56, no. 3, p. 275-370.

James, L. D., 1965, Using a computer to estimate the effects of urban development on flood peaks: Water Resources Research, v. 1, no. 2, p. 223-234.

Lull, H. W., and Sopper, W. E., 1966, Hydrologic effects from urbanization of forested watersheds in the northeast: Upper Darby, Pa., Northeastern Forest Expt. Sta., 24 p.

McGauhey, P. H., and Krone, R. B., 1954, Report on the investigation of travel of pollution: California State Water Pollution Control Board Pub. 11, 218 p.

Mallmann, W. L., and Mack, W. N., 1961, Biological contamination of ground water: Robert A. Taft Sanitary Eng. Center Tech. Rept. W61-5, p. 35-43.

Martens, L. A., 1966, Flood inundation and effects of urbanization in metropolitan Charlotte (North Carolina): U.S. Geol. Survey open-file rept., 54 p.

Musgrave, G. W., 1947, Quantitative evaluation of factors in water erosion—First approximation: Jour. Soil and Water Conserv., v. 2, no. 3, p. 133-138.

Olson, G. W., 1964, Application of soil survey to problems of health, sanitation, and engineering: Cornell Univ. Agr. Expt. Sta. Mem. 387, 77 p.

Pluhowski, E. J., 1968, Urbanization and its effect on stream temperature: Baltimore, Md., Johns Hopkins Univ., Ph. D. dissert. (in preparation).

Wark, J. W., and Keller, F. J., 1963, Preliminary study of sediment sources and transport in the Potomac River Basin: Interstate Comm. on Potomac River Basin, Washington, D.C., Tech. Bull. 1963-11, 28 p.

Wayman, C., Page, H. L., and Robertson, J. B., 1965, Behavior of surfactants and other detergent components in water and soil-water environments: Federal Housing Adm. Tech. Studies Pub. 532, 136 p.

Wiitala, S. W., 1961, Some aspects of the effect of urban and suburban development upon runoff: U.S. Geol. Survey open-file rept., 28 p.

Wilson, K. V., 1966, Flood frequency of streams in Jackson, Mississippi: U.S. Geol. Survey open-file rept., 6 p.

Wolman, M. G., 1964, Problems posed by sediment derived from construction activities in Maryland—Report to the Maryland Water Pollution Control Commission: Annapolis, Md., 125 p.

Wolman, M. G., and Schick, P.A., 1967, Effects of construction on fluvial sediment, urban and suburban areas of Maryland: Water Resources Research, v. 3, no. 2, p. 451-462.

11. DECEMBER 1964, A 400-YEAR FLOOD IN NORTHERN CALIFORNIA

EDWARD J. HELLEY and VALMORE C. LAMARCHE, JR.

In 1955 and again in 1964, unusually high floods and peak discharges were experienced in northern California. On many streams the peak discharges in both years were greater than any that had occurred during the period of record, and on some streams the 1964 peaks exceeded any that had previously occurred during the period of reasonably dependable observations by local residents; in some instances, more than 100 years. The occurrence of such extreme floods provides one reference point, sometimes a critical one, in the sampling of annual floods. Because the extreme floods sometimes seem to be outliers when viewed in company with data from other floods, the assignment of a reasonable probability of occurrence to such extreme floods is important and at the same time difficult. This difficulty requires an examination of all available hydrologic information that may help deduce the average length of time, or recurrence interval, between floods of similar magnitude.

To define the estimated frequency-magnitude relation, the annual discharges are arranged in order of magnitude. Each flood is assigned a recurrence interval T, by use of the arbitrary formula

$$T = \frac{n+1}{m}$$

where

T = the recurrence interval, in years,

n = the number of years of record, and

m = the rank of the event in the plotting array ($m = 1$ for the maximum and $m = n$ for the minimum event).

Implicit in this method of flood-frequency analysis is the fact that the frequency of the highest observed flow is determined by the length of record. For example, the greatest flood in 100 years of record will be asigned a 101-year frequency interval. This leads to an unrealistic prediction of flood events like the high flows of December 1955 and December 1964 in northern

Reprinted with permission of the authors from *U. S. Geological Survey Professional Paper 600-D*, p. D34-D37, 1968.

California. Prior to 1964, the floods of December 1955 were the second highest reported since 1854 (Rantz, 1964, p. 55) and were the highest flows on record that were actually measured. The 1964 floods, which followed a scant 9 years later, proved to be the highest ever measured. The question then arose as to whether floods of a magnitude equal to those of December 1964 actually occur with a recurrence interval averaging 115 years or do they, in fact, have a longer recurrence interval, perhaps 200 years or more.

Geomorphic and botanical evidence may be useful in extending flood records and can perhaps yield a better estimate of the true long-term recurrence interval of large floods than can be obtained by conventional methods. Distinctive types of sedimentary deposits, for example, are direct evidence of past floods (Jahns, 1947; Stewart and LaMarche, 1967). These deposits may be dated by radiocarbon analysis of included organic material or they may be assigned minimum ages by dendrochronologic study of associated trees. Dating of other deposits that were undisturbed prior to erosion by recent floods can give a minimum date for the last previous flood of comparable magnitude. Tree-ring dating of flood damage to vegetation (Sigafoos, 1964) is another promising source of information, particularly in areas where many trees reach ages of several hundred years.

Flood evidence of this type has already been described on Coffee Creek, a tributary to the Trinity River in northern California (Stewart and LaMarche, 1967). Radiocarbon dating of organic material buried in preflood deposits along the valley margin indicated that the flood of December 1964 exceeded any that had occurred in at least 200 years. That fact implies a recurrence interval much greater than that obtained from conventional methods of flood-frequency analysis.

In 1967, geomorphic and botanical evidence of a major prehistoric flood was investigated on Blue Creek, a tributary to the Klamath River. There, deposits of poorly sorted, obscurely bedded, coarse gravel underlie a high terrace.

These old deposits were deeply eroded by the floods of December 1964 which just overtopped the terrace surface as is evidenced by flood debris and high-water marks. The flood erosion revealed stumps of redwoods, *Sequoia sempervirens* (D. Don) Engl., which had previously been buried in the terrace deposit to a depth of about 20 feet above the root crown. It was further established that the trees were dead and limbless snags when they were logged in 1958-59. The cutting of those snags at the then-existing ground level accounts for the fact that all the stumps now project to approximately the same height, about 21 feet above the present bed of Blue Creek. Tree-ring counts on six of the largest stumps indicated that the trees were 500-600 years old when they died.

The texture and structure of the deposits underlying the terrace indicate that the gravel may have been laid down in a single catastrophic flood. Similar deposits buried standing trees along Coffee Creek (Stewart and LaMarche, 1967) to depths of more than 5 feet in 1964. Another feature suggesting catastrophic burial of the older redwood trees is the simple pancake form of their root systems, some of which have been partly exposed by the 1964 erosion. Stone and Vasey (1968) showed that redwoods deeply buried by deposition of successive thin layers of sediment at long intervals develop new root systems at progressively higher levels from adventitious buds in the lower parts of their stems. The root system in the Blue Creek stand did not show such successive levels of root formation; this is strong evidence that the trees were killed as a consequence of rapid burial of their root system to a depth of 20 feet.

The terrace surface supports a mixed stand of redwoods and Douglas-fir (*Pseudotsuga menzieii* [Mirb.] Franco) whose maximum age does not exceed 90 years, as determined by tree-ring counts of increment cores from the 10 largest trees growing on the terrace surface near the buried trees. One of the redwood stumps displaying 560 rings and buried by the terrace deposit has been dated by radiocarbon analysis. The radiocarbon date of 850±100 years before present was established on wood 100 rings from the center of the tree; hence, this established that the older trees began growth about A.D. 1000 and lived to about A.D. 1560±100 years. If the older trees were killed by rapid deposition of flood deposits, then the floods responsible for their death must have occurred approximately 400±100 years ago. Because the floods of December 1964 just overtopped the terrace deposit they are probably of the same order of magnitude as the event that deposited the terrace material. Thus, at least one or more floods equal to, or greater than, the flood of December 1964 have occurred in the past 400 years; that is, since A.D. 1560±100 years.

A test of the acceptability of this hypothesis may be made by comparison with the results of conventional flood-frequency analysis. The Klamath River, to which Blue Creek is a tributary, has an unusually long record of flood events. Data on the major peak flows dating back to 1862 have been computed by Rantz (1964) on the basis of floodmarks and the hydraulic properties of the channels. A major peak flow of unknown magnitude is also known to have occurred in the 1853 water year. Annual flood data for the period 1911-67 have been used to compute a frequency-magnitude relation based on a log Pearson type-3 distribution (Fig. 1). Data for the historic floods of 1862, 1881, and 1890 are also shown in Figure 1 at recurrence intervals based on knowledge of the relative magnitude of all major floods since 1854. The flood of December 1964 is shown by a dashed line. Extension of the flood-frequency curve from the base period and historic data would seem to support the hypothesis of an approximate 400-year recurrence interval for the flood of December 1964, although the agreement may be fortuitous.

Botanical and geomorphic evidence of past flood events can probably be useful in assigning a more meaningful recurrence interval to floods of large magnitude.

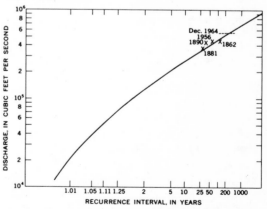

Figure 1. Annual floods on the Klamath River at Klamath, Calif. plotted for base period 1911-67 by log Pearson type-3 method.

REFERENCES

Jahns, R. H., 1947, Geologic features of the Connecticut Valley as related to recent floods: U.S. Geol. Survey Water-Supply Paper 996, 158 p.

Rantz, S. E., 1964, Surface-water hydrology of coastal basins of northern California: U.S. Geol. Survey Water-Supply Paper 1758, 77 p.

Sigafoos, R. H., 1964, Botanical evidence of floods and flood-plain deposition: U.S. Geol. Survey Prof. Paper 485-A, 35 p.

Stewart, J. H., and LaMarche, V. C., Jr., 1967, Erosion and deposition produced by the flood of December 1964 on Coffee Creek, Trinity County, California: U.S. Geol. Survey Prof. Paper 422-K, 22 p.

Stone, E. C., and Vasey, R. B., 1968, Preservation of coast redwood on alluvial flats: Science, v. 159, p. 157-161.

12. HAZARDOUS DAMS IN MISSOURI

MISSOURI MINERAL INDUSTRY NEWS

The following editorial reflects the concern of the Missouri Geological Survey about the responsibilities and complexities of impounding large volumes of water. Much of the editorial was adapted from a talk given by Mr. James H. Williams before a meeting of the American Society of Civil Engineers, Kansas City Section. Mr. Williams, Chief of the Engineering Geology Section of the Missouri Survey, and his staff have examined a total of more than 1,000 potential lake sites in Missouri.

Three lives were lost, and $3 million in property damage occurred in Los Angeles, California when the Baldwin Hills Reservoir failed on December 14, 1963. Such a tragedy *can* happen in Missouri. In 1966, the Missouri Geological Survey published a map showing 1300 lakes five acres or larger in size, compared with 1052 in California as of January, 1967. Many of these 1300 structures were built with the intent of getting the highest dam at the lowest cost, with no professional engineering advice and without regard to safety in dam construction. Safety costs money, but is far cheaper than even one of the dam disasters surely in Missouri's future.

Since 1958 there have been at least 12 dam failures in Missouri, primarily due to overtopping with partial or total destruction. The dams ranged in height from 35 feet down to 15 or 20 feet. No lives were lost and there was little property damage because the dams that failed fortunately were downstream from population concentrations. A recent survey identified 21 Missouri dams that are in danger of failure.

The chain of events resulting in dam failure begins with site selection. Good lakes obviously enhance the value of property, and owners may disregard such factors as foundation stability, inadequate spillways, unsuitable borrow, and insufficient storage capacity in their haste to turn a profit. In most cases, the land is purchased with lake construction in mind before considering whether it is *feasible* to build a lake there. The

Reprinted with permission of Jerry D. Vineyard, editor, *Missouri Mineral Industry News,* v. 8, no. 2, p. 16-19, February 1968, Missouri Geological Survey.

builder may never have seen a small valley in flood, so it is not hard to understand why he might build a dam with a watershed-to-lake ratio of 100:1; safe ratios range from 10:1 to perhaps 40 or 50:1, depending upon many factors, especially spillway design. There are lakes (temporary?) in Missouri with a 1000:1 ratio!

Dams fail because they are improperly located, constructed, or maintained. Inexperienced landowners frequently rely entirely on contractors, who may be equally inexperienced or without adequate equipment to build lakes. Obvious consequences follow, such as the use of improper fill, poor compaction, unstable foundations, and poorly designed spillways. A common result is a leaking lake, which is perhaps fortunate, because a structure that will not hold water can hardly be considered hazardous. However, small but persistent leakage problems over a period of years can weaken structures to the point of failure.

Spillways are designed to safeguard dams from overtopping during excessively heavy rains. Spillways must be designed to carry away stormwater and relieve the danger to the dam from overtopping. Many Missouri dams have inadequate spillways and some have no spillways at all. A typical, chilling example is a dam 70 feet high with one spillway that is only two feet below the crest of the dam. Even this spillway is blocked so that it is only a narrow swag at the end of one abutment. In another part of the state, a similar structure is downstream of several other dams, poised like dominoes to fail in sequence because they have equally poor spillways.

Safe dam construction requires adequate earthmoving equipment capable of proper compaction. But construction practices are extremely lax. Inexperienced builders may rely on the weight of a bulldozer for compaction, yet the compaction pressure per square foot exerted by a bulldozer is less, for example, than that of an automobile because the weight of the dozer is spread over its wide metal treads, while the weight of a car exerts pressure through the small area of the four tires in contact with the ground.

Inadequate foundation exploration is a fellow-traveler with poor construction practices, because the builder who uses inadequate equipment is also unlikely to spend money on foundation studies. For example, the Cape Girardeau region has intensely faulted bedrock, poorly consolidated near-surface materials, and noticeable earthquakes at least once a year. Building a dam in this area without determining its relation to faults and unstable foundations is definitely irresponsible. Or consider parts of northeastern Missouri where massive earthslides frequently occur. Windblown soil deposits (loess) on the uplands along the Missouri and Mississippi rivers make poor foundations for dams because the loess — highly stable when dry — loses strength when wet. A more dramatic foundation hazard exists in the central and southern Ozarks where extensive caverns occur. Sinkholes frequently form when weakened cave roofs collapse because of earthquake shocks, heavy rains, or excessive loading. One needs little imagination to see the consequences of building a dam over a weakened cavern roof.

Nor can we assume that a dam that has stood well for 10, 15, or even 20 years is proven safe. Assuming improper construction in the beginning, the statistical probability of failure increases with age. In addition, the periodic cycle of major storms increases the likelihood that the dam will have to weather an unprecedented flood.

The scope of the problems of hazardous dams in Missouri is well illustrated by the following findings of the U.S. Committee on Large Dams:

1. Thirty-three states participate in the design and construction of dams; Missouri *not* included.
2. Seventeen states provide on-site inspection during construction; Missouri *not* included.
3. Twenty-nine states review the preliminary plans and designs; Missouri *not* included.
4. Thirty-two states require that contract plans and specifications be reviewed; Missouri *not* included.
5. Twelve states have a roster of dams readily available for public inspection; Missouri *not* included.
6. Some states have no record or list of dams at all. (Missouri has "Lakes and Reservoirs Map of Missouri," published by the Missouri Geological Survey in 1966.)
7. Five states require no permit or license for construction of a dam; Missouri included.
8. Eleven states require no construction supervision; Missouri included.
9. Nine states require no supervision or review of any kind; Missouri included.
10. Thirteen states require no filing of application for construction; Missouri included.
11. Fifteen states have no control over dams once they are built; Missouri included.
12. Ten states do not require that the design of a dam be supervised or approved by a registered professional engineer; Missouri included.

It is evident that anyone may build a dam in Missouri at any time, in any place, and with complete disregard for safety if he has the funds, owns the land, and chooses to do so.

It is not our intent to imply that all dams in Missouri are suspect. The majority of dams are well constructed and many were designed and construction was supervised by qualified engineers. Since 1958 the Engineering Geology Section of the Missouri Geological Survey has investigated 824 potential sites to determine the geological feasibility of lake construction.

An additional important factor is that natural foundation materials in many parts of Missouri are inherently stable, and earthen dams may be at least partially stable even with lackadaisical construction practices. But being "half safe" is not enough.

It is tragic that so many dams are built today without benefit of geological and engineering know-how when both are available. Missouri has no laws to protect the public interest in dam construction. Should builders be permitted to construct dams without benefit of geological and engineering certification? Would *you* like to live *downstream* from such a structure? Many Missourians already find themselves in such situations.

13. CHANNELIZATION: A CASE STUDY

JOHN W. EMERSON*

Channelization means straightening of a stream or the dredging of a new channel to which the stream is diverted. The purpose is to minimize local flooding by shortening the distance traveled and thereby moving the floodwaters downstream more rapidly. This technique has been practiced for many years by private drainage districts, the Army Corps of Engineers, and, more recently, the Soil Conservation Service under Public Law 566 (U.S. Statutes, 1954). Recently several articles concerning channelization have appeared in newspapers and magazines (Creighton, 1970; Miller and Simmons, 1970; and Bagby, 1969). The detrimental effects on game and fish populations and on landscape esthetics have been widely described, but there has been a paucity of data about changes in stream channel geometry. This report documents the increase in erosion caused by channelizing a stream and thereby increasing its gradient.

The headwaters of the Blackwater River are in northwest Johnson County, Missouri, about 65 km east of Kansas City. The river flows east to join the Missouri River just west of Boonville, Missouri. A local drainage district was formed in 1909, and in 1910 a new channel was dredged for the lowland portion of the Blackwater River eastward nearly to the county line.

The pre-1910 river in Johnson County had an average of 1.8 meanders per kilometer, with a meander radius ranging from 60 to 140 m. This former channel is now blocked off, silted up, full of vegetation, and used as a dump wherever the original bridge remains in use. These bridges over the former channel are from 15 to 30 m wide, the majority being of the smaller width. The length of the old channel, from the beginning of the new ditch to the county line, was 53.6 km, and the gradient was 1.67 m per kilometer.

Reprinted with permission of the author and publisher from *Science*, v. 173, p. 325-326, July 23, 1971. Copyright 1971 by the American Association for the Advancement of Science.

*Department of Geology, Central Missouri State College, Warrensburg.

County Circuit Court records state the dimensions of the new Blackwater ditch, those of the dredged tributaries, and the length of new bridges to cross the dredged channels (Stanley, 1909). The new Blackwater channel was 9 m wide at top, 1 m at bottom, and 3.8 m deep, giving a cross-sectional area of 38 m^2.

Length and elevation measurements for the former and present channels were made on topographic maps. Channel widths were taken by taping across bridges on straight portions of the present river. Channel depth was obtained by lowering a lead line, marked in meter increments, from the bridge. A hand level was used to sight from one bank to the other, and the height of the intersection of the line of sight with the lead line was noted. At the same time, bottom elevation was obtained by measuring the length from the bridge floor to the stream bed and subtracting this distance from the bridge elevation given on the topographic map. The measurements are given in Table 1 and in the stream profile (Fig. 1).

The present Blackwater River is 29 km long from beginning of channelization to the county line and has a gradient of 3.1 m per kilometer. The dredging shortened this portion of the river by 24.6 km and nearly doubled the gradient. The present channel has increased from a cross-sectional area of 19 m^2 when newly dredged to a size now ranging from 160 to 484 m^2. The maximum figure represents an area increase of 1173 percent in 60 years. For a comparison of the present channel width with the width of the old abandoned channel, measurements of the bridges that cross both are useful. At location c, the old channel bridge is 15.2 m wide; the present channel bridge, originally 15.2 m, has been extended to 60.9 m. At location g, the old channel bridge is 15.2 m wide; the present channel bridge, originally 22.8 m, is now 124.2 m wide.

The dredged lower reaches of the tributary streams have also increased in size. Honey Creek, one such tributary, has gone from a cross-sectional area of 12 m^2 when newly dredged to

255 m² today. Along the channelized portion of several tributaries, parts of the predredging channels are preserved about 3.5 m above the present stream bed. In the unchannelized reaches of the tributaries, meanders have become en-

trenched. This condition is also evident in the unchannelized parts of the Blackwater.

The widening and deepening of the streams have caused serious erosional problems along their banks and headward erosion of gullies that

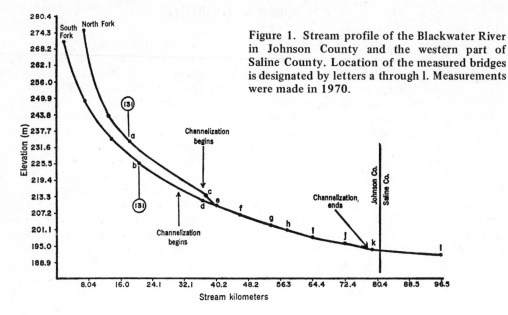

Figure 1. Stream profile of the Blackwater River in Johnson County and the western part of Saline County. Location of the measured bridges is designated by letters a through l. Measurements were made in 1970.

TABLE 1. DIMENSIONS OF THE PRESENT BLACKWATER RIVER IN JOHNSON AND SALINE COUNTIES, MISSOURI. SIZE OF THE ORIGINAL DREDGED CHANNEL: WIDTH AT TOP, 9 m; WIDTH AT BOTTOM, 1 m; AND DEPTH, 3.8 m.

	Present channel dimensions			
Bridge location	Top width (m)	Bottom width (m)	Depth (m)	Cross-sectional area (m²)
a. North Fork, Route 131	21.9	7.0	4.7	67.9
b. South Fork, Route 131	20.1	5.0	4.1	51.2
c. North Fork	67.6	9.2	9.2	353.2
d. South Fork, Route 50	45.7	12.2	9.4	280.1
e. Elevation, 729 feet (222 m)	53.3	12.8	10.9	360.2
f. Elevation, 711 feet (217 m)	60.9	11.6	10.0	362.5
g. Elevation, 696 feet (212 m)	64.0	22.8	10.0	434.0
h. Bear Creek	71.0	12.5	11.6	484.3
i. Valley City	51.8	15.8	8.2	277.1
j. Route J	35.0	15.2	6.4	160.6
k. Dunksburg	29.8	15.2	5.8	130.5
l. Sweet Springs	42.7	15.3	5.8	168.2

lead to the tributaries. Most bridges in Johnson County have been replaced or lengthened and have had vertical extensions added to the lower supports. In most cases the ends of the present bridges are threatened by bank erosion. An example of this rapid widening is illustrated by the experience of a local farmer. A county bridge spanning the Blackwater had collapsed, owing to bank erosion, and was replaced with a chain bridge constructed by area farmers in 1930. The new bridge was 27 m wide. That bridge had to be replaced in 1942 and again in 1947. The final bridge had a span of 70 m, but it too has collapsed because of erosion. Channelization increased the gradient of the Blackwater River and initiated a degradational regimen, which is still in progress. The present channel has displayed no tendency to resume meandering, and so it apparently has not yet reached equilibrium. For the central part of the county (locations c through i), erosion since channelization has averaged 1 m in width and 0.16 m in depth per year.

The lithology in most of Johnson County consists of thin-bedded Pennsylvanian shale, coal, sandstone, and limestone. Continual degradation on easily eroded stream beds have produced a smooth chutelike condition, which is not conducive to bottom fauna. Preliminary observations indicate a negative correlation between channelized portions of the stream and density of macroinvertebrates (Fox, 1971). These observations are reinforced by the work of the Missouri Department of Conservation, which reports 256 kg of fish per acre in unchannelized portions of the Blackwater but only 51 kg per acre in the channelized portions (Creighton, 1970).

The low resistance of the Pennsylvanian rocks made dredging nearly to the county line economically possible. In Saline County to the east, the change in lithology to Mississippian limestone made dredging unfeasible, and the project was abandoned. Channel constriction as a result of the lithology change causes a large difference in the amount of water that can be transported without flooding. The channelized part of the Blackwater in Johnson County has a capacity of 280 to 850 m^3 per second, whereas the downstream reaches in eastern Johnson County and in Saline County have a capacity of 170 to 255 m^3 per second (Army Corps of Engineers, 1960). The Blackwater drainage basin

in Johnson County receives 102 cm of rainfall yearly, with frequent cloudbursts from April to September. The stream gauging station on bridge i near Valley City recorded maximum flows during these months of 198 to 1840 m^3 per second for the water years 1960 to 1965 (U.S.G.S., 1960). Owing to the abrupt decrease in cross section in the unchannelized part of the Blackwater River, flooding is extremely common in the adjoining parts of Johnson and Saline counties. Long-time residents of the area near bridge k stated that there was no extensive flooding prior to channelization. Since the channelization upstream, two successive generations of fence posts have been buried by overbank deposits on the floodplain near bridge k. This would amount to about 2 m of deposition in 50 to 60 years. A number of public hearings conducted in the 1940s indicated that flooding in Saline County had greatly increased since channelization and that the effectiveness of the lower end of the new channel is being reduced by channel sedimentation, which is slowly progressing upstream (Army Corps of Engineers, 1960). The area now affected most by flooding extends from Valley City (bridge i) to U.S. Highway 40 in central Saline County, a distance of about 70 km of stream.

Channelization has enabled more floodplain land to be utilized in the upper reaches of the Blackwater River. This benefit must be weighed against erosional loss of farmland, cost of bridge repair, and the downstream flood damage resulting from termination of the dredging project.

REFERENCES

Public Law 566, 1954, Watershed Protection and Flood Prevention Act, U.S. Statutes at Large 68, 1.

J. H. Creighton, Dec. 8, 1970, Setting Our Streams Straight, St. Louis Post-Dispatch.

J. N. Miller and R. Simmons, 1970, Crisis on Our Rivers, Readers Dig. 97, 584; G. T. Bagby, 1969, Ga. Game Fish 4,7.

T. O. Stanley, 1909, Final Report of Engineer on Blackwater Drainage District No. 1, Johnson County, Missouri. I wish to thank D. Stous for locating this document in the County Archives.

R. Fox, 1971, thesis, Central Missouri State College, Warrensburg.

Review of Report on Lamine and Blackwater Rivers, Missouri, 1960, (Army Corps of Engineers, Kansas City District).

Surface Water Supply of the United States 1961-65, 1960, U.S. Geol. Surv. Water-Supply Pap. 1919, part 6.

Mass Movement

14. LANDSLIDES

DOUGLAS M. MORTON and ROBERT STREITZ

At first, for people camped along the margins of the valley, it was only a momentary awareness, not a true realization—then it came, a violent rock-shattering shake. Loose debris, along with great slices of bedrock cleaved from the mountain core, came tumbling and vaulting toward the valley floor in a tremendous landslide. Campers in its path felt a horrifying blast of air that was pushed aside by the falling debris—they clung desperately to trees or anything within reach. Some had their clothes torn from them, others were blown beyond the surge of advancing rock; and, unfortunately, some were engulfed. After a few minutes only the dull clacking of a few spent rock fragments could be heard and then it was once more quiet on the valley floor. The landslides following the 1959 Hebgen Lake earthquake, in a remote part of Montana, killed 28 people and changed the face of the landscape by creating lakes and altering the shape of the mountains.

To those in the vicinity of this landslide it was a major catastrophe; in the realm of geology it was an isolated occurrence of a normal geologic process. Landsliding is an important agent shaping the earth's surface and it has been active as long as there have been natural slopes. As canyons are cut by running water, or as mountains are thrust upward, the force of gravity periodically pulls down masses of earth materials from exposed slopes. This process produces much of the debris that is later carried away by streams and rivers to be deposited as sediments in intermontane basins and on the ocean floor.

Technically, landslides are part of a more general category of erosional processes called mass-wasting—the term applied by geologists to the process of downslope movement of earth materials, primarily by gravity. This movement, either slow or rapid, occurs when the strength of the material is exceeded by the force of gravity. Creep is that part of mass-wasting in which earth

Reprinted with permission of the authors and publisher from *Mineral Information Service*, v. 20, no. 10, p. 123-129, and no. 11, p. 135-140, 1967. California Division of Mines and Geology, Sacramento, California.

materials with poorly defined bounds move at imperceptibly slow rates. When a discrete unit (or units) of earth materials moves perceptibly, it is termed a landslide.

Ancient deposits that may represent landslides are found in the geologic record as far back as Precambrian time. Chester R. Longwell (1951) described breccias, which he termed megabreccias, that also resembled landslide debris—these from rocks of Late Cretaceous (?) age in the Lake Mead area of Nevada and Arizona. Breccias of post-Cretaceous age, resembling "modern day mud-flow and debris-flow accumulations" were reported in several areas of southern California by R. H. Jahns and A. E. Engel in 1950.

The ability to distinguish between geologically old and modern-day landslide deposits is of considerable practical value. For instance, geologists Richard H. Jahns and George B. Cleveland, working in the Palos Verdes Peninsula area in Los Angeles County, report that there Miocene breccia and submarine slump deposits greatly resemble modern landslide deposits—but with one important difference: the ancient materials are relatively stable. Thus, if a Miocene breccia deposit were confused with a modern-day landslide deposit, unnecessary concern about the stability of an area could result—or perhaps even the unnecessary rejection of a site for building construction.

The most destructive series of landslides in recorded history occurred in Kansu Province, China. During an earthquake in 1920 gigantic masses of loess (unstratified deposits of silt) were shaken loose, and moved down mountain sides, inundating populated valley areas up to 3 miles in length. More than one hundred thousand persons were killed in this catastrophe. The Chinese aptly described the extensive landslide area as "where the mountains walk." Smaller landslides by many orders of magnitude are more common and generally represent no serious threat to life; but they are, nevertheless, costly where they affect the activities or works of man. Rockwell Smith (1958), in his study of the economic and legal aspects of landslides, estimated that they cost the nation hundreds of millions of dollars annually.

Though landslides are generally considered a detriment to the works of man, a number of dams have been built in river courses at constrictions caused by landslides. For example, the Farmer's Union Reservoir on the Rio Grande River is located at a narrow portion where the river's course is three-quarters blocked by a landslide. The Bonneville dam site on the Columbia River was formed by the deflection of the river by an ancient landslide. The Cheakamus Dam, British Columbia, was founded on a landslide and the dam, an earth-and-rock-fill structure, was constructed of landslide and landslide-derived materials. In such instances, however, intensive geologic and engineering investigations are a necessary safety measure.

In California, interest in landslides has increased markedly because of the great influx of people and the concomitant expansion and development of new public facilities and enlarged areas of private housing. As flat land is used up, urban development is becoming more extensive in hilly and mountainous areas. Hillside development can "trigger" old landslides and initiate new ones, if the project is improperly managed or designed. Either natural or man-induced landslides can occur in areas where development is not properly controlled.

NATURE OF LANDSLIDES

Landslides take place in widely differing rock types and are of almost every conceivable size and shape. They are found at elevations ranging from lofty mountain peaks to the sea floor, and occur in every climate from frigid Arctic to humid tropic and arid desert. The resulting wide range of variables produces many different kinds or types of landslides. Geologists have therefore found it helpful to group them along useful parameters. Of the various classifications, the one proposed by C.F.S. Sharpe in 1938, and the one proposed by D. J. Varnes in 1958, are probably the most widely accepted.

The following classification (Table 1) is, in essence, the one developed by Mr. Varnes, with slight modification. Here the principal division of landslides is based upon the type of landslide movement—fall, slide, or flow, and within each type of movement is a subdivision designating the material involved (i.e., rock, soil, mixtures, etc.). In addition, for the flow type of landslide, the

water content of the material (ranging from dry to saturated) is considered. A complex landslide consists of any combination of the three basic types.

Falls are limited to the free falling of earth material of any size. The name "fall" is modified depending upon the principal material involved: rock fall, debris fall, and soil fall. Falls may take

TABLE 1. EXAMPLES OF VARIOUS TYPES OF LANDSLIDES

Location	Reference
ROCK FALLS	
Elm, Switzerland	Büss and Heim, 1881; Heim, 1882
Flimserstein, Switzerland	Putnam, 1964
Saidmarreh, Iran	Harrison and Falcon, 1937; Kent, 1966
Frank, Alberta, Canada	Daly, et al., 1912
San Juan Mountains, Colorado	Howe, 1909
Mount Rainier, Washington	Crandell and Fahnestock, 1965
Sawtooth Ridge, Montana	Mudge, 1965
Blackhawk Canyon, San Bernardino	Woodford and Harriss, 1928;
County, California	Shreve, 1959
SOIL FALLS	
New Madrid area, Missouri	Fuller, 1912
Amazon River, Brazil	Bates, 1875
COASTLINE FALLS	
Norway	Brigham, 1906
Northern California coast	Lawson, et al., 1908
PLANAR SLIDES	
Goldau, Switzerland	Heim, 1932
Bellinzona, Italy	Holmes, 1964
Vaiont Dam, Italy	Selli, et al., 1964
La Pota, Panama	Nat'l Acad. Sci., 1924
Gros Ventre, Wyoming	Alden, 1928
Hebgen Lake, Montana	Hadley, 1964
Kettle Falls, Washington	Varnes, 1958
Point Fermin, California	Miller, 1931
ROTATIONAL SLIDES	
Telluride and Montrose, Colorado	Varnes, 1949
Toreva, Arizona	Reiche, 1937
Echo Cliffs and Vermillion Cliffs, Arizona	Strahler, 1940
Cape Fortunas, California	Lawson, et al., 1908
Orinda, California	Herling and Stafford, 1952
Pacific Palisades, California	McGill, 1959
Portuguese Bend, California	Merriam, 1960
SLOW FLOWS	
Stockport, New York	Sharpe, 1938
New Philadelphia, Ohio	Sharpe and Dosch, 1942
San Juan Mountains, Colorado	Howe, 1909
Horseshoe Bend, Idaho	Peebles, 1962
Sourdough Peak, Wrangell Range, Alaska	Holmes, 1964
Grand Coulee Dam, Washington	Legget, 1962
Lassen Volcanic Park, California	Sharpe, 1938
Gilroy, California	Krauskopf et al., 1939
San Clemente, California	Blanc and Cleveland, in preparation
FAST FLOWS	
Kansu Province, China	Close and McCormick, 1922
Gunong Keloet, Java	Scrivenor, 1929
Zinal, Switzerland	Bonney, 1902
St. Thuribe, Quebec, Canada	Dawson, 1899
Yamaska River, Quebec, Canada	Clark, 1947
Greensboro, Florida	Jordan, 1949
Slumgullion Gulch, Lake City, Colorado	Howe, 1909
Thunder Mountain, Roosevelt, Idaho	Bumgarten, 1910
Parish County, Utah	Woolley, 1946
Stillwater Range, Nevada	Blackwelder, 1928
Montrose, California	Troxell and Peterson, 1937
Wrightwood, California	Sharp and Nobles, 1953
UNDERWATER FLOWS	
Zug, Switzerland	Heim, et al., 1888
Atlantic Ocean	Heezen and Ewing, 1952
Hawaiian Ridge, Pacific Ocean	Moore, 1964
	Service, vol. 19, No. 3, p. 50.)

place in any material that can stand in a vertical slope for even a short time. Some of the most spectacular and largest landslides have been of this type or were complex landslides which included initial free fall. Talus, common in mountainous and desert areas, is usually the result of numerous individual rockfalls.

Slides (rock slides, debris slides, and soil slides) occur where movement takes place on one or more shear or slip surfaces and the affected mass consists of single to numerous segments bounded by slip surfaces. The movement is commonly rapid, though it does not attain the velocities reached by falling materials.

Planar slides involve translatory (non-rotational) movement of the slide mass. Some such slides consist of single or several undeformed masses termed block glide, and others consist of numerous units such as debris slides. Slump slides involve a rotational movement of the slide mass. Slumps may consist of single undeformed blocks, as in lateral spreading, or multiple partly deformed units termed compound slumps. Slumps combined with considerable internal deformation of the slide mass are quite common in the Coast Ranges of California.

Flows, the third general type of landslide movement, occur where the displaced mass is deformed and moves like a viscous fluid. No discrete slip or shear surfaces are discernible within the landslide mass. The intra-landslide movements generally occur on the scale of individual grains or particles. Flows occur on slopes which range from very gentle to steep and consist of materials which range from well sorted to mixed. They encompass a wide range of water content and may display a turbulent or laminar flow structure.

Creep, here considered the slow end-member of flow movement, is an important mass-wasting agent. It has a very significant relationship to landslides, in that it prepares slope debris for more rapid mass-movement. This is accomplished by increasing permeability, reducing shear strength, oversteepening slopes, and developing downslope structure in soil and detritus.

Dry flows are termed rock, sand, and silt flows, depending upon the materials involved. Wet flows, including mudflows, commonly result from torrential runoff following cloudbursts.

RECOGNITION OF LANDSLIDES

Certainly no one has any difficulty in recognizing a landslide that blocks a highway or carries a neighbor's yard or home away. These landslides are obviously out-of-the-ordinary features in a backyard or on a highway. The anomalous nature of landslide slopes is one of their most characteristic features, regardless of whether they occur in back yards or entirely removed from civilization on far off mountain sides. As a geologist maps landslides, he looks first for physiographic features which are anomalous in a particular geologic and geomorphic setting. To do this, therefore, the geologist must be familiar with the "normal" physiographic development of a given region. What is physiographically anomalous in one setting may be "normal" in another setting.

No difficulty is experienced in the recognition of the most recent landslides because of the bare scarp of the source area and the disturbed surface of the material which has moved. As time passes, erosion and vegetation modify the scarp and the landslide deposit, but the characteristic landslide form is still generally recognizable. Later the surface-altering agencies obliterate the anomalous form, bringing it into equilibrium with the regional landforms. Finally, regional geologic processes can completely remove or integrate the landslide mass into the geomorphology of the area. The recognition of a landslide whose form has been largely masked by subsequent alteration is a problem to the geologist. The anomalous form may be gone or subdued and in its place may be a smoothed-over surface. In this case the geologist must rely on other and often indirect evidence, such as the state and type of the earth material, and presence of a slide surface (slip-surface), or some other local feature.

Commonly, in the course of general geologic mapping in urban areas, the lack of definitive field evidence forces the geologist to outline areas of possible landslides. This action "flags" these areas as potential trouble sites. The substantiation of these landslides remains unresolved until engineering geologists perform a detailed examination of the site to determine the relationship of the landslide or landslide materials to a particular engineering structure or development plan.

Relatively intense stresses may develop within a landslide body during the period of its movement. These stresses give rise to a thoroughly fractured deposit of low strength, though individual blocks in the landslide mass can, and often do, retain their original strength. This state of the material is a criterion suggestive of a landslide. Suggestive only, because other geologic processes may give rise to similar-appearing material.

In some landslides, such as a single slumped block, little if any deformation is developed within the slide mass, and other techniques of identification must be used. These include: 1) the detection of the actual slide surface, or 2) the presence of rocks out of their normal stratigraphic sequence, and 3) the nonconformity of the dip in the slide with that of the surrounding rocks. An example of a landslide that contains large unfractured and undeformed blocks is the Vaiont Dam landslide that took place in 1963 in Italy. The blocks in this slide are so large and relatively undisturbed that various rock types can be differentiated over much of the landslide mass. Such a slide, in an area of poor exposures, could remain undetected except for direct observation of a slide surface, the out-of-sequence nature of the rocks, or deduction based upon suspicions of a trained observer.

SIZE AND MOVEMENT OF LANDSLIDES

The volume of material involved in individual landslides ranges from less than a cubic foot, such as a single falling rock, to 4 to 5 cubic miles, such as the Saidmarreh landslide of Iran (Table 2).

TABLE 2.   AGE AND VOLUME OF SOME LARGE LANDSLIDES

Landslide	Date	Volume (million cu. yds.)
Riviere Blanche, Quebec, Canada	1898	3.5
Elm, Switzerland	1881	10–11
St. Albans, Quebec, Canada	1894	25
Frank, Alberta, Canada	1903	35–40
Gros Ventre, Wyoming	1909	50
Blackhawk, California	Prehistoric	370
Vaiont, Italy	1963	390
Tin Mountain, California	Prehistoric	2,350
Flims, Switzerland	Prehistoric	15,000
Saidmarreh, Iran	Prehistoric	21–27,000

Landslide velocities range from an arbitrarily chosen lower limit such as 1/5 of a foot per year to the terminal velocity in air of particular fragments. A landslide that attained high velocity is the Elm, Switzerland, landslide which covered a distance of 2500 meters in 50 seconds (about 100 miles per hour mean velocity); its maximum velocity was probably about 200 miles per hour. Albert Heim, who investigated the Elm slide, believed velocities of 50 to 150 meters per second, or about 100 to more than 300 miles per hour, to be the rule for falls with which he was familiar.

Recently a mechanism for the rapid transport of some large landslides has been proposed. In a thorough investigation of the Blackhawk landslide, San Bernardino County, California, in 1959, R. L. Shreve showed that this landslide could only have come about by being transported on a layer of compressed air. He further demonstrated that such a mechanism is physically possible from a theoretical standpoint. He later, in 1965, indicated that this hypothesis accounts for many aspects of similar large landslides elsewhere in the world. Apparently, the same transportation mechanism later was suggested independently by P. E. Kent (1966).

CAUSES OF LANDSLIDES

The causes of landsliding can be traced to the inherent properties of the rocks, and to external factors related to the geologic setting. These terms, "inherent" and "external," correspond in general to other twofold divisions of the causes of landsliding, such as "real" and "immediate," as proposed by D. P. Krynine and W. R. Judd (1957).

The inherent properties of a rock unit which may lead to a "slide-prone" condition include low strength minerals, such as kaolinite; minerals possessing perfect cleavage, such as gypsum and some serpentine minerals; rocks that swell, such as montmorillonite-bearing and anhydrite-bearing rocks. Another inherent property that may lead to sliding is the orientation of planar elements of rocks such as bedding planes, joints, and other regular surfaces. Low-strength materials are commonly restricted to one or several lithologic units in an area.

External conditions that cause landslides range from gravity, which is always present, through erosion and rainfall, which are commonly or periodically present, to earthquakes, which are infrequent. Commonly a landslide results from two or more inherent properties plus two or more external conditions. A simplified example of this would be: A sequence of sedimentary layers, one of them a bed of volcanic ash, is deposited in a basin. As time passes, the ash bed is altered to bentonite (a montmorillonite-bearing altered volcanic ash) and the sedimentary sequence is elevated and tilted. At this point two potentially slide-prone inherent properties have been developed—the bentonite bed and its tilted condition. Later, erosion cuts a canyon exposing the bentonite bed, which is so oriented as to be very susceptible to sliding (the erosion is an external cause, as is gravity). Failures could follow either without additional external causes, or by the introduction of water which would expand and weaken the clay, or perhaps by shaking as a result of an earthquake.

Probably the most obvious of the external causes, other than gravity, is seasonal rainfall. In coastal California this takes place in the winter months. Landslides in the San Francisco area, for instance, are almost exclusively a winter-month phenomenon, manifested particularly during the seasons of above-normal rainfall. In the Los Angeles area, too, landslides usually increase in number during a season of great rainfall.

Earthquakes are probably the most prominent mechanism that directly triggers landslides. Earthquakes and landslides go hand in hand in California, particularly near earthquake epicenters. The area of sliding is related to the magnitude of the earthquake, the distance from the epicenter, and the state and kind of rock materials involved.

Landslides are common during earthquakes. The 1811 earthquake at New Madrid, Missouri, resulted in "severe" landslides in an area of more than 5,000 square miles along the Mississippi River Valley. There was apparently almost continuous landsliding for a distance of 40 miles along the Chickasaw Bluffs, east and south of New Madrid. The 1899 Yakutat Bay, Alaska, earthquake resulted in innumerable avalanches. One was reported at a distance of 430 miles from Yakutat Bay!

The 1906 San Francisco earthquake triggered numerous landslides over an area of approximately 13,000 square miles. The most extensive of these was a slump at Cape Fortunas which measured almost a mile in length and a quarter to half a mile in width. Most of the landslides resulting from this earthquake occurred on steep slopes or in soft alluvium along stream courses.

The Kern County earthquake of 1952 resulted in the formation of many hundreds of large and small landslides. Most of them were near the White Wolf fault, movement on which was responsible for the earthquake. Many other landslides occurred at distances of 50 to 60 miles from the fault. Rock falls partly blocked the Angeles Crest Highway between Pasadena and Vincent, in the San Gabriel Mountains. Near the White Wolf fault on Bear Mountain, landslides continued for at least two months after the main shock: "Whenever one of the numerous aftershocks was felt, clouds of dust from landslides would be seen rising out of the canyons shortly afterwards," reported geologists J. P. Buwalda and Pierre St. Amand (1955).

In terms of property damage, the most devastating features of the Alaska earthquake of 1964 were the landslides in Anchorage, some 80 miles from the earthquake's epicenter.

Faults cause landslides by means other than movement during earthquakes. Faults or fault zones, being the sites of crushed and fragmented rock, are of low strength—an inherent cause for erosion and landsliding. Geologic maps of numerous California areas show a preponderance of slides along faults; in a few cases the only landslides shown are along faults. Along much of the infamous San Andreas fault zone landslides are readily visible.

Reverse faults in certain circumstances appear to be very favorable sites for landslides. Drs. Buwalda and St. Amand state that, in the Tehachapi area, ". . . an active reverse fault with numerous branches, creating a high scarp, is a very favorable zone for landsliding on a large scale." The spectacular Blackhawk landslide on the north face of the San Bernardino Mountains owes its origin to low-angle reverse faulting. Turtle Mountain, the site of the Frank, Alberta, landslide, consists of Paleozoic limestone thrust over Mesozoic shale, sandstone, and coal beds. Several large slides along the northeast side of the Avawatz Mountains, in the Mojave Desert, may be due to oversteepening of slopes resulting from reverse faulting.

Obviously oversteepened topography caused by faulting is not limited to reverse fault movement. Scarps produced by normal faulting are the most spectacular in the state. The steep eastern face of the Sierra Nevada is the site of constant rock falls. The high scarp of the San Jacinto fault, north of the town of San Jacinto, appears rather thoroughly covered by large landslides.

Differential erosion gives rise to over-steepened topography and vertical faces, as in the Oroville area, where basalt overlies barely consolidated sediments. Erosion by running water and slumps undermine the basalt cap and produce extensive rockfalls and rockslides. Above much of the California shoreline, wave action produces steep cliffs which result in recurring landslides.

Mudflows, generally, the result of canyon scour following torrential downpour in arid or semiarid areas, are common features in California. A special case of this type of flow accompanies volcanism and can occur in any climate. Some volcanic mudflows reach considerable size, such as those that took place at the start of the 1919 eruption of Gunong Keloet in Java. This eruption and attendant activity killed more than 5,000 people. Such mudflows are common in other parts of the world, though very infrequent in California. The eruption of Mt. Lassen—one of the few historically recorded volcanic eruptions in California—was accompanied by extensive mudflows. Especially notable were those that occurred in conjunction with the explosions of May 19-22, 1915; these were the greatest explosions of the 3-year period of activity.

The activities of man must be considered an external cause contributing to the triggering of some spectacular landslides. Slate quarrying has been cited as a cause for the landslide at Elm, Switzerland; coal mining has been suggested as a contributing factor in the Canadian landslide at Frank, Alberta.

Landslides, which killed 11 people near Menton, France, were blamed on the cultivation of carnations. The farmers of the region, unaware of the element of stabilization created by roots of olive trees, removed the trees in favor of the more profitable but less stabilizing carnations.

LANDSLIDES IN CALIFORNIA

Within the boundaries of California is almost every imaginable type of rock, structure, physiography, and climate. Unfavorable elements within each of these factors are generally considered to be basic causes of landsliding. As a result, landslides are found in most of the vastly different environments of California.

The coastal areas of California appear to contain the most landslides. A prime factor in these areas is the relative instability of some of the rocks of Tertiary and late Mesozoic age. As these areas of the state show the most rapid population growth, the recognition and understanding of landslides in them is of paramount importance.

In the northern coastal ranges of California, landslides appear to be a pervasive feature, especially in the rocks of the Franciscan Formation and associated serpentine. Andrew Lawson, as early as 1908, indicated that landslides were important ". . . in the evolution of the geomorphology of the Coast Ranges of California to an extent equaled in few other regions . . ." This fact was re-emphasized by W. P. Irwin in 1960: ". . . landslides" he wrote, "are most common and widespread throughout the central belt of Franciscan Formation where they are perhaps the foremost mode of degradation of the landscape." Some landslides or landslide areas mapped by him are nearly 10 miles long.

C. B. Beaty (1956) found that, in the central Coast Ranges of California, ". . . landslides may well be the major agent in the processes at work which move material from higher to lower elevations." In this region slides occur on slopes as gentle as 3° to 5°, as well as on steeper slopes.

The coastal areas of southern California are similarly very susceptible to landsliding. Landslides, such as the Portuguese Bend landslide on the Palos Verdes Peninsula in Los Angeles County, have resulted in losses aggregating many millions of dollars.

Recent geologic mapping indicated numerous landslides adjacent to and within the Los Angeles area. Even the "solid" crystalline basement rocks of the Santa Monica and San Gabriel Mountains are literally covered with landslides.

High mountain ranges, such as the Sierra Nevada, Klamath, and San Gabriel, are areas of extensive mass-wasting. Quantitatively the most important landslides, yet the least impressive, are probably the innumerable rock falls which form the widespread talus deposits of these mountains. Many lakes in the Sierra Nevada, such as Mirror Lake in Yosemite Valley and Kern Lake in Kern River Canyon, originated from landslides that blocked the canyons. Close relatives of landslides, the slowmoving rock glaciers, are found in parts of the Sierra Nevada. Some of these attain a maximum dimension of at least a mile.

Landslides are common within the semi-arid or arid deserts of the state; talus is very widespread in the high mountains, and mudflows are in evidence in many areas. Interlayered with alluvial fan deposits in the intermontane basins throughout the Basin and Range physiographic region are sheets of unsorted debris interpreted as ancient mudflows. These are similar—in the nature of their material—to those of present-day mudflows. On the flanks of the desert ranges, such as the Santa Rosa or San Bernardino Mountains, are scattered large landslides; mudflows are found in the San Gabriel Mountains . . . .

URBAN HILLSIDE DEVELOPMENT

Intensive hillside development can lead to landsliding if the geology is not thoroughly understood and considered prior to development. In many areas of California undergoing hillside development at this time, detailed geologic mapping is a basic prerequisite for the formulation of grading plans. Proper grading practices will minimize the possibility of initiating landslides, both during and after grading.

Knowledge of geologic features, such as the orientation of bedding planes or joint systems, the presence of structurally weak units, and the presence of expansive or clayey beds, will aid in determining the proper orientation of cut slopes and proper cut-slope angles. This knowledge also enables an engineer to determine whether preventive or corrective measures, such as buttressing of known or suspected trouble sites, are needed.

Related directly to landslide problems in artificially cut slopes are problems in areas being filled. The placing of a hillside fill, unless done properly on a suitably stable and amenable surface, can readily lead to failure of the fill.

Probably the most familiar and most troublesome man-induced landslides are the small landslides in road cuts or, less commonly, in road fills. Though most man-caused landslides are here termed small, they do not appear to be small to the home owner when his backyard disappears and his property value is halved. The occurrence of such "small" landslides can be a crushing financial loss to both developers and home owners. When just a few of these small landslides occur together, the resultant loss is a disaster; and so it has been declared in western Los Angeles County.

To what extent man and his activities have influenced the triggering of a landslide can, in many cases, be debated. Such apparent subtleties as lawn water, sewage effluent, or street drainage discharged into already "precarious" geologic situations have been singled out as the causes, or as the renewing agents, of landsliding.

A recent court ruling found the County of Los Angeles to be party to the reactivation of part of an ancient landslide at Portuguese Bend, Palos Verdes Hills, California. The eastern part of this old landslide, which covers 300 to 400 acres, began moving in the summer of 1956 and has continued to move. In the period between the beginning of the movement and September 1959 damage to the property was estimated to be in excess of 10 million dollars. Possible causes considered to have led to the reactivation of this slide include: (1) increased ground water due to surface watering and sewage effluent, (2) increased natural precipitation and, (3) loading at the landslide head by highway fill.

A court judgment against the County of Los Angeles for their supposed role in the landslide reactivation was $5,360,000. This sum gives the landslide a tangible connection to all Los Angeles County taxpayers.

LANDSLIDE PREVENTION— KNOWLEDGE OF THE TERRANE

In the past it was common, when studying the general geology of a region, to give only cursory attention to landslides. Some geologists faithfully recorded the presence of landslides, but gave only slightest mention to them in their text. Others discussed their existence in the text but did not map them. Striking cases of lithologic, structural, or geomorphic control of landslides have gone entirely unmentioned.

Today, especially in the regions of urban or expected urban growth, intensive studies are being made of the distribution of landslides, as well as of other geologic features pertinent to urban development. This work has been identified periodically as engineering geology, urban geology, or environmental geology, by the various agencies engaged in the efforts.

The U.S. Geological Survey was the first governmental agency to initiate regional detail mapping in urban areas within California. This work was initiated in the San Francisco Bay area just before 1950; and, in the late 1950s, work was begun in the Baldwin Hills and Pacific Palisades areas of southern California. Currently the U.S. Geological Survey is mapping a large part of the Santa Monica Mountains in the

Malibu area in cooperation with the Los Angeles County Engineer. These studies are in large part concerned with surficial materials, their distribution, composition, origin, and relationship to geologic framework. One goal of these studies is to provide a map and text useful in planning future urban development. They do not replace the detailed site investigations made by engineering geologists, but rather draw attention to large regional features pertinent to the local problem. Recognition of the fact that a particular rock unit is prone to fail in one area and not in another, or is prone to slide under certain conditions, can be an invaluable aid in long-range planning and in the evaluation of a specific site. Since 1960 the State Division of Mines and Geology has undertaken an ever-widening program of urban geologic studies. A paramount concern in these investigations is the origin of landslides and their geologic setting .

LANDSLIDE PREVENTION—
ENGINEERING TECHNIQUES

In the prevention and correction of landslides, various engineering techniques have been employed, with different degrees of success. A prerequisite is the recognition of landslide or potential landslide areas.

In regions where cuts are to be made in unstable materials several possible alternatives exist. In areas of unfavorably oriented planar structures or materials of low strength the stability of the slope may be increased merely by flattening the cut-slope angle or benching the slope. Construction of retaining structures such as fill buttresses, concrete walls or slopes, cribbing, and pilings can be effective. Gabrons, used in Great Britain to stabilize slopes, are steel wire crates filled with handsize rocks. These are very strong structures and have the added advantage of being permeable. The use of piles, which is often ineffective as a remedial measure, must be advised only after a thorough examination, because vibrations produced during the driving of piles can induce failure in sensitive materials, or accelerate slow-moving landslides. During some highway construction the problem has been avoided entirely by bridging over unstable areas. Partial or complete removal of unstable materials or landslides is also used as a positive remedial measure. Rock bolts, bolts inserted and wedged in holes drilled through unstable or potentially unstable rocks into stable rocks, were extensively used at the Glen Canyon

Dam on the Colorado River. At the Howard A. Hanson Dam, on the Green River, Washington, rock bolts as much as 40 feet in length were used to secure the slopes.

Commonly, stability can be increased by decreasing groundwater pressure in the unstable area. This, in part, can be accomplished by increasing surface runoff or by sealing the surface. Excessive groundwater can be successfully withdrawn by a subdrain system in the interior of the landslide area.

The Ventura Avenue oil field, Ventura County, a very important source of petroleum in the state, has extensive landslides which have caused considerable damage to producing oil wells. To increase the stability of the problem area, the cover of vegetation was removed and the area covered with macadam. This technique, together with extensive systems of horizontal subdrains to the interiors of the slides, has been quite effective in decreasing landslide movement.

A unique remedial system was used in the Pacific Palisades area of southern California. After several landslides in 1932, two exploratory tunnels were dug to drain water believed to be perched on a clay stratum. No free water was encountered. Therefore, as simple draining methods could not be used, additional tunnels were dug and hot air was circulated to dry out the clay. This apparently successful operation continued for 6 years. An estimated 3000 pounds of water was evaporated daily during the first 6 months of operation.

To stabilize a landslide threatening to impede construction of Grand Coulee Dam, another unusual corrective measure was used. The landslide which was composed of water-laden silt was stabilized by freezing the silt-water mixture. This was done using 377 freezing points and a refrigeration system circulating a brine-ammonia solution. The system was able to make 160,000 pounds of ice a day. A frozen dam 40 feet high, 20 feet thick, and 100 feet long was formed during construction to prevent further landslide movement.

LANDSLIDE PREDICTION

A new and interesting field of study is landslide prediction: that is, either to forecast an immediate failure, or to ascertain where landslides will occur. A beginning on forecasting landslides has been made by the Norwegian Geotechnical Institute. In Norway, rock falls on the steep faces of fjords have caused huge waves, which in turn have destroyed shoreline villages. The Institute designed and installed automatic sensing extensometers, which relay any slight differential rock movements which might precede a rock fall.

The second type of slope failure prediction entails an intensive geologic investigation of the entire region in question. With the knowledge of the basic geologic conditions, the inherent rock properties, and the external causes which give rise to landslides, predictions of the locations, or the most likely locations for sliding can be made.

REFERENCES

Alden, W. C., 1928, Landslide and flood at Gros Ventre, Wyoming: American Institute of Mining and Metallurgical Engineers Trans., v. 76, p. 347-361.

Bates, H. W., 1875, The naturalist on the River Amazon. London, John Murray, p. 249-250.

Beaty, C. B., 1956, Landslides and slope exposure: Journal of Geology, v. 64, p. 70-74.

Blackwelder, Eliot, 1928, Mudflow as a geologic agent in semiarid mountains: Geological Society of America Bull., v. 39, p. 465-484.

Bonney, T. G., 1902, Moraines and mud-streams in the Alps: Geological Magazine, v. 9, p. 8-16.

Brigham, A. P., 1906, A Norwegian landslip: Geographical Society of Philadelphia Bull, v. 4, p. 292-296.

Bumgarten, Karl, 1910, Thunder Mountain landslide (Idaho): Mining and Scientific Press, v. 101, p. 698-699.

Buss, Ernst, and Heim, Albert, 1881, Der Bergsturz von Elm: J. Wuster und Cie, Geographischer Verlag, p. 163.

Buwalda, J. P., and St. Amand, Pierre, 1955, Geological effects of the Arvin-Tehachapi earthquake: California Division of Mines Bull. 171, p. 41-56.

Clark, T. H., 1947, Two recent landslides in Quebec: Royal Society of Canada Trans., v. 41, p. 9-18.

Close, Upton, and McCormick, Elsie, 1922, Where the mountains walked: National Geographic Magazine, v. 41, p. 461-464.

Crandell, D. R., and Fahnestock, R. K., 1965, Rockfalls and avalanches from Little Tahoma Peak on Mount Rainier, Washington: U.S. Geological Survey Bull. 1221-A, 30 p.

Daly, R. A., Miller, W. G., and Rice, G. S., 1912, Report of the commission appointed to investigate Turtle Mountain, Frank, Alberta: Canada Geological Survey, Mem. 27, 34 p.

Dawson, G. M., 1899, Remarkable landslip in Portneuf County, Quebec: Geological Society of America Bull, v. 10, p. 484-490.

Fuller, M. L., 1912, The New Madrid earthquake: U.S. Geological Survey Bull. 494, 119 p.

Hadley, J. B., 1964, Landslides and related phenomena accompanying the Hegben Lake earthquake of August 17, 1959: U.S. Geological Survey Prof. Paper 435-K, p. 107-138.

Harrison, J. V., and Falcon, N. L., 1937, The Saidmarreh landslip, southwest Iran: Geographical Journal, v. 89, p. 42-47.

Heezen, B. C., and Ewing, Maurice, 1952, Turbidity currents and submarine slumps, and the 1929 Grand Banks earthquake: Journal of Science, v. 250, p. 849-873.

Heim, Albert, 1882, Der Bergsturz von Elm: Deutsche geol. Gell., Zeitschr., v. 34, p. 74-113, 435-439.

Heim, Albert, 1932, Bergsturz und Menschen Leben: Fretz und Wasmuth Verlag A. G., 218 p.

Heim, A., Moser, R., and Bürkli-Ziegler, A., 1888, Die Catastrophe von Zug 5 Juli 1887: Zurich, Hofer und Burger, 49 p.

Herling, E. W., and Stafford, Gifford, 1952, Orinda slide: California Highways and Public Works, v. 31, nos. 1 and 2, p. 45.

Howe, Ernest, 1909, Landslides in the San Juan Mountains, Colorado, including a consideration of their causes and their classification: U.S. Geological Survey Prof. Paper, 67, 58 p.

Irwin, W. P., 1960, Geologic reconnaissance of the northern Coast Ranges, California, with a summary of the mineral deposits: California Division of Mines Bull. 179, 80 p.

Jahns, R. H., and Engel, A. E., 1950, Chaotic breccias in southern California; tectonic or sedimentary? (abstract): Geological Society of America Bull., v. 61, p. 1474.

Jordan, R. H., 1949, A Florida landslide: Journal of Geology, v. 57, p. 418-419.

Kent, P. E. 1966, The transport mechanism in catastrophic rock fall: Journal of Geology, v. 74, p. 79-83.

Krauskopf, K. B., Feitler, S., and Griggs, A. B., 1939, Structural features of a landslide near Gilroy, California: Journal of Geology, v. 67, p. 630-648.

Krynine, D. P., and Judd, W. R., 1957, Principles of engineering geology and geotechnics. McGraw-Hill Book Co., Inc., New York, 699 p.

Lawson, A. C., et al., 1908, The California earthquake of April 18, 1906 (Report of the State Earthquake Investigation Commission): Carnegie Institute of Washington Pub. 87, v. 1, pt. 2, p. 384-401.

Legget, R. F., 1962, Geology and engineering. New York, McGraw-Hill, 884 p.

Longwell, Chester R., 1951, Megabreccia developed downslope from large faults: American Journal of Science, v. 249, p. 343-355.

McGill, J. T., 1959, Preliminary map of the landslides in the Pacific Palisades area, City of Los Angeles, California: U.S. Geological Survey, Misc. Geol. Inv., Map 1-284.

Merriam, Richard, 1960, Portuguese Bend landslide, Palos Verdes Hills, California: Journal of Geology, v. 68, p. 140-153.

Miller, W. J., 1931, The landslide at Point Fermin, California: Scientific Monthly, v. 32, p. 464-469.

Moore, J. G., 1964, Giant submarine landslides on the Hawaiian Ridge: U.S. Geological Survey Prof. Paper 501-D, p. D95-98.

Mudge, M. R., 1965, Rockfall-avalanche and rockslide-avalanche deposits at Sawtooth Ridge, Montana: Geological Society of America Bull., v. 76, p. 1003-1014.

National Academy of Science, 1924, Report of the

Committee of the National Academy of Sciences on Panama Canal slides: National Academy of Science, Washington, Mem., v. 18, 84 p.

Peebles, J. J., 1962, Engineering geology of the Cartwright Canyon quadrangle (Idaho): Idaho Bureau of Mines and Geology Pamphlet 127, 68 p.

Reiche, Parry, 1937, The Toreva block—a distinctive landslide type: Journal of Geology, v. 45, p. 538-548.

Scrivenor, J. B., 1929, The mudstreams ("lahars") of Gunon Keolet in Java: Geological Magazine, v. 66, p. 433-434.

Selli, R., Trevisan, L., Carboni, G. C., Mazzanti, R., and Ciabatti, M., 1964, La frana del Vaiont: Annale del Museo Geologico de Bologna, serie 2, vol. 32, 154 p.

Sharp, R. P., and Nobles, L. H., 1953, Mudflow of 1941 at Wrightwood, southern California: Geological Society of America Bull., v. 64, p. 547-560.

*Sharpe, C. F. S., 1938, Landslides and related phenomena. New York, Columbia University Press, 137 p.

Sharpe, C. F. S., and Dosch, E. F., 1942, Relation of soilcreep to earthflow in the Appalachian Plateaus: Journal of Geomorphology, v. 5, p. 312-328.

Shreve, R. L., 1959, Geology and mechanics of the Blackhawk landslide, Lucerne Valley, California: California Institute of Technology, unpublished Ph.D. thesis, 79 p.

Shreve, R. L., 1965, Air-layer lubrication of large avalanches: Geological Society of America Annual meeting, Kansas City, p. 151.

Smith, Rockwell, 1958, Economic and legal aspects: Chapter 2, in Eckel, E. B., ed., Landslides and engineering practice: National Research Council, Highway Research Board, Special Rept. 29. p. 6-19.

Strahler, A. N., 1940, Landslides of the Vermillion and Echo Cliffs, northern Arizona: Journal of Geomorphology v. 3, p. 285-301.

Troxell, H. C., and Peterson, J. Q., 1937, Flood in La Canada Valley, California January 1, 1934: U.S. Geological Survey Water-Supply Paper 796-C, p. 53-98.

Varnes, D. J., 1958, Landslide types and processes: Chapter 3, in Eckel, E. B., ed., Landslides and engineering practice: National Research Council, Highway Research Board, Special Rept. 29, p. 20-47.

Varnes, H. D., 1949, Landslides problems of southwestern Colorado: U.S. Geological Survey Circ. 31, 13 p.

Woodford, A. O., and Harriss, T. F., 1928, Geology of Blackhawk Canyon, San Bernardino Mountains, California: University of California Pub., Department Geological Sciences Bull., v. 17, p. 265-304.

Woolley, R. R., 1946, Cloudburst floods in Utah: U.S. Geological Survey Water-Supply Paper 994, 120 p.

15. SOME ESTIMATES OF THE THERMAL EFFECTS
OF A HEATED PIPELINE IN PERMAFROST

ARTHUR H. LACHENBRUCH

As one means of transporting crude oil from oil fields on the Alaskan Arctic coast to a year-round ice-free port, a large pipeline traversing most of the state of Alaska from north to south has been proposed. Plans call for a pipe 4 feet in diameter, which will be buried along most of the route in permafrost. According to preliminary estimates the initial heat in the oil plus frictional heating in the pipe are expected to maintain oil temperatures in the neighborhood of 70° to 80°C (158° to 176°F) along the route when full production is achieved. Such an installation would thaw the surrounding permafrost. Where the ice content of permafrost is not high, and other conditions are favorable, thawing by the buried pipe might cause no special problems. Under adverse local conditions, however, this thawing could have significant effects on the environment, and possibly upon the security of the pipeline. It is important that any potential problem be identified prior to its occurrence so that it can be accommodated by proper pipeline design. Identifying a problem in advance depends upon an understanding of the conditions under which the problem will occur. If the pipeline system is properly designed, and if it is constructed and maintained in compliance with the design, problems will not occur. Perhaps "proper design" in some areas will involve abandoning plans for burial or changing the route; in others it might involve burying the pipe and invoking special engineering designs or monitoring procedures. These are matters to be determined by much additional study and an intensive program of field and laboratory measurements of conditions along the route.

In this study a few basic principles were applied to simplified models of permafrost regimes to identify some effects of a heated pipe, the conditions that control them, and the approximate ranges of physical properties for which these effects are likely to result in problems. The computations are approximate, and

Extracted with the author's permission from *U. S. Geological Survey Circular 632*, 23 p., 1970.

the problems discussed are only illustrative examples. Comprehensive discussions of these and related effects, taking account of physical and theoretical refinements, are beyond the scope of the report. Refined studies will probably be needed, however, to form an adequate basis for engineering design.

It is difficult to summarize these effects briefly, but a few will be mentioned. The reader is urged to consult the full text for a more complete statement of the conditions under which they are likely to occur. It should be emphasized that whether or not such conditions exist is a matter yet to be determined by measurements on permafrost materials along the pipeline route. Such measurements are essential for predictions of the interaction between the pipeline and its environment.

A 4-foot pipeline buried 6 feet in permafrost and heated to 80°C (176°F) will thaw a cylindrical region 20 to 30 feet in diameter in a few years in typical permafrost materials. At the end of the second decade of operation, typical thawing depths would be 40 to 50 feet near the southern limit of permafrost and 35 to 40 feet in northern Alaska where permafrost is colder. Except for special materials near the northern end, equilibrium conditions will not be reached and thawing will continue throughout the life of the pipeline, but at a progressively decreasing rate. If the thawed material or the water within it flows, these amounts of thawing can be increased several fold. If the pipeline temperature were only 30°C (instead of 80°C), the depth of thawing would probably be reduced by only 30 or 40 percent. The principal effect of insulating the pipe would be to increase oil temperatures rather than to decrease thawing.

If permafrost sediments have excess ice and a very low permeability when thawed, melting below the pipe could generate free water faster than it could filter to the surface. As a result the material in the thawed cylinder could persist as a semiliquid slurry. Where permeabilities are very low and excess ice contents are moderate, thawing rates could be sufficient to maintain this state for decades.

If the strength of these slurries is less than 1 pound per square foot, they will flow with substantial velocities on such imperceptible slopes as are characteristic of "flat" basins. The entire thawed cylinder would tend to flow like a viscous river and seek a level. As an extreme example, if these slurries occured over distances of several miles on almost imperceptible slopes, the uphill end of the pipe could, in a few years, be lying at the bottom of a slumping trench tens of feet deep, while at the downhill end, millions of cubic feet of mud (containing the pipe) could be extruded out over the surface. Where the pipe settled to the bottom of the trench, it would accelerate thawing and flow, and the process could be self-perpetuating. The pipeline could be jeopardized by loss of support in the trench and by displacement in the mudflow, and the disruption to the landscape could be substantial. Where such extreme conditions might occur, these problems could normally be anticipated by observations prior to or during construction. Less extreme conditions leading to partial liquefaction might be more difficult to identify in advance.

Where the pipe passed from strong material into a liquefied region, it would tend to float or sink, depending on the density of the slurry. It could be severely stressed by the resulting forces.

Almost imperceptible systematic movements of the thawed material can accelerate the thawing process locally by as much as a thousand times. Hence if flow occurs the ultimate amount of thawing can be very great and difficult to predict.

Seismic vibrations can cause loosely packed saturated sands and silts to liquefy. Hence where such material occupied the thawed zone around the pipe, the flow, buoyancy, and convective effects just discussed could also be caused by an earthquake. The southern part of the pipeline route lies in an active seismic zone.

Differential settlement causing shearing stresses in a pipe can result from a variety of processes—the most conspicuous of which is probably the thawing of ice wedges. These massive vertical veins of ice form tight polygonal networks, commonly invisible from the surface and difficult to delineate with borings. They are widely distributed in northern Alaska. A pipeline crossing ice-wedge networks at random angles would thaw the wedges quickly and could there-

by lose support over considerable spans. A statistical calculation suggests that in typical ice-wedge terrain, conditions which might exceed the design stress of the pipeline could occur on the average of once every mile. Most of these conditions could be anticipated by observations made during trenching.

Settlement of the pipe due to thawing is a cumulative effect of all of the thawed material beneath it. Only a negligibly small fraction of this material will be directly observed in separated bore holes. Rather small and subtle changes in porosities, moisture content, and other properties occurring over lateral distances of tens of feet could cause differential settlement resulting in excessive stress on the pipe. Such changes may be difficult or impossible to detect in advance by trenching and boring, even if holes were drilled every 1,000 feet along the route.

Where the sediments are saturated or oversaturated, a trench one or more feet deep and tens of feet wide will probably develop over the pipeline in a few years; it will deepen and widen somewhat as time progresses. Where the trench is discontinuous it could create a series of ponds which could enlarge by thermal processes under certain conditions. Indiscriminate drainage of these ponds could create excessive stress on the pipe by removing buoyant forces that might be partially supporting it in these differentially settled zones.

Where the trench above the pipeline is continuous, it could become a stream channel, altering drainage patterns and creating erosion problems along the pipeline.

Heat conducted from the pipe to the surface will have a significant effect on surface temperatures and plant-root temperatures over a band not more than about 60 feet wide. Directly over the pipe snow will probably remain on the ground only after the heavier storms.

The inflow of water into the depression likely to develop over the pipe will probably more than supply the heat requirements for excess evaporation, and in general conditions will probably remain wet. However, if the material overlying the pipe should be very permeable, thermal convection of water in the sediments could probably increase heat loss from the pipe to the surface one-hundred fold. Under these conditions evaporation would probably exceed the rate of local water supply and the region above the pipe could eventually become desiccated. Heat and moisture transfer above the pipe could have a significant effect on the formation of local ground fog.

This study was not exhaustive. Potential problems certainly exist that have not been considered, and some that have been considered may be shown not to exist by further studies.

The report represents one perspective on an overall problem that transcends many disciplines and requires the perspectives of many for an optimal solution. It is hoped that the report will provide one reference point for objective discussion between the people of many backgrounds who must communicate effectively on this issue.

16. LAND SUBSIDENCE DUE TO WITHDRAWAL OF FLUIDS

J. F. POLAND and G. H. DAVIS

INTRODUCTION

Principal causes of land-surface subsidence are removal of solids or fluids from beneath the land surface, either naturally or artificially; solution; oxidation; compaction of soil or sediments under surface loading, vibration, or wetting; and tectonic movement. This paper discusses subsidence believed to have been caused chiefly, if not wholly, by fluid withdrawal by man.

The two types of fluid withdrawal by man that have caused noticeable subsidence under favorable geologic conditions are (1) the withdrawal of oil, gas, and associated water and (2) the withdrawal of ground water. The withdrawal of steam for geothermal power has caused subsidence; also, the withdrawal of brines, reportedly, has caused subsidence.

Regardless of the nature of the fluid removed, the principles involved are the same; therefore, the separation of subsidence phenomena due to fluid withdrawal into those caused by exploitation of oil and gas fields and those caused by pumping of ground water may seem highly arbitrary. On the other hand, there are marked differences in the character and dimensions of the two types of reservoirs and in the magnitude of man-made stresses involved. Oil and gas commonly are produced from rocks that are older, at greater depth, more consolidated and have lower permeability and porosity than most ground-water reservoir rocks. Also, oil and gas come from fields of relatively small extent, mostly from 1 to 50 square miles; whereas ground-water reservoirs may be many hundreds of square miles in area. Fluid pressures in deep oil- or gas-producing zones in a fully exploited field may be reduced as much as 2000-4000 pounds per square inch, from initial hydrostatic to approximately atmospheric pressure. Rarely has the fluid pressure in a ground-water reservoir

Extracted from a longer report of the same title, with the permission of the authors and The Geological Society of America, from *Reviews in Engineering Geology,* D. J. Varnes and G. Kiersch (eds.), v. 2, p. 187-269, 1969. Copyright 1969 The Geological Society of America.

been reduced more than 200 pounds per square inch (about 460 feet). One of the extreme declines of artesian head in the United States has been in the Chicago area where drawdown of head in the principal confined aquifer of Cambrian and Ordovician age has exceeded 600 feet since 1864 (Walton and Walker, 1961.

Fuller (1908, p. 33) was the first to theorize that withdrawal of fluids and decrease of fluid pressure cause sinking of the land surface (because of the removal of the hydrostatic support). The first published descriptions of subsidence, by Minor (1925) and Pratt and Johnson (1926) were for the Goose Creek oil field in Texas. The first specific observation of subsidence due to ground-water withdrawal—that in the Santa Clara Valley in California—was published in 1933 (Rappleye). Most of the major subsidences described in this paper have developed as a result of intensified withdrawal of fluid resources during and since the second World War in order to satisfy the needs of the burgeoning world population. Thus, most of the problems and damage due to subsidence have developed in the past two decades; these have spurred several intensive investigations of causes and possible remedial measures. Still more intensive and widespread exploiting of fluid resources, especially ground water, in the future will multiply the incidence of subsidence. Therefore, it appears particularly appropriate at this time to summarize available information on subsidence due to fluid withdrawal.

SUBSIDENCE OF OIL AND GAS FIELDS

Major subsidence of three oil fields has been reported in the literature. These are Goose Creek oil field in Texas; the Wilmington oil field in the harbor area of Los Angeles and Long Beach, California; and oil fields on the shore of Lake Maracaibo in Venezuela. Although the Lake Maracaibo subsidence has been known since the early thirties (Kugler, 1933, p. 758, discussion, p. 769), little has been published on that subsidence. Each of these subsiding areas is at sea level, and the subsidence was obvious because of submergence of the land surface. Although local subsidence of as much as 40 feet occurred within the Sour Lake field, Hardin County, Texas, in 1929 (Carpenter and Spencer, 1940, p. 4), this subsidence was attributed to solution of salt and development of a cavity.

Minor subsidence has been noted at several California oil fields, such as Venice-Playa del Rey (Grant, 1944, p. 136) and Long Beach (Signal Hill), Huntington Beach, and Santa Fe Springs (Gilluly and Grant, 1949, p. 525-527). Undoubtedly, many oil fields away from the ocean or other large water bodies have subsided as much as several feet, but without repeated precise leveling such subsidence may pass unnoticed.

Gas fields at Niigata, Japan, and in the Po Delta, Italy, experienced rapid subsidence in the late fifties. The Niigata field is at sea level, and the Po Delta field borders the sea. Many other gas fields above sea level and not subject to inundation probably have experienced subsidence, but with no marked deleterious effects; thus, they have not been publicized.

Goose Creek Oil Field, Texas

The subsidence of Goose Creek oil field in Harris County, Texas, was the first subsidence due to fluid withdrawal described in the literature (Minor, 1925; Pratt and Johnson, 1926; Pratt, 1927; Snider, 1927). According to Pratt and Johnson (1926), development of the field began in 1917. By 1918, Gaillard Peninsula, which was at the mouth of Goose Creek and overlay part of the oil field, began to subside and soon was covered by the waters of San Jacinto Bay. The maximum subsidence, shown by periodic leveling, was more than 3 feet by 1925, and the area affected was about 2.5 miles long by 1.5 miles wide and conformed with the approximate limit of the producing oil wells (Fig. 1). No change in elevation of the land surface had occurred outside the affected area. Cracks developed at the north edge of the oil field, and by 1925, recurrent movement on these small faults had dropped the ground surface on the oil field (south) side as much as 16 inches. Similar faults developed on Hogg Island along the south edge of the field, and downward displacement of 3-12 inches occurred on the north side of these faults.

The State of Texas claimed title to the lands submerged by the subsidence and sought to recover the value of oil and gas removed subsequent to submergence. The court, however, decided in favor of the defendants, accepting

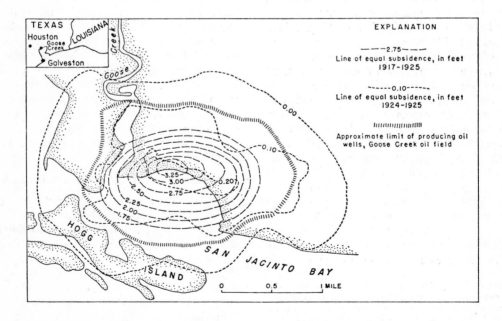

Figure 1. Subsidence, 1917-1925 and 1924-1925, at Goose Creek oil field, Harris County, Texas. *(Generalized after* **Pratt and Johnson, 1926, Fig. 77.)**

their contention that the subsidence was caused by an act of man, namely the removal of large volumes of oil, gas, water, and sand. If the subsidence had been shown to be a natural process, presumably, title to the submerged lands and the underlying oil would have passed to the State of Texas.

The oil at Goose Creek is withdrawn chiefly from lenticular deposits of relatively unconsolidated sand and clay of Oligocene to Pliocene age between depths of 700 and 4500 feet. The structure in the beds of Miocene and younger age is a gentle dome; the Oligocene sediments, beneath an unconformity, are intensely faulted. The volume of oil, gas (at 1000 pounds per square inch), water, and sand extracted from 1917-1926 exceeded 100 million barrels, about five times the calculated subsidence volume. The original reservoir pressures of 1000-1200 pounds per square inch had been reduced to atmospheric pressure by 1926.

Pratt and Johnson (1926) concluded that the subsidence was due to extraction of oil, water, gas, and sand because the area of subsidence corresponded with the area of extraction, because the time of subsidence and extraction corresponded, and because continued extraction was accompanied by continued subsidence.

Wilmington, California

A spectacular and costly land subsidence, first noticeable in 1940 and 1941, has occurred at the Wilmington oil field in the harbor area of Los Angeles and Long Beach, California. By August 1962, the subsidence had increased to 27 feet at its center and included an area of about 25 square miles that had subsided 2 feet or more. Much of the subsiding area initially was only 5-10 feet above sea level and is intensively industrialized, containing many costly structures, such as port facilities, industrial plants, oil wells, pipe lines, and a major naval shipyard.

The subsidence at the Wilmington oil field is particularly noteworthy for three reasons: (1) the vertical settlement of 27 feet at the center is the greatest subsidence due to fluid withdrawal known to have occurred to date anywhere in the world; (2) many fields yielding oil from deposits of similar age and from an equivalent depth range, of approximately similar lithology, and with comparable decrease in fluid pressure have *not* experienced subsidence of more than a few feet; and (3) corrective remedial action taken

since 1958 by repressuring of the oil zones had stopped the subsidence in much of the field by the end of 1962.

The first major published reports describing the subsidence (Harris and Harlow, 1947; Gilluly and Grant, 1949), both based on consulting reports made in 1945, concluded that it was caused primarily by the decrease in fluid pressure in the oil zones, due to removal of oil, gas, and water, which increased the grain-to-grain load and caused compaction. Those reports have been followed by many others, chiefly of the consulting type and reproduced in relatively few copies. To the authors' knowledge, these subsequent reports have concurred with the findings of the initial reports on the primary cause, which has been proven incontrovertibly by the results of the periodic casing collar logs and the repressuring.

Geology. The Los Angeles-Long Beach harbor area is underlain by sediments of Recent to Miocene age about 6000 feet thick that unconformably overlie a basement schist of pre-Tertiary age.

Seven productive oil zones have been developed, extending from a depth of about 2500 feet to 6000 feet.

The Wilmington field is a gently arched anticlinal fold plunging to the northwest. Five main faults that trend roughly north and south divide the oil field into six structural blocks. The faults divide the oil zones into semiseparate pools because of the barrier effect to movement of fluids although the effectiveness of the faults as barriers is reported to be highly variable. The per cent of sand in the several zones ranges from 23 to 70; the average porosity ranges from 24 to 34 per cent; and the weighted average permeability ranges from 100 to 1000 millidarcys (Murray-Aaron and Pheil, 1948, p. 11).

Development of the field. Oil production began in 1936 (Bartosh, 1938, p. 1052), reached a peak average rate of about 140,000 barrels a day in 1951, and declined to about 70,000 barrels a day by 1959. By March 1962, however, production increased to 82,000 barrels per day, due to the repressuring by water flood. Cumulative production through December 1962 was 913 million barrels of oil, 484 million barrels of water, and 832 million MCF of gas (data from Long Beach Harbor Dept.; gas volume at atmospheric pressure; MCF = 1000 cu feet). The developed productive area is about 10 square miles, but an undeveloped part of the field extends several miles to the southeast beneath the harbor.

Land subsidence. The subsidence of the Wilmington oil field began in 1937 (Gilluly and Grant, 1949, p. 464, 479) but was first definitely recognized in the summer of 1941 when the U.S. Coast and Geodetic Survey releveled lines between San Pedro and Long Beach that had been run in 1933-1934. Subsidence along Seaside Boulevard was 0.2 foot at the west boundary of Long Beach and reached a maximum of 1.3 feet at the east end of Terminal Island. Subsequent leveling by the U.S. Coast and Geodetic Survey in 1945 (July) indicated an increase in maximum subsidence to 4.2 feet and in 1946 (March), to at least 4.5 feet.

Because of the problems caused by the accelerating subsidence, the Long Beach Harbor Department established almost 300 bench marks in 1945, and since 1946, the Department has made level surveys to these marks every 3 months. In 1948, the U.S. Navy began quarterly surveys on a net of bench marks on the Naval base on Terminal Island; these surveys have been continued to date. The data from these surveys have been utilized by the Long Beach Harbor Department in preparing maps each year showing total and annual subsidence. These surveys are the basis for the lines of equal subsidence on Figure 2.

Gilluly and Grant (1949) attributed the subsidence of the Wilmington field to the compaction of the oil-bearing sands; whereas Harris and Harlow (1947) concluded that the subsidence was caused by compaction of the shales in the oil zones. As pointed out by Poland and others (1959, p. 143):

The publication of these two conflicting concepts on the mechanics of land subsidence emphasizes the need for careful research to resolve the relatively unexplored question of whether subsidence of the land surface associated with the withdrawal of large quantities of fluid is caused primarily by compaction of the permeable reservoir beds or of the relatively impermeable but porous silt, clay, and shale members which are interbedded with or confine the permeable beds, and which, in effect, are a part of the reservoir system. The authors of this paper surmise that most of the compaction has occurred in the siltstone interbeds (texture silty clay to clayey silt) so prevalent in the Wilmington oil zones. This surmise is based, in part, on

the results of consolidation tests on samples of sand and siltstones (silt and silty clay texture) from the Wilmington oil zones.

Horizontal movement. The vertical subsidence has been accompanied by horizontal movement directed inward toward the center of subsidence. This horizontal movement has been measured by surveys of a triangulation network of the Los Angeles County Engineer's office. In 1951, when subsidence at the center was 16 feet, horizontal movement since 1937 had been as much as 6.2 feet (Grant, 1954, Fig. 1). By 1962, some points on the east end of Terminal Island had moved as much as 9 feet, according to the Long Beach Harbor Department.

The compressional and tensional stresses and the horizontal movements caused by the bending of the sedimentary plate overlying the compacting oil zones have resulted in failure of many surface structures (Shoemaker, 1955; Shoemaker and Thorley, 1955; Neel, 1957). Sheared bridge columns of a lift bridge and buckled railroad tracks and pipe lines are representative examples.

Remedial measures. Extensive remedial measures have been necessary to keep the sea from invading the subsiding lands and structures (Shoemaker, 1955; Coxe, 1949). These measures have been chiefly in the form of construction of levees, retaining walls, fill, and raising of structures. Methods of repairing the sheared, deformed, or collapsed oil-well casings have been described by Frame (1952) and Allen (1959). The cost of remedial work to maintain structures and equipment in operating condition and to repair the several hundred ruptured oil wells had exceeded $100 million by 1962. This remedial work was passive although it was necessary in order to keep facilities operating; it did not reduce the subsidence or eliminate the cause.

Repressuring. Estimates of ultimate subsidence of 30-45 feet made in the middle 1950s spurred joint constructive action directed toward active remedial work. Findings of consulting reports in 1957 that repressuring of the oil zones by water injection would not only control subsidence but also increase oil recovery by about one half billion barrels furnished both a method and economic justification. Many difficult legal, economic, and engineering problems had to be overcome before water injection could be done on a field scale. Probably the greatest of these was unitization of the 117 producers (Anonymous, 1959b). By concerted action, most of these problems have been solved, and repressuring, which had been initiated on a pilot scale in 1953 by the City of Long Beach, was undertaken on a large scale in 1958.

Injection water is obtained from supply wells tapping shallow aquifers. In large part, it has essentially the composition of ocean water and in general is chemically compatible with the oil-zone waters. It is treated chemically to inhibit corrosion and prevent bacterial growth. Then, it is injected into the oil zones at casing-head pressures ranging from 850 to 2000 pounds per square inch (Anonymous, 1960). By August 1960, the rate of repressuring was 370,000 barrels per day through 136 injection wells; by October 1962, the rate had increased to about 530,000 barrels per day through 203 injection wells, and total injection had been about 575 million barrels. The Long Beach Harbor Department has estimated that a total of 300 injection wells and an injection rate of at least 1 million barrels per day will eventually be required. The estimated cost of the repressuring installations is about $30 million (Anonymous, 1959a).

TABLE 1. REBOUND TO 1963 OF SEVEN BENCH MARKS IN WILMINGTON OIL FIELD THAT RECOVERED FROM 6 TO 15 PER CENT OF THEIR INITIAL SUBSIDENCE

Bench mark	Approximate subsidence* (feet)	Rebound to May 1963 (feet)	Rebound in per cent of subsidence
Line 1			
364	4.0	0.49†	12
360R	5.7	.40†	7
Line 2			
M 22	2.7	.40†	15
1525	8.0	.45†	6
Line 3			
927D	3.7	.39	11
1786	5.3	.53	10
1790	6.0	.54	9

*Interpolated from map of subsidence, 1928-1960
†Rebound to August 1963

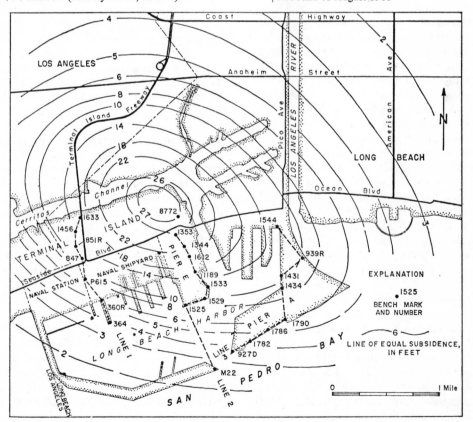

Figure 2. Subsidence from 1928 to August 1962 and location of selected bench marks at Long Beach Harbor area, California. (*Lines of equal subsidence from* Long Beach Harbor Department.)

Effects of repressuring on subsidence. The initial repressuring was concentrated largely in the southern part of the field for the purpose of slowing down and arresting subsidence in the waterfront area. In order to show the effect of repressuring on subsidence, the relative change of elevation has been plotted for bench marks along three north trending lines, shown on Figure 2.

The bench marks at the southern end of each line have experienced appreciable rebound. Table 1 shows the approximate rebound to May (or August) 1963 of seven bench marks that have recovered from 6 to 15 per cent of their initial subsidence. The maximum rebound has been 0.54 foot at bench mark 1790 (line 3), equivalent to about 9 per cent of the overall subsidence at that place.

Lake Maracaibo, Venezuela

Kugler (1933) first reported subsidence of oil fields along the eastern shore of Lake Maracaibo, Venezuela. In 1935, Collins described a seawall built in 1932 on the east shore of Lake Maracaibo to protect an extensive oil-field development from flooding. According to Collins (1935, p. 405), a drainage program was begun in 1923, coincident with the start of oil-field development, to drain the swamps and marshes adjacent to the village of Lagunillas on the lake shore. Several years later, the shore was sinking 1 foot a year. To protect the oil fields on land, a continuous wall almost 3 miles long was built using reinforced concrete sheetpiles.

Although various aspects of the subsidence have been under study at the University of Illinois and elsewhere for a number of years, no papers describing the subsidence have come to the attention of the authors. A paper by D. J. L. Kennedy (1961, Ph.D. thesis, University of Illinois, 251 p.), however, which reports on a study of well-casing failures associated with compaction of oil-producing strata in the eastern-shore fields, furnishes some information on the subsidence.

Oil was discovered in 1917 in the so-called Bolivar Coastal Fields on the northeast shore of Lake Maracaibo. Figure 3 shows the three main oil fields of this area. Much of the oil is produced from off-shore wells. The Tia Juana and Lagunillas fields were discovered in 1926, and the Bachaquero field was discovered in 1930. According to Kennedy (1961, Ph.D. thesis, p. 1), much of the oil has been produced from inter-

Figure 3. Flood-frequency curve for partial-duration series, West Branch Brandywine Creek at Coatesville, Pa., based on data for 1942, 1944-51.

bedded sands, hard clays, and silts of Miocene age, and the decrease in reservoir fluid pressure has caused compaction of these unconsolidated strata. He stated further that:

Evidence indicates that the consolidation of the shale layers within the producing stratum due to the increase in effective pressure is the chief cause of the subsidence; however, the compaction of the sands may contribute a considerable amount to the subsidence. He concluded that, in general, the greatest subsidence coincides with the greatest pressure decline and with the thickest Miocene producing zones.

As a result of the detailed study of liner or casing damage, Kennedy (1961, Ph.D. thesis, p. 104) concluded that the major cause of damage is the compaction of the producing strata because "casing damage occurs almost exclusively within the producing stratum or can be attributed to movements in the producing interval."

Po Delta, Italy

The Po Delta, on the Adriatic coast in northeastern Italy, subsided from various causes at a slow average rate of 1-3 mm a year from about 1890-1950, based on precise leveling by the Institute of Military Geography. Releveling in 1956, however, revealed a great increase in the rate of subsidence after 1950. The average annual subsidence from 1950-1951 to 1956 was a maximum of about 30 cm (1 foot) a year at the River Po, 16 km west of the coast. The shape of the subsiding area was oval, and the 5-cm-per-year subsidence line included an area about 20 km wide (north-south) by 40 km long, extending west from the coast. Flooding and damage caused by the subsidence has led to large expenditures for remedial work, such as construction and raising of levees and reclamation of flooded lands.

Methane gas is produced from this area in large quantities and is an important industrial resource. Commissions have been formed to study the causes of subsidence, and many papers have been published citing causes contributing to the subsidence. Suggested causes include compaction under natural overburden load, tectonic adjustment, rising sea level, and drying out of reclaimed lands (some of which contain peat beds).

The Po River delta (Venetian Po) has been built up very rapidly in Quaternary time. This has resulted in a thickness of 1000 m or more of relatively unconsolidated Quaternary deposits over most of the Delta—in synclinal areas, the thickness exceeds 2000 m (Dal Piaz, 1959). The deposits are chiefly marine (littoral with some lagoonal layers), sandy, and highly calcareous, but they contain some clay layers. According to Dal Piaz (1959, p. 450), Selli has distinguished five well-defined methane-bearing horizons. The gas accumulations are related to gentle undulations in the Quaternary strata or to breaks in the monoclinal dip. Methane also is produced from underlying deposits of Pliocene and Miocene age, but apparently, the major production is from the beds of Quaternary age. The saline and brackish waters in the methane layers have a chemical composition qualitatively similar to sea water.

The methane development began in 1938, and by 1956, gas production from the Delta area was at least 200 million m^3 (about 7 billion $feet^3$) a year. The ratio of gas to water is about 1 to 1. This methane is of great value to the economy of the region.

The rate of subsidence, which accelerated so sharply from 1951 to 1956, continued to increase after 1956. According to Gortani (1961), the area included between the lines of 20-25 cm of annual sinking increased from 8000 hectares (19,800 acres) in 1957-1958 to 17,000 hectares (42,000 acres) in 1959.

Analysis of the relationship between withdrawal of methane-bearing water and the subsidence did not lead to a clear cause and effect conclusion (Puppo, 1957); nevertheless, the costs of attempting to protect the subsiding lands from flooding became so great (about $33 million in 1960) that it was decided to carry out a crucial experiment—stop all the gas and water removal in an experimental area of 10,000 hectares (24,700 acres), including the area of most rapid subsidence. According to Gortani (1961), pumping in this area, which had been about 50 million m^3 (40,000 acre-feet) of water a year was stopped on February 20, 1960. Special bench-mark surveys were made every 3 months, and fluid levels in wells were measured weekly.

After 6 months of shutdown, several instructive developments could be reported. The piezometric level recovered rapidly in the closed-in area, and in general, the deeper the aquifer the greater the pressure recovery (as much as 15 m in 4 months). The bench-mark releveling showed that the maximum subsidence from February 20 to August 20, 1960, was 7.4 cm (annual rate about 15 cm). The rate of subsidence for bench marks in the area of no pumping decreased noticeably after February 20; whereas, for those outside, it continued unchanged (Gortani, 1961, Fig. 12).

A well 714 m deep near the center of subsidence was filled with concrete and used to record compaction. During the period of record, the observed sinking of the land surface with reference to the top of the concrete-filled casing indicated that the compaction of the deposits within the well depth was equal to the subsidence.

The results of the experimental shutdown of wells supported the conclusion that the extraction of the methane waters is the principal cause of the rapid sinking of the Po Delta (Gortani, 1961, p. 13). It was proposed to extend the shutdown over all the Delta area, which would stop the annual extraction of 250 million m^3 (200,000 acre-feet) of water from more than 850 gas wells yielding at least 200 million m^3 (about

7 billion feet[3]) of methane. The revoking of mineral rights is being considered (Anonymous, 1961). Thus, the great cost and difficulty of protecting the sinking area from the sea and from the river floods may close down a major industry. This closure poses economic and social problems as well as legislative problems relating to indemnity for losses suffered.

SUBSIDENCE DUE TO GROUND-WATER WITHDRAWAL

For many years, major subsidence of the land surface has been observed in certain areas of intensive ground-water withdrawal. Areas of major subsidence in California are the San Jose area in the Santa Clara Valley and the Los Banos-Kettleman City, Tulare-Wasco, and Arvin-Maricopa areas in the San Joaquin Valley. Elsewhere, the best-known subsidences are in Mexico City, Mexico, and in the Houston-Galveston area of Texas. All of these areas are underlain by confined aquifers, and in all, the artesian head has been drawn down at least several tens of feet by heavy withdrawal. Doubtless, subsidence has occurred in many other ground-water basins where artesian head of compressible confined aquifers has been drawn down 50-100 feet or more, but it has gone undetected because of lack of repeated leveling.

Mexico City, Mexico

Mexico City is in southeastern Mexico, in the west central part of the Valley of Mexico, a closed basin at an elevation of about 7500 feet surrounded by high mountains. The relatively flat part of the valley underlain by alluvial deposits is about 100 km long (north-south) and 15-40 km wide (Mooser, 1961, unnumbered geologic map). Many small rivers flow into the valley, and under natural conditions, the rivers formed a series of shallow lakes, the largest of which was Lake Texcoco.

Roberto Gayol (1929) presented the first specific evidence on the subsidence of Mexico City and pointed out the need for continuing observation. By 1959, subsidence exceeded 4 m (13 feet) beneath all the old city (extent of city in 1891) and was as much as 7.5 m (25 feet) in the northeast part (Fig. 22). This great and long-continued sinking has caused many problems in water transport, drainage, and in the construction of buildings and other engineering structures in the heart of a great and growing

city; consequently, this subsidence has been studied more intensively in its soil-mechanics aspects than has any other subsidence due to ground-water withdrawal.

Geology. At the end of the Cretaceous Period, crustal deformation of the Cretaceous limestone was accompanied by intensive volcanic activity, which has continued to Recent time but at a decreasing rate. The volcanic sequence has been andesite, rhyolite, and finally basalt. Only 2000 years ago, a basaltic lava flow drove the inhabitants from the valley (Zeevaert, 1949, Ph.D. thesis, University of Illinois, p. 20, 26).

In late Pliocene time and during most of the Pleistocene Epoch, inflowing streams brought coarse andesitic detritus into the valley. Logs of water wells show that sand and gravel containing some interbeds of clayey silt occur almost continuously from a depth of 50-60 m to more than 500 m. They constitute the highly productive aquifer underlying Mexico City (Zeevaert, 1949, Ph.D. thesis). This aquifer is overlain chiefly by soft fine-grained lake deposits of late Pleistocene age—volcanic ash and water-transported sediments.

The depositional units from the land surface to the top of the productive aquifer at about a depth of 50 m vary in thickness from place to place in the city. However, their character and thickness can be generalized as follows: artificial fill and water-laid silt and sand from the land surface to a depth of 6 m; then an upper soft bentonitic and diatomaceous silty clay about 30 m thick; then a coarse cemented sandy bed about 5 m thick; and then a second bentonitic silty clay 5-10 m thick, stiffer than the upper clay bed. Both of the bentonitic clay beds are highly compressible.

In the upper bentonitic clay, the natural water content ranges from 200 to as much as 500 per cent of the solids by weight, depending on location and loading history. The average value is about 300 per cent. The void ratio ranges from about 5 to 9; the average value is about 7. Thus, the porosity of this upper clay ranges from 84 to 90 per cent; the average is about 88 per cent. In the lower bentonitic clay, the natural water content is 200-300 per cent by weight. The void ratio generally is 4-5, indicating an average porosity of about 82 per cent.

Hydrology. Until the last few years, most of the water supply for Mexico City has been obtained from wells within the city. As early as

1854, 140 artesian wells had been constructed. According to Loehnberg (1958), water was supplied from 3000 privately owned wells 30-100 m (100-325 feet) deep and from about 220 municipal wells 100-300 m (325-1000 feet) deep in 1957. Private wells yielded about 2.5 m³/second (90 cubic feet per second), and municipal wells yielded about 6.5 m³/second (230 cubic feet per second). This discharge of these wells far exceeded the natural recharge. The great increase in demand for water was a result of the rapid increase in population, which grew from about one half million in 1895 to 1 million in 1922 and to 5 million people by 1960.

The artesian head in deep wells initially was a few feet above the land surface, but by 1959, the pressure at 50 m depth (at the top of the main aquifer) had decreased 20-35 m (65-110 feet) (Comision Hidrologica de la Cuenca del Valle de Mexico, 1961, p. 338).

The water table stands 1-2 m below the land surface beneath much of the old city, and its level has not changed appreciably throughout the historic record.

Land subsidence. Local subsidence first occurred owing to loading by the large Aztec structures and later by Spanish buildings. The principal subsidence, however, began in the late 1800s as a result of development of artesian water, the consequent decline of artesian head, and the increase in effective stress.

Between 1898 and 1938, subsidence was not defined by leveling; it probably was not uniform, but the average rate was about 4 cm per year (Marsal, and others, 1952, p. 3). The rate of subsidence increased sharply in 1938 and again in 1948, presumably as a result of increased withdrawal from municipal wells beginning in those years. From 1938 to 1948, the rate of sinking was about 15 cm per year; from 1948 to 1952, the rate increased to 30 cm (1 foot) per year in the central part of the city and to 50 cm per year locally (Marsal and Sainz-Ortiz, 1956, p. 3). After 1952, the rate decreased slightly to about

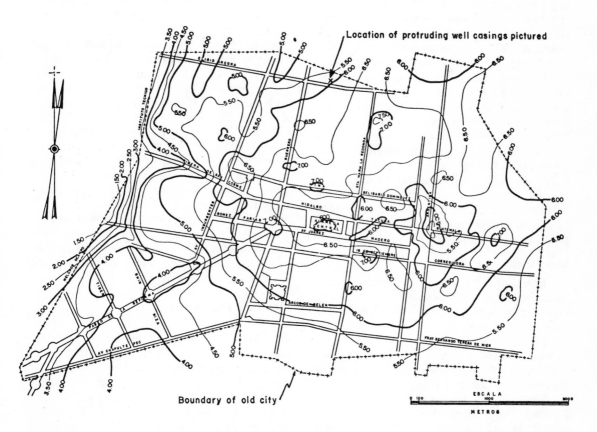

Figure 4. Subsidence, 1891-1959, of Mexico City, Mexico. Lines of equal subsidence in meters. (*After* Comision Hidrologica de la Cuenca del Valle de Mexico, 1961, p. 47.)

25 cm per year. The total subsidence from 1898 to 1956 was 5-7 m (16-23 feet).

Figure 4 shows the magnitude and distribution of subsidence in the old city from 1891 to 1959 as determined by leveling. Maximum subsidence was 7.5 m (25 feet), and subsidence exceeded 4 m (13 feet) in all but the western edge of the old city.

Protrusion of well casings is a common occurrence in the subsiding area and is a graphic demonstration of the decrease in thickness (compaction) of the sediments within the casing depth.

Cause of the subsidence. Investigators of the subsidence in the Mexico City area agree that the principal cause of the regional subsidence is the reduction in artesian pressure that has occurred—most rapidly since 1938.

Estimates of the proportion of subsidence caused by compaction of the upper 50 m of deposits that include the two bentonitic clay beds range from about two-thirds to 85 per cent, depending partly on location and the increase in effective stress (Zeevaert, 1953a). Evidence from the protruding casings suggests that at some places, at least, the compaction of the top 100 m of sediment is about equal to the subsidence.

Recognizing that the artesian-head decline can be stopped only by reducing the local ground-water draft, comprehensive plans have been made for importing water to the city. Since 1952, several new projects have been completed to bring water into the city, and others are under construction. In addition, reservoirs and recharge wells have been constructed for the purpose of injecting flood waters into the aquifer system. According to Quintero (1958), 13 recharge wells have been installed since 1953, and others are planned.

Eloy-Picacho Area, Arizona

Robinson and Peterson (1962) reported land subsidence of as much as 3.6 feet due to withdrawal of ground water in the Eloy-Picacho area about 50 miles northwest of Tucson, Arizona.

Precise leveling by the U.S. Coast and Geodetic Survey in 1905, 1934, 1948-1949, 1952, and 1960 indicates a maximum cumulative subsidence of 3.6 feet along a level line that parallels the main line of the Southern Pacific Railroad. Almost all the subsidence has occurred since 1934 and has been most widespread and rapid in the period 1952-1960. As of 1960,

cumulative subsidence in excess of 2 feet had occurred along 8 miles of level lines centering at Eloy.

In the Eloy-Picacho area, unconsolidated alluvial deposits occur to a depth of 500-600 feet and are underlain by fine-grained sediments—locally called lake-bed sediments—that are as much as 800 feet thick; the fine-grained deposits are underlain by coarse materials. The older wells were 500-700 feet deep and tapped the upper alluvial deposits. Beginning about 1952, wells were drilled into or through the fine-grained sediments to depths of as much as 2000 feet.

Intensive pumpage of ground water for irrigation began in 1936. In 1937, the pumpage was 64,000 acre-feet and increased rapidly during and after World War II to 360,000 acre-feet in 1948; it totaled 300,000 acre-feet in 1952 and 330,000 acre-feet in 1960. This intensive pumpage has resulted in a general decline of water levels in wells of 100-200 feet below the head prior to development.

A definite relationship of subsidence to decline in head is indicated by the fact that (1) there was virtually no subsidence in the period 1905-1934 before pumping of ground water for irrigation began, and (2) the point of maximum subsidence has shifted southeastward in each leveling since 1948-1949, which is in agreement with a similar shift in the center of the pumping depression (Robinson and Peterson, 1962).

As stated, subsidence was negligible in the period 1905-1934 and probably for several years after 1934. The leveling of 1948-1949 indicated maximum subsidence since 1934 of 0.4 foot about 2½ miles northwest of Eloy. The maximum for the period 1948-1949 to 1952 was 1.3 feet at a bench mark about 1 mile northwest of Eloy. By 1960, the point of maximum subsidence had shifted to 2 miles southeast of Eloy where slightly more than 3 feet of settlement was recorded for the period 1952-1960.

Areas in California

Development of ground water has been intensive in California. Most of the water is withdrawn for irrigation although ground water is also pumped extensively for domestic and industrial supply. In 1955, about 13 million acre-feet of ground water was pumped for irrigation from ground-water basins in California, slightly more than one-third of the total pumpage for irrigation in the United States.

Figure 5. Areas of land subsidence in California. Major subsidence due to fluid withdrawal shown in black; subsidence in Delta caused by oxidation of peat.

The ground-water withdrawals in California are chiefly from intermontane basins in which the valley fill of late Tertiary and Quaternary age is chiefly alluvial deposits but also, in places, is of lacustrine and shallow marine origin. In many of the basins, the water bodies tapped are semi-confined or confined below depths ranging from 100 to 600 feet, and, thus, much of the withdrawal is from confined aquifer systems.

The intensive and long-continued pumping has drawn down water levels more than 100 feet in many of the basins—maximum drawdown of 400-500 feet has been on the west side and in the southern end of the San Joaquin Valley. Thus, in California, substantial lowering of water level has occurred in young, unconsolidated, compressible deposits that contain extensive semiconfined to confined aquifer systems. It is not surprising, therefore, that land subsidence due to ground-water withdrawal has developed in many areas. Subsidence in all areas shown on Figure 5, except for those in the Wilmington oil field and in the Sacramento-San Joaquin Delta, is due to ground-water withdrawal and decline of artesian head.

Subsidence in most of these areas has been described briefly by Poland (1958). About 11,000 square miles (7 million acres) of land in California is irrigated, and nearly two-thirds of this is irrigated wholly or in part by ground water. Of this 11,000 square miles, at least 30 per cent has subsided 1 foot or more due to artesian-head decline. Doubtless, many other areas in addition to those shown on Figure 5 have subsided at least a few tenths of a foot, but leveling control is not available to define the magnitude and extent of subsidence in most of these.

The peat lands in the Sacramento-San Joaquin Delta have subsided as much as 15 feet in the last century as a result of drainage (lowering of the water table) for cultivation (Poland, 1958, p. 1774-1775). The primary cause of this subsidence, however, is oxidation of the peat (Weir, 1950), rather than compaction of an aquifer system due to increase in effective overburden load.

In the San Joaquin Valley, about 3000 square miles or 30 per cent of the valley floor is subsiding. The three principal subsiding areas are the Los Banos-Kettleman City area, the Tulare-Wasco area, and the Arvin-Maricopa area (Fig. 5). Maximum rates of subsidence in these areas range from 0.5 foot to 1.5 feet a year. Lands between the Los Banos-Kettleman City area and the Tulare-Wasco area are also subsiding but at a lesser rate. The areas of appreciable subsidence coincide generally with the areas in which ground water is withdrawn chiefly from confined aquifers.

Land subsidence in the central part of the Santa Clara Valley (Fig. 5), beneath the southern part of San Francisco Bay and south past San Jose, has been recognized for 30 years (Rappleye, 1933; Tibbetts, 1933). It was first noted when releveling in 1932-1933 of a line of first-order levels established by the U.S. Coast and Geodetic Survey in 1912 showed about 4 feet of subsidence at San Jose (Tolman and Poland, 1940, p. 29). Tolman and Poland described the subsidence to 1939 and concluded that decline in artesian head due to intensive and continued ground-water withdrawal was the principal cause. Poland and Green (1962) reported on the subsidence through 1954 and confirmed the earlier conclusions concerning the principal cause of subsidence.

SUMMARY

(1) Decrease in hydrostatic pressure in confined systems, such as oil and gas zones or artesian aquifers, results in increased grain-to-grain load on the sediments. The sediments compact in response to the added load, and the land surface subsides.

(2) Damage from subsidence and compaction has totaled hundreds of millions of dollars throughout the world and takes many forms. In tidal areas, flooding by sea water has been a major problem. Changing gradients have seriously affected the capacity of canals, drains, and sewers, and even the channel capacity of streams has been changed materially. Structural failure of buildings, pipe lines, railroads, and other engineering structures at the land surface has occurred due to tensional or compressional stresses caused by flexure of the sediments. Compaction and flexure of sediments at depth have caused extensive damage by compressional or shear failure of oil- and water-well casings. In compressible aquifers, such as micaceous sand, the loss of ground-water storage capacity through compaction is a subtle but, in part, a permanent damage.

(3) Subsidence of the surface can be measured by precise leveling from stable reference points and, in tidal areas, by observing the change with respect to sea level. Compaction at depth can be measured by the use of anchored cables or pipes and by surveys in wells of reference points, such as casing collars and radioactive markers. Protrusion of well casings indicates that compaction has occurred but supplies only a minimum value for subsidence, not an absolute measure.

(4) The ratio of subsidence to head change depends upon the thickness and lithologic character of the compacting sediments. Chief controlling factors are the number, thickness, compressibility, and permeability of fine-grained interbeds and confining beds, clay mineralogy, geochemistry of pore fluids in aquifers and aquitards, initial porosity, previous loading history, and cementation. The most compressible materials are loosely consolidated, clayey sediments of Tertiary and Quaternary age, particularly those of volcanic provenance, that contain montmorillonite as the predominant clay mineral. In subsidence areas overlying these sediments, the range in ratio where known is about 0.01-0.2. The only known marked exceptions are at London and Savannah where water is produced from soft marine carbonate sediments associated with clays. In both of these areas, the ratio of subsidence to head decline is relatively small (less than 0.005).

(5) Continuous measurements of compaction indicate quick response to pressure changes in many areas although, commonly, some residual compaction or lag due to slow drainage of clays may continue long after the pressure decline has ceased.

(6) If artesian head declines over a period of years, then recovers and declines again, compaction will not recur until a previous pressure low is exceeded, provided all residual compaction from the previous drawdown phase has been completed (excess pore pressure has decayed).

(7) In a confined aquifer system, if the overlying water table remains unchanged, increase in effective pressure is equal in magnitude to the decrease of artesian pressure, and the sediments will compact in accord with this increase in stress. If the artesian pressure is wholly depleted and drawdown is continued, the fluid is

yielded by dewatering of the sediments. Once the pressure at the top of the aquifer system (base of upper confining bed) declines to atmospheric pressure, further decline in fluid level will cause compaction at a decreased rate; this is in accord with the effective stress increase under .water-table (unconfined) conditions, which is due to loss of buoyancy.

(8) Subsidence problems have been or are being alleviated in several ways: (1) cessation of withdrawal of petroleum, gas, or water due to depletion of the supply, legal action, or replacement with substitute supply; (2) increase or restoration of reservoir pressure due to reduction in production rate or to increase in recharge (water); (3) repressuring by injection of water. The last method has been highly successful in the Wilmington, California, oil field where it has stopped subsidence and has caused some rebound of the land surface.

REFERENCES

Allen, Dennis, 1959, Wilmington subsidence problems: Houston, Tex., World Oil, v. 149, no. 2, p. 86-88.

Anonymous, 1959a, Water buoys land that sank as oil was removed: Eng. News-Rec., v. 163, no. 20, p. 26-27.

———1959b, Wilmington unitization is moving fast: Tulsa, Okla., Oil and Gas Jour., v. 57, no. 18, p. 94-95.

———1960, The world's largest water flood: Western Oil and Refining Mag., v. 57, no. 1, 8 p.

———1961, Chiusi definitivamente I pozzi metaniferi del Polesine e del Delta Padano [Closing of gas wells in the Po Delta] : Riv. Mineraria Siciliana; no. 67, Gennaio-Febbraio, p. 42-43.

Bartosh, E. J., 1938, Wilmington oil field, Los Angeles County, California: Am. Assoc. Petroleum Geologists Bull., v. 22, no. 8, p. 1048-1079.

Carpenter, C. B., and Spencer, G B., 1940, Measurements of compressibility of consolidated oil-bearing sandstones: U.S. Bur. Mines Rept. Inv. 3540, 20 p.

Carrillo, Nabor, 1948, Influence of artesian wells in the sinking of Mexico City: Rotterdam, Internat. Conf. Soil Mech. and Found. Eng., 2nd, Proc., v. 7, p. 156-159.

Clark, W. O., 1924, Ground water in Santa Clara Valley, California: U.S. Geol. Survey Water-Supply Paper 519, 209 p.

Collins, J. J., 1935, New type seawall built for subsiding lake shore in Venezuela: Eng. News-Rec., v. 114, no. 3, p. 405-408.

Comision Hidrologica de la Cuenca del Valle de México, 1953, Recopilacion de datos del Valle de México, hasta el año de 1953 [Compilation of data on the Valley of Mexico to 1953] : Secretaria de Recursos Hidraulicos, Comision Hidrologica de la Cuenca del Valle de México, Bol. Mecanica de Suelos, no. 1, 217 p.

———1958, Recopilacion de datos del Valle de México, 1953-1956 [Compilation of data for the Valley of Mexico, 1953-1956]: Secretaria de Recursos Hidraulicos, Comision Hidrologica de la Cuenca del Valle de México, Bol. Mecanica de Suelos, no. 2, 337 p.

———1961, Boletin de Mecanica de Suelos, no. 3, June 1956-June 1959: Secretaria de Recursos Hidraulicos, Oficina de Estudios Especiales, 344 p.

Coxe, L. C., 1949, Long Beach Naval Shipyard endangered by subsidence: Civil Eng., v. 19, no. 11, p. 44-47, 90.

Dal Piaz, G., 1959, Il bacino Quaternario Polesano-Ferrarese e i suoi giacimenti gassiferi [The Quaternary Polesano-Ferrarese basin and its gas-bearing layers], in Atti del Convegno di Milano su I Giacimenti Gassiferi dell'Europa Occidentale, Milan 1957: Rome, Academia Nazionale dei Lencei, v. 1, p. 433-474.

Davis, G. H., and Poland, J. F., 1957, Ground-water conditions in the Mendota-Huron area, Fresno and Kings Counties, California: U.S. Geol. Survey Water-Supply Paper 1360-G, p. 409-588.

Frame, R. G., 1952, Earthquake damage, its cause and prevention in the Wilmington oil field, in Summary of Operations, California Oil Fields: California Dept. Nat. Res., Div. Oil and Gas, v. 38, no. 1, p. 5-15.

Fuller, M. L., 1908, Summary of the controlling factors of artesian flows: U.S. Geol. Survey Bull. 319, 44 p.

Gayol, Roberto, 1929, Breves apuntes relativos a las obras de Saneamiento y Desague de la Capital de la República de las que, del mismo genero, necesita con grande urgencia: Mexico, D. F., Rev. Mexicana de Ingeniería y Arquitectura, v. 7.

Gilluly, James, and Grant, U.S., 1949, Subsidence in the Long Beach Harbor area, California: Geol. Soc. America Bull., v. 60, p. 461-530.

Gortani, M., 1961, L'estrazione delle acque Metanifere e il Delta Padano (Extraction of methane waters and the Po Delta): Natura e Montagna, ser. 2, v. 1, no. 1, p. 4-13.

Grant, U.S., 1944, Subsidence and elevation in the Los Angeles Region, p. 129-158 in Science in the University, by members of the faculties of the University of California: Berkeley and Los Angeles, California Univ. Press, 332 p.

———1954, Subsidence of the Wilmington oil field, California, p. 19-24 in Jahns, R. H., Editor, Geology of Southern California: California Dept. Nat. Res., Div. Mines Bull. 170, 700 p.

Green, J. H., 1962, Compaction of the aquifer system and land subsidence in the Santa Clara Valley, California: U.S. Geol. Survey Prof. Paper 450-D, art. 172, p. D175-D178.

Harris, F. M., and Harlow, E. H., 1947, Subsidence of the Terminal Island-Long Beach area, California: Am. Soc. Civil Engineers Proc., v. 73, no. 8, p. 1197-1218.

Kugler, H. G., 1933, Contribution to the knowledge of sedimentary volcanism in Trinidad (with discussion): Inst. Petroleum Technologists Jour., v. 19, p. 743-772.

Leonards, G. A., 1962, Engineering properties of soils,

p. 66-240 in Leonards, G. A., Editor, Foundation Engineering: New York, McGraw-Hill Book Co., 1136 p.

Lockwood, M. G., 1954, Ground subsides in Houston area: Civil Eng., v. 24, p. 370-372.

Loehnberg, Alfred, 1958, Aspects of the sinking of Mexico City and proposed countermeasures: Am. Water Works Assoc. Jour., v. 50, no. 3, p. 432-440.

Lofgren, B. E., 1961, Measurement of compaction of aquifer systems in areas of land subsidence: U.S. Geol. Survey Prof. Paper 424-B, art. 24, p. B49-B52.

———1963, Land subsidence in the Arvin-Maricopa area, California: U.S. Geol. Survey Prof. Paper 475-B, art. 47, p. B171-B175.

Marsal, R. J., and Sainz-Ortiz, I., 1956, Breve descripción del hundimiento de la Ciudad de México [Short description of the sinking of Mexico City]: Bol. Soc. Geol. Mexicana, p. 1-11.

Marsal, R. J., Hiriart, Fernando, and Sandoval, L. Raúl, 1952, Hundimiento de la Ciudad de México, observaciones y estudios analiticos [Sinking of the City of Mexico, observations and analytical studies]: Ingenieros Civiles Asociados, S. A. de C. V., Serie B Ingenieria Experimental, no. 3, 26 p.

Minor, H. E., 1925, Goose Creek oil field, Harris County, Texas: Am. Assoc. Petroleum Geologists Bull., v. 9, no. 2, p. 286-297.

Murray-Aaron, E. R., and Pfeil, A. W., 1948, Recent developments in the Wilmington oil fields, in Summary of Operations, California oil fields: California Dept. Nat. Res., Div. Oil and Gas, v. 34, no. 2, p. 5-13.

Neel, Charles H., 1957, Surface subsidence and remedial measures at the Long Beach Naval Shipyard, Long Beach, California: Rept. to Long Beach Naval Shipyard, 90 p.

Poland, J. F., 1958, Land subsidence due to ground-water development: Am. Soc. Civil Engineers Proc., Jour. Irrigation and Drainage Div., Paper 1774, v. 84, no. IR3, 11 p.

———1960, Land subsidence in the San Joaquin Valley, California, and its effect on estimates of ground-water resources: Internat. Assoc. Sci. Hydrology, Comm. Subterranean Waters, Pub. No. 52, p. 324-335.

———1961, The coefficient of storage in a region of major subsidence caused by compaction of an aquifer system: U.S. Geol. Survey Prof. Paper 424-B, art. 25, p. B52-B54.

Poland, J. F., and Davis, G. H., 1956, Subsidence of the land surface in the Tulare-Wasco (Delano) and Los Banos-Kettleman City areas, San Joaquin Valley, California: Am. Geophys. Union Trans., v. 37, no. 3, p. 287-296.

Poland, J. F., and Green, J. H., 1962, Subsidence in the Santa Clara Valley, California—A progress report: U.S. Geol. Survey Water-Supply Paper 1619-C, 16 p.

Poland, J. F., Garrett, A. A., and Sinnott, Allen, 1959, Geology, hydrology, and chemical character of ground waters in the Torrance-Santa Monica area, California: U.S. Geol. Survey Water-Supply Paper 1461, p. 142-146.

Pratt, W. E., 1927, Some questions on the cause of the subsidence of the surface in the Goose Creek field, Texas: Am. Assoc. Petroleum Geologists Bull., v. 11, no. 8, p. 887-889.

Pratt, W. E., and Johnson, D. W., 1926, Local subsidence of the Goose Creek field: Jour. Geology, v. 34, no. 7, p. 577-590.

Puppo, A., 1957, L'estrazione delle acque metanifere nel territorio del Delta Padano e l'affondamento del suolo [The production of methane in the area of the Po Delta and the subsidence of the ground]: Metano, Petrolio, e Nuove Energie, v. XI, no. 11, p. 1-12.

Quintero, Andres Garcia, 1958, Recharge wells in Mexico City, Mexico: The Texas Engineer, v. 28, no. 2, p. 6-10.

Rappleye, H. S., 1933, Recent areal subsidence found in releveling: Eng. News-Rec., v. 110, p. 848.

Robinson, G. M., and Peterson, D. E., 1962, Notes on earth fissures in southern Arizona: U.S. Geol. Survey Circ. 466, 7 p.

Shoemaker, R. R., 1955, Protection of subsiding waterfront properties: Am. Soc. Civil Engineers Proc., v. 81, no. 805, p. 805-1—805-24.

Shoemaker, R. R., and Thorley, T. J., 1955, Problems of ground subsidence: Am. Water Works Assoc. Jour., v. 47, no. 4, p. 412-418.

Snider, L. C., 1927, A suggested explanation of the surface subsidence in the Goose Creek oil and gas field [Texas]: Am. Assoc. Petroleum Geologists, v. 11, no. 7, p. 729-745.

Tibbetts, F. H., 1933, Areal subsidence: Eng. News-Rec., v. 3, p. 204.

Tolman, C. F., 1937, Ground Water: New York, McGraw-Hill Book Co., p. 341-345.

Tolman, C. F., and Poland, J. F., 1940, Ground-water, salt-water infiltration, and ground-surface recession in Santa Clara Valley, Santa Clara County, California: Am. Geophys. Union Trans., pt. 1, p. 23-34.

Walton, W. C., and Walker, W. H., 1961, Evaluating wells and aquifers by analytical methods: Jour. Geophys. Research, v. 66, no. 10, p. 3359-3370.

Weir, W. W., 1950, Subsidence of peat lands of the Sacramento-San Joaquin Delta, California: Hilgardia, California Univ. Agr. Expt. Sta., v. 20, no. 3, p. 37-56.

Zeevaert, Leonardo, 1953a, Pore pressure measurements to investigate the main source of surface subsidence in Mexico City: Switzerland, 3rd Internat. Conf. on Soil Mech. and Found. Eng. Proc., v. 2, p. 299-304.

17. SUBSIDENCE — A REAL OR IMAGINARY PROBLEM?

AUGUST E. VANDALE

Mining of the Freeport and Pittsburgh coal seams in the Pittsburgh vicinity dates back more than 100 years, and Consolidation Coal Co., or its predecessor, Pittsburgh Coal Co., has been actively mining in the area since 1900. Over the years, Consol has acquired good legal title to the coal lands purchased from individual farm owners, with broad mining rights, and in 98% or more of its title holdings, the company has a complete waiver of surface damage or the right to subside the surface land. (Titles in Pennsylvania can be in three forms: title in fee; title to the mineral; or mining rights permitting the removal and extraction of the mineral with or without waiver of surface damage.)

In the early history of Consol, individual farms overlying the seams were purchased from land owners. Many of these titles severed the coal estate from the "in fee" title, and mining rights with waiver of surface damage were conveyed in the original severance deed. In this manner, Consol was able to put together its large mineable coal reserves.

Consol has practiced "full recovery" mining as far as practical from its early years of hand loading to the recent era of mechanization.

Contrary to public opinion, full recovery of the coal seam is not new with modern fully mechanized mining, but in the Pittsburgh district is as old as mining itself. However, the great change which has transpired is that in the past mining was conducted under farm land and the results of surface subsidence were soon remedied by natural forces. With the influx of suburban housing coming over active coal mines, the result of full recovery mining has taken on an entirely new complexion (Fig. 1). Thus, as the cities and towns have spiraled outward, as modern transportation has made it attractive to live outside of town, the builders of housing developments have moved out over the mines faster than the coal companies could extract their coal.

Reprinted with permission of author and publisher, from *Mining Engineering*, v. 19, no. 9, p. 86-88, September, 1967. Copyright 1967 American Institute of Mining, Metallurgical, and Petroleum Engineers, Inc.

From 1900 to 1957 Consol offered home owners the opportunity to protect their homes from damage which might be caused from full recovery mining under them by purchasing from Consol an agreement to leave coal (usually 50% of the seam) in place in the ground in the form of ribs, stumps and pillars. Several hundred agreements were completed during these years with no warrant guaranteeing against subsidence damage but warranting only to leave the coal in place.

In the summer of 1957, Consol's mining centered in Upper St. Clair Township, Allegheny Co., and in Peters Township, Washington Co., Pa., in areas where many new homes had recently been constructed over active mines. Many home owners had not understood the "Exception and Reservation" clauses in their deeds pertaining to coal and mining rights. A number of developers and house builders had failed to apprise the new home purchaser of the significance of the coal reservation paragraph in his deed or in back title deeds and had avoided an explanation of the impact of such on the structure being purchased.

In 1957 Consol reviewed its policy as it related to public relations with home owners. The support agreement was revised to warrant to a home owner that, should his house be damaged as the result of mining for a period of 10 years after mining had passed his support area, Consol would repair, or pay for repair, of damage caused by mining subsidence. Also, the policy was revised to permit the purchase of a coal support agreement to be paid for either in cash or over 120 monthly payments if the home owner so desired. Interest on installment payments is charged at the current FHA interest rate. A mortgage (usually a second mortgage) is taken on the property as security for payment.

From September 1957 to April 27, 1966, Consol entered into support agreements with 635 individual home owners. The average cost of these 635 agreements amounted to slightly over $1000 per house; 40% of the home owners elected to pay cash while 60% preferred the installment payment plan. The price per house is computed by an engineering formula and is based

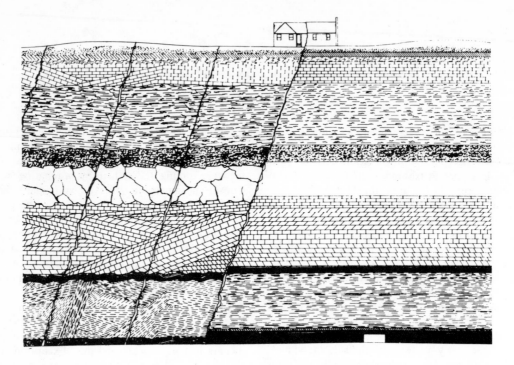

Figure 1. The results of full recovery coal mining, shown in the diagram above, have taken on an entirely new complexion with the growth of suburban housing.

on tons of coal required to support each individual structure. The house is located by survey and plotted onto Consol's mining map. The computation of the support coal is based on a rock fracture angle of 15° on all four sides of the house foundation after providing a 15-ft-wide safety area around the foundation (Fig. 2). In most instances, 50% of solid coal in place is considered proper to support the structure (Fig. 3). The coal support area is in the shape of a truncated pyramid and depends on the size of the house pad or foundation as well as on the depth of cover from the surface to the bottom of the coal seam. Consol has been charging 35¢ per ton for this support coal, which represents approximately the cost of the coal to the company plus taxes over the years of ownership. If Consol could mine the coal to full recovery and not support the house, it could realize three to four times the price being charged the home owner.

During these ten years of warranting the support of houses, the incidence of houses damaged from mining has been approximately 2%. In the early years, some damage occurred as a result of experimentation with the proper spacing between houses wherein new rib lines could be

begun. It was found that when new rib lines were started without sufficient space for a good break to occur, it resulted in rock bending instead of rock breaking. Now this problem is under control but coal is lost between one supported house on a butt entry and the next supported house if there is not sufficient room to do full recovery between them.

Over the years there have been a number of attempts to control by legislation the exercise of the full mining rights which Consol had previously purchased. On July 2, 1937, Act No. 579 was passed, regulating the mining of bituminous coal in certain counties; prescribing duties for county commissioners; and imposing penalties.

The act was never used by Allegheny Co. because many felt that the constitutionality of the Act was very doubtful.

In 1949 the Koehler Act providing means for acquisition of support coal by political subdivisions was enacted into law. So far as is known, no political subdivision ever availed itself of the use of this Act. In 1957 a few localities considered applying the Act, but the problems of administering it to a whole or part of a municipality became too involved. Besides, the elected officials feared the public reaction to an assessment or tax to resolve subsidence questions.

In July 1957, Act No. 431, called "Notice of Right of Surface Support," was enacted. This bill provided clear notice in all deeds that the document does not sell, convey, transfer, include or insure the title to the coal and right of support underneath the surface land described or referred to therein, that the owner or owners of such coal have the complete legal right to remove all of such coal and, in that connection, that damage may result to the surface land and any house,

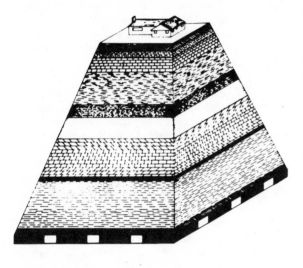

building or other structure on or in such land. This Act has served as a flag-waving notification to those who are not aware of coal mining in the region.

In 1965 another movement began to legislate new subsidence regulations which would deprive the coal companies of their rights to recover the minerals they have owned and on which they have been taxed for many years. Unfortunately, much of the impetus for this legislation came as the result of a few incidents rather than from a general practice of the coal industry. Poor public relations on the part of the industry as a whole permitted these few incidents to be publicized far beyond their true significance. A good plan of subsidence protection supported by most of the coal companies could have prevented the 1966 legislation. Realizing the uncertainty of the attitude of our present-day courts and being fully aware of the amount of time and expense which might be involved in drawn-out court procedures to defend their legal rights, the companies under duress united to negotiate this problem with certain representatives of the legislature and agreed to House Bill No. 13. This Bill was signed into law and took effect on April 27, 1966.

The Bituminous Mine Subsidence and Land Conservation Act of 1966 is comprised of twenty-one sections and basically provides for the protection of the public health, welfare and safety by regulating the mining of bituminous coal; declaring the existence of a public interest

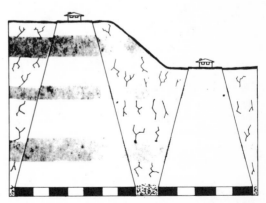

Figure 3. In most instances, 50% of solid coal in place is needed to support a house. The coal support area is in the shape of a truncated pyramid and depends on the size of the house foundation and the depth of cover from the surface to the bottom of the coal seam.

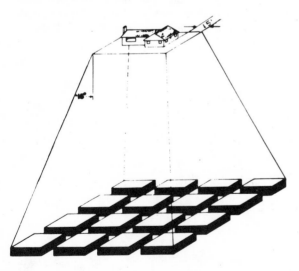

Figure 2. Computation of the necessary support coal is based on a rock fracture of 15° on all four sides of a house foundation after providing a 15-ft-wide safety area around the foundation.

in the support of surface structures; forbidding damage to specified classes of existing structures from the mining of bituminous coal; requiring permits, and in certain circumstances bonds, for the mining of bituminous coal; providing for the filing of maps or plans with recorders of deeds; providing for the giving of notice of mining operations to political subdivisions and surface land owners of record; requiring mine inspectors to accompany municipal officers and their agents on inspection trips; granting powers to public officers and affected property owners to enforce the act; requiring grantors to certify as to whether any structures on the lands conveyed are entitled to support from the underlying coal and grantees to sign an admission of a warning of the possible lack of any such right of support; providing for acquisition with compensation of coal support for future structures and existing structures not protected by this act; and imposing liability for violation of the act.

The new Act of 1966 requires much mapping and paper work preparing the requests for permits to mine. The Act will also require semiannual additional mapping and filing of supplemental notices of areas to be mined. The home owner or prospective home buyer now has additional sources of information on mining and potential house support.

The Act of 1966 alone has caused an estimated one hundred million tons of never-to-be-recovered valuable coal to be left in the ground for support of structures without compensation to the owner of the coal. Over and above the loss of coal, all mines that find it necessary to support houses are being greatly hindered in their mining because of the loss of production and increase in mining production costs incurred because of interruption of a normal mining pattern in order to support the houses. In full recovery mining systems, each house support area necessitates the starting of a new rib line.

Is subsidence, then, a real or imaginary mining problem? Unfortunately, it is a *real* problem, brought about in the present because industry in the past has failed to recognize and live up to its moral responsibility. In the past, many coal operators have tried to sweep subsidence under the rug and hide it. They treated it as an imaginary everyday mining problem and, as a result, in the public mind it developed into a highly emotional matter.

The public news media—press, magazines and TV—have taken up the public cause and promoted the emotional aspects. The conservationists championed the cause and made a political issue of it during 1966. Now, along with air pollution, stream pollution, strip reclamation, safety and welfare, federal and state regulatory bodies will police subsidence, enforcing major regulations to be lived with and lived up to. The Subsidence Act of 1966 emphasizes the need for the coal industry to be fully aware of all of its problems and, beyond being aware, to act to meet the needs of society. This obviously requires a balancing of economic *vs.* social pressures and a voluntary action before punitive laws are enacted to meet an emotional demand.

Part Three
ENVIRONMENTAL HEALTH: GEOLOGIC ASPECTS

The relationship between geology and medicine probably appears very remote or even nonexistent to most people. Recent interest in mercury and mercury poisoning from foods, however, has stimulated scientists to do additional research on trace elements and their relationship to health and disease. Geologists, like many other scientists and laymen, are coming to realize that there is a connection between the natural abundance of some elements in the bedrock and soils of an area and the incidence of certain deficiencies and diseases in that area. The terms Environmental Geochemistry and Medical Geology are now frequently used to designate areas of interest and study that relate geology and health.

One of the best-known examples of the importance of trace elements in health is the connection between some types of goiter and deficiency of iodine in many soils of the Great Lakes region. Another fairly well-known example involves the overabundance of selenium in the soils of certain parts of the northern Great Plains that has resulted in "alkali disease" or "blind staggers" in cattle. Disease also develops if there is a deficiency of selenium in the diet. Thus, there appears to be a limited range within which animals utilize trace elements to maintain health. The range in many cases is apparently very small—too little creates a deficiency in the body; too much results in toxicity; both situations may cause disease. Pettyjohn (Selection 20) notes that "Poison is in everything and no thing is without poison."

The number of studies involving trace elements and health is rapidly increasing. Interdisciplinary cooperation between geologists, medical scientists, nutritionists, and others should produce more meaningful results. A cautionary note in studies in this area is suggested by Underwood (Selection 21), who maintains that an association of trace-element abundance with a disease does not necessarily establish causation. Testimony to the importance and growth of Medical Geology is the recent establishment of the Society for Environmental Geochemistry and Health, formed to promote research and information on trace elements and environmental health.

The relationship between geology and health is not restricted to trace elements, as evidenced by the following two examples. Women living in a silver mining area in Bohemia used to outlive three or more husbands who worked in silver mines which are now used as a source of uranium. These miners were working in an environment in which they were subjected to excessive concentrations of radioactivity and silica, resulting in radiation poisoning and silicosis. Results of a recent study (*Science,* vol. 173, p. 1141) show that the high incidence of stomach cancer in Japanese men is probably due to the eating of rice which is customarily coated with glucose and mineral talc prior to cooking. The study revealed that the talc which is used contains asbestos, and the investigator believes that the sharp fibrous nature of asbestos makes it a cancer-producing substance.

History is undoubtedly replete with unsolved mysteries of death and disease which relate in some way to geologic aspects of the physical environment. Increased studies may solve some of these mysteries of the past, in addition to contributing to better health in certain areas of the world.

18. MEDICAL GEOLOGY

HARRY V. WARREN and ROBERT DELARAULT

At first thought one might be tempted to assume that there can be little to relate the sciences of geology and medicine. However, a few moments of reflection should be enough to permit the most skeptical to realize that an association between geology and medicine is a natural one. After all, most people are prepared to accept, at least as a hypothesis, the possibility that man's health is determined, to some extent, by the food he eats. The quality of food reflects the makeup of the soil which, in turn, is determined, in part, by the chemistry of the rocks and vegetal life on the Earth's crust, which, between them, contribute much to the makeup of soil.

It is not difficult to find medical men who can point out how different communities have different ailments. Some of these ailments probably have little or nothing to do with geology, but a few of them may. For generations, the more fortunate members of our society have enjoyed a change of air, food, and water by going each year for a holiday. For some of those who are not too sophisticated, a change of food may come as a delight. Perhaps a change of trace elements is involved in a holiday. At all events, as society gets more and more removed from close contact with the soil, and more and more closely tied to the supermarkets of today, the ties that surely do exist between man and the earth's crust will become more and more tenuous. Even today, it is difficult to find communities suitable for simple epidemiological studies in which trace elements may be involved. However, with care it is still possible to find some communities suitable for trace element epidemiological studies: such communities do exist in some of the undeveloped countries, but they can also be found in conservative and comparatively long-established settlements in Western Europe and North America.

It has long been known that an iodine deficiency can affect whole communities, although we now realize that the problem of goiter

Reprinted with permission of the authors and publisher from *Geotimes,* p. 14-15, September, 1965.

is much more involved than was originally realized. Human beings can be affected by poisonous materials in soils when those soils contribute to a large proportion of the diet of a community. In parts of the Dakotas, not only cattle but humans were affected by the selenium that was found in some specific soils. Drinking water may also be the vehicle by which undesirable elements may be introduced into a diet: arsenic and fluorine are two elements that may be present in harmful amounts in local water supplies.

To most geologists, lead is merely lead when it is reported in food or drinking water. Actually, there is one isotope of lead, namely lead 210, derived from uranium by way of radon 222, which is a gas slightly soluble in water. Lead 210 is radioactive with a half-life of some 22 years. However, lead 210 itself breaks down and yields polonium 210, which is a strongly radioactive and poisonous element, particularly dangerous because it finds a resting place in the soft tissues of human bodies.

There may be some good reason, but superficially it seems strange that agriculturists have not done more than they have done to draw doctors and geologists together. It is literally an article of faith with agronomists that soils are related on the one hand to their parent material, and, on the other, to the quality of the food they produce. Nevertheless, doctors and nutritionists alike still publish books that contain tables showing the amounts of various elements, such as copper and iron, that are to be found in different foodstuffs. One may search these medical journals, and all too rarely find any evidence that the significance of geology in relation to food is appreciated. It is equally true that one can search geological literature for a long time before finding any analyses of foodstuffs in relation to their geological background. It is easy to forecast that all this will change before long. Already, in Scandinavia, in Australia, in Great Britain, and in Canada, foresters are realizing more and more how the productivity of their forests is governed, in some areas to a significant extent, by the bedrock involved. It may surprise some geologists to learn that there are areas in the world where foresters would not dream of planting new trees before consulting with their geological confreres.

What makes biogeochemistry such a fascinating subject for a geologist is that appropriate quantities of such elements as copper, zinc, and molybdenum are now known to be just as vital to the health of some plants and animals as they are to the success of mining operations: the concentrations of a specific element needed for the fulfillment of these different needs naturally varies considerably. However, zinc, in appropriate concentrations, is as essential to a diabetic patient as it is for the farmer trying to produce a maximum poundage of pig from each pound of food, and for a forester who is attempting to cultivate a forest. Humans, pigs, and trees would all die if no zinc were available, and equally they can all be adversely affected if they are given too much zinc. The problem yet to be solved in most instances is that of knowing just what is the optimum concentration of zinc needed by a human, a pig, or a tree, as the case may be.

Unfortunately, it is much more difficult to solve equations where there are two variables instead of one, and with each additional unknown element, the complexity of the inquiry increases. A comparatively short time ago only some dozen elements were known to be essential to plant and animal health, but today it may be said that nearer 40 than 30 are thought to play some part in nutrition. Some elements that are always present in plants and animals are not yet known to serve any useful purpose: in the fullness of time it may be found that even these elements, such as lead, mercury, and silver, which are now considered as inhibitors or poisoners of enzyme systems, may actually, if present in appropriate concentrations, act as useful moderators, or regulators, of specific metabolic processes. A word coming more and more into use by biogeochemists is "imbalance." For maximum health in both plants and animals, it is desirable not only that the elements should be present in appropriate concentrations, but also that there should be harmonious relationships between the concentrations of the different elements. It has taken hundreds of millions of years for life to evolve as we now have it on our planet. Surely it is reasonable to assume that life today represents a complex synthesis of the energy and the elements present on the crust of the earth? Thus we might expect to have an infinite variety of living cells representing responses to the different facies extant on the earth's crust. Some forms of life are able to adapt to a sharply different environment, but others perish. Some species of grass have been found to adapt in two generations to a high lead content in soil, but sheep eating this grass could not adapt themselves so promptly: fortunately, it seems that the shepherds in the area involved with this lead soon learned just how long their sheep could tolerate this leaded herbage. Interestingly enough, sheepherders for generations seasonally have moved their flocks. Sometimes this was done merely to ensure a supply of food, but occasionally these moves were dictated by the necessity of avoiding poisonous concentrations in herbage of such elements as molybdenum and selenium.

If it be accepted that variety is the spice of life, then, indeed, biogeochemistry should attract many geologists in the years ahead. However, the number of subjects with which a biogeochemist may become involved is large. Biology, botany, agriculture, bacteriology, virology of the life sciences, and physics and chemistry of the physical sciences all have much to offer to the biogeochemist who must sample them with prudence and wisdom if he is not to be overwhelmed with a mental flatulence likely to be neither congenial nor stimulating but merely frustrating.

At the 1964 meeting of the AAAS in Montreal, there was a symposium on Medical Geology and Geography. The participants included a geologist, a pharmacognosist, a biochemist, a general practitioner, and a geological engineer. It might be a moot question as to whether each one of these persons appreciated fully all the finer points raised by their fellow participants in the panel. Nevertheless, the participants, themselves, seemed to find the interdisciplinary exercise well worthwhile and, judging from the reactions of the press and the audience, cross-fertilization experiments of a similar nature may be expected to attract increasing attention in the future. Biogeochemistry is, to many, an uninspiring name: perhaps we should change the name to "Geological ecology," which would relate this field of study to that of life in relation to its geological environment.

19. MINOR METALS OF THE GEOCHEMICAL ENVIRONMENT, HEALTH AND DISEASE

HELEN L. CANNON and HOWARD C. HOPPS

The possibility of causal relationships between environmental factors and the occurrence of many degenerative diseases is slowly being recognized. One aspect of the environment—that concerned with the geochemistry of the rocks, soils, plants, and water—should be studied carefully and the distribution of minor elements be compared with geographic patterns of animal and human health and disease. We know that calcium, phosphorus, iron, copper, and all the other important inorganic nutrients somehow make their way from a never-ending source in the rocks that form our continents to the soils and waters, and from there into plants, animals, and finally man. But many questions come to mind. How is this transport accomplished and how easily do the various elements move into and through the food chain? What effects do climate and time have on this movement? What sort of interactions go on between the various elements as they come in contact with one another to enhance or hinder this process? How are these elements utilized by different kinds of organisms and what effects do even small excesses or deficiencies of any one ion have on the health of the plants or animals? These questions involve many complex interrelationships that cannot be solved by many scientists working in one field or by one scientist working in many fields. These questions should involve many environmental scientists in many parts of the world, and if we are to answer these questions it will require the rapid and effective exchange of information between workers in many disciplines. Answers to these questions are of much more than academic interest because

Reprinted with permission of the authors and the publisher from *Science,* v. 170, p. 1232, December 11, 1970. Copyright 1970 American Association for the Advancement of Science. Originally published as part of an article announcing a forthcoming AAAS Symposium to be held December 30, 1970.

*U. S. Geological Survey, Denver, Colorado.

**University of Missouri, Columbia.

they will pinpoint areas that might be changed or regulated to improve the health of man.

The geochemist knows the quantities of the elements that occur in the different kinds of rocks and sediments in different areas; the hydrologist, the composition of ground and surface waters; the soil scientist, the formation and composition of soils under different climatic conditions; the plant physiologist, the effects on plants of the ions available in the soil; the medical biochemist and physiologist, the use of the ions in physiological processes; and the veterinarian and physician, the effects of excesses and deficiencies in health and disease. But, again, there are broad gaps in this knowledge. Probably the greatest unknown in every area under consideration is that of ion availability in each transfer from one medium to another. How is the basic chemical behavior of the element at each step in the chain affected by the physical and chemical microenvironment in which it occurs? Some elements are released from rock-forming minerals during weathering more readily than others and some cations are bound more tightly than others in residual clays. Especially important in the physical environment are the behavior of iron and manganese in water under different conditions of pH and eH and their profound effect on the availability of a large suite of other metals. As more sensitive chemical tests become available, areas of anomalous geographic distribution of many minor metals are being recognized and the possible health effects of deficiencies of many metals, previously recognized as harmful only in large excesses, are being studied. Deficiency of selenium, for instance, causes white muscle disease in animals in interior and eastern states whereas, at the same time, the element is readily absorbed and accumulated in toxic amounts by plants growing on soils containing an excess of selenium in certain western states. The possibility of causal relationships between naturally occurring concentrations of minor metals (such as cadmium, chromium, molybdenum, strontium, arsenic, fluorine, and lithium) and the occurrence of many degenerative diseases in man is slowly being recognized.

With the appropriate multidisciplinary teamwork, the geographic patterns of element distribution in the physical environment can be compared with those of animal and human disease. We stand, then, on the threshold of discovery in an exciting area of multidisciplinary science that offers promise of constructive regulation of the environment of mankind.

20. NO THING IS WITHOUT POISON

WAYNE A. PETTYJOHN

Near the close of World War II the badly damaged Japanese industrial machine was attempting to keep production in pace with military losses, and as a result good industrial waste-disposal practices were largely ignored. Throughout several regions of the country mining operations for heavy metals were proceeding with great haste. Along the upper reaches of the Zintsu River basin, milling wastes from a mine producing zinc (Zn), lead (Pb), and cadmium (Cd), were dumped into the river. Downstream the contaminated water was used by streamside farmers for domestic purposes, such as drinking, cooking, and washing, as well as for irrigation of rice fields. In a relatively short time, the yield from rice paddies irrigated with the contaminated water began to decrease and many of the rice plants showed evidence of stunted growth.

Sometime later, it was recognized by Japanese health authorities that many people throughout several mining regions were suffering from what appeared to be a strange, unusually painful disease that caused the bones to become so thin and brittle that they easily snapped. Since World War II, the disease has proven fatal to many people. The affliction became known as "itai-itai," which literally means ouch-ouch. The causes of the disease were completely unknown.

In 1960 J. Kobayashi (1969), apparently by accident or curiosity, examined bones and tissues of itai-itai patients; found in them large concentrations of lead, zinc, and cadmium and, consequently, began to carry out various experiments testing the effect of these heavy metals on soil, plants, and rats.

Analytical analyses of rice, roots, and soil showed that plants selectively absorbed the heavy metals from the polluted soil. For example, 5 soil samples contained an average of 6 ppm (parts per million) of Cd, roots contained 1,250 ppm and 17 samples of rice averaged 125 ppm.

Reprinted with the permission of the author from *The Ohio State University Chapter Phi Delta Kappa News Letter,* April 1970.

Thus plants continued to absorb dangerous heavy metals from the contaminated soil long after the source of pollution had been removed.

Ingestion of the contaminated, heavy metal-rich rice caused osteomalacia. Rats fed 0.01% Cd mixed with food lost 200 mg of Ca; those fed a ration containing 0.003% Cd, 0.03% Zn, 0.015% Pb, and 0.015% Cu lost an equivalent of 2 g of bone or 1/3 of their total bone tissue. Additional tests strongly suggested that it was mainly the ingestion of Cd that produced symptoms of osteomalacia.

Similar studies were made on Tsushima Island, between Japan and Korea, where Cd, Zn and Pb are mined; itai-itai was discovered there also, although it had not been recognized previously. Here one of the patients used well water containing 0.225 ppm of Cd, 13.37 ppm of Zn, and 0.41 ppm of Pb.

Of special significance is the unusually low concentration of heavy metals in contaminated water as compared to that in soil, mud, or plants. Of 60 river water samples from the Zintsu basin, most of them contained *less* than 1 ppm of Cd and less than 50 ppm of Zn, although concentrations ranged from 0-410 ppm and 0.7-2050 ppm, respectively. Twenty-three mud samples, however, had a Cd range from 0-620 ppm and Zn from 68-62,000 ppm, but generally the samples contained less than 10 and 1000 ppm, respectively.

It would appear then since heavy metals tend to accumulate in river sediments and become highly concentrated by plants that the determination of the presence of excessive concentrations requires the analyses of samples of mud and plants, and not necessarily the water itself.

Many industries throughout the world dispose of wastes containing heavy metals by pumping them into water ways. Most, if not all, of the governmental agencies that analyze surface waters in order to determine the presence of toxic contaminants, test the water but not the plants or sediment. Consequently, elements that are needed by the body in minute quantities but which become highly toxic in excessive concentrations, could possibly accumulate in soil, mud and plants from which they could enter the food chain. This in turn might affect humans, but an accurate diagnosis of the possible resulting illness would probably be accidental.

"Poison is in everything, and no thing is without poison. The dosage makes it either a poison or a remedy."   Paracelsus

REFERENCES

Kobayashi, J., 1969, Investigations for the cause of the itai-itai disease. Kagaleu (Science), v. 39, no. 6, p. 286-293. (In Japanese)

21. GEOGRAPHICAL AND GEOCHEMICAL RELATIONSHIPS OF TRACE ELEMENTS TO HEALTH AND DISEASE

E. J. UNDERWOOD

There is now abundant evidence that the growth, health and well-being of man and his domesticated animals are determined, among other things, by the amounts and proportions of the various trace elements to which they are exposed. Intakes of these elements come from ingestion with the food and drinking water and from inhalation of the environmental air. In most circumstances the food provides an overwhelming proportion of total exposure. This does not mean that the water supply and the atmosphere cannot be significant sources of these elements in some areas, or that these sources should not be critically considered in any overall assessment of geographical and geochemical factors affecting health and disease. Indeed, high natural levels of fluoride in the water supplies in many parts of the world have been incriminated as the cause of endemic fluorosis in man and animals and controlled artificial fluoridation of the water supplies has been exploited widely as a means of reducing the incidence of another disease condition in man, dental caries. The position with another halogen, iodine, is quite different. The incidence of simple goiter in man has been inversely correlated with the level of iodine in the drinking water. It should nevertheless be emphasized that, in goitrous and non-goitrous areas alike, 90% or more of total iodine intakes come from the food. The correlation with the level of iodine in the water supplies is therefore interesting as it reflects the iodine status of the rocks and soils from which the water comes but it is not of itself a significant factor in the extent or severity of the goiter. Recent evidence obtained by Hadjimarkos (1967) of the concentration of 17 trace elements in the public water supplies located in 44 States of the United States suggests a similar position for other elements. From these data it was calculated that the proportion of the total daily intakes, which came from

Reprinted with the permission of the author and editor from *Trace Substances in Environmental Health - IV*, p. 3-11, D. D. Hemphill, Ed., Pub. by The University of Missouri, Columbia, Missouri, 1971.

the drinking water, ranged from 0.3% for tin to 10.1% for zinc.

Even less significant quantities, compared with the amounts in foods, are also normally contributed by the atmosphere, except in areas adjacent to mines and factories where substantial atmospheric pollution can occur, or in highly urbanized and motorized areas where injection of quantities of certain elements such as lead and cadmium into the air present possible long-term dangers to human health. This question is considered later.

FACTORS AFFECTING THE TRACE ELEMENT CONTENT OF PLANTS

Since the food consumed in most areas constitutes the major source of most trace substances, it is appropriate at this point to consider the basic factors that determine their levels in the materials consumed as foods. In foods of plant or vegetable origin these factors are now well established. They are the genus, species or variety of the plant, the soil and climatic conditions under which the plants have grown and the stage of maturity or the parts of the plant under consideration. The relative importance of these interacting variables varies with different elements and can be greatly modified by man in his efforts to increase yields and control weeds and pests.

An examination of the significance of genetic differences among edible plants to the supply of trace elements to animals and man lies largely outside the scope of the present paper. However, I would like to make two points in this connection. Firstly, genetic differences can be very large. Thus Beeson and co-workers (1947), in an investigation of 17 grass species grown together on a sandy loam soil and sampled at the same time, found their cobalt concentration to range from 0.05 to 0.14 p.p.m., the copper from 4.5 to 21.1 and the manganese from 96 to 815 p.p.m. on the dry basis. Butler and co-workers (1961, 1957), working in New Zealand, observed tenfold differences in the iodine content of different strains of rye-grass growing on similar soils and showed that herbage iodine concentration is a strongly inherited character. The second point is that any consideration of geographical relationships of trace elements to health and disease must take into account such genetic or varietal differences, from area to area, in the plant materials consumed as food. Such differences could greatly modify any geochemical effects. Furthermore, genetic effects upon trace element levels could be modified further by man in his attempts to increase yields through plant breeding and selection. Yield increases in crops and pastures obtained by these means could be obtained at the expense of lowered concentrations of trace substances vital to the health of man and his domestic animals. With animals the effect on trace element intakes would be a direct one. With man it would be direct and indirect—direct through the foods of plant origin consumed and indirect through the foods of animal origin consumed because the trace element concentrations of muscle and organ meats and of milk and eggs are known to reflect, to varying degrees, the level of dietary intakes of the animal.

I felt it important to draw attention to these considerations despite the fact that soil composition is the basic and overriding environmental factor determining the levels of trace elements in plants and their capacity to supply adequate, and at the same time nontoxic, amounts for consumption. Edible plants growing on soils subnormal in available supplies of a particular element react either by reducing their growth, by lowering the concentration of the element in their tissues, or more usually by doing both at the same time. Similarly, plants growing on soils abnormally high in available supplies of a particular element react either by decreasing growth, *increasing* the concentrations of the element in their tissues to above-normal levels, or both together. The marked variation in the chemical composition of the soil which occurs in different geographical areas is thus a major determinant of the levels of intakes of trace elements in those areas. With grazing animals which are limited to locally grown pastures and forages, these intakes can be too high or too low for satisfactory growth, health and fertility depending upon the nature of the local soils. This is the basis for the well-established "area" problems in animals, such as cobalt, copper and selenium deficiencies and molybdenum and selenium toxicities.

Since the composition of the soil is influenced primarily by the nature of the rocks from which

the soil is derived, the geographical variations just cited are largely of geochemical origin. Different parent rocks not only contain the various trace elements in different amounts and proportions, they contain these elements in differing degrees of stability and are subject to varying influences over varying periods of time during the soil-forming processes. In this way elements initially present in the parent rock can be lost, concentrated or changed in chemical form. Soils derived from granitic rocks—rocks characteristically low in the ferro-magnesium minerals which contain many trace elements in their crystal-lattice structure—would therefore be expected to be low in these elements. If soils derived from granitic rocks have been subjected to losses by leaching over long periods, as in podsolized soils, the expectation of sub-normal levels in the soils and therefore in the plants growing upon them, is even higher. In this case we have two geochemical factors, low initial levels in the parent rocks and heavy leaching losses during the long process of soil formation, contributing to geographical differences in the trace element status of particular areas.

The geographical distribution of goitrous and non-goitrous regions present some unique geochemical features. Iodine occurs on low concentrations in the rocks of the earth's crust, compared with most trace elements of nutritional interest, and has a relatively high solubility. It would therefore not be readily concentrated during the process of soil formation from these rocks. Despite this fact, normal mature soils on which goiter incidence is low or entirely absent, contain about 10 times the iodine concentration of the rocks from which they are derived. It seems that this soil iodine enrichment comes from iodine borne in on ocean winds over long periods of time. It has been suggested by Goldschmidt (1954) that the low iodine status of the soils of goitrous areas frequently results from the removal of iodine-enriched surface soils by recent glaciation, coupled with insufficient time for replenishment with post-glacial air-borne oceanic iodine during the subsequent soil-forming period. On this basis regional differences in the iodine status of soils, and hence in the iodine status of the edible plants and potable waters, would clearly be influenced by geochemical and geographical factors, notably recent glaciation, distance from the sea, and mean, annual rainfall. These are obviously not the only factors concerned because iodine-deficient goitrous areas exist in which recent glaciation has not taken place and which are quite close to the sea. Much has therefore to be learned of the factors influencing soil and plant iodine levels. There is no doubt, however, that subnormal levels of iodine in the soils from which the food and drinking water are derived correlate well in many areas with the incidence of simple goiter in man and animals. This observation was made by that great French botanist, Chatin, over a century ago and has been substantially confirmed by other workers in other countries since that time. In fact, the relationship between iodine and goiter is by far the most convincing link yet established between the composition of the soil and human disease.

SOIL RELATIONS IN HUMAN HEALTH

Earlier I stated that various "area" problems in animals, such as cobalt, copper and selenium deficiencies and molybdenum and selenium toxicities, can be related back to the nature and composition of the soils on which the herbage consumed by these animals is grown. Trace element deficiencies and toxicities are much more difficult to relate to the soil in man than they are in farm stock, with the possible exception of iodine deficiency and endemic goiter, as just mentioned. Copper and selenium deficiencies have never been reported in human populations, although extensive areas exist in which a severe deficiency of these elements occurs in stock. Even in the severely seleniferous area of North America and Ireland convincing evidence of selenium poisoning in man has not been produced, although an apparent positive association between high or relatively high dietary intakes of selenium and the prevalence of dental caries in children has been presented by Hadjimarkos (1969) and Ludwig and Bibby (1969).

There are many reasons why the effects on man of soil-induced variations in the trace element contents of foods are minimal. In the first place, the geographical sources of human foods and beverages are now extremely wide in most modern communities, so that the overall diet comprises materials grown on a variety of soil types. In the second place, the directness of the relationship between the soils of a particular area and the actual intakes of trace elements by man is being increasingly reduced by modifications in food composition resulting from technological developments. For instance, the pasteurization and drying of milk, where these processes involve contact with metal containers, can considerably increase the levels of iron and copper, two elements naturally low in milk. The milling of wheat into white flour results in substantial losses of the minerals originally present in the grain. This could be quite important with elements such as zinc and chromium, for which there is some evidence of marginal intakes by sections of the population. It is important to realize that the losses of minerals in flour-milling applies with equal significance to elements initially abnormally high in the element, as for wheat grown in seleniferous areas. In fact, this effect, coupled with the high proportion of cereals consumed in refined form, may be one of the factors contributing to the absence of signs of selenosis in man in those areas, as mentioned earlier. In addition, rising standards of cleanliness and hygiene at both the domestic and retail level and in storage and processing of foods are tending to reduce trace element contamination of foods compared with earlier years. With iron, the decreasing use of iron cooking vessels and containers is a further factor contributing to reduced intakes of this element.

The directness of the relationship between the soil and human health, and therefore of geochemical influences upon human health, is being further reduced by other technological changes involving the injection of large quantities of certain trace elements into the environment. In this connection I need only mention lead, cadmium and mercury, all potentially highly toxic elements. In highly urbanized and motorized communities the amounts of lead and cadmium coming from motor exhausts and other industrial sources are considerable and impose increasing human body burdens of these elements. The long-term effects of such increasing body burdens upon human health have yet to be evaluated but they clearly call for further critical study.

In parts of Sweden the position in respect to mercury is already causing serious concern. Abnormally large amounts of mercury are now present in the fish and other marine life of lakes, estuaries and rivers in parts of that country. These arise from industrial effluents containing mercury as a result of the use of organic mercury compounds as industrial fumigants. Very little is yet known of the maximum long-term intakes of mercury compatible with optimal growth, health and well-being in man or in his domesticated animals.

THE QUESTION OF 'NATURAL' ENVIRONMENTAL LEVELS OF TRACE ELEMENTS

In the preceding section I gave some examples of how the activities of industralized and motorized man could alter the natural environmental cycling of various trace elements and posed the question as to whether such interventions are necessarily harmful. This raises the further question as to what in fact are "natural" levels, i.e., those which prevailed long ago when human and animal physiological responses to particular trace elements were presumably created and evolved. This problem has been ingeniously examined by Patterson (1965) in a paper entitled "Contaminated and Natural Lead Environments of Man." From geochemical considerations, involving the assumption that the chemical composition of the biosphere is determined to a significant degree by the composition of the environment in which it evolved, Patterson compared the relative abundance of various metals in the earth's crust and in the human body and calculated that the "natural" uncontaminated levels of lead should be only about 2 mg Pb/70 kg body-weight and 0.0025 p.p.m. of blood. Data from several studies of western industrialized man indicate actual average body burdens some 100 times these levels, namely 200 mg Pb/70 kg body-weight and 0.25 p.p.m. Pb in blood. Patterson refers to these as "contaminated" levels which have been elevated above his estimated "natural" levels by man's industrial and technological activities which result in massive injections of lead into the environment.

These calculations undoubtedly indicate the need for a closer examination of the possible deleterious effects of a chronic lead insult of this magnitude and of finding means of controlling the dispersion of industrial lead into the food chain, but they do not of themselves show that this lead insult is as yet producing any harmful effects. In fact, the critical data of Goldwater and Hoover (1967) on blood and urine lead concentrations suggest that these concentrations have changed little over several decades and differ little between urban and rural dwellers in most countries. In fact, New Guinea natives, living under conditions completely divorced from industrialization and motorization, revealed average levels comparable with those of highly industrialized communities. These findings illustrate the difficulty of defining "natural" levels in the manner proposed by Patterson, or at least in applying them with much confidence to particular geographical locations. In certain geographical areas the natural level of environmental lead is much higher than it is in other areas, for geochemical reasons, just as certain areas are higher or lower in other trace elements, such as iodine and selenium, and also for geochemical reasons.

GEOGRAPHICAL VARIATIONS IN THE PREVALENCE OF HUMAN DENTAL DEFECTS

Regional differences in the incidence of dental caries and of mottled enamel are well established. These differences have most clearly been related to the distribution of fluoride levels in the drinking water and are therefore of geochemical origin. However, broad relationships have been demonstrated between caries prevalence and the nature of the soils which occur in particular geographical areas in the United States and in New Zealand which cannot be explained on the basis of differing fluoride intakes. In a study of 1876 children, 12-14 years old and lifelong residents of 19 communities in eastern United States, situated on four different soil types and all using water containing 0.3 p.p.m. F, or less, significant differences in caries prevalence were observed by Ludwig and Bibby (1969). Prevalence was highest on the podzol soils of New England, was of descending prevalence on grey-brown and red-yellow podzols, and was of lowest prevalence on the sub-humic clay soils of the south Atlantic States. Comparable differences in caries incidence were earlier reported from New Zealand (Ludwig et al., 1960; Losee et al., 1960). The adjacent cities of Napier and Hastings were shown to have significantly different caries incidence rates, despite similar socioeconomic conditions, dietary habits and fluoride content of the drinking water. In addition to these studies, an alkaline soil area has been identified in the Sepik River region of. Papua-New Guinea in which the native people show a complete absence of dental decay.

The geographical variations just outlined cannot yet be explained in geochemical terms. In fact, a direct cause and effect relationship between the precise geochemical status of a particular area, and therefore the level of intake from the food and the drinking of a particular trace element and the prevalence of dental caries, has yet to be conclusively established, except in the case of fluoride. A higher molybdenum intake by children of Napier has been suggested as a likely factor in the lower prevalence in that city compared with the city of Hastings. This suggestion receives limited support from some studies of the influence of molybdenum on caries incidence in rats but not from other studies with this element. Furthermore, a study of 553 children from high and low selenium soils in the northwestern United States revealed a higher caries prevalence in the towns in the higher selenium areas than in the lower (Ludwig and Bibby, 1969). These findings support those of Hadjimarkos (1969), mentioned earlier, although in this case unknown factors in addition to selenium appear to be involved. It seems, therefore, that significant geographical variation in caries prevalence do exist and that they reflect geochemical variations. The exact nature of these variations in a causal sense in most cases remain for future research to determine.

ASSOCIATION OR CAUSATION

The relationships between the environment and human health and disease, notably between iodine levels and goiter incidence and between water fluoride levels and the prevalence of dental caries and mottled enamel, which were cited earlier, are highly convincing and are supported by abundant experimental evidence. Numerous other links between the environment and disease of a more tenuous nature have been proposed, in addition to those involving dental caries which I have just mentioned. Differential mortality from cancer of the stomach in different parts of England (Smith, 1960) and Holland (Tromp and Diehl, 1955) has been correlated with soil type and the highest prevalence of total cancer and stomach cancer has been related to particular types of soil in New Zealand (Saunders, 1945). More recently Shamberger and Frost (1969) have demonstrated a high inverse correlation between the selenium status of several states of the United States, as indicated by the average selenium content of different forage crops, and the age and sex-adjusted death rates of the populations of those States. It should be emphasized that these associations rest heavily upon correlation rather than causation. This raises the pertinent question of when an association becomes a causation and what criteria should be applied in passing from one to the other. In other words, what justification is there for claiming that a particular environmental variation is a causal variation or that because A changes with B, A causes B.

The question just posed has been examined with great thoroughness and conviction by Hill (1965) in an outstanding paper in the Proceedings of the Royal Society of Medicine. In this paper Hill maintains that an association needs to be studied from nine different viewpoints before we begin to cry causation. These are strength, consistency, specificity, temporality, biological gradient, plausibility, coherence, experiment and analogy. None of these provides indisputable evidence for or against the cause and effect hypothesis and none can be regarded as a *sine qua non* but together they help to answer the question as to whether there is any other explanation of the association equally or more likely than cause and effect. These points are so important to the whole problem of environmental or possible environmental effects involving the trace elements that I propose to explain them a little further.

The strength and consistency of the association is clear enough. It means is the correlation high and has it been repeated by different people in different circumstances and times? The question of specificity also needs no elaboration. Temporality refers to the old cart and the horse question—which of the associated variables comes first? Biological gradient relates to a possible dose-response curve. Does disease condition B increase as environmental factor A increases? If it does, as with fluoride concentration in the drinking water and the incidence and severity of mottled enamel, then a cause and effect relationship becomes more likely. Similarly we should ask, is the suspected causation biologically plausible. This is a difficult one and should not be taken too seriously because biologically plausibility depends upon the biological knowledge of the day and the researcher may be dealing with something new to science. We should remember Sherlock Holmes' advice to Dr. Watson, "when you have eliminated the impossible, whatever remains, *however improbable,* must be the truth." The requirement of coherence follows naturally from plausibility. It refers to the need to ensure that the suspected cause and effect relationship does not conflict with known and established relevant data. The eighth condition, namely experiment, needs little clarification. Can the proposed association be modified by experimentally changing one of the variables, or can the hypothesis be supported by controlled experimental evidence? Evidence from such sources can provide the strongest support for a causation hypothesis. For instance, the epidemiological evidence linking cadmium with human hypertension is of itself far from convincing but the relationship is made less unattractive and more worthy of further investigation by the experiments of Schroeder and co-workers (1964, 1962, 1969) with this element with rats. Finally, there is the question of analogy. Is there any analogous evidence with some other element or some other disease condition which makes the suspected association more acceptable?

By now I imagine that some of you must be saying to yourselves, 'this is all very well but it is straying rather far from my original topic. I am afraid that I must disagree. Geographical and geochemical relationships of trace elements to human health and disease, and indeed the whole problem of trace substances in environmental health, are growing in importance and studies involving correlation and association, claimed all too often to be causation, are growing in number in almost every country. I would like to make a special plea for a more critical examination of the criteria that are applied, along the lines just outlined. If this is done I have every confidence that the role and significance of trace substances in environmental health will achieve the status and the revelation for the future benefit of mankind that they so richly deserve.

REFERENCES

Hadjimarkos, D. M., 1967, J. Pediat. 70, 967.

Beeson, K. C., Gray, L. C., and Adams, M. G., 1947, J. Am. Soc. Agron. 39, 356.

Butler, G. W., and Johns, A. T., 1961, J. Austral. Inst. Agr. Sci. 27, 123.

Johnson, J. M., and Butler, G. W., 1957, Physiol. Plant 10, 100.

Goldschmidt, V. M., 1954, 'Geochemistry', Oxford Univ. Press, London.

Hadjimarkos, D. M., 1969, Caries Res. 3, 14.

Ludwig, T. G., and Bibby, B. G., 1969, Caries Res. 3, 32.

Patterson, C. C., 1965, Arch. Environ. Health 11, 344.

Goldwater, L. J., and Hoover, A. W., 1967, Arch. Environ. Health 15, 60.

Ludwig, T. G., Healy, W. B., and Losee, F. L., 1960, Nature 186, 695; Losee, F. L., Healy, W. B., and Ludwig, T. G, 1960, U. S. Naval Med. Inst. Res. Rept., No. 9.

Smith, S. W., 1960, Soil and Cancer, Medical Press, London.

Tromp, S. W., and Diehl, J. C., 1955, Brit. J. Cancer 9, 349.

Saunders, J. L., 1945, Trans. Roy. Soc. New Zealand 75, 57.

Shamberger, R. J., and Frost, D. C., 1969, Canad. Med. Assoc. J. 100, 682.

Hill, A. B., 1965, Proc. Roy. Soc. Med. 58, 295.

Schroeder, H. A., 1964, Am. J. Physiol. 207, 62; Schroeder, H. A., and Winton, Jr., W. H., 1962, ibid. 202, 518.

Kanisawa, M., and Schroeder, H. A., 1969, Exptl. Molec. Path. 10, 81.

Part Four
WASTE
DISPOSAL

A story that illustrates an all-too-common manner of attacking the waste disposal problem tells of an old man who lived in a small house in a clearing in Maine. This was no ordinary house, for it was mounted on runners and could easily be moved with a tractor. To dispose of his garbage and waste, the man heaved it out the window until the pile reached the level of the window sill. Then to rid himself of this nuisance, he had his house pulled to a new location in the field. Many people still possess this throw-away, move-on attitude toward waste disposal. Living within a closed finite system, which is rapidly reaching its capacity, man no longer has the resources to squander nor the available space to continue in this manner.

Today, disposal of solid wastes in developed areas is largely by dumping in landfills and by incineration. Composting of garbage, as well as feeding of waste organic material to swine, is practiced in some parts of the world. Liquid waste is most frequently diluted with fresh water, usually after limited treatment, and returned to the surface waters of the earth. We generally dilute gaseous waste products by emission to the atmosphere. Many currently used methods present problems that must be resolved in arresting degradation of the environment.

Some encouraging alternatives to present waste disposal methods are beginning to appear. For example, a newly developed plant for disposal and reclamation of municipal wastes is being used in Franklin, Ohio, a relatively small community north of Cincinnati. When fully operational, this plant will treat municipal sewage and refuse, industrial waste water, and nonaqueous liquid wastes on the same site. It will recover paper fiber, iron, nonmagnetic metals, and glass, all in recyclable condition, with minimal pollution of the air or land. A Swedish-developed disposal system, for use in the central city, utilizes a central incinerator which is fed solid waste materials through vacuum tubes from apartment buildings. The energy produced from burning the trash, which is almost as great as that obtained from burning some coals, is used for heating and for generating electrical power.

One approach to the problems of waste disposal and pollution, which is gaining at least token support, is the recovery and reuse of the useful constituents of waste materials. Much of what is regarded as worthless trash is actually of considerable value if properly handled. Recycling will not only reduce the problems of waste disposal, but will also help relieve the strain on mineral resource supply, providing we are able to stabilize population. A system of disposal of sewage that is receiving a great deal of attention (see Selection 23) is one in which the liquid refuse is sprayed on agricultural lands. The sewage will provide fertilizer and irrigation water for the land, and the land in turn will act as a filter in what could be an effective waste treatment system.

Several selections in this section deal with nuclear wastes and the problems that are inherent in their disposal. Radioactive waste materials are highly toxic and radioactive decay takes place slowly in terms of human time; thus these wastes should be permanently sealed from interaction with physical and biological systems at the earth's surface. With the use of nuclear energy multiplying rapidly, and the likelihood that this will become the dominant form of energy at some time in the future, it is becoming increasingly important to intensify research to solve the problem of nuclear waste disposal.

A note of caution is required regarding the development of new methods of disposing of wastes. Great care must be taken to consider every possible environmental implication in the development of any new system. What may appear to be the ideal solution today, may in fact prove to be tomorrow's environmental headache. Careful research and thorough investigation into the impact of all methods of waste disposal on the environment are necessary, along with well-executed management and control of the systems which are ultimately utilized.

Consideration of geologic factors should be absolutely compulsory in evaluating the development of waste disposal facilities, and yet they are seldom considered at all. Geologic factors control the extent to which ground and surface water will be contaminated by landfills, a type of waste disposal facility which will apparently be utilized for years to come. Deep-well disposal may provide a satisfactory method for disposal of certain liquid wastes but, without thorough knowledge of geologic structures and the bedrock, they could prove unsatisfactory. Indiscriminate location of water wells and waste disposal facilities frequently present problems in safeguarding health, which could be avoided if geologic studies were undertaken prior to locating these facilities.

22. GEOLOGIC CONSIDERATIONS IN DISPOSAL OF SOLID MUNICIPAL WASTES IN TEXAS

PETER T. FLAWN, L. J. TURK and CAROLYN H. LEACH

INTRODUCTION

In past decades, science fiction (horror) writers used to spawn monsters from putrifying garbage dumps—usually the creature was catalyzed by a violent electrical storm acting on the rotting mass of waste. Our time has a way of making science fiction come true—the monster is there. One arm is the sheer volume of solid wastes, the other is the environmental contamination resulting from improper interment of wastes in landfills, and the third arm is the rising cost of disposal.

In the United States the average citizen produces 6 to 8 pounds of solid wastes per day—this includes his personal contribution plus his pro-rata share of industrial and agricultural wastes. A city of 200,000 to 300,000 people is faced with collecting, transporting, and disposing of about 400 tons to 500 tons of solid wastes every day. This is the amount produced by the residents and small businesses—it does not include the wastes from big industrial operations. Costs of solid waste disposal range from $10 to $30 per ton depending on local labor costs, the distance the material must be transported, and the costs of acquisition and operation of disposal sites. In Texas, cost of landfill operations alone averages $1.10 per ton (Gazda and Malina, 1969, p. 23). The practice of open burning of wastes at the disposal site has been discontinued in many areas because of air pollution control legislation. This increases the volume of material that must be buried. In some areas the volume of solid wastes is reduced by high temperature incinerators prior to ultimate disposal, in others controlled burning of wastes produces by-product steam. Currently in Texas some four municipal incinerators are in operation.

SANITARY LANDFILL

Considerable research is in progress to develop new, economic methods of collecting,

Reprinted with permission of the authors and publisher from *Texas Bureau of Economic Geology Circular*, 70-2, 22 p., March 1970.

transporting, and disposing of wastes. The Solid Waste Disposal Act of 1965 (Public Law 89-272, Title II) gave considerable impetus to this effort. The average city dump contains substantial quantities of metals and other potentially valuable substances that might be recovered. Wastes might be converted to a useful building material by high-temperature, high-pressure conversion to a kind of brick or block. Purification or sterilization of wastes by atomic radiation is under investigation. Long distance transport of solid wastes to fill abandoned mines and quarries in sparsely inhabited areas is contemplated by some large cities.

However, notwithstanding the new ideas and research in progress, the most satisfactory economic means of disposing of solid municipal wastes (excluding the large volume of wastes produced by mines, smelters, and other large industries) is the sanitary landfill. Unfortunately, in Texas there are still more open dumps than sanitary landfills.

What makes the landfill "sanitary" is the practice of compacting and covering each day's accumulation of waste with a compacted layer of earth so that gases and fluids produced by chemical and biological action are restrained from escaping into the atmosphere or surface water and ground-water systems, and so that insects, rodents, and other animals are denied continued access to the wastes. The objective is to contain and isolate the fill; it should not be allowed to drain into surface or ground-water systems.

The pollution potential of a landfill depends on (1) the reactivity of the waste itself as measured in content of organic matter, soluble inorganic constituents, easily oxidized substances, etc.; (2) the physical stability of the refuse in terms of volume change (mostly shrinkage) as decomposition advances; (3) the geological and hydrological parameters of the site—the porosity and permeability of the formation in which the fill is located, topography, and whether or not the water table intersects the fill; (4) how efficiently the upper surface of the fill is protected from insects, animals (mainly rodents), and exposure to wind and rain; and (5) climate—chemical reactions are inhibited by low temperatures; in areas with little rainfall leaching of fills is slight.

The surface of the fill must be graded to insure good drainage and eliminate depressions that might trap rain. Ponded rainfall serves as a source of water to leach the fill. Subsidence within landfills is common so that an original well-graded surface may be converted to one containing small water-filled sinkholes. Periodic inspection is necessary for many years after a sanitary landfill has been properly closed and abandoned to determine if regrading is required.

The most permeable earth materials are sand, gravel, jointed and fissured rocks such as limestone and dolomite, and some vesicular lavas; least permeable are unjointed clays and shales. Wastes from incinerators where much of the original refuse has been gasified are less subject to biological action than wastes which have not been so processed, but they may contain substantial amounts of soluble constituents. Where there is an original separation of food wastes (garbage) from non-food wastes (trash or refuse) the resulting non-food accumulation is more stable than a mixture of the two. Where the landfill is located well above the water table in a relatively impermeable formation, fluids produced by leaching of the fill by rainfall do not percolate downward into the ground-water system. Where daily accumulations are compacted and protected by a well-compacted earth layer the amount of rain percolating downward is reduced and the volume of leachate is reduced. A well-compacted cover also cuts down on production of gases by oxidation and decomposition of organic matter. However, compaction alone will not protect the fill from rain if the covering material used is permeable. A compacted clayey layer is much less permeable than a compacted sandy layer. A flat-surfaced fill in England was covered by 18 inches of soil and compacted by a vibrating roller to a depth of 5 feet. Nevertheless, some 10 inches of rainfall out of a total of 25 inches penetrated the fill and produced a leachate (Hughes, 1967, p. 7). If the fill cover is impermeable, gas produced in the fill will be forced to move laterally into the surrounding formations instead of escaping into the air.

Hughes (1967) summed up investigations of the production and movement of pollutants from landfills that have been made in Great Britain, New York, California, and Illinois and presented a useful bibliography. Studies have been made of contaminants produced in ash dumps, leachates from domestic garbage landfills, the effects of refuse fills on ground water, the composition and shrinkage of refuse, the gases produced in landfills, comparisons of saturated and unsaturated fills, and the efficiency of filtering of leachates passing through natural formations and engineered gravel systems. The following discussion is condensed from Hughes (1967).

Decomposition of fills begins in contact with air and processes are aerobic; after burial anaerobic processes predominate. Rainwater or ground water moving through the fill dissolves the soluble components including CO_2 produced by decomposition. The weak acid thus produced increases the solvent power of the solution. Principal gases produced are CO_2 and methane. Gas production is at a maximum early in the deposition of the fill and decreases as the fill ages. Table 1 presents the composition of some leachates. Natural purification occurs by filtering of contaminants in sand and gravel formations and by ion exchange in clay formations. If contaminating leachates do reach the ground-water system, they may remain undetected for years because of the generally slow movement of ground water. Thus, a large reservoir of contaminated water may build up before corrective action can be initiated. Putrescent organic material that escapes from improperly designed fills is commonly a noxious brown sludge that may contain bacteria and viruses. The writers have observed such foul-smelling emissions entering streams 4 to 5 years after a fill was abandoned.

Figures 1-4 are diagrammatic illustrations of sanitary landfills in several common geologic environments; they attempt to show the effects of seasonal variations in the position of the water table. In Figure 1 the fill is in a permeable formation but generally above the water table; contaminants move into the stream during periods of heavy rainfall when high water tables intersect the fill. In Figure 2 the low permeability host prevents contaminants from moving away from the fill, and there is no ground-water contamination from a practical point of view. The fill in Figure 3 above the water table in an impermeable host is secure and results in the least contamination. Figure 4 represents an environment common in Trans-Pecos Texas where the principal danger lies in cloud-burst destruction of the fill's cover and consequent flushing out of accumulated contaminants.

Generally, a satisfactory site would be above the water table or zone of saturation. The permeability of earth materials should be low enough to retard movement of contaminants, and the contaminants produced either should be unable to reach any ground-water reservoir or should be removed or attenuated to acceptable levels before entering such a reservoir.

Although clays offer the best sites in terms of low permeabilities, effluents or leachates of some kinds can change the physical properties of clays. Work by the Illinois Geological Survey demonstrated that soaps, detergents, water softeners, starches, and fabric softeners changed plasticity and shrink-swell potential (White and Kyriazis, 1968). The overall result is to affect the stability of the clay. An old landfill placed in clay that is to be used as a building site should be examined to determine whether or not the physical properties of the clays have been significantly affected by leachates from the decomposing clay. If the terrain is characterized by steep slopes, the slide potential of the filled area should be checked periodically to determine if the leachates have reduced slope stability.

The depth to the water table is more important in porous formations, such as sands and jointed limestones where ground water moves

TABLE 1. PERCENTAGES OF MATERIALS LEACHED FROM REFUSE AND ASH—BASED ON WEIGHT OF REFUSE AS RECEIVED (FROM HUGHES 1967, P. 6, TABLE I)

Materials leached	Percent leached					
	1*	2*	3*	4*	5*	6*
Permanganate value						
30 min.	0.039					
4 hr.	0.060	0.037				
Chloride	0.105	0.127		0.11	0.087	
Ammoniacal nitrogen	0.055	0.037		0.036		
Biologic oxygen demand	0.515	0.249		1.27		
Organic carbon	0.285	0.163				
Sulfate	0.130	0.084 (as SO_4)		0.011	0.22	0.30
Sulfide	0.011					
Albuminoid nitrogen	0.005					
Alkalinity (as $CaCO_3$)				0.39	0.042	
Calcium				0.08	0.021	2.57
Magnesium				0.015	0.014	0.24
Sodium			0.260	0.075	0.078	0.29
Potassium			0.135	0.09	0.049	0.38
Total iron				0.01		
Inorganic phosphate				0.0007		
Nitrate					0.0025	
Organic nitrogen	0.0075	0.0072		0.016		

*Source of data and conditions of leaching:
1. Ministry of Housing and Local Government [Gt. Brit.], 1961, p. 117. Analyses of leachate from domestic refuse deposited in standing water.
2. Ministry of Housing and Local Government [Gt. Brit.], 1961, p. 75. Analyses of leachate from domestic refuse deposited in unsaturated environment and leached only by natural precipitation.
3. Montgomery and Pomeroy, 1949, pp. 4 and 19. Refuse from Long Beach, California. Material leached in laboratory before and after ignition.
4. Engineering-Science, Inc., 1961, p. 39. Estimate based on data reported in "Final Report on the Investigation of Leaching of a Sanitary Landfill" (Sanitary Engineering Research Laboratory, 1954). Domestic refuse in Riverside, California, leached by water in a test bin.
5. Engineering-Science, Inc., 1961, p. 73. Based on data reported in "Investigation of Leaching of Ash Dumps" (Sanitary Engineering Research Laboratory, 1952). Leaching of California incinerator ash in a test bin by water.
6. Engineering-Science, Inc., 1961, p. 73. Based on data reported in "Investigation of Leaching of Ash Dumps" (Sanitary Engineering Research Laboratory, 1952). Leaching of southern California incinerator ash in a test bin by acid.

FIGURES 1-4
Surface waste disposal and ground-water contamination

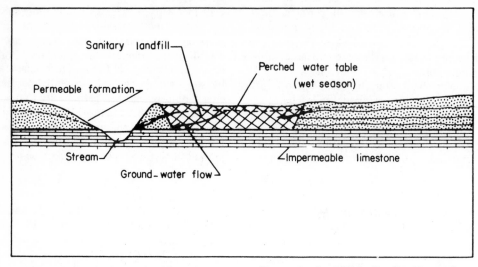

Figure 1. Perched water table, near stream. (Example: landfill in Burditt Formation, near Austin, Travis County.) Permeable sites near streams should be avoided unless special measures are taken to protect the surface water. Ground water is dynamic—always moving: the hydrologic situation at any given site is subject to seasonal and long-term variations.

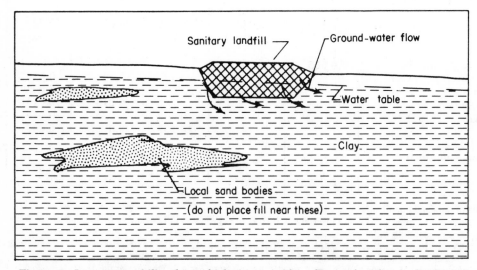

Figure 2. Low permeability host, high water table. (Example: clay in Beaumont Formation, Gulf Coast.) Fill placed below water table causes local contamination, but extremely slow movement of the ground water precludes widespread distribution of the contaminants. Typical ground-water flow rates through clayey sediments under small hydraulic gradients are 0.1 to 0.5 foot per year. Thus, in fifty years, the leachate would move only 5 to 25 feet from the fill. On-site investigation is required to locate and avoid sand bodies. Major risk of this type of fill is contamination of surface water. While active, the fill should be isolated from surface water, and before abandonment, it should be re-compacted and covered with several feet of impermeable material.

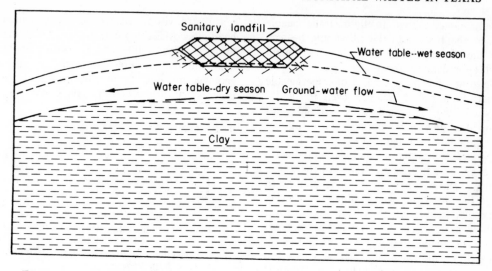

Figure 3. Low permeability host, moderate climate. (Example: clay in Taylor Formation, near Austin, Travis County.) Fill placed on a topographic rise (preferably on a broad, relatively flat area) is secure. In wet season, if water table intersects the landfill, contamination of a small area around the landfill occurs, but the low permeability of the host prevents extensive movement of the contaminants. Typical rates of ground-water movement away from the fill would be less than 1 foot per year.

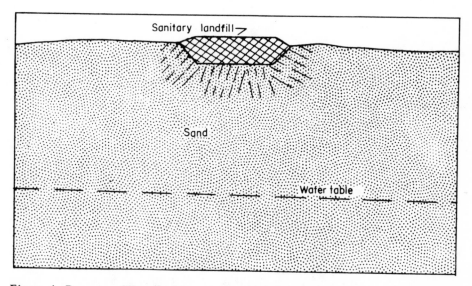

Figure 4. Dry area, fill well above water table. (Example: bolsons of West Texas.) This type of fill is secure during dry years, but a single heavy rain may flush contaminants to the water table, particularly if the host rock and cover are permeable. Security is improved considerably by lining the pit before filling, and mounding the compacted, impermeable cover of the fill before abandoning it.

relatively rapidly, than in tight, impermeable clays. In the first cases the fill should be well above the water table and the base of the fill should be separated from the aquifer or permeable zone by at least 50 feet of impermeable material. In a clay formation—even if the fill intersects the saturated zone—ground-water movement is slow and the clay acts to filter or fix the pollutants through ion exchange. If a site in impermeable materials cannot be secured within an economically attractive range of the waste-producing center, then special engineering to protect the site is necessary. Impermeable clay layers can be used to line the fill site and to cover it. Sub-surface barriers to movement of leachates can be constructed, and where gases and leachates are thus impounded they can be diverted to a collection point and treated (Landon, 1969). If favorable sites are rare, it is possible to reuse proven sites by excavating old stabilized non-reactive wastes and using them as fills in more

sensitive environment. Of course, this increases handling costs. Decomposition and stabilization proceed most rapidly where moisture content is high and temperatures are warm. In any case, geologic and hydrologic investigation of the site is necessary for protection of the public.

REFERENCES

Gazda, F. P., and Maline, T. F., Jr., 1969, Land disposal of municipal solid wastes in selected standard metropolitan statistical areas in Texas: Univ. Texas, Environmental Health Engineering Research Lab., Pub. EHE-69-B, 114 p.

Huges, G. M., 1967, Selection of refuse disposal sites in northeastern Illinois: Illinois State Geol. Survey, Environmental Geol. Notes No. 17, 26 p.

Landon, R. A., 1969, Application of hydrogeology to the selection of refuse disposal sites: Groundwater, v. 7, no. 6, p. 9-13.

White, W. A., and Kyriazis, M. K., 1968, Effects of waste effluents on the plasticity of earth materials: Illinois State Geol. Survey, Environmental Geol. Notes no. 23, 23 p.

23. REVIVING THE GREAT LAKES

JOHN R. SHEAFFER

The death of Lake Erie has been announced. Premature aging, brought on by excessive intake of powerful stimulants, is given as the cause. And it is said that the whole Great Lakes system is rapidly being brought to the end of its life by the same malady.

This calamitous news should not be accepted as the final word. The Great Lakes have been grievously abused, but the effects are not irreversible. Technology competent to restore a fondly remembered past is available. All we lack is the will to use it.

The revival could be started by one simple official order: "No direct discharge of any wastes into any water-course."

There are those who will say that such a directive would be meaningless for practical purposes because alternate means of waste disposal either are not available or are far too expensive to contemplate. But the Federal Water Quality Administration of the U.S. Department of the Interior is gambling the biggest single project grant in its history on the conviction that a workable substitute for indiscriminate dumping into the lakes is at hand. FWQA is committed to spend $2-million on the opening phase of a research project intended to demonstrate that sewage and factory effluent presently being poured into Lake Michigan can be diverted to fertilize barren land in Michigan. If all projections for the scheme prove out, this new waste disposal system will pay for itself and net a profit, perhaps even stimulate the economy of Michigan by building up an agro-industrial complex of respectable size.

Michigan's Muskegon County, fronting on the eastern shore of the lake directly opposite Milwaukee, is the scene of this precedent-setting experiment, which is built around acceptance of the principle that nature is a closed ecological system and that wastes, when properly cycled back into the system, are valuable resources. Wastes become liabilities only when they lose

Reprinted with permission of the author and publisher from *Saturday Review*, v. 53, no. 45, p. 62-65, November 7, 1970. Copyright 1970 Saturday Review, Inc.

their rightful place in the cycle. Human and animal excrement, emptied into watercourses, stimulates aquatic plant growth and turns lakes into bogs. When spread upon the land, however, the same chemical constituents of waste give nutriment to food grains and vegetables.

Historically, the closed-system principle, though recognized by professional ecologists, has been ignored in practice in this country. We have dumped our wastes into rivers and lakes for generations. As long as the human population remained a statistically insignificant factor in the system, oxygen and bacteria in the water decomposed the waste and redistributed the chemicals in the purifying process. A certain amount of acceleration occurred in the rate of eutrophication (a geological process through which lakes gradually fill up and become first marshes and then dry land) but not enough to be distressing.

However, as cities and towns multiplied and grew and as household conveniences such as detergents were added to the burden of sewage, the amount of waste rose to flood proportions. Phosphorus, potassium, and nitrogen released into the water encouraged proliferation of colonies of plants to choke streams and lake beds, exhaust the oxygen supply, and overwhelm the restorative microorganisms. Idyllic watercourses deteriorated into stagnant, stinking pools.

Eight years ago, public-spirited members of the faculty of Pennsylvania State University reminded us of the intelligent way out of this dilemma. Long before then, the university had built a sewage disposal plant to serve the school together with the borough of State College, which existed chiefly as a dormitory community. The plant was designed in two stages: the first a sedimentation basin in which solid waste particles were separated out by gravity, the second a biological trap in which microorganisms digested organic matter in the wastes. The chlorinated effluent from the plant emptied into nearby Duck Pond and thence into Spring Creek, a tributary of the Juniata River, which flowed into the Susquehanna and on to Chesapeake Bay.

As the town and the school expanded, the amount of effluent added to the water rose from a million gallons a day to 3.5 million gallons a day, and the university faculty anticipated the time when the volume might reach six million gallons a day. Ultimately, if matters continued in that direction, Spring Creek would no longer be a body of water carrying away the liquid residue of human waste but a torrent of human waste carrying unrecognizable water through the beautiful Nittany Valley.

The geological structure of the valley was underlaid with limestone, which formed aquifers for storage of water underground all the way from Bellefonte to Scotia Mine. The water level in these subterranean reservoirs had been falling at the rate of 75 feet a year for a period of years. Being followers of the land grant college tradition, the Penn State faculty members were well aware of the remarkable filtering properties of the soil. They decided to test whether it would be possible to divert the sewage effluent from Duck Pond and spread it instead on adjacent crop land, open fields, and woods owned by the university. A network of irrigation pipes was spread out from the pond (thus avoiding Spring Creek) to the test plots, and sewage effluent was driven through these pipes and sprinkled onto the soil summer and winter for a period of six years.

At the end of the test period, it was found that the water level in the underground aquifers had dropped only a few feet each year in contrast to the precipitous annual decline previously experienced. Corn and hay grown on the irrigated land yielded three times the harvest of fields not involved in the experiment. Wheat planted in the test plots retained the same yield as before, but the protein content of the wheat rose. Northern pine trees grew as rapidly as southern pines usually do. The bird and animal population of the test area thrived on the new regime [for further details see "The Crisis in Water—What Brought It On?" SR, Oct. 23, 1965].

One of the inspirations for this experiment was work that had been done at Seabrook Farms in New Jersey by the late Professor Warren Thornthwaite, who was associated with the geography department at the University of Chicago while I was a graduate student there. I remember listening to his descriptions of the Seabrook project and wondering why he did not propose its application on a grand scale. Con-

sequently, when I began to receive personal reports of the Penn State project from one of its prime movers, Dr. R. R. Parizek, I pondered more deeply than ever the implications of the idea's application to widespread urban areas.

Parizek, a young geologist who had taken his Ph.D. at the University of Illinois before going to Penn State, had been a college roomate of Dr. Arthur J. Zeizel, my assistant during my tenure as resource planning officer at the Northeast Illinois Planning Commission. Parizek visited Zeizel periodically and would tell us about what he was doing in Pennsylvania. The information he conveyed went into momentary storage at the back of my head through the three years during which I was occupied—first at the Northeast Illinois Planning Commission and then as research associate at the Center for Urban Studies of the University of Chicago—with problems of flood plain management. But in the spring of 1968, the subject moved to the front of my mind in response to a plea from Roderick Dittmer, director of planning for Muskegon County.

Dittmer dropped in at the Center for Urban Studies one day and said he would welcome some guidance in drawing up a policy to govern Muskegon County's planning for the future use of the county's water resources. Muskegon County was party to a four-state (Wisconsin, Michigan, Illinois, and Indiana) pact calling for an 80 per cent reduction in phosphates discharged into Lake Michigan by the end of the year 1972. It was Dittmer's responsibility to recommend how this cleanup could best be done in his county. My research associate and I agreed to help him in return for what the experience could teach us about managing urban environments. Muskegon County had about every modern problem we could imagine—racial, economic, educational, environmental—yet it encompassed an area small enough to study in everyday operation. A population of 170,000 is contained within 512 square miles.

Our initial investigation identified an interrelationship between two major causes of Muskegon County's economic woes. The county had never developed an agricultural economy to balance its industrial strength, nor had it capitalized on the recreational resource potential represented by Muskegon, Mona, and White Lakes. Popular use of the lakes was inhibited by pollution of the water, while the poor agricultural yield was caused by low fertility of the soil. Obviously, a waste-water irrigation system similar in its fundamentals to the one demonstrated at Penn State could fertilize the barren land with chemicals recovered from sewage diverted from the lakes.

Why had such an eminently sensible concept not been pushed to a stage that would give it national prominence? Was it because no set of elected officials had ever laid down a sufficiently demanding policy to suggest the notion to public appointees responsible for municipal water and sewage works? Acting on that probability, we wrote Dittmer a statement of policy that could be effectuated only by banning discharge of pesticides, insecticides, phosphates, and other pollutants into the rivers and lakes. Dittmer courageously endorsed the statement and presented it to the Muskegon County Planning Commission. The commission, rallying behind its fighting chairman, Michael Kobza, added its approval. And then we encountered trouble.

The Michigan State Water Resources Commission did not like our point of view. What we proposed would meet any situation anyone could think of up to the year 2000. Why go to all that expense? It was costly enough to try to think in terms of 1980.

If the United States Supreme Court had not delivered its famous legislative reapportionment decision—the "one man, one vote" edict—we very probably would have lost our case right there. The old forty-man board of Muskegon County commissioners almost certainly would have bogged down in endless rounds of precinct politics. Fortunately, a reapportioned board of only fifteen members took office on January 1, 1969. With a remarkable disregard for partisan considerations, the nine Democrats and six Republicans (with F. Charles Raap sitting as chairman) voted in February to support the County Planning Commission in the face of the state Water Resources Commission's displeasure. We were thus authorized to come up with a plan to carry out the policy we had enunciated.

In earlier efforts to break through the conventional restraints that have kept politics so far behind technology in the handling of waste disposal, I had formed a professional liaison with William J. Bauer, founder of the Bauer Engineering Company of Chicago. I now proposed that Muskegon County hire Bauer to draw up engineering specifications for a comprehensive sewage disposal system that would leave no environmental after-effects for future generations to worry about. A contract with Bauer was underwritten jointly by the county and U.S. Department of Housing and Urban Development.

Bauer worked out a system far more sophisticated that Penn State's experimental project. He proposed coupling of the sewage outlets of twelve cities and townships into one great outlet pipe that swung away from Lake Michigan, Muskegon Lake, Mona Lake, and White Lake—traditional sinks for the wastes in these communities—and fifteen miles inland to virtually uninhabited sandy barrens of the eastern part of the county (Fig. 1). There the pipe would empty into three aerated lagoons, each covering eight acres. These man-made basins, agitated continually by streams of air from mechanical mixers to minimize odor while bacterial colonies in the waste matter decomposed their host, would be big enough to hold the waste flow up to three days. This would enable accommodation of sudden surges of water such as occur after storms. And, because of the volume of water contained at one time, toxic industrial spills could kill the restorative bacteria and yet remain under treatment long enough for a new bacterial colony to grow and do its necessary work.

The enormous advantage represented by the latter circumstance may not be widely appreciated because most people do not realize that the conventional sewage treatment system in use in most American communities suffers regular spells during which the helpful bacteria are dead and the sewage simply passes through the system in an almost raw state. These spells last anywhere from seven to ten days. If six of them happen each year (one Midwestern state suggests that as an average), almost raw sewage is dumped into watercourses about one day in every week.

The system Bauer designed for Muskegon County called for two storage lagoons to hold the waste after it had passed through the aerating lagoons. Each of these storage receptacles would occupy 900 acres. Their purpose would be to hold the waste during the winter months when the ground would be too hardened by cold to absorb the effluent. After being withheld until the return of milder weather, the waste might be used as fertilizer during the remainder of the year.

Bauer's system finally called for the effluent to be piped from the storage lagoons to rotary irrigation rigs, which would spray the liquid with its suspended solids over almost 6,000 acres of now unproductive but potentially valuable sandy soil.

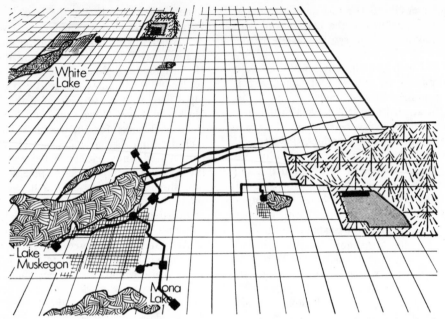

—Doug Anderson following Muskegon County Planning Commission sketch

Figure 1. Artist's sketch above shows how sewage from Muskegon County communities will be piped away from lakes and taken inland to fertilize now barren but potentially profitable sand-dune country. Lower piping system covers Muskegon and Mona Lakes; upper system covers White Lake. The entire collection and irrigation network is designated.

One appendix to the plan estimated a profit of $740,000 a year from sale of corn that could be grown on the irrigated fields, a quadrupling of the value of the land because of the irrigation, opening of at least 1,200 new jobs, recreational development of shorelines now useless because of uglification caused by water pollution, and construction of a 200-boat marina. Another appendix described a new industrial complex that might be built around the corn crop. Among its suggested products were feed for cattle, oil for the human diet, charcoal for use in Muskegon's existing paper mill, starch for the paper mill and for a foundry, carbon dioxide gas for a carbonate mill, calcium hydroxide for use on the irrigated land, and furfuryl alcohol for the finishing of office furniture.

Apart from its dollars and cents aspect, the Bauer system offered an intangible human bonus of inestimable value. This arises from a growing suspicion among public health physicians that many rapidly spreading diseases in this country are transmitted by viruses. How do the viruses travel? Their presence is not sought by any water quality tests now in use. Studies have been made of viruses in sewage, however, and thirteen different viruses have been found in raw sewage, in effluent from primary (one-step) sewage treatment plants, and in effluent from secondary (two-step) treatment plants as well. A month-long sequestration of the effluent in oxidation ponds kills 70 per cent of the viruses. But only after the effluent is filtered through soil do the viruses disappear altogether. Researchers have discovered that soil particles possess an electrical affinity for viruses, which allows the viruses to be grabbed by the soil and held long enough to be dismembered into innocuous protein.

Students of irrigation had one serious question about the Muskegon plan. It had to do with the established fact that elsewhere, in the past, prolonged irrigation saturated the land and created within it a mound of water that in time destroyed the enterprise. Because the thick layer of glacial debris—sands and gravel—underlying Muskegon County is incapable of holding water for long, the danger here was not great. Nevertheless, the Bauer system eliminated it by providing a network of drainage wells through which any water could be pumped back into the county's rivers and lakes.

The very farsightedness of the plan frightened some people away from it. They just could not believe it would perform as promised. The cities of Muskegon and Muskegon Heights already had drafted plans for systems that would continue dumping treated sewage into the water. From a short-range perspective, these systems looked cheaper than ours. Consequently, they seemed more desirable to the local politicians, who not unnaturally followed the advice of sanitation consultants they had known and trusted for years: men who were still working with technologies no longer competent to anticipate the needs of an exploding population.

The continuing absence of approval from the Michigan Water Resources Commission encouraged this local opposition. To counter it, we invited Parizek to come out from Penn State and show a short documentary movie of the Penn State project in operation. Dittmer, Kobza, Raap, and Muskegon County Administrator Ray Wells responded by rounding up their colleagues and chartering an airliner to take them to Penn State to inspect that experiment personally.

The political struggle surged back and forth, with the outcome unpredictable, until N. J. Lardieri, corporate director of air and water pollution for the S. D. Warren Paper Company, a division of Scott Paper—one of the three dominant industries in Muskegon County (Ott Chemical, a division of Corn Products, and Continental Motors, a division of Teledyne, are the other two)—asked to be shown the facts on which our policy decisions had been based. Although we figured his company would have to pay more than half the operating costs of the disposal system Bauer had planned (because charges for the system would be allocated according to the flow rate, and effluent from the S. D. Warren factory would make up 55 per cent of the total discharge into our system), Lardieri saw that our concept had the advantage of solving the water pollution problem once for all; the costs could be amortized with businesslike predictability. When the other Muskegon industries followed S. D. Warren, our opposition began to crumble. But we still lacked the approval of the state of Michigan.

Michigan Congressman Guy Vander Jagt is the ranking Republican member of the Conservation and Natural Resources Subcommittee of the Government Operations Committee of the U.S. House of Representatives. On one of his frequent trips home to consult with his constituents, he heard of the furor we had raised. After meeting with us at dinner, he said: "It appears that our present efforts [in handling sewage disposal] are headed in the wrong direction." Later he added, "I will predict that the Muskegon County facility will be the focal point for the nation's battle to solve water pollution problems." He returned to Washington to make this prediction come true.

From David Dominick, head of the Federal Water Quality Administration, the Congressman went to Russell Train, chairman of the White House Council on Environmental Quality, and from Train to President Nixon's assistant for domestic affairs, John Ehrlichman, and Ehrlichman's environment specialist John Whittaker. The President must have heard about this round of visits, for he wrote me a letter expressing interest in the development of Muskegon's "new and promising approach to sewage disposal." Train voiced his enthusiasm to Dominick, who wrote glowingly to Congressman Vander Jagt. The Congressman personally carried Dominick's letter to Michigan Governor William Milliken. The Governor thereafter announced that he would make an environment tour of Michigan, with Muskegon as one of the stops. After his return to the capitol in Lansing at the end of this tour, the approval we had awaited from the Michigan Water Resources Commission came through.

In mid-September U.S. Interior Secretary Walter J. Hickel announced that FWQA, which operates within his Cabinet jurisdiction, had awarded a $1,083,750 research and demonstration grant and an additional $981,650 construction grant to the Muskegon project. These sums cover only the first year of a seven-year commitment. Secretary Hickel fixed the total cost at approximately $30-million. Of this, the federal government will pay 55 per cent, the state of Michigan 25 per cent, and Muskegon County the balance. Design specifications are now being prepared for bids. Construction will be awarded about January 1, 1971, and the system ought to be in operation in 1972.

"If this project is completely successful, there will be many more opportunities to utilize similar systems in the Great Lakes region," Secretary Hickel said in his September announcement. This is unquestionably true. The Great Lakes basin is made up of glacial outwash plains. Large stretches of well-drained soil suitable for irrigation lie within reach of urban centers but beyond commuting zones and thus are susceptible to purchase at unexploited farmland prices (Fig. 2). If we take the Muskegon irrigation tract as a model, simple mathematics tell us that a billion gallons of waste water per day (that is the flow rate of Chicago's sewage disposal system, the largest in the country) can be disposed of on 260,000 acres of land. A preliminary survey of the major metropolitan areas in the United States suggests that all of them could be served in this manner by using marginal lands equivalent to no more than 2 per cent of the acreage on which fifty-nine principal crops were harvested in 1968.

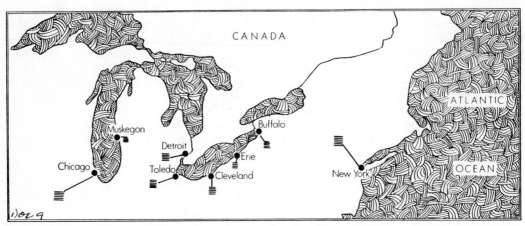

Figure 2. Map indicates feasible inland irrigation sites for disposal of sewage now polluting Great Lakes.

24. OCEAN DUMPING: A NATIONAL POLICY

COUNCIL ON ENVIRONMENTAL QUALITY

The Council on Environmental Quality concludes that there is a critical need for a national policy on ocean dumping. It is not a serious, nationwide problem now, but the decisions made by municipalities and industries in the next few years could lead to dramatic increases in the level of dumping. Once these decisions are made and ocean dumping proceeds, it will be costly and difficult to shift to land-based disposal at some future date.

Ocean-dumped wastes are heavily concentrated and contain materials that have a number of adverse effects. Many are toxic to human and marine life, deplete oxygen necessary to maintain the marine ecosystem, reduce populations of fish and other economic resources, and damage esthetic values. In some areas, the environmental conditions created by ocean disposal of wastes are serious.

The Council study indicates that the volume of waste materials dumped in the ocean is growing rapidly. Because the capacity of land-based waste disposal sites is becoming exhausted in some coastal cities, communities are looking to the ocean as a dumping ground for their wastes. Faced with higher water quality standards, industries may also look to the ocean for disposal. The result could be a massive increase in the already growing level of ocean dumping. If this occurs, environmental deterioration will become widespread.

In most cases, feasible and economic land-based disposal methods are available for wastes currently being dumped in the ocean. In many cases, alternatives to ocean dumping can be applied positively for purposes such as land reclamation and recycling to recover valuable waste components.

Current regulatory activities and authorities are not adequate to handle the problem of ocean dumping. States do not exercise control over ocean dumping, and generally their authority

Extracted from "Ocean Dumping: A National Policy" Report to the President prepared by the Council on Environmental Quality, 45 p., October, 1970. U. S. Government Printing Office, Washington, D. C.

extends only within the 3-mile territorial sea. The Army Corps of Engineers authority to regulate ocean dumping is also largely confined to the territorial sea. The Corps has responsibility to facilitate navigation, chiefly by dredging navigation channels. As such, it is in the position of regulating activities over which it also has operational responsibility. The Coast Guard enforces several federal laws regarding pollution but has no direct authority to regulate ocean dumping. The authority of the Federal Water Quality Administration does not provide for issuance of permits to control ocean dumping. And the Atomic Energy Commission has authority only for disposal of radioactive materials. The Council believes that new legislative authority is necessary.

Finally, this report recognizes the international character of ocean dumping. Unilateral action by the United States can deal with only a part—although an important part—of the problem. Effective international action will be necessary if damage to the marine environment from ocean dumping is to be averted.

POLICY AND REGULATORY RECOMMENDATIONS

The Council on Environmental Quality recommends a comprehensive national policy on ocean dumping of wastes to ban unregulated ocean dumping of all materials and strictly limit ocean disposal of any materials harmful to the marine environment. In order to implement the policy, new regulatory authority is necessary. The Council on Environmental Quality recommends legislation that would:

- Require a permit from the Administrator of the Environmental Protection Agency for the transportation or dumping of all materials in the oceans, estuaries, and the Great Lakes.
- Authorize the Administrator to ban ocean dumping of specific materials and to designate safe sites.
- Establish penalties for violation of regulations.
- Provide for enforcement by the Coast Guard.

The Administrator of the Environmental

Protection Agency would be guided by the following principles in exerting his authority:

- Ocean dumping of materials clearly identified as harmful to the marine environment or man should be stopped.
- When existing information on the effects of ocean dumping are inconclusive, yet the best indicators are that the materials could create adverse conditions if dumped, such dumping should be phased out. When further information conclusively proves that such dumping does not damage the environment, including cumulative and long-term damage, ocean dumping could be conducted under regulation.
- The criteria for setting standards for disposing of materials in the ocean and for determining the urgency of terminating disposal operations should include:
    1. Present and future impact on the marine environment, human health, welfare, and amenities.
    2. Irreversibility of the impact of dumping.
    3. Volume and concentration of materials involved.
    4. Location of disposal, i.e., depth and potential impact of one location relative to others.
- High priority should be given to protecting those portions of the marine environment which are biologically most active, namely the estuaries and the shallow, nearshore areas in which many marine organisms breed or spawn. These biologically critical areas should be delimited and protected.

The Council on Environmental Quality recommends the following policies relating to specific types of wastes currently being dumped in the ocean, in estuaries, and in the Great Lakes:

- Ocean dumping of undigested sewage sludge should be stopped as soon as possible and no new sources allowed.
- Ocean dumping of digested or other stabilized sludge should be phased out and no new sources allowed. In cases in which substantial facilities and/or significant commitments exist, continued ocean dumping may be necessary until alternatives can be developed and implemented. But continued dumping should be considered an interim measure.
- Ocean dumping of existing sources of solid waste should be stopped as soon as possible. No new sources should be allowed, i.e., no

dumping by any municipality that currently does not do so, nor any increase in the volume by existing municipalities.
- Ocean dumping of polluted dredge spoils should be phased out as soon as alternatives can be employed. In the interim, dumping should minimize ecological damage. The current policy of the Corps of Engineers on dredging highly polluted areas only when absolutely necessary should be continued, and even then, navigational benefits should be weighed carefully against damages.
- The current policy of prohibiting ocean dumping of high-level radioactive wastes should be continued. Low-level liquid discharges to the ocean from vessels and land-based nuclear facilities are, and should continue to be, controlled by Federal regulations and international standards. The adequacy of such standards should be continually reviewed. Ocean dumping of other radioactive wastes should be prohibited. In a very few cases, there may be no alternative offering less harm to man or the environment. In these cases ocean disposal should be allowed only when the lack of alternatives has been demonstrated. Planning of activities which will result in production of radioactive wastes should include provisions to avoid ocean disposal.
- No ocean dumping of chemical warfare materials should be permitted. Biological warfare materials have not been disposed of at sea and should not be in the future. Ocean disposal of explosive munitions should be terminated as soon as possible.
- Ocean dumping of industrial wastes should be stopped as soon as possible. Ocean dumping of toxic industrial wastes should be terminated immediately, except in those cases in which no alternative offers less harm to man or the environment.
- Ocean dumping of unpolluted dredge spoils, construction and demolition debris, and similar wastes which are inert and nontoxic should be regulated to prevent damage to estuarine and coastal areas.
- Use of waste materials to rehabilitate or enhance the marine environment, as opposed to activities primarily aimed at waste disposal, should be conducted under controlled conditions. Such operations should be regulated, requiring proof by the applicant of no adverse effects on the marine environment, human health, safety, welfare, and amenities.

RESEARCH NEEDS

In the long term, additional information is required in the implementation of this policy. Serious information deficiencies exist, and research is required in the following major areas:

- Broad-based ecological research is needed to understand the pathways of waste materials in marine ecosystems. Such studies should be directed to a better understanding of the food chain from microscopic plants and animals to high predators; how pollutants concentrate in the food chain; the origin and ultimate fate of pollutants in the oceans; and the effects of concentration on the marine environment and eventually man.

- Marine research preserves should be established to protect representative marine ecosystems for research and to serve as ecological reference points—baselines by which man-induced changes may be evaluated.

- Oceanographic studies of basic physical and chemical processes should be directed toward gaining a thorough understanding of the marine environment, with special emphasis on estuaries and coastal areas.

- Toxic materials should be identified and their lethal, sublethal and chronic long-term effects on marine life investigated. Information is needed on the persistence of toxic substances; how pollutants are degraded chemically and biologically; the effects of radioactivity on the marine environment and man; and the capacity of waters to assimilate waste materials.

- More information is needed about public health risks from ocean pollution. Studies should determine what pathogens are transported in marine ecosystems and how. Better methods of measuring public health dangers are also needed.

- Research is needed on the recycling of wastes and the development of alternatives to ocean dumping. Technical problems must be solved, but there is also a great need to study the social, institutional and economic aspects of waste management.

- Effective national and international monitoring systems need to be developed. Research is necessary to develop improved methods and technology so that alternations in the marine environment may be detected. But there is also a need for data coordination so that data gathering and analysis efforts are not duplicated.

ALTERNATIVES TO OCEAN DUMPING

This chapter sets forth alternatives, both interim and longer term. The interim alternatives discussed are practical, available disposal techniques which can be used now to reduce or prevent damage to the marine environment without shifting the problem to another part of the environment. Long-term alternatives look toward recycling, resource conservation, and more economic and environmentally safe techniques of waste management. Costs and capacity are estimated to indicate the impact of the alternatives.

The types of wastes for which alternatives are presented include: solid waste, sewage sludge, dredge spoils, industrial wastes, construction and demolition debris, radioactive wastes, and explosive and chemical munitions.

Although dredge spoils and industrial wastes are the two largest sources of ocean dumping, solid waste is discussed first because the alternatives are largely applicable to the other wastes dumped in the ocean.

Solid Waste[1]

The amount of solid waste dumped in the ocean is not yet significant, less than 1 percent of all wastes disposed of in the ocean. Only about 26,000 tons were dumped in the ocean in 1968, (Smith and Brown, 1970) compared to the 190 million tons of municipal solid waste collected and disposed of on land. (Dept. of Health, Education, and Welfare, 1970) However, many communities are beginning to look to the ocean as a place to dispose of solid waste in light of increasing population; increasing per capita rates of solid waste generation; and the declining capacity, increasing costs, and lack of nearby land disposal sites. If many coastal cities were to dump solid waste in the ocean, many millions of tons would be introduced annually into the marine environment. Although little research has been done on how solid waste affects marine ecology, it is known that improper disposal of solid waste on land seriously contaminates ground water. Further, floating materials from the solid waste dumped in the ocean would be unattractive, especially when carried to shore. Accordingly, the policy recommended would prohibit new sources of solid waste in the ocean and call for phasing out existing sources.

[1]Includes residential, commercial, industrial, institutional, and agricultural solid wastes.

Interim Alternatives. Nationwide, landfill capacity is generally adequate. The average time remaining for currently used landfills in all metropolitan areas is 16 years, although some large metropolitan areas will soon exhaust their current sites. (Dept. of Health, Education, and Welfare, 1970) Only 10 percent of land disposal operations are sanitary landfills, in which the wastes are covered daily by soil. The other 90 percent are open dumps, which create many health and esthetic problems. Rodents and insects breed and carry infectious diseases, and ground water often becomes polluted. Esthetically, open dumps are unattractive and malodorous. Converting open dumps to sanitary landfills can be accomplished relatively quickly and inexpensively.

There are two alternatives to ocean dumping of solid waste. New sites can be developed, but often at a considerably increased distance. Or incinerators can be constructed. By reducing the volume, possibly up to 90 percent, they can prolong the use of existing sites by many years.

The barriers to acquiring new sites are political and financial. Communities are reluctant to be the dumping ground for the wastes of large metropolitan areas, and transport to distant sites increases costs. Transfer stations and rail or transfer truck operations make these longer hauls more costly than collection vehicles' traveling only a few miles to the disposal area. But they provide more flexibility in site selection. The barriers to the construction of new incinerators are largely financial. They are expensive to build and to operate. More stringent air pollution standards will add to both capital and operating costs.

Comparative costs for various alternative methods of disposal are shown in Table 1. As it indicates, the additional costs for use of rail haul and land disposal instead of ocean dumping are not so high when the distances are comparable. For example, when the wastes are transported 50 or 100 miles by either method, the costs of land disposal are less than 10 percent higher.

If conducted correctly, rail haul and land disposal offer an economically attractive method of disposing of solid waste. However, the political problems are a significant barrier to a good economic and environmental solution. A stronger regional approach to waste management, better disposal operations, and adequate payment for the use of land could well overcome these barriers.

One possible alternative deals with the problems of both solid waste disposal and abandoned strip mines. Because of the small incremental costs involved in rail haul, large coastal cities could haul their wastes to these mines economically.

Available acreage within range of the three coastal areas has been estimated. In the mid-Atlantic States of Ohio, Pennsylvania, West Virginia, Virginia, New York, and New Jersey, over 660,000 acres of unreclaimed surface-mined land are available. Over 300,000 additional unreclaimed acres are available in the Gulf Coast States, Texas, Alabama, Mississippi, Louisiana, and Florida. On the West Coast, California and Nevada have approximately

TABLE 1. COMPARISON OF ESTIMATED SOLID WASTE DISPOSAL COSTS*

(On a cost-per-ton basis)

Unit process	Sanitary landfill at nearby site	Incineration at central city site	Rail haul and landfill			Baling and ocean dumping			Incineration ship-based
			50 ml.	100 ml.	150 ml.	20 ml.	50 ml.	100 ml.	
Collection[1]	$15.00	$14.00	$14.00	$14.00	$14.00	$14.00	$14.00	$14.00	$14.00
Transfer operation[2]	0	0	4.05	4.05	4.05	4.20	4.20	4.20	0
Haul	0	0	2.65	3.00	3.45	.60	1.30	2.25	0
Disposal[3]	1.25	10.50	.65	.65	.65	0	0	0	10.89
Total	$16.25	24.50	21.35	21.70	22.15	18.80	19.50	20.45	24.89

*Dept. of Health, Education, and Welfare, 1970, and Massachusetts Institute of Technology, 1970.

[1] Higher cost of collection for nearby landfill due to lack of central city site.

[2] Higher cost of ocean baling due to higher density requirements.

[3] Lower cost of landfill operation due to baling.

150,000 acres of available, unreclaimed surface-mined land.

Nationwide, surface mining has disturbed over 3.2 million acres of land. The Department of the Interior estimates that over two-thirds of this acreage is completely unreclaimed. This 2 million acres represents 3,300 square miles of potential solid waste disposal sites (Dept. of Interior, 1967).

These figures do not consider suitability of terrain, amount of cover material, volume in need of fill, or other limiting factors. Nevertheless, there are access roads and rail lines to almost all this land, and if legal and social barriers can be removed, the problems both of providing large disposal areas and of reclaiming the land would be solved.

Containerizing wastes—that is enclosing them in plastic or other material to prevent interaction with the sea—raises a number of potential problems. First, any containment system will still allow leaching of the wastes, some of which are toxic. Second, containment systems will probably not isolate the wastes from the ocean environment indefinitely. Plastics and other floatables are likely to be released eventually. As indicated in Table 1, the economics of containerizing wastes are not significantly better than for land disposal, assuming that solid waste would have to be dumped some distance from shore.

Ship-based incineration has also been suggested as an alternative disposal technique. It appears, however, to have little economic or environmental advantage. As Table 1 indicates, the costs are higher than for rail haul or land-based incineration. And difficulties of systematically locating and using sea dump sites may be a problem compounded by the difficulties of operating during bad weather. Further, many of the materials are noncombustible, and the effects of large amounts of ash residue on the ocean environment are not clearly known.

Longer-Term Alternatives. Although ship-based incineration may not be practical, other advances in incineration may have long-term benefits for solid waste management. A new type of incinerator, the CPU-400, is being developed under a Bureau of Solid Waste Management contract. Shredded and dried refuse is burned in a fluidized bed reactor to produce gas for turboelectric power generation. A 400-ton-per-day modular unit will produce up to 15,000 kilowatts of electric power. Total annual cost is projected at between $4.27 per ton for a municipal utility and $5.99 per ton for private ownership; the difference is a function of the interest rate. (Combustion Power Co., Inc., 1969) (Current incineration costs are $10.50 per ton.) Depending on revenues from the sale of electricity and residue by-products, the net cost could be reduced. Soon in the pilot plant stage, this incinerator may provide a low-cost, environmentally sound method of dealing with solid waste.

Recycling may also become general practice. Technology exists to recycle many types of paper, glass, aluminum, and ferrous metals, among others. Currently, 19 percent of the materials used to manufacture paper products in the United States are recycled rather than virgin materials. (Dept. of Health, Education, and Welfare, 1970) Eighty-five percent of all automobiles taken out of service are recycled and used in steelmaking, and tires and aluminum cans are beginning to be recycled. (Dept. of Health, Education, and Welfare, 1970) The problems and associated costs of separation; transportation; poor secondary markets; and other legal, economic, and social barriers have limited recycling. However, with new approaches to these barriers, new technology, and the need to conserve resources, recycling may become practical on a broad scale in the future. And as more materials are reused, disposal needs will lessen. It is important to note that inexpensive but environmentally unsound practices such as ocean dumping discourage waste reuse and recycling, which are desirable in the long term.

Sewage Sludge

In 1968, about 200,000 tons of sewage sludge on a dry basis were disposed of at sea, compared to about 3 million tons disposed of by other means. Increasing population and the higher levels of treatment required to meet water quality standards will generate even more sludge. Given the difficulties of sludge disposal and the high costs involved, pressures to use the oceans will necessarily increase. The environmental problems from sludge disposal in the ocean are significant, in terms both of volume and of the toxic and sometimes pathogenic materials involved. Accordingly, the policy recommended would phase out ocean disposal of sewage sludge and prevent new sources.

Alternatives (Interim and Longer Term). Sewage sludge is primarily disposed of by much lesser degree, by incineration. The costs of using it as a soil conditioner or landfill and, to a present ocean disposal operations are generally far below costs for land-based disposal. Ocean disposal a few miles from shore costs an average $1 per ton. (Smith and Brown, 1970) Table 2 contains more detailed data on the per-ton-mile costs for longer hauls.

TABLE 2. BARGE HAUL COSTS FOR SEW-AGE SLUDGE DISPOSAL*

City	Distance (miles)	Cost per-ton-mile	Cost per ton
New York City	25	$0.30	$ 7.50
Elizabeth, Md.......	30	.23	6.90
Baltimore, Md.	230	.08	18.40
Philadelphia, Pa.	300	.04	12.00

*Dept. of Interior, Federal Water Quality Adm., 1970.

Depending on distance, actual barge haul costs range from $1 to $12 per ton. Thickening, a process preparatory to barging, can add $2 to $6. Digestion can raise total ocean disposal costs by $5 to $18 per ton. Total ocean dumping costs can range from $3 for undigested sludge deposited nearshore to perhaps $40 per ton for digested sludge dumped several hundred miles offshore. The current average is low because most communities that use the ocean for disposal dump undigested sludge nearshore. Table 3 summarizes costs for land and ocean disposal of sewage sludge.

TABLE 3. ESTIMATED COSTS OF LAND-BASED SEWAGE SLUDGE DISPOSAL*

Location	Method	Cost per ton
Land	Digestion and lagoon storage (Chicago)	$45
	Digestion and land disposal**	22
	Composting	35-45
	Processing into granular fertilizer (net cost)	35-50
	High temperature incineration	35-60
Ocean	Barging undigested sludge	3-18
	Barging digested sludge	8-36
	Piping disposal	12-30

*Dept. of Interior, Federal Water Quality Adm., 1970, and Metropolitan Sanitary District of Greater Chicago, 1970.
**At Chicago, with a 7-mile pipeline to the land disposal site.

These data indicate that land-based sewage sludge disposal is more expensive than nearshore ocean disposal. But when sewage is digested and barged a distance from shore, the costs become comparable, and land-based disposal may even be cheaper. As indicated in the discussion on solid waste disposal alternatives, the capacity does exist to handle more sewage sludge. But current land-based operations are often not adequate to protect the environment.

Pipeline disposal of treated sewage sludge, used by Los Angeles, has been proposed for other areas. Because piped and barged sludge materials are the same, the same policy is recommended. Further, the potential savings for piping are not significant in light of the potential environmental impact.

Piping digested sewage sludge 7 miles from Los Angeles costs an estimated $1.55 per ton. (Dept. of Interior, FWQA, 1970) FWQA estimates that current costs on the East Coast would double the net cost—a function of both increasing costs since the Los Angeles pipeline was constructed and the higher construction costs on the East Coast. Costs for longer pipelines to limit environmental damage would increase at a linear rate, and perhaps even faster, as the distance increased because of construction and pumping difficulties. A 30-mile pipeline might raise the cost to $12 per ton and a 50-mile pipeline to perhaps $20 to $30 per ton.

More promising is the use of digested sludge for land and strip mine reclamation and for a supplemental crop fertilizer. As discussed earlier, many strip mines are in need of reclamation. Sewage sludge is high in nutrient value and can be used to improve lands low in organic matter.

The Metropolitan Sanitation District of Chicago has intensively researched the environmental impact and potential of using digested sewage sludge as a crop fertilizer and in land reclamation. Their studies document the nutrient value, lack of odor, and safety when used on all types of land, including clay, sand, and acid strip mine tailings. Depending on crops and soil condition, other nutrients may be needed, but the sludge can supply much of the needed nutrients and moisture. Chicago now spends over $20 million annually to dispose of 900 tons (on a dry weight basis) of sewage sludge per day, using incineration, lagoon storage, and other methods. (Metropolitan Sanitary District of Greater Chicago, 1970) The District is prepared to initiate a program of rail or barge haul for sludge disposal and land reclamation within a year. The program should cost approximately the same amount as current operations and has potential for large savings if pipe transport becomes feasible. Use of sludge for land reclamation looks promising, but it must be carefully controlled and monitored to assure no environmental harm.

In this discussion of land-based sewage sludge disposal, the alternatives to ocean dumping do not involve significantly greater costs. However, a phase-out period is required because of substantial commitments by some communities and the lead time necessary to develop the alternatives.

Dredge Spoils

Disposal of dredge spoils—38 million tons—represents 80 percent of all ocean dumping in 1968. (Smith and Brown, 1970) Removed primarily to improve navigation, spoils are usually redeposited only a few miles away. About one-third is highly polluted from industrial and municipal wastes deposited on the bottom. (Dept. of Army, Corps of Engineers, 1970a) Their disposal at sea can be a serious source of ocean pollution. The recommended policy to phase out ocean disposal of polluted dredge spoils recognizes that the speed of implementation depends almost entirely on available alternatives.

Interim Alternatives. Disposing of all dredge spoils on land is not possible simply because of the vast tonnage. The Corps of Engineers esti-

mates that of the total dredge spoils removed from each coastal region, 45 percent, or approximately 7,120,000 tons, on the Atlantic Coast are polluted; 31 percent, or 4,740,000 tons, on the Gulf Coast, are polluted; and 19 percent, or 1,390,000 tons, on the Pacific Coast are polluted.

Until land-based disposal facilities can handle these quantities, the following interim operational techniques are recommended: First, the pollutant level of dredge spoils should be determined by sampling and analysis for such key factors as BOD and concentration of heavy metals. If the spoils are not polluted, they can be disposed of in the ocean. However, care must be taken in the location of disposal sites and in the method of disposal in order to minimize turbidity and to protect marine life.

For polluted dredge spoils, current disposal practices are not adequate, but mitigation of damage to the environment is possible without recourse to sophisticated and/or expensive processing techniques. The estimated cost increases for hauling polluted spoils farther from the dredging site are presented in Table 4.

Most spoils are now deposited within a few miles from shore in less than 100 feet of water. Table 5 summarizes the additional costs for

TABLE 4. ESTIMATED DREDGING COSTS PER CUBIC YARD*

Method	1 mile	3 miles	10 miles	20 miles	50 miles
Hydraulic pipeline dredging	$0.95	$1.30	(^{1})	(^{1})	(^{1})
Dipper dredging and dump scows	1.10	1.25	$1.50	$1.80	$3.60
Hopper dredging	0.28	0.34	0.54	0.81	1.66

*Dept. of Army, Corps of Engineers, 1970b.

[1] Pipeline dredging operations beyond 3 miles are usually not practical because of problems in handling long floating pipelines and the extra pumping equipment involved.

TABLE 5. ESTIMATED COSTS FOR DISPOSAL OF POLLUTED SPOILS USING HOPPER DREDGE

Costal area	Tons	3 miles	10 miles	20 miles	30 miles
Atlantic Coast	7,120,000	$2,421,000	$3,845,000	$5,767,000	$11,819,000
Gulf Coast	4,740,000	1,612,000	2,560,000	3,839,000	7,868,000
Pacific Coast	1,390,000	473,000	751,000	1,126,000	2,307,000
Total	13,250,000	4,506,000	7,156,000	10,732,000	21,994,000

disposing of polluted dredge spoils farther out to sea using a hopper dredge.

As the table indicates, the additional cost for dumping polluted dredge spoils 10 miles rather than 3 miles out is $2.7 million annually. For 20 miles, the additional cost is $6.2 million; for 50 miles, it is $17.5 million.

Diking is another interim alternative for disposing of polluted dredge spoils. Briefly, a dike is constructed to hold the dredge spoils nearshore or at the shoreline. Its effectiveness depends on the prevention of contaminated spoils' interaction with surrounding waters. At Cleveland, diking was successful in containing over 99 percent of the contaminants in dredge spoils removed from Lake Erie. (Dept of Army, Corps of Engineers, 1969)

Estimates for 35 dike projects on the Great Lakes indicated that the costs of diking and depositing dredge spoils vary greatly—from $0.35 to over $6 per cubic yard. (Dept. of Army, Corps of Engineers, 1969) The increased cost for disposal by diking over open-lake disposal ranged from $0.03 to almost $5.50 per cubic yard, with an average increase of $1.50 per cubic yard.

Diking is not without environmental problems. Dredge spoils would not provide fill of sufficient strength to allow use of the diked area for many years. Hence, areas of the coastal zone, already in high demand, would be unusable. Further, diking is unattractive and may cause greater environmental problems than controlled dispersal of pollutants.

Longer-Term Alternatives. Reduction in the volume of sediments requiring dredging and higher levels of treatment of wastes will both lessen the problem of polluted dredge spoils. Erosion control through improved construction, highway, forest, and farm planning and management will reduce future dredging needs. One example is the recently completed stream bank stabilization project on the Buffalo River, which reduced maintenance dredging requirements 40 percent. (Dept of Army, Corps of Engineers, 1969) The level of pollution in dredge spoils will be reduced by the higher levels of treatment of municipal and industrial wastes required by federal-state water quality standards within a few years.

High-temperature incineration of contaminated dredge spoils is a longer-term alternative requiring further development and testing. Such incineration can render spoils an inert ash, safe for land disposal. Processing costs are a function of the size of the plant, the percent of total solids, and the percent of volatile solids. Figure 1 illustrates disposal costs per cubic yard for incinerating dredge spoils whose total solid content ranges between 30 percent and 45 percent (a normal range) and volatile solids between 10 percent and 20 percent (a normal range). Also shown are costs for aerobic stabilization, a process similar to that used for sewage treatment. These costs can range from $2 to $12 per cubic yard or roughly 4 to 24 times current ocean disposal costs. Compared to disposal 20 miles out to sea, however, incineration is 3 to 15 times as costly. But compared to disposal at 50 miles, incineration may cost the same or it may be as much as 8 times more costly.

Special treatment to remove toxic materials so that the sludge may be used as a fertilizer either on arid lands or for ocean farming is possible. An approach similar to that discussed for use of digested sewage sludge as a fertilizer may be feasible.

Industrial Wastes

Industrial wastes vary widely, but they usually contain nutrients, heavy metals, and/or other substances toxic to marine biota. Although the volume of industrial wastes is 10 percent of all wastes disposed of in the ocean, it is minor compared to the quantities of industrial wastes treated at land-based facilities.

The policy recommended would call for termination of ocean dumping of industrial wastes as soon as possible. Ocean dumping of toxic industrial wastes should be terminated immediately, except in those cases in which no alternative offers less harm to man or the environment.

Interim Alternatives. Many industries utilize ocean disposal because it is cheaper and easier than other disposal processes. Table 6 shows costs for bulk and containerized wastes.

The costs of discharging bulk wastes directly

TABLE 6. INDUSTRIAL WASTES DISPOSAL COSTS*

Method	Average cost/ton	Range of cost/ton
Bulk wastes	$1.70	$0.60-$9.50
Containerized wastes . .	24.00	$5-$130

*Smith and Brown, 1970.

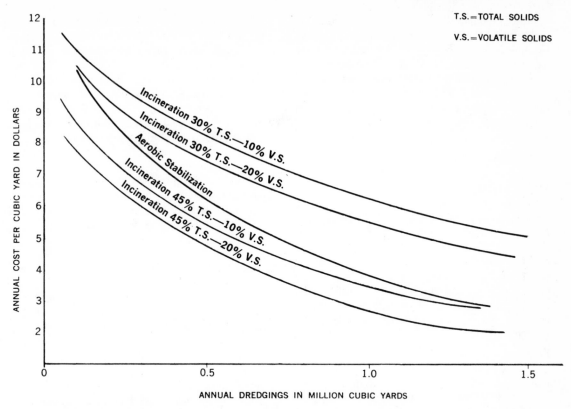

T.S. = TOTAL SOLIDS

V.S. = VOLATILE SOLIDS

ANNUAL DREDGINGS IN MILLION CUBIC YARDS

Figure 1. Total annual cost per cubic yard for complete treatment using incineration and aerobic stabilization (Dept. of Army, Corps of Engineers, 1969)

into the sea are significantly lower than for other disposal techniques. Containerization, used mainly for toxic materials, is much more costly than dumping bulk wastes.

Industrial wastes can be treated and disposed of on land, or they can be incinerated. Whichever technique is used, it is necessary to assure that the environment is protected. Treatment of wastes should not add to stream pollution, and incineration should not add to air pollution. Deep-well disposal of toxic wastes is generally undesirable because of the danger of ground water pollution.

Unlike the other categories discussed, industrial wastes are not homogeneous. Hence, interim disposal methods will vary not only among the different types of wastes but also according to process, location, local practices, and other factors. The costs of using some alternatives will be significantly higher than for ocean dumping, but as a portion of total production costs, generally they will not be great. Total industrial pollution control costs, as a percentage of gross

sales, are well under 1 percent, although costs for some industries are much higher.

Longer-Term Alternatives. In the long term, changes in industrial production processes and recycling offer great promise for reducing or reusing industrial wastes. For example, the average waste from modern sulfate paper plants is only 7 percent of wastes in the older sulfite process. In some cases, recycling will be an alternative to ocean disposal. Two West Coast refineries are now recycling oil wastes instead of disposing of them at sea.

Toxic wastes present a more difficult problem. They cannot be stored indefinitely, but allowing ocean disposal is a disincentive to development of adequate detoxification and recycling techniques and of production processes with fewer toxic by-products. But highly toxic wastes will continue to be produced, and many will not be amenable to land disposal.

One alternative worthy of further study is the establishment of regional disposal, treatment, and control facilities. Federally or privately operated, the facilities could conduct research on and provide for waste detoxification and storage. Complicated disposal processes that are too expensive or complex for a single company could be used jointly to dispose of wastes. Fees would need to be sufficiently high to encourage development of private solutions, except in the most troublesome cases or when significant economies would result from shared use of facilities.

Construction and Demolition Debris

Construction and demolition debris, less than 1 percent of all wastes dumped in the ocean, (Smith and Brown, 1970) are composed mainly of dense and inert materials. Because of the small amounts dumped and their character, these wastes are not a threat to the marine environment. Moreover, amounts dumped in the ocean are not expected to increase significantly because of their high value as landfill. The recommended policy assumes continued ocean dumping, but with care to prevent damage to the marine ecosystem.

Radioactive Wastes

Since 1962, no significant quantities of radioactive wastes have been dumped at sea. Rather, they have been stored at several sites operated or regulated by the Atomic Energy Commission or at sites regulated by the states. Increasing demands for electricity and for use of nuclear power portend a dramatic increase in the amounts and kinds of nuclear wastes produced. Hence, it is important to develop policy to prevent contamination of the ocean.

The policy recommended would continue the practice of prohibiting high-level radioactive wastes in the ocean. Dumping other radioactive materials would be prohibited, except in a very few cases for which no practical alternative offers less risk to man and his environment.

Alternatives (Interim and Longer Term). The quantity of nuclear wastes is not large, and the technology for storing and treating them is well developed. However, the AEC estimates that the amount of high-level liquid radioactive wastes will increase approximately sixtyfold between 1970 and the year 2000. High-level wastes, usually liquid, are now stored on an interim basis in large, well-shielded tanks. In the long run, the wastes will be solidified, reducing their volume by a factor of ten, for eventual storage in special geological formations, such as salt mines. As new nuclear facilities are constructed, provision is being made for parallel construction of storage tanks and treatment facilities to handle the wastes.

Solid radioactive wastes have been buried in carefully controlled landfill sites. In 1970, about 40,000 cubic yards of solid radioactive wastes will be buried in approximately 15 acres. (U. S. Atomic Energy Commission, 1970) The increase in the amount of these wastes in the next decade will require about 300 acres. This figure could be reduced with compaction and incineration, which are currently being used or planned.

Low-level liquid wastes from nuclear power generation, medical facilities, etc., are treated and/or stored to reduce radioactivity. A small amount is eventually released to the environment under controlled conditions.

Large radioactive structures, chiefly reactor vessels and associated parts, have heretofore not presented a significant problem. With the exception of ocean disposal of the SEAWOLF submarine reactor vessel, obsolete reactor vessels and associated parts have been decontaminated, dismantled, and stored on land. Sixteen nuclear power plants are now operating, and 80 are either under construction or permit applications are pending. There may be as many as 1,000 plants by the year 2000. When reactor vessels are taken out of service, each used structure is a source of high-level induced radiation.

There are three alternative ways to dispose of these vessels and associated parts: ocean disposal; entombment in place, with final disposition after radioactive decay; and dismantling and burial. Ocean disposal is the cheapest method when the facility is on the coast or when waterborne transporation is available. Entombment provides an opportunity to monitor disposal operations carefully but occupies valuable land during the period of radioactive decay. Dismantling and burial is the most expensive of the alternatives.

Because of the need to keep all sources of radioactivity at the lowest possible level, ocean disposal of the wastes should be avoided except when no alternative offers less harm to man or the environment. These cases should be carefully examined to assure that no safe and practical alternatives do exist. If ocean disposal is necessary, it should be carefully controlled.

Explosives and Chemical Munitions

Large quantities of explosives and some chemical warfare agents have been disposed of at sea. No biological warefare agents have been disposed of at sea. The policy recommended would prohibit ocean disposal of chemical and biological warfare agents and phase out disposal of explosive munitions.

Alternatives (Interim and Longer Term). Ocean disposal of munitions was developed as an alternative to burning them in the open. That practice is often hazardous, is noisy, and creates air pollution.

Other alternatives to ocean dumping are available and should be used. In some cases weapons can be dismantled and critical components, such as gunpowder, lead, etc., either disposed of safely or sold for reuse. Centralizing the disposal of obsolete munitions may be desirable to provide efficient dismantling. Alternatively, portable disposal facilities, under development by the Department of Defense, offer promise. When salvage value is significant, commercial contracting for disposal services may be possible. Mass underground burial or detonation is another alternative.

The alternatives used for disposal of munitions will depend on ability to train people for disposal operations, relative costs, available sites, and their environmental impact. Dismantling and recycling the materials is the preferable alternative from an environmental point of view, but facility and manpower constraints may dictate the use of other alternatives to ocean dumping.

For chemical warfare agents and munitions, the alternatives to ocean disposal are neutralization and incineration. Toxic chemical warfare agents can be separated from munitions or containers and then treated. Facilities are currently being modified at the Rocky Mountain Arsenal near Denver, Colo., for disposal of toxins. Similar facilities for treatment of chemical warfare agents are needed elsewhere. (Dept. of Defense, 1970)

References

Combustion Power Company, Inc. 1969. Combustion Power Unit—400. Prepared for Department of Health, Education, and Welfare, Public Health Service, Bureau of Solid Waste Management under contract No. PH 86-87-259. (mimeograph)

Department of the Army, Corps of Engineers. 1970a. Information supplied to the Council.

Department of the Army, Corps of Engineers, Buffalo District. 1969. Dredging and Water Quality Problems in the Great Lakes. Vol. 1.

Department of the Army, Corps of Engineers, New York District. 1970b. Information supplied to the Council.

Department of Defense, Office of the Assistant Secretary of Defense for Health and Environment. 1970. Information supplied to the Council.

Department of Health, Education, and Welfare, Bureau of Solid Waste Management. 1970. Information supplied to the Council.

Department of the Interior. 1967. Surface Mining and the Environment.

Department of the Interior, Federal Water Quality Administration. 1970. Information provided to the Council.

Massachusetts Institute of Technology. 1970. Economic Aspects of Ocean Activities. Vol. III.

Metropolitan Sanitary District of Greater Chicago. 1970. Information provided to the Council.

Smith, D. D., and Brown R. P. 1970. An Appraisal of Oceanic Disposal of Barge-Delivered Liquid and Solid Wastes from U.S. Coastal Cities. Prepared by Dillingham Corporation for Department of Health, Education, and Welfare, Bureau of Solid Waste Management under contract No. PH. 86-68-203. (mimeograph)

U.S. Atomic Energy Commission. 1970. Information provided to the Council.

Nuclear Wastes

25. A NUCLEAR GRAVEYARD

NEWSWEEK

Lyons, Kans., is a small, pleasant town of some 5,000, situated close to the geographic center of the state and superficially indistinguishable from hundreds of other little wheat-growing communities in the American Midwest. But down below—deep down below—Lyons is special. For at the end of Fifth Street is an abandoned salt mine and there, 1,000 feet below the surface, the U.S. Atomic Energy Commission proposes to build the nation's first nuclear cemetery—a repository for radioactive wastes produced by the agency itself and by the fast-growing number of nuclear-power plants (29 will be in operation by the end of this year) throughout the country.

Last week, in hearings before the Joint Congressional Committee on Atomic Energy, it was obvious just how much planning the AEC had poured into the Lyons mine—and just how uneasy a significant part of the U.S. public remains over the problem of how to dispose of the nation's inexorably accumulating mass of lethal radioactive wastes. Republican Rep. Joe Skubitz, whose Pittsburg, Kans., district is 200 miles east of Lyons, echoed the fears of many when he told the JCAE that the mine would become a dump for the "most dangerous garbage in the knowledge of mankind."

"The experts tell us this is the safest place in the world to put these wastes," countered JCAE chairman Rep. Chet Holifield. "I don't doubt your sincerity, but this committee is sincere, too. For 24 years, we've been studying all these problems and have put hundreds of millions of dollars into these problems."

Holifield and other supporters of the proposal profess themselves generally satisfied with the results of experiments conducted by the AEC in the Lyons mine from 1965 to 1967 as part of Project Salt Vault. Then cans of radioactive material, simulating nuclear wastes, were buried

Reprinted with permission of the publisher from *Newsweek,* March 29, 1971, p. 60. Copyright 1971 Newsweek, Inc.

in pits in the 300-foot-thick subterranean salt layer and the burial chambers heavily instrumented to detect the spread of heat and radioactivity from the containers, and also any geological movement of the salt deposits. Salt, AEC scientists point out, is a good blanket with which to smother radioactivity because of its density, its high melting point (about 1,400 degrees Fahrenheit, or more than twice the temperature of most radioactive wastes), and its seismic stability.

LABYRINTH

Encouraged by the results of Project Salt Vault, the AEC now seeks $3.5 million to start what ultimately will be a $25 million, 1-square-mile underground complex at Lyons. Like the interior of the ancient pyramids, the salt mine is divided into a series of tunnels and chambers; currently, there are fewer than a dozen of these burial chambers, but the AEC estimates that there could be as many as 500 rooms by the end of the century.

Each of the rooms is to contain eight or ten pits cut into the solid salt. Stainless-steel cylinders containing radioactive wastes will first be lowered down the mine shaft onto a special carrier vehicle and then driven to one of the chambers. There, from inside his heavily shielded cab, the driver will operate remote-control hoists to lower the too-hot-to-handle cylinders (about 600 degrees Fahrenheit) into the pits, like coffins into a grave. The pits then are to be refilled with crushed salt, as will be each room when, in turn, all of the graves are filled. The exact coordinates of each pit, however, will be carefully noted should the need ever arise in the future to exhume the deadly wastes. The AEC thinks that the only event that could conceivably create such a need would be an unexpected shift in the geological structure of the area, and officials note that the salt strata beneath Lyons have not changed position in something more than 250 million years, and are not expected to at any time in the foreseeable future.

CORROSION

As for the cylinders housing the wastes at the time of burial, they are expected to corrode in some six months to ten years as a result of the combined effects of the salt itself and the heat of the nuclear trash. The wastes themselves, however, will be in solid form, and AEC officials say they will not move—or migrate, in the technical phrase—by more than a hairbreadth in the course of 1,000 years.

Most of the waste will be ash from civilian nuclear-power plants, plus some other waste from the AEC's nuclear-weapons factories. These include such isotopes as strontium-90, cesium-137 and plutonium-239, which require anywhere from several centuries to 500,000 years before they decay sufficiently to be no longer hazardous to humans. Already, the AEC is holding more than 80 million gallons of liquid, extremely radioactive wastes at plants near Idaho Falls, Idaho; Richland, Wash., and Aiken, S.C. In addition, there is a private, but AEC-licensed, fuel-reprocessing plant near Buffalo, N.Y., and a second about to begin operation in Morris, Ill.

To date, there have been some leaks in a few of the AEC's storage tanks, mostly at the Washington facility, and though the agency insists that no radioactive wastes have entered either water tables or food chains, it does concede that the huge steel-and-concrete containers currently in use are only interim measures. Even now, the AEC is evaporating and condensing the pool of liquid radioactive wastes into blocks or granules of solid material—some of which will be eventually transferred to the Lyons Nuclear Park, as the vaults have been officially designated—presumably by an AEC press agent now in debt to those wonderful folks who gave us Forest Lawn.

A.D. 2000

By the end of the century, if AEC estimates are borne out, there will be nearly 1,000 nuclear-power plants operating in the U.S. in addition to the agency's own installations—and approximately 3,000 metric tons of radioactive ashes will be hauled out to the Lyons graveyard each year.

So far, this prospect doesn't seem to perturb the stolid burghers of Lyons unduly. They accept the AEC's claims that the radioactive-storage project will not be dangerous and they even look forward to the 200 or so full-time jobs that will be required in the continuing operation of the mine. One fairly typical reaction came from John Johannes, manager of the local Kansas Power & Light Co. office. "What it boils down to is education," he says. "You're afraid of anything until you have knowledge of it."

26. RADIOACTIVE WASTES IN SALT MINES*

W. C. McCLAIN and R. L. BRADSHAW

Many industries are currently facing problems in the treatment and disposal of their waste materials. However, none of these problems is likely to be of the scope and magnitude of the problems associated with the wastes from nuclear fuel-reprocessing plants. These materials are initially produced in the reactor fuel when the uranium nucleus disintegrates and subsequently appear as a waste when the spent fuel is chemically processed in order to recover the unburnt fissionable and fertile material. This processing generates several waste streams, but this paper will be concerned only with the high-level wastes; that is, those which contain nearly all of the fission products. These wastes will be produced in quantities of about 250 gal/tonne (metric) of fuel processed.

Approximately 80 different primary fission fragments are formed when the uranium nucleus splits (Glasstone, 1955). Since nearly all of these are radioactive and decay through an average of three stages before a stable isotope is formed, the high-level waste will contain over 200 radioactive species. Each of these species has a different half-life; some are short, some very long. Since the total concentration of fission products in the waste is about ¼ lb/gal, this radioactivity makes it extremely hazardous and heat producing. Table 1 gives an average activity and heat-generation rate of each gallon of high-level waste as a function of time since the fuel was discharged from the reactor. Any disposal system or repository for these wastes must be capable of removing heat and at the same time it must completely isolate the materials from any contact with the biological environment. More importantly, this total containment must be maintained for periods approaching geologic time. Although radioactive decay will have signif-

icantly reduced the hazard associated with these materials after 1000 years, complete isolation must be maintained for even longer periods. This is much longer than any governmental institution has existed and approaches the duration of what historians call "civilizations."

Recently published predictions (Civilian Nuclear Power, 1967) of the growth of nuclear power generation in the United States indicate that the installed capacity will increase from 11,000 Mw (electrical) in 1970 to 734,000 Mw (electrical) by the year 2000. The production of high-level wastes associated with this evolving nuclear power economy is shown in Table 2. These waste volumes are not large compared with the wastes produced by many other industries, but when their hazard, and heat generation are considered, the volumes become quite appreciable.

CONCEPT OF SALT MINE DISPOSAL

Research has been in progress for many years on the development of methods to safely and economically handle and dispose of these high-level wastes. One of the more promising of these methods is solidification of the wastes followed by disposal in the floor of specially mined caverns in deep, fairly thick, bedded salt formations. The advantages of salt for this purpose were first pointed out in 1955 by a National Academy of Sciences–National Research Council Committee (Committee on Waste Disposal, 1957) which was formed to consider radioactive waste-disposal problems. Some of these advantages are:

1. Salt deposits are essentially impermeable and are completely isolated from circulating groundwater. Furthermore, any fractures tend to heal due to the plastic properties of salt. This means that materials deposited in salt formations are unlikely to come into contact with leaching solutions over very extended periods of time.
2. Salt is widely distributed and abundant. Disposal sites can be chosen in many

Reprinted with permission of the authors and publisher from *The Mines Magazine,* August 1969, p. 11-14. Copyright 1969 Colorado School of Mines Alumni Association.

*Research sponsored by the U.S. Atomic Energy Commission under contract with the Union Carbide Corp.

TABLE 1. RADIOACTIVITY AND HEAT GENERATION
OF 1 GALLON OF HIGH LEVEL WASTE

	Time Since Reactor Discharge		
	4 Months	1 Year	30 Years
Combined Activity (curies/gal.).	14,500	5,300	516
Heat Generation (Btu/hr. gal.)	200	70	5.5

TABLE 2. PROJECTIONS OF UNITED STATES NUCLEAR POWER
GENERATION AND WASTE PRODUCTION*

	Calendar Year		
	1970	1980	2000
Installed Nuclear Capacity . . . . [Mw (electrical)]	11,000	95,000	734,000
Volume of High Level Waste . . Annual (gal./year)**	23,000	510,000	3,400,000
Accumulated (gal.)	45,000	2,400,000	39,000,000

*Blanco et al., 1967.
**Based on 100 gal. of high-level waste per 10,000 Mwd (thermal) irradiation and a
  3-year lag between dates of power generation and waste production.

locales, and utilization of salt for this purpose will not sterilize a valuable natural resource.

3. Salt formations are, in general, located in regions of low seismicity, thereby reducing the chances of breaching the containment.
4. Excavation in salt is a well-developed technology and low-cost operation.
5. Salt has a high thermal conductivity for removing heat from the wastes and approximately the same structural and shielding physical properties as concrete.

In concept (Bradshaw et al., 1968) the wastes would be solidified at the processing site by one of the several processes currently in pilot-plant testing. These processes, which involve either direct calcination or fixation of the nuclides in a glassy slag, produce about 1 ft^3 per 100 gal of liquid waste (or 2.5 ft^3 of solid waste per (metric) tonne of fuel processed). These wastes, sealed in containers 6 to 24 in. in diameter and up to 10 ft long, would be interim cooled, probably in water-filled canals, for periods of several years. The containers would then be shipped to the salt mine disposal site in specially designed shielded shipping casks.

The size of an actual disposal facility would

waste itself will be limited by the conductivity of be determined by an economic balance of the capital investment and the operating costs. A 1-square-mile area was chosen for the size of this example, one quadrant of which is shown in Fig. 1. The mine space would be developed in such a way that concurrent excavation and disposal operations are completely isolated and that the mine personnel never enter a ventilation air stream after it has passed a filled disposal area.

At the mine, the waste containers would be removed from the shipping cask by remote operations in a hot cell located at the top of a special waste shaft leading to the underground workings. After inspection and any necessary decontamination or recanning, the containers would be lowered, one at a time, into a shielded underground transporter positioned under the waste shaft. The transporter would then move to the current disposal area, deposit the waste container into a hole drilled in the floor of the room, and backfill the hole with crushed salt. All operations, except those when the container is completely inside the shielded transporter would be carried out by remote control.

The spacing of the holes in the floor of the disposal rooms will be designed so that the maximum temperature of both the salt and the

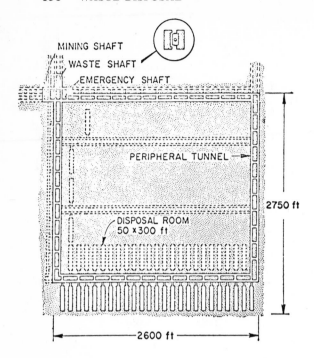

Figure 1. One quadrant of 1-square-mile disposal facility.

the salt. After all the holes in a given room have been filled, the room itself would be backfilled with crushed salt obtained from the excavation operations and sealed from the ventilation air. The design of the entire operation, including the sizes of the disposal rooms and the support pillars, would be such that plastic flow, accelerated by the elevated temperatures, will cause a consolidation and recrystallization of the salt, thus returning the salt bed to very nearly its undisturbed state within a few decades after disposal operations have ceased. It is felt that this method will safely and completely contain the wastes throughout their hazardous lifetime even if events precluded surveillance and radiological monitoring of the site by future generations.

A study (Bradshaw et al., 1968) of the costs associated with the disposal of high-level solidified wastes in salt mines has been carried out by assuming a constant nuclear power economy of 15,000 Mw (electrical) installed capacity. This study showed that the cost of disposal and the life of a 1-square-mile mine were highly dependent upon the age of the waste at burial. If disposal takes place when the waste is 1 year old, the heat-generation rate is high and the con-

tainers must be widely spaced. With this waste, the mine will last about 12½ years and disposal costs will be about 0.019 mills/kwhr of electricity produced. If the waste is interim cooled for 30 years, the containers can be placed much more closely together, extending the life of the mine to about 70 years and reducing the cost of disposal to about 0.003 mills/kwhr. These costs are a relatively small and quite acceptable portion of the 2 mill/kwhr cost of competitive nuclear power.

DEMONSTRATION EXPERIMENT

In order to advance the development of this attractive disposal method, a demonstration experiment was undertaken in an inactive salt mine at Lyons, Kansas. The principal objectives of this experiment were to "demonstrate" the feasibility and safety of both the technique and the waste-handling equipment and to obtain data on the properties of in-situ salt which would permit rational design of an actual disposal facility. In this experiment, which was carried out from November 1965 to October 1967, irradiated fuel assemblies from the Engineering Test Reactor at Idaho Falls were used to provide sources of intense radioactivity while electrical heaters supplemented the decay heat generated by wastes.

The experimental area consisted of five rooms newly mined at a level approximately 15 ft. above the existing mine floor which is about 1000 ft. deep (Fig. 2). This increase in elevation was necessary to assure that the holes in the floor into which the radioactive material was deposited would be in the purest available salt strata. The main part of the experiment was carried out in the two end rooms of the experimental area. The first room contained the main radioactive array of seven specially lined 12-ft. deep holes in the floor, laid out in a circular pattern on 5-ft. centers. Each of these holes contained auxiliary electrical heaters and two ETR fuel assemblies sealed in a 7-ft.-long canister. The end room contained an electrical array which was identical with the main array in every way except for the absence of radioactivity. This array provided a control for the main array, and any unexplainable differences in the behavior of the salt of these two rooms could be ascribed to the effects of radiation. The two center rooms of the experimental area contained a part of the experiment which was designed especially and exclusively to obtain additional information on the

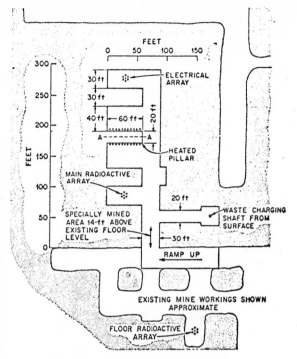

Figure 2. Layout of experimental area.

deformational properties of the salt at elevated temperatures. A row of electrical heaters was installed in the floor along both sides of the intervening pillar which was narrower than a usual support pillar. These heaters simulated the heat flowing into the base of the pillar from a room filled with waste. In addition to this experimental area, one room of the existing mine was incorporated into the experiment. This room contained the floor radioactive array which was identical to the main radioactive array. The array holes in this room were drilled into salt which contained appreciable quantities of interbedded shale and therefore significant moisture. This part of the experiment was undertaken to investigate the possibilities of using old, mined-out areas for disposal rather than mines specifically designed and excavated for the purpose.

The various operations involved (Schaffer et al., 1966) in the handling of the radioactive materials began in a hot cell at Idaho where two reactor fuel assemblies were placed in each canister. Seven of these canisters were then loaded into a shielded shipping cask which was transported to the Kansas mine by truck, along with its self-contained cooling system. At the mine, the cask was removed from the truck and

erected in a vertical position over the 20-in. shaft leading to the experimental area. The canisters were then lowered, one at a time, into the underground transporter at the mine level. This transporter, which is similar to the equipment which might be used in an actual disposal operation, carried the canister to the experimental room and deposited it into an awaiting hole.

In order to increase the radiation dose delivered to the salt and to gain additional experience with the handling equipment and techniques, the canisters were exchanged for fresh ones every 6 months. Each set of canisters was placed first in the main radioactive array for 6 months, then moved to the floor radioactive array for 6 months before being removed from the mine and returned to the National Reactor Test Station. Over the 19-month course of the experiment, three different sets of seven canisters each were handled three separate times. Each of these canisters contained approximately 200,000 curies of activity when first received at the mine. All handling operations were performed by remote control without the aid of hot cells. Hot cells would be required in a disposal facility. The experiment was completed without any accidental exposure of mine personnel or releases of activity to the off-gas system. The experiment successfully achieved the objective of demonstrating the feasibility of salt mine disposal and the operation of the handling equipment.

Temperature distributions in the salt, as measured on the more than 500 thermocouples throughout the experimental area, reconfirmed the validity of the theoretical heat transfer calculations (Bradshaw et al., 1966; Empson et al., 1966). These calculations make it possible to predict with reasonable accuracy the temperature rise to be expected at any point in the salt around any geometrical configuration of heat-generating wastes.

The deformation of the salt in the experimental rooms and pillars and throughout the existing mine was measured on a rock mechanics instrumentation network consisting of over 800 gage points. Although laboratory tests indicated that some alternation of the mechanical properties of salt occurs at radiation doses above 5 x 10^8 rad., (Gunter and Parker, 1961) such changes had no discernible effect in the mine even though the maximum total dose to the salt around the main radioactive array was nearly 10^9 rad. However, the mechanical behavior of salt is strongly temperature dependent. Laboratory studies on model pillars of salt from the Lyons mine have yielded much information on this property which can be summarized in the empirically determined strain rate equation (Lomenick, 1968)

$$e = 0.39 \times 10^{-37} \, T^{9.5} \, s^{3.0} \, t^{-0.7}$$

where

  e = vertical (convergence) strain rate (in./in./hr.),
  T = absolute temperature ($^{\circ}$K),
  s = average pillar stress (psi), and
  t = time (hr).

However, because of scaling problems, this model work does not furnish any information on the transient thermal stresses and the effects of thermal gradients.

Some of the more interesting results from the rock deformation instruments are shown in Figs. 3 and 4. The first figure illustrates the strange effects which can be produced by the transference of thermal stresses over much larger than anticipated distances. When the heating at the arrays in the center of the rooms was begun, thermal expansion of the salt caused an immediate uplift (expansion) of the floor of the room. Part of this movement and the thermal stresses causing it, extended beyond the walls and resulted in an increment of pillar stress, expecially at their edges. This increased vertical stress caused an accelerated horizontal deformation of pillar edges toward the room which, in turn, applied an axial load to the 2-ft.-thick bed of salt making up the roof of the experimental area. This axial load on the roof bed produced a fivefold increase in

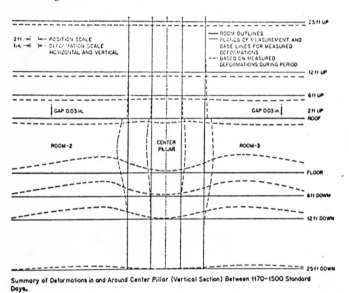

Summary of Deformations in and Around Center Pillar (Vertical Section) Between 1170–1500 Standard Days.

Figure 3. Mechanism of thermal stress transference from floor to ceiling.

Figure 4. Total deformation of center pillar during 1-year heating period.

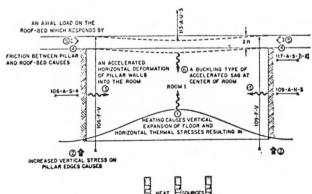

Mechanism of Stress Transference from Floor to Ceiling; Numerical Sequence.

the rate of deformation (sag) of the roof. All of these deformations occurred immediately after the heaters were turned on and could not have a consequence of thermal alteration of the rock properties. Therefore, they represent transmission of the thermal stresses from the center of the floor of the room to the center of the ceiling of the room.

Figure 4 shows the total deformation which occurred during the heating of the center pillar, a period of about 1 year. It is included to illustrate the amount of detail which could be detected with the extensive instrumentation network throughout the experimental area. In most rock mechanics investigations in operating mines, it is both impossible and impractical to collect this amount of data in a small area over a long period of time. It is felt that the information obtained on the creep and plastic flow characteristics of salt will make it possible to arrive at a suitable mine design for a disposal facility.

The results of the demonstration experiment were so encouraging that burial in salt mines is now considered to be one of the better, if not the best, currently available methods for the ultimate disposal of high-level solidified wastes. It should also be noted that this work illustrates a case where the solution of a waste-disposal problem was obtained before the waste became a "problem," indeed, before the waste became available. Perhaps, more importantly, it is a demonstration of the fact that a reasonable and economically feasible solution of any waste-disposal problem, no matter how difficult, can be found if the incentive is high enough.

REFERENCES

Samuel Glasstone, Principles of Nuclear Reactor Engineering, D. Van Nostrand Company, 1955, 861 pp.

Civilian Nuclear Power—1967 Supplement to the 1962 Report to the President, USAEC, 1967.

R. E. Blanco, J. O. Blomeke, and J. T. Roberts, Solving the Waste Disposal Problem, Nucleonics 25(2), 58-61 (February 1967).

Committee on Waste Disposal, Division of Earth Sciences, Disposal of Radioactive Waste on Land, NAS-NRC Publication 519 (1957), 142 pp.

R. L. Bradshaw, J. J. Perona, J. O. Blomeke, and W. J. Boegly, Jr., Evaluation of Ultimate Disposal Methods for Liquid and Solid Radioactive Wastes: VI. Disposal of Solid Waste in Salt Formations, ORNL-3358 (1968), 89 pp.

W. F. Schaffer, Jr., W. J. Boegly, Jr., F. L. Parker, R. L. Bradshaw, F. M. Empson, and W. C. McClain, Project Salt Vault: Design and Demonstration of Equipment, Proceedings of International Symposium on Solidification and Long-Term Storage of Highly Radioactive Wastes, Richland, Washington, February 14-18, 1966, CONF-660208, 685-706 (Nov. 1966).

R. L. Bradshaw, T. F. Lomenick, W. C. McClain, W. J. Boegly, Jr., F. M. Empson, and F. L. Parker Project Salt Vault: Effects of Temperature and Radiation on Plastic Flow and Mine Stability, Proceedings of International Symposium on Solidification and Long-Term Storage of Highly Radioactive Wastes, Richland, Washington, February 14-18, 1966, CONF-660208, 707-722 (Nov. 1966).

F. M. Empson, R. L. Bradshaw, W. J. Boegly, Jr., W. C. McClain, F. L. Parker, and W. F. Schaffer, Jr., Project Salt Vault: Design and Operation, Proceedings of International Symposium on Solidification and Long-Term Storage of Highly Radioactive Wastes, Richland, Washington, February 14-18, 1966, CONF-660208, pp. 671-684 (Nov. 1966).

B. D. Gunter and F. L. Parker, The Physical Properties of Rock Salt as Influenced by Gamma Rays, ORNL-3027 (March 6, 1961).

T. F. Lomenick, Accelerated Deformation of Rock Salt at Elevated Temperature and Pressure and Its Implications for High Level Radioactive Waste Disposal, ORNL-TM-2102 (March 1968).

27. SUBSURFACE GEOLOGY AT THE PROPOSED SITE OF THE NATIONAL RADIOACTIVE WASTE REPOSITORY AT LYONS, KANSAS

EDWIN D. GOEBEL

A burial site for the nation's radioactive waste is proposed for construction in the Hutchinson Salt Member of the Wellington Formation (Lower Permian) at Lyons, Kansas. At the proposed site the Hutchinson Member is about 800 feet deep, 300 feet thick, and is an evaporite sequence containing about 70 percent clayey salt and about 30 percent anhydrite, clay and shale in thin interbeds. The overlying 800 foot section is dominantly shale.

Detailed study of the cores and wire-line logs of Permian and Cretaceous rocks helped to identify key thin units of variable thicknesses but with a high degree of lateral continuity. Moreover, photographs of the cores show a wide diversity of sedimentary microstructures.

The distribution of pre-Pennsylvanian Paleozoic rocks shows the presence of the structurally complex but relatively stable southeastern flank of the Kansas Uplift beneath the Lyons area. Structures of lesser magnitudes and areal extents are shown by an isopachous map of the Stone Corral Formation which lies above the Hutchinson Salt Member.

Reprinted with permission of the author and publisher from Geological Society of America, *Abstracts with Programs,* v. 3, no. 3, p. 237, 1971.

28. PROBLEMS OF HEAT TRANSFER
AT THE LYONS, KANSAS SITE

JOHN HALEPASKA

The effects of placing radioactive wastes in a salt environment, such as the Lyons, Kansas site, have been examined by members of ORNL. Preliminary examination of the temperature distribution expected from heat-generating radioactive canisters has been made. While the type of calculations performed by ORNL personnel are correct, a realistic answer may not have been reached for the following reasons:

1) The stratigraphic section has been oversimplified. As an example, in a hypothetical 100-foot laminated section of salt and shale, all the shale and all the salt are lumped for computational purposes. This type of calculation will give a distribution in time and space markedly different from the real case.

2) The strength of the source terms (heat flow rate per canister) is not presently accurately known. While this is understandable since the canisters have not been manufactured, it should be kept in mind that assuming all canisters to be of equal and constant strength may be unrealistic. The temperature distribution as found by the heat flow calculations can be considered as maximum values only if maximum source values are chosen.

3) The assumption that the thermal properties of the media are independent of temperature has not been substantiated.

4) An analytic solution for the heat-flow distribution is of little value as it assumes a *single* homogeneous and isotropic medium.

5) The numerical solutions to the differential equations were performed in one and two dimensions for both the steady and unsteady cases. While it is readily conceded that one- and two-dimensional calculations are quite good in problems that exhibit symmetry, it is not conceded that this particular problem exhibits any symmetry. The three-dimensional nonsteady or steady state problem has not been solved to date.

The temperature distribution and its overall relation to the structural system considered at Lyons is of vital importance. The net change in volume of the system is dependent upon the temperature distribution. The rate and total amount of subsidence cannot be determined accurately without knowing the volume change.

Reprinted with permission of the author and publisher from Geological Society of America, *Abstracts with Programs,* v. 3, no. 3, p. 237-238, 1971.

29. ENERGY STORAGE IN SALT AND ITS EFFECT ON WASTE DISPOSAL SITES

EDWARD J. ZELLER

One of the least investigated facets of the problems of the storage of radioactive wastes in salt mines is the effect of high energy radiation upon the salt. Some data has been obtained about the alteration of the mechanical properties of highly irradiated salt and it is known that an increase in volume of up to 10 per cent can occur. This condition results in a significant alteration in heat conductivity and mechanical strength. In addition, experimental measurements have shown that irradiated salt can store appreciable quantities of energy. The release of this energy can be triggered by any process which heats the salt above the temperature at which the initial irradiation takes place. Stored energy amounts as high as 80 cal/g have been measured in salt irradiated by high energy particles. Lesser amounts are found in gamma irradiated samples.

Sudden release of energy stored in the salt may result in the development of local hot zones in the mine. These zones will remain at high temperature for a few minutes to a few hours, and it is unlikely that they will contribute significantly to the overall heat budget of the mine. Nevertheless, such thermal excursions might permit considerable movement by the waste canisters and could alter further the heat flow patterns within the mines. As long as the waste containers maintain their integrity, the main volume of salt will be exposed only to gamma radiation. After disintegration, however, the salt will come into direct contact with isotopes which emit high energy alpha particles and protons. Particle radiation is capable of producing radiation damage at a much higher level and will be the dominant process causing energy storage in the latter stages of the mine area history. Fortunately, this is a period of slowly falling temperatures and thus chances for local heat sources serving to trigger excursions are reduced. The total amount of material involved and the amount of heat released would be substantially larger than in the earlier stages of the history of the disposal area.

Reprinted with permission of the author and publisher from Geological Society of America, *Abstracts with Programs*, v. 3, no. 3, p. 248-249, 1971.

30. NUCLEAR WASTE: KANSANS RILED BY AEC PLANS FOR ATOM DUMP

CONSTANCE HOLDEN

Plans by the Atomic Energy Commission (AEC) to set up its first graveyard for radioactive wastes in the middle of Kansas have met with objections from Kansans who believe the safety of the project is doubtful and who resent being selected without being thoroughly informed and consulted on the matter.

The dump, which the AEC plans to make out of an abandoned salt mine in Lyons, is billed as a "demonstration project." It would be a permanent repository for solid, high-level radioactive matter imported from commercial nuclear power plants, and for alpha wastes, which are low-level, from the AEC's Rocky Flats, Colorado, plutonium refining plant.

The plan has raised a good deal of controversy in the state, fueled by reports from the Kansas State Geological Survey, which doesn't want the AEC to purchase the 1000-acre site and the 1700 acres of underground rights until further studies prove that all risks have been eliminated.

The AEC's Oak Ridge National Laboratory has been performing the studies. It insists that all conceivable problems are under control and that what is needed now is "confirmatory data," best supplied as work progresses on the site. The AEC has asked the Joint Committee on Atomic Energy, which last month held 2 days of hearings on the subject, to authorize a $3.5-million appropriation for purchase of the site, architect and engineering services, and further detailed investigation of the salt beds. The total cost is estimated at $25 million.

SURVEYS FAVOR LYONS SITE

The AEC has had its eye on the Lyons bed since 1955, when it was surveyed as a possible repository by the National Research Council of the National Academy of Sciences (NAS). Salt has been found to be the best material available for this purpose because of its seismic stability,

Reprinted with permission of the publisher from *Science*, v. 172, p. 249-250, April 16, 1971. Copyright 1971 American Association for the Advancement of Science.

compressive strength, ability to conduct heat, high melting point (1450° F), self-sealing ability, and nuclear shielding property, which is similar to that of concrete. The Lyons salt field, 1000 feet down and 300 feet thick, has emerged from studies carried on through the years as an ideal final resting-place for nuclear-age garbage, which must "cook" for a half a million years before the radioactivity of the longest-lived plutonium isotopes has been spent.

The AEC has more than 80 million gallons of high-level wastes stored underground in concrete-encased, million-gallon, stainless steel vats at its defense installations in Richland, Washington; near Idaho Falls, Idaho; and at the Savannah River plant in South Carolina. The AEC is experimenting with ways to solidify this waste and bury it in various geological formations, but it will be many years before its final disposition is decided on.

It is the proliferation of civilian commercial plants, of which there will be 29 by the end of this year, that is creating the urgent need for the big new dump. Lethal wastes just from these sources will amount to an average of 58,000 cubic feet per year by 2000 A.D. At present, there exists no technology for neutralizing the wastes or hastening the radioactive decay process.

Thus, the AEC is eager, after 16 years of planning and studying, to get the show on the road. Some Kansans, however, are saying, "Not so fast."

For months, Representative Joe Skubitz (R–Kans.) has been speaking out for his state's rights in letters to the Commission. He and William H. Hambleton, director of the state geological survey, have asked that the $3.5 million be used for more research and development rather than for purchase of the land.

At the hearing, they cited the survey's report, released last December, which insisted that serious questions remained unanswered. They have to do with possible migration of waste containers through the salt, the possibility that thermal expansion of the salt might cause overlying layers of rock to crack and allow ground-water to seep in, and possible surprises brought about by unforeseen radioactive interactions. The report also criticizes the AEC's transportation plans as "completely inadequate," and says that no retrieval plan for the wastes "exists at all."

Skubitz further pleaded for the AEC to stop "playing God" and to pay more attention to the wishes of the state's residents. "Kansas has some rights," he said plaintively. "We are not country bumpkins who can be taken for granted."

AEC WANTS TO GET MOVING

The position of the AEC, represented at the hearing by Milton Shaw, director of reactor development, and Floyd Culler, associate director of Oak Ridge National Laboratory, was that all necessary data have been accumulated, and the only way to confirm the safety of the installation is through actual work on the site. Three-dimensional studies—which Hambleton repeatedly called for in his testimony—could be carried on concurrently with the development of the site, said the Oak Ridge men.

Shaw said the AEC's Salt Vault project, conducted in Lyons over a 19-month period ending in 1967, had proved beyond any doubt that the Lyons salt could contain the wastes effectively. In this project, radioactive fuel elements were inserted in core samples of salt to monitor radioactivity and heat distribution and to test waste handling techniques. The NAS Radioactive Waste Committee reaffirmed the suitability of the salt mine in a 1970 report, he added. Shaw and Culler fired off highly polished rounds of statistics to prove that the Kansas people have nothing to worry about hydrologically, geologically, thermally, or radioactively. As for transportation, they invoked the Commission's 20-year history of hauling wastes around with no serious accidents.

On the subject of retrieval, they said they could conceive of no circumstance that might necessitate removing the wastes, but if one arose, there would be plenty of time to design and build the remote-control mining machinery needed for such an operation.

According to the plan, canisters of the hot, solidified, high-level wastes, which range from the size of firewood logs to 18 feet long and 2 feet in diameter, will be brought to the mine in railroad cars and lowered down shafts into large rooms that have been carved in the salt. There,

drivers operating heavily shielded, motorized vehicles will use remote-control hoists to insert the canisters into holes drilled about 22 feet apart in the floor of the mine. When each vault has its complement of containers, it will be filled in with salt. The pressure of the salt and the heat of the cylinders—ranging from 600° to $900^{\circ}F$—will cause the natural plastic action of the salt, which has the consistency of very hard wax, to move in and seal around the containers. Within a period of 6 months to 10 years, the steel-covered ceramic canisters will disintegrate, leaving the salt to hold the wastes in place.

Shaw emphasized the flexibility that has been built into the plans: If heat or radioactivity projections prove inaccurate, the energy can be diluted by reducing the amount of material in each container or by placing the canisters farther apart.

Skubitz and his friends in Kansas are still not buying. Several members of the Kansas state legislature, backed by Governor Robert Docking, have introduced bills asking for postponement of AEC's land purchase plans until further studies have been made. The AEC is well aware that it will have to make greater efforts in public relations if it wants its plans realized on schedule. As Senator Joseph Pastore (D–R.I.) warned at the hearing, "you are not going to stuff this down the Kansas governor's throat."

Oak Ridge, in response to Hambleton's complaint that it was not furnishing information promptly to the state geological survey, has offered to let a state representative sit in at Oak Ridge as planning continues. Further efforts at communication will probably be needed to overcome the appearance of an attitude that Skubitz characterizes as "leave it to us ... we're great scientists." Ironically, the 5000 citizens of Lyons—who have been reassured at public meetings with AEC officials, and who may gain 200 permanent jobs manning the dump—appear not to be perturbed at all by the prospect of being the country's nuclear waste capital.

The Lyons Nuclear Park, as it is called, is designed to hold all the non-defense atomic refuse this country will have accumulated by the end of the century—a total of 770,000 cubic feet, or 38,000 tons. So it will not be long before the AEC will be scouting around for a new repository; probably somewhere in the extensive salt beds underlying New York, Michigan, and states along the Gulf coast. But even if the AEC can prove the safety of its plans beyond the doubts of the most skeptical Kansan, it seems likely that there will always be psychological objections to the idea of a half a million years' worth of man-made hell simmering under the earth's surface.

Disposal Wells

31. DISPOSAL OF LIQUID WASTES
BY INJECTION UNDERGROUND

ARTHUR M. PIPER

Injecting liquid wastes deep underground is an attractive but not necessarily practical means for disposing of them. For decades, impressive volumes of unwanted oil-field brine have been injected, currently about 10,000 acre-feet yearly. Recently, liquid industrial wastes are being injected in ever-increasing quantity. Dimensions of industrial injection wells range widely but the approximate medians are: depth, 2,660 feet; thickness of injection zone, 185 feet; injection rate, 135 gallons per minute; wellhead injection pressure, 185 pounds per square inch.

Effects of deep injection are complex and not all are understood clearly. In a responsible society, injection cannot be allowed to put wastes out of mind. Injection is no more than storage—for all time in the case of the most intractable wastes—in underground space of which little is attainable in some areas and which is exhaustible in most areas.

STATUS OF KNOWLEDGE AND
STEPS TO BE TAKEN

Admittedly, injecting liquid wastes deep beneath the land surface is a potential means for alleviating pollution of rivers and lakes. But, by no stretch of the imagination is injection a panacea that can encompass all wastes and resolve all pollution, even if economic limitations should be waived. Limitations on the potentials for practical injection are stringent indeed—physical, chemical, geologic, hydrologic, economic, and institutional (including legal) limitations. A general appraisal of certain principal limitations, and of our state of knowledge concerning them, follows.

Categories of Waste

The very wide range in volume and in concentration and kind of noxious constituents in liquid wastes all but precludes meaningful generalization as to practicality of disposal by

Extracted with the author's permission from "Disposal of Liquid Wastes by Injection Underground—Neither Myth nor Millennium" by Arthur M. Piper, *U. S. Geological Survey Circular 631*, 15 p., 1969.

deep injection. Uniform and specific criteria are urgently desirable for categorizing wastes in this regard, principally according to type, quantity, and persistence of critical constituents. Such criteria have been proposed recently in one small part of the field of concern, wastes from the nuclear-energy industry (American Institute Chemical Engineers, 1967). Specifically, five categories or classes of radioactive waste would be defined with respect to "maximum permissible" concentration, exposure, and intake as established previously by the International Commission on Radiological Protection. The five classes, and their parallels for industry in general, can be summarized as follows:

At one extreme, class A wastes would be those whose radionuclide concentration is so low as to justify dispersal without restriction. The parallel from general industry would be those liquid products to which an unnatural property has been imparted, but not to a degree that conceivably would be harmful to human beings, in the food chain, or indiscriminately in the biosphere. An appropriate general standard would be analogous to, and ordinarily close to the maximum allowable concentrations that numerous public-health agencies have set for various chemical constituents in drinking water. Such limits of concentration are known in the main; they need only to be collated and promulgated through suitable channels. It is highly desirable that the general standard be equally comprehensive the nation over. For certain limits, however, some variation from one region to another would seem appropriate, according to the variable concentration of the particular constituents in local native waters. Vexatious questions would arise in regard to appropriate limits for the almost overwhelming array of new products from the chemical and pharmaceutical industries—for one common example, the very stable insecticide DDT which, along with other chlorinated hydrocarbons, is causing so much concern nowadays.

Class B radioactive wastes would be those whose radionuclide concentration is greater than that of class A wastes, by a factor not greater than 10. The class would have force only in "controlled areas," where personnel would be exposed only during working hours and where suitable safety precautions could be enforced. In the general industrial parallel, an appropriate concentration factor between classes A and B probably would be neither 10, nor uniform among all waste constituents, nor uniform either regionwide or nationwide. Rather, the factor might relate to the acceptability of zoning under which dispersal of the waste would be so controlled as to time or place, or the waste would be so diluted, that the cumulative exposure of human beings to the waste was substantially as though the class A standard was satisfied. In this connection, dilution probably would be acceptable only transiently, until precluded by the ever-greater demand for water of highest purity.

In regard to general industry, liquid products of classes A and B would of course not require disposal underground. However specific definition of the two classes is desirable to discriminate wastes that, even in the distant future, need not preempt the limited space in which injection would be feasible.

Nuclear-waste class C would be more concentrated than class B by a factor not greater than 10^4. In general it would be amenable to a treatment converting a major fraction to class B or class A, and a minor fraction to class D or class E. In the general parallel the concentration factor between the analogs of waste classes B and C commonly would be much less than 10^4 and might relate more to chemical stability of the principal waste constituent than to its concentration. The general class C might comprise those wastes that are produced in volumes exceeding the underground space available for long-term storage but which might either (1) be reduced to a smaller volume or converted to a less concentrated class, or (2) be suitable for injection into the relatively shallow zone of rapid circulation or the underlying zone of delayed circulation [zones to be described], in which residence time would suffice for disintegration of the noxious constituents. A common example of the first type would be spent pickling acid, which might be neutralized and filtered, and possibly otherwise treated, to yield an effluent of class B or class A. An example of the second type would be septic-tank effluent, that common product of rural and some suburban communities, or certain

unstable products and wastes of organic chemistry.

Nuclear class D wastes would be more concentrated than class C, again by a factor not exceeding 10^4. Alternatively, these would be either stored indefinitely in suitable containers on the land surface, incorporated into a bituminous matrix or into concrete, or reduced to a solid residue. The solid forms of converted waste would be held on the land surface. The general analog of class D might be those wastes which are produced in, or can be reduced to, relatively small volumes; which are relatively stable; and which are of such kind or concentration that on the land surface they would constitute a persistent but ordinarily a nonlethal, nuisance. Examples among organic substances would be certain oils and solvents; among inorganic substances, numerous highly soluble salts. Such are the wastes generally suitable for deep injection into the zone of lethargic circulation [to be described] where a residence time of many decades or even centuries, could be assured and would suffice. Alternatively, analog class D wastes might be incorporated into concrete or otherwise converted to solid form, and retained on the land surface.

Nuclear class E waste is that whose concentration exceeds that of class D—that is, the class C concentration is exceeded by a factor greater than 10^4. It would be stored indefinitely in suitable containers on the land surface unless it can be converted to, or incorporated in, a radiation-stable solid. We must acknowledge, and face up to, the analog of class E in industry—that is, waste of such persistent intractability and concentration that (in the words of de Laguna, 1964) its "future disposition must be known unequivocally and in detail," and it must be excluded from the biosphere for virtually all time. Since absolute immobility cannot be assured underground, the analog class E waste would be unthinkable for injection. Included in the category would be stable substances so highly toxic as to be potentially lethal if dispersed in the biosphere, even at slight concentrations. Certain pesticides and chemical-biological warfare agents are potentially of this general sort.

The writer feels strongly that orderly management of liquid wastes by injection deep into the ground will prove elusive until general waste categories such as those just outlined have been defined, in terms of specific concentrations for each of numerous kinds or groups of waste constituents. Magnitude of the limiting concentrations seems less urgent than specific limits drawn so conservatively that the several categories might receive early and virtually universal acceptance. Adequate standards for the categories would be more comprehensive, but inherently no more complex, than those of the nuclear industry. As has been alluded to, drafting such standards would be largely a task of discriminately collating existing knowledge. Principal disciplines involved include chemistry, medicine, and public health.

Chemical and Physical Aspects

Background. Injection underground would of course put wastes out of sight but, in a responsible society, cannot be allowed to put them out of mind. Injection does not constitute permanent disposal. Rather it detains in storage and commits to such storage—for all time in the case of the most intractable wastes—underground space of which little is attainable in some areas, and which definitely is exhaustible in most areas. These precepts have been stated or implied repeatedly in diverse contexts, by numerous writers.

Wastes underground cannot be managed responsibly in the absence of comprehensive knowledge as to their character and expected history. The responsiblity is in part, but only in part, separable into two phases: First, an agency creating wastes must know or determine, and fully disclose to a suitable public institution, the character and amount of wastes committed to underground storage. Second, and conversely, public institutions must know or determine, and maintain a suitable record of, where wastes are dispersed underground (in three dimensions, specifically), what their chemical characters are, and how those characters may change with time. Further, an agency creating and injecting a waste must constrain that waste within the land-surface boundaries of its real property, unless or until custody of the waste passes to a responsible agency, private or public, having wider jurisdiction. The restraints here outlined or implied are strict and in some respects novel. To relax them substantially, however, would disclaim reality.

Raw wastes. Physical and chemical character must be known for each raw waste that is a candidate for injection. Information should be specific as to: (1) Rate of production and anticipated aggregate volume; (2) temperature and thermal stability; (3) viscosity, pH, and density; and (4) concentration and stability of the several entrained, suspended, or dissolved constituents. If dissolved, suspended, or entrained constituents are nuclides, radiometric properties should be known in terms such as specific radioactivity; percentage distribution of the nuclides according to the kinds and energies of their radiations, or according to their half lives; and radioactivity due to key nuclides. (See Nace and others, 1962.) Any of or all these properties may determine whether a particular waste is suitable for injection. Thermal and chemical stability may be especially critical—for example, wastes from the nuclear industry commonly generate heat as they disintegrate or "decay," at rates greater than would dissipate through the rock matrix of an injection zone (Birch, 1958; Skibitzke, 1961). Chemical stability must be considered over not only the short term, but also the long term—possibly indefinitely long—of potential storage underground (injection). In this regard, the very feasibility of injection may hinge on the life of a noxious constituent in relation to predictable residence time of the waste in the particular injection zone. (More will be said concerning this.) Physical stability must be considered likewise—for example, the rate at which a suspension may convert to a gel.

Information such as just outlined is a product of the chemist, physicist, and laboratory technician. Commonly that information is known to the waste-creating agency, but may be considered by the agency to be of concern to it alone. If wastes are to be managed effectively, however, the writer considers such information to be everybody's concern, expressible through a public agency having appropriate responsibility and authority. The authority should include the prerogatives of requiring from the producing agency, and verifying, analytical data on all raw wastes.

Compatibility and interaction. Even though comprehensive, information as to chemical and physical character of a waste does not, of itself, determine suitability for injection. Additional information is required as to compatibility among (1) a particular waste as it might be injected, (2) other wastes with which it might make contact in the injection zone, (3) fluids native to the injection zone, and (4) both mineral and organic (perhaps including bacterial) constituents of the injection-zone matrix. The possibilities of interaction are many and complex. The environment in which interactions might occur is unlike that of the land surface, particularly in respect to temperature and pressure. The pH of waste and native fluid may differ little or much. All these environmental differences influence the kind and rate of potential interactions. Residence time of the waste in the injection zone may be indefinitely long, so that interactions that are slow in rate may be major factors in waste behavior.

The reactions of potential concern are diverse in kind—chemical reaction that results in a precipitate, diminishing pore space of the injection zone; separation of a gel with like effects; flocculation or deflocculation (dispersion) of clay minerals, with an influence on permeability; dissolution of mineral matter from the injection-zone matrix, with or without further reaction; base-exchange and sorption reactions between waste constituents and minerals of the zone matrix; buffer action inhibiting or modifying reaction between other constituents.

Exchange and sorption reactions may involve, not the dominant minerals of the injection-zone matrix, but only minerals which occur in minor quantity—for example, a clay-mineral fraction in a sandstone that is dominantly of quartz. Even so, these reactions may be of far-reaching effect, and even the principal factor in managing a waste.

Compatibility and potential interaction between waste and injection zone have for some years been studied intensively, but largely in general terms, by numerous persons. Much of this effort has been in regard to potential deep injection of radioactive wastes. Warner (1966) summarizes current knowledge, and undertakes experimental and theoretical analysis.

There is an urgency to proceed soon from general to specific consideration of interactions between potential wastes and injection zones, collating dispersed experience and information now available with future experience that would be assessed systematically. First stages of this effort well might be in conjunction with the canvass of major injection provinces, which will be outlined. The primary disciplines involved would be those of geochemistry and geohydrology.

Pretreatment of wastes. Certain wastes, otherwise incompatible with a potential injection zone, can feasibly be pretreated. Possibly the most common step would be to adjust pH of the waste to the ends of chemical stability and minimum reaction in the injection zone. Conceivably a dilute waste might be concentrated to diminish its volume, where the available injection zone has only small capacity and where compatibility problems would not be worsened by the concentration.

Beyond these highly general considerations, pretreatment seems largely a matter of matching a specific waste to a specific injection zone. Such becomes a task of chemistry and geochemistry, in detail much too diversified for specific treatment here.

CANVASS OF INJECTION PROVINCES

To the end that injection as a means of waste management shall be planned effectively and administered in orderly fashion, there is here proposed a comprehensive canvass of all the United States to discriminate injection provinces according to their diverse potential capacities to accept wastes. Through identification and definition of such provinces, meaningful administration and regulation of injection would be facilitated, according to limitations peculiar to each province. Oversimplified, the alternative would seem to be spot-by-spot consideration under a dilemma of standards either impractically complex if all diversities of "injectability" were served, or generalized to the point of becoming ineffective.

First steps toward defining such injection provinces have been made, under sponsorship of the Atomic Energy Commission—specifically, in summary descriptions of salt deposits and major sedimentary basins over the United States (Griggs, 1958; Pierce and Rich, 1958; Repenning, 1959 and 1960; de Witt, 1960; Love and Hoover, 1960; Colton, 1961; Beikman, 1962; LeGrand, 1962; Sandberg, 1962; and MacLachlan, 1964). Most of these summaries considered only geologic aspects—stratigraphy and structure. In some respects more comprehensive, but in other respects more selective, than the summaries just listed is a review by the American Association of Petroleum Geologists (1964; also Galley, 1968).

A more comprehensive basis for discriminating injection provinces is necessary and, in preliminary scope, can be formulated from information at hand. More definitive classification by subprovinces could follow as data and experience accumulate. Both the preliminary and the ultimate canvass of provinces would involve numerous disciplines, chiefly those of geology (in an all-inclusive sense, including, in particular, geophysics and seismology), geochemistry, and hydrology (including hydrodynamics in particular). The preliminary canvass would assess the following aspects.

Zones of Circulation

The manner of waste management underground may range widely indeed. A chemically stable, dilute waste may require only to be injected into, and dispersed thoroughly in, a body of rapidly circulating ground water that is recharged continually or copiously. Alternatively, a biochemically unstable effluent may require only a residence time, within the injection zone, of sufficient duration that disintegration proceeds to completion; dispersion into the native ground water may or may not be desirable and residence time of a few days or weeks may suffice. At another extreme, a persistently intractable or a very concentrated waste may require the longest possible residence time, with or without dispersion into the native water. Thus, freedom of native-water circulation is a primary criterion by which to scale "injectability." In this connection, Nace and others (1962) recognize a functional succession of ground-water zones, generally downward, in which circulation is respectively rapid, delayed, lethargic, and stagnant. The latter two are subzones of the so-called noncyclic zone, which includes a dry subzone also. Over much of the United States, information at hand should suffice for a general description of such zones and their potentials for injection of wastes—specifically, their depth and thickness, lithology, extent and continuity, and transmissibility (and other properties to be considered). The several zones are as follows (adapted from Nace and others, 1962).

Zone of rapid circulation. The zone of rapid circulation extends from land surface downward some tens, or a few hundreds, of feet; the aerated zone and the uppermost part of the saturated zone are included. Here, generally or commonly, the native soil water and ground water are unconfined, fresh, and largely or exclusively of meteoric origin; residence time is from a few hours to a few years; and the environment is oxidizing. Natural discharge from the zone of rapid circulation is the principal source of water sustaining the dry-season flow of streams; thus, injection of chemically stable wastes into it is precluded commonly although not universally. as will be outlined.

Injection of waste into the zone of rapid circulation could be feasible in a quantity so small, and at a site so placed, that the waste would be adequately diluted by dispersion, or stabilized by disintegration, before it could reach a point of discharge to a stream or of withdrawal for use. Feasibility of such injection, therefore, would depend on hydrodynamics of the area involved; hydrodynamic factors would need be established explicitly and monitored adequately.

Most common among wastes injected into the zone of rapid circulation probably is septic-tank effluent, to which reference has been made. Reference has been made also to successful management of certain wastes in this way on the Hanford reservation of the Atomic Energy Commission. Here dispersal of the waste within the zone has been monitored rather intensively, the path of waste travel within the reservation is some 20 miles, and adequate residence time appears to have been assured. Elsewhere, however, indiscriminate injection into the zone has led to the contamination of usable ground waters in numerous scattered areas, as described by Deutsch (1961, 1963, 1965) for Michigan.

Zone of delayed circulation. In the zone of delayed circulation, native ground water is also largely or exclusively of meteoric origin, is generally fresh, and may be unconfined and oxidizing at the shallower depths but commonly is confined and nonoxidizing at the greater depths. The water circulates continually and comparatively freely, but is retarded sufficiently that natural residence time within a given zone is a few to many decades, or even a few centuries. Depth to or through the zone may range from no more than a few hundred feet, in some geologic and geographic situations, to thousands of feet at other places.

The zone of delayed circulation being the principal source of water supplies drawn from the ground, injection of wastes into it is generally not advisable, as in the case of the overlying zone of rapid circulation. However, locally and under suitable monitoring, wastes have been injected successfully, as at the National Reactor Testing Station, Idaho (Jones, 1961a,b; Morris and others, 1965).

Subzone of lethargic flow. The subzone of lethargic flow is the common locus of so-called salaquifers—that is, in that subzone the native liquid is commonly saline. Much of, or even all, the water is of ultimate meteorologic origin, but its residence time in the subzone—in isolation from the normal hydrologic cycle—has been in the order of hundreds or even thousands of years. The very slow movement is considered generally to be hydrodynamic, but possibly in part is by geochemical osmosis. The environment commonly lacks free oxygen. Saline water and lethargic flow may occur within the upper few hundred feet of the earth's crust and are common at depths of a few thousand feet, but are generally at depths greater than 5,000 feet.

The subzone of lethargic flow is the chief potential locus for storing (disposing of) the more concentrated and moderately intractable wastes by injection (excepting wastes so intractable and noxious that absolute containment is required for virtually all time). Thus, delimiting and describing these subzones is largely tantamount to defining injection provinces. Description is needed, in terms as specific as is possible, for all principal factors that influence injectability. Fairly comprehensive and extensive data are at hand from oil fields, of which most are in the subzone here of concern. Aside from such fields, and a few commercial brine fields, the descriptive data at hand may not be definitive, but preliminary guides for injection may be inferable.

Stagnant subzones. In stagnant subzones the rocks are porous but the interstitial liquid (generally brine) appears to be hydrodynamically trapped and so essentially without Darcy-law flow. A very small movement may take place by geochemical osmosis or some other process that is not understood clearly. Pressure of the interstitial liquid ranges greatly: it may be considerably less than in overlying zones, but on the other hand may equal or even exceed the geostatic pressure for the depth of occurrence. With few exceptions, if any, stagnant subzones are at least several thousand feet below land surface.

Because by definition its native liquid is virtually motionless over a very long interval of time, a stagnant subzone would seem to afford the ideal locus of injection for intractable waste. However, the existence of such subzones is inferred commonly from sparse or weak evidence; proof of existence would be difficult and certainly costly. Injection, necessarily under pressure, would immediately change the stagnant state to one of local hydrodynamic movement;

the reach of such an effect could be difficult to predict with certainty from the data attainable by ordinary effort. Thus, the capability of a stagnant subzone to accept and retain an injected liquid should be assessed with extreme caution.

Dry subzones. Within depths that would be fully practicable for injection, dry subzones are in a sense anomalous. A common type would be a salt bed or plug (dome), in which free water is virtually nonexistent and which may be impermeable in a finite sense. Depth to such subzones ranges from a few tens to thousands of feet. Thickness and horizontal extent are likely to be conjectural except, for example, for salt domes that have been delimited in connection with extraction of petroleum or sulfur.

A waste injected into a dry subzone of the sort just described, by hydrofracturing or otherwise, would in principle be wholly isolated from the natural hydrodynamic circulation. However, injection would create a hydrodynamic potential, conceivably sufficient to induce movement of the injected fluid if the hydrofractures should extend to a boundary of the subzone. Thus, performance of a dry subzone under injection should be assessed cautiously; absolute containment of injected liquid cannot be assumed.

Dry (unsaturated) subzones do occur in permeable strata, but not commonly. Waste injected into such a subzone would move down dip until it reaches a saturated zone, then would come under local hydrodynamic forces. In detail, its behavior could be most difficult to foresee.

Hydrodynamics; Potentiometric Levels and Gradients

In general, virtually all movement of ground water and behavior of an injected liquid are hydrodynamic processes. Unfortunately, in a large fraction of the relevant current literature, effects of injection have been assessed only in terms of hydrostatics and of injection wells under hydraulic equilibrium. As a result, the assessment has not always been adequate.

It is contemplated that the canvass of injection provinces would seek to generalize, for each zone or subzone of circulation, the patterns of regional hydrodynamic circulation so far as these can be inferred. Two examples of regional circulation in the subzone of lethargic flow are described by McNeal (1965) and Hoeger (1968), respectively for the Permian basin and for the eastern half of the Denver basin. Data to delineate other analogous areas is expected to rest largely in the petroleum industry. Outside the oil fields, current information may not be definitive.

Potentiometric (fluid) levels and gradients should suggest relative rates of fluid movement. These must be assessed not only for the natural condition, but especially for the conditions of injection, when levels and gradients may change transiently or progressively, perhaps greatly, and commonly will fluctuate considerably. Under such conditions, only nonequilibrium concepts and formulas seem appropriate for analyzing and anticipating the fluid movements (Ferris and others, 1962). Prototypes for the conditions of waste injection doubtless rest in the experience with brine injection, in the petroleum industry.

A zone whose potentiometric level is substantially below those of overlying zones or in which the potentiometric gradients are locally centripetal, seems, on casual consideration, especially favorable for injection. Such zones or areas should, however, be assessed cautiously for reasons that include these: First, fluid levels for deep zones are not easy to measure accurately, so that any isolated unverified level may be considerably in error. Second, centripetal gradients imply an anomalous hydrodynamic circulation that may have been misinterpreted. Third, the greater the depth of the potential level, the greater the degree to which injection pressure would diminish the friction across fracture planes in the injection-zone matrix (see Healy and others, 1968, p. 1306)—that is, other factors being the same, the greater the potential for injection-triggered earthquakes.

Hydrofractures; Safe Injection Pressure

Experience of the petroleum industry with brine-injection wells indicates that as injection pressure increases, the rate of brine acceptance increases proportionally until, at a so-called critical pressure, the rate of brine acceptance quickens notably. At injection pressures greater than critical, the rock "hydrofractures" so that its permeability increases. At least approximately, however, if injection pressure then is diminished to less than critical, brine acceptance diminishes to its antecedent rate. Accordingly, it is reasoned that hydrofractures do not permanently modify the permeability of the rock matrix. (In this connection see American Petroleum Institute, 1958; Cleary, 1958; Dickey and Andresen, 1945; Grandone and Holleyman, 1949; Hubbert and Willis, 1957; and Yuster and Calhoun, 1945.)

Generally it has been assumed, expressly or tacitly, that the critical pressure determines the safe maximum injection pressure at a particular well. On this basis, safe pressure falls commonly between 0.6 and 1.0 psi per foot of depth (the higher of these limits is the common value of the so-called geostatic or lithostatic pressure—that is, the pressure exerted by overlying rock at 2.3 average density). Existing waste-injection wells operate at pressures as much as 2.1 geostatic— that is, at about twice the pressure necessary to "float" the rocks overlying the injection zone. Yet the brief reports available do not note excessive hydrofracturing at the maximum pressure cited.

Again, there is involved here a seeming paradox—specifically, a safe pressure less than critical pressure would, in general, foreclose hydrofractures and the greater injectivity they cause. Yet hydrofractures would, at some places and times, be both permissible and desirable. At Oak Ridge National Laboratory, for example, certain radioactive waste liquids are made into a slurry with cement, the slurry is injected into shale by hydrofracturing, and the radioactive constituents become sensibly immobile once the slurry hardens (de Laguna, 1962). Definitive criteria are lacking, by which to constrain hydrofractures appropriately.

In another context, a "safe" injection pressure would be less than that which could "trigger" an earthquake. The quakes originating near the Rocky Mountain Arsenal well were contemporaneous with injection pressures ordinarily not greater than about 0.53 psi per foot of depth—that is, somewhat less than that at which hydrofracturing is considered generally to start, and about half the ordinary upper limit of critical pressure which has been cited. Here, injection pressure is but one of numerous relevant factors. Involved are the stress in the injection zone due to overburden, that due to active tectonic forces, and that which is residual (D. J. Varnes, written commun., 1969); hydrodynamic and thermodynamic fluxes; geochemical processes; and mechanical properties of the injection-zone matrix. Injection of an extraneous liquid (waste) distorts the balance among the natural forces. Oversimplified, if the natural balance is delicate, a small distortion can trigger an earthquake; in detail, current theory and techniques of observation are little more than rudimentary (R. W. Stallman, written commun., 1969).

It seems necessary, therefore, to develop a

fully comprehensive and wholly general concept of "injectivity" at a "safe" injection pressure, to serve as the ultimate basis for classifying potential injection provinces and their subzones. To that end it is proposed that the brine-injection experience of the petroleum industry, related theory, and the separate theory of injection-induced earthquakes all be reviewed critically and reexpressed as necessary in criteria generally applicable to waste injection. (See Healy and others, 1968; Kehle, 1964; and Scheidegger, 1960.) Here, there is particular need to discriminate clearly between wellhead pressure, the incremental pressure equivalent to weight of fluid between wellhead and natural water level, and total pressure on the zone. Further, it is emphasized that in some areas, brine injection has dealt with a fluid system in which one component (gas) is readily compressible, whereas generally all the fluids of a waste-injection system would be liquid—that is, none of the fluid components would be highly compressible. The comprehensive and general concept here outlined probably will not be realized easily.

Geochemical Aspects

Allusion has been made to chemical compatibility among injected waste, materials of the injection-zone matrix, and native interstitial water of the zone. Possible combinations of the variables involved are numerous indeed, as are the relevant analytical data at hand—chemical analyses of brine, other native waters, rocks, and earth materials; temperature and pressure gradients; fluid densities; sparse but suggestive values of exchange capacities. In all the complexities and wealth of data it should be possible to isolate some criteria for classifying injection subzones according to broad types of chemical problems that could be anticipated with various categories of waste. A search for general criteria of this kind is suggested. The primary discipline involved would of course be geochemistry, with close support required by geohydrology.

Incidental allusion has been made to geochemical osmosis as a possible driving force acting between two aquifers that contain waters of unlike chemical concentrations at unlike pressures, and that are separated by a confining bed acting as a semipermeable membrane. That such a force acts at depth in the subzones of lethargic circulation and of stagnation has been suggested by several investigators, presumably from the spatial analogy of certain aquifer and confining-bed systems to the laboratory environ-ment of unlike concentrations of fluid on either side of a semipermeable membrane. If strictly valid, the analogy to fluid transfer by osmosis, in the laboratory, anticipates the long-term history of certain deeply injected wastes. To the writer the analogy has not been, but if possible should be, demonstrated from rigorously screened field data, by theoretical analysis.

LEGISLATIVE AND INSTITUTIONAL CONSIDERATIONS

Three of the 50 States—Missouri, Ohio, and Texas—have enacted statutes specifically to regulate disposal of waste liquids by injection into the ground. Provisions of the statutes in the latter two states, are generally alike; very greatly simplified, they may be summarized as follows: (1) A permit is required of any person who drills, modifies, or uses a well "for the injection of sewage or any liquid used in or resulting from any process of industry, manufacture, trade, business, or agriculture" [Ohio's language, disposition of oil-field brines is regulated by another statute in both Ohio and Texas], (2) application for such a permit is made to a named administrative agency, the application locating and describing the proposed injection facility and stating composition of the liquid intended to be injected, (3) an application may be denied only on a determination of "unreasonable risk [of] waste or contamination of oil or gas in the earth, . . . unreasonable risk of loss or damage to valuable mineral resources, . . . [or] pollution [of water]" [Ohio's language]; otherwise, a permit must be issued, (4) the permit may include conditions necessary to protect health, safety, conservation of resources, or purity of water supplies, (5) a permit may be suspended or revoked for infraction of the statute, of regulations promulgated under the statute, or of conditions attached to the permit, and (6) a permit may be suspended and, after a hearing, revoked if warranted by information disclosed after that permit was first issued [Ohio only].

The two statutes just summarized are concise, reasonably explicit as to intent, quite explicit as to placement of relevant responsibility and authority, and free from technical restrictions that would be tantamount to prejudgments of field conditions. In a "legalistic" sense they are perhaps ideally workable. To the writer, however, the two statutes share three substantial inadequacies: First, they require of the administering agency a binding judgment as to effectiveness of the proposal for injection whereas, in the present state of injection art, available information commonly does not suffice for a fully reasoned judgment. All uncertainty must be covered into conditions attached to the permit. This could lead to dilemma: futility for the administrator versus frustration for the injector. Second, the statutes admit only two parties to an injection—the individual who injects and the state agency that administers. Reasons will be advanced that this grossly oversimplifies and restricts the interests concerned. Third, the statutes neither establish, nor provide for promulgation of, "off-limit" zones or areas—the entire "subsurface" of each state is declared open for injection except where specific inimical effects are anticipated. Limitless injectability at any point seems to be implied. The art of injection being ill understood, and the effects of injection being irrevocable, a policy so open-handed verges on rashness.

The brief Missouri statute provides that (1) "any individual wishing to use underground wells or depositories for the injection of liquid waste" must apply for a permit, (2) a permit is granted provided the "health or property of others" will not be harmed, and (3) a "reasonable" bond may be required of the permittee to assure that the injection facility, if and when its use ends, is plugged or sealed.

Other states impose various degrees of constraint on injection of liquids underground, under as many as three regulatory agencies in a particular state (Warner, 1965, p. 23, 36-37). The diversity of these constraints is suggested by the following generalizations. Nearly all the states regulate the cementing of casings in wells drilled for petroleum or natural gas; only by implication and, so far as the writer is informed, in no instance by specific wording of statute would such regulation apply to injection wells. A few states prohibit all injection; several prohibit injection of liquids other than salt water or oil-field brine. Others require that oil-field brine be returned underground; among these, some require that the return be to the very stratigraphic zone from which the brine was extracted. California specifically prohibits disposal of waste into strata that are used, or are usable, as a source of domestic water supply. In respect to these diverse constraints, there are similarly diverse requirements as to application for a permit; preconstruction submittal of statement of location; postconstruction filing of a statement of location, plans, or log of a well; or filing of a record of facilities abandoned. All degrees of public involvement are represented.

The writer feels strongly that the current order in waste disposal by injection—in essence a private individual or corporation versus a state—is inherently and woefully insufficient. Principal reasons follow, in addition to others already implied.

Exploration to prove feasibility and absolute safety, together with adequate construction of a well and related facilities to accomplish deep injection, commonly would be exceedingly costly. For example, at one installation of the Atomic Energy Commission, somewhat more than a million dollars was expended on definitive exploration in an area of a few square miles, to depths of only about 800 feet, over a 3-year term. Construction of injection facilities and continuing monitoring have about equaled the exploration cost. Even so, some potentially critical questions remain unanswerable. Few private agencies have, or can command, the specialized technical skills and the financial resources necessary for demonstrably sound performance, when injection is to be at depths of thousands of feet. Should the skills and resources be at hand, full disclosure of findings by a pioneer injector could grant an unearned "free ride" to the competitors. The urge to shortcuts in exploration and construction, and to avoidance of disclosure, would seem all but irresistible. A joint injection facility, with cost of exploration and construction shared among several private agencies, would be advantageous to the participants but would aggravate the tendency to avoid disclosure.

At the opposite pole in the current order, the general public should have the inalienable rights to be spared harm from, and to reap the benefit of accrued experience with, deep injection. Few, if any, state agencies currently have the staff skills, centralized authority, and financial resources to assure these general-public rights. Some new, fully competent institutional arrangement appears to be essential. As suggestive means to that end:

1. An agency or commission of government or a public corporation, either designated from among existing institutions or created for the purpose, might be vested with exclusive authority and responsibility to (1) delineate provinces and stratigraphic zones suitable for

injection, and (2) maintain a continuing record of waste storage in the several provinces and zones—both capacity occupied and capacity unused, both volumes and chemical character and concentration of wastes injected. As required, such institutions might exist in en echelon scope—nationwide, single state or major province, subprovince, and local zone. Staff capability and financial support, both commensurate with responsibility, would be presumed at each echelon. Each subprovince or local zone would constitute a hydrodynamic whole and would be administered as a whole; if any such unit had parts in more than one state, a single jurisdiction would be negotiated or otherwise arranged.

2. Each of the above governmental or public entities might (1) construct injection facilities and offer waste-storage service at a suitable fee or, alternatively (2) license a private agency or an association of such agencies to construct and operate an injection facility for its exclusive use. The fee charged for injection service might be scaled according to volume, concentration, and compatibility of the waste delivered to the public agency. Such a policy would create incentive for the waste producer to minimize his demand on the space available for waste storage. The license would require full disclosure of all information originating with the waste producer but required for orderly long-term management of the injection province or zone. The license might also grant to the private agency or association the prerogative of exploring and delineating a suitable injection zone or zones.

3. Among its prerogatives, the public agency would be authorized to: (1) so regulate the construction and casing of injection wells that wastes are excluded, completely and permanently, from the zone between the land surface and the injection zone into which they are released, (2) promulgate and enforce "safe" injection pressures and rates of injection; these should be variable as hydrodynamic conditions might require, (3) prescribe an aggregate volume of waste permitted to be injected into a particular province, subprovince, or zone, (4) require any waste to be treated before injection, as may be necessary to render it chemically compatible or stable, (5) prohibit injection

of chemically incompatible or excessively noxious wastes, (6) declare any province, subprovince, or zone to be "off limits" to injection, either permanently or temporarily, as may be necessary to achieve or maintain suitable hydrodynamic and geochemical balances, (7) as warranted, reserve any particular zone or subzone for a declared resource-management purpose—for example, as a source of fresh water by desalination, or for gas storage, (8) preserve the integrity of the confining layer above any designated waste-injection zone, by requiring that all wells or other openings drilled into that layer for any purpose be adequately cased, and plugged if abandoned, and (9) continually search for alternative and economically competitive methods of waste handling, to the ends of minimizing encroachment on the land-surface environment, while prolonging capacity for injection underground.

In the concept just suggested, the public agency having only a local jurisdiction would, in principle, act as an agency of one particular state, possibly in the form of a utility or conservancy district. To implement the concept fully would require legislation establishing the proper federal role and approaching a uniform state role, both roles to encompass the full scope of technical and management problems discussed or implied.

Advisedly, the concept is concerned only with injecting wastes underground. Even in perfected form, it resolves only in part the necessity that mankind learn to manage the wastes it produces.

References

American Association of Petroleum Geologists, 1964, Radioactive waste-disposal potentials in selected geologic basins—A reconnaissance study: U.S. Atomic Energy Comm. rept. SAN–413–2, 31 p.

American Institute of Chemical Engineers, 1967, Proposed definition of radioactive waste categories: Approved, United States of America Standards Institute, June 7, 1967.

American Petroleum Institute, 1958, Problems in the disposal of radioactive waste in deep wells: Dallas, Tex., American Petroleum Inst., Div. of Production, 27 p.

Beikman, H. M., 1962, Geology of the Powder River Basin, Wyoming and Montana, with reference to subsurface disposal of radioactive wastes: U.S. Geol. Survey TEI–823, 85 p.

Birch, Francis, 1958, Thermal considerations in deep disposal of radioactive waste: Natl. Acad. Sci.–Natl. Research Council Pub. 588. (Report for

Committee on Waste Disposal, Div. of Earth Sciences.)

Cleary, J. M., 1958, Hydraulic fracture theory—Part 1, Mechanics of materials; Part 2, Fracture orientation and possibility of fracture control: Illinois Geol. Survey Circs. 251 and 252, p. 24 and 19, respectively.

Colton, G. W., 1961, Geologic summary of the Appalachian Basin, with reference to the subsurface disposal of radioactive waste solutions: U.S. Geol. Survey TEI—791, 121 p.

de Laguna, Wallace, 1968, Disposal of medium-level radioactive waste by hydraulic fracturing: Paper presented at annual meeting Natl. Water Well Assoc., Sept. 24, 1968, Washington, D.C.

Deutsch, Morris, 1961, Incidents of chromium contamination of ground water in Michigan in Groundwater contamination: U.S. Dept. Health, Education, and Welfare, Proc. 1961 Symposium, Tech. rept. W 61-5.

———1963, Ground-water contamination and legal controls in Michigan: U.S. Geol. Survey Water-Supply Paper 1691, 79 p.

———1965, Natural controls involved in shallow aquifer contamination: Ground Water, v. 3, no. 3.

de Witt, Wallace, Jr., 1960, Geology of the Michigan Basin with reference to subsurface disposal of radioactive wastes: U.S. Geol. Survey TEI—771, 100 p.

Dickey, P. A., and Andresen, K. H., 1945, The behavior of water-input wells in Drilling and production practice: Am. Petroleum Inst., p. 34-58.

Ferris, J. G., Knowles, D. B., Brown, R. H., and Stallman, R. W., 1962, Theory of aquifer test: U.S. Geol. Survey Water-Supply Paper 1536—E, p. 69-174.

Galley, J. E., ed., 1968, Subsurface disposal in geologic basins—A study of reservoir strata: Am. Assoc. Petroleum Geologists Mem. 10, 253 p.

Grandone, P., and Holleyman, J. B., 1949, Injection rates and pressures for water flooding Mid-Continent oil sands: U.S. Bur. Mines Rept. Inv. 4600, 30 p.

Griggs, R. L., 1958, The Silurian salt deposits of the northeastern United States: U.S. Geol. Survey TEI—710.

Healy, J. H., Rubey, W. W., Griggs, D. T., and Raleigh, C. B., 1968, The Denver earthquakes: Science, v. 161, no. 3848, p. 1301-1310.

Hoeger, R. L., 1968, Hydrodynamic study of the western Denver basin, Colorado: Colorado School Mines Quart., v. 63, no. 1, p. 245-251.

Hubbert, M. K., and Willis, D. G., 1957, Mechanics of hydraulic fracturing: Am. Inst. Mining Metall. Engineers Trans., p. 153-168.

Jones, P. H., 1961a, Hydrology of radioactive waste disposal at the Idaho Chemical Processing Plant, National Reactor Testing Station in Short papers in the geologic and hydrologic sciences: U.S. Geol. Survey Prof. Paper 424—D, p. 374-376.

———1961b, Hydrology of waste disposal National Reactor Testing Station, Idaho; an interim report: U.S. Geol. Survey open-file rept. IDO—22042, 82 p.

Kehle, R. O., 1964, The determination of tectonic stresses through analysis of hydraulic fracturing: Jour. Geophys. Research, v. 69, no. 2, p. 259-273.

Le Grand, H. E., 1962, Geology and ground-water hydrology of the Atlantic and Gulf Coastal Plain as related to disposal of radioactive wastes: U.S. Geol. Survey TEI—805, 169 p.

Love, J. D., and Hoover, Lynn, 1960, A summary of the geology of sedimentary basins of the United States, with reference to the disposal of radioactive wastes: U.S. Geol. Survey TEI—768, 89 p.

MacLachlan, M. E., 1964, The Anadarko Basin (of parts of Oklahoma, Texas, Kansas, and Colorado): U.S. Geol. Survey TEI—831, 75 p.

McNeal, R. P., 1965, Hydrodynamics of the Permian basin in Fluids in subsurface environments: Am. Assoc. Petroleum Geologists Mem. 4, p. 308-326.

Morris, D. A., Barraclough, J. T., Chase, G. H., Teasdale, W. E., and Jensen, R. G., 1965, Hydrology of subsurface waste disposal, National Reactor Testing Station, Idaho; Annual Progress Report, 1964: U.S. Geol. Survey open-file rept. IDO—22047, 146 p.

Nace and others, 1962, Site requirements for routine liquid waste disposal: Am. Standards Assoc. Working Group N5.2.2.

Pierce, W. G., and Rich, E. I., 1958, Summary of rock salt deposits in the United States as possible disposal sites for radioactive waste: U.S. Geol. Survey TEI—725, 175 p.

Repenning, C. A., 1959, Geologic summary of the San Juan Basin, New Mexico, with reference to disposal of liquid radioactive waste: U.S. Geol. Survey TEI—603, 57 p.

———1960, Geologic summary of the Central Valley of California, with reference to disposal of liquid radioactive waste: U.S. Geol. Survey TEI—769, 69 p.

Sandberg, C. A., 1962 Geology of the Williston Basin, North Dakota, Montana, and South Dakota, with reference to subsurface disposal of radioactive wastes: U.S. Geol. Survey TEI—809, 148 p.

Scheidegger, A. E., 1960, On the connection between tectonic stresses and well fracturing data: Geofisica pura e applicata, v. 46, p. 66-76.

Skibitzke, H. E., 1961, Temperature rise within radioactive wastes injected into deep formations: U.S. Geol. Survey Prof. Paper 386-A.

Warner, D. L., 1965, Deep-well injection of liquid wastes—A review of existing knowledge and an evaluation of research needs: U.S. Dept. Health, Education, and Welfare, Public Health Service, pub. 999-Wp-21, 55 p.

———1966, Deep well waste injection—Reaction with aquifer water: Am. Soc. Civil Engineers, Jour. Sanitary Engineering Division, v. 92, no. SA4, Proc. Paper 4881, p. 45-69, August 1966.

Yuster, S. T., and Calhoun, J. C., 1945, Pressure parting of formations in water flood operations: Oil Weekly, v. 117, no. 2, p. 38, no. 3, p. 34, 35, 38,

32. DESIGN OF DISPOSAL WELLS

JOHN H. MARSH

This paper is concerned with the design of high and low capacity wells for the disposal of very corrosive waste liquids. Parts of the design criteria are applicable to other types of wells used for injecting liquids, such as surface runoff, fresh water, salt water, or other wastes into saline or otherwise useless formations. Sketches are included of two designs for disposal wells recently completed 2,000 feet below the surface in the massive, unconsolidated fine sand of the Gulf Coastal Plain.

Construction of waste disposal wells is not new to the Gulf Coast area. The oil and related industries have used disposal wells for perhaps 30 to 40 years. A significant thing is that a large percentage of the disposal wells have been, and are still being constructed with oil well completion techniques. These completions, when compared to modern water well completions are usually inferior from the standpoint of efficiency, injection capacity, operating costs, maintenance, and well life.

The typical oil field type completion would be to first drill through the injection zone plugging the sands with bentonite drilling mud; then install casing through the injection zone; pressure grout the annulus further plugging the sands and losing completely the access to the formation. The next step is to partially regain access to the formation by gun-perforating through the casing, cement and mud cake. (A typical perforating schedule for 6-inch casing would be four one-half inch diameter perforations per foot, which equals about 0.3 percent open area, or 0.8 inch^2 of open area per foot of perforated zone.) Last, the task of cleaning the plugging agents from the formation must

Reprinted with the permission of the author and publisher from *Ground Water*, v. 6, no. 2, p. 4-8, 1968. Copyright 1968 National Water Well Assoc., Inc. John H. Marsh is President of Engineering Enterprises, Norman, Oklahoma, a consulting firm specializing in ground water development, pollution control, and irrigated agricultural systems. This paper was written in 1967 when the author was on the staff of the Johnson Division of Universal Oil Products.

be accomplished via a very limited access. This development work must be done in such a manner so the sand will bridge the perforations to prevent its flowing into the well bore. Sometimes consolidating agents are forced through the perforations out into the formation to glue the sand grains together. This can arrest the flow of sand, but it further decreases the permeability of the formation in the vicinity of the well bore. The mud, the perforated casing, the cement grout, and the sand consolidation material are all barriers to the flow of liquids into and out of the formation. More important, they are a larger barrier to the well development or restoration of permeability.

The result of this type completion is usually an inefficient well which is likely to fill with sand when being backwashed or pumped in a flushing cycle. The cost of cement, casing, perforations and development work is high in proportion to the efficiency and reliability of the structure.

The completion technique for disposal wells need not be different from that for efficient water production wells. Drilling muds with automatic viscosity reversion properties can be used to minimize or eliminate permanent plugging of sands. Precision made screens can be set in the open hole by means as simple as setting casing. With screens there certainly is no need to extend the cement grout barrier into the injection zone.

It is logical that the degree to which the plugged formation can be developed, or cleaned, and made permeable, is related directly to the amount of exposure of the formation to the well bore. Therefore, development can be much more complete through wire wound screens which provide grossly more open area than perforated pipe. (A 6-inch Johnson Screen with a 0.010-inch slot opening has 12.5 percent open area—forty times that of the aforementioned perforation schedule).

In addition to the increased open area, precision screens with the correct slot opening provide absolute sand control, eliminating any need for consolidation techniques.

The design requirements for waste disposal

wells in unconsolidated sands generally are the same as those for water production wells (Edward E. Johnson, Inc., 1966) with the following five additional considerations:

1. Absolute steps must be included to prevent intrusion of waste liquids into fresh-water aquifers. This requires that an impermeable boundary, such as a massive clay layer or other aquiclude must separate the injection zone from any fresh-water aquifers.

2. Casing must be pressure grouted or otherwise positively sealed well into, preferably through, the aquiclude. Cementing agents resistant to deterioration by the waste or formation liquid should be used when available.

3. If the waste is corrosive to the casing used, then a separate injection string of corrosion resistant or replaceable pipe must be used to prevent contact of the waste with the casing. Also, the annulus between the injection string and the casing must be sealed or pressurized to prevent the injection fluid from entering the annulus at the bottom. Figures 4 and 6 illustrate two methods of protecting the casing from injected fluids. The screen also must be resistant to corrosion attack.

4. The injection rate should be planned for no more than one-half the production capability of the well. Theoretically, the formation should take fluid at the same specific capacity that it will produce fluid. However, there are factors other than permeability which have bearing on the specific injection capacity. Some of them are: suspended solids in injection fluid, mineral precipitation due to oxidation, changes in temperature and in pressure; growth of slimes and air binding. Experience has shown that all disposal wells require periodic cleaning. Therefore, provisions should be made so the flow can be reversed to remove plugging solids as conveniently as possible by flushing (backwashing) the well. When backwashing, the well should be pumped at twice the injection rate. This will allow the cleaning flow velocity to be twice the velocity which carried the plugging particles into the formation. This is consistent with good practice for cleaning other types of intake screens and filters.

5. The screen should have enough open area to pass the design injection flow at a velocity of 0.05 ft/sec or less.

DESIGN EXAMPLE NO. 1

In the summer of 1966 two screened wells were completed for the disposal of refining waste in an unconsolidated artesian, salt-water zone of the Gulf Coastal Plain. The injection stream contained high concentrations of chlorides and hydrogen sulfide. Figure 1 shows the chemical analyses of the waste stream and the formation water. Both of these wells were gravel packed. They were designed for an injection rate of 700 gpm each. Here we will discuss one of them in detail.

	Waste Stream		Formation Water	
pH	6.00 – 8.00		6.30	
Turbidity (Jackson unit)	10.00		10.00	
Total dissolved solids	6300	ppm	125,000	ppm
Total alkalinity	35	ppm	70	ppm
Chlorides	3500	ppm	100,000	ppm
Total hardness	800	ppm	24,000	ppm
Hydrogen sulfide (H₂S)	4200	ppm		
Sodium (Na) & potassium (K)	2300	ppm		
Phenols	70	ppm		
Total suspended solids	10	ppm		
Sediment			700	ppm
Iron & aluminum as oxides			510	ppm

Figure 1. Disposal well water analysis,
Gulf Coast area.

A test hole was drilled to a depth of 2,300 feet. Formation samples were collected and an electric log was run measuring the formation spontaneous potential and resistivity. Figures 2 and 3 show the E-log from 600 to 1,300 feet and 1,300 to 2,100 feet respectively. The E-log shows layers of fresh-water sand to about 900 feet. Below this level the water is saline. A 270-foot thick clay aquiclude is present from 1,550 to 1,820 feet. This clay stratum serves as the confining layer for the injection zone.

Because hydrogen sulfide and chlorides are so corrosive, a double casing was planned with the outer casing cemented and the inner casing as a replaceable injection string. A packer near the bottom of the injection string seals the annulus. The injection string controls the diameter of the well. It was sized to transmit the design injection rate at 1.5 feet of head loss per 100 feet of pipe. The 13-3/8 OD casing permits access to the annulus, which was filled under pressure, with water containing a corrosion inhibitor. Figure 4 shows the well design. Notice that the injection tubing was internally coated for corrosion protection and that it was also replaceable.

Sieve analyses of sand samples from 1,820 to 2,060 feet and the E-log indicated the most permeable strata to be from 1,955 to 2,060 feet.

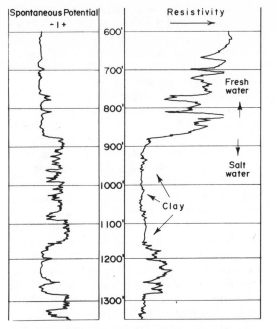

Figure 2. Electric log: disposal well for liquids with high H_2S and chloride content, Gulf Coast area. Log interval, 600 feet to 1350 feet.

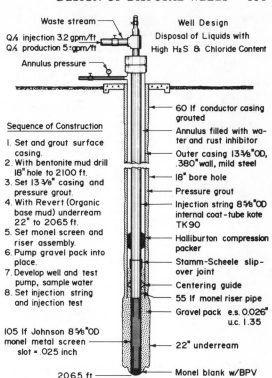

Figure 4. Well design: disposal of liquids with high H_2S and chloride content.

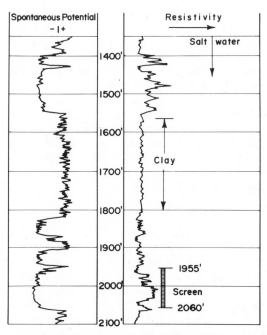

Figure 3. Electric log: disposal well for liquids with high H_2S and chloride content, Gulf Coast area. Log interval, 1350 feet to 2100 feet.

This then was selected as the injection zone. To develop maximum hydraulic efficiency the screen length (105 feet) was selected to penetrate the full thickness of this strata. Full penetration eliminates vertical flow in the formation near the well bore. An even larger specific injection capacity could have been obtained by placing screen in the strata from 1,830 to 1,860 feet and 1,910 to 1,940 feet, but in this case it was not required.

Sieve analyses of the sand from the injection zone, and the gravel pack material, are shown in Figure 5. The formation was a fine, uniform sand. The gravel pack material was designed to control the finest sample by selecting a very uniform graded pack having a 70 percent retained size about five times that of the sample (Edward E. Johnson, Inc., 1966). The well screen slot opening of .025 inch retains more than 95 percent of the gravel pack.

Monel 400 metal was selected for fabrication of the wire wound, welded Johnson well screen. The screen, end fittings, riser pipe and tail pipe were all made of Monel. Monel is the most economical screen material having the required

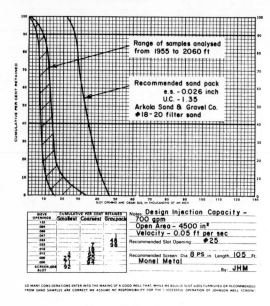

Figure 5. Sand analysis

strength for a 2,000-foot setting, and having adequate resistance to corrosion from hydrogen sulfide and chloride solutions. Monel 400 is approximately 65 percent nickel, 32 percent copper, with small amounts of carbon, iron, manganese and silica. It has a modulus of elasticity of 26 x 10⁶ psi (304 stainless steel, a very strong material commonly used for well screens, has a modulus of elasticity of 30 x 10⁶).

With the screen slot of .025 inch set by the gradation of the gravel pack and the screen length set by the formation thickness, the remaining screen dimension to be set was the diameter. The proper diameter was selected so the total open area of the screen would transmit the 700 gpm at a velocity of 0.05 feet per second. In this case an 8-inch ID, 8-5/8-inch OD screen conveniently met the requirement.

The sequence of construction is outlined on Figure 4. Two of the construction steps are of particular interest. The contractor used conventional bentonite drilling mud to drill to 1,950 feet where the 13-3/8 OD outer casing was set and cemented. The hole was then drilled through the injection zone to 2,065 feet and under-reamed to 2,060 feet using an organic mud with an additive of formaldehyde. This particular mud, "Johnson Revert" has the basic property of building viscosity, holding the viscosity for three to four days before it breaks down or reverts

back to a viscosity about the same as water. The contractor's schedule was such that the hole was to be open for more than four days so a small amount of formaldehyde was added to the organic mud to extend the life (time before break down) to one week.

Another interesting point about the construction was the method used to place the gravel pack material (Procedures Used in Gravel Packing Wells, 1966). The screen and riser assembly was set with drill stem. A left hand thread on top of the riser pipe facilitated breaking the joint for retrieval of the drill stem after the gravel packing was complete. A retrievable stinger pipe extended to near the bottom of the screen. A water and gravel mixture was pumped down the annulus between the drill stem and the casing. The gravel was deposited around the screen and the water was circulated through the screen and back up the drill stem. When the gravel level rose above the screen, the system pressure suddenly increased indicating the screen was covered. An additional measured amount of gravel was then pumped down to raise the gravel level to near the top of the Monel riser pipe.

After both wells were completed, one was pumped and the saline water produced was injected into the second well and vice versa. The formation water contained 510 ppm iron and aluminum (see Figure 1 for the formation water quality). Consequently, a closed system was required during testing to prevent the precipitation of metal oxides from aeration of the water. The metal oxides would plug the injection well very rapidly. The specific injection capacity of the well discussed here was 3.2 gpm per foot of head compared to the pumping specific capacity of 5 gpm per foot of drawdown.

The cost of each well, including the well casing head assembly, but not including the surface concrete work, or surface piping, was approximately $105,000.

DESIGN EXAMPLE NO. 2

A well screen made of another exotic metal was installed this summer in a well for the disposal of a chemical process waste stream containing 32 percent hydrochloric acid. The temperature of the water was 115 degrees F. The design injection rate was 30 gpm. The well was a naturally developed design. It is located in the Gulf Coastal Plain. Figure 6 shows the well as constructed.

On the basis of an E-log and formation

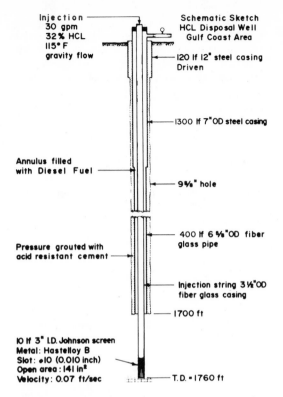

Injection
30 gpm
32% HCL
115° F
gravity flow

Schematic Sketch
HCL Disposal Well
Gulf Coast Area

120 lf 12" steel casing
Driven

1300 lf 7"OD steel casing

Annulus filled
with Diesel Fuel

9⅝" hole

Pressure grouted with
acid resistant cement

400 lf 6 ⅝"OD fiber
glass pipe

Injection string 3½"OD
fiber glass casing

1700 ft

10 lf 3" I.D. Johnson screen
Metal: Hastelloy B
Slot: ⌀10 (0.010 inch)
Open area : 141 in²
Velocity: 0.07 ft/sec

T.D. = 1760 ft

Figure 6. Schematic sketch of HCL disposal well, Gulf Coast area.

metal. It has good corrosion resistance to hydrochloric acid and is very strong. (Hydrochloric acid is corrosive to mild steel and all the common screen metals and even Monel metal.) Hastelloy B is composed of roughly 62 percent nickel, 28 percent molybdenun, 5 percent iron and other trace elements. The modulus of elasticity is 26.4 x 10^6 psi.

Sieve analyses of sand samples from the injection zone (Figure 7) show that for a naturally developed well the screen should have a 0.010-inch slot. The owner requested the screen to be 3-inch ID, 10 feet long, with a special thread to match the threaded coupling on the injection string. The 10 slot screen provides 147 square inches of open area, and will transmit the design flow of 30 gpm at a velocity through the slots of 0.07 ft/sec.

The well receives the acid waste solution by gravity flow, even though the formation's static water level is 20 feet above ground. This is possible because the acid solution is heavier than the formation water.

Incidentally, before the well was put into

samples from the test hole, the injection zone with an overlying confining layer was selected.

The combination of two materials used for the outer casing is of unique design. Seven-inch steel casing extends to 1,300 feet and corrosion resistant fibre glass pipe, connected to the steel casing, extends from 1,300 feet to 1,700 feet. Acid resistant latex cement was used to grout the outer casing from 1,700 feet to the surface. The separation injection string, also fibre glass, was connected to the screen.

The static level of the formation water was 20 feet above ground surface so by filling the annulus between the injection string and the casing with diesel fuel under pressure, the injection liquid cannot come in contact with the steel outer casing. The 400 feet of fibre glass outer casing provides a buffer zone should the acid begin to rise up the annulus. Also, if the acid attacked the latex cement grout, it would have to deteriorate a 400-foot thickness of it to reach the corrodable steel outer casing.

Hastelloy B was selected as the proper screen

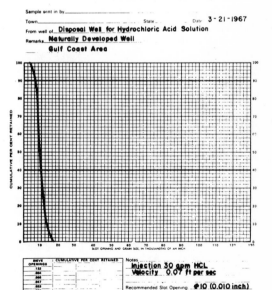

UOP JOHNSON DIVISION
315 North Pierce Street
Saint Paul, Minn. 55104

Sample sent in by
Town   State   Date 3-21-1967
From well of Disposal Well for Hydrochloric Acid Solution
Remarks Naturally Developed Well
Gulf Coast Area

Notes
Injection 30 gpm HCL
Velocity 0.07 ft per sec
Recommended Slot Opening ⌀10 (0.010 inch)
Recommended Screen Dia 3" I.D. Min. Length 10 Ft.
Hastelloy B
Setting 1750-1760 ft   By JLM

SO MANY CONSIDERATIONS ENTER INTO THE MAKING OF A GOOD WELL THAT, WHILE WE BELIEVE SLOT SIZES FURNISHED OR RECOMMENDED FROM SAND SAMPLES ARE CORRECT WE ASSUME NO RESPONSIBILITY FOR THE SUCCESSFUL OPERATION OF JOHNSON WELL SCREEN

Figure 7. Sand analysis.

operation it was charged with four barrels (168 gallons) of saturated salt water which killed the flow and held the water level low enough for two weeks until the gravity injection of the waste stream could be started. The brine was also heavier than the formation water. That the brine held the static level down for two weeks gives emphasis to the fact that the dispersion of liquids into each other is relatively slow, particularly in a porous media. Therefore, the addition of buffer solutions may serve to keep injected wastes from coming into contact with formation water thereby preventing chemical reactions that could cause precipitation of plugging materials. This has been discussed at length by others (Warner, 1966).

These examples of design are typical of efficient disposal wells that can be constructed using modern completion techniques. Equally important, the examples emphasize that materials are available which can be incorporated into the disposal well design to handle very corrosive wastes simply and efficiently.

REFERENCES

Johnson, Edward E., Inc. 1966. Ground water and wells. Chapter 10.

Procedures used in gravel packing wells. 1966. The Johnson Drillers Journal, March-April, UOP Johnson Division.

Warner, Don L. 1966. Deep well waste injection-reaction with aquifer water. Journal ASCE, Sanitary Engineering Division, August.

33. DISPOSAL OF WASTES: EXAMPLES FROM ILLINOIS

ROBERT E. BERGSTROM

DISPOSAL OF RADIOACTIVE WASTES

The state of Illinois and the U. S. Atomic Energy Commission have recently licensed a private company to operate a burial ground for low-level, solid, radioactive wastes. The wastes are encased in steel drums or concrete containers and buried in trenches 20 to 25 feet deep. The operation is similar to a sanitary landfill, but required considerable preliminary testing and proving. Figure 1 illustrates the conditions at the site. Some 40 or 50 feet of loess and till overlie Pennsylvanian bedrock. The till has some lenses of sand and gravel but overall permeability is very low. In only one test well in six could any water be pumped (5 gpm). From the pumped well a permeability of 4 gpd/ft^2 was determined for the more permeable part of the site. Water levels in the test wells ranged from a depth of about 40 feet on the ridge to about 20 feet in the dry valley bottoms. Ground-water discharge appears to be to the strip mine pond about 800 feet from the burial site. A flow velocity of 0.01 ft/day was estimated from the permeability and gradient data.

Investigation for the project brought out several scientific and technological problems of interest to ground-water practitioners; among them:

1. The fine-textured glacial sediments did not lend themselves to the methods of hydrologic testing and analysis that are employed in dealing with aquifers; yet field permeability measurements, with groundwater velocities, were requested by A.E.C. reviewers. The determinations finally made and submitted may be high for the actual burial zone.

2. The details of possible saturation and water movement above the so-called water table are not known. Our experience with piezometers installed in sanitary landfills and various glacial drift terranes in northeastern Illinois (Hughes,

Extracted with permission of publisher from "Disposal of Wastes: Scientific and Administrative Considerations" by R. E. Bergstrom in *Environmental Geology Notes,* no. 20, 12 p., January, 1968. Published by Illinois State Geological Survey, Urbana, Illinois.

1967) suggests that fine-grained tills are usually saturated closer to the surface than is shown here by water levels in test wells. If this is true for the area tested, it could modify the actual burial conditions from what are shown here. Furthermore, the piezometer response to precipitation at various depths in glacial till suggests that some ground-water movement takes place rather quickly through joints rather than through intergranular openings (Williams and Farvolden, 1967). If this occurs here, it could affect the velocity of ground-water movement and travel time to the pond.

DISPOSAL WELLS

Figure 2 illustrates conditions at four disposal well sites in Illinois. The two on the left are in the Illinois Basin and the two on the right are in northern Illinois. Lithology is shown on the left of each well, and quality of ground water is shown on the right. The rocks shown as shales are considered good confining beds. Fresh water (less than 1000 ppm total dissolved minerals) and brackish to saline water (more than 5000 ppm) are indicated. The figures to the right of the wells show water quality in ppm dissolved minerals at various depths.

At the two sites on the left, fresh water occurs only within a few hundred feet from land surface, and there is considerable shale and brackish to saline water between the disposal zone and upper fresh-water-bearing aquifers. In the Putnam County well, usable water (1000 ppm total dissolved minerals) occurs fairly deep, but there is shale and mineralized water above the disposal zone. In the DuPage County test well at the right, fresh water extends to a depth of about 2300 feet, or into the top 500 feet of a thick sandstone that continues down to the granite basement. The quality of water deteriorates rapidly below 2500 feet; right above granite basement at 4000 feet the water has a dissolved mineral content of 95,000 ppm. The thick sandstone thus contains fresh, brackish, and saline water from top to bottom, with no prominent intervening shale sections, though the sandstone has low permeability. The basal 200

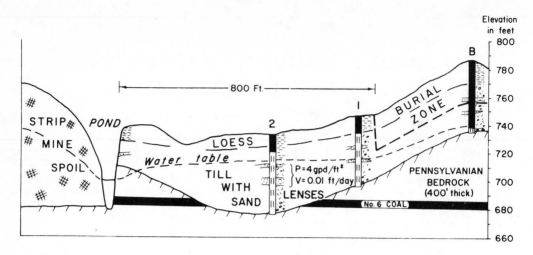

Figure 1. Burial ground for low-level, solid, radioactive wastes in Bureau County, Illinois.

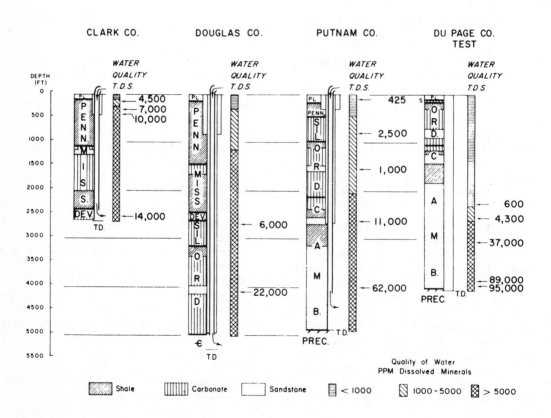

Figure 2. Hydrogeologic conditions at waste disposal well sites. Mineral quality of water is given in parts per million total dissolved solids.

feet of sandstone accepted water at a rate of only 25 gallons per minute at allowable operating pressures. We estimated that nearly 1000 feet of section would be required for injection of waste at 325 gpm. This would bring the injection zone up to about the 3000-foot depth, which we considered too close to the potable water zone.

The main problems were presented by the DuPage County site where there is deep fresh water occurrence and large ground-water development. There is a real need for waste disposal facilities in this part of the state, but it was necessary for state agencies to be very cautious in reviewing the proposal. For example, the State Sanitary Water Board ruled that fracturing of the basal part of the sandstone would not be permitted. Fracturing might have produced the permeability that could have made the project feasible, could it have been accomplished without hazard to potable ground-water supplies.

An additional problem presented by this site was the extent to which water of poor quality might migrate upward as a result of injection of wastes into the lower part of the sandstone and the pumping of potable water from the upper part.

SEWAGE-STORM WATER TUNNELS

Another interesting problem in waste management is the Chicago Sanitary District's proposal (Harza Engineering Company and Bauer Engineering, Inc., 1966) to store combined sewage and storm water temporarily in deep tunnels in the Galena-Platteville Dolomite. The water would enter the tunnels during storms, and after storms would be processed in the Sanitary District's treatment plants and then returned to the Sanitary Canal. At present, during many storms the treatment plants are by-passed and the combined storm water and raw sewage are fed directly into the canal.

A final investigation of feasibility and design has been started. The initial report concluded that storm and sewage water would not pollute the ground-water reservoir because the rock in which the tunnel would be excavated is quite tight, and head relations are such that any water movement would be *into* rather than *out of* the tunnel. The present head is well above the proposed tunnel section. However, by the year 2010, pumpage might have drawn the head down below the tunnel level. To prevent this from occurring, artificial recharge into the St. Peter Sandstone in the tunnel area and distribution of water and head in the Galena-Platteville would keep the head above the tunnel and assure head relations that would keep pollution from entering the dolomite.

CONCLUSIONS

I should like to conclude by mentioning some of the things I believe ground-water practitioners could be doing in waste management.

First, in addition to maintaining a vigilance over pollution hazards connected with waste disposal, we should exercise our knowledge of hydrogeologic conditions to promote sites and environments for waste disposal where there are natural safeguards that will assure protection of health and resources. We should also point out environments where risks of pollution hazard are high. Even the use of fairly broad hydrogeologic generalizations with reference to disposal conditions are useful to the regulatory and planning agencies and to the interested public, and they can keep ill-advised projects from being developed.

Figure 3 shows the hydrogeologic feasibility of deep waste disposal wells in Illinois. Conditions range from very good in the Illinois Basin, where there is a thick geologic section and highly mineralized water below shallow depth, to highly questionable in the northern part of the state, where there is a thinner section and deep fresh water penetration.

Second, in reviewing proposals for specific waste disposal sites in cooperation with other specialists, we are in a position to stimulate the acquisition of useful data on the physical system and to promote the development of criteria for assessing the protection afforded by certain geologic conditions and engineering practices. Decisions should be based on facts rather than on the absence of facts.

Finally, we should delve into investigations that are especially pertinent to waste management problems. There should be studies of saturation conditions and water movement in typical geologic materials and terranes that might be used for disposal of wastes. Methods of investigation and hydrologic analysis should be developed for environments having fine-textured, relatively impermeable sediments. Geochemical factors that may affect attenuation of contaminants should be further considered. And studies should be made of the means by which injected liquid wastes are accommodated in subsurface reservoirs and of the possible role of hydrofracturing in facilitating waste injection into deep, impermeable rocks.

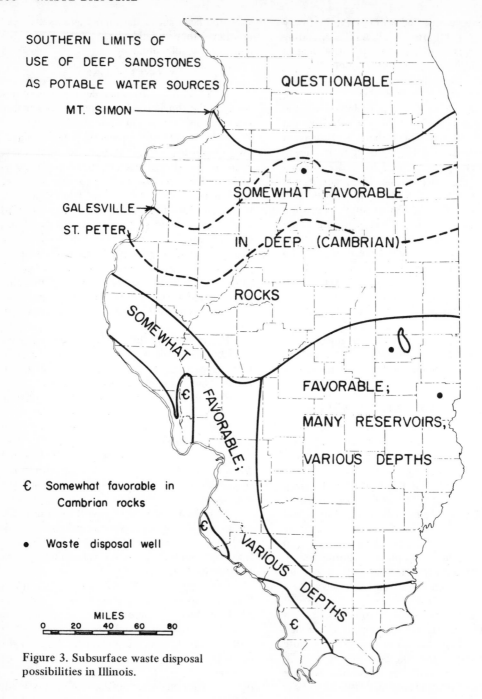

SOUTHERN LIMITS OF
USE OF DEEP SANDSTONES
AS POTABLE WATER SOURCES

MT. SIMON

QUESTIONABLE

GALESVILLE
ST. PETER

SOMEWHAT FAVORABLE

IN DEEP (CAMBRIAN)

ROCKS

SOMEWHAT

FAVORABLE;

FAVORABLE;

MANY RESERVOIRS;

VARIOUS DEPTHS

€   Somewhat favorable in
    Cambrian rocks

•   Waste disposal well

VARIOUS DEPTHS

MILES
0   20   40   60   80

Figure 3. Subsurface waste disposal
possibilities in Illinois.

REFERENCES

Harza Engineering Company and Bauer Engineering, Inc., 1966, Flood and pollution control: A deep tunnel plan for the Chicagoland area: Metropolitan Sanitary District of Chicago Prefeasibility Rept., Chicago.

Hughes, G. M., 1967, Selection of refuse disposal sites in northeastern Illinois: Illinois Geol. Survey Environmental Geology Note 17, 26 p.

Williams, R. E., and Farvolden, R. N., 1967, The influence of joints on the movement of ground water through glacial till: Jour. Hydrology, v. 5, p. 163-170.

Groundwater Contamination

34. MANMADE CONTAMINATION HAZARDS

P. H. McGAUHEY

INTRODUCTION

The activities of man upon the earth may affect the quality of ground water in two major ways: (1) by accelerating the rate of buildup of compounds or ions normally found in ground water, and (2) by adding or increasing the concentration of dissolved solids during beneficial use of water. The first results from plowing of fields, denuding of forest lands, construction of highways, and similar actions which expedite the normal movement of water into soils containing soluble compounds. The second results from discharging to the water which may infiltrate the soil, or to the land through which water may move, inorganic chemicals, biological agents, and organic compounds associated with municipal, industrial, and agricultural use of water. For the purpose of this discussion, only this second type of activity is considered as producing "manmade" hazards; hence specific attention is directed to the significance to ground-water quality of the natural and synthetic fractions which appear in:

1. Wastes from human life processes.
2. Wastes from industrial processes.
3. Agricultural return flows or percolates.
4. Solid residues resulting from the use of resources or industrial products.

WASTES FROM HUMAN LIFE PROCESSES

By far the greatest concern for contamination of ground waters has been directed to human wastes in the form of municipal sewage. Curiously enough, such concern has not generally been expressed over septic tank effluents discharged directly underground. At least such concern is so recent in origin that groundwater quality considerations did not prevent the use of septic tanks in urban subdivisions in the past 25 years on a scale sufficient to run the total of persons served by such systems to more than 30 million. However, from the viewpoint of contam-

ination hazards from human wastes it matters little whether the percolating liquid comes from subsurface leaching fields or from operations involving surface application of sewage effluents, as will presently be noted.

In the practical case municipal sewage contains both domestic and industrial waste products. From the domestic fraction comes wastes from the human body, grease, ground garbage, and residues from commercial products such as soap and detergents. The industrial fraction normally includes a variety of biochemically unstable organic matter and a wide spectrum of common chemicals as well as more exotic organics and toxic ions, generally in concentrations below that critical to waste treatment processes. Therefore, in evaluating contamination hazards involved in municipal sewage the fate of several kinds of material in soil systems must be considered.

For purpose of discussion these materials may be divided into such general classes as:

1. Organic and inorganic particles, other than living organisms.
2. Microorganisms, including bacteria and viruses.
3. Chemical products of degradation of organic matter.
4. Chemicals from industrial wastes or from industrial products in commercial use.
5. Leachings from landfills.

Of this group the organic degradation products may be generated under either aerobic or anaerobic conditions and so develop a variety of intermediate products. All of the group are generated or commonly discarded by man at the earth's surface, with a few rare exceptions, and hence are initially separated from the ground water by the soil mantle of the earth. They are further separated from the user of ground water by the extent of aquifer between the point of outcrop or withdrawal of water. Further, the soil mantle of the earth is biologically active. Under these circumstances the question of manmade hazards to the ground water involves two basic considerations:

Reprinted with permission of the author and publisher from *Ground Water*, v. 6, no. 3, p. 10-13, 1968. Copyright 1968 National Water Well Association, Inc.

1. The nature of contaminants in each of the general classes of material.

2. The fate of each contaminant in water percolating downward through the biologically active mantle of the earth or in water translated laterally as ground water in saturated aquifer sands and gravels.

To these may be added the question of contaminants in water moving through fractured strata or dissolution channels. However, in this latter case the "hazards" of manmade pollution may be directly assumed from the nature of the contaminants in five classes of material listed, for while phenomena such as sedimentation absorption, time-decay, and the like may reduce the concentration of contaminants, the hazard remains. Hazard prevention, therefore, is related to management of wastes above ground—a subject beyond the scope of this paper.

Therefore we turn to the nature of contaminants in the previously mentioned five arbitrary classes of man's wastes, and to their movement with percolating water. In this, more attention is given to what fractions get through than to the scientific aspects of removal, which are discussed elsewhere (McGauhey and Others, 1966).

Organic and Inorganic Particles

The fact that ground water is derived from rain falling through an atmosphere containing dust particles and bacteria, passing through a soil mantle containing bacteria, and organic and inorganic particles, and yet historically has been notable for its clarity tells us that suspended matter is not a ground-water contaminant to be expected from man's activities. Such, indeed, is shown to be the case in numerous experiments with soils and waste waters from cities, industries and agriculture.

Microorganisms

Bacteria: Not only has ground water resulting from percolation or moving through aquifer sands been noted for its clarity, its traditional purity is also well known. This does not mean that all ground water is uncontaminated, because the microgeology of the earth is not always favorable. Certainly, bacteria will flow with water in fissures just as readily as in pipes at similar velocities, although gravity and time are against bacterial contamination of an outcropping ground water. Thus contamination with pathogenic bacteria must always, but not in all situations, be considered as a "hazard" to ground-water quality if nondisinfected sewage effluents are carelessly managed. However, where a protective mantle of soil is involved, bacteria behave as other particulate matter and are removed by such forces as sedimentation, entrapment, and adsorption. Studies of the movement of bacteria with percolating water have been widely reported in the literature. For example, the historic work of A. M. Rawn and associates (McGauhey and Others, 1966, pp. 157-158) in Los Angeles County found bacteria in sewage removed in from 3 to 7 feet of quite coarse soil. Pilot infiltration ponds at Lodi, California (McGauhey and Others, 1966, p. 42) gave the same results for a fine soil. More recently, the well-known Santee Project at San Diego reported the removal of coliform bacteria in 200 feet of travel of water in quite coarse gravel.

When injected directly into a water-bearing stratum, coliform organisms have been found (McGauhey and Others, 1966, p. 135 and p. 180) to travel only limited distances—less than 100 feet at Richmond, California. These are but a fraction of the references that support the conclusion that under any circumstances where normal soil bacteria do not reach the ground water, man's activities do not pose a bacterial "hazard" to ground-water quality. However, where fractures or dissolution channels reach the soil surface and transport water underground, sewage disinfection is necessary if released waters are with certainty to pose no hazard to ground-water quality.

Viruses: Viruses are known to be present in sewage, but until quite recent years there was no evidence in the literature relative to their movement with percolating water. Being more resistant to chlorine than are enteric bacteria, the possibility of viral contamination of ground water has long been entertained. Recently, however, studies at the Santee Project (McGauhey and Others, 1966, pp. 164-165 and pp. 194-195) have shown viruses to be removed in less than 200 feet of flow through a gravel bed. These and other (McGauhey and Others, 1966) data support the conclusion that viral contamination of ground water is no more of a hazard than bacterial contamination.

Chemical Products of Biodegradation

Organic solids in sewage, whether from ground garbage, vegetable and meat trimmings, or from the human body, differ from the natural contribution of organic matter to the soil only in that they are associated with man's activities and may reach the soil in varying degrees of degradation. Fundamentally they are proteinaceous in nature and under aerobic conditions oxidize to normal nitrates, sulfates, carbonates, phosphates. etc. Along the way there may be ammonia, nitrites, and similar unoxidized compounds. Under anaerobic conditions degradation products include amino acids and a considerable spectrum of intermediate compounds of notable fragrance and unpleasant taste. Organic molecules themselves are heavily adsorbed on many soils (McGauhey and Others, 1966, p. 109 and p. 197); hence they behave very much as particulate matter and there is little likelihood of contamination of ground water by migrating undegraded organic matter of sewage origin. The question is then one of the degree of degradation occurring in a soil system and the nature of the products produced.

Biodegradable organic solids applied to a soil quickly develop a heavy growth of bacteria in the top centimeter or so of the soil. This serves as a reactor in which biostabilization of compounds occurs. It also acts as a clogging zone to limit the rate of infiltration. Under aerobic conditions oxidized compounds result. If it becomes anaerobic, ferric sulfide is also produced, which as a particulate matter, helps to clog the soil completely. Therefore, infiltration is essentially precluded and intermediate compounds which might cause tastes and odors and bacterial aftergrowths cannot reach the ground water.

In high rate direct injection experiments at Richmond, California, partially degraded soluble organic compounds were forced into an aquifer beyond the bacterially active zone and traveled with ground water to support bacterial life when again pumped to the surface (McGauhey and Others, 1966, p. 180). Protection against such migration in soil, however, is the normal situation. For example, measurements of degradable material passing through sand and gravel columns reported by Robeck (McGauhey and Others, 1966, p. 211) showed that from a septic tank effluent all BOD and 90 percent of the COD was removed.

Of the decomposition products, ammonia is notably adsorbed on soil, where it displaces calcium, magnesium, sodium and potassium ions which are then carried away by percolating water. Later the ammonia is oxidized to nitrates by microbial activity and so becomes soluble and free to move with water. Phosphates too are adsorbed and taken out in the top horizons of soil. Numerous data show that when sewage is applied to a soil the result is simply an increase in the sulfates, bicarbonates, nitrates and other anions and cations normally found in ground water. Thus in summary it may be said that contamination of ground water by degradable organics is largely confined to an increase in concentration of normal ground-water ions.

Dissolved Chemicals of Industrial and Commercial Origin

Chemicals of industrial and commercial origin may reach the earth with municipal sewage, industrial wastes, agricultural fertilization, and the use of pesticides and herbicides for a number of purposes. Prior to 1965, ABS was the principal example of commercial products used in the household which might reach the ground water with domestic sewage effluents. Although degradable in soil systems, its residence time was not always adequate to prevent migration with percolating water. Adoption of the more degradable LAS, however, removed this problem of contamination. Hence from a commercial formulation the phosphates might be expected to be adsorbed on soil and the detergent biodegraded to an inorganic sulfate, which will travel with percolating water or with moving ground water.

Of the agricultural chemicals, commercial fertilizers are perhaps the most significant. Recently (San Francisco Chronicle, January 25, 1967) the State Health Department of California reported concentrations of nitrate of 176 mg/1 in ground waters in California's San Joaquin Valley and warned against its use for young babies. The recommended (P.H.S.) maximum of 45 mg/1 has been observed elsewhere (Tucker and Others, 1961) in recent years to produce intoxication of livestock on high nitrogen diets.

The effect of fertilization of land can therefore involve both the displacement of alkaline ions by ammonia and the subsequent migration of nitrates derived from residual ammonia or direct application of nitrates.

Perhaps the most serious effect of man's use of water is a buildup in concentration of the salts normally found in surface waters, soils and ground water. Above all others, this seems to be the greatest of manmade hazards to ground-water quality. It begins perhaps with the concentration of salts by evaporation of water from reservoirs, canals, and industrial cooling, plus regeneration of water softeners, water distillation, etc. This concentrate is then applied to the land in irrigation where it leaches out more salts. Percolating downward or flowing as return flows in open channels, some of it percolates to the ground water. Heavy use of ground water recycles an appreciable amount of water and the net result in the semiarid West is a continous increase of the salinity of the ground-water resource. The hazard of manmade contamination here is that although we have learned how to prevent the poisoning of land from our irrigation practice, we may go the way of Mesopotamia by poisoning the water instead.

In addition to the buildup of normal salts, industrial wastes contribute a hazard to ground-water quality by delivering a vast and ever changing spectrum of ions and compounds which move with percolating water. Some of the most commonly deplored are phenols, picric acid, metal ions such as Fe, Mn, Cr, oil field brines, oils, tar residues, weed killer wastes, and a host of miscellaneous chemicals. Instances of long distance travel of such materials are to be found in the literature. Control of discharges is the normal method of preventing ground-water contamination with industrial wastes, but it must be recognized that the wastes from many industrial processes always represent a hazard to ground water through accidental spill, carelessness, or deliberate discharge, as well as through ignorance of the behavior of the waste from some newly developed processes.

Commercial use of industry's products presents a varied picture. Attention has already been called to detergents and commercial fertilizers. Of much concern today are the so-called exotic organics—the refractory compounds—of which pesticides and herbicides are the most cited example. While a great deal of speculation exists concerning the ability of pesticides to move with percolating water, and most of the literature deals with surface-water contamination, there is some evidence of hazard to ground waters. Walton (Proceedings National Conference on Water Pollution, 1960) of the U.S.P.H.S. noted a case near Henderson, Colorado, where ground water contaminated by arsenals which eventually formed 2, 4-D traveled three miles in eight years to affect crops and eventually seriously affect some 60 square miles. At Montebello, California, seepage of 2, 4-D from a manufacturing plant persisted in

water for five years after the plant ceased operation.

Leachings from Solid Waste Fills

When the soil mantle of the earth is looked upon as the infiltrative surface from which ground water derives, it is evident that the necessary concentration of solid wastes in landfills creates a local pocket of potential infection overlying the ground water. Therefore, man's activity in managing his solid wastes must be examined in relation to ground-water contamination.

A hazard to ground-water quality might be created by landfill both directly and indirectly. A direct hazard exists, except in unusual geological situations, in the disposal of old cylinder oil, cleaning fluid, and miscellaneous liquid chemicals within a dump. Although good practice, and local ordinances, prohibits such discharges, one need not become particularly familiar with dump operation to observe that it does occur.

Assuming that contact between ground water and fill material is prohibited—a quite generally valid assumption—an indirect hazard exists in most landfill operations. This is the possibility that poor operation will permit rain water or flood waters to enter the fill and so dissolve soluble dry chemicals which might be present, leach iron and various earth minerals from incinerator ashes, pick up soluble fractions of organic degradation and transport them to the ground-water table. Good operation, involving surface drainage of the finished fill, is unfortunately not enough to remove this indirect threat. Cracking of the fill cover due to shrinkage of the fill, poor maintenance of the finished fill during the first decade or two after its completion, and seismic disturbances are among the ways in which avenues of entry of water may be opened with time.

More recent studies (In-situ investigation of movements of gases produced from decomposing refuse, 1966) of diffusion of gases from fills into the surrounding soil show the possibility of carbon dioxide from the decomposing fill material becoming dissolved in percolating water and so increasing its aggressiveness to the primary rocks from which the content of calcium and magnesium bicarbonates in ground water is normally derived.

SUMMARY

Ground water may derive a wide variety of

materials from man's waste producing activities. Chemicals characteristic of normal ground waters may be increased in concentration from the degradation of organic solids in human and industrial wastes, and from the storage, transport, and use of water, particularly in irrigation and industry. Similar compounds might come from leaching of a solid waste landfill. Toxic, odorous, and bad tasting compounds may reach the ground water with industrial wastes, or with municipal effluents containing such wastes or the residues of industrial products used in commerce. The variety of such wastes is endless but includes all types of liquid or soluble chemicals. Particular concern is felt for the pesticide residues. Chemical residues of various nature may come also from their illegal disposal in landfills or dumps. Disease producing bacteria or viruses are no particular hazard, nor is particulate matter which might produce turbidity. However, if fractures or fissures bypass the biologically active mantle of the earth and lead water directly from the surface to the ground water or spring, microorganisms may join the soluble chemicals as contaminants.

In general, all of man's waste producing activities would create "manmade hazards" to ground water if accident, carelessness, or lack of vigilance and constraint were permitted to prevail. The most serious current hazard of man's activities lies in the buildup of salinity of the ground water to levels inimical to all beneficial uses to which such water is put.

REFERENCES

In-situ investigation of movements of gases produced from decomposing refuse. 1966. Fifth and Final Report. Engineering-Science, Inc., prepared for State Water Quality Control Board, November.

McGauhey, P. H., R. B. Krone and J. H. Winneberger. 1966. Soil mantle as a wastewater treatment system: review of literature. SERL. Report 66-7. Sanit. Eng. Research Lab., Univ. of Calif., Berkeley, September.

Proceedings, National Conference on Water Pollution. 1960. USPHS, Washington, D. C., December 12-14.

Tucker, J. M., D. R. Cordy, L. J. Berry, W. A. Harvey and T. C. Fuller. 1961. Nitrate poisoning in livestock. Circular 506. California Agricultural Experiment Station Extension Service, Univ. of Calif.

35. EFFECTS OF MINE DRAINAGE ON GROUND WATER

GROVER H. EMRICH and GARY L. MERRITT

INTRODUCTION

The large deposits of coal in the eastern United States have been the foundation for the industrialization of the area. These coal deposits extend from northeastern Pennsylvania down to Alabama and as far west as the Great Plain. The deposits were originally developed by deep mining but since the end of World War II have been developed primarily by strip-mining.

One of the major problems in the mining of coal is the occurrence and handling of water. Wherever possible, the deep mines were developed so that this water would drain out of the mine by gravity. After mines were abandoned, the drainage of water continued.

The character of the drainage from coal mines varies from area to area and from coal seam to coal seam (Table 1). It is commonly high in iron and sulfates, low in pH, and high in acidity. When this drainage flows into a stream, it can pollute the stream by destroying aquatic life and making the water unusable for municipal and industrial water supply. Water pollution control programs have been concerned primarily with protecting and cleaning up surface waters polluted by coal mine drainage. A recent study in the Toms Run area indicates that the drainage from the coal mines is affecting not only the surface water, but in many areas also the ground water.

TABLE 1. CHARACTER OF DRAINAGE FROM COAL MINES

pH	2.3 →	7.3
Acidity	0 →	8,000 mg/l
Iron (Fe)	10 →	2,000 mg/l
Sulfate (SO$_4$)	20 →	3,000 mg/l

FORMATION OF ACID MINE DRAINAGE

Associated with the coal beds is the iron sulfide mineral pyrite, commonly also called

Reprinted with permission of authors and publisher from *Ground Water*, v. 7, no. 7, p. 27-32, 1969. Copyright 1969 National Water Well Association, Inc.

fool's gold. This mineral usually occurs in high concentrations in the upper foot to 18 inches of the coal seam and in the overlying black shales. In a few instances it may also occur in sandstones above the coal seam. Because pyrite produces a high sulfur content in the coal, it is commonly left behind in the coal mine or in the refuse banks around the coal mine. This material is the source of the acid, iron and sulfate in mine drainage (Figure 1). Before the mining of coal, the rocks above the coal seam are usually completely saturated with ground water. As the mining progresses, the overlying rocks are fractured and the ground water drains through the rocks (Figure 2). When the pyrite is exposed to air, it begins to oxidize.

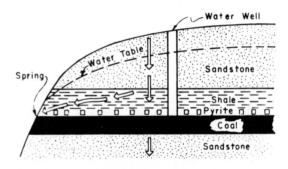

Figure 1. Effects of coal mining on ground water—before mining.

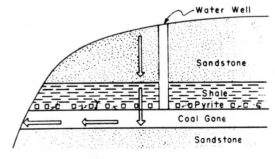

Figure 2. Effects of coal mining on ground water—after mining.

In many cases when mines are first developed, drainage from the mine is slightly alkaline with low iron and sulfate concentrations. As the mining progresses, the pyrite is exposed to air, oxidizes, the oxidized material dissolves, and the drainage from the mine becomes acid. When moisture is present, the oxidation of the mineral pyrite is expressed in the following simplified formula:

$$FeS_2 + H_2O + O_2 \longrightarrow Fe(OH)_3 + H_2SO_4$$

(Pyrite)   (Water)   (Oxygen)   (Iron Hydroxide)   (Sulfuric Acid)

Water flowing over the rocks picks up these salts and carries them out of the mine in the form of acid mine drainage.

In the western parts of Pennsylvania and parts of West Virginia, Ohio, and westward, coal beds are associated with limestone beds. When the mine drainage flows through these rocks, it is neutralized through reaction with the limestones. The drainage that would occur from a mine under these conditions could have a pH up to 7, but would be high in iron and sulfate. Although these conditions do not produce a high acidity in the water, they do increase the mineralization of the water.

POLLUTIONAL PROBLEMS FROM COAL MINING

Acid mine drainage causes pollution by increasing the total mineralization of the water which decreases its ability to support aquatic life or to be used for industrial or public water supplies. Pennsylvania now has over 2,300 miles of streams that are adversely affected by coal mine drainage—which is the result of its topography, the widespread development of coal mining, mining practices, and its hydrogeologic conditions. These streams are normally acid. Many have a pH less than 4.0. In some of these streams, the iron concentration is greater than several hundred milligrams per liter, and the sulfates are greater than 1,000 milligrams per liter.

As a result of amendments to the Pennsylvania Clean Streams Law in 1965, Sanitary Water Board Regulations now require that a discharge from an active coal mine contain no more than 7 milligrams per liter of iron, have a pH between 6 and 9, and have no acidity. Unfortunately, the vast majority of Pennsylvania's mine drainage comes from abandoned coal mines. The cessation of coal mining does not necessarily stop the pollution of the surface water or the ground water. It will take decades before most of these waters again become usable. Programs to abate this form of pollution in the surface waters of Pennsylvania are estimated to cost over one billion dollars.

Coal mining's immediate effect on ground water is generally the lowering of the local ground-water table (Figure 2). In many cases where underlain by the coal measures, ground water occurs under perched conditions. Mining of the coal will fracture the overlying rocks and allow drainage of the perched ground water. All water wells that have been developed in this perched ground water will immediately go dry and, in many cases, will not return even after the coal mining has ceased.

In some cases, when the coal is mined, the underlying or associated ground water is not drained from the rocks. The acid mine drainage formed in the coal mine will then flow into the associated ground water through joints, fractures, or open wells. It will increase the mineralization of the ground water, raise the iron and sulfate concentration, and lower the pH. Special care must be taken by all well drillers in areas that are underlain by coal seams to make sure that the well is cased and grouted through the coal measures, so that it does not serve as a conduit for the downward migration of waters from the coal mines. When oil and gas wells or water wells are abandoned in areas underlain by coal seams, they should be completely grouted and records kept as to their location. The past abandonment of open wells now allows the migration of acid mine drainage downward from one aquifer to another, increasing the probability of ground-water pollution.

TOMS RUN STUDY

There has been much speculation in the past concerning the effect of coal mining on ground water. An intensive local study was conducted in the Toms Run area of Pennsylvania to determine how coal mining has affected the local ground water and its possible connection with surface-water quality.

The Toms Run Basin is located in the northeast portion of Clarion County, Pennsylvania, approximately 63 miles southeast of Erie and 95 miles northwest of Pittsburgh (Figure 3). This basin contains one of the few remaining stands of virgin white pine and has been developed as a State park. Water pollution from springs, flowing wells, and coal mine drainage is inhibiting full use of the park.

Toms Run
Drainage Basin

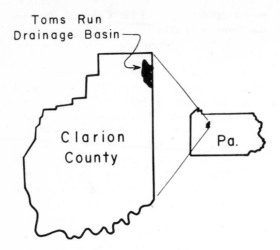

Figure 3. Location of Toms Run Basin.

The area has been mined for coal and drilled for gas and oil for almost 100 years. Gas and oil wells have been drilled throughout the entire basin. Coal mining is limited to two areas in the basin: near the headwaters of Toms Run, and along the southwestern boundary of Toms Run (Figure 4).

There are numerous secondary iron deposits within the drainage basin. All the deposits are in the west half of the basin (Figure 4). Along the East and West Branches of Toms Run there are iron deposits at two flowing abandoned oil and gas wells. Along West Hefren Run is the largest secondary iron deposit around a large flowing spring. All other deposits are associated with small discharges or seeps. All these discharges are rich in iron, sulfate, and acid and were originally attributed to deep flows from abandoned oil and gas wells.

GEOLOGY

Rocks of Devonian, Mississippian, and Pennsylvanian-age underlie the Toms Run area (Figure 5). Oil and gas wells have been drilled to the Bradford Sands (Devonian) at a depth of 2,300 feet. The rocks of Mississippian and Pennsylvanian age form a multiaquifer system—three major aquifers separated by siltstone and shale beds. The Mississippian Burgoon sandstone is the lowermost aquifer in the Toms Run area. It grades up to a shale at the top. The Pennsylvanian-aged rocks are the Conno-

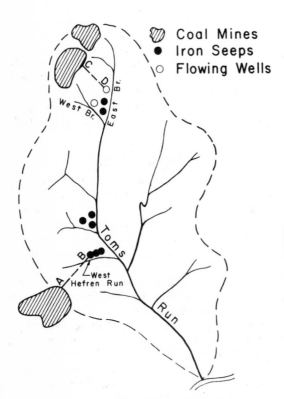

Figure 4. Map of Toms Run Basin.

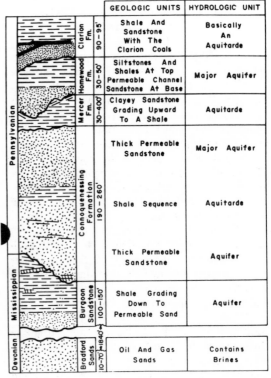

Figure 5. Geologic section and hydrologic units.

quenessing, Mercer, Homewood, and Clarion Formations. The Connoquenessing Formation has two sandstone units that act as aquifers, separated by a shale unit that acts as an aquitarde. The upper unit is one of the two major aquifers for private water supply in the area. The Mercer Formation is mainly shale with local coal stringers and acts as an aquitarde. The Homewood Formation has permeable sandstones at the base with shales and siltstones at the top. This sandstone is the other major source for private water supply in the area. The Clarion Formation contains the only mineable coal in the basin. This coal is underlain by tight sandstone and overlain by shale coal. This unit acts as an aquitarde.

The rocks in the Toms Run drainage basin are folded into a very shallow downwarp or syncline (Figure 6). The strike of the axis of the syncline is North 55 degrees East. Most of the rocks in the basin dip to the south and southeast. Although the coal beds along the southwestern edge are mostly outside the Toms Run drainage basin, they are within the structural basin and strike toward West Hefren Run.

GROUND-WATER QUALITY

The ground-water quality in the Toms Run Basin is the key to understanding the ground-water flow system and the sources of pollution (Table 2).

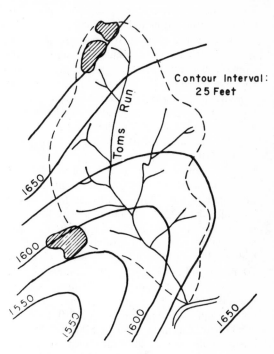

Figure 6. Structure contours on top of Clarion coal.

TABLE 2. GROUND WATER QUALITY IN THE TOMS RUN DRAINAGE BASIN

AQUIFERS	pH	Sulfate (SO_4)	Iron (Fe)	Chloride (Cl)
Burgoon Sandstone and Lower Sandstone Unit of the Connoquenessing Formation	5.2 to 6.8	1 to 10	0.0 to 16.0	4 to 10.0
Upper Sandstone Unit of the Connoquenessing				
Nonmining areas	6.3 to 6.8	4 to 13	3 to 16	1 to 7
Areas near mining	2.9 to 5.4	30 to 620	25 to 160	1 to 7
Homewood Formation				
Nonmining areas	6.5 to 6.7	10 to 15	10 to 15	0 to 2
Areas near mining	3.0 to 5.5	39 to 80	20 to 70	0 to 2
Discharges from Coal Mines	2.6 to 3.3	2450 to 4400	200 to 500	0 to 2
Discharges from Abandoned Oil and Gas Wells	2.9 to 6.3	21 to 678	10 to 140	5 to 8
Brines from Active Gas and Oil Wells	5.3 to 6.1	67 to 253	67 to 253	42,000 to 200,000

The ground-water quality in the Burgoon Sandstone and in the Lower Sandstone unit of the Connoquenessing Formation are the same. The water in these aquifers has a pH from 5.2 to 6.8 and is low in iron and chlorides.

In areas not affected by coal mining ground water in the Upper Sandstone unit of the Connoquenessing Formation has a pH from 6.3 to 6.8, low sulfates (3 to 16 mg/1), chloride (1 to 7 mg/1), and relatively low total iron (4 to 1 mg/1). Areas affected by coal mining have water with a low pH (2.9 to 5.4), low chlorides (1 to 7 mg/1), high sulfates (30 to 620), and total iron (25 to 160).

The ground water in the Homewood Formation in areas not affected by coal mining has a pH from 6.5 to 6.7, low sulfates (10 to 15 mg/1), chloride (0 to 2 mg/1), and relatively low total iron (10 to 15 mg/1). In areas affected by coal mining the water has a lower pH (3.0 to 5.5), higher sulfates (39 to 80 mg/1), total iron (20 to 70 mg/1), and low chlorides (0 to 2 mg/1).

Mine drainage from the coal mines has a very low pH (2.6 to 3.3) and low chlorides (0 to 2 mg/1), and very high sulfate (2,450 to 4,400 mg/1) and total iron (200 to 500 mg/1). Obviously, in the area of the coal mines, the ground water has been degraded by drainage from the coal mines.

Discharges from the abandoned oil and gas wells, the main sources of pollution, were thought to be brines from the deep oil and gas horizons. Water from these wells (in the area of the secondary iron deposits) has a pH from 2.9 to 6.3, high sulfates (24 to 678 mg/1), total iron (10 to 140 mg/1), and low chlorides (5 to 8 mg/1).

In contrast, brine from active gas and oil wells in the Toms Run area has a pH from 5.3 to 6.0, total iron from 100.0 to 1000.0 mg/1, sulfates from 67 to 253 mg/1, and very high chlorides from 42,000 to 200,000 mg/1. Thus, the water from the abandoned oil and gas wells is not coming from the deep brines, but rather from shallow coal mine drainage.

INTERPRETATION

Drainage from coal mines has affected the water quality of various aquifers in the area. Where affected, the iron and sulfate concentrations are too high for drinking water and require extensive filtration, softening, and settling before use.

The drainage in the vicinity of the strip mines moves down to the lower aquifers along joints, fractures, and especially old abandoned gas and oil wells. This can be seen on two cross sections in the basin (Figure 4): cross section A-B in the headwaters and cross section C-D along the west side. Drainage from coal mines at the headwater of Toms Run moves down through wells to the lower units, laterally within the aquifers, then upwards to land surface and discharges from the flowing oil and gas wells (Figure 7a). Along the southwestern boundary of the drainage basin (Figure 7b) the mine drainage moves down to the Upper Sandstone of the Connoquenessing Formation and along the strike of the formation until it discharges as a contact spring along West Hefren Run.

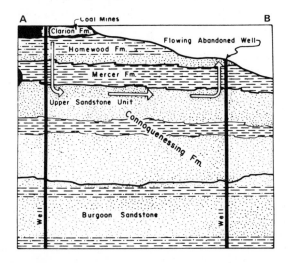

Figure 7a. Cross section A-B—flow from an abandoned well.

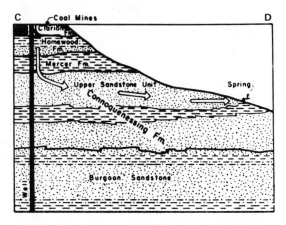

Figure 7b. Cross section C-D—natural seepage.

CONCLUSIONS

The mining of coal in many cases produces an acid drainage with a high concentration of iron and sulfate. This drainage may discharge directly to surface water or move into the ground water and pollute it. In a study of the Toms Run area, Pennsylvania, it was found that the coal mine drainage moved down to underlying aquifers through joints, fractures and abandoned oil and gas wells and polluted the ground water. It moves down the hydraulic gradient of the aquifer and discharges as iron-rich springs or flowing wells.

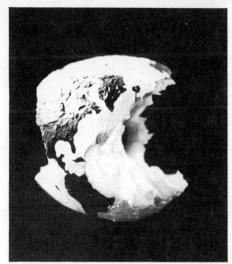

Part Five
RESOURCES
AND CONSERVATION

The fundamental question involving mineral resources is supply. Can we always find enough to supply our needs by increasing the price and mining lower grade ore, or will we exhaust our supply of mineral "X" at 12 noon, January 5, 2048? These two viewpoints are presented by Holman (Selection 37) and Cloud (Selection 39). The article by C. K. Leith (Selection 36), *Conservation of Minerals,* which was written in 1935, contains some time estimates of reserves that have long since been exceeded. This selection provides historical perspective for the question of mineral supply, as does Holman's article of 20 years ago.

The supply of mineral resources available on planet earth is finite. With an increasing population, we can no longer hold to the concept, developed in earlier days, of a boundless supply of minerals. Overconsumption or waste of our finite resources for the current benefit of the people who possess the capability to exploit them cannot be allowed. Present rates of consumption dictate minimal waste, wise use, and reuse of minerals now and in the future. We must learn to recycle mineral resources. This, if accompanied by a static population, will help to solve our resource problem as well as part of the waste disposal problem. The sea may provide a supplemental source of mineral resources, but only for a relatively small number of commodities (Selections 42 and 43).

Man must look with urgency at the energy resources available on earth for present and future use. Fossil fuels are the dominant source of energy utilized in the world today. Although the world's mineable reserves of fossil fuels are large, at the rate at which consumption is increasing, it will not take long to finish off the unconsumed reserves. Of the remaining energy sources, geothermal power offers some promise in certain localities (Selections 44, 45, and 46). Utilization of solar energy does not look promising at this time. This leaves only nuclear energy with enough potential to meet the high-level energy requirements of the future.

In order to obtain the mineral resources required for our standard of living a certain price in environmental damage is usually paid. This price is now often too great, as it has also been in the past. With proper utilization it can and must be kept at a minimum. Selections offered here on land reclamation present some of the problems and costs of reclaiming strip-mined land. Included are two papers written by representatives of industry, a viewpoint which frequently is not considered.

The cost of reclamation may be high, but the price of inaction in the past may be even higher. Strip mining has left many acres of utterly ravaged land, which in many cases will remain "orphan" land. The effects of strip mining frequently extend beyond the boundaries of a mine area and are present for many years after mining is concluded. Examples of these are acid-mine drainage and siltation of streams. In these cases the populace still pays for the neglect of yesterday.

Legislation is being considered and enacted at local, state, and national levels to restrict or ban strip mining. Should all strip mining be banned? This question is one which must be considered very carefully. Assuming that the insatiable demands for energy by an increasing population persist and conversion to another source of energy does not take place immediately, we will have to continue to utilize fossil fuels. The price of a complete switch from surface to subsurface mining may be too high in terms of increased manpower, energy, and cost necessary for underground mining. Surface mining, if accompanied by good reclamation, may in many cases be the best or only method of obtaining the desired mineral resources. Proper reclamation with multiple or sequential land use, particularly in quarries and pits near urban areas, can sometimes provide more valuable property than that which existed prior to mining or quarrying. A special tax should probably be imposed on surface-mined commodities, with proceeds utilized for reclamation and development of orphan lands. At any rate, mining of any kind should not be carried out without careful preplanning, including environmental impact statements which show that every conceivable environmental implication has been thoroughly investigated.

Mineral Resources

36. CONSERVATION OF MINERALS

C. K. LEITH

As an abstraction the idea of conservation of natural resources is widely accepted by the public. In fact, active opposition to the idea is almost nonexistent. It is a safe and attractive phrase for publicists, politicians and party platforms, as well as a plausible caption for many laws. Yet for most people conservation remains a vague profession of faith, not tied down to realities or practical programs. To specialists in forests, parks, game, recreation, soils, water resources and minerals, conservation means many different things. In a recent survey at the University of Wisconsin it was found that conservation was receiving attention in twenty-seven different courses, in nearly as many departments, and that in no two of them was the subject defined in the same terms. The many so-called conservation laws in our state and federal statutes reflect an equally chaotic condition. Text-book definitions of conservation, in the very nature of the case, must be so generalized that they fail to convey any clear notion of the practical problems involved. To illustrate the difficulty of simplifying the concept of conservation I quote to you an attempt made by the twenty-seven units of the University of Wisconsin to agree on a general platform:

> Conservation is the effort to insure to society the maximum present and future benefit from the use of natural resources. It involves the inventory and evaluation of natural resources; calls for the maintenance of the renewable resources at a level commensurate with the needs of society; and requires the substitution, where the conservation of human energy permits, of renewable or inexhaustible resources for those which are non-renewable, and of the more abundant non-renewable resources for the less abundant ones. It not only seeks to eliminate waste of resources if use is economically feasible, but also looks forward to

Extracted with permission of the publisher from "Conservation of Minerals" by C. K. Leith, *Science*, v. 82, no. 2119, p. 109-117, 1935.

improvements in techniques of production and use, and requires that there be prompt and proper adjustments to advances in technology. It thus appears that conservation involves the balancing of natural resources against human resources and the rights of the present generation against the rights of future generations. It necessitates, moreover, the harmonizing of the procedures and objectives of conservation with the conditions of the present or future economic order, and calls for a careful allocation of duties and powers among private and public agencies.

To students of conservation this definition is comprehensive and tangible, but to the public it can scarcely be other than an euphonious abstraction. It is almost inevitable that plans and legislation must be developed piecemeal from many standpoints, and that the synthesis of the parts into a consistent program for natural resources as a whole must be a slow and difficult task on which we have barely started. Even within the special fields there are still large gaps between general concepts and workable plans.

I propose to-day to review briefly the practical problems of conservation of one group of natural resources—our minerals—a field in which we start from a well-established body of facts, sufficiently limited and defined to be studied with some degree of objectivity. Some of the ideas developed from the study of minerals may be found useful in approaching the problems of conservation of other natural resources.

I shall draw freely, but not solely, from the preliminary report recently issued by the Planning Committee for Mineral Policy, which was appointed by the President to formulate a national mineral policy. The Planning Committee is also acting as the Mineral Section of the National Resources Board. Its report was a part of a more general statement by the National Resources Board which was submitted to the President early in the year and by him transmitted to Congress with the statement that it constitutes "a remarkable foundation for what we hope will be a permanent policy of orderly development in every part of the United States."

FACTUAL STATEMENT OF
THE MINERAL SITUATION

First, a few salient facts of the mineral situation bearing on the problem of conservation. Ours is the age of the power machine, and minerals furnish both the power and machine. Minerals are a non-reproducible and exhaustible resource—a one-crop resource; they are limited in quantity; they are fixed geographically for all time; they are not distributed equally among the countries of the world. The United States stands far in front in the amount and variety of its resources, but still depends on foreign sources for part or all of its supplies of about 20 industrial minerals. The flush of discovery in the United States is passed, and the main geographic outlines of the ultimate mineral picture are now pretty well established. Reserves can be approximately measured. Discovery has not stopped, but the rate has been slowing down for a considerable time. Of 33 metal-mining districts that have yielded the greatest wealth to date only five have been discovered since 1900 and none at all since 1907. The coal and iron fields are pretty thoroughly mapped. The chance of finding another Mesabi Range or another Pittsburgh coal field is small indeed. The rate of discovery of oil and gas still continues high, but the geological limitations are pretty well understood, and the chances of finding another East Texas or Kettleman Hills are not promising.

Finally, the United States leads the world in the speed with which it is exploiting and ex-hausting its resources. For the metals and fuels, despite a magnificent endowment, depletion is further advanced than even mining men generally realize. In gold the peak of American production was passed in 1915, and despite the enormous stimulus of falling commodity prices and devalu-ation of the dollar, production to-day is still far below the pre-war level. In silver, also, we seem to have passed the peak. The copper mines of Michigan have gone a mile below the surface, by far the deepest copper mines in all the world, and at those depths, despite the ablest of engineering, they are quite unable to compete with many low-cost districts here and abroad. Mining at Butte has reached deep levels and has long since passed its peak. The great tri-state zinc district of Missouri, Oklahoma and Kansas is no longer expanding, and no notable geographic extensions

are in sight. In the oil industry the glut produced by east Texas makes us forget the hundreds of dead or dying pools in other areas. The South-west gas production hides the decline of many eastern districts and the death of the Indiana gas belt. Even in coal, one of the most abundant of our resources, it is estimated that the anthracite fields of Pennsylvania are 29 per cent. exhausted. While the total supply of bituminous coal is huge, the exhaustion of the best of the bituminous beds, such as the Moshannon, the Big Vein, Pocahontas, New River and Pittsburgh, is well advanced. About half of the known high-grade iron ore of the Lake Superior region has already been produced.

The speed of our attack on mineral resources is indicated generally by the fact that the amount produced since the opening of the century far surpasses the total of all preceding history of the United States. In this respect we are literally digging ourselves into our natural environment on a scale which has no precedent in history.

In terms of years of measured reserves of present commerical grades the United States has supplies of oil, zinc and lead for from 15 to 20 years. Its copper supply is good for about 40 years. The total for iron ore, including its lower grades, such as Alabama, is good for hundreds of years, but the known reserves of high-grade Mesabi ores now supplying about half of our requirements will last about 40 years, and for the rest of the Lake Superior region, supplying about 30 per cent. of our requirements, the figure is less than 20 years. Coal reserves of all kinds, high and low grade, favorably and unfavorably located, will last 4,000 years, but the kinds we are now using in favorable location are measured in a century or two.

Minerals in which the United States is wholly or partly deficient include antimony, asbestos, chromite, manganese, mercury, nickel, tin, tungsten and ten or twelve others.

Further discovery and the use of lower grade resources will extend the life of most of these resources, but the range of possibilities is now pretty well understood, and with maximum allowance for such extensions, the figures are sufficiently small, when compared with what we hope to be the life of the nation, as to be matters of public concern.

The depletion of mineral reserves here sketched has been accompanied by huge losses, some avoidable and some unavoidable. It is estimated that not more than 50 per cent. of oil is recovered from a pool, even under efficient recovery practices; where extraction methods are wasteful of gas and reservoir energy, a commonly accepted average is 10 to 20 per cent. In one field a billion feet of gas are being blown into the air daily—enough to supply the United Kingdom twice over and forty times as much as all the Scandinavian countries use together. In twelve years in California the quantity of gas known to be lost was about one third of that produced for commercial use. The average loss in the recovery of coal is 35 per cent., as estimated by the Bureau of Mines. The mining of iron, copper, lead and zinc—in fact, of most minerals—shows waste, due to the necessity for selective mining to meet competitive price conditions or the burden of excessive taxation. In the Lake Superior region large tonnages of low-grade iron ores have been left behind in the progress of mining, many of which will never be recovered after the operations close down. The list of specific losses could be extended indefinitely. Loss of resource is not a theory or an insignificant incident; it is a demonstrable fact, which can be documented in detail and which runs into large figures.

CONCLUSION

The mineral conservation problem of the United States comes down to the following elements:

(1) Continuance of technological and scientific improvements already under way.

(2) The balancing of supply and demand in our so-called surplus industries at a price level which will permit of proper conservational practice; this to be accomplished by voluntary cooperative efforts of the industry under government supervision, through legislation which will exempt them from the anti-trust law; the exemptions from the anti-trust law in the interest of conservation to be specifically defined and public supervision to be provided to make sure that the wastes on the basis of which exemption is claimed can and will be eliminated.

(3) The legalization of some method of coordinating the highly chaotic efforts of the individual states under their police powers, and support any collective efforts the states may attempt. Much of the authority necessary for production control now exists only in the police powers of the states. Since the Supreme Court decision, Washington is now struggling with the problem of finding authority for any national control. On the outcome of this major issue of federal versus state rights will depend largely the success of any effective program of conservation.

(4) Federal control of interstate shipments of minerals shipped in excess of quotas set by the state police powers.

(5) Possible abolition of ad valorem taxes in favor of taxes of one kind or another on current production.

(6) The use of tariffs for the surplus group which will protect any domestic economy built up in the interest of conservation, which may result in some further sacrifice of our already dwindling export trade because of the necessary maintenance of domestic prices above the world level.

(7) For the deficient group of minerals derived in part or in whole from foreign sources, to desist from a tariff program which merely hastens the exhaustion of our limited high-grade supplies and to substitute direct expenditure by the government on the problem of finding additional supplies.

In the last analysis, the practical basis for mineral conservation is voluntary cooperative effort under permissive legislation, which will carry safeguards against its misuse. The natural evolution of the industry, under the driving power of self-interest, has been in the direction of larger commercial units and cooperation. The relatively few large sources of mineral supply create a situation which lends itself to concentration of commercial control and even monopolies for some of our minerals. As the units of the industry, commercial or cooperative, grow in size and power, there is an inevitable growth of public interest and concern. Cooperation and public supervision are complementary and parallel developments which are not in conflict unless one or the other proceeds too fast. It is the hope and belief of our Planning Committee, based on the history of the few cooperative efforts thus far tried, that in the long run enlightened self-interest of the industries and the public interest may be made to coincide in a common program, which will avoid, on the one hand, the extreme of nationalization now gaining so generally in other countries, and on the other, the extreme of unregulated competition which is proving so disastrous both to the industries and to national welfare.

We recognize the fact that private industry has successfully developed the minerals of the United States to an extent never before approximated in the world; that the job on the whole has been done efficiently and without greater wastes or mistakes than were more or less inevitable under existing conditions of enforced competition and widely scattered ownership of the resources; that the record of the mineral industry in the United States warrants the presumption that it should continue to develop so far as possible under private initiative. However, we also believe that our mineral heritage is vested with a public interest in those specific conditions which are distinctly detrimental both to the public and to the industries themselves and which seem beyond the power of the industries themselves to remedy. To be frank, some of us do not think that the brains exist which are competent to produce a fool-proof plan broad enough to cover all the shifting variables of the problem, but, on the other hand, we are not content with a defeatist or drifting attitude, and hope that cooperative planning will produce some if not all of the desired results. Rugged individualism, with all its merits, seems ill-adapted to realize, unaided, the present political and economic requirements of conservation.

37. OUR INEXHAUSTIBLE RESOURCES[1]

EUGENE HOLMAN[2]

I want to talk with you about a concept concerning the quantities of natural resources available for human use. It is a concept which many, including myself, believe in very strongly and which I think merits thoughtful examination by all of us who are in any way connected with natural resource industries.

The mission of practicing geologists, simply stated, is to help find in the earth the materials man needs for civilized life. These materials have a vitally important place in the pattern of human existence, and people frequently fear that they are going to run out of one or another of them. You see this fear reflected in the terms used to describe the materials geologists seek. Those materials are often referred to as "wasting" resources or as "exhaustible" resources. What I want to suggest to you is that the viewpoint expressed in those terms "wasting" and "exhaustible" is a partial viewpoint It does not see to the heart of geology or, indeed, to the heart of any of the activities in which man displays his intellect.

Let us consider whether under certain circumstances we cannot forget our fears and accept the notion of inexhaustible resources.

Let's begin with a quick glance at material progress in the past—in other words, let's look at the record. It shows that from earliest times men have used minerals drawn from the earth. And we see that the availability of larger numbers of minerals, in greater quantities, has progressed by a kind of steplike process.

Let me enlarge for a moment on the picture of progress by a series of steps.

Reprinted with permission of the publisher from *Bulletin of the American Association of Petroleum Geologists*, v. 36, no. 7, July, 1952, p. 1323-1329. Copyright 1952 American Association of Petroleum Geologists.

[1] Read before the joint annual meeting of the American Association of Petroleum Geologists, the Society of Economic Paleontologists and Mineralogists, and the Society of Exploration Geophysicists, at Los Angeles, March 25, 1952.

[2] President, Standard Oil Company (New Jersey).

Another group of scientists who delve in the earth—the archaeologists—have shown us that prehistoric men used axes, drills, and other implements made of flint and other hard stone. With these tools they were able to create simple societies, which, in turn, made possible the accumulation of knowledge about the natural world.

The Stone age developed both the instruments and the knowledge which enabled men to use certain of the softer metals, especially copper and tin. Humanity then stepped up to the Copper and Bronze age. Now man had more tools and more serviceable ones. He could fell trees faster and thus have more buildings for shelter and more vehicles for transport. He could move more widely than before over the earth.

As the men equipped with bronze tools learned more and more about the world, humanity stepped up again—this time to an age of Iron. Now man began fashioning a really formidable array of tools. He had new power to cut, grind, hammer, and otherwise work materials. He could handle masses of material with stronger levers, wedges, pulleys, gears, hooks, eyes, and pincers.

In modern times the age of Iron has given way to the Steel age. And within our own lifetimes there has been superimposed on the Steel age what we may call the age of lightweight metals, plastics and atomic fission.

From the Stone age to the present so great a wealth of scientific information has been amassed—most of it in the past 100 years—that we now have tools and instruments of a power and precision beyond all previous imagination. We have the means to compound, cast, and grind lenses and mirrors that permit us to peer farther than ever before into matter and into space. We command the strength of engines whose ratio of power to weight is constantly being increased. We have machines to produce millions of glass tubes whose miraculous contents harness a stream of electrons to our service.

A notable feature of the steplike pattern of material progress is that it has proceeded at a geometric rate. Each successive age has been shorter than the one before it. The Stone age lasted several hundred thousand years; the Copper and Bronze age, for 4,000 years; the Iron age, 2,500 years. Steel was first made in commercial quantities 95 years ago; and the past twenty years have seen material developments that are almost incredible. It is as though the stairway of advancement was composed of steps with progressively higher risers and narrower treads.

Another outstanding feature in the history of material progress is that each step has been dependent on the one before it. The use of the materials available in one period—and I emphasize that word "use"—has supported societies in which men could accumulate knowledge. Such knowledge then made new quantities and new kinds of material available.

I emphasize the fact that people used the materials available in any period so a fallacy one sometimes finds in connection with the conservation of natural resources will be crystal clear. This fallacy is the concept of conservation as non-use. I am convinced that non-use results only in hobbling progress. It will not result in more natural resources for men to use but less, because it retards the march of scientific knowledge.

Now it goes without saying that I do not advocate reckless squandering of natural resources. What I do advocate is true conservation—which is not hoarding but efficient and intelligent use.

Increasing knowledge operates in a number of ways to expand the natural resources available to us. It helps us to discover new sources of materials which we are already using and in the raw form that is currently useful to us. For example, new techniques like the airborne magnetometer help us to locate oil fields. New knowledge also enables us to extract a material we are already using from raw forms which we were previously unable to process, such as iron from taconite. It also extends supplies of the familiar materials by developing more efficient methods of use. Improved heating units, turbines and internal combustion engines are cases in point here. More knowledge helps us work out means of using materials which have been known but not usable as, for example, titanium. And it discovers or makes entirely new materials that do not exist in nature, such as plastics.

I'd like to enlarge a bit on these examples, and their significance. Take petroleum.

As you are well aware, a great many new sources of oil have been discovered in just the past several years. To mention only a few, there are the Williston basin in North Dakota, the Uinta basin in Utah, the Alberta fields in Canada, the Scurry and Spraberry fields in Texas, in addition to the fields in central Sumatra, southern Iraq, and the Cretaceous fields of western Venezuela. In some of these areas, geologic explorations had gone on for years without any oil ever having been found before. In others of these areas, oil had been produced before, production had subsequently fallen off, then new sources were tapped.

By producing and using oil we have built a dynamic oil industry and have accumulated the means, both financial and technical, to find more oil. We have developed methods for locating and mapping structures with greater speed and accuracy. We can select where to drill a structure with better odds of success. We can reach deeper strata. As a result, in the United States alone, there has been produced since 1938 as much oil as was known to exist in the country at that time. And despite that great withdrawal, the domestic industry's proved reserves are at an all time high level. It's as though we started out with a tank of oil, used it all up, and had a bigger tankful left. The wisdom of optimistic men in our profession, like Wallace Pratt, is becoming daily more evident.

Besides learning more about finding underground reservoirs of crude, oil men are also learning how to get more of the oil out of the reservoir after it has been located. Since 1935 especially, the science of petroleum engineering, sparked by such men as Morris Muskat of the Gulf Company, M. W. Vietti of the Texas Company, and Stuart Buckley of the Humble Company, has developed ways of forecasting reservoir performance so production can proceed by the most efficient methods. We are finding out how to get maximum yield from large, highly porous reservoirs of the Middle East type, where the water table is important, as we are also learning how to get maximum yield from tricky, tight reservoirs. Repressuring, water-flooding, and other techniques of secondary recovery are also adding greatly to the quantities of oil available for people's use.

The supply of useable oil is increased also by improved practices in its transport and handling, which cut down losses.

New developments in the science of refining

make possible better products. This fact, coupled with improvements in consuming devices, means that we can get more work from a barrel of oil today than we could previously. And I think we've only begun to use the energy potential in a barrel of oil.

Not only are we finding new sources of liquid hydrocarbons in the familiar raw form of crude petroleum, we will be able, when and if it ever becomes necessary, to derive liquid hydrocarbons from oil shales, tar sands, and coal, and other sources not used at present.

Finally, our present use of oil and coal supports an industrial and scientific structure in which men are already learning how to apply atomic power to constructive work and may learn how to harness solar energy. Such developments, of course, would probably displace the fossil fuels in some applications, thus making them available for other use. The overall effect would be to again increase the total amount of energy available to humanity.

Incidentally, in connection with atomic energy, two news items which I recently noticed have a bearing on our subject.

Only a few months ago it appeared that the future use of atomic energy for industrial purposes might be doubtful because of the problem of the radioactive wastes. Yet only a few weeks ago, a Government official reported that the solution is in sight. What he called "atomic garbage" is apparently on the verge of being employed in such a way as to be not just harmless but actually useful.

The second story was about a new atomic plant, called a "breeder reactor," now in operation in one of the western states. As I understand it the object of the process is to use uranium 235, which is rare and costly, to convert nonfissionable materials, which are abundant and cheap, into fissionable material at a faster rate than the uranium 235 itself is consumed. One of the non-fissionable materials they will use is thorium, which previously was used chiefly in the manufacture of mantles for gas lights.

During the past few minutes I have been considering mineral energy resources. Now let us look at the picture for metals, if I may pass from my familiar field of soft rocks into that of hard rock geology. There are 45 metallic elements and some 8,000 alloys of those metals now in commercial use.

As you well know, the world in general and the United States in particular is using metals at a rate never seen before. Two world wars in a quarter century and the present unhappy need to build great quantities of arms have used unheard of amounts of iron and copper—to name but two metals in demand. Our steel expansion program now under way calls for annual production of 120 million tons—15 million tons more than we turned out last year. And, to meet our new needs, we plan to step up our domestic production of copper (which last year was about 1,200,000 tons) by 225,000 tons, of zinc by 230,000 tons, and aluminum by 700,000 tons.

Can we say that what has proved true of fuels will prove true of metals? We have seen that increased knowledge has led to the discovery of new sources of energy which are seemingly unlimited. Does a comparable outcome seem likely with respect to metals?

The metals we use most today—iron and aluminum—are second only to oxygen and silicon in their abundance on our planet. It has been estimated that there is at least 5,000 times as much iron ore, bauxite, and alunite in the earth's crust as the world now uses annually. Furthermore, unlike fossil fuels, most metals can be reclaimed after use and used again.

In the meantime, the discovery of new sources of metal supplies, and the development of techniques for making them economically available go on at a rapid pace.

It wasn't so long ago that people were worrying about imminent depletion of the 50 per cent iron-ore deposits of the Mesabi Range. Today a number of steel companies are planning or building facilites, estimated to cost over three quarters of a billion dollars, for processing taconite. Taconite deposits in Minnesota occur in a 100-mile strip, several miles broad, and are believed to amount to 5 billion tons. The reducing plants will turn out about 1 ton of 60 per cent iron from every 4 tons of taconite.

Rich deposits of iron ore have been found in a number of countries outside the United States and are now being developed, in many cases by American capital. Labrador, Venezuela, and Brazil, for example, are the scenes of some truly epic engineering projects. A 358-mile railroad is being cut through wilderness and wasteland to haul ore from Ungava, Labrador, to water. At Steep Rock Lake, Ontario, 70 million tons of a lake bed are being removed in a four-year dredging operation to get at an iron deposit underneath. In El Pao, Venezuela, one of two projects in that country has been completed after

14 years of work. Ore has to be shipped by a railroad built through jungles, and by barge to the sea on a river whose water level at the loading point fluctuates 43 feet at different seasons.

We take aluminum for granted these days. It costs currently about 18 cents a pound. Yet when the Civil War started it sold for $545 a pound. United States production now amounts to about 800,000 tons per year, and plants under construction will almost double that figure. If it ever becomes necessary to find substitutes for bauxite or alunite ores, chemists seem confident they will be able to produce aluminum oxide from aluminum-bearing clays.

The first plant to extract magnesium from sea water went into operation only 11 years ago with a capacity of 9,000 tons a year. Magnesium production in the United States for 1952 is expected to exceed 100,000 tons. As for the future—there's a lot of water in the sea.

Titanium is one of our most abundant metals and has long been known. What we have not known is how to extract it from the earth's crust at a cost which would make it economic for large-scale use. Up to five years ago, titanium was used chiefly as an ingredient in paint. But it is lighter than steel, stronger than aluminum, and highly heat resistant—hence potentially very useful. Present extraction processes are still expensive, but I have heard that a more economical method is being developed.

With almost every metal the story is repeated—of widening use, of the discovery of new sources and better methods of extraction. Here, as in other fields, research and ingenuity have been great multipliers of our natural resources.

Our supply of metals is being supplemented by other rigid materials—both old ones put to new uses and newly discovered ones. Glass, for example, is an ancient product that has been improved in recent years to the point where it can substitute for many other materials. And it is made of materials whose supply is practically unlimited.

As for plastics—mere infants in comparison with Granddaddy Glass—there seems no limit to the possibilities of synthesizing organic compounds. A hint of some of the things to come may have been contained in a story I read only a month ago of an automobile body made of plastic and layers of glass fiber. It was claimed the body is dent-proof, rust-proof, and, for its weight, stronger than steel. When you consider the large fraction of our steel output that goes into auto bodies you can perhaps imagine what a successful plastic body would mean in terms of metal supply. That's especially impressive when you consider further that plastics can be made from corncobs, oat hulls, the spent fibers of sugar cane and other materials we used to regard as waste.

These benefits are available to us as they become economically feasible, in that orderly natural development characteristic of all true technical progress. We discovered long ago that the real usefulness of any new product or process begins only when its economy in use surpasses the economy of that which it is supposed to replace. We could, for example, grow bananas at the North Pole, but the usefulness of such a project is clouded by considerable doubt.

* * *

For many years, I believe, people have tended to think of natural resources as so many stacks of raw material piled up in a storehouse. A person with this sort of picture in his mind logically assumes that the more you use of any natural resource, the sooner you get to the bottom of the pile. Now I think, we are beginning to discover that the idea of a storehouse—or, at least, a single-room storehouse—does not correspond with reality. Instead, the fact seems to be that the first storehouse in which man found himself was only one of a series. As he used up what was piled in that first room, he found he could fashion a key to open a door into a much larger room. And as he used the contents of this larger room, he discovered there was another room beyond, larger still. The room in which we stand at the middle of the 20th century is so vast that its walls are beyond sight. Yet it is probably still quite near the beginning of the whole series of storehouses. It is not inconceivable that the entire globe—earth, ocean, and air—represents raw material for mankind to utilize with more and more ingenuity and skill.

This conception of limitless raw material is not new. It is held by a number of persons. But it is an idea certainly not familiar to people at large. I notice, though, that Lahee's recent A.P.I. report is receiving wide publication. It's the one that shows that for every barrel of crude oil or cubic foot of natural gas withdrawn from the ground in 1951, two new barrels of oil or cubic feet of gas were found or developed. Perhaps the idea is getting around.

* * *

I would like to close my remarks by pointing out a corollary to this thesis. It is that the concept of unlimited raw materials does not mean that progress is simple and that Utopia is near at hand. On the contrary, raw materials, no matter how vast in amount, do not become available resources until human thought and effort are applied to them. In a very real sense raw materials do not exist, they are created. We know, for example, that in a region of great mineral wealth, people can grind out their lives in poverty and misery if they do not realize the wealth exists or if they do not know how to get at it. It is use that makes it valuable. Even when the wealth is made available through technical means, the accelerating growth of populations and the enormous wastage of war are additional complications to consider.

So the march up the steps of material progress, or from storehouse to storehouse— according to which figure of speech you prefer— depends not alone on the continued expansion of scientific knowledge and on industrial daring and managerial skill, but also on political and social conditions. Those conditions in many parts of the world today are not conducive to progress. In fact, extreme nationalism, government controls and monopolies, currency restrictions, abnormal tariffs, threats of expropriation, wars, and revolutions have sealed the doors to many storehouses of useful raw materials.

The basic requirement for progress is freedom—freedom to inquire, to think, to communicate, to venture. Without these conditions, the human mind and spirit will be so shackled that the availability of natural resources will be limited, and we may exhaust the known sources of some needed material and find nothing to replace it.

So we see, I think, that the most important thing in life is spirit. To the free man, all things are possible. Opportunity is the wand which can change the useless into the useful—waste into raw materials of great value—exhaustible resources into inexhaustible resources. It is the key that unlocks the greatest energy source of all—the infinite power of the human individual.

The longer I live the more convinced I am that material progress is not only valueless without spiritual progress, it is, in the long term, impossible.

38. CONSERVATION, GEOLOGY, AND MINERAL RESOURCES

PETER T. FLAWN

The conservation movement has grown enormously in strength and breadth during the last decade as a result of widespread concern about natural resources and the quality of the environment. The federal leadership broadened the definition of conservation to "applied ecology" and thereby put a meaning into the word that went far beyond its original sense. Conservation now includes all of the physical, social, and legal problems attendant on use of the land. The inclusion of a wide variety of environmental problems under the umbrella of "conservation" caused a great deal of pushing and shoving of traditional "conservationists" to make way for the new "environmentalists." Broadening of the conservation movement to a total-environment movement has brought many new people into it—scientists, engineers, economists, geographers, and ecologists—people that are professionally concerned with the environment on a working-day basis. In Washington, they have taken the leadership from the naturalists that dominated the movement in the past. However, on the local level, part-time conservationists organized into garden clubs, sportsmen's clubs, boating clubs, and heritage or historical societies retain the leadership. In some areas these groups have combined to form conservation federations and congresses. Commonly, there is a dichotomy between the federal leadership which is influenced by scientific, engineering, and economic realities (the need to fix priorities, the need to consider the more urgent problems affecting the largest numbers of people, and the need to resolve conflicts between users of land) and the local conservation groups with a more visceral feeling that one part of the environment must be protected or conserved at any cost. The new conservationists and particularly the federal conservationists commonly include stewardship of the land in the general mission of conservation.

Extracted, with permission of the author and publisher from "Mineral Resources and Conservation in Texas" by Peter T. Flawn, *Texas Bureau of Economic Geology Circular* 70-1, 20 p., February, 1970. The University of Texas at Austin.

There is thereby added to the broad definition of applied ecology the responsibility of management. Management involves planning and decision making. Both of these require data.

Although geology and geologists are commonly associated with mineral resources rather than environmental problems in general, no natural resource can be considered out of its environmental context. Development and production of mineral resources produces an environmental response that must be considered in planning, and where the response results in environmental degradation, steps must be taken to protect the environment and reclaim the land after the mineral resources have been harvested. Thus, geology and geologists can contribute broadly to the mission of conservation.

As long as the owner of the minerals can economically extract them through wells or shafts which occupy only a small area of the surface, the surface owner can farm, ranch, or otherwise develop the surface contemporaneously with the extractive operations and thus *simultaneous multiple use* of the land is possible. Measured in dollars, extraction of minerals gives a much higher yield per acre and a more rapid rate of accrual than most other land uses. Such multiple use is beneficial to society, and indeed the government in administration of the public domain has seen fit to encourage it through legislation.

This happy situation does not prevail, however, where the mineral estate is valuable earth materials at or near the surface and the economic mining method is open-pit or strip mining, which consumes the surface. In fact, the courts and the Congress do not recognize some of the so-called common varieties of earth materials which form the earth's surface as qualifying as a "mineral substance" under the mineral location laws governing the public domain (for example, sand and gravel, stone and cement materials), nor are they included in general grants or reservations of "minerals." In dealing with private property owners who hold valuable deposits of these "common varieties," the mineral producer either buys the land outright in fee simple or buys the minerals under a special agreement which allows him to break up and remove that part of the surface necessary to his mining operation. In this case other beneficial use of the surface—simultaneous multiple use—is impossible while mining is in progress. To add to the problem surface mining for low-unit value earth materials, such as construction materials, is most common in and around urban areas where competition for land is at a maximum, where large numbers of people are affected by nuisances associated with mining effort (noise, dust, vibrations, traffic, ugliness), and where they can effectively bring political pressures to close down the mining operation.

Because of technological developments in earth-moving equipment, surface mining has expanded to include deeper and deeper deposits beneath thicker and thicker overburdens. To those with a short time-perspective, the great open pits with adjacent cast-aside mountains of overburden constitute permanent ruination of the land. The geologist who has studied the changing earth through geologic time has seen evidence that the earth's natural processes have filled much larger basins and leveled much higher mountains. He understands better than most that nothing is permanent. But the living do not want to wait half a century or more for natural reclamation—and properly so. What man has done, he can undo.

After the extractive operation—or after any exclusive land use—the land can be restored for subsequent use—at a cost. This is *sequential multiple use.* If the principle of sequential multiple use—as contrasted to simultaneous multiple use—is accepted, the solution to the problem of mineral resources and multiple land use can be stated in term of three elements:

1. Creation of a legal structure that will require industrywide performance in land-use practices on an equitable basis.
2. Creation of an economic structure that will not only permit but encourage the mineral industry to reclaim and restore the surface, prevent subsidence, and pre-

vent deleterious environmental effects from solid, liquid, and gaseous wastes.
3. Creation of a social attitude that includes a long-term *sequential* view of land use and recognizes that in certain areas containing mineral deposits needed by society, exclusive land use is required during the extractive period. All of the mines and quarries cannot be in another township, county, state, or country.

The legal structure is now being built on both the state and federal level. The geologist must help build it so the structure will be sound and compatible with geological reality.

The economic consequences of that legal structure are and will be increased costs. These increased costs are coming at a time when costs are rising due to inflation, and the changes in the tax structure threaten to lower mineral industry net earnings through cuts in the depletion allowances. The government, as the chief steward of the land who is establishing land-use criteria while deploring price increases and at the same time encouraging industrial development and economic growth, cannot ignore this economic problem. The least that the government can do is to formulate and publicize a rational mineral and mining policy so that within the Federal Establishment there will be some coordination and consistency in policies. If we are to preserve our industrial society and the opportunity it gives to support large numbers of people at a high standard of living, mineral resources must continue to flow. However, through informed conservation practices, the environment must be protected against the impact of this industrial society. Surface mining scars the land and produces great quantities of solid wastes. Oil production produces enormous quantities of waste brines. We must have minerals; we must have a habitable environment. The government is the ultimate *steward* of the land; it must look at its trust in terms of centuries and it must follow an educated regional environmental plan—a patchwork with industry-by-industry variances will not produce the kind of environment that society wants.

39. REALITIES OF MINERAL DISTRIBUTION

PRESTON E. CLOUD, JR.

"Is there intelligent life on earth?" —Anonymous astronomer (Annual Report, Travelers Research Center, Inc., Hartford, Conn., 1966, p. 4)

INTRODUCTION

Optimism and imagination are happy human traits. They often make bad situations appear tolerable or even good. Man's ability to imagine solutions, however, commonly outruns his ability to find them. What does he do when it becomes clear that he is plundering, overpopulating, and despoiling his planet at such a horrendous rate that it is going to take some kind of a big leap, and soon, to avert irreversible degradation?

Dr. Weinberg, with his marvelous conception of a world set free by nuclear energy sees man at this juncture in history as comparable to the frog who was trying, unsuccessfully, to jump out of a deep rut. A second frog came along, and, seeing his friend in distress, told him to rest awhile while he fetched some sticks to build a platform from which it would be but a short leap to the top of the rut. When frog number two returned, however, his friend was nowhere to be seen. A glance around soon revealed him sitting at the top of the rut. "How did you get up there?" the second frog exclaimed. "Well," said the first frog, "I had to—a hell of a big truck came down the road." In this story we are the first frog, the truck is overpopulation, pollution, and dwindling mineral resources, and the extra oomph that gets us out of the rut is nuclear power—specifically the breeder reactor, and eventually contained fusion.

The inventive genius of man has got him out of trouble in the past. Why not now? Why be a spoil-sport when brilliant, articulate, and well-intentioned men assure us that all we need is more technology? Why? Because the present crisis is exacerbated by four conditions that reinforce each other in a very undesirable manner: (1) the achievements of medical technology

Extracted with permission of the author and publishers from "Limitations of the Earth: A Compelling Focus for Geology" Bureau of Economic Geology, University of Texas at Austin, 1968, p. 103-126. Also published in *Texas Quarterly*, v. 11, no. 2, 1968.

which have brought on the run-away imbalance between birth and death rates, to which Dr. Erlich addresses himself; (2) the hypnotic but unsustainable national dream of an ever-increasing real Gross National Product based on obsolescence and waste; (3) the finite nature of the earth and particularly its accessible mineralized crust; and (4) the increased risk of irreversible spoilation of the environment which accompanies overpopulation, overproduction, waste, and the movement of ever-larger quantities of source rock for ever-smaller proportions of useful minerals.

Granted the advantages of big technological leaps, therefore, provided they are in the right direction, I see real hope for permanent long-range solutions to our problems as beginning with the taking of long-range views of them. Put in another way, we should not tackle vast problems with half-vast concepts. We must build a platform of scientific and social comprehension, while concurrently endeavoring to fill the rut of ignorance, selfishness, and complacency with knowledge, restraint, and demanding awareness on the part of an enlightened electorate. And we must not be satisfied merely with getting the United States or North America through the immediate future, critical though that will be. We must consider what effects current and proposed trends and actions will have on the world as a whole for several generations hence, and how we can best influence those trends favorably the world over. Above all, we must consider how to preserve for the yet unborn the maximum flexibility of choices consistent with meeting current and future crises.

Rhetoric, however, either cornucopian or Malthusian, is no substitute for informed foresight and rational action or purposeful inaction.

What are the problems and misconceptions that impede the desired progress? And what must we invest in research and action—scientific, technological, *and* social—to assure a flexibility of resource options for the long range as well as for the immediate future? Not only until 1985, not only until the year 2000, not only even until the year 2050, but for a future as long as or longer than our past. In the nearly five billion years of earth history is man's brief stay of now barely a million years to be only a meteoric flash, and his industrial society less than that? Or will he last with reasonable amenities for as long as the dinosaurs?

NATURE AND GEOGRAPHY OF RESOURCES

Man's concept of resources, to be sure, depends on his needs and wants, and thus to a great degree on his locale and place in history, on what others have, and on what he knows about what they have and might be possible for him to obtain. Food and fiber from the land, and food and drink from the waters of the earth have always been indispensable resources. So have the human beings who have utilized these resources and created demands for others—from birch bark to beryllium, from buffalo hides to steel and plastic. It is these other resources, the ones from which our industrial society has been created, about which I speak today. I refer, in particular, to the nonrenewable or wasting resources—mineral fuels which are converted into energy plus carbon, nuclear fuels, and the metals, chemicals, and industrial materials of geological origin which to some extent can be and even are recycled but which tend to become dispersed and wasted.

All such resources, except those that are common rocks whose availability and value depend almost entirely on economic factors plus fabrication, share certain peculiarities that transcend economics and limit technology and even diplomacy. They occur in local concentrations that may exceed their crustal abundances by thousands of times, and particular resources tend to be clustered within geochemical or metallogenic provinces from which others are excluded. Some parts of the earth are rich in mineral raw materials and others are poor.

No part of the earth, not even on a continent-wide basis, is self-sufficient in all critical metals. North America is relatively rich in molybdenum and poor in tin, tungsten, and manganese, for instance, whereas Asia is comparatively rich in tin, tungsten, and manganese and, apparently, less well supplied with molybdenum. The great bulk of the world's gold appears to be in South Africa, which has relatively little silver but a good supply of platinum. Cuba and New Caledonia have well over half the world's total known reserves of nickel. The main known

reserves of cobalt are in the Congo Republic, Cuba, New Caledonia, and parts of Asia. Most of the world's mercury is in Spain, Italy, and parts of the Sino-Soviet bloc. Industrial diamonds are still supplied mainly by the Congo.

Consider tin. Over half the world's currently recoverable reserves are in Indonesia, Malaya, and Thailand, and much of the rest is in Bolivia and the Congo. Known North American reserves are negligible. For the United States loss of access to extra-continental sources of tin is not likely to be offset by economic factors or technological changes that would permit an increase in potential North American production, even if present production could be increased by an order of magnitude. It is equally obvious that other peculiarities in the geographical distribution of the world's geological resources will continue to encourage interest both in trading with some ideologically remote nations and in seeking alternative sources of supply.

Economic geology, which in its best sense brings all other fields of geology to bear on resource problems, is concerned particularly with questions of how certain elements locally attain geochemical concentrations that greatly exceed their crustal abundance and with how this knowledge can be applied to the discovery of new deposits and the delineation of reserves. Economics and technology play equally important parts with geology itself in determining what deposits and grades it is practicable to exploit. Neither economics, nor technology, nor geology can *make* an ore deposit where the desired substance is absent or exists in insufficient quantity.

ESTIMATED RECOVERABLE RESERVES OF SELECTED MINERAL RESOURCES

Consider now some aspects of the apparent lifetimes of estimated recoverable reserves of a selection of critical mineral resources and the position of the United States with regard to some of these. The selected resources are those for which suitable data are available.

Figure 1 shows such lifetimes for different groups of metals and mineral fuels at *current* minable grades and rates of consumption. No allowance is made for increase of populations, or for increased rates of consumption which, in the United States, tend to increase at twice the rate of population growth. Nor is allowance made for additions to reserves that will result from discovery of submarine deposits, use of submarginal grades, or imports—which may reduce but will not eliminate the impact of growth factors. Data are from the U. S. Bureau of Mines compendia *Mineral Facts and Problems* and its *Minerals Yearbooks,* as summarized by Flawn *(Mineral Resources,* Rand McNally, 1966). The thin lines represent lifetimes of world reserves for a stable population of roughly 3.3×10^9 at current rates of use. The heavy lines represent similar data for a United States population of about 200 million. Actual availability of some such commodities to the United States will, of course, be extended by imports from abroad, just as that of others will be reduced by population growth, increased per capita demands, and perhaps by political changes. The dashed vertical line represents the year 2038. I have chosen this as a reference line because it marks that point in the future which is just as distant from the present as the invention of the airplane and the discovery of radioactivity are in the past. I might have used 2089, which is only as far from the present as the admission of Texas to the Union in 1845.

The prospect is hardly conducive to unrestrained optimism. Of the nineteen commodities considered, only fourteen for the world and four or five for the United States have assured lifetimes beyond 1984; only ten for the world and three for the United States persist beyond the turn of the century; and only eight for the world and three for the United States extend beyond 2038. I do not suggest that we equate these lines with revealed truth. Time will prove some too short and others perhaps too long. New reserves will be found, lower-grade reserves will become minable for economic or technological reasons, substitutes will be discovered or synthesized, and some critical materials can be conserved by waste control and recycling. The crucial questions are: (1) how do we reduce these generalities to specifics; (2) can we do so fast enough to sustain current rates of consumption; (3) can we increase and sustain production of industrial materials at a rate sufficient to meet the rising expectations of a world population of nearly three and one-half billion, now growing with a doubling time of about thirty to thirty-five years, and for how long; and (4) if the answer to the last question is no, what then?

A more local way of viewing the situation is to compare the position of the United States or North America with other parts of the world. Figures 2 to 4 show such a comparison for sixteen commodities with our favorite measuring stick, the Sino-Soviet bloc. Figure 2 shows the more cheerful side of the coin. The United States is a bit ahead in petroleum, lignite, and phosphate, and neither we nor Asia have much chromium—known reserves are practically all in South Africa and Rhodesia. Figure 3, however,

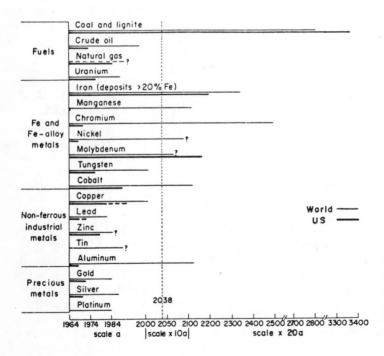

Figure 1. Lifetimes of estimated recoverable reserves of mineral resources at current mineable grades and rates of consumption (no allowance made for increasing rates of consumption, or for submerged or otherwise concealed deposits, use of now submarginal grades, or imports). (Data from Flawn, 1966).

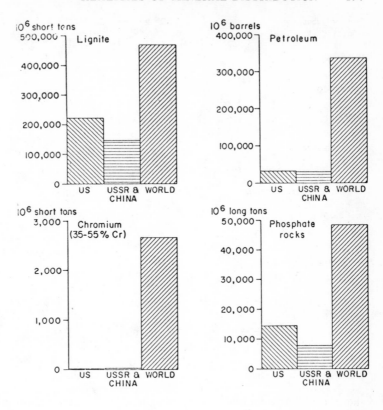

Figure 2. Estimated recoverable reserves of minerals (above sea level) for which US reserve estimates exceed, equal, or fall only slightly below those of the USSR plus Mainland China. (Data from Flawn, 1966).

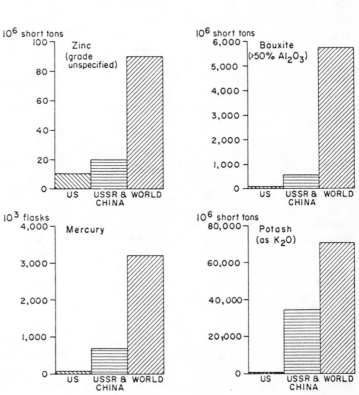

Figure 3. Estimated recoverable reserves of minerals (above sea level) for which US reserve estimates are less than those of the USSR plus Mainland China. (Data from Flawn, 1966).

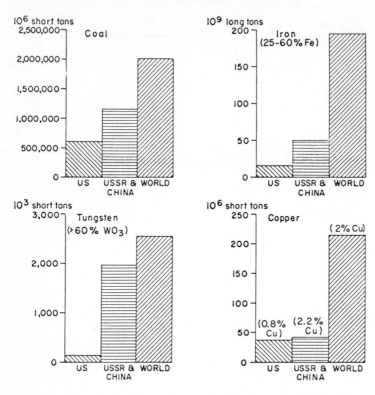

Figure 4. Estimated recoverable reserves of minerals (above sea level) for which US reserve estimates are less than those of the USSR plus Mainland China. (Data from Flawn, 1966).

shows the Sino-Soviet bloc to have a big lead in zinc, mercury, potash, and bauxite. And Figure 4 shows similar leads in tungsten, copper, iron, and coal.

Again there are brighter aspects to the generally unfavorable picture. Ample local low grade sources of alumina other than bauxite are available with metallurgical advances and at a price. The United States coal supply is not in danger of immediate shortage. Potassium can be extracted from sea water. And much of the world's iron is in friendly hands, including those of our good neighbor Canada and our more distant friend Australia.

No completely safe source is visible, however, for mercury, tungsten, and chromium. Lead, tin, zinc, and the precious metals appear to be in short supply throughout the world. And petroleum and natural gas will be exhausted or nearly so within the lifetimes of many of those here today unless we decide to conserve them for petrochemicals and plastics. Even the extraction of liquid fuels from oil shales and "tar sands," or by hydrogenation of coal, will not meet energy requirements over the long term. If they were called upon to supply all the liquid fuels and other products now produced by the fractionation of petroleum, for instance, the suggested

lifetime for coal, the reserves of which are probably the most accurately known of all mineral products, would be drastically reduced below that indicated in Figure 1—and such a shift will be needed to a yet unknown degree before the end of the century.

THE CORNUCOPIAN PREMISES

In view of these alarming prospects, why do intelligent men of good faith seem to assure us that there is nothing to be alarmed about? It can only be because they visualize a completely nongeological solution to the problem, or because they take a very short-range view of it, or because they are compulsive optimists or are misinformed, or some combination of these things.

Let me first consider some of the basic concepts that might give rise to a cornucopian view of the earth's mineral resources and the difficulties that impede their unreserved acceptance. Then I will suggest some steps that might be taken to minimize the risks or slow the rates of mineral-resource depletion.

The central dilemma of all cornucopian premises is, of course, how to sustain an exponential increase of anything—people, mineral products, industrialization, or solid currency—on a finite resource base. This is, as everyone must realize, obviously impossible in the long run and will become increasingly difficult in the short run. For great though the mass of the earth is, well under 0.1 per cent of that mass is accessible to us by any imaginable means (the entire crust is only about 0.4 per cent of the total mass of the earth) and this relatively minute accessible fraction, as we have seen and shall see, is very unequally mineralized.

But the cornucopians are not naive or mischievous people. On what grounds do they deny the restraints and belittle the difficulties?

The five main premises from which their conclusions follow are:

Premise I—the promise of essentially inexhaustible cheap useful energy from nuclear sources.

Premise II—the thesis that economics is the sole factor governing availability of useful minerals and metals.

Premise III—the fallacy of essentially uninterrupted variation from ore of a metal to its average crustal abundance, which is inherent in Premise II, and from which emanates the strange and misleading notion that quantity of a resource available is essentially an inverse exponential function of its concentration.

Premise IV—the crucial assumption of population control, without which there can be no future worth living for most of the world (or, worse, the belief that quantity of people is of itself the ultimate good, which, astounding as it may seem, is still held by a few people who ought to know better—see, for instance, Colin Clark, *Population Growth and Land Use,* Macmillian, 1967).

Premise V—the concept of the "technological fix."

Now these are appealing premises, several of which contain large elements of both truth and hope. Why do I protest their unreserved acceptance? I protest because, in addition to elements of truth, they also contain assumptions that either are gross over-simplifications, outright errors, or are not demonstrated. I warn because their uncritical acceptance contributes to a dangerous complacency toward problems that will not be solved by a few brilliant technological "breakthroughs," a wider acceptance of deficit economy, or fall-out of genius from unlimited expansion of population. They will be solved only by intensive, wide-ranging, and persistent

scientific and engineering investigation, supported by new social patterns and wise legislation.

I will discuss these premises in the order cited.

Premise I

The concept of essentially inexhaustible cheap useful energy from nuclear sources offers by all odds the most promising prospect of sweeping changes in the mineral resource picture. We may be on the verge of developing a workable breeder reactor just in time to sustain an energy-hungry world facing the imminent exhaustion of traditional energy sources. Such a development, it has been persuasively stated, will also banish many problems of environmental pollution and open up unlimited reserves of metals in common crustal rocks. There are, unhappily, some flaws in this delightful picture, of which it is important to be aware.

Uranium 235 is the only naturally occurring spontaneously fissionable source of nuclear power. When a critical mass of uranium is brought together, the interchange of neutrons back and forth generates heat and continues to do so as long as the U^{235} lasts. In the breeder reactor some of the free neutrons kick common U^{238} over to plutonium 239, which is fissionable and produces more neutrons, yielding heat and accelerating the breeder reaction. Even in existing reactors some breeding takes place, and, if a complete breeding system could be produced, the amount of energy available from uranium alone would be increased about 140 fold. If thorium also can be made to breed, energy generated could be increased about 400 fold over that now attainable. This would extend the lifetime of visible energy resources at demands anticipated by 1980 by perhaps 1000 to 3000 years and gain time to work on contained nuclear fusion.

The problem is that it will require about 275,000 short tons of $6.00 to $10.00 per pound U_3O_8 (not ore, not uranium) to fuel reactors now on order to 1980, plus another 400,000 tons to sustain them until the turn of the century, burning only U^{235} with currently available enrichments from slow breeding (Charles T. Baroch, U. S. Bureau of Mines, oral comment). Only about 195,000 of the 675,000 tons of uranium needed is known to be available at this price, although known geologic conditions indicate the possibility of another 325,000 tons. Thus we now appear to be about 155,000 tons short of the U_3O_8 needed to produce the hoped-for 150,000 megawatts of nuclear energy on a sustained basis from 1985 until the end of the century without a functioning breeder reactor. Unless we find a lot more uranium, or pay a lot more money for it, or get a functioning complete breeder reactor or contained nuclear fusion within ten or fifteen years, the energy picture will be far from bright. There is good reason to hope that the breeder will come, and after it contained fusion, *if* the U^{235} and helium hold out—but there is no room for complacency.

If and when the breeder reactor or contained fusion does become available as a practicable energy source, however, how will this help with mineral resources? It is clear immediately that it will take pressure off the fossil "fuels" so that it will become feasible, and should become the law, to reserve them for petrochemicals, polymers, essential liquid propellants, and other special purposes not served by nuclear fuels. It is also clear that cheap massive transportation, or direct transmittal of large quantities of cheap electric power to, or its generation at, distant sources will bring the mineral resources of remote sites to the market place—either as bulk ore for processing or as the refined or partially refined product.

What is not clear is how this very cheap energy will bring about the extraction of thinly dispersed metals in large quantity from common rock. The task is very different from the recovery of liquid fuels or natural gas by nuclear fracturing. The procedure usually suggested is the break-up of rock in place at depth with a nuclear blast, followed by hydrometallurgical or chemical mining. The problems, however, are great. Complexing solutions, in large quantity also from natural resources, must be brought into contact with the particles desired. This means that the enclosing rock must be fractured to that particle size. Then other substances, unsought, may use up and dissipate valuable reagents. Or the solvent reagents may escape to ground waters and become contaminants. Underground electrolysis is no more promising in dealing with very low concentrations. And the bacteria that catalyze reactions of metallurgical interest are all aerobic, so that, in addition to having access to the particles of interest, they must also be provided with a source of oxygen underground if they are to work there.

Indeed the energy used in breaking rock for the removal of metals is not now a large fraction

of mining cost in comparison with that of labor and capital. The big expense is in equipping and utilizing manpower, and, although cheap energy will certainly reduce manpower requirements, it will probably never adequately substitute for the intelligent man with the pick at the mining face in dealing with vein and many replacement deposits, where the sought-after materials are irregularly concentrated in limited spaces. There are also limits to the feasible depths of open pit mining, which would be by all odds the best way to mine common rock. Few open pit mines now reach much below about 1,500 feet. It is unlikely that such depths can be increased by as much as an order of magnitude. The quantity of rock removable decreases exponentially with depth because pit circumference must decrease downward to maintain stable walls.

It may also not be widely realized by non-geologists that many types of ore bodies have definite floors or pinch-out downward, so that extending exploitative operations to depth gains no increase in ore produced. Even where mineralization does extend to depth, of course, exploitability is ultimately limited by temperature and rock failure.

Then there is the problem of reducing radioactivity so that ores can be handled and the refined product utilized without harm—not to mention heat dispersal (which in some but not all situations could itself be a resource) and the disposal of waste rock and spent reagents.

Altogether the problems are sufficiently formidable that it would be foolhardy to accept them as resolved in advance of a working efficient breeder reactor plus a demonstration that either cheap electricity or nuclear explosions will significantly facilitate the removal of metals from any common rock.

A pithy comment from Peter Flawn's recent book on *Mineral Resources* (Rand McNally, 1966, p. 14) is appropriate here. It is to the effect that "average rock will never be mined." It is the uncommon features of a rock that make it a candidate for mining! Even with a complete nuclear technology, sensible people will seek, by geological criteria, to choose and work first those rocks or ores that show the highest relative recoverable enrichments in the desired minerals.

The reality is that even the achievement of a breeder reactor offers no guarantee of unlimited mineral resources in the face of geologic limitations and expanding populations with increased per capita demands, even over the middle term. To assume such for the long term would be sheer folly.

Premise II

The thesis that economics is the sole, or at least the dominant, factor governing availability of useful minerals and metals is one of those vexing part-truths which has led to much seemingly fruitless discussion between economists and geologists. This proposition bears examination.

It seems to have its roots in the interesting economic index known as the Gross National Product, or GNP. No one seems to have worked out exactly what proportion of the GNP is in some way attributable to the mineral resource base. It does, however, appear that the dollar value of the raw materials themselves is small compared to the total GNP, and that it has decreased proportionately over time to something like 2 per cent of the present GNP, as I recall. From this it is logically deduced that the GNP could, if necessary, absorb a several-fold increase in cost of raw materials. The gap in logic comes when this is confused with the notion that all that is necessary to obtain inexhaustible quantities of any substance is either to raise the price or to increase the volume of rock mined. In support of such a notion, of course, one *can* point to diamond, which in the richest deposit ever known occurred in a concentration of only one to twenty-five million, but which, nevertheless, has continued to be available. The flaw is not only that we cannot afford to pay the price of diamond for many substances, but also that no matter how much rock we mine we can't get diamonds out of it if there were none there in the first place.

Daniel Bell (1967, Notes on the Post-industrialist Society II: *in* the *Public Interest*, no. 7, p. 102-118) comments on the distorted sense of relations that emerges from the cumulative nature of GNP accounting. Thus, when a mine is developed, the costs of the new facilities and payroll become additions to the GNP, whether the ore is sold at a profit or not. Should the mine wastes at the same time pollute a stream, the costs of cleaning up the stream or diverting the wastes also become additions to the GNP. Similarly if you hire someone to wash the dishes this adds to GNP, but if your wife does them it doesn't count.

From this it results that mineral raw materials and housework are not very impressive fractions of the GNP. What seems to get lost sight of is what a mess we would be in without either!

Assuming an indefinite extension of their curves and continuance of access to foreign markets, economists appear to be on reasonably sound grounds in postulating the relatively long-term availability of certain sedimentary, residual, and disseminated ores, such as those of iron, aluminum, and perhaps copper. What many of them do not appreciate is, namely, that the type of curve that can with some reason be applied to such deposits and metals is by no means universally applicable. This difficulty is aggravated by the fact that conventional economic indexes minimize the vitaminlike quality for the economy as a whole of the raw materials whose enhancement in value through beneficiation, fabrication, and exchange accounts for such a large part of the material assets of society.

In a world that wants to hear only good news some economists are perhaps working too hard to emancipate their calling from the epithet of "dismal science," but not all of them. One voice from the wilderness of hyperoptimism and overconsumption is that of Kenneth Boulding, who observes that, *"The essential measure of the success of the economy is not production and consumption at all, but the nature, extent, quality, and complexity of the total capital stock, including in this the state of the human bodies and minds included in the system"* (p. 9 *in* K. E. Boulding, 1966, "The economics of the coming spaceship Earth," p. 3-14 *in Environmental Quality in a Growing Economy*, Resources for the Future, Inc., The Johns Hopkins Press). Until this concept penetrates widely into the councils of government and the conscience of society, there will continue to be a wide gap between the economic aspects of national and industrial policy and the common good, and the intrinsic significance of raw materials will remain inadequately appreciated.

The reality is that economics per se, powerful though it can be when it has material resources to work with, is not all powerful. Indeed, without material resources to start with, no matter how small a fraction of the GNP they may represent, economics is of no consequence at all. The current orthodoxy of economic well-being through obsolescence, over-consumption, and waste will prove, in the long term, to be a cruel and a preposterous illusion.

Premise III

Premise III, the postulate of essentially uninterrupted variation from ore to average crustal abundance is seldom if ever stated in that way, but it is inherent in Premise II. It could almost as well have been treated under Premise II; but it is such an important and interesting idea, whether true or false, that separate consideration is warranted.

If the postulated continuous variation were true for mineral resources in general, volume of "ore" (not metal) produced would be an exponential inverse function of grade mined, the handling of lower grades would be compensated for by the availability of larger quantities of elements sought, and reserve estimates would depend only on the accuracy with which average crustal abundances were known. Problems in extractive metallurgy, of course, are not considered in such an outlook.

This delightfully simple picture would supplant all other theories of ore deposits, invalidate the foundations of geochemistry, divest geology of much of its social relevance, and place the fate of the mineral industry squarely in the hands of economists and nuclear engineers.

Unfortunately this postulate is simply untrue in a practical sense for many critical minerals and is only crudely true, leaving out metallurgical problems, for particular metals, like iron and aluminum, whose patterns approach the predicted form. Sharp discontinuities exist in the abundances of mercury, tin, nickel, molybdenum, tungsten, manganese, cobalt, diamond, the precious metals, and even such staples as lead and zinc, for example. But how many prophets of the future are concerned about where all the lead or cadmium will come from for all those electric automobiles that are supposed to solve the smog problem?

Helium is a good example of a critical substance in short supply. Although a gas which has surely at some places diffused in a continuous spectrum of concentrations, particular concentrations of interest as a source of supply appear from published information to vary in a stepwise manner. Here I draw on data summarized by H. W. Lipper in the 1965 edition of the U. S. Bureau of Mines publication *Mineral Facts and Problems.* Although an uncommon substance, helium serves a variety of seemingly indispensable uses. A bit less than half of the helium now consumed in the U. S. is used in pressurizing liquid fueled missiles and space

ships. Shielded-arc welding is the next largest use, followed closely by its use in producing controlled atmospheres for growing crystals for transistors, processing fuels for nuclear energy, and cooling vacuum pumps. Only about 5.5 per cent of the helium consumed in the United States is now used as a lifting gas. It plays an increasingly important role, however, as a coolant for nuclear reactors and a seemingly indispensable one in cryogenics and superconductivity. In the latter role, it could control the feasibility of massive long-distance transport of nuclear-generated electricity. High-helium low-oxygen breathing mixtures may well be critical to man's long-range success in attempting to operate at great depths in the exploration and exploitation of the sea. Other uses are in research, purging, leak detection, chromatography, etc.

Helium thus appears to be a very critical element, as the Department of the Interior has recognized in establishing its helium-conservation program. What are the prospects that there will be enough helium in 2038?

The only presently utilized source of helium is in natural gas, where it occurs at a range of concentrations from as high as 8.2 per cent by volume to zero. The range, however, in particular gas fields of significant volume, is apparently not continuous. Dropping below the one field (Pinta Dome) that shows an 8.2 per cent concentration, we find a few small isolated fields (Mesa and Hogback, New Mexico) that contain about 5.5 per cent helium, and then several large fields (e.g., Hugoton and Texas Panhandle) with a range of 0.3 to 1.0 per cent helium. Other large natural gas fields contain either no helium or show it only in quantities of less than 5 parts per 10,000. From the latter there is a long jump down to the atmosphere with a concentration of only 1 part per 200,000.

Present annual demand for helium is about 700 million cubic feet, with a projected increase in demand to about 2 billion cubic feet annually by about 1985. It will be possible to meet such an accelerated demand for a limited time only as a result of Interior's current purchase and storage program, which will augment recovery from natural gas then being produced. As now foreseen, if increases in use do not outrun estimates, conservation and continued recovery of helium from natural gas reserves will meet needs to slightly beyond the turn of the century. When known and expected discoveries of reserves of natural gas are exhausted shortly thereafter, the only potential sources of new supply will be from the atmosphere, as small quantities of He^3 from nuclear reactor technology, or by synthesis from hydrogen—a process whose practical feasibility and adequacy remain to be established.

Spending even a lot more money to produce more helium from such sources under existing technology just may not be the best or even a very feasible way to deal with the problem. Interior's conservation program must be enlarged and extended, under compulsory legislation if necessary. New sources must be sought. Research into possible substitutions, recovery and re-use, synthesis, and extraction from the atmosphere must be accelerated— *now* while there is still time. And we must be prepared to curtail, if necessary, activities which waste the limited helium reserves. Natural resources are the price-less heritage of all the people; their waste cannot be tolerated.

Problems of the adequacy of reserves obtain for many other substances, especially under the escalating demands of rising populations and expectations, and it is becoming obvious to many geologists that time is running out. Dispersal of metals which could be recycled should be controlled. Unless industry and the public undertake to do this voluntarily, legislation should be generated to define permissible mixes of material and disposal of "junk" metal. Above all the wastefulness of war and preparation for it must be terminated if reasonable options for posterity are to be preserved.

The reality is that a healthy mineral resource industry, and therefore a healthy industrial econ-omy, can be maintained only on a firm base of geologic knowledge, and geochemical and metal-lurgical understanding of the distribution and limits of metals, mineral fuels, and chemicals in the earth's crust and hydrosphere.

Premise IV

The assumption that world populations will soon attain and remain in a state of balance is central to all other premises. Without this the rising expectations of the poor are doomed to failure, and the affluent can remain affluent only by maintaining existing shameful discrepancies. Taking present age structures and life expectan-cies of world populations into account, it seems certain that, barring other forms of catastrophe, world population will reach six or seven billion by about the turn of the century, regardless of how rapidly family planning is accepted and practiced.

On the most optimistic assumptions, this is probably close to the maximum number of people the world can support on a reasonably sustained basis, even under strictly regularized conditions, at a general level of living roughly comparable to that now enjoyed in Western Europe. It would, of course, be far better to stabilize at a much smaller world population. In any case, much greater progress than is as yet visible must take place over much larger parts of the world before optimism on the prospects of voluntary global population control at any level can be justified. And even if world population did level off and remain balanced at about seven billion, it would probably take close to one hundred years of intensive, enlightened, peaceful effort to lift all mankind to anywhere near the current level of Western Europe or even much above the level of chronic malnutrition and deprivation.

This is not to say that we must therefore be discouraged and withdraw to ineffectual diver-sions. Rather it is a challenge to focus with energy and realism on seeking a truly better life for all men living and yet unborn and on keeping the latter to the minimum. On the other hand, an uncritical optimism, just for the sake of that good feeling it creates, is a luxury the world cannot, at this juncture, afford.

A variation of outlook on the population problem which, surprisingly enough, exists a-mong a few nonbiological scholars is that quan-tity of people is of itself a good thing. The misconception here seems to be that frequency of effective genius will increase, even exponen-tially, with increasing numbers of people and that there is some risk of breeding out to a merely high level of mediocrity in a stabilized population. The extremes of genius and idiocy, however, appear in about the same frequency at birth from truly heterogeneous gene pools re-gardless of size (the data from Montgomery County, Maryland, are really no exception to this). What is unfortunate, among other things, about overly dense concentrations of people is that this leads not only to reduced likelihood of the identification of mature genius, but to drastic reductions in the development of potential gen-ius, owing to malnutrition in the weaning years and early youth, accompanied by retardation of both physical and mental growth. If we are determined to turn our problems over to an elite corps of mental prodigies a more sure-fire method is at hand. Nuclear transplant from various adult tissue cells into fertilized ova whose own nuclei have been removed has already produced identical copies of amphibian nucleus-donors and can probably do the same in man (Joshua Lederberg, 1966, *Bull. Atomic Scientists*, v. 22, no. 8, p. 9). Thus we appear to be on the verge of being able to make as many "xerox" copies as we want or need of any particular genius as long as we can get a piece of his or her nucleated tissue and find eggs and incubators for the genome aliquots to develop in. Female geniuses would be the best because (with a little help) they could copy themselves!

The reality is that without real population control and limitation of demand all else is drastically curtailed, not to say lost. And there is as yet not the faintest glimmer of hope that such limitation may take place voluntarily. Even were all unwanted births to be eliminated, populations would still be increasing at runaway rates in the absence of legal limitation of family size, as Dr. Erlich has so passionately argued. The most fundamental freedom should be the right not to be born into a world of want and smothering restriction. I am convinced that we must give up (or have taken away from us) the right to have as many children as we want or see all other freedoms lost for them. Nature, to be sure, will restore a dynamic balance between our species and the world ecosystem if we fail to do so ourselves—by famine, pestilence, plague, or war. It seems, but is not, unthinkable that this should happen. If it does, of course, mineral resources may then be or appear to be relatively unlimited in relation to demand for them.

Premise V

The notion of the "technological fix" expresses a view that is at once full of hope and full of risk. It is a gripping thought to contemplate a world set free by nuclear energy. Imagine soaring cities of aluminum, plastic, and thermopane where all live in peace and plenty at unvarying temperature and without effort, drink distilled water, feed on produce grown from more distilled water in coastal deserts, and flit from heliport to heliport in capsules of uncontaminated air. Imagine having as many children as you want, who, of course, will grow up seven stories above the ground and under such germ-free conditions that they will need to wear breathing masks if they ever do set foot in a park or a forest. Imagine a world in which there is no balance of payments problem, no banks, or money, and such mundane affairs as acquiring a shirt or a wife are handled for us by central computer systems, Imagine, if you like, a world in which the only problem is boredom, all others being solved by the state-maintained system of genius-technologists produced by transfer of nuclei from the skin cells of certified gene donors to the previously fertilized ova of final contestants in the annual ideal-pelvis contest. Imagine the problem of getting out of this disease-free world gracefully at the age of 110 when you just can't stand it any longer!

Of course this extreme view may not appeal to people not conditioned to think in those terms, and my guess is that it doesn't appeal to Dr. Weinberg either. But the risk of slipping bit by bit into such a smothering condition as one of the better possible outcomes is inherent in any proposition that encourages or permits people or industries to believe that they can leave their problems to the invention of technological fixes by someone else.

Although the world ecosystem has been in a constant state of flux throughout geologic time, in the short and middle term it is essentially homeostatic. That is to say, it tends to obey Le Chatelier's general principle—when a stress is applied to a system such as to perturb a state of near equilibrium, the system tends to react in such a way as to restore the equilibrium. But large parts of the world ecosystem have probably already undergone or are in danger of undergoing irreversible changes. We cannot continue to plunder and pollute it without serious or even deadly consequences.

Consider what would be needed in terms of conventional mineral raw materials merely to raise the level of all 3.3 billion people now living in the world to the average of the 200 million now living in the United States. In terms of present staple commodities, it can be estimated (revised from Harrison Brown, James Bonner, and John Weir, 1947, *The Next Hundred Years,* Viking Press. p. 33) that this would require a "standing crop" of about 30 billion tons of iron, 500 million tons of lead, 330 million tons of zinc, and 50 million tons of tin. This is about 100 to 200 times the present annual production of these commodities. Annual power demands would be the equivalent of about 3 billion tons of coal and lignite, or about ten times present production. To support the doubled populations expected by the year 2000 at the same level would require, of course, a doubling of all the above numbers or substitute measures. The iron needed could probably be produced over a long period of time, perhaps even by the year 2000, given a sufficiently large effort. But, once in circulation, merely to replace losses due to oxidation, friction, and dispersal, not counting production of new iron for larger populations, would take around 200,000 tons of new iron every year (somewhat more than the current annual production of the United States), or a drastic curtailment of losses below the present rate of 1 per cent every two or three years. And the molybdenum needed to convert the iron to steel could become a serious limiting factor. The quantities of lead, zinc, and tin also called for far exceed all measured, indicated, and inferred world reserves of these metals.

This exercise gives a crude measure of the pressures that mineral resources will be under. It seems likely, to be sure, that substitutions, metallurgical research, and other technological advances will come to our aid, and that not all peoples of the world will find a superfluity of obsolescing gadgets necessary for the good life. But this is balanced by the equal likelihood that world population will not really level off at 6.6 or 7 billion and that there will be growing unrest to share the material resources that might lead at least to an improved standard of living. The situation is also aggravated by the attendant problems of disposal of mine wastes and chemically and thermally polluted waters on a vast scale.

The "technological fix," as Dr. Weinberg well understands, is not a panacea but an anesthetic. It may keep the patient quiet long enough to decide what the best long-range course of treatment may be, or even solve *some* of his problems permanently, but it would be tragic to forget that a broader program of treatment and recuperation is necessary. The flow of science and technology has always been fitful, and population control is a central limiting factor in what can be achieved. It will require much creative insight, hard work, public enlightenment, and good fortune to bring about the advances in discovery and analysis, recovery and fabrication, wise use and conservation of materials, management and recovery of wastes, and substitution and synthesis that will be needed to keep the affluent comfortable and bring the deprived to tolerable levels. It will probably also take some revision of criteria for self-esteem, achievement, and pleasure if the gap between affluent and deprived is to be narrowed and demand for raw materials kept within bounds that will permit man to enjoy a future as long as his past, and under conditions that would be widely accepted as agreeable.

The reality is that the promise of the "technological fix" is a meretricious premise, full of glittering appeal but devoid of heart and comprehension of the environmental and social problems. Technology and "hard" science we must have, in sustained and increasing quality, and in quantities relevant to the needs of man—material, intellectual, and spiritual. But in dealing with the problems of resources in relation to man, let us not lose sight of the fact that this is the province of the environmental and social sciences. A vigorous and perceptive technology will be an essential handmaiden in the process, but it is a risky business to put the potential despoilers of the environment in charge of it.

THE NUB OF THE MATTER

The realities of mineral distribution, in a nutshell, are that it is neither inconsiderable nor limitless, and that we just don't know yet in the detail required for considered weighting of comprehensive and national long-range alternatives where or how the critical lithophilic elements are concentrated. Stratigraphically controlled substances such as the fossil fuels, and, to a degree, iron and alumina, we can comprehend and estimate within reasonable limits. Reserves, grades, locations, and recoverability of many critical metals, on the other hand, are affected by a much larger number of variables. We in North America began to develop our rich natural endowment of mineral resources at an accelerated pace before the rest of the world. Thus it stands to reason that, to the extent we are unable to meet needs by imports, we will feel the pinch sooner than countries like the U.S.S.R. with a larger component of virgin mineral lands.

In some instances nuclear energy or other technological fixes may buy time to seek better solutions or will even solve a problem permanently. But sooner or later man must come to terms with his environment and its limitations. The sooner the better. The year 2038, by which time even current rates of consumption will have exhausted presently known recoverable reserves of perhaps half the world's now useful metals (more will be found but consumption will increase also), is only as far from the present as the invention of the airplane and the discovery of radioactivity. In the absence of real population control or catastrophe there could be fifteen billion people on earth by then! Much that is difficult to anticipate can happen in the meanwhile, to be sure, and to place faith in a profit-motivated technology and refuse to look beyond a brief "foreseeable future" is a choice widely made. Against this we must weigh the consequences of error or thoughtless inaction and the prospects of identifying constructive alternatives for deliberate courses of long-term action, or inaction, that will affect favorably the long-range future. It is well to remember that to do nothing is equally to make a choice.

Geologists and other environmental scientists now living, therefore, face a great and growing challenge to intensify the research needed to ascertain and evaluate the facts governing availability of raw material resources, to integrate their results, to formulate better predictive models, and to inform the public. For only a cognizant public can generate the actions and exercise the restraints that will assure a tolerable life and a flexibility of options for posterity. The situation calls neither for gloomy foreboding nor facile optimism, but for positive and imaginative realism. That involves informed foresight, comprehensive and long-range outlooks, unremitting effort, inspired research, and a political and social climate conducive to such things.

CONCLUSIONS AND PROPOSED ACTIONS

Every promising avenue must be explored. The most imperative objective, after peace and population control, is certainly a workable breeder reactor—with all it promises in reduced energy costs, outlook for desalting saline waters and recovering mineral products from the effluent wastes, availability of now uselessly remote mineral deposits, decrease of cutoff grades, conservation of the so-called fossil "fuels" for more important uses, and the reduction of contaminants resulting from the burning of fossil fuels in urban regions.

But, against the chance that this may not come through on schedule, we should be vigorously seeking additional geological sources of U^{235} and continuing research on controlled nuclear fusion.

A really comprehensive geochemical census of the earth's crustal materials should be accelerated and carried on concurrently, and as far into the future as may be necessary to delineate within reasonable limits the metallogenic prov-

inces of our planet's surface, including those yet poorly-known portions beneath the sea. Such a census will be necessary not only in seeking to discover the causes and locations of new metalliferous deposits, but also in allowing resource data to be considered at the design stage, and in deciding which "common rocks" to mine first, should we ever be reduced to that extreme. Of course, this can be done meaningfully only in context with a good comprehension of sequence and environment based on careful geologic mapping, valid geochronology, perceptive biogeology, and other facets of interpretive earth science.

Programs of geophysical, geochemical, and geological prospecting should meanwhile be expanded to seek more intensively for subglacial, subsoil, submarine, and other concealed mineral resources in already defined favorable target areas—coupled with engineering, metallurgical, and economic innovation and evaluations of deposits found.

Only as we come to know better what we have, where it is, and what the problems of bringing it to the market place are likely to be will it be feasible to formulate the best and most comprehensive long-range plans for resource use and conservation. Meanwhile, however, a permanent, high-level, and adequately funded monitoring system should be established under federal auspices to identify stress points in the mineral economy, or likely future demands, well in advance of rupture. Thus the essential lead time could be allowed in initiating search for new sources or substitutes or in defining necessary conservation programs.

Practices in mixing materials during fabrication and in disposal of scrap metal should be examined with a view to formulating workable legislation that will extend resource lifetimes through more effective re-use.

Management of the nation's resources and of wastes from their extraction, beneficiation, and use should be regarded in the true democratic tradition as national problems and not left entirely to the conscience and discretion of the individual or private firm. Where practices followed are not conducive to the national, regional, or local welfare, informed legal inducement should make them so.

Research into all phases of resource problems and related subjects should be maintained at some effective level not dependent on political whimsy. It would be a far-sighted and eminently fair and logical procedure to set apart some specific fraction of taxes derived from various natural resources to be ploughed back into research designed to assure the integrity of the environment and the sufficiency of resources over the long term.

Much of the work suggested would naturally be centered in the U. S. Department of the Interior and in various state agencies, whose traditionally effective cooperative arrangements with the nation's universities should be enlarged.

Institutions like the one whose dedication we celebrate today are central to the problem of sustaining a healthy industrial society. For they are the source of that most indispensable of all resources—the trained minds that will discern the facts and evolve the principles via which such a society comes to understand its resources and to use them wisely. The essential supplements are adequate support and a vision of the problem that sweeps and probes all aspects of the environmental sciences the world over. The times cry for the establishment of schools and institutes of environmental science in which geologists, ecologists, meteorologists, oceanographers, geophysicists, geographers, and others will interact and work closely together.

I can think of no more fitting way to close these reflections than to quote the recent words of Sir Macfarlane Burnet (p. 29, *in* "Biology and the appreciation of life," The Boyer Lectures, 1966, ABC, 45p)—"*There are three imperatives: to reduce war to a minimum; to stabilize human populations; and to prevent the progressive destruction of the earth's irreplaceable resources.*" If the primary sciences and technology are to be our salvation it will necessarily be in an economic framework that evaluates success by some measure other than rate of turnover, and in the closest possible working liaison with the environmental and social sciences.

ACKNOWLEDGMENTS

I am obligated to literally scores of people whose brains I have picked and whose ideas, data, and words have influenced me or have even been appropriated in formulating the above statement. Among these I acknowledge a special debt to T. S. Lovering, M. K. Hubbert, Peter Flawn, H. L. James, A. L. Weinberg, Frank Forward, and Walter Hibbard, Jr.

I also had the advantage in preparing this paper of having been the Chairman of a Committee on Resources and Man of the National Academy of Sciences, whose final report was being prepared for publication as I was working on this. The views expressed above, of course, are not the official views of that Committee. They are also cast in a more hortative vein than would be appropriate in a report by such a Committee.

40. CAN OUR CONSPICUOUS CONSUMPTION
OF NATURAL RESOURCES BE CYCLIC?

LEALLYN B. CLAPP

Since a natural resource is never consumed (except for the sun's energy), the answer to the title question has to be yes. Exhaustion of the sun's energy will not be a real limitation for a billion years.

By conspicuous consumption I mean the profligate American use of about 19 tons (per person) of the world's resources each year, compared to 2 tons for everybody else.[1] In 1950 each American was using 18 tons of the world's resources divided into those categories shown in Table 1.

This imbalance in our use of natural resources is recognized by citizens of the world and often resented but seems to be taken as a natural right by unquestioning Americans. The resentment against the imbalance is compounded because the difference between our supply and our demand is made up (in several cases) by importation of other people's resources. To be sure, we pay for the resources with food, tourists, plastics, and pens that write under water, but these are replaceable while the importations (fuels and ores) are irreplaceable resources. Resentment against the Ugly American might be in part relieved if we tried to change these imbalances.

Two ways to do this suggest themselves. We could continue and extend our help to other people in developing their own resources (e.g., by peaceful uses of atomic energy); and we could try to make our own consumption cyclic.

Chemists hold that a natural resource is never consumed[2] but only converted into new forms; e.g., a metal into an oxide (iron rust), fuel into carbon dioxide and water, falling fresh water into a reservoir of seawater, fertilizer into protein, etc. The chemist sees the problem of excessive consumption as one of converting the end product back to resource so that, in fact, there is no "end product" but only a cyclic process. Since any or all the steps in the cycle may consume energy, the bottleneck in excessive consumption of natural resources is, in the end, energy. In the final analysis, the source is the sun's energy, and this is nearly an infinite resource.

To make any resource cyclic, the first requisite is a large supply of the original resource, since a cycle may not be completed for years or even centuries. At present the use of only five resources, nitrogen (Delwiche, 1969), iron, copper, lead, and lumber,[3] is in any sense cyclic. (However, we are beginning to worry about air and water, resources not included in the 19 tons.)

Of the five categories making up the 19 tons, fuel, agricultural supplies, and metallic ores are amenable to the present discussion. The problem of building materials is one of transportation, not supply, so that energy remains the main bottleneck. The problem of food, is partly a matter of agricultural supplies (fertilizer).

TABLE 1. PER PERSON USE OF RESOURCES IN THE UNITED STATES (IN TONS)

Resource	1950	1969*
Fuel	7.2	7.5
Building materials	5.4	5.8
Agricultural supplies	2.1	2.3
Metallic ores	2.55	2.65
Food	0.75	0.75
	18.00	19.00

*Extrapolated

Reprinted with permission of author and publisher from *The Science Teacher,* v. 36, no. 4, p. 35-37, April 1969. Copyright 1969 National Science Teachers Association, Inc.

[1] The figure of 19 tons is a 19-year extrapolation of figures available for 1950 from "Resources for Freedom." U.S. President's Materials Policy Commission. U.S. Government Printing Office, Washington, D.C. 1952. Five volumes. The report was neither pessimistic nor optimistic in outlook.

[2] The one exception is the element helium, which is lost to the upper atmosphere irretrievably when it is allowed to escape from balloons or tanks.

[3] Conservationists have been very effective in making the lumber supply cyclic in character.

Enchantment of the original supply of a resource depends on new discoveries or on the use of slimmer and slimmer reserves of resources. Both sources are available to increase fuel supply. Geologists recognize that oil and gas discoveries even in the United States have surpassed usage by about 3 percent per year since 1920. Slimmer reserves (oil shale in Colorado and Wyoming) are untapped at present but will extend the oil supply 135 years at present consumption rates. Coal reserves (new discoveries are not expected in the United States) will last several centuries (500 years' supply under Utah). The world's supply of oil, gas, and coal will last about 900 years at present rates of use, but only 200 years at rates expected by the year 2000.

After exhaustion of fossil fuels, the combustion products (carbon dioxide and water) may have to be converted back to liquid fuels, first by atomic energy, and finally by the sun's energy. Evidence that carbon dioxide content in the earth's atmosphere is increasing beyond a safe margin may necessitate removal of carbon dioxide from the atmosphere, most happily by recycling it back to a fuel. Alternatively, efficient fuel cells or some new invention may speed the change from present dependence on fossil fuels.

In the field of mineral exploration, the reserves get larger every year, because new discoveries in technology allow use of slimmer and slimmer resources. The two most convincing examples are those of copper and iron.

The first copper ores in Michigan contained about 14 percent copper. The content gradually retreated to 2 percent, and the ores now mined in Arizona and Montana, containing 0.9 percent (even as low as 0.5 percent) copper, are still economic.

A more complete recovery of the metal from its ore also helps to extend the original resource. A recent use of ion exchange in the leach liquors of mine tailings promises a 97 percent recovery of copper from this source (Chem. Eng. News, 1969).

Iron ores were once economically unrewarding unless they contained at least 30 percent iron. Now taconite ores of 15 percent iron are beneficiated and compete with better grade ores from the Mesabi range. Mineral resources ordinarily suffer an orderly retreat to slimmer content as the economic recovery of known resources gradually becomes more expensive.

The story of uranium resources in the past few decades suggests another way in which we have had to change the basis of our thinking about natural resources (Jarrett, 1959). In 1945 our uranium reserves were so low that it was classified information to conceal a military weakness. By 1954 the uranium ore reserves were in the millions of tons. Now we have 80 million tons of proven reserves, and the United States government has not been buying uranium ore since 1962.

How did the change come about in such a short time? The search for uranium ores was turned into a national lottery in which the ticket was a Geiger counter, the prospector rode in an airplane and not on a mule, and the prize was a sizable bonus for discovery and production. It was a very popular lottery. The search provided amusement, adventure, and even a serious patriotic purpose; and it worked. Perhaps the method would not work in the case of other metal shortages, however it is in the realm of possibility. Uranium is not a unique case since half the elements in the periodic table are more abundant than is uranium. Though radioactivity could be used to explore for only two other elements, thorium and potassium, other techniques could be used to locate other ores. Color aerial photography could be used, for example, for exploration for other minerals.

Will available agricultural supplies sustain the world indefinitely? Or each United States citizen at the rate of 2.3 tons of resources per year? The three necessary substances which must be renewed in the soil continually are potash, phosphate rock, and nitrogen (as nitrate or ammonia). The world supply of potash and phosphate rock is on the order of 50 billion tons. At the rate of consumption expected by the year 2000, the supply will still extend for 700 to 1,000 years. Only then will cyclic consumption be necessary. The leaching of these two resources from the soil eventually carries them to the rivers and finally, the ocean. Recovery from the ocean may in the end be a necessity.

The supply of nitrogen is truly inexhaustible since 80 percent of the air is nitrogen gas. Synthetic ammonia, urea, and nitrate have been competing with Chilean nitrate since World War I. The limiting factor in making agricultural supplies undergo cyclic consumption is again energy (and ingenuity). Only recently, better technology cut the cost of ammonia synthesis in half.

To sum up, *scarcity* of natural resources in the United States has actually been *decreasing* by

1/3 of 1 percent per year since 1870 (Fisher and Potter, 1964). Nevertheless, meeting production of metallic ores, to the extent of 2.65 tons per person per year, is fraught with uncertainties because of the importation problem. The United States obtains only two important metals completely from our own sources, magnesium from seawater and molybdenum from Climax, Colorado. Molybdenum is used in steel manufacture, and we have a virtual monopoly of it. The use of other important metals depends more or less on ore importation.

This is especially true of the heavy metals. We import substantial quantities of copper (Murphy), iron, zinc, and lead ores and all the tin that we use. We reached this stage with iron in 1953 when the first iron ore shipments arrived in Philadelphia from Venezuela. In 1969, we are importing 23 percent of our iron ore. By 1975 we will be importing 40 percent of our iron ore—from Venezuela, Labrador, and Liberia. We will soon have to induce foreign countries to double their production of copper, iron, and lead, and almost double zinc output. Among the light metals, we will, by 1975, also need four times as much aluminum and 18 times as much magnesium as we did in 1950. We can supply the magnesium by running more seawater through our plants, but aluminum production will depend on other peoples.

To produce aluminum we need bauxite (an aluminum ore) and cryolite to dissolve the alumina prepared from bauxite. We depend on Jamaica, Surinam, Italy, and Mexico for bauxite. In 1950, we thought there was only a 40-year supply from those four countries. But in 1942 a farmer had discovered a new supply of bauxite in Jamaica, because he wondered why his land was so poor. It took several years to find that he had discovered a 300-year supply. Aluminum production will depend on the willingness of Jamaica to supply our increasing demand for aluminum ore.

If Venezuela decided to keep her iron ore and build her own smelters (or Jamaica decided to keep her bauxite), should we just wave more American dollars to get the iron ore or otherwise make it economically impossible for Venezuela to make an independent decision?

Could we make our consumption of metallic ores more nearly cyclic by solving the problems of scrap metal recovery? (Andersen, 1961) I shall examine the metals separately since the scrap problems are different for each one. To begin we need to reduce this 2.65 tons of metallic ores to

poundage of the metals themselves. Smelting and refining reduces this figure to those given in Table 2.

Shouldn't we attempt to make our steel consumption cyclic by using more scrap iron? How well is the job being done now? Most of the scrap from the steel mills and fabricators gets back into circulation, but of the 72 million tons used for containers, transportation, construction, and durable goods about one-fourth is recovered, one-half goes into a 26.5-year recovery cycle, and one-fourth is considered nonrecoverable. We do a poor job of collecting junk and getting it back as metal into cyclic consumption. Only about 25 percent of scrap iron gets back into circulation.

The aluminum industry is not old enough to have formed a large scrap industry. Two-thirds of all the aluminum ever used was made in the last 10 years, and the 30-year cycle of recovery is not nearly complete. Most of the aluminum is used in the airplane industry, and the scrap problem has not been faced.

Copper gets back into the stream of usefulness more completely than does any other metal—about 75 percent is recycled over a 35-year period. This is because copper is easily identified. It is red, and much of it is in the form of wire. Three percent of copper now in use is recovered annually.

Lead scrap, nearly 500,000 tons per year, comes largely from storage batteries. Lead is the most easily recycled metal, for melting and recasting are all that is necessary. Collection is also easy, for batteries are not conveniently ignored and are commonly left at the point of exchange. The fixed-use period (three years) also makes recovery steady and predictable. Each

TABLE 2.   METAL AND MINERAL EQUIVALENTS (POUNDS) EXTRACTED PER 2.65 TONS OF ORE

Iron	1400
Phosphate	150
Aluminum	98
Manganese	36
Potassium	24
Copper	15
Zinc	15
Lead	8
Calcium flouride	7.4
Sulphur	0.72
Molybdenum	0.33
Gold	0.008

battery contains 25 pounds of lead. At present 50 to 60 percent of the lead in use is recycled.

Are natural resources ever consumed? No, but we can prolong the cycle of recovery, and the entropy of our natural resources can increase so that it takes energy to gather them together again. We do such a good job of scattering our metals that someday we may have to lengthen the 30-hour week back to 40 hours and spend the 10 hours gathering scrap metal.

In conclusion, the total resources of the world might be enough for three times its present population but not at the American rate of consumption and not with our present attitude toward cyclic recovery.

REFERENCES

Andersen, A. T., 1961, Resource and Competitive Significance of Scrap Reclamation. PhD Thesis, Harvard University, Cambridge, Massachusetts.

Chemical and Engineering News 45:62-64, April 1967.

Delwiche, C. C., March 1969, The Nitrogen Cycle. The Science Teacher 36:14-21.

Fisher, J. L., and Potter, N., 1964, World Prospects for Natural Resources. The Johns Hopkins Press, Baltimore, Maryland.

Jarrett, H., 1959, Science and Resources. The Johns Hopkins Press, Baltimore, Maryland.

Murphy, R. P. What is the Future of the Copper Industry? Metals and Controls Division, Texas Instruments, Attleboro, Massachusetts, Private Communication.

41. THE U.S. RESOURCE OUTLOOK: QUANTITY AND QUALITY

HANS H. LANDSBERG

It will soon be sixty years since Gifford Pinchot published *The Fight for Conservation,* as informative and succinct a guide to the Conservation Movement's views and judgments as one can hope to find. With regard to resource adequacy, it presents a generally somber picture, supported by careful projections based on the idea that the volume of economic resources in the United States is defined by their identified physical occurrence. The lesson that only careful husbanding can stretch the supply is the logical sequel. Governor Pinchot summarizes the findings of approaching resource exhaustion as follows:

> The five indispensably essential materials in our civilization are wood, water, coal, iron, and agricultural products. . . . We have timber for less than thirty years at the present rate of cutting. We have anthracite coal for but fifty years, and bituminous coal for less than 200. Our supplies of iron ore, mineral oil, and natural gas are being rapidly depleted, and many of the great fields are already exhausted.

Later in the book, Pinchot points to our "limited supply" of coal, a substance that he holds to be "in a sense the vital essence of our civilization."

> If it can be preserved, if the life of the mines can be extended, if by preventing waste there can be more coal left in this country after we of this generation have made every needed use of this source of power, then we shall have deserved well of our descendants.

On that last point there is unfortunately no direct way of judging how well we have, in fact, done. Not only is the evaluation of resources and reserves a very imprecise art at any point in time, but criteria and methods themselves undergo change. Thus, the nation's first estimate of coal

Reprinted with permission of the author and DAEDALUS, Journal of the American Academy of Arts and Sciences, Boston, Mass., Fall 1967, *America's Changing Environment* p. 1034-1057. Copyright 1967 American Academy of Arts and Sciences.

resources, published by the U.S. Geological Survey in 1909, one year before Pinchot's book, reckoned that 3,200 billion tons had been in existence "when mining first began." This estimate held for four decades but was trimmed to 2,500 billion tons in 1950, and to 1,900 billion tons in 1953, not because of intervening consumption (not more than 40 billion tons or so, a minute fraction of the amount estimated to exist, has been mined in the entire history of the country), but because of more sophisticated and extensive methods of measurement.

Governor Pinchot would probably judge us kindly on the score of coal consumption, for the American of 1966 used about two and a half tons of coal per year where his forebear of 1910 consumed almost twice as much. The decline was not, however, motivated by thrift or avoidance of waste, as the Conservation Movement understood these terms. Rather, the prime reasons were vastly greater efficiency in burning, especially in steam-electric plants, and the emergence of other energy sources that have almost totally replaced coal in ships, railroads, and homes, and partially replaced it in factories and power plants.

Indeed, in the case of coal, we have come full circle. Today the U.S. Department of the Interior is investing millions of dollars a year in research that is aimed not at conserving coal but at developing new uses. Two of them, liquefaction and gasification, could, if successful, increase future coal consumption spectacularly. But few considerations, we may be sure, prey less on the Department's mind than the fact, incontestable as it is, that the country's coal supplies constitute a finite resource and thus are subject to eventual exhaustion.

HOW WE HAVE MADE DO—
THE BIG PICTURE

What has wrought this radical change in our view of things is, of course, the cumulative and joint impact of increased knowledge and improved technology—in short the forces generally lumped under the broad heading "The Scientific Age." (Barnett and Morse, 1963) Change induces change. Diminishing returns from exhaustion of resources with better characteristics are staved off not by lucky discoveries, as was once the case, but by advances that are both systematic and cumulative. Moreover, we have learned the advantages of "disaggregation"—that is, the separate utilization of the different inherent features of natural resources, as opposed to their joint use in the form in which they occur in nature. To illustrate the technique and realize its advantages from a conservation point of view, one need only think of the way in which the chemical industry, prominently including oil and gas processing, typically breaks down its raw-material stream.

We have thus enhanced our ability to upgrade old resources (for example, cropland through the addition of fertilizer), to discover new ones (oil, gas, nuclear fission, and so forth), to utilize them more efficiently (coal in power generation, low-grade copper ore, wood waste for pulp mills and building board, and the like), and to adjust to relative resource availabilities (aluminum replacing copper, or air-cooling replacing water-cooling). Consequently, the relative importance of the country's resources as inputs into the economic hopper has steadily diminished. A few gross examples will suffice to support this statement.

At the end of the Civil War, 6.5 million people were employed by the resource industries, which represent the sum total of the agriculture, forestry, and extractive industries (lack of suitable data prevents inclusion of water-associated activities). By 1910, this figure had climbed to 12 million, but it has now dropped to 5.5 million—one million less than it was ninety years ago. Resources now claim less than one tenth of all the labor in the country, instead of the half of a century ago, but this tenth produces five times as much as the half did.

Almost the same relationship is revealed when the output of resource industries is compared with the output of all goods and services. A quintupling in the resource field has been accompanied by a twenty-five-fold growth in the economy's total output. Not surprisingly, prices of resource commodities have, in general, not risen above prices for all goods and services.

A QUICK RUNDOWN IN SOME DETAIL

One might, therefore, say so far so good. Things have not worked out badly, at least not for the United States. Fossil fuel reserves have held up well, even though we have drawn on them at rates that were unimaginable not so long ago. Because rising yields allow us to grow what

is needed on fewer acres, land in crops has been on the decline. And were it not for booming food exports, partly financed by ourselves, the problem of surplus farm land would loom much larger.

The most recent survey reveals that our forests are adding new growth at a substantially faster rate than that at which the annual cut is removing them. In 1962, when detailed estimates were last made, growth exceeded cut by 60 per cent. To be sure, behind this favorable aggregate comparison lurk problems of quality, species, location, marketing, and so on. For example, we still cut more sawtimber softwood—a highly desirable product—than we grow. Moreover, some of this apparent good fortune derives from improved measurement. This would mean that we were better off in the past than we had thought and that part of the apparent improvement is a mirage, but it would not negate the finding that current growth exceeds cut. The products of new technology—metals, plastics, and other synthetic substances—have reduced the demand for forest products; and in some lines, such as pulp and paper, we have been able to rely extensively on imports to supplement domestic production.

Perhaps nothing reflects so dramatically the changing tide of events as the conditions of timber resources. As Harold J. Barnett and Chandler Morse (1963, p. 86) have pointed out, the Conservation Movement's "sense of impending scarcity derived directly from a concern for the future of America's forests, dating back at least to the 1870s." As early as 1877, Carl Schurz, then Secretary of the Interior under President Hayes, forecast a coming "timber famine," with supplies to last only another twenty years. Today the concern for forests focuses on their role as part of the environment rather than as a source of materials.

In the field on nonfuel minerals, we are intermittently plagued by specific shortages—copper, sulfur, tin, and the like—but a stretch of high prices and concern has never as yet failed to engender successful efforts to locate new deposits, to exploit old ones more efficiently, and to promote substitution of more abundant, natural or man-made, materials, sometimes temporarily, sometimes permanently.

THE ROLE OF TECHNOLOGY

The current condition of ease regarding sufficiency of quantity is rooted largely in advancing technology, with its twin offspring:

efficiency and substitutability. This trend has accelerated in the recent past. Only fifteen years ago, the authors of "Resources for Freedom" (the name under which President Truman's Materials Policy, or Paley, Commission released its findings in 1952) commented that "in the U.S. the supplies of the evident, the cheap, the accessible are running out."

The Commission would probably not phrase it that way today, for there are abundant examples of the nonevident becoming evident, the expensive cheap, and the inaccessible accessible. Broadening scope, increasing variety, and rising volume of man-made products exemplify the nonevident that is becoming evident. So do nuclear power generation and telecommunication by microwave and laser.

Hardness, low-metal content, fine-grained structure, and the nonmagnetic nature of part of the deposits made the extensive iron-bearing ores of Minnesota, Michigan, and Wisconsin that are commonly lumped under the generic heading of taconites too costly to mine until after World War II. New processing technology has since made it not merely possible to extract usable material at acceptable costs but has turned the initial handicap of having to agglomerate the fine particles into pellets into a major advantage, because the pellet feed greatly enhanced the productivity of the industry's furnaces. Similar evidence testifies to the changing circumstances of accessibility. Thus, the deposits of oil in offshore fields, buried under hundreds of feet of water and thousands of feet of ocean bottom, have become accessible. So have many and varied underground ore deposits that have yielded to the search by airborne magnetometer, sensing devices, chemical anomalies, and other new exploration tools.

But while that Commission, from the vantage point of 1967, appears to have underestimated the speed of population growth, of economic growth, and of industrially useful new knowledge and technology, its place in history is secure, for its decisive emphasis was not on the "running out of resources," which had been a popular concept in earlier years, but on resource availability at a cost, on the role of costs as a barometer of scarcity, and on future technology as a factor in determining costs and availability. Thus "running out" becomes a relative matter. Copper may "run out" for fabricator A, but not for fabricator B who, for one reason or another, is able to pay the higher price that reduced

availability engenders. At the same time, the higher price is likely to bring closer the threshold at which deposits with poorer characteristics can be commercially exploited. The "running out" process is a dynamic one, subject to changes in direction, and thus is quite different from the straight-line, down-trending concept current early in the century.

Barnett and Morse (1963, p. 235 ff.) have suggested that a major cause of this development is the flowering of the scientific advances. In such an environment, there are no diminishing returns from improvements, for the improvement is in turn improved upon before its advantages have been dissipated or squeezed to a zero return. We have reached constant cost plateaus, at which increased amounts of resources are available without cost increases.

Others suggest that the curve of technological improvement will soon begin to flatten out and that we may already be moving along the upper leg of the sigmoid development curve. The bigger part of many technical revolutions, says John R. Platt (1966), appears to lie behind us. We have reached "science and technology plateaus." From horse-and-buggy to the current version of the jet plane is a bigger quantum jump than the impending advance to the SST. The invention of the telephone marked a bigger break with past communications methods than will the transition to satellites.

Perhaps this is so, although the odds in speculating on unknown technology are notoriously long. Nevertheless, no amount of speculation on the kind of plateau we may be approaching can relieve us of the need or impair the usefulness of taking a long look ahead for a test of how well, under carefully spelled-out, realistic assumptions, our resource situation is likely to hold up. Such a look involves a wide array of guesses, the worth of which will depend as much on the effort that goes into making them as on the investigator's success in recognizing and overcoming his biases.

A LOOK AHEAD

Resources for the Future has engaged in making and publishing such informed guesses or projections (Landsberg et al., 1963 and 1964). I can, therefore, be brief and summarize the picture that emerges for the balance of this century. It is not one to provoke undue concern, at least not on the score of quantity and for this country.

FARM LAND

Rising crop yields—based both on further advances in agronomy and on a large-scale catching-up of the bulk of the growers with the best—can confidently be expected to keep land from becoming a limiting factor to food production. A few years ago, contemplation of past history led Resources for the Future to project 1970 corn yields at 70 bushels per acre. Because yields ranged between 53 and 55 bushels per acre in the three years preceding 1961, the year in which we had to make our projections, we thought our prediction a little daring; some scholars who were asked to review what was then a manuscript thought we were very daring. But by 1965 the yield had climbed to 74 bushels and had outrun the projection. The average yield in Iowa had jumped above 80 and in Indiana and Illinois above 90 bushels per acre. Our projected yield of 100 bushels in the year 2000, a faraway guess when made, had begun to move into clearer view. This projection and those for other feed grains stand a good chance of being overtaken before the end of the century. Little can as yet be said about other major crops (Brown, 1966).

FORESTS

It is difficult to speak with assurance regarding the long-run adequacy of U.S. forests to supply the domestic market. A few years ago, Resources for the Future had grave doubts that even allowing for a generous drawing on imports, prospective demand could long be satisfied by domestic supply without impairing the size and quality of our forests. These doubts have diminished. Demand continues to lag. Wood prices seem high in comparison with nonwood alternatives, especially when the latter offer advantages in handling and maintenance. Also, there has been a less than buoyant housing market. Moreover, the existing volume of trees now appears larger than was believed a few years ago. The most recent figures (1962) compiled by the U.S. Forest Service show a significantly higher timber inventory than does their previous estimate (1953). For the time being, emphasis has shifted from forest products in the aggregate to adequacy and quality of given species.

OUTDOOR RECREATION

Considerable uncertainty attaches to those uses of land that do not lead to production of commodities. This is true especially for outdoor recreation. Even cautious projections of the use trend of parks and other recreation land translate into very large acreage figures.

On what some might consider quite conservative assumptions regarding both the rate of increase in visits and tolerable density of recreation acreage, Resources for the Future estimated that by 1980 there might be need for 76 million acres for outdoor recreation; and by the year 2000 this need should call for an additional 58 million acres. For comparison, in 1960 there were only 44 million acres of land in national parks, monuments, recreation areas, state parks, and in national forests used primarily for recreation.

In terms of new policies and of magnitude of outlays required, such figures put a wholly new face on a hitherto secondary aspect of land use. On the other hand, until we know more about such factors as the carrying capacity of outdoor acreage for recreation and the potential of private land for such purposes, we must handle these statistics with some sense of detachment. Unfortunately, it will take some time for research to catch up with the speed at which use of this new resource has been growing.

OTHER USES OF LAND

A common complaint of the sixties is the "asphalting over" of America's land. Houses, offices, factories, highways, airports, parking lots, and the like have such high visibility to so many people that their presence and growth tends to distort perspective. It is the view during the occasional airplane ride that restores it.

In cold figures, the 25 million acres or so occupied by the urban population at this time is less than 1.5 per cent of the country's surface. Highways, railroads, and airports take up perhaps 27 million acres, for a grand total of built-up terrain of, say, 50 million acres, not quite 3 per cent of the face of America. By the end of the century, this might grow by 50 per cent, to 75 million acres, due overwhelmingly to expansion of urban land use.

I do not mean to suggest that problems of land use—especially in urban areas—are meaningfully measured in terms of acres. If they were, the task of finding the additional 25 million acres of land that we may need for urban living between now and the end of the century could be entrusted to a child equipped with nothing more than a map and a ruler. Nor does dealing in aggregates, unqualified by reference to land characteristics, do justice to the issue. Pointing to

European population densities that typically run five to ten and, in some cases, fifteen times the U.S. density merely shows that other countries have problems too.

On the other hand, nearly 500 million acres are devoted to commercial raising of trees, and about 700 million acres are primarily grazing land (there is room for arguing over proper land classification here, but these rough figures will do for the purpose). Thus, 75 million acres for urban centers and transportation facilities pose less a problem of "space shortage" due to "asphalting over" than of inventiveness in efficient use of the country's surface.

THE DEMAND FOR ENERGY

The demand for energy is likely to be three times as high in the year 2000 as it is now, but the entry of new or newly derived energy resources (from nuclear reactors to oil and gas from coal, shale oil, oil sands, and so forth), combined with more efficient utilization and conversion of conventional energy sources, is likely to ward off rising costs. Indeed, we may well be entering an era of slowly declining energy costs. There is unprecedented activity in developing new coal technology to widen the scope of our largest fossil fuel resource; research and development leading to a breeder reactor, which may begin to bear fruit by the mid-seventies, will multiply many times over the country's uranium resources as a basis for power generation.

METALS

Enough deposits of the major metals, supplemented by imports and rising amounts of scrap, have been identified that emergence of sustained supply problems due to inadequate resources seems unlikely given our demonstrated ability to handle ever lower-grade material. This does not, however, insure against shortfalls in times of national emergency—to be provided for through special measures, such as stockpiles. Nor does it offset temporary and, perhaps, even prolonged difficulties like those that have in recent years plagued copper, which is mined in major quantities in countries that are subject to political upheavals or uncertainties. Supply cannot always keep up with quickly rising demand, but it has a habit of catching up, sometimes to a greater extent than is required.

Ability to process low-grade material carries one great advantage: Such material usually exists in very large volume. For example, the previously mentioned taconite ores, most of which are

likely to become subject to commercial exploitation during the balance of the century, equal four times the cumulative demand for iron projected through the end of the century. Perhaps a turn to unconventional sources, such as the ocean floor, will help the situation for others, as will substitutions by nonmetallic materials. Thus, despite projected levels of consumption that between now and the year 2000 could cumulate to the equivalent of 60 to 70 times the 1960 consumption for iron, copper, lead, and zinc, 90 to 100 times that for nickel, chromium, and tungsten, and 125 times that for aluminum, it is difficult to envision serious supply problems because of resource limitations.

WATER

Judgments about water are often confusing because of fuzzy concepts and poor terminology and complicated because of the attention that must be given to problems of quality. It helps to realize initially that in many of its uses water is either a free or nearly free good and that incentives for economizing are the exception rather than the rule. Thus, projections of future consumption are based more on what people have been led to take for granted as "needed" than on what they would be willing to buy at prices that more nearly reflect cost.

Another aid to understanding is a clear distinction between *withdrawal* of water with subsequent discharge back into the original source and withdrawal followed by consumption, or *depletion*. All uses have elements of both, but the proportions vary greatly. In municipal use, for example, most water—about 90 per cent—is discharged after it has served its function, while irrigation depletes from 60 to 90 per cent, depending upon the circumstances. Since water can be used over and over again, the item to keep one's eye on is, for most purposes, depletion—not withdrawal. Unfortunately, most popular discussion is conducted in terms of water "use," without further definition of the term.

The need for sharpness of definition applies equally to the supply side. The total supply of surface water—precipitation—is a multiple of what becomes accessible in the form of runoff. The latter is, in turn, normally a multiple of withdrawal, and withdrawal typically exceeds depletion. (Instances where the entire flow is diverted without any return to the source are the exceptions.) Moreover, ground water, as distinguished from annual replenishment, constitutes a separate supply. Finally, there is a variety of techniques for adding to available supply. Some, such as storage, predate the era of recorded history; others, such as desalinization, weather modification, and evaporation control, are undergoing active development. They are paralleled on the demand side by techniques for reducing consumption. Substituting air-cooling for water-cooling, less wasteful irrigation techniques, and a more efficient use generally (for example, having a smaller flow or depletion per unit of service required) belong in this category. As our political and administrative approaches to water management, as well as our costing and pricing mechanisms, receive attention and review, channeling water into the highest-yielding alternatives will assume increasing importance.

Differences in natural endowment and climate have combined with a different mix of use categories to produce a sharp cleavage in situation and outlook between the eastern and western United States, using these geographic terms in the loosest of meanings. Because of the large role played by irrigation, the West (excluding the Pacific Northwest) depletes nearly five times the volume of water depleted in the East. Since it only disposes of about 20 per cent of the runoff available to the East (which is, of course, the reason why the West needs irrigation if it wants to have agriculture), the West depletes about 40 per cent of the water it can count on.

Before long, the West may find water supply a serious obstacle to economic growth if flows are not diverted to uses other than irrigation, prices are not brought into line with costs, and techniques for adding new supplies do not soon become commercially feasible for meeting the needs of cities and industries at prices they can afford.

In sharp contrast, and for the opposite reasons, the East depletes less than 2 per cent of its runoff and faces no long-range physical shortage, provided rainfall deficiencies during the past few years do not represent the beginning of a basic long-term change in climatic conditions. Meteorologists are divided on this issue, and conclusive evidence one way or the other will not be forthcoming for some time. Meanwhile, whatever the ultimate trend, the East faces decisions associated with pricing and allocating water and with encouraging economizing by means other than admonitions and exhortations (though in the face of uncertainty the "muddling-through" approach has the merit of preserving options).

Above all, however, the eastern United States is confronted with growing deterioration of water quality. This increasingly narrows the usefulness of many streams and lakes for purposes that demand clean water. It imposes costs on users that draw their supplies from stretches polluted by others. Moreover, it raises in full not only a host of new technical problems but economic, political, and administrative questions about equitable and efficient remedies to the situation. For those who try to appraise the degree of adequacy of the nation's resources, it opens up a new dimension—the quality of resources.

The size and characteristics of domestic resources, in combination with imports, are such as to exclude any significant limitation to U.S. growth because of resources. This picture would no doubt look different if one were to widen the geographic scope and consider the world, or a major portion of it. The number of critical resource areas would increase, and the time horizon for which one would have a reasonable assurance of adequacy would shrink. Specifically, it is unlikely that these conditions will affect the terms on which the United States obtains its imports sufficiently to alter significantly the general perspective outlined above. Except in the case of food, however, only the most general quantitive appraisals have been made of the resources that the developing countries are likely to need for the decades ahead (See Fisher and Potter, 1964). Analogies of trends and patterns of material use that have prevailed in Western industrialized nations and extrapolations of short trends in the developing countries can both be misleading. Exploration of future development patterns in terms of claims on specific resources is badly needed, however, if we are to gain a realistic picture of what faces this country in its role as a member of the world community.

QUALITY OF RESOURCES:
HOW GOOD?

It would be convenient to deal with the quality problem in much the same fashion as with quantitative adequacy. We would, in other words, assess the degree of past acceptability for each of the resources, project the demand into the future, and judge whether the supply will be forthcoming, or whether, where, and when "quality shortages" will develop.

Unfortunately, we can barely begin to measure the state of adequacy at the present. How good or bad the past has been we can deduce, at best, from the presence or absence of comments and protests. Moreover, we are as yet woefully short of methods that can help us pick our way between those who see the population tobogganing toward physical and emotional decay and those who regard the current concern over quality decline as but another phase of modern life with which common sense and technology will in time come to grips.

TECHNOLOGY—TWO SIDES OF THE COIN

Technology, it seems, has played a cruel hoax on us: It has assured enough, but in the process it has led to degraded quality. Excessive use of the waste-assimilative characteristics of water and air by cities, factories, coal mines, oil wells, chemical-bearing agricultural land, and many other concomitants of life in the industrial age has created a complex technological and economic problem: to devise ways and means other than natural stream and air flow for disposing of waste material, and to determine and apportion the costs and benefits that arise in the process. Undesirable by-products have made their mark on both the rural and the urban landscape. The settings are different but the adverse consequences and the problems of measurement, evaluation, and policy are similar.

Deploring technology's side effects—which range from unpleasant to highly dangerous—is not tantamount to decrying technology as such. In one of his recorded songs, Tom Lehrer, Cambridge's gift to social satire, finds it a sobering thought that at his age Mozart had been dead for two years. Similarly I find it a sobering thought that I would have been less likely to accept the invitation to contribute to this symposium at the turn of the century, for a man in his fifties would at that time have outrun his mean chance of survival. Life expectancy at birth in the United States has since moved from less than fifty to seventy years.

One is apt to view the more disagreeable aspects of modern life, including most prominently those due to the impact of technology, with partiality—often unconsciously. We take for granted that we may drink tap water, eat uncooked fruit or vegetables, and consume milk with no thought of falling victim to a lurking bug. We are reminded of our good fortune only when we travel in parts of the world that require preventive or remedial counter-measures, or when the exceptional case in this country hits the front page. But, customarily, we fail to do much balancing of pluses and minuses. We tend to overlook the fact that the chemical industry produces not only controversial pesticides, but

also antibiotics and vaccines; that the automobile whose incomplete fuel combustion fouls the city air does, at the same time, enable us to escape its boundaries and to know the world in a way available a generation or two ago only to the daring or the rich. We are quick to lament the fallen sparrow, but slow to celebrate the fall of "Typhoid Mary."

This is not the same as inviting, or welcoming, or even being indifferent to the negative aspects and abuses that can be or are associated with technological advance. To reconstruct what is in terms of what could have been is generally a misleading venture, for people commonly engage in such reconstruction for the purpose of excising the obnoxious features while leaving untouched those they sanction. They forget or ignore that both are usually part of one and the same fabric. To show that we could have had one without the other requires more than saying so.

Nor can it be taken for granted that accurate and timely anticipation of the adverse consequences of a particular action necessarily produces decisions to prevent them. For example, the failure of cigarette-smoking to decline or of repeated disasters to discourage occupancy of flood plains raises doubts about the level of individual response. Failure to have acted long ago on such matters as provision of adequate, common-carrier urban transport or nonpolluting incinerators suggests that we act no more wisely in matters of collective response.

Beyond the need of adequate motivation and appropriate institutions, there is the great difficulty of balancing the gains and the losses. Let us look more closely at the cigarette-smoker, and let us assume that he is well informed about the effects. Presumably the smoker has achieved a balance of gains and losses: The gain from inhalation more than offsets the pain from possible illness and shorter lifetime. Arriving at the balance is likely to involve several elements— among them, the weighing of pleasure *now* against pain *later,* with the distant event, as is customary in such situations, heavily discounted; the reluctance and remoteness of applying to oneself a cause-and-effect relationship that is only statistically demonstrated, a reason for additional discounting; the calculating of odds; allowance for personal habits and characteristics; appeasement through change to presumably less harmful brands. Clearly some such calculus underlies the decision to smoke and how much to smoke.

One might go on to speculate that those

smokers who have digested the new knowledge have adjusted to it by setting their daily intake at a level at which they judge reduction would gain them less in future health than they would forego in current pleasure; a level, conversely, at which the improvement in current well-being derived from the extra cigarette, the marginal revenue, is not worth the incremental health hazard, the marginal cost. At that point, the smoker is in equilibrium. This point comes at different levels of smoking for different people, and the motivation—the type of gain extracted—differs widely among smokers. Thus, rationality of decision is not the issue. Rather, what is open to discussion and represents a proper area for education are the value scales on which pleasure from smoking and pain from ill health are traded off.

A serious economic problem arises not when an individual's actions affect adversely only himself (though costs of medical attention will in varying degrees not be defrayed by the individual, and there is, therefore, a public interest), but when those actions affect, primarily and often exclusively, other people. This is the heart of the quality aspect of resources.

QUALITY VERSUS GRADE DIFFERENTIAL

One could argue that to distinguish quality from quantity is merely a semantic nicety; that supply must always be understood as supply corresponding to appropriate specifications; and that if there is not "enough" by whatever the qualitative yardstick, then we have a quantitative shortage, whether it be water, air, iron ore, copper, or softwood sawtimber.

To some extent this is true. For example, within a large excess of aggregate forest growth over aggregate cut, there is too much poor hardwood from small trees and too little good softwood from large ones. Why do we not customarily speak of this as a separate dimension in judging resource adequacy? In part, we do not because there is a market on which poor hardwoods are traded and have, in different uses, found acceptance as satisfactory substitutes for good softwoods. Taconite ores are undoubtedly poorer bearers of iron than the traditional ores, but poor quality did not prevent their acceptance as soon as they could be processed at a cost low enough to make their use lucrative in blast furnaces. Copper mines today go after ores that hold only five pounds of metal per thousand. In the end, there is nothing that distinguishes the copper ingot derived from poor ore from that derived from rich ore; all that matters is that their costs be in a range that finds them a market. These grade differentials are handled satisfactorily by the market that reduces the offerings to quantities of some commonly agreed upon standard or equivalent. Provided we have an appropriate processing technique, six tons of .5 per cent copper ore are neither better nor worse than one ton of 3 per cent copper ore.

But one hundred cubic feet of slightly polluted water or air cannot presently substitute for fifty or ten of clean water or air—at least not for most purposes. Given a choice, one could not be indifferent, as in the case of copper. But above all, the choice is not one the consumer can effectively make, except in the most roundabout way.

Examples of these kinds of quality problems are abundant. There is the discharge of municipal, industrial, and agricultural waste into watercourses, of pollutants into the air; there is disfiguration of the landscape through mining activities, transmission lines, or other symbols of the industrial revolution; there is ugliness along highways, be it beer bottles or billboards, interference with plant life and wildlife through the use of pesticides, disturbance of the atmosphere through vibration caused by fast-flying planes and of the sound waves through indiscriminate use of portable radios.

A new wrinkle in the quantity-quality relationship, best exemplified in the energy field, should be mentioned here. The traditional conservation doctrine maintains that use of natural gas as boiler fuel signifies an "inferior" use of an exhaustible resource. In the past, both the Federal Power Commission and the courts have upheld this viewpoint. As late as 1961, the Supreme Court confirmed the Commission's authority to make end use a factor in deciding upon certification for service (in a case involving shipment of gas from Texas to New York for use as boiler fuel). "One apparent method of preventing waste of gas," said the six-man majority, "is to limit the uses to which it may be put, uses for which another, more abundant fuel may serve equally well."

This was before air pollution became a pressing problem and made natural gas the preferred boiler fuel, given its low pollution quotient. The Federal Power Commission has not yet made this feature a basis for granting electric-utility applications for increased gas deliveries. It does not deny that gas is a less polluting fuel; the "inferior use" argument would sit badly with urban communities today. It does, however, contend that steam-electric plants are not the major villains in the situation and that additional gas would be, at best, a temporary palliative—at worst, a block to more radical remedial action. In any event, appraisal of adequacy can obviously be heavily affected by such changes in judgment.

ECONOMIC CHARACTERISTICS OF SIDE EFFECTS

The "side effect" syndrome has a number of characteristics, all of which distinguish it from simple grade differentiations and make it a highly controversial object of economic analysis and public policy.

Certain effects arise apart from and beyond the primary purpose. Not confined to the user, these affect others. Gains are reaped and costs are incurred, but there is no market that relates the two. Most importantly, the costs that arise are borne not by those that cause them but by others that happen to be around but are outside the process—bystanders, so to speak. Not all the costs of the process end up as costs to the producer; a slice is lodged outside. With inventiveness, but at the peril of losing their non-technical audience, economists refer to these as "external diseconomies" or "externalities"; less elegantly, one might think of them as "someone else's headache."

Unless these headaches are brought home to the originator in such a way that they are included as costs in his profit-and-loss calculations—or "internalized"—private costs will understate total, or social, costs. Consequently, production decisions will lead to misallocation of resources, for the producer will be faced with production costs that are lower than they would be if he had also to foot the bill for the external diseconomies—the unpleasantness, nuisance, or other aggravation caused to his neighbor or environment.

The cause-effect nexus of such phenomena is often difficult to establish. Sometimes this may be due to the low intensity of the degrading substances or activities or to the low degree of quality deterioration that takes place. At other times, damage may be long delayed in appearing, or it may turn up in areas remote from the locus of emission. Finally, effects seldom occur with laboratorylike purity and in isolation, but are intermingled with a variety of other factors. Thus, presumption is more common than proof.

And when the causal relationship can be satisfactorily established, it is often difficult to identify the offender, or when he can be identified, to assess his share in the total effect.

Typically, there is a widely dispersed multiplicity of the offended. In marked contrast to traditional "nuisance" cases that are actionable in the courts, this raises questions of both efficiency and equity in remedial action, if not of the feasibility of starting any action at all.

Changes in the environment are not easily, and often not at all, susceptible to meaningful evaluation in dollars and cents. This impedes comparison with costs incurred or avoided by the producer of the side effect in question, which as a rule lends itself to expression in monetary terms.

There is no answer to "what price beauty?" that would furnish a zoning authority a ready method of weighing the claims of, say, a stone quarry, a wildlife refuge, and a resort hotel where they are competing for the same tract of land. Psychic values are not traded in the market, at least not directly and not obviously. One is, therefore, limited to seeking surrogates and proxies that reflect such values. (For example, movements into and out of specific areas may be prompted by changes in environmental conditions and may be reflected in real-estate quotations.) This search has only just begun. Moreover, there are, as yet, few institutional and administrative arrangements that offer a mechanism for bringing together the offended and the offender, even when both can, in principle, be identified.

For the sake of efficient management it is frequently desirable that measures dealing with questions of environmental quality be considered for large areas at a time. This is almost a necessity where air and water are concerned. Action then tends to become collective and regional, rather than individual and local. The rationale is that the smaller the community considered, the more the costs will be of the "external" kind. As the area widens, they become internal and, therefore, part of the proper economic calculus. If the decision-making unit is my home, then the costs of my dumping trash in my neighbor's backyard are "external" as far as I am concerned. If the unit is my street, then the costs are "internal."

Thus, one way of catching up with side effects is to extend the area within which they cannot be "external." Decisions made on the basis of rather large areas—the community, the river basin—are likely to produce a result closer to the optimum than the sum total of many individual decisions. One consequence of this spatial relationship, incidentally, is that for reasons of both efficiency and equity the role of the federal government as well as that of interstate and regional compacts, commissions, and similar multi-state bodies will inescapably grow larger.

While it may sound as though stressing the size of the decision-making unit as an important element in quality management is a highly academic point, it is actually a very practical one. A good topical illustration is the use of pesticides in crop production. One's balancing of the gains and losses incurred from use of pesticides would differ according to whether one focuses on the individual farmer and his immediate surroundings, the county, the state, a region, the country, or an even larger supranational area. It is one thing to weigh damage to the environment against gains in crop production in a given locality, but quite another to do so in a national or supranational framework. It could be argued that the United States might not now be able to ship one-fourth of its wheat crop to India had it not been for the prolonged application of various chemicals to soil and vegetation. Such chemicals not only raise productivity in their own right but permit many other changes in farm practices and organization that jointly form a tight, almost ecological system. Evaluation of gains and losses from use of pesticides, thus, can be seen to depend greatly on the size of the decision-making unit—on where one draws the line.

THE CASE FOR QUANTIFICATION

The above categorizing makes no claim to either comprehensiveness or uniqueness. But it does serve to bring out the principal difficulties that beset improvement of resource quality: identification of gainers and losers, ascertainment and valuation of gains and losses in the absence of a market, and lack of channels and institutions for arbitration of rival claims. If economists have not yet found many answers, they have begun to bring to this relatively new field of concern the integrating element of a common denominator—cost. Its applicability can be exaggerated, but its neglect surely leaves the field open to pressure and emotion. At the very least, even a rough casting of gains and losses into dollars and cents will convey a sense of magnitude that would otherwise be lacking. There is nothing dehumanizing in the process of monetary quantification (Gaffney, 1965). Where efforts must be expanded to achieve a given objective, they are not available for alternative uses, and it is only fair that we establish at least the magnitude of what we must forego, so we can gain some idea of whether the environmental change contemplated is worth the price tag. This approach suggests a number of areas that call for better understanding. To a degree, they are corollaries of the characteristics discussed above.

We must learn more about the physical characteristics of the desirable objectives, of the undesirable side effects, and of the relationship of the one to the other. In such studies, attention should be directed not to the spectacular, which is usually accidental and ephemeral, but to the pedestrian, which is usually basic and lasting. From the study of physical aspects, we must move to the dollar values associated with them Above all, we must ascertain and analyze cost relationships. We know, for example, that it is extraordinarily expensive to remove the final traces of pollution. In water treatment, costs double and triple as we approach a state of pristine purity. In removing successive amounts of coal dust from power-plant smokestacks, the capacity of precipitators must increase proportionally with the added removal efficiency, measured in terms of the remaining dust. Thus, if removal efficiency is to be raised from 96 to, say, 98 per cent, the increase is not 2, but 50 per cent, and consequently represents a steep rise in equipment size and cost. We must, therefore, ask how we determine the point of equilibrium, beyond which additional purity costs more than is gained in terms of health or aesthetics? Where does one reasonably stop? The more we can learn about cost behavior under different conditions, the easier it will become to establish criteria around which compromises can be built, even in the face of the difficulties that beset ascertainment of corresponding benefits.

Indignation over the manifestations of pollution comes easily; remedies do not. It has been estimated, for example, that it would cost some $20 billion annually to return all watercourses to an unspoiled state. This is about what the country spends each year on primary and secondary education. Will such knowledge affect specific decisions? It might, for decisions will tend to be more in accord with explicit value scales, openly arrived at. And these will frequently differ from what is merely presumed.

We must find ways of measuring society's demands for improving the quality of resources, the environment. The baffingly unmeasurable must be made measurable. There are small beginnings today and much groping for answers, for it is clear that in the absence of acceptable measurements the debate will continue to produce more heat than light. Moreover, since funds will be appropriated and spent without greater guidance from any demand gauge, responsibility will remain above all with the resource manager, who must construe a demand schedule out of his own scale of preferences, what he believes are other people's preferences, and what he thinks ought to be other people's preferences. He will get some help from the political process, but that process is clumsy, especially when it comes to detail. Customarily, it permits choices only between approval and rejection, between yes and no; rarely between more and less, or among a whole spectrum of alternatives. As a consequence, decisions tend to be reached with little factual knowledge of the values that society as a whole puts on the results of the contemplated action.

Nor does the matter end here. Even though the individual consumer's choice is limited to the range of goods and services that are offered in the market, there *is* choice, both in quantity and in kind. This is not so in most decisions that are arrived at politically. As little as I can have a federal government that is part Democratic and part Republican, can I have a river that is both wild and provides storage for water supply and power. Thus, there is a problem of meeting the wants and needs of minorities whose desires are swamped in political decisions.

Finally, we must recognize that the decision-maker can err. Let us assume, for the sake of argument, that cigarette-smoking were considered a form of pollution and its practice made subject to public regulation. In the light of the last few years' experience, there can be little doubt that any restrictions put on smoking would not be in accord with the aggregate of private valuations rationally arrived at—not only, as J. W. Milliman (1962) has suggested, because the political process is no freer from imperfection than the market mechanism, but because there is a real conflict between a theoretical cost-benefit calculus, made in all good faith, and one derived from the summation of an individual's preferences. Only by cranking in society's interest in a healthier population as a plus could one hope to redress the balance toward a net gain from restrictive regulation.

All of this demonstrates the need for greatly increased research efforts directed toward methods of ascertaining where in the hierarchy of rival claims people rank quality improvement and similar intangibles. Even without accurate measurements, however, we are not quite lost. Establishing a range of arbitrary quality standards and estimating the costs their imposition would imply is one way out. To initially recommend itself, the cost of an action would have to be at least commensurate with the value of the improvement that is sought or the deterioration that is to be prevented. With the aid of such calculations of alternatives, we can begin to make intelligent choices among policy decisions—intelligent, but not necessarily easy. The cost tag is an indispensable aid: "No intangible has infinite value. All intangibles have cost." (Milliman, 1962) Nevertheless, it is not the only nor perhaps always the determining criterion for decision. Still, the magnitude of what one has to forego, which is what cost is all about, is always relevant and usually lurks somewhere in the decision-maker's mind. Instead, it should be explicitly and prominently on the decision-maker's agenda.

Calculation of both gains and losses greatly facilitates dealing with quality changes. Whether it is more efficient to allow degradation to stand, or to reduce or suppress it, the course followed should leave nobody worse off and somebody better off than before. Without cost tags, this is hard to judge.

If the effluent from a paper mill muddies the water for the downstream resident, and the cost of removing the cause exceeds the cost of reducing such disturbance by treatment at the intake, it would clearly be efficient to let the offending effluent continue and to treat the water prior to its further use. In that event, the "winner," the paper mill, could compensate the "loser," the municipality, out of the savings that would accrue from not having to treat the effluent. Thus, both efficiency and equity would be served. The added cost (added, that is, in comparison to the previous condition of pollution without compensation) would most likely be reflected in higher costs of paper, at least initially, which only proves that you do not get something for nothing.

As has been pointed out, most situations of this kind are very complex, involving a multitude of participants, actions, and reactions. But it is easy to see the need for finding ways in which the external cost—in the simplified case above, the nuisance to the city residents—can be gauged and added to the private, or internal, cost, with the result that the polluter's cost will fully reflect the social cost of his activity.

Existing institutions and mechanisms need to be modified or new ones invented to facilitate making the cost of side effects a cost to the originator—that is, "internalizing" them. Imposition of taxes, charges, or other financial burdens on the producer is one way. These might be rigid or flexible so that the punishment could fit the crime. Their rationale lies in the consideration that the use of a congested facility, be this a watercourse, the air, a highway, or a park, should be reduced by putting a price on it.

At times, particularly when it is impractical or too costly to bar free access to the resource, a charge can be levied not on the activity itself but on the agent that causes the adverse effect (a pesticide, a detergent, a fuel), in the expectation that this will promote more sparing use of the offending substance and thus lead to a reduction of the noxious side effects. Also, raising the cost may stimulate the development of new technology, and the charges collected can be tapped for remedying the effects of the activity in question. In other situations, collective, administrative action may be more efficient. Unlike taxes, standard-setting regulations will not, however, produce revenue; also, flexibility will be less easily achieved, and policing and enforcement will present major administrative burdens, if not problems.

Technical considerations may, however, suggest collective action of a different sort—not through regulation—but through doing on a large centralized scale what is harder and more expensive to accomplish through the aggregation of a multitude of individual actions. To illustrate, a dollar's worth of aeration of dirty water performed by a public body according to a carefully laid plan is likely to beat a dollar's worth of waste-discharge treatment undertaken separately by a score of users.

When we can compare meaningfully the costs to society—which are, as we have tried to show, the producer's private costs plus costs to others that are not part of his calculus—with the many-sided benefits that are the counterpart of those costs, we shall have taken a long stride toward evolving a workable policy of preserving the quality of the environment without sacrificing the beneficial effects of advancing technology. Only then will we be able to appraise the present and future adequacy of quality of the resources as we have appraised that of quantity. If this means having the best of two worlds, then the time may be at hand to cease calling economics the dismal science. Until then, the economist will have to insist that the frontiers of cost and benefit measurement be vigorously extended—not necessarily to dictate action but to allow it to be shaped in the presence of the newly gained knowledge.

Appreciation is expressed to the Cooper Foundation Committee, Swarthmore College, for permission to utilize material first developed in connection with a talk on conservation presented to a symposium in February, 1966.

REFERENCES

See Harold J. Barnett and Chandler Morse, Scarcity and Growth: The Economics of Natural Resource Availability (Baltimore, 1963).

John R. Platt, The Step to Man (New York, 1966), pp. 185-203.

Hans H. Landsberg, Leonard L. Fischman, and Joseph L. Fisher, Resources in America's Future (Baltimore, 1963); and Hans H. Landsberg, Natural Resources for U. S. Growth (Baltimore, 1964).

A cautionary view of prospects for rising yields in developed countries was advanced by Lester R. Brown at the December, 1966, meeting of the American Association for the Advancement of Science. (See Journal of Commerce, January 3, 1967; no published version as yet available.)

For a recent attempt, see, for instance, Joseph L. Fisher and Neal Potter, World Prospects for Natural Resources (Baltimore, 1964).

Mason Gaffney, Applying Economic Controls, Bulletin of the Atomic Scientists (May, 1965), pp. 20-25.

J. W. Milliman, Can People Be Trusted with Natural Resources?, Land Economics (August, 1962), pp. 199-218.

42. PROGRESS IN THE EXPLORATION AND EXPLOITATION OF HARD MINERALS FROM THE SEABED*

V. E. McKELVEY

Continuing our review of the progress and exploitation of seabed resources since the report of the ad hoc committee was completed, we can say, as we did for petroleum, that while the advances of the past year in the field of hard-mineral seabed mining have been encouraging, they do not change any of the conclusions reached last year. Nevertheless, it may be worthwhile to briefly review some of the highlights of the recent achievements in this area.

RECENT DEVELOPMENTS

Advances in offshore mining of hard minerals have not been nearly as rapid as those relating to petroleum. Progress in solving the difficult problem of prospecting for and evaluating seabed mineral deposits has come in recent years through the development of a detached "boomerang" corer, which is brought to the surface by a float after it has taken its sample; a series of such corers can therefore be dropped from a moving ship on traverse and picked up on its return. A sediment analysis pod has also been developed that will transmit a digitized signal by cable to the surface, giving data on acoustic velocity, bearing strength, temperature, and bulk density. Another new device is a radioisotope-powered acoustic pinger that has a 5-year life, is usable in water as deep as 6,000 feet, and will precisely mark undersea locations, a fundamental need in both mineral evaluation and mining. The advances in geophysical exploration, submersibles, undersea work vehicles and habitats, and deep-drilling techniques already mentioned also contribute to the development of subsea hard-minerals technology.

Reprinted with the senior author's permission from "Subsea Mineral Resources and Problems Related to Their Development" by V. E. McKelvey, J. I. Tracey, Jr., George E. Stoertz, and John G. Vedder, *U. S. Geological Survey Circular* 619, 26 p., 1969.

*Statement by United States Representative before the Economic and Technical Subcommittee of the United Nations Committee on the Peaceful Uses of the Seabed and the Ocean Floor Beyond the Limits of National Jurisdiction, March 13, 1969.

Mining is in progress in waters less than 200 feet offshore in many countries—sulfur in the Gulf of Mexico; sand, gravel, and shell off the United States, Japan, Iceland, and Great Britain; lime mud off the Bahamas; magnetite off Japan; tin off Indonesia and Thailand; diamonds off the southwestern coast of Africa; and rutile and ilmenite off Australia. Exploration underway in other areas includes that for gold and platinum in Norton Sound and the Bering Sea; gold off northern California, the Gulf of Alaska, Nova Scotia, and British Columbia; gold, chromite, and magnetite off the Philippines; gold off the Soviet Union in the Laptev Sea and the Sea of Japan; gold and tungsten off Australia; tin off Malaysia, Borneo, Solomon Islands, and Great Britain; metal-rich mud in the Red Sea; and phosphorite off the United States, Palau, and Mexico. Interest continues in the manganese nodules, particularly for their content of nickel and copper, and research is underway on mining systems that will make their economic recovery feasible. Most of the companies who have investigated the manganese nodules have found the prospects for their development in the next decade or so discouraging. One American company, Deepsea Ventures, Inc., recently announced plans, however, to begin research on the recovery of the nodules, has a vessel equipped to prospect and appraise certain deposits, and believes it will reach production of metals within 5 years.

IMPACT AND OUTLOOK

The exploration in progress may lead to the development of offshore mining in new areas, but none of the developments of the past year constitute breakthroughs that substantially enlarge the scope of marine mining in the near future or that will speed economic access to the sea-floor minerals in deep water.

The drag on the development of hard minerals in deep water has several origins. Ore-finding technology, particularly for bedrock minerals beneath the floor, is poorly developed—as indeed it is for wholly concealed deposits on land—and knowledge of the regional and local geology necessary to guide prospecting is as yet fragmentary. Evaluation technology for most subsea minerals is both weak and expensive. Low-cost systems for deep-sea mining are not much beyond the conceptual stage, and each of the major surficial deposits—the manganese nodules, the phosphorites, and the sulfide muds—poses difficult beneficiation or extraction problems. On the economic side, low-cost onshore sources of most seabed minerals are ample for the foreseeable future, and this dampens the incentive to press the research and development necessary to speed development. They do not kill it, however, and even though the advance of deep-sea-mining technology may be slow, it seems certain to come eventually. And, of course, a real breakthrough that would reduce mining and extraction cost to competitive levels would have a substantial impact on world supplies in the case of the manganese nodules and perhaps also the sulfide muds and an important impact on regional supplies in the case of the phosphorites.

43. IMPLICATIONS OF GEOLOGIC AND ECONOMIC FACTORS TO SEABED RESOURCE ALLOCATION, DEVELOPMENT, AND MANAGEMENT*

V. E. McKELVEY

Many of the questions we have been considering in item 2 of our program of work on the ways and means of promoting the exploitation of seabed resources essentially relate to the requirements of a system for seabed resource allocation, development, and management, regardless of what might be the structure of such a system or its national or international affinity. We have been privileged to hear many cogent observations by several of our distinguished colleagues on what these requirements might be as they are expressed in the terms governing exploration and exploitation. The statements of the distinguished representatives of Australia and Canada, both of whom are experts in this field, are especially pertinent, for the Canadian and Australian systems have been designed to meet the very objective this committee is considering—namely to encourage seabed exploration and development in regions in which it is not already in progress.

In previous discussions of agenda item 2, our delegation has attempted to report relevant U.S. experience and procedures, not as a model by any means, but merely as a description of one set of working procedures. We would be glad to describe also our procedures and experience for resource allocation and development, but frankly neither are entirely relevant to the problem at hand. Our system for leasing on the outer continental shelf was designed in 1953 after offshore petroleum development had already gotten underway in the state waters in the Gulf of Mexico, where extensive exploration and development in the adjacent onshore area had already shown the existence of a most promising

Reprinted with the senior author's permission from "Subsea Mineral Resources and Problems Related to Their Development" by V. E. McKelvey, J. I. Tracey, Jr., George E. Stoertz, and John G. Vedder, *U. S. Geological Survey Circular* 619, 26 p., 1969.

*Statement by United States Representative before the Economic and Technical Subcommittee of the United Nations Committee on the Peaceful Uses of the Seabed and the Ocean Floor Beyond the Limits of National Jurisdiction, March 24, 1969.

petroleum province, and had provided a wealth of information about the nature of occurrence of oil and gas in the gulf province. In the light of this background of interest and experience, our leasing system for oil and gas provided for geophysical exploration under a nonexclusive permit with no subsequent rights, followed by the sale of lease tracts, each not exceeding 9 squares miles in area, by competitive bidding in advance of drilling on a cash bonus with a fixed royalty of not less than one-eighth the value of production. These terms are much stiffer than those described for Australia and Canada. Nevertheless, the offshore industry in the Gulf of Mexico has flourished under them, for since 1954 when production of oil and gas began on the outer continental shelf there, outer continental shelf production has come to make up 7 percent of our national production. Our system has also encouraged exploration off southern California and in the Gulf of Alaska, both of which are extensions of adjacent onshore producing provinces. Other parts of our shelves not adjacent to onshore producing provinces, however, have not received nearly as much attention. No doubt there are several reasons for this, including the greater appeal of the producing provinces and the magnitude of the resource potential in their still unexplored parts. But when we look at the much greater amount of offshore exploration that is in progress on the Canadian Atlantic Shelf compared to that on the U.S. Atlantic Shelf, where the first exploratory well has yet to be drilled, we must recognize that one possible reason for the difference may be the more favorable terms offered under the Canadian system than under our own. Australia has also attracted exploration to areas with no existing onshore production, as have several other countries. At this stage, the systems in effect in those countries may therefore be more applicable than ours to the problem of encouraging seabed petroleum development beyond the limits of national jurisdiction. The same may be true also for nonpetroleum minerals, for except for sulfur we have had little or no offshore exploration for other minerals. Many of our leaders in the mining industry say that one of the reasons for this is that the terms governing exploration and development are unfavorable for such high risk ventures.

For these and other reasons, our policies governing offshore leasing have been undergoing review. These studies are not yet complete, but the fact that they are in progress makes a point that is significant for the deliberations of this committee, namely that the needs to be served by a resource allocation, development, and management system differ from place to place and change from time to time. In seeking the common denominators among existing resource allocation and development systems—several speakers have recommended that we do this—it is well to keep in mind that different systems may serve different purposes, and that widely differing terms may in fact be appropriate in the varied circumstances that will be encountered in the development of seabed resources beyond the limits of national jurisdiction.

It may be helpful at this stage to describe some of the geologic and economic factors that constitute the basic requirements that a resource allocation and development system must meet, for their identification may help to indicate the flexibility that such a system must provide.

GEOLOGIC FACTORS

Two geologic factors are particularly relevant to lease terms: One is that the size and mode of occurrence of mineral deposits vary greatly from one mineral or group of minerals to another. The other is that the presence of concealed deposits, such as oil and gas, can be established only by drilling or other means of underground exploration, and that the quality and recoverable quantity of minerals in individual deposits of nearly all minerals—exposed and unexposed alike—can be determined only by extensive sampling, whether done by drilling or other means, and perhaps even some production experience.

The differences in the characteristics of deposits of different minerals or groups of minerals affect the size of the area that an operator must prospect and hold to achieve an economically viable operation. For example, although some petroleum reservoirs underlie large areas, many producible petroleum reservoirs underlie areas of only a few square miles; the largest kinds of copper deposits—the porphyry

coppers as they are called—generally underlie areas of a square mile or less; and many other workable hard minerals either occur in relatively small deposits or can be profitably mined from units a few square miles in size. Such deposits, however, may be widely scattered, so that even in provinces that are broadly favorable for their occurrence, a far larger area may need to be explored to find a deposit suitable for mining.

For the manganese nodules, however, even the area required to sustain a viable operation might be extremely large. For example, Chester Ensign, the Vice President for Exploration of the Copper Range Co., has calculated from John Mero's estimate that the manganese nodules at the surface of the sea floor in the better areas amount to 30,000 tons per square mile, that a normal large scale mining operation of 20,000 tons per day would mine out the nodules over an area of 235 square miles per year.

Differences in the characteristics of various minerals also influence the time required to bring them into production. Thus, where fixed installations are required, and where special mining systems or extractive processes have to be devised, several years or more may be required to bring a deposit into production after its existence and magnitude have been established.

The terms for resource allocation and development, therefore, must provide for prospecting and exploration over a far larger area than that in which production may take place; and they must take account of differing requirements for individual minerals or groups of minerals, both with regard to the area necessary for viable mining operations and the time required for development.

The facts that the presence of concealed deposits can be established only by drilling and that the quality and recoverable quantity of minerals in both exposed and unexposed deposits can be determined only by extensive sampling also bear on the terms for resource allocation and development, for they make it nearly impossible to appraise the value of seabed resources in advance of exploration, and perhaps even in advance of some production experience. In producing areas, experience may be sufficient to assign a probability factor to discovery that can be used in appraising value, much as one might do in establishing the value of the opportunities on a punchboard. For example, if experience shows that producible petroleum reservoirs in a partly explored area contain an average of about

10 million barrels of oil, and that one out of four structures identifiable from geophysical exploration usually contains oil, the value of a property believed to have such a structure might be estimated as 25 percent that of the in-place value of 10 million barrels of oil, discounted further to take account of the present value of money spent for something that will not be fully recovered for many years. If, however, there is no previous exploration and production experience to give an indication of the size, quality, and frequency of occurrence of mineral deposits in a given area, the chance of finding a producible deposit can hardly be assigned a numerical value. When investigations reach the stage when expensive forms of exploration are required to determine whether or not an economic operation is feasible, the operator, of course, needs an exclusive right to explore and to produce valuable deposits as they are found. Because the value of the deposit cannot be established in advance, particularly in unexplored and nonproducing provinces, the basis for payment for the resource produced should be one that is related to actual production rather than to a predetermined estimate of the value of an unexplored area.

As indicated by the distinguished representative of France, the right to explore need not be granted on an exclusive basis until the stage of expensive exploration is reached; in fact, there is much merit in giving wide opportunity for geophysical and other relatively low-cost means of exploration on a non-exclusive basis in order to encourage prospecting, as is permitted under the Canadian exploration license as well as our own permit for geophysical exploration.

ECONOMIC FACTORS

Now for some observations on the economic side of the problem. Four things are worth discussing here: (1) The sources and effects of risk in mineral exploration and development, (2) the concept of net resource value, (3) alternative means of resource allocation and payment to the resource owner, and (4) the kinds of benefits that result from mineral production.

Mining is well known to be a high-risk activity. Large sums of money may be spent in searching for a producible deposit and evaluating discoveries without any assurance that production will result or be sufficient to pay out the investment. The risk is not confined to the prospecting and evaluation stage, for mining and recovery problems may prove to be insurmount-

able, the mining process or natural forces such as storms may lead to costly accidents, and later developments in the market may reduce prices or demand and make it necessary to close down operations before the investment has paid off. To compensate for the high risk involved, it is necessary to have the opportunity for a higher rate of profit from mining investments than is expected from other kinds of enterprises. Thus, if only one out of 10 ventures is likely to be successful, profits received from the successful one must be sufficient to cover the losses on the other nine. Although several factors contribute to risk, its magnitude is generally reduced by increasing knowledge about the occurrence of recoverable minerals in a given area and by increasing experience in producing them. Thus, even though risk in petroleum exploration and exploitation in a producing province is high, it is much lower than it is in a nonproducing area, such as that beyond the limits of national jurisdiction, where there is little knowledge of the occurrence of specific minerals and no experience in production.

Let me speak now of net-resource value, which I will define as the surplus remaining after the mineral product has been sold and the costs of production plus a normal profit on risk investment have been paid. This value is sometimes referred to as economic rent—the amount earned by land as a factor of production over and above returns to all other production factors, that is, wages to labor, interest to capital, and profits to management—and it is the amount that the resource owner can hope to receive in return for the production of his resources. Because the price at which the product can be sold is generally established externally, its level is beyond the control of either the owner or the producer. The amount that remains as net-resource value at any given time is thus largely a function of production costs and the profit that must be returned to management and to risk investment. If exploration and production costs are high, if the risk of discovery and successful production is so high that the investor insists on a high rate of return on invested capital, and if prices are relatively low, net resource value may be zero; and if costs exceed prices, the operation would not be economic even if no payment needs to be made for the resource itself. These situations are the ones that often prevail at the outset of exploitation in unexplored provinces or in the exploitation of minerals in forms of environments from which they have yet to be produced economically, and it is these situations that may be expected to prevail for seabed resources beyond the limits of national jurisdiction in the early stages of their development. As exploration, however, shows the existence of workable deposits, as costs are reduced, and as accumulating knowledge and experience reduce risks, net resource value may increase, particularly if prices do not decrease.

Now a word about the means of allocating seabed resources and the terms of payment for them. As the distinguished representative of Australia pointed out, the means of allocation must be impartial. Among the systems now in operation, the means for achieving this have included competitive bidding, assignment by lottery, assignment to the first to file a claim, or assignment on the basis of a judgment of the qualification and the plans of the operator. As I mentioned earlier, the United States Government uses competitive bidding as the means of assigning title to offshore leases; although this has many advantages, it probably would not be applicable now to the seabed beyond the limits of national jurisdiction, for it involves a predrilling estimate of value. The question as to which of the other systems is most desirable may not be significant now, for the first to propose mining in this environment should be welcomed with open arms, but the question will have to be posed eventually.

The most commonly used forms of payment of net-resource value are a lump-sum cash payment made at the time title is assigned, royalty on production, and profit sharing. Each of these forms of payments has advantages and disadvantages. The advance cash payment is an incentive to prompt development, it does not add to marginal cost, and is easy to administrate. But it offers a high-capital barrier to entry, requires predrilling appraisal of value, and offers no means of sharing windfall gains and losses by the operator and the resource owner. It is most suitable for the payment for resources where the risk is comparatively low and conversely is least suitable where risks are likely to be extremely high as they are in mining on the deep ocean floor. The royalty payment reduces the capital barrier to entry and relates payment directly to production. It may invite irresponsible operators, however, who may later plead for a lower royalty rate in order to initiate or continue production, and it increases the marginal costs of production;

if royalty is established at a fixed rate, it may therefore lead to premature abandonment of the property when these costs can no longer be borne by the operator. Profit sharing also reduces the capital barrier to entry and because it does not add to marginal cost it is less of a deterrent to recovery than is a fixed royalty. It is difficult to administer, however, because it requires close control of accounting procedures, and it does not assure that title will be assigned to the most efficient producer. In contrast to the advance cash payment, which is most suitable where the risk is relatively low, profit sharing is most applicable where the risk is extremely high. These systems of payment can be modified in various ways, including combinations with each other, to make them more suitable to individual situations, but the important thing to note is that each of them has advantages and disadvantages that determine its suitability for individual operations.

In examining these various forms of payment we all have a tendency to view them in terms of the revenue they are likely to yield to the resource owner. As the distinguished representative of Australia pointed out, however, the direct revenue from the development of seabed resources is only one of two general forms of benefit to mankind that may come from their exploitation. The other is the addition to the world's inventory of useable minerals. For the developed countries, this is now by far the most important form of contribution that mineral production makes to their economies. Built as they are on the extensive use of minerals and energy in machines, in industrialized agriculture, in housing and construction, in transportation and communications systems, and in manufactured and processed goods of nearly all kinds, it is the use of minerals and fuels that supports their economies and it is in their use that they benefit most from mineral production. The direct revenue that comes to them from the sale and production of minerals may not be insignificant, of course. For example, revenue to the United States from petroleum on the outer continental shelves has been both substantial and welcome, for it has already amounted to about $4.4 billion. But the value of the raw products, the production of which adds directly to gross national product, is four to five times that of the revenue to the federal government; the total economic activity surrounding production and stimulated directly by it may be 10 times this amount; and far greater value—100 times or more that of the direct revenue from production—is represented in the chain of activities beginning with the processing and manufacture of petroleum products and ending with their use. The value that comes from the use of minerals in an industrial society is thus far greater than those that come merely from their sale and production, and it is these greater values, as I emphasized to the ad hoc committee last year, that we hope the developing countries and the peoples of the world will eventually come to share. When we think of means to promote seabed exploitation in the long run, then, we must recognize the fundamental importance of encouraging production for the materials it will yield rather than merely for the direct revenue that may come from the sale of seabed resources.

RESOURCE MANAGEMENT

In addition to the problem relating to the selection of terms for allocating and developing seabed resources, there is the very important responsibility of government to supervise many aspects of the exploration and exploitation processes. Some of these aspects we have already discussed in connection with the prevention of ill effects from mineral exploration and exploitation, and because the time available for our discussion is now drawing to a close, I will not elaborate on the other problems involved in resource management. I may mention, however, that in addition to maintaining safe practices and preventing damage to other values and interference with other uses of the sea, it is necessary for government to concern itself with the problem of conservation to see that minerals are extracted with maximum ultimate recovery. The requirements here also depend on the kind of mineral that is being produced, the environment in which it is found, and the mining system that is being used. The responsibility on supervisory authority in this area is not only heavy, but requires superior technical competence in its execution.

SUMMARY

In summarizing the implications of geologic and economic factors to seabed allocation, development, and management, I may list the following points:

1. The terms appropriate for mineral resource allocation and development vary from place to place and time to time.

2. The geologic characteristics of minerals that may be exploited from the seabed differ from one mineral or group of minerals to another, and influence the size of the area required for viable operation and the time required to achieve production for various minerals. For nearly all minerals a far larger area may need to be explored to find a deposit suitable for mining than is finally selected for exploitation.

3. The presence of concealed deposits can be established only by drilling or other means of exploration, and the amount and quality of both exposed and unexposed deposits can be determined only by extensive and expensive forms of sampling and may even require some production experience. At the stage when such expensive forms of exploration are reached, the operator needs an exclusive right to explore and to produce if workable deposits are found. Because the value of such deposits cannot be determined in advance, particularly in wholly unexplored areas, the basis for payment for such right should be one that is related to actual production rather than a predetermined estimate of the value of an unexplored area.

4. The high investment risks characteristically associated with mining must be compensated for by the opportunity for higher profits than are acceptable in many other enterprises. The risks stem from uncertainty of discovery, uncertainties concerning the feasibility of mining and recovery systems, possibility of loss from mining accidents, storms, and so on, and from uncertainties concerning future prices, demand, and other externalities. Although the high risk in mining cannot be eliminated altogether, it tends to reduce with increasing knowledge about the occurrence of recoverable minerals in a given area and with increasing experience in producing them.

5. Net-resource value—the surplus remaining when the mineral has been sold and after production costs and profits on risk investment have been paid—is the amount the owner can hope to receive from the sale and production of his resources. Limited as it is on one side by production costs and the amount of risk involved and on the other by a price that is fixed externally, net-resource value varies considerably from place to place and time to time. At the outset of seabed exploitation, it may be nearly zero, but if

exploration shows the existence of workable deposits, if production costs can be reduced, if environmental hazards can be controlled, and if prices do not decrease, net-resource value may increase over time.

6. Several alternatives exist in the methods of impartial allocation of resources and the means of payment of net-resource value, each of which has advantages and disadvantages that influence its suitability for individual operations.

7. Direct revenue from the production of minerals is welcome to all governments, and to developing countries it may be the principal benefit to be derived from production of seabed resources in the immediate future. The chief value of minerals, however, is in the chain of economic activities that surround their production and follow on their use, and in the future these benefits should come to be shared by all the people of the world. In the long run, therefore, our goal should be to encourage subsea production for the raw materials it will make available rather than merely for the direct revenue that may come from the sale of seabed resources.

8. Resource management entails not only responsibility to maintain safe practices and prevent damage to other resources and uses of the sea, but also for conservation in production to see that minerals are extracted with maximum ultimate recovery.

Geothermal Energy

44. BRIEFS ON GEOTHERMAL ENERGY

U. S. GEOLOGICAL SURVEY

Geothermal energy is a practically untapped natural resource that may provide heat, electric power, and water for certain parts of the United States. The environmental effects of geothermal power production are local in extent, and the use of geothermal power reduces the severity of pollution problems inherent in many other conventional methods of energy production, especially those involving fossil fuels.

The term "geothermal resources" is generally used to include energy plus any associated mineral products which can be extracted from steam and hot water emitted from the earth. The most important item—and one of greatest current interest—is geothermal energy, which is electric power generated by releasing steam from naturally hot areas through drill holes, and channeling it to a generator unit.

The earth is a tremendous reservoir of heat, and its surface displays "hot spots" that generally occur near areas of "recent" volcanic activity. In the western United States, particularly along the Pacific Coast, widespread and intense volcanic activity has occurred during the past 10 million years; thus, the western states hold promise for geothermal power development. Over 5 percent of the world's resources of geothermal energy are in the United States, most of it stored in rocks in the upper 6 miles of the crust.

The U.S. Geological Survey estimates that as much as 1.3 million acres of land, mostly within the western portions of the United States, including Hawaii, and possibly Alaska, may be potentially attractive for geothermal development and may provide an energy source of from 15 to 30 thousand megowatts. Most of the sites that appear promising for geothermal development are on federal or public lands.

World production of power using the earth's natural heat as an energy source has now reached about 1 million kilowatts, and can probably be increased at least 10 times under present economic conditions. This increase would be about

From U. S. Department of Interior "news release," January 27, 1971.

equal to the energy produced by burning 1 billion tons of coal. Those nations possessing a minimal reserve of fossil fuels are among those leading in the development of geothermal energy. Italy at Larderello heads the production list (over 400,000 kilowatts produced); New Zealand is second (over 170,000 kilowatts); and the United States is third (83,000 kilowatts). Numerous other countries have stepped up research activities, including Algeria, Chile, Columbia, Czechoslovakia, Hungary, Indonesia, the Philippines, Iceland, China (Taiwan), El Salvador, Nicaragua, France (Fr.W.I.), Turkey, Ethiopia, Kenya, Mexico, and the USSR. Several other nations are in the process of gathering geothermal energy information, and in some instances— Japan is an example—geothermal energy development has a high priority in national planning.

Volcanoes produce the most dramatic displays of natural steam. Water that comes in contact with molten lava (temperatures of 2,000 degrees F. and higher) near the earth's surface can exist only as steam. The rapid expansion of steam and other gases below the surface causes some of nature's most violent and explosive eruptions. In September, 1965, an eruption of Taal Volcano in southwest Luzon, Philippine Island, killed nearly 200 persons, and blasted houses and vegetation 3-1/2 miles away. A series of explosions, believed to have been caused by water gaining access to the volcanic conduit, ejected huge quantities of ash and cinders that formed a thick blanket over more than 25 square miles.

For years man has viewed with awe the spectacular bursts of natural steam from volcanoes, geysers, and boiling springs. Early records note the widespread use by the Romans of natural hot waters in Italy and other countries. Similar use was made of hot springs—now referred to as "health spas"—in Germany, Austria, and Czechoslovakia. Although the use of hot springs for baths dates to ancient times, the use of natural steam for the manufacture of electric power did not begin until early in the 20th century.

The first commercial use of geothermal

resources took place in Larderello, Italy, in 1777 when borax was recovered from numerous natural steam and hot water vents; to this day, the Larderello district continues to produce borax as well as sulfur, boric acid, and a number of other chemicals for industrial purposes. In 1905 the world's first power-generating station using natural steam energy was established at Larderello.

Hot water energy was used for space heating in Iceland in 1925. By 1930, hot water was being supplied to homes and industries in Reykjavik. In 1925, also, attempts were made to harness geothermal steam in New Zealand, although no serious developments occurred there until 1946, when the government took over development of that nation's natural steam deposits.

In the United States, interest in geothermal resources began in the early 1920s, but it was not until about 1955 when The Geysers area, located about 75 miles north of San Francisco, was redrilled, and four wells began producing from depths of less than 1,000 feet. In 1958, the owners of the wells and the Pacific Gas and Electric Company signed a contract arranging for the wells to supply steam to a plant erected for generation of electricity. Power production was started in 1960 at a rate of 12,500 kilowatts, and the capacity has since reached more than 83,000 kilowatts.

Locating a promising geothermal system is often a difficult problem. A system is apparent only when it is defective—when it is "leaking" hot water or steam to the surface. These areas of hot springs and geysers are currently being explored, but experts have said that the state of our knowledge regarding geothermal resources is comparable to that regarding petroleum resources at the turn of the century. Current exploration, based on modern geologic, geochemical, and geophysical methods, is likely to discover new fields. The recent discovery of a new field at Monte Amiata, Italy—where there were only meager surface manifestations of geothermal energy—was based on the use of such methods.

Disposal of waste products is a serious problem encountered in the development of some hot water systems. This is particularly true

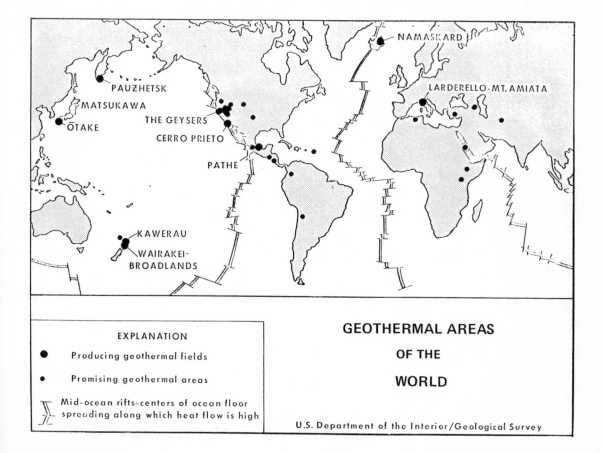

GEOTHERMAL AREAS

OF THE

WORLD

EXPLANATION

● Producing geothermal fields

• Promising geothermal areas

⊥ Mid-ocean rifts-centers of ocean floor spreading along which heat flow is high

U.S. Department of the Interior/Geological Survey

in the Salton Sea area of California where the mineral content of the brine is quite high—about 25 percent in total weight of dissolved salts, or nearly 10 times higher than sea water.

All natural geyser areas of the world are potential sites for the commercial development of geothermal energy, yet it is to be remembered that development of these areas for the recovery of steam may destroy the geysers themselves. Although the need to develop new sources of energy may become urgent, every reasonable effort must be made to protect these scenic wonders of nature.

45. RESOURCES OF GEOTHERMAL ENERGY AND THEIR UTILIZATION

DONALD E. WHITE

DOMESTIC AND WORLD RESOURCES OF GEOTHERMAL ENERGY

The total amount of heat above surface temperatures stored in the outer 100 km of the earth is on the order of 2×10^{28} cal, which is equivalent to the heat content of 3×10^{18} short tons of coal. Heat stored under the United States to a depth of 10 km is about 6×10^{24} cal or equivalent to the heat content of 9×10^{14} short tons of coal. Most of this heat is in areas of "normal" geothermal gradient and is contained in rocks that are extremely low-grade sources of energy.

Areas of abnormally high geothermal gradient can be classified into three types, at least in part overlapping: (1) areas in which geothermal gradient is significantly higher than "normal" but where notable hydrothermal activity is absent; in some of these areas, molten magma may exist within accessible depths; (2) hot spring areas, in which natural thermal fluids are discharged at the surface; and (3) hydrothermal areas of composite type that have little surface expression but with high-temperature fluids that exist beneath capping rocks of low permeability.

In the first type of geothermal area, heat contents and thermal conductivities are so low, and drilling costs for very deep wells so high, that heat is probably not recoverable economically even at 10 times present values. In the future, with research and experience, some energy probably can be recovered from heated rocks or magma if the value of the energy is sufficiently high, but no attempt is made here to compute resources of this type.

The hydrothermal areas mentioned, including both types 2 and 3 offer the greatest immediate possibilities for economic development because high temperatures occur relatively near the surface and hot natural fluids are present as energy-transporting media. Geothermal heat is now competing successfully with

Extracted, with permission of the author, from "Geothermal Energy" *U.S. Geological Survey Circular* 519, 17 p., 1965.

other sources of energy in Italy, New Zealand, Iceland, and The Geysers in the United States. Experience at some localities indicates that heat can be withdrawn at rates of four to more than 10 times the natural rate of heat flow for at least 10 years without serious effect. The heat withdrawn in excess of the natural flow is derived from reservoirs of previously heated rocks. However, many other geothermal areas, especially of the hot-water type in rocks that are at least in part of low mass permeability, have not been tested adequately; serious degradational effects may become evident in shorter times and at lower withdrawal rates.

The total heat flow from hot spring areas for which estimates of natural heat flow have been made is about 2.7×10^9 cal/sec (or 1×10^{17} cal/yr). Information is probably reasonably complete for Iceland, New Zealand, and El Salvador but in most other countries only a few of the known areas are included. Almost none of the thousands of hot spring areas of low to moderate surface temperature (Waring, 1965) are considered, and hydrothermal systems of the composite type that are much more difficult to recognize are very inadequately represented. The world's total natural heat flow from all hydrothermal areas is probably at least 10 times that of the estimated areas, or about 3×10^{10} cal/sec (or 1×10^{18} cal/yr).

The total stored heat of the crudely "measured" hot spring systems (excluding the composite type) is estimated to be about 2×10^{20} cal to a depth of 3 km.

Total heat stored in other hot spring systems is difficult to estimate. Some systems of high discharge and low temperature may have less stored heat than comparable volumes of "normal" earth. Others may prove to be hydrothermal systems of composite type, having meager surface discharge of fluid but high geothermal gradients in near-surface caprocks of low permeability.

Heat reservoirs of hydrothermal systems of the composite type may be relatively large because their heat has been largely preserved by good natural insulation rather than dissipated by convective discharge at the surface. The heat content of the Salton Sea geothermal area is crudely estimated to be 2×10^{19} cal to a depth of 3 km (or 10,000 ft), and the Larderello system may be similar in magnitude. No sound basis exists for predicting how many large undiscovered systems of the composite type exist in the world, but 40 of the magnitude estimated for the Salton Sea area is not unreasonable. In addition, some hot spring systems of shallow circulation may be underlain at intermediate depth by rocks of low mass permeability, and these rocks in turn may be underlain by one or more circulation systems of composite type.

A very crude estimate of 2×10^{21} cal is suggested as the total stored heat of all hydrothermal systems to depths of 3 km, and 1×10^{22} cal to 10 km.

Geothermal energy has been utilized for such a short period of time that estimates of the proportion of heat commercially recoverable from hydrothermal reservoirs are of doubtful value, but 1 percent is viewed as a conservative estimate. On this basis, estimated recoverable reserves are:

Heat content (calories)

Potential reserves to depths of 3 km, recoverable at or near present costs . . . . 2×10^{19}

Additional resources to depths of 10 km, recoverable at much more than present costs . . . . 1×10^{22}

Existing worldwide utilization equivalent to about 1 million kw, or 7.5×10^{15} cal/yr, probably can be increased at least 10 times under present economic conditions and maintained for at least 50 years. The author may be too conservative in these estimates, but many technical and scientific problems are not yet solved, and great optimism is not warranted until these problems clearly can be solved. Although geothermal heat is now only of minor importance as an energy source, the quantities available in hydrothermal systems are large and with additional research and development, recovery is likely to increase greatly.

The western half of the conterminous United States, Hawaii, and parts of Alaska are particularly favorable for local concentrations of geothermal energy. Of the total global resources of geothermal energy underlying land areas, probably 5-10 percent is in the United States.

GENERAL PROBLEMS OF UTILIZATION

At the present time, the geothermal areas of the earth that can most hopefully compete economically with other sources of energy are the "hot spots" that discharge steam or hot water as the heat-transporting medium or that have a permeable reservoir of hot fluids beneath near-surface rocks of low mass permeability. The essential requirements are relatively high temperature and permeable structures that can yield heat-transporting fluids to a well. Hot volcanic rocks or magma chambers at or near the surface but lacking heat-transporting fluid are also possible commercial sources of energy; however, effective recovery of heat from such reservoirs has additional problems not yet solved commercially.

The very low thermal conductivity of rocks imposes a restriction on effective recovery, especially if mass permeability is also low. The heat immediately adjacent to a well drilled in impermeable rocks can be withdrawn easily by circulating a cold fluid, but the amount of heat recovered is small and steadily decreases as rocks adjacent to the well are cooled. This low yield of heat is comparable to the low flow of an oil-test well in impermeable shale of high fluid hydrocarbon content. In contrast, large amounts of oil are obtainable from a single well in an oil pool in very permeable rocks. The possibilities for finding or creating high thermal "permeability" in reservoir rocks of low mass permeability seem limited to the following:

1. Each well is drilled deep enough to intersect one or more highly permeable channels or aquifers that, in total, will yield commercial quantities of the hot water already present in the rocks; however, in most crystalline rocks and many sedimentary rocks, permeable channels are narrow or widely spaced and are likely to be less numerous at great depth than near the surface.

2. The rocks adjacent to a well are artifically fractured to such an extent that the heat of a large volume of rock can be tapped. Natural permeable channels in the surrounding area must be made accessible to the newly broken ground to permit adequate discharge of existing deep water, or a transporting fluid must be introduced from the surface to recover the heat. Fracturing by

buried nuclear explosion has also been proposed (Carlson, 1959), the nuclear energy providing additional heat.

Most deep waters are saline and are likely to contain high but uneconomic concentrations of elements such as boron, arsenic, sodium, and chloride; these elements constitute disposal problems. Some elements, including boron, potassium, lithium, cesium, and iodine have been considered for recovery to pay for part of the costs, but actual quantity and value of these elements are generally much below costs of recovery. The Salton Sea area of California is an outstandingly promising exception (White and others, 1963), and other similar areas may be found.

In some developed geothermal fields, heat is being withdrawn in considerable excess over the natural heat flow. Computed rates of withdrawal are four times the natural flow for Wairakei, New Zealand (Banwell, 1964a), three times for Reykir, four times for Hengill, and nine times for Reykjavik, Iceland (Bodvarsson and Zeöga, 1964), and at least 10 times for Larderello (calculations based on data from Boldizsar, 1963). McNitt (1963) estimated an excess withdrawal of 170 times for The Geysers, Calif. This excess over the natural heat flow is far greater than the indicated overdrafts of other geothermal areas; thus, additional studies should be made.

The quantity of stored heat that can be withdrawn from a reservoir without serious decline in quantity or quality of the heat-transporting fluids will be very different for each area, depending on the magnitude of the whole reservoir, the overdraft relative to natural heat flow, and the physical characteristics of the reservoir rocks. Yield from a large volume of rocks of high porosity and mass permeability, as in much of the Wairakei and Larderello fields, should decline less quickly than that from a heat reservoir in crystalline or sedimentary rocks of low permeability. In crystalline and sedimentary rocks, circulation of fluids is localized in faults, fractures, or the more permeable sedimentary layers; the total surface area of rocks in direct contact with migrating fluids thus is relatively small, and recoverable stored heat of the reservoir must be transferred to the circulating fluids by conduction through relatively large distances.

Bodvarsson and Palmason (1964) suggested that recovery of only 10 percent of the stored heat is a reasonable assumption for Iceland's heat reservoirs, which consist largely of plateau basalts

having few permeable channels. Banwell (1964a), however, concluded that recoveries of 70-90 percent can be achieved over drawoff times of 20-100 years, provided that channel spacing is less than about 200 feet. Banwell's theoretical discussion of this subject is very useful, but several of his important assumptions need comment:

1. Efficiency and percent of heat recovery refer only to heat stored above 100°C (rather than to that stored above mean surface temperature, which is commonly used by others). Banwell's calculated efficiencies are therefore correspondingly high.
2. Banwell's idealized models assume all faults and fractures to be so permeable that permissible rates of fluid withdrawal or circulation have no restrictive upper limit; his model also assumes a uniform rate of flow across all surfaces.

Geologists familiar with permeability variations along veins, faults, and fractures in ore deposits will recognize the danger of accepting the latter assumption without modification. Flow rates are not stated for Banwell's models, but if 80 percent of stored heat is to be recovered in 20-100 years from a reservoir of heat content equal to at least 1,000 years of natural heat flow, fluid must be withdrawn at rates at least 10-50 times that of the natural discharge of the system. Any increase in circulation rate will be localized along interconnected channels of highest permeability and will result in excessive withdrawal of stored heat adjacent to these few channels and eventually in degradation in heat content of the recovered fluids.

A hot spring system prior to development probably approximates a steady-state equilibrum relative to its recharging water supply, the pressure drive from recharge to discharge parts of the system, and frictional resistance along its channels of circulation. A highly permeable spring system that has unlimited recharge potential will have achieved a steady state characterized by very high discharge and relatively low temperature; the latter is a consequence of the low thermal conductivities of rocks. A high-temperature geothermal system, on the other hand, can persist for thousands of years only if the recharge potential or the permeability of the most restrictive parts of the system is low. If the most impermeable part of a geothermal system is near its discharge end, as seems probable for the Larderello and the Salton Sea fields, wells can be drilled through the caprocks into the underlying more permeable rocks and the rate of through-flow of fluids can be increased significantly. In a thermal spring system in competent crystalline rocks, however, high permeability is likely to occur near the surface, and channels of lower permeability are characteristic of deep parts of the system. Compare, for example, the open textures of most shallow epithermal ore deposits with the tight structures of most mesothermal and hypothermal ore deposits. The tightest restrictions or bottlenecks, along channels of flow are likely to be deep in a hot spring system, below the shallow reservoir. Production at rates that exceed the natural discharge of fluids may prove to be short lived. Water levels, temperatures, and pressures are then likely to decline, and the accelerated withdrawal may be balanced only in small part by increased circulation through the system.

The hydrodynamics of hot spring systems are very complicated and not yet well understood. Each system differs in at least some respects from all others. Until testing proves otherwise, it is hazardous to assume that the natural discharge of many hot spring systems can be as much as doubled for more than short periods of time. In the testing of a new field, nonproducing observation wells are essential to monitor and evaluate changes in water level, temperature, pressure, and water composition. The adequacy of fluid supply is likely to be more critical than adequacy of the heat reservoirs in limiting future utilization of geothermal energy.

Other engineering problems related to utilization of geothermal energy are discussed in excellent reviews by Smith (1964; Bodvarsson 1964b). Total cost of geothermal power is presently considered to be about 8 mills per net kwhr in Iceland, and abour 4.5 mills in New Zealand. G. Facca and A. Ten Dam (written commun., 1964), computed total generating costs for Italy as about 2.4-3.0 mills per net kwhr. At The Geysers, Calif., the cost of steam delivered at the powerplant is 2.5 mills per net kwhr of electric energy delivered to the transmission line (Bruce, 1964), but the overall cost, including power generation, has not been published.

Corrosion of equipment and deposition of mineral matter constitute problems in utilizing the heat of many thermal areas (Smith, 1964). Corrosion is likely to be more serious than deposition in the dry steam areas, but this problem evidently has been solved or adequately controlled in Italy and at The Geysers, Calif. Deposition of calcium carbonate or silica is characteristic of many, if not most, of the hot water areas. The chemistry of deposition has been discussed by Ellis (1964), White (1964), and others.

ASSUMPTIONS, STATISTICS, AND CONVERSION FACTORS

Surface area of earth, 5.1×10^{18} cm^2; surface area of United States, 9.3×10^{16} cm^2.

Assumed temperature at 100 km depth, 1,100°C; average temperature of the outer 100 km of earth, 550°C above surface temperature; average volumetric specific heat, 0.8 cal/cm^3; latent heats of any phase transitions are disregarded.

Temperature gradient of outer 10 km, 20°C/km (or 1°C/160 ft); average temperature in the outer 10 km, 100°C above average surface temperature; average volumetric specific heat assumed 0.6 cal/cm^3. The assumed gradient is probably too low for orogenic areas and is almost certainly too high for stable continental areas having low heat flow and higher than average thermal conductivities.

Global average heat flow about 1.5×10^{-6} cal/cm^2/sec or 2.5×10^{20} cal/yr from the earth's surface. For geothermal considerations, heat flow in the range of $0.8\text{-}2.0 \times 10^{-6}$ cal/cm^2 sec may be considered within the "normal" range. Thermal conductivities of most rocks range from about 3 to 10×10^{-3} cal/sec/cm °C. Within these extreme limits, temperatures could increase with depth at rates ranging from 50 to 410 feet per 1°C; the average is about 160 feet per degree.

1 cal (mean)=0.001 kcal (kilocalories)=0.00116 watt hr = 1.16×10^{-6} kwhr = 0.00397 BTU (British thermal unit) (mean) = 4.186 joules.

1 year = 365 days = 8,760 hrs = 5.26×10^5 min = 3.5×10^7 sec.

Coal is assumed to have a heat content of 13,000 BTU/lb = 6.5×10^9 cal/short ton = 7.2×10^3 cal/g.

Average rock of outer crust is assumed to contain 4 ppm uranium and 12 ppm thorium; uranium and thorium in 1 ton of such rock is equivalent in heat content to 50 tons of coal (Brown and Silver, 1956, p. 95).

Solar energy striking earth, 17×10^{14} kw or 1.3

x 10^{24} cal/yr (Weinberg, 1959); United States assumed to be average.

Heat available from granite magma, assumed liquid at 900°C, then crystallizing and cooling to 500°C, is about 175 cal/g or 4.7 x 10^{17} cal/km^3. If cooled to mean earth-surface temperature, nearly 300 cal/gm or 7 x 10^{17} cal/km^3 is available. Heat content of molten basalt at 1,100°C is about 375 cal/g, relative to surface temperatures.

References

Banwell, C.J., 1964, Thermal energy from the earth's crust. Pt. 2: The efficient extraction of energy from heated rock: New Zealand Jour. Geology and Geophysics, v. 7, p. 585-593.

Bodvarsson, Gunnar, 1964, Utilization of geothermal energy for heating purposes and combined schemes involving power generation, heating, and/or by-products, in Geothermal energy, II: United Nations Conf. New Sources Energy, Rome 1961, Proc., v. 3, p. 429-436.

Bodvarsson, Gunnar, and Palmason, G., 1964, Exploration of subsurface temperature in Iceland, in Geothermal energy, I: United Nations Conf. New Sources Energy, Rome 1961, Proc., v. 2, p. 91-98.

Bodvarsson, Gunnar, and Zoëga, Johannes, 1964, Production and distribution of natural heat for domestic and industrial heating in Iceland, in Geothermal energy, II: United Nations Conf. New Sources Energy, Rome 1961, Proc., v. 3, p. 449-455.

Boldizsar, Tibor, 1963, Terrestrial heat flow in the natural steam field at Larderello [Italy]: Geofisica Pura e Appl., v. 56, p. 115-122.

Brown, Harrison, and Silver, L.T., 1956, The possibilites of obtaining long-range supplies of uranium, thorium, and other substances from igneous rocks, in Page, L.R., and others, Contributions to the geology of uranium and thorium by the United States Geological Survey and Atomic Energy Commission for the United Nations International Conference on Peaceful Uses of Atomic Energy, Geneva, Switzerland, 1955: U.S. Geol. Survey Prof. Paper 300, p. 91-95.

Bruce, A.W., 1964, Experience generating geothermal power at The Geysers power plant, Sonoma County, California, in Geothermal energy, II: United Nations Conf. New Sources Energy, Rome 1961, Proc., v. 3, p. 284-298.

Carlson, R.H., 1959, Utilizing nuclear explosive in the construction of geothermal power plants: U.S. Atomic Energy Commission, 2d Plowshare symposium, San Francisco 1959, Proc., pt. 3, p. 78-87.

Ellis, A.J., 1964, Geothermal drillholes; Chemical investigations, in Geothermal energy, I: United Nations Conf. New Sources Energy, Rome 1961, Proc., v. 2, p. 208-218.

McNitt, J.R., 1963, Exploration and development of geothermal power in California: California Div. Mines and Geology Spec. Rept. 75, 45 p.

Smith, J.H., 1964, Harnessing of geothermal energy and geothermal electricity production, in Geothermal energy, II: United Nations Conf. New Sources Energy, Rome 1961, Proc., v. 3, p. 3-57.

Waring, G.A., 1965, Thermal springs of the United States and other countries of the world: U.S. Geol. Survey Prof. Paper 492, 383 p.

Weinberg, A.M., 1959, Energy as an ultimate raw material: Physics Today, v. 12, p. 18-25.

White, D.E., 1964, Preliminary evaluation of geothermal areas by geochemistry, geology, and shallow drilling, in Geothermal energy, I: United Nations Conf. New Sources Energy, Rome 1961, Proc., v. 2, p. 402-408.

White, D.E., Anderson, E.T., and Grubbs, D.K., 1963, Geothermal brine well — mile-deep drill hole may tap ore-bearing magmatic water and rocks undergoing metamorphism: Science, v. 139, no. 3558, p. 919-922.

46. THE SALTON-MEXICALI GEOTHERMAL PROVINCE

JAMES B. KOENIG

Recent decisions to produce sodium and calcium chlorides at Niland, Imperial County, and to generate electric power at Cerro Prieto, south of Mexicali, Mexico, have brought renewed attention to the Salton-Mexicali geothermal province (figure 1).

Morton International, Inc., through its subsidiary, Imperial Thermal Products, announced plans in January to construct facilities this year for the recovery of sodium and calcium chlorides from geothermal brines. In early February the Mexican Federal Electricity Commission (C.F.E.) revealed its decision to contract for an electric power plant with the generating capacity of 75,000 kw. Power is to be generated from steam separated from geothermal brines of the Cerro

Prieto field. These two developments will be the first commercial operations utilizing the extremely hot, saline fluids of the Salton-Mexicali geothermal province. No attempt will be made at present to recover chemicals at Cerro Prieto, and there will be no immediate generation of electric

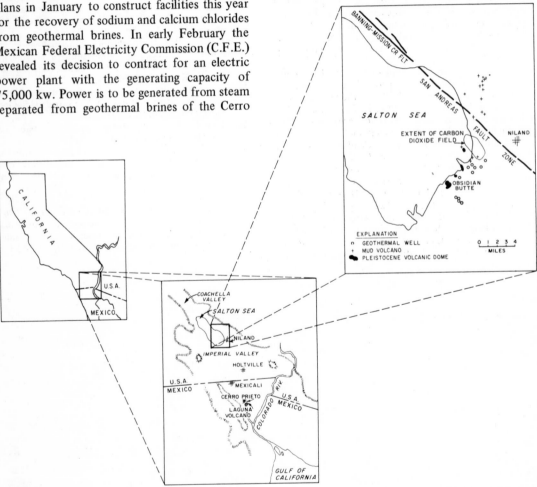

Reprinted with permission of the author and publisher from *Mineral Information Service*, v. 20, no. 7, p. 75-81, 1967. California Division of Mines and Geology, Sacramento, California.

Figure 1. Index map to Salton-Mexicali geothermal trough, with details of geothermal field at Niland, Imperial County, California.

power on a commercial basis at Niland. Morton will continue research into methods of commercial recovery of potash and perhaps lithium and manganese.

At this time the only commercial operation in North America involving use of geothermal resources is at The Geysers, Sonoma County, California, where Pacific Gas and Electric generates electric power from superheated natural steam produced from wells (see bibliography, McNitt, 1963, revised 1965). At Niland and Cerro Prieto, however, an extremely hot (over 600° F.) brine, rather than superheated steam, is produced. This brine in part flashes to steam, and in part remains as a hot saline solution. The percentage flashing to steam is dependent upon the temperature and chemistry of the fluid. In practice, at Niland approximately 15 to 20 percent of the brine by weight flashes to steam; at Cerro Prieto the percentage is somewhat higher, reflecting the lower salinity of the fluid.

At The Geysers, and at Larderello, Italy, relatively pure, superheated steam is fed to turbines and then either evaporated into the atmosphere or condensed into pure water. Corrosion, contamination and disposal problems are minimal as compared to the problems encountered at Niland and Cerro Prieto. However, the brine fields of the Salton-Mexicali trough offer the possibility of establishing a major extractive chemical industry, a possibility not clearly present at The Geysers.

STRUCTURAL SETTING

The Salton-Mexicali structural and topographic trough extends from Coachella Valley north of the Salton Sea, through Imperial and Mexicali Valleys to the Gulf of California. On the north it is terminated by the Transverse Ranges. To the south it opens out into the Gulf of California. On the west it is bordered by mountains of the Peninsular Range, and on the east by the Colorado and Sonoran deserts. Structurally, the trough is characterized by very high heat flow locally through the earth's crust (see Rex, 1966); by thinning of the crust (see Biehler, Kovach, and Allen, 1964); by the accumulation of several thousand feet of Upper Tertiary and Quaternary sediments in a low-lying plain, part of which is below sea level; and by major northwest-trending faults, which in places serve as east or west boundaries of the trough (Rusnak, Fisher, and Shepard, 1964). In essence, there is a

thick, fault-bounded and fault-cut prism of water-saturated, relatively unconsolidated sediments lying upon a granitic-metamorphic basement that in turn rests upon dense, crystalline mantle material (see figure 2). Estimates of the thickness of the sedimentary prism, and of the total thickness of the crust, have come from seismic refraction profiles, from deep drilling, and from interpretation of gravity studies. Sediment thickness is known to exceed 13,000 feet in wells, and is believed to exceed 20,000 feet at its greatest, with the maximum reached in an area immediately southeast of Mexicali. This estimate is based on seismic refraction studies. By the same method, it is estimated (Biehler, Kovach, and Allen, 1964) that the total crust is only 12 to 15 miles thick beneath the Salton Sea, and is still thinner to the southeast beneath the Gulf of California. However, crustal thickness in the northern part of the region (the Salton Sea-Coachella Valley) is known to be appreciably less than in the mountains of the bordering Peninsular and Transverse Ranges (Biehler, 1964). Thus, the crust beneath the Salton-Mexicali trough is from 6 to 10 miles less thick than the crust beneath the surrounding mountain ranges.

Heat flow measurements reported by Rex (1966) are abnormally high in the Obsidian Buttes (Niland) and Cerro Prieto areas, but are not unexpectedly high in most intervening areas. There is, however, appreciable variation in the heat flow pattern across the length and breadth of the trough. This may suggest a pattern of local "hotter spots" in the trough, where thermal effects are concentrated. Assuming that the heat source lies within the deeper crust or uppermost mantle, the "lack" or absence of 6 to 10 miles of granitic-metamorphic basement beneath the Salton-Mexicali trough may shorten the time needed for conductive transfer of heat upward from the deep source, relative to the surrounding ranges. Additionally, the 4 miles of water-saturated sediments above the granitic basement provide a near-perfect environment for development of hot water convection cells. These cells speed the transfer of heat from the granitic-metamorphic basement toward the surface. Where relatively impermeable clays, shales, volcanic tuffs, and flows occur, the upward movement of these heated fluids is impeded. Such confined heat fields may have little or no expression at the surface. However, where there are major faults cutting through the permeable

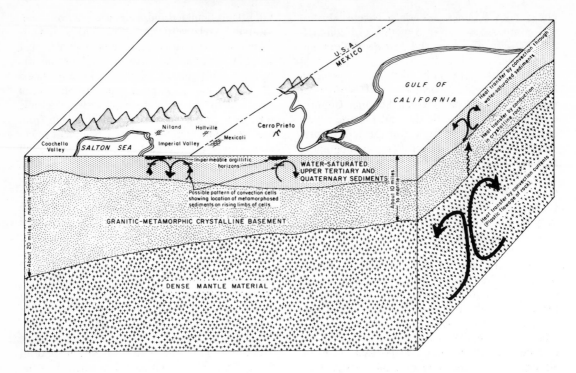

Figure 2. Schematic block diagram northwest-southeast along Salton-Mexicali trough showing possible methods of heat transfer and development of geothermal fields.

and impermeable layers, heat seeps and other evidences of the convection cell system may show clearly at the surface.

The map of ground-water temperatures of the Mexicali Valley (figure 3) prepared by the geologists of the C.F.E. shows such a pattern of relatively high and low temperature zones along the projected trace of the San Jacinto fault zone in Baja, California. It is possible that this is the surface expression of convection-cell activity beneath the Mexicali Valley. The "highs" may represent the upward, "rising" limbs of convection cells; the "lows" the descending limbs. Elsewhere in that valley the water-temperature picture reveals no striking pattern. A possible alignment of weak highs and lows may be seen near the trace of the Imperial fault; another weak series parallels the trace of a possible extension of the San Andreas fault zone in Mexico. These indistinct patterns probably reflect the presence of relatively impermeable beds near the surface; only where there is appreciable leakage as a result of fault-cutting of the impermeable layers is the convection cell pattern clearly seen at the surface. Therefore, one possible conclusion is that permeability is greater along the San Jacinto fault than along the Imperial or San Andreas faults. In places the intense hot-water activity is sufficient to cause metamorphism of sediments

in the Salton-Mexicali trough. White, Anderson, and Grubbs (1963) discuss metamorphism of Upper Tertiary sediments found in geothermal wells in the Niland area. Evidences of metamorphism of young sediments also are found in wells at Cerro Prieto (Bernardo Domínguez, C.F.E., oral communication, 1967) and near Holtville, in the Imperial Valley (Rex, 1966). These metamorphosed zones lie, apparently, on the rising or hotter limbs of convection cells. Such a pattern of local metamorphism and convection "hot spots" is suggested by Biehler, Kovach, and Allen, (1964) in analyzing the travel-time pattern of seismic refraction data, although they acknowledge that seismic profiles have been run for only limited areas.

Both Harold Helgeson (oral communication, 1966) and Bernardo Domínguez (oral communication, 1967) suggested that the thick, relatively impermeable shale or clay and volcanic units near the surface of the trough serve as an insulator and thermostat preventing the dissipation of the major portion of the geothermal fluid — and therefore the heat — to the surface. At Niland,

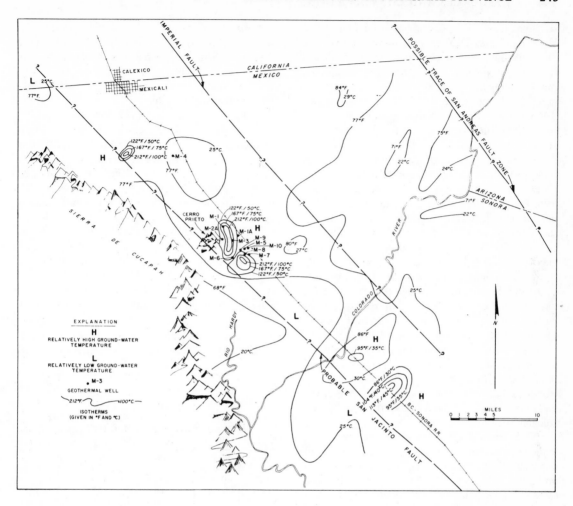

Figure 3. Ground-water isotherms, Mexicali Valley, Baja, California, Mexico. Modified from map of Comision Federal de Electridad de Mexico, July 1965.

the shales of the Borrego Formation and minor Pleistocene rhyolitic flows form the impermeable cap. The Borrego Formation becomes increasingly sandy at depth and gradually interfingers with and merges into the Palm Spring Formation. This largely sandstone sequence is the reservoir rock at Niland. Similarly, a metamorphosed argillitic cap overlies sandy beds — the reservoir — at Cerro Prieto. Metamorphism may reduce permeability of the shaly cap-rock still further. Significantly, as presently known, each geothermal field is limited to areas overlain by these relatively impermeable beds. Those wells drilled where the shale cap is thinner or almost absent reveal lower fluid temperatures and pressures (B. Domínguez, oral communication, 1967). At Niland, there is a central zone of high temperature and salinity of fluid of about 3 miles in radius. Beyond this zone there is a rapid

dropoff in temperature, heat content, and salinity of fluid. A similar pattern appears to exist at Cerro Prieto.

The presence of Quaternary volcanic rocks at Niland and at Cerro Prieto has suggested the possibility of the existence of a magma chamber at a relatively shallow depth. The local gravity high at Niland and metamorphism of sediments at Niland and Cerro Prieto are cited as supporting evidence. However, metamorphism was encountered in the deep well at Holtville, without Quaternary volcanic rocks being present at the surface.

A magnetic anomaly — or, rather, a cluster

of small magnetic highs – has been mapped in the Niland area (Kelley and Soske, 1936). This anomaly corresponds closely to the outcrops of Quaternary volcanic rocks, and to the positive gravity anomaly at Niland. This association is considered by some (Biehler, 1964; McNitt, 1963) as evidence of a buried, cooling, magmatic mass that is the source of heat for the geothermal field.

The magnetic anomaly is due, at least in part, to the presence of magnetite in the volcanic domes (Matti Tavela, oral communication, 1967), and to the probable presence of magnetite in volcanic flows or sills encountered in the sedimentary section. There are no published results of magnetic traverses across the other gravity anomalies of the Salton-Mexicali trough.

It is thought by the writer that the high rate of upward flow of heat through the thinned crust has been the cause of the metamorphism, and of partial melting of the granitic basement, as well as providing the source of the geothermal anomaly. The local gravity highs may be due to the increased density of the metamorphosed sediments. Therefore, the thin crust of the trough is the "chicken," and the hot brine, the metamorphosed sediments, and the Quaternary volcanic rocks are the "eggs."

The origin of the trough is the subject of appreciable controversy and research. The Gulf of California to the south has been described as a probable extension of the East Pacific Rise (Menard, 1960), a submarine ridge extending for 8,000 miles to the south beneath the surface of the Pacific Ocean. This ridge is the locus of high heat flow, and of earthquake activity, and is considered to represent the surface expression of major convection-current forces causing uplift from within the mantle. The suggestion is that the crest of the rise is represented on land in California by such tectonically active zones as the San Andreas fault, the Owens Valley, and the Salton-Mexicali trough. The crest of the rise is believed to consist of fault-bounded ridges and troughs, with a central trough being the site from which outward-spreading of the crust occurs. Relating this to the Salton-Mexicali trough, it appears possible that major right-lateral displacement along several strike-slip faults, or rifting and rotation westward into the Pacific of the Baja California peninsula, or a combination of these, may have begun in Late Mesozoic or Early Tertiary time, and have continued to the

present. (The trough is extremely active seismically. For example, there occurred up to 12 feet of right-lateral displacement over a 36-mile zone during the El Centro earthquake of 1940.) It is possible that this continuing rifting and lateral displacement has caused thinning of the crust by rupture and by plastic flowage.

Biehler, Kovach, and Allen (1964) commented on the problems arising from the attempt to reconcile the presence of a series of *en echelon* right-lateral faults with rifting or rotation of crustal blocks. Obviously, more work is needed before the origin of the trough is clearly understood.

Quite probably the geothermal fluids at Cerro Prieto and Niland have a common mode of origin. Concentration of salts is much higher at Niland (Table 1) than at Cerro Prieto, but there is remarkable agreement in the ratios of ionic concentrations at both sites (Table 2). Analyses

TABLE 1. ANALYSES OF FLUID FROM GEOTHERMAL WELLS AT NILAND AND CERRO PRIETO, P.P.M.

Element	Niland			Cerro Prieto
	I.I.D. #1 White, 1965a	I.I.D. #2 Helgeson, 1967	Sportsman #1 McNitt, 1963, revised 1965	M-3 Alonso E. and Mooser, 1964
Na	51,000	53,000	70,000	5,610
K	24,000	16,500	24,000	1,040
Ca	40,000	27,800	34,470	320.4
Li	300	210	149.9	13.6
Mg	35	10	18	–[1]
Sr	740	440	–[1]	27.4
Ba	200	250	–[1]	57.0
Rb	168	70	–[1]	–[1]
Cs	22	20	–[1]	–[1]
Fe	3,200	2,000	4,200	–[1]
Mn	2,000	1,370	–[1]	–[1]
Pb	104	80	–[1]	–[1]
Zn	~300	500	–[1]	–[1]
Ag	–[1]	–[1]	–[1]	0.05
Cu	10	–[1]	–[1]	0.09
SiO$_2$	~100	400	5	
Cl	185,000	155,000	201,756.7	9,694
B	520[2]	390	~149[3]	12.4[4]
F	18[2]	–[1]	–[1]	0.88
ΣS	~20	30	–[1]	~10
Total dissolved solids . .	309,887	259,000	334,987	~17,000

[1] Not reported.
[2] From D.E. White, 1965, Saline waters of sedimentary rocks, *in* Fluids in subsurface environments: American Association of Petroleum Geologists Memoir 4, pp. 342-366.
[3] Recalculated from B$_4$O$_7$.
[4] Recalculated from H$_3$BO$_3$.

TABLE 2. RATIOS, BY WEIGHT, OF ELE-
MENTS PRESENT IN GEOTHERMAL FLUIDS
AT NILAND AND CERRO PRIETO.

Element	Niland			Cerro Prieto
	I.I.D. #1 (White, 1965a)	I.I.D. #2	Sports-man #1	M-3
Ca/Cl	0.22	0.18	0.17	0.03
Mg/Cl	0.0039	0.00006	0.00009	—[1]
Na/Cl	0.28	0.34	0.35	0.58
K/Cl	0.14	0.11	0.12	0.11
L/Cl	0.0016	0.0013	0.0007	0.0014
B/Cl	0.0028	0.0025	0.0007	0.0013
SO_4/Cl	0.0003	<0.0006	—[1]	0.0014
F/Cl	0.0001	—[1]	—[1]	0.0001
$\Sigma Alkalis/Cl$	0.638	0.634	>0.632	0.729
$\Sigma Aklali$/Alkali earths/metals	0.545	0.408	~0.37	0.061
K/Na	0.49	0.30	0.34	0.19

[1] Not available.

will vary with temperature of sample, depth in
reservoir to production zone, manner of sampling,
and source of sample.

Also it must be noted that the analysis of
I.I.D. #2 (Helgeson, 1967) represents "hundreds
of analyzed samples" (Helgeson, written communication, 1967) and has been corrected for
steam separation. The other analyses in Table 1
are of post-flash brine. Total dissolved solids
reported for I.I.D. #2 are less than for I.I.D. #1
or for Sportsman #1, reflecting the additional
water flashing off as steam.

Still, the agreement among analyses is
notable; the Cerro Prieto analysis corresponds
closely to those from Niland when multiplied by
a factor of 10 to 20, except for calcium which
remains relatively low, and sulfur which appears
surprisingly high. Barium relatively is high, too,
at Cerro Prieto. Silica is anomalously low in one
analysis from Niland.

It is generally agreed (Berry, 1966; White,
1965a) that the water of the brine is almost
entirely of meteoric origin, entering the ground
as run-off from adjacent mountain ranges. Very
little (less than 5 percent) magmatic or connate
water is believed to be present. The dissolved
salts of the brine are believed to be derived from
the sedimentary rocks of the reservoir. Isotopic
studies of several elements present in the brine
(Doe, Hedge, and White, 1966; Craig, 1966) have
tended strongly to confirm this. The source of

the extremely high concentrations of chlorine in
the brine is still being investigated. White (1965a)
proposed that chlorine is obtained by solution
"from evaporites in the sediments of the basin."
Berry (1966) suggested that chlorine is concentrated by "hyperfiltration of dilute hydrothermal
solutions" through semi-permeable membranes
consisting of clays abundantly present in the
reservoir sediments. In either case, the sedimentary rocks of the trough are considered to be
the source of the salts of the brine.

DEVELOPMENTS AT NILAND

Since 1927, there have been several attempts
to exploit the heat and carbon dioxide seeps at
the south end of the Salton Sea (McNitt, 1963,
revised 1965). Surface manifestations include a
zone of mud pots and mud volcanoes discharging
hot water, mud, steam and carbon dioxide.
Additionally, at the surface, partially inundated
by waters of the Salton Sea, are five rhyolite-
pumice-obsidian domes of Late Quaternary age.
In the 1930s a commercial carbon dioxide field
was developed to the northeast of these domes,
at depths of between 200 to 700 feet. Production of carbon dioxide gas continued until 1954,
when a continuing rise in the level of Salton Sea
caused abandonment of the field.

In 1957 geothermal exploration began anew.
Since that date at least eleven wells have been
drilled in the vicinity of Niland, four of these
wells being on the 34,000-acre leasehold of
Joseph I. O'Neill, and associates, of Midland,
Texas. In January 1965, Morton International
entered into an agreement with the O'Neill group
to allow Morton's subsidiary, Imperial Thermal
Products, to conduct pilot operations of chemical recovery and electric power generation on
the geothermal leasehold. This pilot operation
(Phase 1) terminated January 3, 1967 with the
announcement that Morton, with the O'Neill
group as minority participants, would construct a
plant for commercial recovery of specific commodities (Phase 2). Similar pilot operations set
up by Earth Energy, Inc., a subsidiary of Union
Oil Company, on property adjacent to the
Morton-O'Neill property, are presently inactive.

Morton will recover sodium and calcium
chlorides by a solar evaporation process; steam
from the wells will be utilized in the recovery
operation. Morton has a 3,000 kw generating
plant on its property, which has been used in
pilot operations, but will not attempt to generate

electric power at this stage. Problems concerning corrosion of generating equipment, sale of electric power, and optimum plant size remain to be solved. Estimates of power capacity of these steam wells range up to 5,000 to 10,000 kw each, and a figure often mentioned for a geothermal power plant at Niland is 27,500 kw. The Imperial Irrigation District is a potential purchaser of electric power.

Morton plans to begin construction later this year of a plant with estimated annual capacity of about 100,000 tons of sodium chloride and about 20,000 tons of calcium chloride. Potassium chloride, valuable for use in chemical fertilizers, will be precipitated late in the evaporation process and will remain stockpiled as bedded layers at the bottom of evaporation ponds, pending a decision regarding construction of facilities for commercial extraction of potash. At one point Morton had indicated that an integrated plant capable of producing potash as well as sodium and calcium chloride, and perhaps lithium and manganese, would cost in the neighborhood of $30,000,000 to construct. Present construction costs will be much less. Ultimately, the market for potash — and perhaps lithium — will determine whether Morton will invest the larger sum. Reserves of potash are probably great; recoverable potash will in part depend upon the production characteristics of the reservoir rocks. Assuming[1] the reservoir to be 3 miles long at Niland, with a producing zone 2,000 feet thick, given a KCl content of perhaps 2 percent in the reservoir fluid, and assuming that interconnected pore spaces represent 10 percent of the rock by volume, an estimate of several tens of million tons of potash is not excessive.

The Morton time schedule calls for commercial production of sodium and calcium chlorides in 1968. Plans also call for drilling of an additional well in 1967 or early 1968.

Steam produced from the wells will be used in the final evaporation step in the recovery of sodium chloride. Sodium chloride will first be precipitated from the brine in solar evaporation ponds. It will then be re-dissolved and processed for removal of impurities. Then it will be flashed to dryness by natural steam. Calcium chloride will be recovered by solar evaporation, and will

be marketed as an accelerant for use in the concrete industry. Ponds of approximately 200 acres in total area are currently used for precipitation, experimentation, and ponding of wastes prior to re-injection. Special precautions are taken to ensure that no contamination of surface water or shallow ground-water occurs.

At Niland, where the post-flash brine runs as high as 330,000 parts per million of dissolved solids, a 1,500 foot deep well has been constructed for re-injection of fluid remaining after extraction of commercially valuable chemicals. This fluid will be residually enriched in iron chloride, and will be extremely corrosive. Pumping tests appear to have established that the re-injected fluids do not contaminate existing ground-water supplies. Very little is known, however, about the long-term nature of water circulation at that depth. Discharge from the well will be into a sandy layer of the shaly Borrego Formation of Plio-Pleistocene age. Shale beds above the sandy horizon will confine the flow, and prevent upward seepage into the near-surface water table. There may, however, be displacement upward of water presently contained in these sands. Morton will probably need more than one re-injection well to dispose of the large volumes of brine produced.

DEVELOPMENTS AT CERRO PRIETO

Cerro Prieto is a double-peaked basaltic volcano of Quaternary age, not known to be active presently. Immediately to the southeast is Laguna Volcano, a playa of perhaps 4 square miles in area. Laguna Volcano is the site of intense fumarolic and solfataric activities, and is marked by the development of mud volcanoes and by periodic phreatic explosions. Both Laguna Volcano and Cerro Prieto lie along a probable extension of the San Jacinto fault zone. Isothermal maps of ground-water temperatures, mentioned earlier, show several distinct high-temperature cells along this lineament in Baja California. Highest ground-water temperatures — boiling — are found at Laguna Volcano and 1 mile to the east of Cerro Prieto.

In 1960, on the basis of these heat manifestations, a geothermal drilling program was begun. The first wells (M-1, M-1A, M-2) were drilled in the zone of high ground-water temperature to the east and northeast of Cerro Prieto. Successive wells, with the exception of M-4, have been located to the southeast, entering into the area of Laguna Volcano.

[1] These figures are arbitrarily chosen from published locations and descriptions of wells at Niland, published analyses of the geothermal brine, and a rough estimate of permeability made by the writer.

The pilot operations of Morton International, Inc. at Niland, showing evaporation ponds and steam discharge from a geothermal well; low in the background at right are Quaternary volcanic domes partially inundated by the waters of the Salton Sea. Photo by Morton International, Inc.

Six wells currently are considered to be production wells, or capable of becoming production wells. These are numbers M-3, M-5, M-7, M-8, M-9, and M-10 (figure 3). Well M-4 drilled some 8 miles to the northwest, along the projected trace of the San Jacinto fault, was unsuccessful. The earlier wells (M-1, etc.) were not considered commercially successful, although M-1 was reported (Facca, 1965) to have produced 900 tons per hour of a mixture of steam and hot water. De Anda and Paredes (1964) report a temperature of 291°F. and wellhead pressure of 107 psi for M-1. These early wells were completed to depths of about 1,300 to 2,300 feet. With well M-3 a program of deeper drilling began. Well M-3 (Alonso E., and Mooser, 1964) was drilled to 8,000 feet, and tested at 200 tons per hour of steam and water at 410°F. from a zone at 1,900-2,900 feet. The *Oil and Gas Journal* of June 1, 1964 reported wellhead temperature of 358°F., wellhead pressure of 280 psi, and a potential capacity of 5,500 kw for well M-3. This estimate may be very conservative.

Data for this and subsequent wells are incomplete, partially because testing of the field is still continuing. However, for wells M-5 through M-10 certain generalizations can be made. Depths have varied between 3,000 and 4,500 feet. These are appreciably shallower than M-3, and reflect the fact that well M-3 was planned as a deep probe. Its results, and those of subsequent wells, have confirmed a zone of high flow and maximum temperatures at depths averaging 2,000 to 3,500 feet. Surface temperature measurements of the effluent are commonly in the range 300-400°F., while maximum downhole temperatures have reached as high as 620°F. for M-10. During pumping tests held at M-10 at the end of January, rates of flow of steam and hot water were about 1,000 tons per hour, at pressures of about 390 psi through a 3-inch orifice, with the percentage of the fluid flashing over to steam reaching perhaps 35 percent or more. Shut-in pressures are great, being estimated at 1,600 psi for M-10.

In general, as exploration has progressed to the southeast, higher temperatures and pressures, and greater enthalpies have been encountered in the successive holes. This has led Bernardo Domínguez of the C.F.E. to believe that the hottest, most productive part of the field may not yet have been reached. Facca (1966) writes that the Cerro Prieto field is presently the largest known geothermal field of the world, in terms of linear extent and estimated reservoir volume.

Continuing pumping tests at Cerro Prieto indicate that two of the wells have an estimated power-generating capacity of 20,000 to 25,000 kw each, and that two others are in the vicinity of 10,000 kw each. Thus, the six probable production wells are considered easily capable of supplying steam to generate the planned 75,000 kw; perhaps not all six will be needed at first.

The plant is to be located alongside the tracks of Baja California-Sonora Railroad, adjacent to well M-10. Steam will be removed mechanically from the brine, and carried in insulated lines to the plant. The residual brine, having a chemical composition somewhat similar to sea-water both in amount of total dissolved solids, and in that it is rich in sodium chloride, will be piped into the Gulf of California via the Rio Hardy. No re-injection wells are planned. As at Niland, corrosion and scaling are problems to be solved. At very high temperatures, rates of chemical reactions are greatly accelerated. One estimate is that the rate of reactivity effectively doubles with every increase of 20°F. in temperature. Therefore, corrosive reactions that proceed extremely slowly at ordinary temperatures are a potential hazard in geothermal fields. Also, fresh-water supplies and crop-growing areas must be protected from contamination. It is not known what precautions will be taken at Cerro Prieto.

The plant to be constructed will have two 37,500 kw generating units, and is to be completed by 1970. Additional power plant units will be constructed as the steam reserves are proven and as the power needs of the region increase. Presently, as in the Imperial Valley, there is a peak power demand in summer with high power consumption for irrigation pumping and air-conditioning (de Anda and Paredes, 1964). However, during winter it is believed that there will be excess power capacity.

Cost analyses indicate that power can be produced at Cerro Prieto for perhaps a quarter to half the cost of power produced by the thermo-electric plant at Rosarito, near Ensenada. Therefore, it may prove more economical to install lower-cost geothermal power plants to augment and to replace the existing electrical generating capacity.

CONCLUSIONS

The infant geothermal industry will be greatly expanded by the developments at Niland and Cerro Prieto. At Niland the potential exists for a major extractive chemical industry; while at Cerro Prieto the potential for electric power generation appears great. Both fields are part of the Salton-Mexicali geothermal province, and have a common origin, which is a function of thinning of the crust and of establishment of convection cells for transfer of heat through water-saturated sediments.

Continued prospecting for heat fields in the Salton-Mexicali geothermal province might, therefore, center on the following: 1) zones of gravity highs (indicating lesser depth to mantle, and presence of metamorphosed sediments); 2) thick impermeable beds in the shallow subsurface; 3) anomalously high pressures and rates of heat flow in shallow wells; and, perhaps incidentally, 4) surface heat manifestations.

References

Alonso Espinosa, H., and Mooser, F., 1964, El pozo M-3 del campo geotérmico del Cerro Prieto, B.C., México: Bóletin de la Asociación Mexicana de Geólogos Petroleros, v. 16, no. 7-8, pp. 163-178.

Berry, F.A.F., 1966, Proposed origin of subsurface thermal brines, Imperial Valley, California (abs.): American Association of Petroleum Geologists, Bull., v. 50, no. 3, pp. 644-645.

Biehler, S., 1964, Geophysical study of the Salton trough of southern California, Ph.D. thesis, California Institute of Technology. (Unpublished).

Biehler, S., Kovach, R.L., and Allen, C.R., 1964, Geophysical framework of northern end of Gulf of California structural province, in Marine geology of the Gulf of California: American Association of Petroleum Geologists Memoir 3, pp. 126-143.

Craig, H., 1966, Isotopic composition and origin of the Red Sea and Salton Sea geothermal brines: Science, v. 154, no. 3756, pp. 1544-1547.

de Anda, L.F., and Paredes, E., 1964, La falla de San Jacinto y su influencia sobre la actividad geotérmica en el valle de Mexicali, B.C., México: Bóletin de la Asociación Mexicana de Geólogos Petroleros, v. 16, no. 7-8, pp. 179-181.

Doe, B.R., Hedge, C.E., and White, D.E., 1966, Preliminary investigation of the source of lead and strontium in deep geothermal brines underlying the

Salton Sea geothermal area; Economic Geology, v. 61, no. 3, pp. 462-483.

Facca, G., 1965, Recent development of geothermal energy: reprinted by Worldwide Geothermal Exploration Co., Los Angeles, California.

Facca, G., 1966, La energía geotérmica: Revista Mexicana de Electricidad, no. 315, December, pp. 12-15, 35-38.

Helgeson, H.C., 1967, Solution chemistry and metamorphism, in Researches in geochemistry, P.H. Abelson, ed., John Wiley and Sons, New York (in press).

Kelley, V.C., and Soske, J.L., 1936, Origin of the Salton volcanic domes, Salton Sea, California: Journal of Geology, v. 44, pp. 496-509.

McNitt, J.R., 1963, revised 1965, Exploration and development of geothermal power in California: California Division of Mines and Geology Special Report 75, 45 pp.

Menard, H.W., 1960, The east Pacific rise: Science, v. 132, no. 3441, pp. 1737-1746.

Rex, R.W., 1966, Heat flow in the Imperial Valley of California (abs.): American Geophysical Union, Transactions, v. 74, no. 1, p. 181.

Rusnak, G.A., Fisher, R.L., and Shepard, F.P., 1964, Bathymetry and faults of Gulf of California, in Marine geology of the Gulf of California: American Association of Petroleum Geologists Memoir 3, pp. 59-75.

White, D.E., 1965a, Metal contents of some geothermal fluids: Symposium, Problems of postmagmatic ore deposition, Prague, Czechoslovakia, v. 2, pp. 432-443.

White, D.E., 1965b, Geothermal energy: U.S. Geological Survey Circular 519, 17 pp.

White, D.E., Anderson, E.T., and Grubbs, D.K., 1963, Geothermal brine well — mile-deep drill hole may tap ore-bearing magmatic water and rocks undergoing metamorphism: Science, v. 139, no. 3558, pp. 919-922.

Some Environmental Considerations of Resource Utilization

47. NATURE, NOT ONLY MAN, DEGRADES ENVIRONMENT

U. S. GEOLOGICAL SURVEY

Natural earth processes are by far the principal agents in modifying our environment, according to Dr. William T. Pecora, Director, U.S. Geological Survey, Department of the Interior. In a commencement address yesterday at George Washington University, Washington, D.C., Pecora said that "the ability to maintain an acceptable environment can be hindered by failure to recognize basic earth processes and quality patterns beyond our control. Environmental degradation is a natural process on earth; with the intellectual development now achieved by man, it is inexcusable that we should fail to predict responses of nature consequent to our own actions. Better 'housekeeping' of the earth must be practiced as man continues to take from the earth the things he needs and uses.

"From a humble beginning in which ancient man lived in harmony with nature, evolved our present society which indicts man for all environmental ills and assumes that nature can be shaped to meet his every need. If we must take from the earth to provide for ourselves, we must employ value judgment and trade-off concepts in deciding how much to take from our environment, where to take it, and how to leave it in the taking and using. Take and use we must, or we cannot survive as a species on earth."

In an address that pointed up the conflict between the need to develop our resources and the need to preserve our environment, Pecora listed a "staggering amount of mineral resources upon which the sustenance of the nation depends," and noted that "this imposes a tremendous task of new discovery and new development."

In listing the resource needs of the nation, the USGS Director said that within the life span of 200 million people now living in the United States, resources to meet their needs will include 6-1/2 quadrillion gallons of water; 7-1/2 billion tons of iron ore; 1-1/2 billion tons of phosphate rock; and 100 million tons of copper. Water

From U.S. Department of the Interior "news release" of June 8, 1970.

usage and energy requirements will triple by the year 2000, and by that time, we will have to construct as many houses and other facilities as now exist in the United States.

"If the earth shall provide the materials for the survival of man's society," Pecora said, "then a prudent society must provide for an intimate understanding of the earth; inquiry must be made into the geologic processes that have operated over the span of earth history and operate today; an inventory of current and potential resources must be continued; and efforts must be made to develop new techniques for information-gathering systems."

The Survey Director scorned what he termed an "environmental myth" — the belief by many people that man alone is degrading and polluting his environment by our modern society. "Some myths need to be destroyed, because if man is to tackle the many complex problems of environmental degradation effectively, he must first understand its forces. This is not to excuse or put aside what man has done, but rather to put man's actions in proper natural perspective. Those who speak about restoring our inherited environment to pristine states, often ignore the inevitability of nature."

To demonstrate that natural processes are principal agents in modifying the environment, Pecora cited the following:

- It has been estimated that more than 100 million tons of fixed nitrogen in the form of ammonia and nitrates is annually deposited from the atmosphere to the earth as part of a natural precipitation process. In the United States alone, more than 4 million tons of table salt, 2-1/2 million tons of sodium sulphate, and 36 million tons of calcium compounds, fall upon the land surface — all in rain water.

- Particulate matter and natural gases dispersed from volcanoes is a continuing phenomenon. From three eruptions alone — the Krakataua eruption in Java (1883), the Mount Katmai eruption in Alaska (1912), and the Hekla eruption in Iceland (1947) — more dust, ash, and combined gases were ejected into the atmosphere than from all of man's activities.

- Many have long believed that water issuing from natural springs is pure and beneficial to health because of its purity. The springs issuing into the Arkansas and Red Rivers carry 17 tons of salt per minute. In the Lower Colorado River, salt springs carry 1,500 tons of salt per day. The Lemonade Springs in New Mexico carry 900 pounds of sulphuric acid per million pounds of water, which is 10 times the acid concentration of most acid mine streams in the nation. Hot Springs in Yellowstone Park is likewise many times more acidic than the typical acid stream in a coal-mining district. The Azure Yampah spring in Colorado contains 8 times the radium that Public Health Service sets as a safe limit.

- Lakes and ponds throughout geologic history have gone through a life cycle of birth, maturity, old age, and disappearance. No lake is truly permanent. Some of our inland lakes during their mature stage become more salty than the ocean itself. The Great Salt Lake is nearing its dying stages. Once 20,000 square miles in area (Lake Bonneville), it is now only 950 square miles. Many thousands of years ago, it was essentially a fresh water lake, fed during the Great Ice Age, and now it is about 10 times as salty as sea water.

- Lake Erie is not "dead," as is heard frequently. It's the shallowest of the Great Lakes, and was created about 10,000 to 20,000 years ago. Barring another Ice Age, it has several thousands of years yet to go before senility. The western part of the lake is extremely shallow, and receives a large amount of natural organic material transported from the surrounding terrain. This is where algae growth has always been present. Lake Erie has continually produced about 50% of the fish catch of the entire Great Lakes system, consistently over the past 100 years. This is not the mark of a dead lake. Green Bay, Michigan, so named by the first settlers because of the green color of the algae so prevalent in the Bay is, like the western shallow part of Lake Erie, the source of a great amount of organic matter. The food supply for aquatic life is high in these environments. The oxygen supply, unfortunately, diminishes as algae growth increases, as this portion of the lake becomes more and more shallow and as organic material is swept into the water, whether from natural or human sources. Every lake or pond, whether natural or man-made, faces a similar life history.

- The nation's rivers are called dirty because of the works of man. River systems, however, are the natural transport systems for sediment washed downhill by the rains that fall upon the land. It is estimated that the Mississippi River carries into the Gulf a load of more than 2 million tons of sediment a day — equivalent to the load of 40,000 freight cars. The Colorado carries about 40,000 tons a day into Lake Mead. The Paria River in Arizona is probably the dirtiest river in the world. It carries 500 times as much sediment as the Mississippi per unit volume of water. Chemicals are also transported by streams in phenomenal amounts. The Brazos River of Texas, for example, transports 25,000 tons of dissolved salt per day. Peace Creek in Florida carries twice the concentration of fluoride that is harmful to teeth. Many rivers and streams throughout the nation have natural qualities that do not meet the Public Health standards for drinking water.

In looking to the future, Dr. Pecora said that "we find ourselves in the midst of a conflict between the need to develop the earth's resources, and the desire to preserve the earth's environment — both, presumably, for the salvation of mankind.

"Must one choose between the two concepts or can one seek balance as we move into the future? The first judgment must distinguish between danger and aesthetics because change is inevitable in any developing society. The pace of change is a function of the choice of the people, as it should be."

48. RESTORATION OF A TERRESTRIAL ENVIRONMENT —
THE SURFACE MINE

RONALD D. HILL

INTRODUCTION

The very concept of disturbing the surface of the earth by removing, turning over, and exposing it to remove the mineral wealth entombed therein, dictates that changes and possible damages will result to the environment. The damages can be permanent or held to a minimum and eventually restored to a condition approaching that existing before mining. A certain price in environmental damage usually must be paid to obtain the minerals required for our standard of living. The basic question is: What price are we willing to pay? We might outlaw certain types of surface mining resulting in an increase in cost of consumer products, or a reduction in the standard of living. A strict environmental control policy might produce the same effects.

In this paper, I will try to describe damages caused by surface mining (with emphasis on coal mines), to outline techniques that can be utilized to hold damage to a minimum, and procedures to restore the land after surface mining has occurred.

As of 1965, according to the best estimates, in excess of 3.2 million acres of land had been disturbed by surface mining in the United States. (Figure 1 illustrates land disturbed by commodities.) Open-pit mining accounted for about 35 percent and strip mining for 56 percent of the disturbed land. Two-thirds of the disturbed land (2.0 million acres) required some form of treatment to prevent environmental pollution (Figure 2). Approximately 800,000 of these acres requiring treatment were strip mined (Udall, 1967).

Water pollution associated with strip mines is due to mine drainage and siltation resulting from erosion. Mine drainage is usually characterized by a low pH and high iron, calcium, magnesium, sulfate, and total dissolved solids. High concentrations of aluminum, sodium, manganese, and other heavy metals may also be present. Mine drainage quality varies from mineral seam to mineral seam, and even within the same mine. Examples of water quality from several coal surface mines are presented in Table 1.

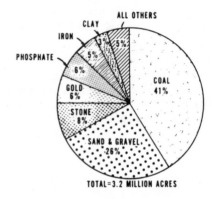

Figure 1. Percentage of land disturbed by surface mining of various commodities as of January 1, 1965.

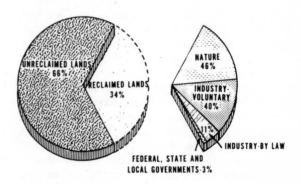

Figure 2. Status of land disturbed by surface mining as of January 1, 1965.

Reprinted with permission of the author and publisher from *The ASB Bulletin,* y. 18, no. 3, July 1971, p. 107-116. Published by the Association of Southeastern Biologists, Inc., at Philadelphia, Pa. Originally published as "Restoration of a Terrestrial Environment — the Surface Mine" by Ronald D. Hill, Environmental Protection Agency, Water Quality Office, Publication no. 14010, 22 p., April, 1971.

TABLE 1. EXAMPLES OF MINE DRAINAGE
FROM COAL SURFACE MINES

	Southwestern Indiana	Western Pennsylvania	Southeastern Illinois	Northern West Virginia
pH	5.7	3.2	2.7	3.0
Acidity, mg/1	0	152	1,620	870
Alkalinity, mg/1	170	0	0	0
Hardness, mg/1	1,780	—	—	—
Iron, mg/1	0.4	9.4	130	75
Sulfate, mg/1	850	499	—	1,742
Chloride, mg/1	7	—	—	—
Manganese, mg/1	7.8	—	—	—
Calcium, mg/1	328	—	—	—
Aluminum, mg/1	—	—	—	60

ACID MINE DRAINAGE

One of the most troublesome mine drainage problems is caused by acidity. Although the exact mechanism of acid mine drainage formation is not fully understood, it is generally believed that pyrite (FeS_2) is oxidized by oxygen (equation 1) or ferric iron (equation 2) to produce ferrous sulfate and sulfuric acid (Hill, 1968).

$$2FeS_2 + 2H_2O + 7O_2 \rightarrow 2FeSO_4 + 2H_2SO_4 \quad (1)$$
(Pyrite)   (Ferrous Iron) + (Sulfuric Acid)

$$FeS_2 + 14Fe^3 + 8H_2O \rightarrow 15Fe^{2+} + 2SO_4^{2-} + 16H+ \quad (2)$$
(Pyrite)+(Ferric Iron)   (Ferrous Iron) + (Sulfate)   (Acid)

The reactions may proceed to form ferric hydroxide and more acid:

$$4FeSO_4 + 2O_2 + 2H_2SO_4 \rightarrow 2Fe_2(SO_4)_3 + 2H_2O \quad (3)$$

$$Fe_2(SO_4)_3 + 6H_2O \rightarrow 2Fe(OH)_3 + 3H_2SO_4 \quad (4)$$

A low pH water is produced (pH 2-4.5). At these pH levels the heavy metals such as iron, magnesium, manganese, copper, zinc, and calcium are more soluble and enter into the solution to further pollute the water. Water of this type supports only limited water flora, such as acid-tolerant molds and algae; it will not support fish life, destroys and corrodes metal piers, culverts, barges, etc., increases the cost of water treatment for power plants and municipal water supplies, and leaves the water unacceptable for recreational uses.

ALKALINE MINE DRAINAGE

Alkaline mine drainage may result where no acid producing material is associated with the mineral seam or where the neutralization of that acid is produced by alkaline material. Alkaline mine drainage may be, but is not usually, as bad as acid mine drainage. Drainage from freshly exposed strata usually has a higher mineral content than that from undisturbed land because the strata has high levels of readily leachable minerals. These minerals were leached from the surface material centuries before. Reports of increased runoff concentrations of aluminum, iron, manganese, sulfate, magnesium, sodium, and potassium have been made (Curtis, 1969; Collier et al., 1966). These ions, in general, decrease the usability of the water for domestic and industrial uses.

Some alkaline waters have high concentrations of ferrous iron and, upon oxidation and hydrolysis, form acid which lowers the pH and changes the drainage to the acid type. These types of discharges are more common to underground mines than surface mines.

SEDIMENTATION AND EROSION

The removal of the vegetation and the loosening and breaking up of the overburden by blasting, shovels, draglines, and dozers creates materials and conditions conducive to erosion. Curtis (1969) and Collier, et al., (1966) have documented the increased sediment and suspended solid loads from surface mined areas.

Sediment fills creek beds destroying fish habitat and creating flooding conditions. Suspended solids increase treatment cost for industrial and municipal supplies.

Erosion is influenced by the soil type (sand, clay, salt, infiltration rate, and percolation rate), the climate (temperature and amount and type of rainfall), the topography (steepness, length of slope, land configuration and exposure), and the vegetation cover. Each of these factors should be considered in the planning, development and reclamation of a surface mine to prevent erosion.

TYPES OF SURFACE MINES

To better appreciate the problems associated with strip mining, it is imperative that the stripping operation be understood. Strip mining can be divided into two general types — area and contour.

Area strip mining is practiced on relatively flat terrain. A trench (called a cut) is made through the overburden to expose the deposit of mineral or ore to be removed (Figure 3). The first cut is extended to the limits of the property or the deposit. The overburden from the first cut is placed on unmined land adjacent to the cut. The mineral or ore is then removed. Once the first cut is completed, a second cut is made parallel to the first; however, the overburden from the succeeding cuts is deposited in the cut just previously excavated. The deposited overburden is called spoil. The final cut leaves an open trench equal in depth to the thickness of the overburden and the mineral bed removed, bound on one side by the last spoil pile and on the other by the undisturbed highwall. The final cut may be up to a mile or more from the starting point, and the overburden from the cuts, unless graded or leveled, resembles the ridges of a gigantic washboard. Shovels (with capacities to 160 cubic yards), draglines (up to 220 cubic yards), and wheel excavations are used to remove

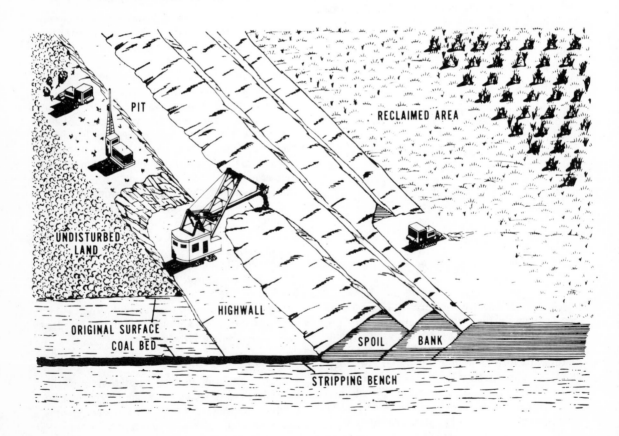

Figure 3. Area strip mining with concurrent reclamation.

the overburden. The nature of the spoil, the surface features, and characteristics depend to some extent upon the type of equipment used.

In general, the pollution from area mines is not as severe as that from contour mines. Silt from erosion can often be confined to the mining area. The overburden can be graded and revegetated to prevent erosion. Final cuts can be filled with water to prevent oxidation of the pyrite. The acid-producing material can be buried and thus prevented from being oxidized. A dragline or wheel excavator can perform this selective placement better than a shovel. A dragline, which sits on top of the overburden can selectively remove layers of overburden, placing the acid producing material on the bottom and the better material on top. Similarly, a wheel excavator has the ability to remove different layers. A shovel, on the other hand, sits in the cut and generally removes a section of overburden from the bottom to the top, thus mixing all of the various materials. In spite of these potentially beneficial actions, pollution does occur. Corbett and Agnew (1968) have shown that during periods of high rainfall, acid mine drainage can be flushed from spoil piles. Siltation of streams in area stripping regions is sometimes evident.

Contour stripping is practiced on rolling to very steep terrain. It consists of removing the overburden from the mineral seam, starting at the outcrop and proceeding around the hillside (Figure 4). The cut appears as a contour line, thus the name. The overburden is deposited along the outer edge of the bench. After the uncovered mineral seam is removed, successive cuts are made until the depth of the overburden becomes too great for economical retrieval of the ore. This type of mining creates a shelf or bench on the side of the hill. On the inside it is bordered by the highwall, ranging in height from a few feet to more than 100 feet, and on the outer side by a high ridge of spoil material. The spoil may be piled on the bench or pushed down the side of the hill. In either case, on steep slopes a more or less precipitous downslope is formed which is subject to severe erosion and landslides. Plass (1967) made a survey of eastern Kentucky and found that 12 percent of the outslope area had failed (landslides). Because of the landslide problem, West Virginia has limited the bench width on steep slopes and forbids mining on slopes greater than 65 percent (Reclamation Handbook, 1969). Even with these precautions, landslides still occur. Many water problems arise from this type of mining. The highwalls and spoil piles, because of their long, bare, steep, uninterrupted slopes are subject to severe erosion. Sediment coming off these slopes has been known to clog

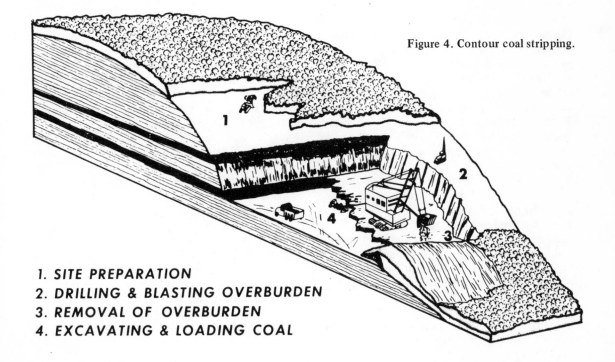

Figure 4. Contour coal stripping.

1. SITE PREPARATION
2. DRILLING & BLASTING OVERBURDEN
3. REMOVAL OF OVERBURDEN
4. EXCAVATING & LOADING COAL

stream channels, cover highways, settle on cultivated land and kill crops, cover fish spawning beds, fill water courses, and thus, subject adjacent land to flooding, etc.

A study of watersheds draining to Beaver Creek, Kentucky (Collier et al., 1966; Musser, 1963) showed that a partially stripped watershed (6.4 percent of area) had an average erosion rate of 5.9 tons per acre per year as compared to 0.7 tons per acre per year for an unmined area.

Even when spoil piles are graded, problems occur. If the grading is toward the highwall, the water may accumulate in an area of poor quality spoil (i.e., a spoil high in pyritic material) and may therefore be degraded in quality. When underground mines are located behind the highwall, grading toward it often causes water to flow into the underground mine. This flow often flushes toxic material from the mine.

When spoil piles are graded away from the highwall, erosion may be as bad or worse, unless good water management practices are followed, such as diversion ditches across the top of the highwall, ditches or terraces across the slope to break the slope length and control structures to remove the water from the mining area.

Grading alone is not enough. A cover crop must be established to protect the bare surface and hold the surface in place. First consideration of a cover crop should be given to one that covers and holds the soil; a crop that will give a commercial return may also be possible. Neither planting nor grading alone is a satisfactory answer to the spoil bank problem, but a combination of the two can be very beneficial.

Another problem inherent in contour strip mining is that of toxic materials, i.e., pyrites, acid, soluble metals, etc., in the overburden. During the normal stripping operation, the high quality overburden near the surface is placed on the bottom of the spoil pile and then covered with low quality and often toxic overburden, leaving toxic material exposed to weathering and conversion to soluble acids and minerals which are carried away by water. However, for a small extra cost, the high quality overburden can be set aside to cover the toxic material after grading and/or during excavation. By this means, the toxic material is not subject to weathering and pollution can be reduced. Moreover, cover crops are difficult to establish on toxic overburdens and therefore, erosion damages occur. Erosion serves to prolong the mineral pollution problem

by continuing to reveal new surfaces to weathering. However, when the toxic material is covered with a good material, cover crops can be grown to protect the surface.

The final cut in a contour strip mine can also be troublesome. Materials adjacent to the ore seam are often toxic. A final cut left uncovered is a potential pollution source. When covered, the danger from this source of pollution is reduced or eliminated.

Highwalls can also lead to pollution problems. An unstable highwall that sloughs off can ruin the natural drainage in a strip area. Material falling off the highwall can dam up channels and thereby prolong the contact between water and toxic material or even force the water to seep through toxic spoil piles. Sloughing highwalls can open up new toxic material to weathering. Highwall problems such as these can often be overcome by grading the spoil back against the highwall and "knocking off" the top of the highwall.

Often in the excavation of a strip area, a natural drainageway is cut across. Unless the water is diverted around the mine workings, the water enters the mine area where it may become polluted. Problems such as this have been averted by not stripping the drainageway or by placing control structures such as drop boxes and concrete flumes.

RECLAMATION

If pollution from surface mines is to be held to a minimum, then reclamation must consist of a four prong attack: preplanning, proper mining, water control during mining, and reclamation after mining.

Preplanning is the first step in reclamation. The operator should determine not only the quality and quantity of the deposit, but also the quality of the overburden material, the water pattern within the area (both surface and subsurface), the location of adjacent abandoned or inactive underground mines, the adjacent land and water uses, and the topography.

Analysis should be made of the overburden materials to determine their texture (sandy, clay, silty) and their chemical makeup (i.e., which strata are acid producers, have nutrient value for vegetation, and contain toxic material). This information should serve as a guide for planning the mining operation and water control. The less toxic, more fertile, and less acid producing materials should be selectively placed so that they will be on top when grading is performed. If the overburden contains acid producing strata, the installation of a system to treat any acid water should be developed. Water quality of discharges from nearby mines in the same seam is a valuable reference to estimate water quality from the proposed operation. If the texture analysis indicates that the overburden is highly susceptible to erosion, special erosion control measures should be taken.

An evaluation of the surface and subsurface water pattern should lead to a sound water management plan. Mining can be planned around natural drainage ways or control structures designed. Interception of ground water can be avoided or control planned. The location of treatment facilities, such as sediment ponds, mechanical water control structures, and diversion ditches, can be determined. Quantity and quality of water can be estimated.

It is critical that all efforts be made to locate underground mines adjacent to the surface mines. Cutting into abandoned or inactive underground mines can result in the discharge of large volumes of polluted water stored in underground mines. The resultant continued underground discharges into surface mining works during and following mining, can result in water passing from the surface mine into the underground mine and aggravating that problem. These conditions often make complete reclamation impossible, and in steep terrain the underground mine can supply the water necessary for the development for slippage planes in the spoils. Where underground mines are adjacent to the proposed surface mines, barrier pillars should be left. When a deep mine is breached, the opening should be sealed as soon as possible by clay compaction, concrete, or any other method deemed necessary.

Adjacent land uses and present use of the area before mining should be taken into consideration in planning the type of grading to be performed. In most cases, the area should be returned as nearly as possible to the topography existing before mining. The possible exceptions are the very steep contour mines and those situations where better land use and less environmental problems would result by not returning it to the natural contour.

Silt structures and treatment facilities should be designed before mining ever starts.

The mining method itself should be evaluated to determine how the area could best be mined with the least environmental damage.

Mining the area is the next important step in environmental control. Before mining ever begins, the water control structures should be constructed. Well designed and constructed silt structures should be built following good design criteria for small impoundments, including compacted dams, mechanical overflow structures, emergency spillways, and adequate sediment storage. The pond should be designed to provide one hour of detention time at maximum flow and a minimum of short circuiting. Basically, it should remove all settleable solids and reduce the suspended solids to approximately 200 mg/1. Where the overburden contains clay that will not settle from water, additional treatment with lime, alum, etc., will be required.

A treatment facility to assure that the water has a pH of 6 to 9, a net alkalinity, and an iron concentration of less than 7 mg/1 should also be installed.

The haulage road, which is often a source of erosion, should be properly designed and installed. Proper grades and water control should be followed.

Care should be taken in cleaning and grubbing, cutting roads for drilling machinery and during blasting to protect the environment.

Diversion ditches with good controlled outlets should be constructed along the top of the highwall to keep water out of the workings. Drainage ways should be protected or control structures built.

Water that does enter the pit should be properly handled. In most cases this means rapid removal and discharge to a siltation pond or treatment plant. Under some conditions, where a workable system can be developed, it might be better to catch the water on the bench and control the discharge to the treatment facilities. Drainage patterns should be established in the pit to facilitate water removal. Water discharge from the pit area should be through well-designed outlets and should not overload the natural drainage way. Proper management of water on the bench can markedly reduce the siltation and acid mine drainage problem.

Removal and placement of the overburden are critical in environmental control. The nontoxic, nonacid, and fertile material should be stockpiled for later spreading or placed on top of the less desirable spoils already mined. The placement of the spoil should assure that long steep slopes are avoided, that it is not on material subject to slippage and that it does not produce high peaks difficult to regrade. In very steep terrain, such as in eastern Kentucky and southern West Virginia, the spoil should not be placed on the outslope, but hauled to a fill area designed for that purpose or placed on the bench behind the operation.

Reclamation should follow closely behind the mining operation. The bare spoil and pit should be reclaimed as fast as possible because the freshly moved material is easier to grade and handle than older compacted material. In addition, bare spoils and pits are more susceptible to acid formation and erosion.

Area mines should be graded back to the original contour. Where the final cut can be permanently flooded above any acid producing strata, it can be left to form a lake. It may also serve as a silt trap. Care should be taken to assure that it has a properly designed discharge facility.

These types of backfills might be used on contour mines: contour, pasture, and swallow-tail.

For a contour backfill, the edge of the highwall is "knocked-off" and the spoil is graded back toward the highwall to approximate the original contour (Figure 5). This method is the closest approach to returning the area to its original topography and produces the most pleasing aesthetic effect. Long steep slopes can be formed that are subject to erosion. However, the erosion problem can be solved by the construction of a diversion ditch at the top of the slope, of terraces, or of a series of diversions or ridges across the slope. Each of these measures should have a controlled outlet. Rapid vegetation with grasses and legumes is critical for this type of backfill. Contour backfills are preferred wherever possible.

Pasture backfilling calls for the grading of the spoil to cover the pit and any acid-producing strata, but not the entire highwall (Figure 6). The slope of the graded spoil should be away from the highwall and the slope of the "outslope" should be reduced to control the water running off the bench. Diversion ditches should be constructed along the top of the highwall to reduce the water entering the pit.

Where it is necessary to grade the spoil

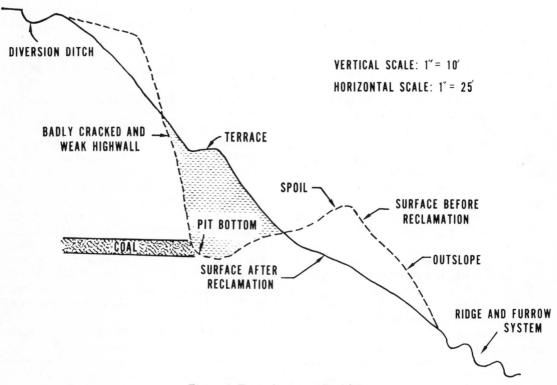

VERTICAL SCALE: 1" = 10'

HORIZONTAL SCALE: 1" = 25'

Figure 5. Typical contour backfill.

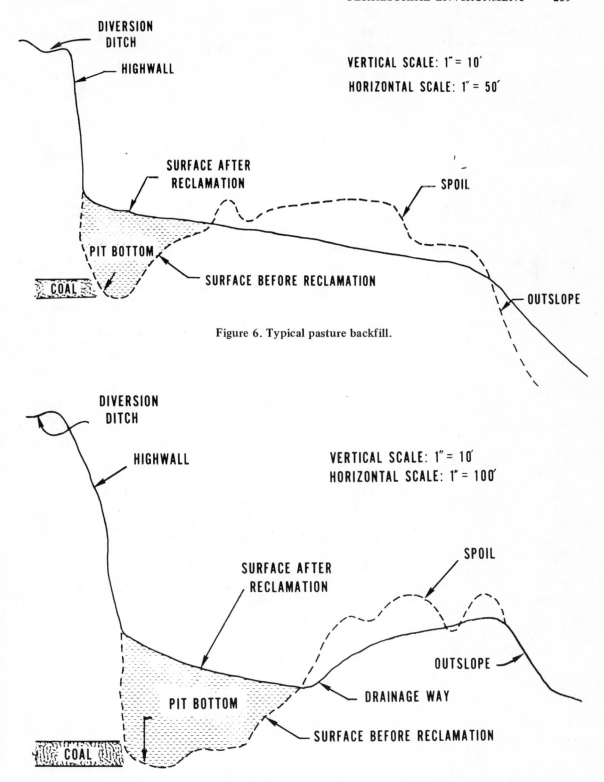

Figure 6. Typical pasture backfill.

Figure 7. Typical swallow-tail backfill.

toward the highwall, a swallow-tail backfill should be used (Figure 7). In this case a drainage ditch parallel to the highwall is constructed. This ditch is of sufficient distance from the highwall to assure that any material falling off it will not obstruct the drainage way. It should also be away from the final cut. The ditch should carry the runoff to a properly designed discharge structure.

Revegetation should follow the grading as soon as planting conditions are favorable. Grasses and/or legumes should be planted on all areas. Trees may be planted in combination with grasses, but not alone as they require excessive periods of time to be effective for erosion control. Soil samples should be taken to determine the limestone and fertilizer requirements. Where possible, the ground should be loosened and the fertilizer and limestone worked in, then the grass seed planted. On steep slopes hydroseeders and airplanes can be used to seed the area. A mulch may also have to be used. The type of grasses, legumes, and trees to be planted will depend on the local conditions and the long-term use of the land.

SUMMARY

Surface mining almost always causes damages to the environment. These damages manifest themselves in the form of degraded water quality, resulting in the water being unusable for domestic, industrial, and recreational uses, an aesthetic eyesore, decreased real estate value, and a wasteland. However, surface mining does not have to produce these detriments. With proper preplanning, mining, water control, and reclamation as outlined in this paper, environmental damages can be held to a minimum. This is not to say that these procedures will be easy or inexpensive; however, if we wish to preserve our environment, a price must be paid.

REFERENCES

Udall, Stewart L., 1967, Surface Mining and Our Environment, U.S. Department of the Interior, Washington, D.C..

Curtis, Willie R., 1969, The Effects of Strip-Mining on the Hydrology of a Small Mountain Watershed in Appalachia, U.S. Forest Service Paper, Berea, Kentucky.

Collier, C. R., et. al., 1964 and 1966, Influence of Strip Mining on the Hydrological Environment of Parts of Beaver Creek Basin, Kentucky, U.S. Department of the Interior, Geological Survey, Prof. Paper 427-B, and Geological Survey, Prof. Paper 427-C.

Hill, Ronald D., December 1968, Mine Drainage Treatment—State of the Art and Research Needs, Federal Water Pollution Control Administration, Mine Drainage Pollution Control Activities.

Corbett, D. M., and Agnew, A. F., 1968, Hydrology of the Busseron Creek Watershed, Indiana, Indiana University Water Resources Research Center, Report, Invest. No. 2, Bloomington.

Reclamation Handbook, 1969, Department of Natural Resources, Division of Reclamation, Charleston, West Virginia.

Porges, R., Van Den Berg, L. A., and Ballinger, D. G., February 1966, Re-Assessing an Old Problem—Acid Mine Drainage, Journal of the Sanitary Engineering Division, Proc. of the American Society of Civil Engineers, Vol. 92, No. SA 1.

Bullard, W. E., 1965, Acid Mine Drainage Pollution Control Demonstration Program Uses of Experimental Watersheds, International Association of Scientific Hydrology, Symposium of Budapest, Extract of Publication No. 66, Budapest, Hungary.

Musser, John J., 1963, Description of Physical Environment and of Strip-Mining Operations in Parts of Beaver Creek Basin, Kentucky, U.S. Department of the Interior, Geological Survey, Prof. Paper 427-A.

Plass, William T., 1967, Land Disturbances from Strip Mining in Eastern Kentucky, U.S. Forest Service Research Notes, Berea, Kentucky.

Thrush, Paul W., 1968, A Dictionary of Mining, Mineral and Related Terms, U.S. Department of the Interior, U.S. Bureau of Mines Special Publication, Washington, D. C.

Struthers, P. H., and Vimmerstedt, J. P., 1965, Rapid Strip Mine Reclamation, Ohio Report, 50 (c), Ohio Agriculture Research and Development Center, Wooster, Ohio.

49. PLANNING AND ENGINEERING DESIGN OF SURFACE COAL MINES: LAND RECLAMATION

J. CROWL and L. E. SAWYER

As surface mining spreads into more and larger areas, land reclamation is assuming an increasingly important role in overall mine planning. In fact, many of the major surface mining companies now employ qualified technical men to plan and carry out the reclamation of their properties.

EFFECTS OF SURFACE MINING

Following surface mining, the resultant material has lost all resemblance to soil. There are no soil horizons and the material has no soil structure. On a mined area, the land is an unorganized mass of parent material (rock, slate and shale) combined with whatever soil that covered it in the undisturbed state. Given enough years to weather, these parent materials may form a completely new type of soil. Innumerable combinations of extremes in physical composition and chemical content must be considered in establishing vegetation on areas disturbed by surface mining. The potential productive capacity of the overburden must, therefore, be determined largely by its texture and acidity.

END USES FOR DISTURBED AREAS

The use for which a mined area can best be reclaimed depends, as a general rule, upon several factors that can be determined in the field, including the following: (1) the percentage of hard rock or shale in the overburden, (2) the amount of sulfides or other materials toxic to plant growth in the rock or shale, (3) the percentage of soil-size particles and (4) the amount of lime, phosphate and potash available for plant growth.

Farm Land

The highest forms of agricultural yield for which mined areas can be reclaimed are row crops, orchards and forage that can be mechanically harvested. To be suitable for one or all of

Reprinted with permission of publisher from *Mining Engineering,* v. 19, no. 10, p. 121-122, October, 1967. Copyright 1967 American Institute of Mining, Metallurgical, and Petroleum Engineers, Inc.

these uses, the overburden should be relatively free of large rocks and coarse, hard shale. It should contain a high percentage of soil-size particles and adequate lime, phosphate and potash to support the growth of grasses and legumes. It should be free of materials that would form chemicals toxic to plant growth when oxidized. As a rule, this means materials with a pH of 6.0 or above. For all of the aforementioned purposes, the surface must be completely graded so that it can be traversed with agricultural equipment.

Range Land

In areas where large quantities of rock preclude grading, the surface may be reclaimed for pasture or range land if it has suitable chemical characteristics. For such reclamation, topping the banks to a width of 15 to 20 ft has been found to be beneficial. This flattened surface presents a seed bed which may be disced prior to seeding, thereby giving a better initial stand than ungraded banks. The topping shortens the slope between the flattened ridges and at the same time retains the depressions formed by the valleys to retard runoff and minimize erosion. Seeding on ungraded banks without any preparation has often left the upper parts of the ridges or peaks only partially covered for the first two or three years. By following the above grading and seeding practices, thousands of acres have been successfully reclaimed for pasture, for the mechanical harvesting of forage crops, and for the production of row crops.

Reforestation

Areas where the overburden consists of a much higher percentage of rock and hard shale that contain a small amount of soil-size particles can be successfully reforested, providing the pH lies between 4.0 and 7.0. Below 4.0 very few species of herbaceous vegetation have been found to survive, although a few will persist down to a pH of 3.5. Above a pH of 7.0, very few of our native deciduous trees and practically no coniferous trees will thrive.

The reclamation of mined overburden by

reforestation has been a common practice for almost 40 years. The different types of material on which different species can be planted is known. A wide range of native conifers and deciduous species are well adapted to planting and growth on mined areas, as are several exotic types that have become adapted to the climatic conditions.

Play Areas

Recreation is another use for reclaimed mine areas that has grown into prominence in the last ten years. The lakes created by the final cuts in the mined areas are providing excellent fishing, swimming and areas for water sports. The areas of reclaimed land adjacent to these lakes are in great demand for the erection of summer homes and permanent homesites.

COST CONSIDERATIONS

The cost of completely grading an area varies considerably from one site to another. One factor which enters into this is the method of mining. Overburden cast with a shovel is normally much easier to grade than overburden produced with a dragline. A shovel will usually deposit its material in the form of a somewhat continuous ridge, while the dragline tends to deposit the overburden in mounds of varying sizes. Another available cost item is the amount of rock in the material to be handled.

Under ideal operating conditions some complete grading has been accomplished for as little as $100 per acre; under adverse conditions grading has cost more than $1000 per acre. Striking off the tops of ridges to a width of 15 to 20 ft can be accomplished for as little as $25 per acre under ideal conditions, and can exceed $100 per acre under adverse conditions. The use to be made of a mined area, as determined by the factors previously mentioned, and the results that can logically be expected from that area should be the primary factors in determining the amount of grading that will be done.

THE PRICE OF INACTION

The ultimate use of disturbed areas should be decided on the basis of research and experience, the wishes of the landowner, the use of the surrounding land and the ability of the land to produce. Because of emotional and political pressures that exist in the supercharged atmosphere of some surface mining areas, unsound practices of reclamation have provoked mandatory punitive laws in some states. As a part of its operations, industry must voluntarily accept the responsibility of good land reclamation practices or be prepared to suffer restrictive legislation in future years.

50. CURRENT RESEARCH TRENDS IN MINED-LAND CONSERVATION AND UTILIZATION

G. DON SULLIVAN

Although the first application of strip mining dates back to 1866, the true origin of today's problem of land reclamation is found in World War II, when the yawning war machines demanded more and faster fuel production. To meet the new wartime demands, the strip coal mining companies that had been producing coal for the normal needs of industry and commerce during peacetime worked to the full extent of their capacities but were unable to satisfy the voracious demand.

To supplement the production of the established mining firms, a host of temporary, make-shift coal strip operations came into being — road contractors, ditchers and foundation excavators, earth movers of every type became strip coal operators. Unfortunately, many were of the here-today-gone-tomorrow category and showed little concern for the condition of the land after mining. Likewise, the land owners of the mined properties (most of the land was on royalty lease or tonnage contract) showed little concern. Land owners realized from their acreages more income during the war years of coal production than could have been obtained in two or three lifetimes of conventional farming or other land uses. Most of these mined lands were submarginal with little productive promise. As a result the wartime stripping produced most of what are known today as "orphan banks" or "abandoned strip pits." It is of these that so much of the present-day complaints about strip mine reclamation are being made.

Most of the research on mined land reclamation has been done by the individual mining companies and through financial support by companies and cooperative industry programs with state agricultural experiment centers and educational institutions which feature schools of agriculture, forestry or the like. The basic research categories involving mined land conserva-

Reprinted with permission of author and publisher from *Mining Engineering,* v. 19, no. 3, p. 63-67, March, 1967. Copyright 1967 American Institute of Mining, Metallurgical, and Petroleum Engineers, Inc.

tion, reclamation and utilization fall into five categories, cited below.

REVEGETATION

Primarily, this type of research is intended to develop vegetative species that will provide quick cover on mined land areas, and also to provide plant species that will be sufficiently hardy to provide permanent growth under difficult conditions. Very little of the land involved in surface mine land reclamation is capable of supporting superior vegetative species. In several studies, it has been established that from 90-99% of all of the surface land affected by surface mining had been land that was forest or had been worked to such exhaustion that it was incapable of supporting lush vegetative growth. Since most of the lands are marginal and minerally deficient, reclamation must be adapted to the types of plant life that can be accommodated by such soils. Research has established that soil characteristics are so varying, it is practically impossible to establish a uniform plant selection to provide ground cover in all areas. The mineral imbalances found in strip spoils demand that combination seedings are necessary on most mined land areas. Although generally accepted as a criterium to satisfactory plant survival and growth, acidity of the soil has been found to be only one of a number of factors affecting satisfactory ground cover. Mineral deficiencies and imbalances, along with proper moisture ratio have equally important parts in the assurance of proper land reclamation.

CHEMISTRY OF OVERBURDEN AND SPOILS

Among the results sought in this phase of study is pyritic material identification, soil and rock mixtures, soil and water characteristics and chemical weathering properties. One of the most important developments in these investigations has been that favorable compounds and nutrients are released as a result of disturbance of the surface in mining operation. These favorable materials are conducive to plant growth after natural assimilation and breakdown of inhibiting chemical compounds. It has been determined that the favorable compounds and nutrients become available for plant assimilation at a faster rate on mine bank spoils than on the original undisturbed soils.

The great percentage of spoil soils were found capable of sustaining plant growth eventually. A study by TVA determined that less than 4% of all highwall material produced by surface mining was of such high acidity that it was toxic to all plant life. Studies also determined that fertilization of the mined land spoil materials had a very limited effect on the ability to produce vegetative cover.

Another determination is pertinent, particularly in the light of recent urging for reclamation of mined lands abandoned years previously. The reshaping of spoil bank surfaces that have, through the years, weathered and stabilized, can re-expose detrimental and harmful materials and re-create a surface toxicity that can inhibit plant growth until the redisturbed materials are again neutralized.

HYDROLOGY

The study of water and drainage effects is an important adjunct of mined land reclamation research. Included in considerations covered in this phase are storm water runoff, geochemistry of stream flows, sedimentation, ponds and water impoundments on mined land areas, and ground water movements and storage. Important findings in this area revealed that less than 25% of all the pollution attributable to mine drainage may be charged to the effects of surface mining and land reclamation. It has been found that very little acid develops from storm runoff on mined land spoils.

A 1964 study of the Patoka River area in Indiana by Indiana University Water Resources Research Center determined that whereas the "cast overburden" areas, during October, contributed an average of 7 cu ft per sec of water, or 4,524,200 gals daily to the Patoka River, "all watersheds where original overburden remained undisturbed, – were dry during October 1964 as well as during all of September and most of November." The study area included some 270 sq miles of Patoka River watershed. The precipitation in the southwestern Indiana, during October 1964, was the most deficient since records began. The conclusions were that the mined spoils land provided areas with substan-

tially better water containment than undisturbed or cultivated lands.

EARTH MOVEMENT AND PLACEMENT

This category involves studies in geology and exploration of surface mine areas; engineering practices and methods, including preplanning of operations to include reclamation; new equipment; adaptations of equipment and development of techniques in earth moving, and soil mechanics.

Overburden placement studies involved identification of, planning for, and handling of acid-bearing materials. Although bone coal and rider coal seams compose only a small proportion of the strip overburden materials handled, they account for practically all of the toxicity created in the spoil banks.

Most interesting developments have come from the investigations into handling of overburden and spoil materials. The most widely quoted is the conclusion that excessive grading of mine spoils retards vegetative growth and prevents moisture absorption so essential to plant growth and survival. It is advocated that when grading is required, it be done when the soil is dry or on fresh banks before seeding or weathering takes place. Tests revealed that in controlling stabilization of the soil, vegetation of any density had little effect on massive slides. A variety of causes of soil movement have been developed but no real solution has been found. Solid densities of spoil materials were 40-80 lbs per cu ft compared with 110-130 lbs per cu ft on original overburden. Official reports state that there is actually no difference between strip coal spoils or highwalls, highway cuts or natural cliffs as far as reclamation is concerned.

In handling vegetative cover, one thing has been apparent – planted seedlings have distinct advantages over direct seeding. However, in the seeding of grasses for grazing, particularly on rough lands, aerial seeding is becoming more popular. Although not as effective as hand seeding, it has proved substantially cheaper in rough terrain.

In this field, significant contributions are being made by the manufacturers of equipment used in the mining of surface coal and the reclamation of the mined lands.

Marion Power Shovel Co. is currently cooperating with strip mining companies in developing methods and equipment for dirt handling in the strip mining industry that are expected to revolutionize the processes of overburden removal and dirt placement for land reclamation and surface contouring. William Boyle, president of Marion, says that although the results are as yet indefinite, they are encouraged and optimistic about an early breakthrough.

Another large equipment manufacturer, the Bucyrus-Erie Co. has established as an integral part of its manufacturing organization an Advance Products Division. The major thrust of this group is to develop new concepts to aid the surface coal mining industry to do better and more economical jobs of reclamation. Generally, the fields of research ventured by Bucyrus-Erie APD are: (a) new types of equipment to resolve the reclamation problem cheaply and efficiently, and (b) development of additional attachments to present conventional equipment that will solve the problem. E.P. Berg, Bucyrus-Erie president, has indicated that his researchers feel that the second category of investigations offer "excellent possibilities for early results."

It is predicted that in the not-too-distant future the surface mining industry will be operating with draglines carrying booms of 500 ft in length, increasing the digging and despoiling areas two to three times. At the same time, shovels with 250 to 300 yds operating ranges are coming. Soil stability problems offer a bright prospect for the future of large draglines. A limited future for wheeltype excavators is also foreseen. In dirt moving it was indicated that computerized analysis of mining problems will probably greatly accelerate the preplanning operation and assure positive programs of mining and land reclamation.

In another area important to surface mining, are rotary drilling rigs equipped for laser beam drilling, use of chemical rock softeners and development of jet pierce drilling. Research being carried on by some of the drill manufacturing companies interested in auger mining hope to produce an auger recovery unit which can be utilized in long hole mining by which the auger can be directed far back into the hillside to bring out coal by use of multiple heads and conveyors in tandem. Still other research is being done by coal treatment equipment concerns. Coal washers have been an important adjunct to strip coal progress. McNally-Pittsburgh Manufacturing Co. is building closed-circuit washing systems for coal preparation, in which the water is conserved and reused with the pollutant elements adequately provided for in the settling and neutralizing processes. Roberts and Schaefer, another important producer of preparation plants, promises equally interesting research developments.

HAULAGE ROADS

Transportation in the surface mining industry is a major part of operations. This phase of research takes into account development of equipment, tires and accessories, as well as access roads; roads and haulage ways in the strip pits proper; road construction and maintenance, and drainage. Most of the haulage at surface mine operations is of the off-the-highway type. As a result, cost of haulage becomes a sizeable item in the mining company's operations. With the development of gigantic haulage units, privately maintained roadbeds on which these oversize carriers operate must of necessity be more substantial than ordinary highway construction. Because of the toxic materials sometimes used in the mine road construction, plus the toxicity of materials hauled, the drainage of these roads to eliminate acid runoff or drainage becomes as important as the construction or maintenance of the roads. In this field, almost unbelievable developments by equipment manufacturers have taken place — not only in the size of the haulage units themselves, but the development of rubber on which the units operate economically and efficiently.

There are a number of other worthwhile research projects that could be treated in this paper, but neither time nor space would permit. However, some undertakings are worthy of additional note.

One of the most current of all research reports involving mined land reclamation is a Technical Report published by the Southeastern Illinois University giving a 1966 evaluation of research plots that were originally established by the Central States Forest Experiment Station of the Department of Agriculture in 1937. The current report is by Dr. A. G. Chapman, former chief of the Central Forest Experiment Station. Originally, this study involved techniques and species of trees for planting on mined land areas, where, when and how to plant trees on mined lands, and refining the tree planting techniques. An early report on this project was contained in *Agricultural Handbook 166* entitled "Forestation of Strip Mined Land," by Dr. Chapman and G. A. Linstrom. The strip coal mine industry cooperated with the agency in establishing and maintaining test areas. The test plots covered areas in Ohio, Indiana, Kentucky and Kansas. In summary, the findings are that growth and survival on ungraded spoils are better than on graded areas.

Another interesting research report is contained in a publication by the Eastern Region, U.S. Forest Service, Department of Agriculture, entitled *Digest-Strip Mine Reclamation.* This report has come up with several very interesting findings, among which are "delay in planting of mined land in order to permit weathering of materials produces advantages through better plant growth and the elimination of plant failures when freshly mined spoils of questionable consistence are planted . . . Success of spoil reclamation depends to a great extent on the quality and hardiness of the stock planted . . . Most attempts at direct seeding of tree species have resulted in poor survival or complete failure. The objections to direct seeding are drying out of germinating seedlings due to lack of moisture, washing away of seed materials in melted snows and heavy rains, and burial of seeds by siltation."

The report noted that "Few spoil bank sites are naturally favorable to profuse seed germination and survival, although natural or volunteer vegetation in many cases will provide some cover. Generally, however, the natural seeding is not sufficient and must be supplemented by man sown material. Researchers agreed that natural vegetation can supply an important aid to artificial seeding . . . Mixed plantings are preferred to single species because the mixture accommodates abrupt variations in topography and soil moisture requirements of species planted . . . Fall plantings had lowest rate of survival of all seasonal seeding . . . Grading of clay and limestone spoils had very detrimental effect on survival and growth of planted tree species. It was found that soil drought was more common on fine textured soils and limited the survival rate. . . ."

Most of the other states where surface mining of coal has been an important contributor to the welfare of the area's economy, have supported research endeavors for many years. Indiana maintains a number of projects. Purdue University is now studying desirable wildlife habitat and the game carrying capacity of reclaimed mined lands on 3000 acres of mined land

donated by Indiana strip producers. Purdue, in cooperation with the State Departments of Forestry and Conservation and Agricultural Economics, is also studying the effects of strip mining on the local economies, timber resources, wildlife, water and recreational opportunities, as well as the adequacy of present reclamation practices. This two-year project is financed by the Indiana Coal Association. In addition, Indiana coal producers — Ayrshire, Enos and Peabody companies, have underway studies as to the water holding capacity and water quality of strip mine impounds in strip mines of southwestern Indiana.

The Indiana Coal Association is also cooperating with the Carbondale, Ill., branch of the U.S. Forest Experiment Station in developing new planting materials for strip-mined land.

Ohio is another state where a wide variety of research is being directed to the reclamation of mined lands. One of the foremost and pioneer projects in mined land uses for wildlife propagation has been supervised by Dr. Charles Riley of Kent State University. He has been conducting studies for more than 20 years to determine the utilization of reclaimed mined land by waterfowl, fur-bearing game, game fish and other wildlife. In another experiment to assess wildlife food and cover, he has worked with more than 100 different species of plants, shrubs and grasses. At the same time, he is developing more modern management techniques applied to reclaimed mined land to produce more beneficial game habitat. Aside from wildlife studies, Dr. Riley has been interested in the alleviation of acid mine water in coal strip pits. He has studied the physiochemical characteristics of mine water impounds as related to fish management and recreational use, as well as work in erosion control and aesthetic values of land reclamation.

Another state, Pennsylvania, has a unique arrangement in operation. A Research Committee on Coal Mine Revegetation is composed of representatives of Penn State University's School of Forest Resources, the State Department of Forests and Waters, State Department of Mines and Mineral Industries, Pennsylvania Game Commission, the Pennsylvania Coal Mining Association and the Izaak Walton League of America.

Among the projects which this Committee has developed are:

1. Evaluation of native tree growth and adapta-

tion to spoil bank revegetation, originally begun in 1946 at The Pennsylvania State University.

2. Study of soil characteristics and a 10-year tree-survival-and-growth study on 22 selected test plots in spoil areas. This study analyzed 16 species – 6 good, 5 fair, 5 poor. It was found that tree growth was variable within the spoil areas and between the spoil banks. Soil content, slope position and acidity were prime influences on tree survival and growth. One of the earliest determinations was that grading of spoils had a depressing effect on tree growth, and tree growth on upper slopes of the banks was not as good as on the lower slopes.

3. Tests also revealed that a species of hybrid poplars showed great promise. The clones grew on all but the most acid of soils (-pH 4) and test trees attained a 30-ft growth in five years. These plantings also prevented erosion on the steepest of slopes.

4. Another test involved crown vetch. Direct seeding of this grass showed poor results, but planting on lime-treated surfaces produced outstanding results.

In the far western states outstanding research is in progress. In Kansas, the State Forestry, Fish and Game Commission has acquired a large number of strip mine lakes created in the mining process and has converted them into public fishing areas. The commission is currently conducting research on improved fish species for these lakes and management techniques to better adapt areas to public recreation spots. Kansas attained nationwide prominence through articles in sportsmen's publications extolling the virtues of the state's strip mine lakes as the finest bass fishing in the nation. More recently, development of camping sites at these lakes was noted in the trade publication of the camping fraternity.

In North Dakota, a study is underway, supported by the large strip coal producers in the state, to develop adaptable plant species for the arid conditions of North Dakota and make evaluation of the economic benefits therein.

In Wyoming another ambitious program has been undertaken by Dr. Morgan May of the University of Wyoming, under the sponsorship of the state's largest coal producer, to establish adaptable species for the arid and partially mineral-deficient soils of that state, as well as

determining satisfactory techniques for attaining vegetative cover on the spoils. The project, underway for two years, is being continued with a high note of optimism.

West Virginia University, under the direction of the Governor and with the cooperation of the West Virginia Surface Mine Association, is conducting a comprehensive study of the economic impact of coal strip mining and the contributions which are derived both from the production of strip coal and the reclamation of mined lands.

Perhaps the most recent of the research activities in the field of strip mining and mined land reclamation is that which is being undertaken by the University of Kentucky under a grant by one of the larger coal mining companies of eastern Kentucky. The company is providing all of the funds for a study not only of the reclamation practices and techniques, but also looking into the economics of the program.

Research of more general nature is being carried on by other groups and institutions of national and regional prominence. The work being done by the Ohio Agricultural Research and Development Center is one of these. Tests here indicated that efforts to develop plants more tolerant to strip mine soils showed little promise, because of the wide variation in soil characteristics. The real need was reported to be methods to alleviate conditions in spoil banks adverse to the vegetative growth. It was found that accumulation of mineral salts in spoil areas could amount to as much as 20 tons per acre. Rainfall is essential to leach out the excess soluble salts on the surface layers. The results indicated that percolating rainfall diluted the salts and provided greater moisture retention for plant growth. Sustained plant life was found to be more satisfactory with the multiple planting of trees and low forage plants, including alders and locusts with orchard grass, trefoil and bluegrass. It was determined that five years are needed to develop and spread plants and ten years to provide reformation of a layer of top soil.

Other tests, conducted by the TVA on Tennessee's mined lands also have provided interesting information. The TVA indicated that best results were obtained with a minimum amount of grading except along highways where the aesthetic benefits were a more important consideration. Work on handling drainage control and use of siltation ponds also revealed beneficial results. The project indicated that planting costs are running about $80 per acre. Direct seeding by plane was tried but with only mediocre results.

The U.S. Department of Agriculture, through the Northeast Forest Experiment Station at Berea College, Berea, Ky., is working in cooperation with the U.S. Bureau of Mines in conducting 46 various projects related to strip mining and mined-land reclamation. The studies incorporate not only plant species and planting methods, but also mining techniques and dirt placement techniques. In addition to the projects now in progress, these government agencies anticipate inaugurating an even more expansive program beginning next month.

Of important consideration is a project dealing with the problem of mine drainage from both deep and surface mines. The Coal Industry Advisory Committee to the Ohio River Valley Water Sanitation Commission, which is financed totally by industry contributions, has established a center for acid mine drainage information at Bituminous Coal Research, Inc., Monroeville, Pa. Here, all written and printed materials on the subject are collected, annotated and classified. Almost 500 published items have already been catalogued, and more are being added daily. Supplementing the work in the library project, the Advisory Committee is currently undertaking establishment of a technical office on mine drainage, with a qualified expert in charge to study, evaluate and coordinate all mine drainage research projects. This is expected to be a most profitable contribution to general industry knowledge on mine drainage in the surface mine industry.

Currently, there is much discussion about the interest of the federal government in regulation of surface and strip mine operations and mined land reclamation. The industry has felt that regulation of strip and surface mining, because of the widely varying conditions in both land and soil conditions and mineral extraction techniques, is best handled at the local level. The federal government can make major and effective contribution, in the field of research by providing grants, or other incentives for research efforts, as they have done in the field of water pollution control, health and other aspects of general public benefit.

The industry is conscientious in its efforts. They warrant the consideration that such dedication to a worthy cause deserves. What is needed is understanding and encouragement by agencies of government, whether federal, state or local, as well as by the press and other media, but more importantly by the public itself.

51. COST OF RECLAMATION AND MINE DRAINAGE ABATEMENT — ELKINS DEMONSTRATION PROJECT

ROBERT B. SCOTT, RONALD D. HILL, and ROGER C. WILMOTH

Acid mine drainage, discharging from coal beds, has polluted our streams and rivers since early time. These pollutants affect water quality by lowering the pH, reducing natural alkalinity, increasing total hardness, and adding undesirable amounts of iron, manganese, aluminum and sulfates. The tangible damages are the costs involved in replacing equipment corroded by the acid water, additional treatment costs at municipal and industrial water treatment plants, and damages resulting from corrosion of steel culverts, bridge piers, locks, boat hulls, steel barges, pumps, and condensers. Intangible damages, which are real and important, include destruction of biological life of the stream, reduced property values, and streams rendered undesirable for recreational uses (Committee of Public Works, U.S. House of Representatives, 1962).

The major problems of mine drainage occur in the anthracite and bituminous coal regions in Appalachia. However, many of the western mining states have significant mine drainage problems in specific areas, but the overall problem is not as great as in the eastern states.

Pollution studies in Appalachia have revealed that inactive underground mines contribute 52 percent of the acid, active underground mines 19 percent, inactive surface mines 11 percent, and active surface mines 1 percent. Most of the remaining sources are in combination surface-underground mines (Federal Water Pollution Control Adm., 1969).

A conclusive report on acid mine drainage was issued by the Committee of Public Works of the U.S. House of Representatives in 1962. The report pointed out the extent of the problem and stated that elimination of this form of pollution would restore vast quantities of water for munici-

pal and industrial use, propagation of fish, aquatic life, wildlife, and recreational purposes. Previously, methods to abate acid mine drainage had been abandoned because of high costs and technical failure. The committee concluded that mine sealing was the most promising method (Hill, 1970).

The report recommended: (1) a sealing program directed at sealing abandoned mine shafts and other drainage openings, (2) stepped-up research programs by federal, state, and interstate organizations to develop other abatement measures, and (3) a stream and acid flow regulation program employed where sealing or other methods are unable to sufficiently reduce the acid content of the stream to meet water quality requirements for all legitimate purposes. Funds for a demonstration program were authorized by Congress in 1964.

In March 1964 the first demonstration project site was selected in the Roaring Creek-Grassy Run watersheds near Elkins, West Virginia. The project was a cooperative effort between federal agencies and the State of West Virginia. The selected watersheds lie side by side. One, Roaring Creek, covers about 28 square miles and the other, Grassy Run, about 4 square miles. Both drain into the Tygart Valley River in the Upper Monongahela and Ohio River Basins (Porges et al., 1966).

The site is roughly a rectangular area at elevations from 1,850 feet at the mouth of Grassy Run to 3,660 feet on the southeast rim of the Roaring Creek watershed. The topography is hilly and rough.

SUMMARY

During reclamation of the Roaring Creek-Grassy Run watershed, 651 acres of surface mines were reclaimed, 709 acres revegetated, 55 masonry seals constructed, and 41 clay seals installed.

The average overall surface mine reclamation cost was $2,236/acre including $330/acre for clearing and grubbing, $1,658/acre for reclamation, and $248/acre for revegetation. Overall cost

Abstracted from a paper presented at the Society of Mining Engineers meeting, St. Louis, Missouri, October 21-23, 1970. Printed with permission of the authors (Robert A. Taft Water Research Center, Environmental Protection Agency), and The Society of Mining Engineers.

269

for masonry seals was $4,138 each and clay seals $1,479.

The high costs were due primarily to unknown conditions of the abandoned mines, exploration which was necessary to locate the high-wall fractures and openings intercepting the deep mine, and multiple moving of spoil to bury toxic material.

Indirect costs on the reclamation contract appear high due to the inclusion of vehicle rental and foremen's salaries. Because of the data collection system, it was necessary to include these charges, normally considered direct, in indirect costs. A more comprehensive report, to be published at a later date, will present cost data in greater detail.

Stability of the reclaimed area has been exceptional as only eight small subsidence holes have occurred since 1967. Total maintenance costs have been less than $2,000 in the past three years or less than 0.03 percent per year of the construction cost.

REFERENCES

Committee of Public Works, U.S. House of Representatives, 1962, Acid Mine Drainage, House Committee Print No. 18, 87th Congress, Second Session, U.S. Government Printing Office, Washington, D.C.

Stream Pollution by Coal Mine Drainage in Appalachia, 1969, Federal Water Pollution Control Administration, Cincinnati, Ohio.

Hill, Ronald D., May 1970, Elkins Mine Drainage Pollution Control Demonstration Project, Third Symposium on Coal Mine Drainage Research, Pittsburgh, Pennsylvania. Copies available from Environmental Protection Agency, Cincinnati, Ohio 45226.

Porges, Ralph, Lowell A. Van Den Berg, and Dwight G. Ballinger, February 1966, Reassessing an Old Problem—Acid Mine Drainage, Journal of the Sanitary Engineering Division, Proceedings of the American Society of Civil Engineers, v. 92, no. SA 1.

52. POTENTIAL ILL EFFECTS OF SUBSEA MINERAL EXPLOITATION AND MEASURES TO PREVENT THEM*

V. E. McKELVEY

Subsea mineral exploitation inevitably carries the potential to create hazards to other uses of the sea and to damage other marine resources. The nature of some of these dangers is already known from experience gained in coastal waters, but others, particularly as viewed with respect to the deep-sea floor far from land, are as yet poorly understood. Experience thus far indicates that the hazards and damages stemming from subsea mineral exploitation can be largely avoided if it is properly managed, but at this stage it is essential to recognize that some of the problems to be faced and overcome are as yet unknown and that the dimensions of others are as yet not defined.

The potential ill effects of subsea mineral exploitation relate to (1) safety of personnel, (2) damage to living resources, beaches, and other installations from pollution, (3) interference with navigation and fishing, and (4) aesthetic and recreational values. These ill effects may be associated with each phase of the exploration-exploitation process. In areas under national jurisdiction, government should establish procedures and practices governing the exploitation and extraction of the subsea mineral resources so as to insure, to the extent feasible, that the operations are at all times safe, do not interfere with the other uses of the sea, and do not in any way damage the other resource values. Under any international arrangement agreed to relating to the seabed beyond the limits of national jurisdiction, it will be necessary to insure that seabed operations there are conducted in a manner that will avoid damage to other values.

At this stage in our deliberations, it may be helpful to review the nature of the potential ill effects of subsea mineral operations and the approaches taken to prevent them by regulatory authorities. Most of what is known of these topics comes from experience with petroleum exploration and production. It is this experience in U.S. waters and the U.S. regulatory procedures that govern these operations that form the primary basis for the following review. Several other governments represented here also have procedures to cope with these problems, and we hope they will report their experience also.

HUMAN SAFETY

Subsea mineral exploration and exploitation undertaken from floating vessels combine the hazards to the safety of operating personnel related to shipping and fishing and those associated with onshore drilling or dredging. In U.S. waters and vessels the U.S. Coast Guard, advised by a Merchant Marine Council, maintains a Merchant Marine Safety Program, providing for safety inspection and regulation of vessels, their construction, repair, and their equipment, and for the investigation and review of marine casualties and acts of incompetency and misconduct. The Coast Guard also maintains a search and rescue program to provide assistance to ships at sea. Experience in these activities is sufficient to form the basis for safety regulations and practices, which nevertheless deserve continuing review and improvement.

Marine operations undertaken from submersibles and from platforms attached to the bottom introduce some hazards not encountered in vessels. The submersibles that might be used in conjunction with subsea mineral exploration, evaluation, and exploitation are almost entirely in the experimental stage, and much research will be required in several fields — e.g., in materials and structural engineering, in physiology and medicine, and in oceanography — to make them operational under acceptable licensing, and operation of submersibles and the training and licensing of pilots are currently under consideration by the Congress of the United States.

Reprinted with permission of the senior author from "Subsea Mineral Resources and Problems Related to Their Development" by V.E. McKelvey, J.I. Tracey, Jr., George E. Stoertz, and John G. Vedder, *U.S. Geological Survey Circular* 619, 26 p., 1969.

*Statement by United States Representative before the Economic and Technical Subcommittee of the United Nations Committee on the Peaceful Uses of the Seabed and the Ocean Floor Beyond the Limits of National Jurisdiction, March 17, 1969.

271

Fixed platforms are also undergoing continual changes in design, and entirely new types are in the design or construction phase. An excellent safety record has been achieved by those already in use, but nevertheless several have toppled over or have been otherwise destroyed during hurricanes and other storms. The danger comes not only from the direct force of high winds and heavy seas, but also from the effects of scouring on the sea bottom. The experience gained thus far about these effects is being taken account of in new designs and modification of older structures. Another danger to operating personnel in petroleum exploration, whether undertaken from a fixed or mobile platform, comes from fire, particularly that resulting from gas or oil blowouts, such as that which destroyed the Little Bob rig offshore Louisiana last summer and took 10 lives. In U.S. waters, state agencies have regulatory authority over fixed platforms in state waters, and the U.S. Geological Survey is responsible for design approval and inspection in federal waters.

The millions of tons of ordnance explosives that have been dumped in the sea constitute a hazard to subsea mining that may prevent it altogether in some areas (a phosphorite lease off southern California was cancelled for this reason) and may be an uncertain threat elsewhere.

POLLUTION

Pollution stemming from subsea mineral exploitation may be of three types: (1) oil, gas, brines, or fluids released directly from the well, from production or storage facilities, and from pipelines, (2) particulate matter stirred up from the sea bottom in mining or discharge as waste in the course of onsite beneficiation, and (3) human waste and refuse. The last of these is readily controllable and needs no further discussion.

Not enough is known yet about the effects of seabed mining to assess adequately the hazards stemming from the release of particulate matter even in shallow water (the U.S. Bureau of Mines is beginning an investigation of the effects of dredging that will define the problem in coastal waters), much less in deep water far from shore. Locally, dredging in such waters may be expected to pose some hazard to marine life, but on the whole particulate matter released in the course of deep-sea mining should have no ill effects on other resources or the environment. In fact, over much of the ocean beyond the limits of national jurisdiction, the capacity of the sea to receive locally generated solid waste without producing any harmful effects may well prove to be a valuable advantage compared to mining either in coastal waters or on land.

Pollution from offshore petroleum exploration and production in the past has resulted from blowouts during drilling, from rupture of well casing as the result of hurricanes or of ship collisions, from spillage of oil in storage at the surface, and from pipeline leaks. Earthquakes are a potential source of rupture of well casing and pipelines, although thus far no offshore spills are traceable to them.

The procedures and equipment to prevent release of oil and gas from all of these sources are already available. Drilling technology, for example, already provides for control of unexpected oil or gas pressure through the use of heavy drilling mud, well casing, and automatic blowout preventers. Storm chokes close the well automatically if wellheads are broken by storms or ship collision. Valves in surface lines shut off flow when loss in pressure signifies a leak. Electronic navigational devices are used to guide ships through shipping lanes in which oil and gas operations are not permitted, offshore platforms are equipped with navigational devices to warn ships that for one reason or another ply the water around producing fields, and navigation charts are periodically updated to show the location of new installations. Weather services are employed to provide advance storm warnings and thus allow exercise of safety precautions and evacuation of personnel if necessary. The surprise and the unexpected elements in many of the events leading to release of oil and gas set the stage for the "accident," but in view of the state of development of both prevention procedures and equipment, the accident itself must be attributed to human error or equipment failure or a combination of the two.

Parallel in importance to procedures and equipment to prevent unwanted release of oil and gas are those necessary to regain control of the flow and dissipate and clean up that already released. As shown by the Santa Barbara incident, the technology for stopping the flow also is available. Means to dissipate and clean up a large spill are as yet poorly developed, but many valuable lessons have been learned as a result of the *Torrey Canyon* and Santa Barbara incidents.

In the United States, State agencies are responsible for the supervision of exploration, drilling, and production offshore, and the Secretary of the Interior, and under his direction the Geological Survey, are responsible for operations on the outer continental shelf. On the outer continental shelf, regulations governing procedures have been further supplemented by specific orders issued by the Regional Oil and Gas Supervisors of the Geological Survey, who must also approve proposed plans for exploration, production, and related operations and who also inspect operations in progress. That the regulations, procedures, and practices generally have been effective in preventing pollution is shown by its very low incidence in offshore operations over the years, but the entire process requires further improvement.

Although government, of course, bears the responsibility of insuring that safe procedures and practices are followed at all times in offshore operations, the public purpose in the prevention of offshore pollution is also served by industry, which is largely reponsible for the development of the highly effective safety technology already in use and which is continuing to improve both the technology and its practice.

INTERFERENCE WITH NAVIGATION AND FISHING

As already indicated, the establishment of sea-lanes and use of modern aids to navigation have largely eliminated interference with navigation by offshore mineral operations in coastal waters, and the hazard should be diminished further in waters beyond the limits of national jurisdiction. There is no denying, however, that the increase in the number of fixed or stationary installations increases the number of obstacles shipping must face and calls for increasing attention and vigilance on the part of both shipping crews and authorities. In the U.S. waters the Corps of Engineers is responsible for the delineation of sea-lanes and for preventing obstruction to navigation, and the Coast Guard is responsible for other aids to navigation.

In addition to the damage that may be done to marine life by pollution, mineral exploration and extraction may interfere with fishing. The use of dynamite as an energy source in seismic exploration may kill fish locally, and obstructions in the form of gear or debris piles not visible from the surface may cause damage or loss of fishing gear. The development in recent years of seismic methods of exploration that utilize nonexplosive energy sources, however, has nearly eliminated the use of dynamite, and in water

below a depth of several hundred meters, it seems unlikely that other mineral operations still interfere much with fishing.

The 1958 Geneva Convention on the Continental Shelf recognizes the need for multiple use and provides for it in several specific terms in Articles 4 and 5. In the United States, the Fish and Wildlife Service advises the Geological Survey on the issuance of exploration permits and other problems related to fishing and, through state agencies and the Department of the Army, reviews proposals and plans for marine undertakings that affect fisheries and other values. The Geological Survey requires operators to remove all litter and obstructions from the sea bottom on the abandonment of a well site.

RECREATION AND AESTHETIC VALUES

Nearshore mineral operations may adversely affect sports, fishing, and boating, and it may damage aesthetic values as well, although the sign on the balance sheet is by no means clearly negative on either point. Many fishermen are of the opinion that oil and gas platforms attract fish, others find that they serve as navigational aids and emergency ports, and the number of boats that visit platforms on a summer weekend suggest that they offer some attraction to sportsmen. Be this as it may, coastal preserves have been set aside in certain areas, and in certain other areas in U.S. waters the Geological Survey requires that the platforms be camouflaged and that as many wells as possible (20 or more) be drilled from a single platform to reduce their number.

In waters beyond the limits of national jurisdiction, the damage to recreational and aesthetic values will be negligible in most areas.

CONCLUSIONS

All of the ill effects that may result from subsea mineral exploitation in coastal waters seem at this stage to be subject to satisfactory control. Technologic improvements in both prevention of cause and remedy of effect are necessary in many areas and will come, but of equal if not greater importance is improvement in the practice of prevention procedures, particularly fail-safe procedures that guard against human and equipment failures.

The potential ill effects of mineral exploitation in waters beyond the limits of national jurisdiction are much less well understood at this stage and will require both further study and caution. The danger to operating personnel may prove to be greater in certain deep-sea undertakings than it is in coastal waters, but the ill effects from pollution and the hazard to navigation, fishing, recreation, and aesthetics very likely will be less in deep water far from land than they are near shore.

Marine industries and operators can be counted on to pursue aggressively the development of safe practices and equipment — accidents are costly in terms of both life and capital and they work hard to avoid them. Nevertheless, it is government's responsibility to set and enforce safety standards, and this function must be provided for in mineral exploitation beyond the limits of national jurisdiction.

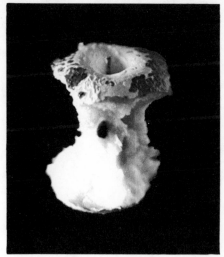

Part Six
GEOLOGY AND
REGIONAL PLANNING

The time-worn adage "an ounce of prevention is worth a pound of cure" is particularly appropriate when man interacts with the physical environment. A sound regional plan based on the geologic information of the area can do much to prevent problems of waste disposal and loss of valuable mineral and aesthetic resources, and to reduce geologic hazards. If we consider that one geologic map or aerial photograph properly used could prevent a large landslide, we might restate the above adage as, "an ounce of prevention is worth a megaton of cure."

In the field of land-use planning the geologist can produce some of the greatest benefits for mankind. Unfortunately, it is this field in which he may experience the greatest frustration, since in many situations he will not only have to sell his plan but also the need for considering the physical environment in planning. Geologic reports for land-use planning will be read by non-geologists such as architects, engineers, sociologists, realtors, and legislators and hence must be written in a simple, jargon-free style. These reports should contain not only basic surficial geologic maps but also interpretive land-use maps based on the geology of the region. The traffic-stop-light system, developed for presenting soils information and much used by the Illinois Geological Survey (see Selection 56) currently is well suited for displaying the "most suitable," "moderately suitable," and "least suitable" areas for ground-water, waste disposal, mineral resources, agriculture, recreation, industry, and residential use.

Several urban areas in the United States are now undergoing intensive study of the physical environment for purposes of planning. In San Francisco a large U.S. Geological Survey-Department of Housing and Urban Development (USGS-HUD) program has as objectives the development of geologic techniques applicable to urban development, preparation of data in formats useful for planners, and improvement of communication between geologists and users of their products.

53. ENVIRONMENTAL GEOLOGY AND THE COAST — RATIONALE FOR LAND-USE PLANNING

PETER T. FLAWN, WILLIAM L. FISHER, and L. FRANK BROWN, JR.

The term "Environmental Geology" was first used to describe some of the applied geological activities of the Illinois Geological Survey in and around the Chicago area. We are informed that Jim Hackett and John Frye coined the term, but in any case the Illinois Geological Survey's "Environmental Geology Notes" gave it substance. The term is commonly used synonymously with "urban geology," but it isn't the same thing. Environmental geology deals with the entire spectrum of man's use of the earth both in cities and in rural and primitive regions — it includes the location and exploitation of natural resources, the disposal of wastes, the effects of both mass movements and tectonic movements on structures, and the effects of subtle variations in the composition of earth materials on health. It involves the oceans and atmospheres as well as the solid earth — the effects on the earth of the great columns of heat and smoke produced by massive concentrations of people and industry fall within its domain. The key word in environmental geology is *application*. It is the application of geology to problems arising out of the interaction of the human colony and the earth. Clearly these problems are more acute where there are more people. Clearly an industrial society has more impact on the earth than a pastoral society.

Urban areas are currently the prime focus of environmental geology for good and sufficient reasons which do not need to be labored here.

The purpose of this paper is to direct attention to an equally important area for environmental geology — the Coast.

1. The coastal zone is the locus of very rapid geological change. It is a dynamic zone of high energy. Earth materials are moving in complex erosion-transportation-deposition systems that respond quickly to man's modifications of the coastal zone. It is, therefore, a zone of continuing engineering problems.

2. The population of the coastal zone is growing rapidly both in and outside of the great port cities. The growth outside of the cities is perhaps the more spectacular. In many parts of the United States there are long strips of high-population density that conform to the coastal zone.

3. Industrial nations consume large quantities of raw materials and most highly industrialized nations sustain a high volume flow of imports and exports through their port cities. Because of the economic differential between cheap ocean transport and more costly land transport, the trend more and more is to construction of benefication, processing, and refining facilities to treat imported raw materials in the coastal zone. Great steel and aluminum complexes are growing along the coasts. This is particularly true in the United States because the Middle Atlantic Coast is close to large coal reserves and the Gulf Coast has large natural gas reserves.

4. Where there are concentrations of people and industry there are large volumes of wastes. Solid waste disposal in the coastal zone requires geological study if the wastes are to be securely contained. It is in many areas the practice to use wastes to fill marsh and shallow bays to create new land — with marked ecological consequences. Noxious wastes are barged out and dumped in deep water. High water tables and permeable coastal plain sediments make it difficult to find secure sites for sanitary land fills.

5. Competition for land and water use in the coastal zone is intensified because of its varied use potential. For example, the bays, estuaries, marshes and near off-shore Gulf Coast — particularly in Texas and Louisiana — are and have been used simultaneously by various groups for transportation, for commercial fishing, for sport fishing, for recreation, for shell dredging, for oil and gas well locations, for pipelines, as a source of fill for real estate developments, and as part of a

Reprinted with permission of the authors and publisher from *Journal of Geological Education*, v. 18, no. 2, p. 85-86, 1970. Copyright 1970 by the National Association of Geology Teachers, Inc.

*Bureau of Economic Geology, The University of Texas at Austin.

waste disposal system. These uses have been increasing in intensity except perhaps commercial fishing which has been forced into a decline as other users became more active. Conflicts between users have increased in number and severity. Users with grievances have turned to state and federal agencies and to the courts for redress.

6. The coastal zone includes a fundamental legal boundary. Commonly, the shore zone is in private ownership whereas the bays, estuaries, and off-shore area are in public ownership. Because the legal boundary is also a high-energy geological boundary, actions taken by one proprietor have an immediate and significant effect on other proprietors.

In recent years the federal government and the coastal states have increasingly been concerned with planning and management of the public lands that constitute such a large part of the coastal zone. Their concern has been forced by the increasing conflicts between land users and the rapidly deteriorating nature of some of the public lands under their stewardship. In order to formulate a regional long-range plan for the use of the coast in the public interest, these institutions must find out something about the coast. They must know what they have, what is happening to it, and how fast. Fundamental to any planning study is mapping.

The Bureau of Economic Geology of The University of Texas at Austin has undertaken to compile as a basic document for planning purposes an Environmental Geologic Atlas of the Texas Gulf Coast. It is not a conventional geologic map. The map units are land-forms and depositional units. Six Holocene depositional systems are being mapped — these include about 100 map units. The units selected are those that best depict present processes (mainly depositional) along the coastal area, though other features are considered (for example, units with particular engineering, navigation, pollution, and reclamation significance; resources such as clays, oyster reefs, and gravels). Relic features, chiefly sand units (meander belts, abandoned channels, barrier bar nuclei) are being mapped in the late Pleistocene (Upper Beaumont) of the coastal area. Examples of units are given in Table 1.

It is difficult to predict the wide variety of nongeologic uses for such an atlas. To cite just a few examples — the Texas Parks and Wildlife Department will use the maps to calculate the number of acres of various kinds of marsh lands important for water fowl nesting; attorneys and the Attorney General's office are interested in areas, processes, and rates of accretion that increase or diminish the size of tracts of land; fishermen and other conservationists are concerned with areas of bay filling; hotel and motel owners are looking for sand sources. It will not be too great a task, using aerial photos, to revise the map at appropriate intervals to provide a quantitative measure of a changing coast line.

TABLE 1. MAP UNITS FOR ENVIRONMENTAL GEOLOGIC ATLAS OF TEXAS GULF COAST.

Barrier Bar System (15 units)	*Lagoon-Bay System* (8 units)
Foreshore (shoreface)	Marginal sand flat and grass flat
Beach	Shelly bay-center mud
Foredune ridge	Nonshelly bay-center mud
Vegetated barrier flat	Landslide with tidal flats
Tidal channel	Oyster reefs
Tidal delta	Serpulid reefs
Wind tidal flat	Marsh
Storm channel	Storm berm
Washover fan channel	
Washover fan interchannel	
Back island dune	
Barrier bar nucleus	
Runway or runnel	
Marsh	
Beach ridge	

Chenier-Strandplain System (5 units)	*Eolian System* (4 units)
Beach ridge	Active dune
Foreshore	Stabilized or vegetated dune
Mudflat	Clay dune
Pond	Playas
Marsh	

Pleistocene (relic features) (6 units)	*Delta System* (8 units)
Meander belt	Distributary channel (active)
Channel (abandoned)	Distributary channel (abandoned)
Lagoonal muds	Delta plain (undifferentiated)
Delta plain muds	Levee
Barrier bar sands	Delta floodbasin
Undifferentiated	Destructional bars
	Lake
	Marsh

54. PUT HYDROGEOLOGY INTO PLANNING

DAVID A. SOMMERS

The effective planning of our environment requires close teamwork among many diverse professions and organizations. Proper planning must relate the economic, social, and *physical* considerations responsive to the needs of our society. The individuals who contribute significantly to this planning process are called planners. Today, nearly every community in the nation has a body of planners called a planning board and practically every county has a planning and development commission with supporting technical staffs. In addition, there are various regional, district, and national planning commissions, river basin planning boards, and watershed planning boards. If there is any single important group of people with whom the hydrogeologist should make contact and become acquainted, it is the planners.

The planning boards, commissions, and the planning consultants play a very important role in shaping today's policies that effect development and management of ground-water resources. If hydrogeology is a factor to be considered in these policies, it must be represented. Consider the appalling fact that in New York State the Office of Planning Coordination, an agency which disperses millions of dollars throughout the state for local and regional planning, including mineral and water resource planning, has a central staff of over 200 people directly responsible to the governor, yet does not have a single geologist or hydrologist on its staff. This situation is no doubt similar in other states and clearly illustrates the challenge to the hydrogeology profession.

WHY HYDROGEOLOGY IS IMPORTANT TO PLANNERS

The rapid rate of the population growth and the consequent shifting patterns of urban and suburban expansion have given rise to almost overwhelming problems of city and regional

Reprinted with permission of the author and publisher from *Ground Water,* v. 8, no. 6, p. 2-7, 1971. Copyright 1971 by the National Water Well Association.

planning. Fundamental to these problems is the evaluation of the relative advantages and disadvantages of one land use in contrast with another. How the land can be most effectively and safely utilized depends, to a significant degree, on the topography, the hydrology, and the geology of a particular area. The hydrogeologic considerations are becoming more important to the planner as the more desirable sites are depleted and the suburban expansion is forced into the outlying, marginal and less desirable areas. Cooperation between the planner and hydrogeologist can assure careful evaluation to reduce the likelihood that land use will conflict with natural limitations imposed by geologic and hydrologic conditions.

WHEN THE PLANNER NEEDS THE HYDROGEOLOGIST

Whenever a planner is dealing with water and earth materials, whether he is planning the location of sanitary landfills, choosing areas to be zoned for sand and gravel operations, or designing hillside apartment complexes, he can profitably use the services of a hydrogeologist.

Frequently, hydrogeologists are sought for advice *after* a problem has developed, usually during the construction phase of a project. Ideally, a study should be completed before the planner formulates his design. The hydrogeologist and a planner, engineer or architect should then confer at the design stage of a project; thus, costly future problems can be foreseen and avoided.

THE VALUE OF HYDROGEOLOGIC MAPS IN ENVIRONMENTAL PLANNING

One of the hydrogeologist's most valuable tools is the hydrogeologic map, a graphic classification of rocks, water and water-bearing earth materials which have certain characteristics in common. Special symbols and geologic sections permit three-dimensional interpretation. By interpretation, hydrogeologic maps become the basis for new maps showing such items as foundation conditions, surface and subsurface waste disposal sites, mineral resource locations, landslide locations, potential industrial sites, and areas of potential ground-water contamination. Surficial hydrogeologic maps are especially useful for planners, architects, and engineers, who generally are concerned mainly with the upper few feet of the earth's surface.

The scale of hydrogeologic maps must vary — depending on their use. General-purpose maps for regional planning, with a scale of 1" = 2,000 feet, can serve as guides for land-use planning, zoning and future detailed, local studies. A scale of 1" = 100 feet, or larger, is commonly used for special purpose mapping in hillside subdivisions or specific engineering projects. The most useful maps for urban planning are those emphasizing hydrological and engineering characteristics of geologic materials that are significant in land use and engineering projects.

In a pilot study of land-use planning and environmental geology in Kansas, maps of physical environmental factors were prepared for planning purposes (Kansas Geological Survey, 1968). These included maps of slopes, drainage basins, vegetation, soils, bedrock geology, mineral resources, land use, and historic and aesthetic factors. Each factor map alone offers valuable information for specific land usage. Many times, however, land uses are dependent on several different factors and planning decisions may be based on a combination of physical and environmental factors. Thus, two or more factor maps often can be combined into a single-purpose map called a "suitability map." Suitability maps are of great value to planners during initial stages of development.

The use of suitability maps can be illustrated by a situation in which a land developer might seek areas for construction of one- and two-story buildings with full basements. A slope factor map could be used to find the areas with slopes of less than 15 percent. The depth to bedrock maps show those areas where the bedrock is 5 to 10 feet below the land surface. The bedrock map can then be superimposed on the slope factor map. A drainage-water table depth factor map also could be used to show the developer where to avoid construction in areas with high water tables and subject to frequent flooding. Thus, a suitability map, a combination of these different factor maps, would allow the builder alternative choices of topographically suitable construction sites for buildings with full basements in areas not subject to flooding.

HOW HYDROGEOLOGY IS USED FOR EFFECTIVE PLANNING

The role of geologic and hydrologic factors with the physical aspects of community development were neatly emphasized by a recent planning study for the City of Naperville, Illinois (Hackett, 1968). The geologic and hydrologic characteristics considered in this study included the nature of the streams and rivers that drain the surface, the characteristics of the slope and relief that determine the landscape, the deposits of clay, gravel and rock that underlie the surface of the land, and the sources of ground water that supply the water needs of the community. Areas subject to flooding were recommended for open-space for public or private use, while areas with slopes in excess of 6 percent were designated for low density construction or open-space uses. It was found that in the northern part of the community extensive deposits of sand and gravel suitable for use as construction material occurred. Because the deposits exist below the normal river level, multiple-use benefits might be realized if properly controlled excavation of the mineral aggregate were followed. Public recreation lakes doubling as storage basins for surface flow and ground-water recharge pits could be developed.

Transportation

Knowledge of hydrogeologic conditions is of major importance in the design and construction of transportation facilities such as highways, railroads, airports, pipelines, and utility installations. In highway design, the geologic factors of soil, bedrock, water and topography are extremely important. Detailed knowledge of the watershed hydrology is essential in order to design the routes to avoid flooding and possible destruction, and to minimize changes in ground-water recharge and alteration of water-supply systems.

The engineering geology maps of the Northeast Corridor of the United States, prepared by the U.S. Geological Survey, provide excellent examples of the usefulness of geologic studies for the advanced planning of transportation facilities. These reports delineate and describe the engineering and hydrologic characteristics of the bedrock and surficial deposits as well as indicate earthquake epicenters and geothermal gradients which would affect construction of a proposed highspeed ground transportation system between Washington, D.C. and Boston, Massachusetts.

Water Resources

Surface-water resources and, to a lesser extent, ground-water resources have been extensively described by state and federal agencies for many years. A tremendous amount of hydrologic information has been compiled and published. However, the data are usually technical in nature and exist in an undigested form which cannot be readily utilized by planners. Hydrogeologists can provide an extremely valuable service to planners, engineers and community officials by taking such information and reinterpreting it for the specific purpose of water resource planning. The data can then be integrated with overall planning needs.

In New York State, studies are being made, under contract with the New York Department of Health, to anticipate the need for water in local areas and to relate this need to the availability of water. Many of these studies are predominantly surface-water oriented. For the most part, the careful evaluation of the valuable subsurface water resources that exist in the many deeply-buried preglacial drainage channels in the state has been neglected. Planners anticipating needs of a large water supply should be advised by hydrogeologists of the many advantages of ground water over surface water. It is well documented in many areas of the country that ground water, where available, can be developed for *one-tenth the cost* of surface water. The desirable characteristics of ground water such as its nearly constant temperature and quality and freedom from biological and radiochemical contaminants often need to be explained to planners and developers. Also, ground water frequently is available to communities and industry in areas lacking surface water.

Regional planners and water-resource management personnel will be especially interested in the recent application of the zoning concept for managing subsurface ground-water supplies for several counties in Maryland (Hansen, 1970). This concept could help the planner relate the requirements of individual water users to the productivity and quality of specific aquifers.

The hydrologic effects of urbanization should be of utmost concern to the planner. Urbanization is, by far, the most forceful of all land-use changes affecting the hydrology of an area (Leopold, 1968). Some of the major effects of urbanization on the hydrology of an area are increases in the stream runoff and frequency of flooding and decreases in ground-water recharge

and the chemical and biological quality of the water (Guy, 1970; Sheaffer, et al., 1970; and Thomas and Schneider, 1970).

Waste Disposal

Mankind is constantly producing more diverse types and greater quantities of waste products which may virtually overwhelm the land environment in and around highly populated areas. Consequently, the effective management and disposal of these wastes is extremely urgent and demands considerable attention from planning officials and hydrogeologists.

Solid Wastes — Sanitary Landfills. Available locations of acceptable sites for disposal of solid wastes in sanitary landfills are becoming increasingly difficult to find. The selection of sanitary landfill sites is largely a hydrologic and geologic problem due to (1) the possibility of detrimental effects on the quality of aquifers and nearby lakes and streams; and (2) the need for large local sources of inexpensive mineral aggregate to use as cover material.

An example of how design and proposed operational methods of a large sanitary landfill are related to the distribution of geologic units is shown in the Capitol District Region of New York State. It was determined that the direction of the ground-water movement was away from the nearby local water wells and that these wells were safely protected from possible contamination by a thick layer of impermeable, glacial-lake clay and till underlying the proposed site. As a by-product of the investigation, sources of suitable cover material were located on the site, and a sequential excavation plan was developed to assure optimum usage of the land.

Individual Septic Systems. Not generally appreciated is the large number of septic tanks in use for disposal of sewage. If individual water wells and septic tanks are to be used in rural developments, a minimum size of lots must be determined by investigating surface drainage and permeability of subsurface geologic materials. Where such factors are not considered, the effluent from individual septic systems may contaminate water wells and nearby lakes and streams. Perceptive use of hydrogeologic maps and consultation between health department officials and hydrogeologists before design approval of individual septic systems, can likely alleviate many such problems. However, it will be up to the hydrogeologist to educate the local health department accordingly.

Surface Spreading of Waste Water. Hydrogeologic maps can be prepared to indicate those areas where the surface and subsurface conditions are most suitable for surface spreading of waste water and least susceptible to ground-water pollution. This information can be used in selecting potential industrial sites in rural areas lacking central sewage systems. These same maps also can be used to indicate minimum lot sizes for rural septic systems and to select other waste disposal sites.

Underground Liquid Waste Disposal — Injection Wells. Hydrogeologists can play an extremely important role in evaluation of potential environmental risks from injection wells. They should help analyze objections to injection wells, such as the potential hazard of contaminating potable ground water and subsurface mineral resources.

The risks of deep-well disposal are exemplified by the problems of some existing injection systems. For instance, an injection well "blow-out" occurred at a paper company on the shore of Lake Erie in 1968. As a result, waste liquids poured into Lake Erie at a rate of 200 gallons per minute for several days before the well could be capped. The Rocky Mountain Arsenal injection well, near Denver, is believed by some geologists to be the cause of the nearly 2,000 minor earthquakes that have shaken the Denver area since 1962. However, subsurface injection of liquid wastes had been used successfully for a wide variety of applications. For these reasons, it is important for the hydrogeologist to inform the planners and other officials of his valuable knowledge, so in their initial evaluation of potential industrial sites, they will seek the advice of hydrogeologists regarding the geologic and hydrologic subsurface conditions for waste disposal in their evaluation of potential industrial sites.

HOW HYDROGEOLOGIC INFORMATION IS APPLIED

It is the responsibility of the hydrogeologist to make recommendations to the planner, engineer, architect, and proper institutional authorities based on the realities of geologic and hydrologic conditions. Once the data are available to them, any deviation from the hydrogeologist's recommendations must be made cautiously with the foreknowledge of the possible risks.

Planning policies and zoning ordinances must recognize the importance of the physical environment. Specifically, desirable codes and ordinances must be formulated to protect water and mineral resources, to take advantage of geologic conditions in engineering projects, and to promote measures to protect lives and property against geologic hazards. In hazardous areas, construction and development must be controlled by strict regulations and open-space uses of the land should be adopted.

Areas containing mineral deposits should be treated as the special features that they are; some planning and zoning bodies have created specific "natural resource" zones. Surface and underground water should be treated as complete systems, affected and altered by everything that man does. It is the hydrogeologist's professional responsibility to inform and educate the people who propose the planning policies and zoning ordinances to make certain that geologic concepts are adequately considered. It is his social responsibility to assist in the formulation of laws and regulations relating to the protection and use of water and mineral resources.

How to Improve Communications Between Hydrogeologists and Planners

Improve the Hydrogeologist's Image. Our first undertaking should be to improve the public image and increase the public's recognition of hydrogeologists. Basically, there are two ways to receive recognition as a profession: (1) the production of good scientific and professional work, and (2) public relations.

There is no doubt that hydrogeologists are making valuable contributions to society, but the small size of our membership and the limited capabilities of our technical organizations limit our impact. Hydrogeologists, like other geologists, need to rally under the sponsorship of a larger, *professional* organization like the American Institute of Professional Geologists (AIPG), a national organization dedicated to the advancement of the entire profession of geology. Economically and politically it is practical for hydrogeologists to unite as a subgroup within the auspices of AIPG and create a movement not only to advance the recognition of hydrogeologists specifically, but to elevate the status of the entire geologic profession.

Secondly, an extensive educational campaign is required to rid our profession of the stigma of the water witch. Disparaging news articles like: "Ninety-One Years Old and Still Witching"

(August, 1970 issue of Ground Water Age) can no longer be tolerated. National television programs like the one on "Mayberry, RFD" (Summer, 1970) that make mockery of hydrogeologists, are derogatory and set our profession back a hundred years.

Hydrogeologists Must Become Involved. The third effort required to improve communications between hydrogeologists and other disciplines is more active involvement on the part of the hydrogeologist in state, local and national issues in which his participation and expertise may serve the best interests of society. It is a neglect of professional responsibility for knowledgeable hydrogeologists (whether federal employees, university staff or private consultants) to sit back and offer no public criticism or alternatives to proposed grandiose multimillion dollar schemes; for example, coastal desalinization plants proposed to supply expensive (\$.35/1,000 gallons) fresh water to communities when uncontrolled lateral discharge of millions of gallons of potable fresh water occurs at the proposed location each day. In such instances, hydrogeologists should be heard.

Our profession of hydrogeology has been too long dominated by an apolitical conservative attitude. We must shed this image and accept political reality if we hope to gain the popular support which we need to bring our scientific insight into active social planning.

Hydrogeologists Must Become Active. Fourthly, hydrogeologists must enter into the organizations and societies of planners, engineers, and architects. Most urban areas have local associations of planners or engineers or architects that welcome "outsiders" to join their ranks. The American Institute of Planners (AIP) and the American Society of Planning Officials (ASPO) are national planning organizations with local chapters in major urban centers. The American Institute of Architects (AIA) and the American Society of Civil Engineers (ASCE) have local chapters in many cities and near most major universities; ASCE even offers an affiliate membership for nonengineers for which professional hydrogeologists can qualify. Hydrogeologists should affiliate with these organizations, attend their conventions, join their ranks, and participate in their local project work in order to expand their "sphere of influence." At the local level, every hydrogeologist must make efforts to *promote* his profession and "politic" to become associated with the local, county and regional planning boards.

The University Curricula Must Be Improved. The challenge to our educational system is clear cut — provide curricula that will graduate hydrogeologists who can work effectively with planners and the real problems of the world. Undergraduate geology curricula must be made more flexible to allow students time for more interdepartmental study. Courses in economics, communications, political science, law, resource management, and government administration need to be incorporated into the basic undergraduate geology curricula. Graduate education of hydrogeologists should include more interdisciplinary study relevant to planning such as urban geography, engineering, and practical field study in regional and local planning.

PERSPECTIVE

Only a few of the many uses of hydrogeology for planning purposes have been defined in this editorial; the included reference list provides sources of additional information regarding the application of hydrogeology and, more broadly, environmental geology. Reference to these publications will provide the practicing hydrogeologist with useful concepts and ideas applicable to particular needs and adaptable to local conditions.

Admittedly, hydrogeology is one of many factors to be appraised for effective planning of our environment and the economic and social considerations must also be evaluated. I have stressed the importance of improving communications between the hydrogeologist and the planner in this editorial because, at a great cost to our society, hydrogeologic conditions have been grossly overlooked.

References

Cartwright, Keros and Paul Kraatz. 1967. Hydrogeology at Shelbyville, Illinois — a basis for water resources planning, Environ. Geol. Notes No. 15, Illinois State Geol. Survey.

Dougal, Merwin D., Editor. 1969. Flood plain management — Iowa's experience. Papers presented at the Conf. on Flood Plain Management, 6th Water Resources Design Conf., Iowa State Univ., Iowa State Univ. Press, Ames, Iowa, 270 pp.

Flawn, Peter T. 1970. Environmental geology — conservation, land use planning and resource management. Harper & Row, New York, 313 pp.

Frye, John C. 1967. Geological information for managing the environment. Environ. Geol. Notes No. 18, Illinois State Geol. Survey.

Gates, Gary R. 1962. Geologic considerations in urban

planning for Bloomington, Indiana. Geol. Survey Report of Progress No. 15, Indiana Dept. of Conservation.

Guy, H.P. 1970. Sediment problems in urban areas. U.S. Geol. Survey Circular 601-E.

Hackett, James E. 1968. Geologic factors in community development at Naperville, Illinois. Environ. Geol. Notes No. 22, Illinois State Geol. Survey.

Hackett, James E. and Murray R. McComas. 1969. Geology for planning in McHenry County, Circular 438, Illinois State Geol. Survey, Urbana, Ill.

Hansen, Harry J. 1970. Zoning plan for managing a Maryland coastal aquifer. Journal of American Water Works Assoc., v. 62, no. 5, June.

Hayes, William C. and Jerry D. Vineyard. 1969. Environmental geology in town and country. Education Series No. 2, Missouri Geol. Survey and Water Resources, Rolla, Mo.

Hughes, G.M., R.A. Landon and R.N. Farvolden. 1969. Hydrogeology of solid waste disposal sites in northeastern Illinois, An Interim Report on a Solid Waste Demonstration Grant Project, U.S. Public Health Service, Cincinnati, Ohio, 137 pp.

Kansas Geological Survey. 1968. A pilot study of land-use planning and environmental geology. University of Kansas, Lawrence, Kansas.

Leopold, Luna B. 1968. Hydrology for urban land planning — a guidebook on the hydrologic effects of urban land use. U.S. Geol. Survey Circular 554.

McHarg, Ian L. 1969. Design with nature. The Natural History Press, Garden City, New York, 197 pp.

Richards, C.A. 1970. How the geologist can help your city. The American City Magazine, June issue, pp. 82-86.

Sheaffer, J.R., D.W. Ellis and A.M. Spieker. 1970. Flood hazard mapping in metropolitan Chicago. U.S. Geol. Survey, Circular 601-C.

Sommers, D.A. 1970. Geology plus planning equals progress. The New York State Planning News, v. 34, no. 5.

Thomas, H.E. and W.J. Schneider. 1970. Water as an urban resource and nuisance. U.S. Geol. Survey Circular 601-D.

U.S. Geological Survey. 1967. Engineering geology of the northeast corridor, Washington, D.C. to Boston, Mass. Misc. Geol. Investigations Map 1-514A-C.

55. FLOOD INFORMATION FOR FLOOD-PLAIN PLANNING

CONRAD D. BUE

INTRODUCTION

Where flood damages have been relatively minor, they are usually permitted to continue. In some places this choice has been arrived at by a study which showed that the cost of flood protection was greater than the anticipated reduction in damage. Where flood damages become unbearably high, something is ultimately done to lessen them. Just what is done depends upon the nature of the developments on the flood plain and the physical and economic feasibility of providing protection.

By the Flood Control Act of 1936, the federal government first assumed responsibility for flood control on a national scale. At that time the Congress stipulated that the federal government would participate only in projects designed to protect cities and communities against catastrophic floods. But subsequent flood-control acts became progressively broader in scope, and now these acts, although still referred to as flood-control acts, constitute the main body of federal law dealing with the development, utilization, and conservation of the nation's water resources. "Flood-control law has become the legislative basis for the broadest and greatest programs of public works and resource development ever undertaken by the United States" (U.S. Senate, 1960).

In the last two or three decades much thought has been given to flood zoning as a means of abating flood losses and of reducing the mounting requirements for flood control. "Flood zoning" is the general term applied to the various measures designed to control the use of the land within the flood plain. Flood zoning reduces damage by requiring that the flood plain be used for purposes not subject to flood damage, and by providing for an unobstructed floodway. The flood-inundation maps of the U.S. Geological Survey are intended to aid those engaged in planning the best use of a river flood plain.

The purpose of this circular is to give the

Extracted from *U.S. Geological Survey Circular* 539, 10 p., 1967.

reader a broad view of the flood problem and to acquaint him with the nature and use of the flood-inundation maps of the U.S. Geological Survey.

THE FLOOD PROBLEM

Floods have always been recurrent events; they are natural and normal phenomena. Floods become a problem to man only when he competes with rivers for the use of the flood plains, the high-water channels of rivers. This competition between man and the rivers has been long and costly.

There is no complete record of flood damages that includes the effects of both the great and the ordinary floods. However, White (1958) gives an estimate of $329 million as an average annual loss for the period 1936-55, based on figures from the U.S. Weather Bureau adjusted to the 1957 index. Loss of life as a consequence of floods has diminished during the past half century, owing to improved communication facilities, greater and more immediate availability of medical aid and rescue operations, the Weather Bureau's warning system, and perhaps a greater awareness of the flood hazard on the part of the public.

Property damage, on the other hand, is generally increasing, despite the expenditure of several billion dollars for flood control since the enactment of the Flood Control Act of 1936. Hoyt and Langbein (1955) found evidence of increased flooding during the past half century, but were mindful of the "long-term though irregular cycles in river behavior of which the past fifty years may represent a rising phase, which may again be reversed." Of the increase in reported flood damage, they ascribe about 45 percent to the increase in property values, 25 percent to an increase in flooding, and 30 percent to an increase in building and other uses on flood-hazard lands.

Flood problems, like our problems of water supply, are without any clear-cut solution. There are various approaches to the flood problem, all of which have been used and found effective to a degree. But no one measure is adequate in itself, except perhaps in minor floods, and if the flood is of rare magnitude all measures fail as a solution.

Solutions to flood problems fall into two broad categories — structural and nonstructural. Structural solutions include reservoirs, levees, floodways, and channel improvement; nonstructural consists mainly of flood-plain regulation. This report is concerned with flood-plain regulation and with the use of Geological Survey maps and reports in defining flood risk.

FLOOD-PLAIN REGULATION

The purpose of flood-plain regulation is to obtain beneficial use of flood plains with a minimum of flood damage and a minimum of expense for flood protection. In other words, the objective of flood-plain regulation is to promote uses of the flood plain so that the benefits derived from its use exceed the flood damage plus the cost of providing a specified degree of protection. Indiscriminate use of flood plains invites great property damage and human suffering, including loss of life, whereas at the other extreme, complete abandonment of flood plains would be a sacrifice of a valuable national resource; the answer lies somewhere between those extremes, depending upon circumstances.

The techniques of flood-plain regulation include (1) land-use zoning, and (2) flood proofing. Application of these techniques depends on delineation of flood zones on a map. A subsequent section entitled "Hydrologic Investigations Atlases" describes how Geological Survey maps can aid in defining flood zones.

Nonstructural measures may be used effectively and profitably in conjunction with structural measures. For example, land-use zoning and flood proofing might be practiced in conjunction with a flood-control reservoir; a smaller reservoir might thus be required, or, a certain amount of potential reservoir storage might be released for other uses.

LAND-USE ZONING

Land-use zoning is the restriction of the use of flood-prone lands to minimize flood damage. "Zoning has been the most widely advocated of all the methods of regulating development in flood plains. This method has been proposed repeatedly for the past thirty years, but probably no more than eight communities had effective flood-plain zoning before 1955. . . . The reasons

for non-use revolve mostly around (1) lack of basic data and (2) questionable legality" (Murphy, 1958). The lack of basic data is rapidly being corrected through the flood-information activities of the Geological Survey, the Corps of Engineers, and the Tennessee Valley Authority, and the question of legality has largely ceased to be a valid argument against zoning.

Flood protection can seldom be complete. There is always a probability that a greater flood will occur than has been experienced in recorded history. The provision of even a degree of flood prevention invites continued and increased use of the protected area; people tend to confuse a degree of protection with complete protection. Then when a flood occurs in excess of that for which protection has been provided, damage may be greater than if there had been no protection. Logically, then, some limitations should be placed on the type and degree of use of a protected area (Leopold and Maddock, 1954).

As discussed by Hoyt and Langbein (1955): "The primary goal of flood zoning [that is, land-use zoning] must be to prevent unwarranted constrictions that reduce the ability of the channel to carry water and thereby add to the height of floods. Thus there should be maintained a channel with capacity adequate to carry the discharge of a certain specified flood depending on local conditions. Where this is to be done 'encroachment lines' beyond which no structure may extend, must be established after suitable field surveys. This is not to protect the structures, but so that the structures will not cause damage to other property. . . . In general, therefore, the practice of setting encroachment limits is a balance between the principle of complete exclusion and no restrictions whatever. Coupled with regulations for flood-plain use outside the encroachment limits, it provides a fully economic arrangement."

Zoning, as described by Hoyt and Langbein, requires ". . . consideration of flooding as a guide to the use of land. Most agriculture, grazing particularly, represents justifiable use of flood lands. So do parks and lakes built to replace channel storage lost when buildings and protective works were put up on the flood plain. . . Home building, on the other hand, is an example of the most unwise use of flood land. The use of flood land must be based, first, on what effects a particular use may have on flood heights, i.e., whether it aggravates the flood problem for users and others. . . ."

The uses of the flood plain relate directly to the frequency of flooding, and regulations usually recognize certain "flood zones," defined as bands within which floods occur with comparable frequency. Permissible land uses within each flood zone would then correspond to the frequency of flooding in that zone. For example, a flood zone whose upper limit is the 1.5-year flood would correspond to the channel itself, since the bankfull stage is reached with an average frequency of once in a 1.5-year period. In this flood zone, no obstructions would be permitted that would interfere with the free flow of water, and particularly bridges would be designed so as not to cause back water. A flood zone comprising the range from the 1.5- to 10-year floods would also be kept free of fixed obstruction, and reserved for such uses as agriculture, parks, and roads. In a flood zone for the 10- to 100-year interval, buildings might be permitted, either with first floor above the 100-year level or flood proofed. These possibilities are only examples of the application of flood maps to the delineation of flood zones, and of flood zones to flood-plain regulation.

According to Hogan (1963), "The constitutionality of zoning as a proper exercise of the police power has been established for some time. . . . While their [zoning ordinances] application to particular situations is sometimes held so arbitrary as to violate the due process clause, zoning ordinances have been held valid in virtually every case in which the zoning was reasonably related to the public health, safety, or general welfare."

In further discussing the legal aspects of flood-plain zoning, Hogan states: "In the final analysis each ordinance setting up a land-use regulation must, in the words of the courts, 'be reasonable and not arbitrary.' The principal criterion as to the reasonableness of flood-plain zoning ordinances involves a determination of the extent of the flood hazard. In other words, the regulations must bear a reasonable relation to the engineering data. In order to be reasonable the area, extent and elevation determinations of the land placed in the flood-plain zone should be based upon: historical evidence of flooding; a computed frequency of floods; an engineering study of flood potential; an analysis of the degree of flood protection afforded by other methods of regulation; the degree of flood protection offered by engineering structures and whether or not development in the immediate

future will increase or lessen the runoff. The uses to be permitted on the land subject to flooding should also take into consideration the anticipated growth of the area and the availability of non-flood land sufficient for the needs of the community. Once a legislative finding of fact as to flood hazard has been made, although not conclusive upon the courts, it will be accorded judicial consideration and deference. Therefore, there appears to be no legal reason why flood-plain zoning is any different from any other type of zoning except for the rather extensive amount of engineering research which must be conducted in order to determine the area and elevation of the land to be included in any such district."

FLOOD PROOFING

Flood proofing is defined as adjustments to structures and contents to reduce flood damage. In some small flood-damage reduction programs, flood proofing alone may suffice; in most flood-damage reduction programs, flood proofing can be used effectively in conjunction with other measures.

Sheaffer (1960) gives three main classes of flood-proofing measures: permanent, contingent, and emergency. Permanent measures provide permanent protection against the flood for which they were designed, such as permanently closing openings in outer walls with impervious material or installing automatic gate-valves on sewer lines in such a manner that when flood waters back up, the back pressure closes the valve. Contingent measures require action to make them operative, such as a sewer valve that must be closed manually, or a show window equipped with a removable bulkhead that must be installed when a flood is imminent. Emergency measures are either improvised when needed or carried out according to prior emergency plans, such as temporary removal of merchandise from a threatened level, or rescheduling freight shipments to reduce the amount of damageable goods on hand.

FLOOD FORECASTING

Flood forecasting, although not a measure in itself, plays an important role in flood-damage reduction. It may save lives by enabling residents to evacuate the flood plain, and save property by enabling residents to put flood-proofing measures into effect.

Flood forecasting was started in the United States in 1871 by the Signal Service of the U.S.

Army. In 1890 that activity was transferred to the then newly established U.S. Weather Bureau, and it is now performed at many River Forecast Centers of the Weather Bureau in the basins of large rivers. It is not possible to evaluate the dollar benefits of forecasting with any degree of accuracy, but Hoyt and Langbein (1955) estimated that the savings accredited to this service approximated 10 percent of the total annual flood loss. Undoubtedly many lives, too, have been saved through forecasting, although experience has shown that many people prefer to remain at home and face the flood rather than to move out.

Forecasts that are made public must be dependable; a poor or misleading forecast is worse than none. As pointed out by Hoyt and Langbein, a forecast that is too low catches many unprepared who might otherwise have been ready, and a forecast that is too high requires costly and unnecessary expenses and anxiety, and may result in the next forecast being greatly discounted. Decisions facing a forecaster may be exceedingly difficult to make. If, for example, as a flood is nearing its crest it threatens to overtop a levee or flood wall, a small difference in level may mean the difference between no flooding and disastrous flooding.

HYDROLOGIC INVESTIGATIONS ATLASES

The Geological Survey started its series of flood-information atlases to provide information on flood hazards in easily read form. These atlases are published in the series entitled "Hydrologic Investigations Atlases." The flood-information atlases contain, briefly, a map showing the area inundated by one or more known floods, graphs showing frequency of flood discharges and flood stages at a gaging station in the area, a graph showing the height of annual floods above some specified elevation at a gaging station for the period of record, and profiles of one or more known floods on one or more principal streams in the area. Some show cross sections through the river channel and flood plains. The flood-frequency curves are generally for periods ranging from 25-50 years. The text on the map explains how depth of flooding at points in the area can be estimated.

The primary purpose of the Survey's flood-information atlas is to present historical documentation of flooding by one or more floods that are known to have occurred. It must be emphasized, however, that the mere supplying of information as to where flood water has reached, and when, does not necessarily lead people to avoid flood danger. Buildings are constructed in fair weather when no flood hazard is evident. In the absence of clear and present danger, the typical citizen may not be easily persuaded by a map to protect himself from a danger that seems remote. The information can, however, be transformed into action by land-use planning.

Flood damages begin with decisions to build on flood plains — often in disregard of the facts of flooding. Flood-damage abatement begins with definition of the flood hazard, that is, presenting information on flooding of specific areas. Figure 1 is an example of how such information can be presented on a map.

Because the flood boundaries shown on the flood-inundation map are for a known flood, the fact must be recognized that the flood might be exceeded at some time in the future. Sufficient data are shown to enable the user to determine, at a gaging station, the probable frequency of the flood that is mapped, unless the flood was of such magnitude that it is beyond the range through which frequency has been established by existing data. But the recurrence interval determined at a gaging station does not necessarily apply to the flood level at all points on the map. For example, if the data indicated a 50-year recurrence interval at a gaging station on the main stream, that recurrence interval would not necessarily apply to the main stream above an upstream tributary or below a downstream tributary, or to the tributary itself. However, as the atlas presents a stage-frequency chart for the gaging station (or stations) and profiles for one or more floods, a profile of the desired frequency can be drawn parallel to the nearest profile with reasonably reliable results.

Flood-information atlases of the Geological Survey present hydrologic data concerning the extent, depth, and frequency of flooding that are essential for an appraisal of the hazards involved in occupancy and development of flood plains. They are intended to be a tool for individuals, governmental agencies, and others delegated with the responsibilities of solving existing flood problems and of formulating effective flood-plain regulations that would minimize the creation of new flood problems. The maps are useful for, but not limited to, preparing building and zoning regulations, locating waste disposal facilities, purchasing open space, developing recreational areas, and managing surface water in relation to

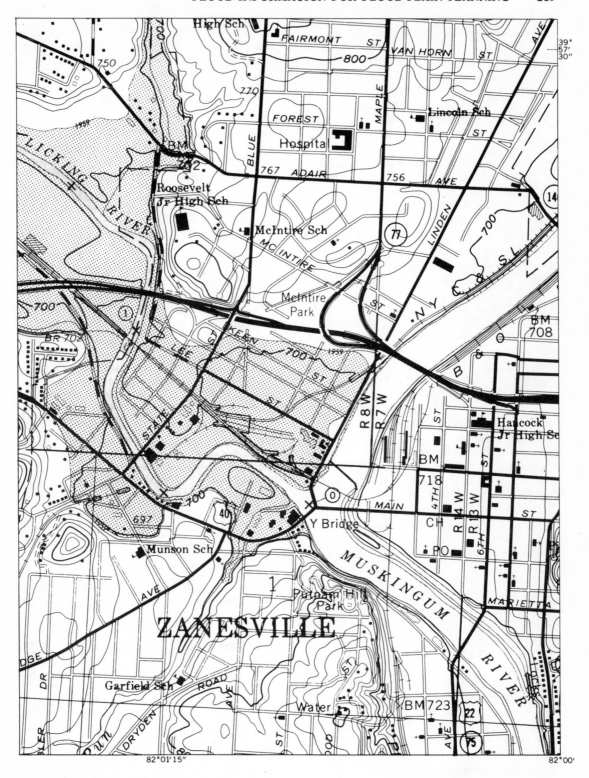

Figure 1. Part of a flood-inundation map, showing how the flooded area is delineated.

the ground-water resources. Examples of the use of flood-hazard information are:

Flood-plain regulations: Establishment of reasonable controls over development of flood plains by local, regional, or state authorities requires information outlining the extent and degree of flood problems. Controls must be based on sound, impartial definition of the facts if they are to stand up in court as reasonable and fair.

Mortgage underwriting: Efforts by bankers or private lenders to consider flood hazard in writing mortgages usually falter because of the lack of proper information. The availability of loans usually controls construction.

Flood insurance: In order that premium rates may reflect the actual degree of risk, it is necessary to have accurate information concerning area, frequency, and depth of inundation.

Flood warning: Local authorities, civil defense workers, corporations, and individuals require precise advance information if they are to benefit from flood warnings. When, for example, there is a forecast that a flood will crest at 18 feet, it must be known precisely which homes, factories, and other structures may be affected.

Some examples of the uses of these flood atlases in northeastern Illinois, where 31 have already been completed, are: The communities of Highland Park, Wheeling, Harvey, Northfield, and Rolling Meadows have established zoning for residential buildings on basis of atlases. The DuPage County Forest Preserve, the Cook County Forest Preserve, and the Park District of Highland Park have used the atlases in acquiring land subject to flooding in order to prevent encroachments on the flood plains that would result in property damages. Real estate appraisers for the Chicago office of the Veterans Administration have to refer to any available atlas to determine possible flood potential of property on which VA loans have been applied for. After some recent flooding in south Cook County, the Northeastern Illinois Planning Commission was requested by the County Board president to prepare a flood-control plan for an area in the Harvey quadrangle; the hydrologic atlas for the Harvey quadrangle which had previously been prepared (Allen and May, 1964) was used as a basis for the commission's plan. Scheaffer (1964) estimated that the flood mapping in northeastern Illinois had a benefit-cost ratio of 40:1.

Twelve atlases have been completed to date

(August 1966) for communities in Ohio. These atlases have been used for such purposes as highway design, flood-insurance studies, and approval by FHA of proposed housing developments.

BASIC DATA ON FLOODS

The Geological Survey began to compile streamflow records from a few gaging stations before 1890. The number of gaging stations increased steadily, and now more than 8,000 gaging stations are operated continuously in the conterminous United States and 225 in Alaska and Hawaii. Flood information is also available at an additional 7,000 stations or more that have been operated for periods of various lengths.

The earliest published records consisted mainly of monthly discharges, daily gage heights, and rating tables whereby the user of the records could compute daily discharge if he wished to. After a few years the publication of daily discharge was started, and beginning with the 1914 streamflow reports annual extremes of discharge were added. Figure 2 is a map of the 48 conterminous states showing areas covered by the parts of the yearly reports on surface water supply of the United States. Since 1951, Parts 1, 2, 3, and 6 have been divided into subparts A and B. Part numbers have not been assigned to Alaska and Hawaii, for which similar reports also are published.

As a supplement to the annual streamflow reports, descriptions of major floods have been reported in nearly 100 water-supply papers. Flood reports contain detailed information on stages and discharges not presented in the annual streamflow reports, in addition to descriptive material and other pertinent data.

Regional flood-frequency reports are being prepared in a series of 19 water-supply papers, 1671-1689 inclusive, that will cover the conterminous United States. Each volume will be for a part, or subpart, as now used for publishing streamflow records. As of August 1966, 12 have been published — Parts 1-A, 2-A, 3-A, 3-B, 4, 7, 8, 9, 10, 12, 13, and 14 — and those for Parts 2-B, 6-A, and 11 are in process of publication. These reports are titled "Magnitude and frequency of floods in the United States," with an areal designation, for example, "Part 7, Lower Mississippi River basin."

The public is, however, usually more interested in extent, depth, and probably frequency of flooding than in discharge rates. Hence,

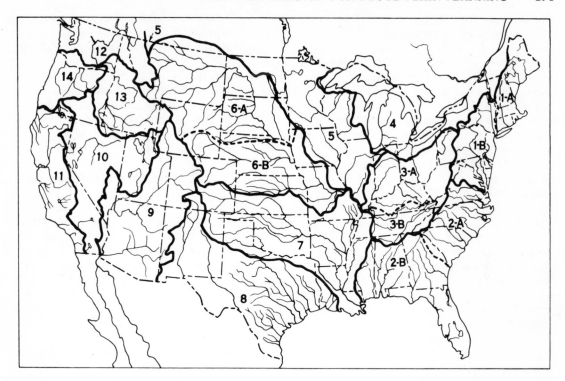

Figure 2. Division of the 48 conterminous states into parts and subparts.

flood-inundation maps are one of the most satisfactory and useful ways of presenting flood information for urban areas to the public.

The earliest flood-inundation maps were those that appeared in flood reports. The first Geological Survey flood report was Water-Supply Paper 88 by G.B. Hollister and M.O. Leighton (1903) describing the flood of 1902 on the Passaic River in New Jersey; this paper contained such a map. Many subsequent flood reports have contained maps showing areas inundated by the subject flood.

In 1959 the Geological Survey started a new series of flood-inundation maps published as hydrologic atlases, the first of which was Hydrologic Investigations Atlas HA-14, "Floods at Topeka, Kansas." The tempo of this program is accelerating in response to wide demand. As of November 1966, 63 atlases in 13 States and Puerto Rico have been published and others are in preparation. The greatest concentration of atlases is in the environs of Chicago, where the Geological Survey is preparing a series of atlases in cooperation with the Northeastern Illinois Metropolitan Area Planning Commission. Twelve atlases have been prepared for communities in Ohio.

A manual for the guidance of those engaged in flood-plain planning, titled "Hydraulic and Hydrologic Aspects of Flood-Plain Planning," by Sulo W. Wiitala, Karl R. Jetter, and Alan J. Sommerville, was prepared by the Geological Survey in cooperation with the Commonwealth of Pennsylvania and published in 1961 as Water-Supply Paper 1526. It is a study of Chartiers Creek at Carnegie, Pa. The manual gives much the same type of information as the flood-inundation maps, but is much more comprehensive and describes the techniques used in considerable detail.

The Corps of Engineers and the Tennessee Valley Authority also collect and disseminate data of immediate application to flood-plain planning.

ZONING BY LOCAL GOVERNMENTS
John E. McCall

Flood-plain studies are made to assist local communities in delineating or recommending zones to which specific regulations should be applied.

Difficult problems and a series of technical

decisions are thus left to the state and local official. Frequently these officials and their staffs have no closely comparable experience to guide them in the hydrologic engineering and legal phases of flood zoning. Nevertheless, positive actions must be taken by the local officials if the potential benefits of flood-plain studies are to be fully realized. Fortunately, steadily growing numbers of engineers, lawyers, planners, and economists are becoming qualified to advise local government officials on the specific steps needed to institute flood-plain zoning. Likewise, a considerable body of precedents is slowly building up in many states that furnish a model for others to follow.

It is not possible or practical to outline herein a specific course of action by local officials because state laws on property rights and "police powers" for zoning are quite variable and local ordinances even more so. Likewise, some but not all states have encroachment statutes that regulate building in the river channel or floodway, the provisions of which are far from uniform across the country. Perhaps even more importantly, differing local conditions of flooding, relative values of flood-plain lands, and attitudes of the citizens of the community prohibit any standard solution. However, one or more of the following suggestions may prove helpful in putting into use the results of a flood-plain study.

1. Request the engineer or planning director of the municipality to contact officials of the state agency concerned with flood control and stream-channel encroachments. Usually this agency will also be coordinating the flood-plain studies by the several federal agencies to arrange priorities and to prevent duplication of effort. This state agency will likely be the best source of guidance on encroachment statutes, as well as specific state laws relating to flood zoning, and may be able to outline the steps to be taken and to furnish other staff assistance. Hopefully this agency can name other municipalities within the state which have already adopted flood-zoning codes or ordinances and may be able to suggest desirable modifications or alternatives based upon experience.

2. Consider retaining a firm of engineering or planning consultants with experience in the field of flood zoning. Such firms can develop the details quickly and formulate a recommended ordinance, making full use of the information contained in the completed flood-plain study. A consulting firm will be especially useful if the municipality has only a small technical staff or if that regular staff is fully committed on other work.

3. Request the cooperation and assistance of a river-basin planning commission, a watershed association, or a regional-planning group, if any exist within the area. Frequently such organizations can furnish staff assistance and advice and may be especially helpful in sponsoring public meetings to gain public understanding and endorsement of flood zoning.

4. Contact officials of state and federal agencies concerned with urban redevelopment and acquisition of land for parks, recreation, and other open-space uses. Federal and state funds may be available to assist the municipality in obtaining development rights, easements, or fee title to flood-prone areas or long-range planning for conversion of land use on the flood plain.

5. Refer to published reports listed in the references contained herein. A section on "Implementation of Flood-Plain Regulations" is given, for example, on pages 98-106 of the American Society of Civil Engineers Task Force report cited in the references.

6. Invite representatives of the federal agency that has prepared the flood-plain study and representatives of appropriate state, regional or other federal agencies to appear before the municipal officials, including the planning and zoning boards, to present a brief summary of the work accomplished and to discuss its further implementation. These representatives may also be helpful in presenting background information at public meetings, provided that their testimony be restricted to their sphere of knowledge and assigned agency functions.

7. Recent developments pertaining specifically to flood-plain management are Executive Order 11296, signed by the President on August 10, 1966, and House Document 465, 89th Congress, 2d session, transmitted by the President to the Speaker of the House of Representatives by letter dated August 10, 1966. The Executive Order directs federal agencies to evaluate flood hazard in locating federally owned or financed buildings, roads, and other facilities, and in disposing of federal lands and properties. The House

Document is a report by a Task Force on Federal Flood Control Policy; it recommends specific action (1) to improve basic knowledge about flood hazard, (2) to coordinate and plan new developments on the flood plain, (3) to provide technical services to managers of flood-plain property, (4) to move toward a practical national program for flood insurance, and (5) to adjust federal flood-control policy to sound criteria and changing needs.

References

Allen, Howard E., and May, V. Jeff, 1964, Floods in Harvey quadrangle, Illinois: U.S. Geol. Survey Hyd. Inv. Atlas HA-90.

Burton, Ian, 1961, Education in the human use of flood plains: v. 60, no. 8, p. 362-371.

Dalrymple, Tate, 1960, Flood-frequency analyses: U.S. Geol. Survey Water-Supply Paper 1543-A, 80 p.

Goddard, James E., 1963, Flood-plain management improves man's environment: Jour. Waterways and Harbors Div., Am. Soc. Civil Engineers, v. 89, no. WW4, Proc. Paper 3702, Nov. 1963, p. 67-84.

Hogan, Thomas M., 1963, State flood-plain zoning: Chicago, DePaul Law Rev., v. 12, no. 2, p. 246-262.

Hoyt, William G., and Langbein, Walter B., 1955, Floods: Princeton, Princeton Univ. Press, 469 p.

Leopold, Luna B., and Maddock, Thomas Jr., 1954, The flood control controversy: New York, The Ronald Press Co., 278 p.

Sheaffer, John R., 1960, Flood proofing: Chicago, Chicago Univ. Dept. Geog. Research Paper 65, 190 p.

———— 1964, The use of flood maps in northeastern Illinois: Highway Research Board of the National Academy of Sciences, National Research Council, Highway Research Record no. 58, p. 44-46.

U.S. Congress, 1966, A unified National program for managing flood losses: House Doc. 465, 89th Cong., 2d sess., 47 p.

U.S. Senate, Select Committee on Water Resources, 1960, Floods and flood control: Committee Print 15, 86th Cong. 2d sess., 77 p.

White, Gilbert F., and others, 1958, Changes in urban occupance of flood plains in the United States: Chicago, Chicago Univ. Dept. Geog. Research Paper 57, 235 p.

Wood, Wilmer H., 1965, Federal flood hazard mapping in the United States: Chicago, Chicago Univ. Dept. Geog., Master's thesis, 34 p.

56. EVALUATION OF DE KALB COUNTY AREA FOR SOLID-WASTE DISPOSAL AND GENERAL CONSTRUCTION

DAVID L. GROSS

SUITABILITY OF AREA FOR SOLID-WASTE DISPOSAL

Both the location of a site for solid-waste disposal and the operational procedures to be employed must be approved by the Illinois Department of Public Health. Solid wastes may be disposed of by contained high-temperature incineration, sanitary landfill, composting, and feeding garbage to swine. The sanitary landfill is the most frequently used disposal technique.

The primary consideration in approving a sanitary landfill site is the possibility of polluting either ground or surface water. According to regulations set up by the Illinois Department of Public Health (1966), sites shall be located so that:

1. no disposal takes place in standing water;
2. no disposal takes place in areas having high ground-water tables unless preventive measures are taken to safeguard the ground water;
3. no surface runoff flows into or through the operational or completed fill area;
4. no disposal takes place unless the subsoil material affords reasonable assurance that leachate from the landfill will not contaminate ground or surface water.

For evaluation of a waste disposal site, information is needed about the type and thickness of unconsolidated material at the site, the type of bedrock present, present sources and potential sources of water, and the topography of the site (Cartwright and Sherman, 1969, p. 7-13). In general, at least 30 feet of relatively impermeable material must occur between the base of any landfill operation and the top of any existing or potential ground-water aquifer. In De Kalb County, only the areas covered by clayey

Extracted with permission of publisher from "Geology for Planning in De Kalb County, Illinois" by D. L. Gross in *Environmental Geology Notes*, no. 33, 26 p., April 1970. Published by Illinois State Geological Survey, Urbana, Illinois.

glacial till appear to meet this requirement consistently.

The preparation of interpretative maps for this study involved a color coding system first developed by Quay (1966) for presenting information about soils. The system borrows from the traffic stop light the scheme of using green for go (favorable conditions), yellow for caution, and red for stop (unfavorable conditions or severe problem areas). In this report the colors are represented by the letters G, Y, and R. Three shades (numbered 1, 2, and 3) of each of the basic colors may be used to represent different kinds of limitations within the color group. For example, a classification of G-1 (Green-one) indicates either an area with the fewest limitations or the best resources, whereas R-3 (Red-

---

EXPLANATION FOR FIGURE 1.

SUITABILITY OF DE KALB COUNTY AREA FOR SOLID-WASTE DISPOSAL

G Suitable disposal sites probably available; areas of glacial till where there are no data suggesting the occurrence of sand or sand and gravel.

Y-1 Suitable disposal sites may be available; extremely varied material; primarily till with many inclusions of sand or sand and gravel.

Y-2 A few suitable disposal sites probably available; isolated sand or sand and gravel deposits; usually associated with extremely varied till.

R-1 Disposal sites are likely to pose pollution hazards unless special engineering precautions are taken; surficial silt, sand, or sand and gravel underlain by till at less than 20 feet.

R-2 Disposal sites are liable to pose pollution hazards unless special engineering precautions are taken; less than 50 feet of glacial drift over the bedrock surface; surficial material varies from sand to till.

R-3 Disposal sites are liable to pose pollution hazards unless special engineering precautions are taken; upper 20 feet of surficial material consists of silt, sand, or sand and gravel.

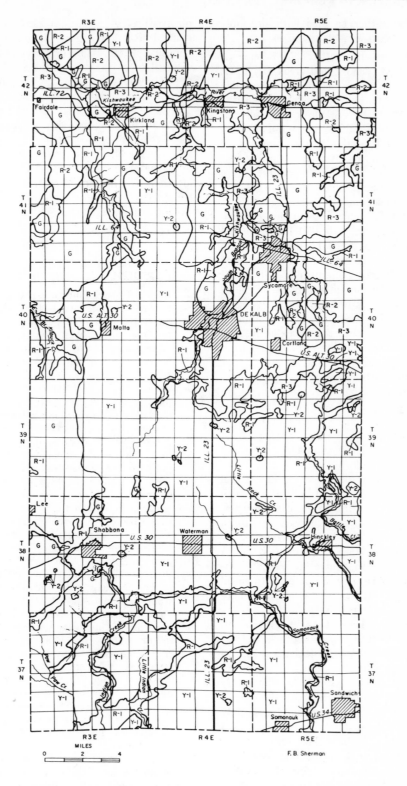

Figure 1. Suitability of De Kalb County area for solid-waste disposal.

three) indicates either an area with the most problems or the least valuable resources.

Figure 1 uses the traffic light scheme of designating as red, yellow, and green (R, Y, G) the relative probabilities for locating a suitable sanitary landfill site. Much of the area labelled G on the map should be suitable for landfill use. These areas are believed to have more than 50 feet of glacial till overlying any aquifer unit. Sand and gravels are relatively rare. One or two test borings would probably be required at a proposed site because reliable subsurface data are not available for every area.

The lack of favorable areas in the southern part of the county suggests that less favorable areas (Y-1, Y-2, Y-3) must be used for waste disposal. These areas commonly contain layers of sand, or sand and gravel, interbedded with glacial till and silt. Acceptable sites can be found in these areas, but the varied nature of the earth materials means that a very careful preliminary investigation will be required. An extensive test boring program would be necessary to find areas where sand and gravel is absent. Thin sand and gravel layers might be acceptable if there were reasonable assurance that they would never be developed as a source of water and that they would not serve as a path for leachate to reach surface streams.

Considerable difficulty should be expected if attempts are made to locate landfills in the R-1, R-2, and R-3 areas. In the R-1 areas, the surficial material is silt, sand, or sand and gravel. Such areas are along the existing surface drainageways, and the possibility of surface water pollution must be considered. Relatively impermeable till is usually found at a depth of less than 20 feet. A location where relatively impermeable silt overlies till would probably be acceptable for landfill purposes, but a rather extensive preliminary investigation would be necessary.

R-2 areas are believed to have less than 50 feet of glacial drift over the bedrock. As the bedrock in the country is generally capable of supplying enough water for individual residences, the requirement that at least 30 feet of relatively impermeable material occur between the base of any landfill and any underlying aquifer severely limits the landfill potential of these areas. Test borings to bedrock would be required at a potential site, and only if the unconsolidated materials overlying the bedrock proved to be clay till or silt would the site be safe to use.

Areas where the upper 20 feet of earth materials is silt, sand, or sand and gravel are marked R-3. Of these materials only thick deposits of silt might be acceptable for waste disposal sites. As much of the area is adjacent to the Kishwaukee River, it seems unlikely that suitable sites could be easily located.

Some locations that are naturally unfavorable can be improved by proper engineering. Laying out diversion ditches, tiling, diking, installing clay liners, and collection and treatment of leachate are possible approaches to be used at locations where natural safeguards are lacking. However, construction work of this kind can be expensive and is rarely employed.

EXPLANATION FOR FIGURE 2.

SUITABILITY OF THE DE KALB AREA FOR GENERAL CONSTRUCTION

G-2 Areas of low to medium plasticity; medium to high compressive bearing strengths adequate for nearly all construction; moderate to low shrink-swell characteristics; water table generally low; sand and silt lenses may be encountered during excavation; till unit 13 may be difficult to excavate.

G-3 Areas of thin till having low to medium plasticity; bearing strengths adequate; moderate to low shrink-swell characteristics; exposed or near-surface bedrock will increase costs of excavation; underlying rock units should be protected from surface pollutants. The map unit also includes some areas of granular deposits with good internal drainage.

Y-1 Areas of varied material; may be granular with little or no plasticity; free-draining; low shrink-swell characteristics; water table may be less than 10 feet deep. Clayey silts with high plasticity, high dry strength, high shrink-swell characteristics, subject to frost heave. Drainage conditions and depth to stable material will affect the suitability of construction sites. Artesian water conditions in local sand deposits may cause foundation or excavation problems. Areas of gentle slopes generally provide adequate bearing strengths.

Y-2 Areas of varied materials like those in Y-1; depth of undesirable materials generally more than 10 feet; some areas subject to high water table or possible flooding; materials have poor drainage and low bearing strengths.

R-2 Areas of highly compressible organic materials or muck; ground-water levels at or near ground surface; interior drainage; very poor foundation material.

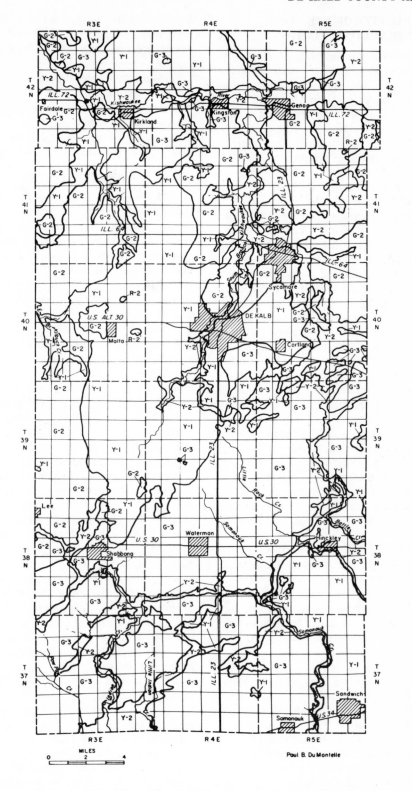

Figure 2. Suitability of De Kalb County area for general construction.

SUITABILITY OF AREA FOR GENERAL CONSTRUCTION

General construction refers to development of a subdivision, erection of small business structures, road building, and other construction projects of similar size. Although planners of such construction projects are primarily interested in the surficial materials, they must also be concerned with subsurface materials encountered in excavations for sewerage systems, basements, and water distribution systems.

Water conditions, composition of the soil unit, and the character of the slope are the principal factors influencing the selection of construction sites. Regions that are topographically low and areas that have a high water table and a potential for frequent flooding should be avoided. Quicksand or sandboils may develop when water under pressure is exposed at the surface or in an excavation.

Generally speaking, well-graded, compacted till deposits and coarse, well-drained alluvial deposits provide suitable construction sites, whereas fine-grained, clayey or silty, poorly drained deposits are less desirable. Organic materials and clays can be squeezed and are termed "compressible." Such materials often cause foundations to settle, with resultant damage to the structures. Clays are the chief cause of the shrinking and swelling characteristics of soils, which also may prove detrimental to foundations. Water-saturated clay or silt zones provide a sliding surface, which may result in a landslide. A silty texture contributes to the frost susceptibility of soils because it allows water to move through them.

Most landscapes, unless adjacent to areas actively being eroded, such as stream banks, lake borders, or steep moraine fronts, develop natural, stable slopes. If, prior to construction, it becomes necessary to alter the natural slope of the land, careful consideration should be given to the settlement and stability of the resultant graded slopes.

Characteristics of the surficial materials in De Kalb County that affect engineering projects are listed in the explanation for figure 2. These units are coded G, Y, and R according to their engineering characteristics. The data used for evaluating the construction suitability of land in De Kalb County include the surficial geology map of De Kalb County, sand and gravel resource studies, and logs of borings made by the Illinois

Division of Highways. No new samples were collected or tested for this study. Additional reports were used as a guide for descriptions of engineering properties.

Figure 2 indicates that most areas in De Kalb County are free from serious construction problems. A competent foundation engineer, however, should be engaged to evaluate construction sites, as his knowledge and experience can be invaluable in avoiding the less suitable areas.

DISCUSSION OF THE MAPS

The map of the surficial deposits was basic to the study of environmental geology in De Kalb County, inasmuch as the interpretative maps were partly, or in some cases wholly, derived from it. The surficial deposits map delineates the deposits that occur within 20 feet of the surface and is based on the texture, mineralogy, color, weathering characteristics, and degree of compaction of the deposits.

Surficial geology is the most important but not the only consideration in evaluating the county for solid-waste disposal sites (fig. 1). The thickness of the glacial drift, the character of the underlying bedrock, the general hydrologic flow system, and the regional use of ground water are all considered in evaluating conditions for solid-waste disposal. Therefore, the resultant waste-disposal map resembles, but does not directly coincide with, the surficial deposits map.

All boundaries shown on the map indicating suitability for general construction (fig. 2) match boundaries on the surficial deposits map, although not all boundaries on the surficial deposits map are relevant to construction conditions. The engineering properties of a geologic unit depend on the physical character and composition of the deposit as well as on its geologic history (including degree of compaction by overriding glacial ice and subsequent weathering). The physical and compositional factors are considered in the surficial deposits map; therefore, the engineering interpretation requires an evaluation of each of the units shown in the surficial deposits map but does not require remapping the boundary lines.

In the preparation of an environmental geology report, the map scale almost always represents a compromise. A county planner would prefer maps on a very large scale that have exceptionally accurate boundaries, but for two reasons this is not always practical. First, the map scale must be based on the accuracy and quantity of the available geologic data. Second, geologic deposits are naturally gradational and do not lend themselves to arbitrary boundaries. In many cases the sharp lines on geologic maps are actually dividing a single sequence that is continuously gradational in composition or thickness. Photographic enlargement of a geologic map is not the answer to the scale problem. Although photographic reduction is acceptable, photographic enlargement may introduce inaccuracies and result in an unwarranted extrapolation of the data.

The accuracy of the surficial geology map is the limiting factor in the application of environmental geology in De Kalb County. The United States Department of Agriculture, Soil Conservation Service, is currently preparing a modern soil map for the county. Close cooperation between soil scientists and geologists can result in improved accuracy in both the resultant soil and geologic maps, which in turn will allow more accuracy in the various environmental maps of this area.

References

Cartwright, Keros, and F.B. Sherman, 1969, Evaluating sanitary landfill sites in Illinois: Illinois Geol. Survey Environmental Geol. Notes, no. 27, 15 p.

Illinois State Department of Public Health, 1966, Rules and regulations for refuse disposal sites and facilities: Illinois Dept. Public Health, Sanitary Eng. Div., 7 p.

Quay, J.R., 1966, Use of Soil surveys in subdivision design, in Soil surveys and land-use planning: Soil Sci. Soc. of America and American Soc. of Agronomy, p. 76-87.

57. LAND: MAKING ROOM FOR TOMORROW

JOHN LEAR

Within thirty years from now, demographers say, more than half the population of the United States will be packed onto less than one-twelfth of all the available land in the country. According to these predictions, about 200 million persons will occupy four great corridors of space: one stretching along the Atlantic seacoast from Maine to Virginia, another spanning the length of Florida, a third skirting the southern shores of the Great Lakes from Buffalo and Erie to Chicago, and a fourth bordering the Pacific Ocean from the top to the bottom of California.

The prospect is infinitely dreary. The nuclei of these so-called megalopolises are already bowed down with poverty, disease, hunger, crime, and filth. Stuffing more people into them can only deepen the misery.

Must we accept so sordid a future?

Can't we make room for a cleaner, more pleasant, and exciting tomorrow?

Wouldn't it be possible to settle tens of thousands happily in the almost empty 2,000 miles between San Francisco and Chicago?

How much serious effort has been made to revive dying towns on the great prairies?

How profoundly have we considered the potential of land within the few hundred miles surrounding places like Denver, Minneapolis, Omaha, and Troy?

Is there any good reason why what happened to Tucson and Phoenix couldn't happen just as well to any of scores of towns elsewhere?

Look at Las Vegas. It was hardly more than a railway crossing just a generation ago.

Stanford University Environmental Studies Professor Rolf Eliassen has pointed out how fantastically disjointed it is to talk about transporting excess water from the Columbia River across several states to the Colorado Basin in order to enable the Southwest to hold more people when the polluted air of Los Angeles is already notorious for its effects hundreds of

miles eastward. Why not encourage people to move to where the water is, where the air is clean and the land is hospitably open? Idaho, Oregon, Washington, and even Canada are reasonable possibilities to Eliassen's logical mind. He applauds the citizens of Texas for exercising exceptional wisdom in refusing to approve a plan that would have carried water from the Mississippi River to the overgrown megalopolitan Dallas-Ft. Worth-Houston complex. He prefers to keep the water in the Mississippi Valley and use it there to found new types of agriculture that would stop the migration of farm workers from Alabama, Louisiana, and Mississippi to the poverty-infested slums in Northeastern, Midwestern, and Southwestern cities.

Up to now, scholars like Eliassen haven't been paid much heed by the practical men who swing the real estate deals that in the end decide where most people live. Decisions about land use are made by hundreds of thousands of town and country officials who too often grab at promises of new taxes from industrial and commercial developers and only later realize their piecemeal responsibility for misshaping the heritage of America. These local politicians sit on disparate bodies deriving their power from the states, which withheld it from the federal government in the debates that forged the Declaration of Independence and the Constitution of the United States of America roughly two centuries ago.

Although Congress meanwhile has granted parcels of public land for use as transcontinental railroad rights-of-way and sites for centers of learning in all states, not once between the writing of the Consitution and the year 1971 did any President formally propose that the use of these and of all other lands should conform to a national pattern and contribute to attainment of the freely chosen goals of the American people.

Last February 8, President Richard M. Nixon set an unexpected precedent. Less than a year before he had talked of vetoing Washington Senator Henry Jackson's bill creating a White House Council on Environmental Quality. Now, in a special message on the state of the environ-

Extracted with permission of the author and publisher from *Saturday Review*, v. 54, no. 10, p. 45-48, March 6, 1971. Copyright 1971 Saturday Review, Inc.

ment, he endorsed CEQ's revised version of Senator Jackson's land use act, the original of which had died aborning in the 91st Congressional session last year.

As Mr. Jackson had done before him, Mr. Nixon suggested federal subsidies to encourage the states to recapture from local zoning authorities at least enough of the previously delegated power to require that land usage throughout a state meet the whole state's needs. In other words, the President gave his blessing to state efforts to determine where people could settle with the greatest benefit to the state and to themselves.

In fact, the scheme Mr. Nixon outlined surpassed Mr. Jackson's in boldness. Where the Senator from Washington would have allowed cities with 250,000 or more residents – or those that accounted for 20 per cent or more of the state's population – to be exempted from the statewide plans, the President offered no exemptions.

Although his message did not explicitly say so, its contents plainly implied the President's recognition that the chances of success for any statewide plan for land use would diminish in proportion to the length of time over which local real estate interests could manage to stretch inevitable quibbling over details. Instead of providing that every state should conduct an inventory of land use and fix zones for all the land under its jurisdiction – as Senator Jackson's bill had done – the Nixon proposal asked the states only to guarantee that certain key matters were covered by each plan. Included among these matters were:

- A method for state control over location of all focal points of growth, such as highway interchanges, major airports, and major recreational centers such as Disneyland.

- A method for state control over the location of all new communities.

- A method for state control over all large-scale developments of property.

- A method for state control over local attempts to block property developments of regional benefit. Such properties might be schools, hospitals, community centers, or multi-dwelling residential settlements capable of providing good housing for the poor.

- A method to ensure state protection of existing property identified as being of "critical environmental concern." Such property includes coastal zones and estuaries; lakes, rivers, and smaller streams and their flood plains; homes of important ecosystems; and areas embodying historical, cultural, or esthetic values beyond the ordinary. "Critical" in this context can also mean hazardous and hence closed to unrestricted development.

To protect the states from being encumbered above while they are disengaging themselves from entanglement below, the President stipulated that all federal-aid expenditures affecting land use must be shaped or redesigned to conform with the state land-development plans.

Mr. Nixon's critics complained that his seemingly comprehensive legislative proposal actually avoided grappling with the most ubiquitous of all mutilations of natural beauty: the highway corridor. The drafters of the bill at CEQ defended their work, observing that highway interchanges are the real foci of speculative land booms and that location of interchanges is reserved to the states under the Presidential scheme. The bill drafters also pointed out that preservation of areas of "critical environmental concern" will require highways to go around beauty spots they now too often carve up and sometimes obliterate. Furthermore, although this fact has not been publicly discerned, the Nixon revenue-sharing proposal will give to all the states sizable blocks of transportation subsidy that once would have been committed almost entirely to proliferation of roads to carry private automobile traffic, but in future may be apportioned as individual states wish to build fumeless buses, modernize railways, and initiate subway lines as well.

Electric power generating stations constitute another major force in population distribution that is not directly covered by the Nixon land use proposal. The President advocated a separate power plant siting law to establish within each state "a single agency with responsibility for ensuring that environmental concerns are properly considered in the certification of specific power plant sites and transmission line routes." Again, the drafters of the President's environmental message and its supporting legislation defended the separation as being more apparent than real. They pointed out that there is nothing to prevent any state from giving authority over land use in general to the same state agency that is authorized to plan power plant siting in particular. In any case, the principal demand of the President's power-siting suggestion was on the public utilities, requiring them to identify needed power facilities ten years prior to construction of those facilities, to identify the actual power plant sites and transmission routes five years before their construction, and to apply for certification of both sites and routes two years in advance of construction. Public hearings were specified, these to be conducted in ample time for all interested parties to express their views. Given these precautions, there would seem to be little opportunity for either power plant sites or transmission line routes to transgress areas critical to preservation of the environment.

The true measure of Mr. Nixon's determination to harmonize land use with national goals lay, his environmental aides said, in subsidiary proposals included in the environmental message of February 8. Among these was a Mined Area Protection Act " . . . to regulate the environmental consequences of surface and underground mining." Here the principal objective was restoration of millions of acres of land scarred by strip mining, and an intensity of purpose broke through the text of the message in these words: "In any state which does not enact the necessary regulations or enforce them properly, the federal government would be authorized to do so." Preservation and restoration of historic architecture "from Boston and Washington to Charleston, New Orleans, San Antonio, Denver, and San Francisco" were also provided for through tax incentives and federal insurance of improvement loans for historic residential properties. Still further concern for a more pleasant tomorrow was expressed by Presidential advocacy of additional national parks, wilderness areas, and neighborhood parks within cities — all in apparent preparation for the time when people will work only four days a week, perhaps even less, and will need the periodic solace of nature.

Part Seven
ENVIRONMENTAL PROGRAMS

In this final part we have assembled material in which a number of groups and individuals look to the future. Two papers discuss the training that should be included in the education of an environmental geologist and the role that geology can and should play in environmental concerns. Other articles look at general environmental education and the responsibility and challenge to the public. Certainly we must recognize that the overriding factor permeating nearly every environmental problem is that of too many people. Since these problems, be they physical, biologic, social, economic, or political, are rooted in overpopulation, we believe that one of the basic requirements for the solution of all environmental problems is a stable population. Death control continues to improve (although increased pollution and resulting diseases may alter this situation). The idea of population control has now emerged and is discussed openly, but it still faces strong opposition from many groups.

Many scientists are reaching the conclusion that the carrying capacity of "spaceship" earth is limited. Geologists realize that energy and mineral resources are finite, biologists see the extinction of species that have been unable to adapt to new polluted environments, sociologists find that strange things happen to humans as well as rats in crowded conditions, and the old-style conservationists have known the importance of pristine areas for decades. Some people are gregarious and prefer to take the risks of living in large cities where they enjoy many cultural advantages. For these people there are enough cities like New York and Los Angeles; for those who desire the other end of the spectrum, including wilderness areas, there is little hope if world population continues to increase. Famine, war, or disease will limit population if man does not. The question is when and by what means will the human population be stabilized?

Environmental programs must develop that strive to improve the total environment for all people. The poor and minority groups, whether from the most highly developed or the most undeveloped countries, must be brought into the environmental movement. This can only be done by improving their quality of life. The scope of environmental problems is world-wide and new international programs are necessary. Hopefully, the United Nations *Conference on the Human Environment* in Sweden, in 1972, will initiate meaningful environmental programs for all people.

58. THE PRESENT IS THE KEY TO THE FUTURE

A. GORDON EVERETT

As one who spent many years being a professional student, I am delighted with this opportunity to beard you lions in your own dens. Last night when I checked into my hotel room, still wondering what to say to you people today, I noticed that the Gideon's *Bible* was open. Curious as to the message the previous occupant had thought so worthwhile, I decided to take a look, hoping for a bit of inspiration. To my delight the passage was:

> And surely the mountain falling cometh to nought, and the rock is removed from his place.

> The waters wear the stones; thou washest away the things which grow out of the dust of the earth, and thou destroyed the hope of man.

Well, if that doesn't speak to the problems of environmental geology, what does? Hence, my remarks today.

All levels of government have found themselves faced with the environmental issue on short notice without prior institutional arrangements or traditions to easily meet the problems. The problems have frequently been caused by the tunnel-vision emanating from single discipline solutions to multifaceted problems. Our traditional educational approach has been to fragment the broad spectrum of life into artificial subdivisions in order to simplify and analyze, thus to better understand. Our oversimplification and broad generalizations are justifiable, but our failure to resynthesize our artificial categories back toward a spectrum having some approximation of reality is not. I feel that this latter failing of education has led, in part, to the present generation of students' charges of "lack of relevance" in traditional disciplines. Myopically,

Reprinted, with permission of the author and publisher from "Environmental Geology and Higher Education," *Journal of Geological Education,* v. 19, no. 3, p. 137-139, May, 1971. Copyright 1971 by National Association of Geology Teachers, Inc. Presented at "Colloquy '70" sponsored by the Council on Education in the Geological Sciences, Milwaukee, Wisconsin, November 10, 1970.

we have also adhered to narrow discipline lines in professional endeavors outside of the boundaries of academia — in the so-called "real world." In the past, relatively few educators have pressed for more integrated education through multidisciplinary programs. Although multidisciplinary programs have received a great deal of lip service in higher education, there has generally been little real acceptance of such programs or encouragement of students or faculty to pursue these new paths in earnest. That widespread, effective, multidisciplinary academic programs are still in the future has been thoroughly documented by the report of Steinhart and Cherniak.

Geology has traditionally required a broad science base, however. Since 1950, geology departments have continually broadened and strengthened the supporting science and mathematics backgrounds of students, frequently at the expense of geology courses themselves. It is customary for undergraduate geology majors to have mathematics through calculus as well as a minimum of the introductory-level courses in chemistry, physics, and biology. Yet these additional science courses have often raised questions in the students' minds when they fail to see the application of these supporting sciences within their advanced geology courses. Part of the problem lies in the fact that the *level* of the supporting courses may not be sufficiently advanced for the student to see the applicability. The basic courses in biology do not cover the necessary material to allow ready transposition of principles to paleoecology and paleontology; yet it is rare that undergraduate geology students take ecology or comparative anatomy from which the transposition to the geologic subdisciplines is relatively easy, even if not brought out by the geology instructor. Similarly, chemistry short of qualitative and quantitative analysis has little apparent applicability to mineralogy and petrology; calculus short of differential equations often seems inapplicable to the qualitative variables interrelated in dynamic geologic processes. Thus, it may be that, as educators, you need to consider partitioning supporting sciences so as to include less breadth but greater depth in those sciences to stay within the constraints of the limited number of courses required for graduation.

Quantification in geology has produced numerous stresses, even to the point of creating factions within departments and within subdisciplines throughout the science. Students have frequently questioned the need for mathematical analysis when the bulk of the science and the majority of textbooks are still largely descriptive. Unfortunately, we have not adequately used the technique of semiquantification of interrelated factors. Clearly, surficial processes are ideally suited to analysis in terms of variables, both dependent and independent. In fact, this is a necessary step in the transposition from mathematically-rigorous empirical formulae to physically significant dependent and independent factors that relate to geologic reality. As we move to increased quantification of geology, as we surely must, let us not lose sight of the necessity of translating empirical results into significant, interrelated, physical parameters. It was Lord Kelvin, often quoted in support of quantification, who cautioned against its overuse because, as he said, the student is often tempted to accept the symbol as the reality where empirical quantification is overemphasized.

It has been mentioned frequently here today that geology is essentially a historical science. That is true, but not exclusively so. The historical aspects of our science have long been influenced by the uniformitarian doctrine that "the present is the key to the past." For geology to make significant contributions as an environmental science, it must also be true that "the present is the key to the future." The geological record is evidence of that doctrine as well. Thus, I would encourage you to take a new approach to old and new courses alike. Traditionally, we have related present *processes* to the *forms* they produce, but we have stressed the historical significance of the *forms*. Let us put some new emphasis on the *process* with the form as evidence that, as the process has operated in the past, so will it operate in the future; as variables have altered the process — and thus the form — in the past, so will they alter these processes in the future. The successful application of engineering geology to environmental problems has been based upon this doctrine of "the present as

the key to the future." It is equally applicable across the spectrum of geology that is applied to environmental problems — to geomorphology, marine geology, hydrology, and geochemistry, to mention but a few subdisciplines.

Several environmental geology curricula with which I am familiar and some that I have heard discussed here today have had one surprising omission. That is the absence of geomorphology as the keystone course on which the remainder of the geologic curriculum is based. I am not referring to any dusty, dry course full of rote recitation of land-form terminology, but rather of a course concerned with *"dynamic surficial processes."* These processes are the geologic life movements of the earth itself. They incorporate the physics, chemistry, and biology associated with dynamic geology. Such a course dealing with modifications of surficial morphology is the academic foundation on which more detailed and specialized courses can be built. Such a course is also a critical early course in geology for those in other environmentally applied sciences and fields of engineering.

For the past ten years or more, there has been a vigorous debate over whether or not the future of geology lies with increased specialization. From my experience in environmental geology as presently being applied by federal and state governments, I can assure you that the best environmental geology specialist is the one with the broadest possible background. That should not be construed to mean that the breadth can be superficial — it must be substantial in both geology and supporting sciences; it must be quantitative, for the environmental geologists *must* work closely with engineers, economists, and others who need to know not only the direction of change, but also the magnitude.

The environmental geologist deals constantly with the chemical systems of nature and of man's modifications thereof, with the physics of materials ranging from discrete particles to large three-dimensional masses under a wide variety of stresses, and with the impact of geologic changes on the biology of the earth. He is frequently called upon to assess the impact of a given change on ecology.

Thus, breadth is required in the ability to generalize quickly, using sound scientific principles and to coordinate and interpret the detailed findings of diverse specialists within and without the field of geology. One must have a feel for the many diverse techniques for problem-solving available throughout our science. It will not do to attack problems with but one pet approach and, when that fails, then to declare the problem technically insoluble. I have seen that done on several recent occasions and it is not impressive.

The applied geology courses — petroleum, mining, and economic geology — which have received shabby treatment in our burst of effort to purge geology into a pure science, have great utility to the prospective environmental geologist. He will be an applied geologist, one who will deal with the environmental problems caused in part by the extractive nonrenewable resources industry but probably without the firsthand knowledge gained through mineral industry employment.

Of *greatest* importance is field experience, however; as much as a student can get. It has applicability to all specialties in geology, of course, but is critical to the environmental geologist. I had the opportunity to participate in the organization and teaching of an introductory-level physical and historical geology course taught in the field among the mountains, deserts, canyons, and plateaus of Utah. The impact of such early exposure to full-scale geology, to both processes and products, has a dramatic effect on both student interest and, later, student performance. After having spent a long, cold winter in the laboratory with our generalizations and simplifications, we have all experienced that first shock at seeing the inhomogeneity and complexity of rocks on the first field excursion of the season. The applied geologist makes his living on the adequacy of his solutions to problems involving real rocks and real water bodies. Statistical approximations and mathematical models have significance only as they approach the reality of large, three-dimensional masses of material. A geologist who idealizes subsurface reservoirs into homogeneous, geometrically-packed arrangements of spheres or treats stressed earth materials as homogeneous, time-rate independent media has a limited future in environmental applications. Encourage your students to gain as much field experience as possible in all aspects of geology. This familiarity with the reality of geologic materials, processes, and systems will mean the difference between success and failure in dealing with environmental problems.

There is no curriculum that offers a panacea in the education of an environmental geologist but all curricula need to stress dynamic geologic processes — in the present and in the future.

As a last comment on scientific curricula, I would like to express concern about the tendency to create a *"degree caste system"* through the "liberal arts B.A. option" and the "science B.S. option." In the long run, the development of strong and widely available courses open to geology minors as well as majors will probably be of the greatest benefit to the development of science-based liberal arts education. Many departments discourage minors in geology and numerous colleges and universities have abolished the concept of a minor program. At this time, with the reality of student concern for the ability of the earth to continue to endure man's use and abuse, the stage seems set for minors in all of the environmental sciences. Let us not price ourselves out of the market with an insistence on a liberal arts B.A. in geology in place of the option of a geology minor.

In addition to the breadth in supporting sciences that we have been encouraging for the past two decades, let us look as well to additional strength in nonscientific subjects. In the solution of environmental problems, we are constantly faced with economic, social, and political factors that must be integrated with the technical alternatives. All too often, the excuse is given that the technical factors are separate and discrete, thus we find scientists unwilling to participate in the final solution which involves judgments on these nonscientific parameters as well. This position of scientists is historical with many geological surveys and is defensible. It has been their role to supply scientific data and research free of bias and uncontaminated, insofar as possible, with nonreproducible nonscientific data or judgments. But you are not educating only future personnel for the various geological surveys. Among your students you have many that are concerned with the multifaceted problems of today's world. Encourage those who seek breadth in economics, the social and political sciences, and other nonscience fields. The management levels of government and business have a crying need for broadly-trained scientists who can function effectively in positions that link technology to the nonscientific world. The geologist is well-suited to this by virtue of a broad scientific training and, given additional breadth and interest, can participate very effectively in these problem-oriented management positions. Geologists are rarely sought for these positions today because few are available or express interest. Their backgrounds and abilities are poorly understood by the man in the street. As many of you have commented here today, geology at the undergraduate level can be an excellent preparation as a liberal arts and liberal science background as well. However, you must encourage and develop in students an awareness that they must create the need for their viewpoint and background in environmental matters. They will frequently have to displace engineers and even nonscientists who are there before them.

At present, positions for environmental scientists are filled predominantly by biologists and engineers. It is absurd to insist that geologists have been deprived of adequate representation in a field for which we are so well qualified. We are the Johnny-come-latelys to active public participation in the environmental issue for the most part and are still customarily thought of by the public only in association with museums and mineral exploration. The use of geology as a factor in the solution of environmental problems will develop only as the relevance of geology to the problem develops in the minds of other participants in the environmental issues.

As geologists and educators, you will help mold the attitudes and influence the direction of the solutions to our environmental problems by the manner in which you educate *all* of the undergraduates of today and tomorrow. The burden is now upon education at all levels to make people realize that, political furor or no, our use of the environment dictates not only the quality of man's life but the length of his civilized existence as well.

REFERENCES

14 Job 18, 19, The Holy Bible (King James Version), published by Gideons International, 1963 edition, p. 503.

Steinhart, John S., and Cherniak, Stacie, 1969, The Universities and Environmental Quality—Commitment to Problem Focused Education. Government Printing Office, Washington, D.C.

59. EDUCATION FOR ENVIRONMENTAL GEOLOGY

WILLIAM R. DICKINSON

As educators, we have a duty to conduct our affairs in a way that will prepare students to help the world surmount these kinds of problems. They are as tough and challenging as any that a person can face. Our first challenge is to educate ourselves, for few of us have enough background in biology, meteorology, sociology, psychology, economics, politics, or engineering to be complacent. To be honest, we will never, given the pressures of life and the scope of the problems, fully catch up. We must plan to graduate students who are better environmental geologists than many of us will ever be. I find this an exciting thought. At the same time, we must gird ourselves for feasible self-improvement. Each of us, in his own way, building on his own background and interests, can help build a solid structure for environmental geology. Nothing could be more arrogant than to suppose that we have all the answers, and need only good will and popular support to set the world right. We need ideas most of all.

I look upon education for environmental geology as an interdisciplinary effort on four levels. At the first level are beginning courses in geology for general students in high school or college. At the second level are curricula for undergraduate majors in environmental earth sciences. At the third level are programs for professional training and the master's degree. At the fourth level are research programs leading to a doctorate. Let us consider each in order.

General courses in geology can be transposed to an environmental approach at once, and I think they should be. Every topic in geology can be treated in its relation to man, his history, and his works. I think there are no exceptions. Even plutonic activity can be discussed in its relation to the underpinnings of volcanism, which arises naturally from considerations of volcanology and its impact on man. What is needed now in

Extracted with permission of the author and publisher from "Geology for the Masses" *Journal of Geological Education*, v. 18, no. 5, p. 194-197, Nov. 1970. Copyright 1970 by National Association of Geology Teachers, Inc.

concrete terms is a concerted effort to pull from the record enough pertinent information to bolster this kind of course with facts. Let us forget introducing volcanism in general, but let us rather teach of lava flows covering plantations, of harmonic tremor and lava fountains, or tiltmeter surveys on swelling mountains, of hot spring temperatures, and lava lakes in Hawaii. Let us talk of eruption warnings in Japan, of mudflows in Indonesia, of ashflows in the Mediterranean and the Caribbean. Let us move from broken cables to subsea fans built by turbidity currents. Let us study deltaic sedimentation in Louisiana and the Persian Gulf where the effects are graphic. Let us show that slope stability problems in California stem plainly from the environment of recent uplift. Let us press equations and numbers on our students, not just to stretch their hands and make them think, but because they are the only way to understand the problems of groundwater recharge, ground response to earthquake shaking, the prediction of flood discharges, the production curves of non-replenishable resources, and a host of other real problems in the real world.

At the level of undergraduate curricula for earth science majors, we have more spadework to do to set ourselves in motion, but the outlines are clear. We must remove some of the encyclopedic clutter of specific applications that grace our present courses. We have to identify valuable principles without regard to whether they have been called geology, geophysics, geochemistry, mineralogy, paleontology, meterology, oceanography, or whatever in the past. These we must hammer home at whatever cost to our concepts of traditional instruction, and then concentrate on fostering the ability to define and attack specific illustrative problems. The focus on problem-solving is vital because many of the problems our students must face in the coming decades are unknown to us now in any precise form. Our curricula must also encourage breadth of training, and we have yet to define closely what balance to strike among a host of disciplines. I think we should allow wide variations in this aspect of individual study programs because our students will move in diverse directions after graduation. Some will continue scientific education, but others will seek professional training that may lead them partly outside science into a planning career of some kind. Even undergraduate curricula in environmental earth science must include a thorough grounding in the philosophy and methods of planning for geological hazards, natural resources, and land use.

At the level of professional graduate training for environmental geology, master's degree programs have two potential benefits. On the one hand, we will need more solid professionals in fields that overlap engineering. These include groundwater geologists, engineering geologists, mining geologists, and the like. At the same time, we need imaginative new thinking about varied constraints on urban development, and I think our large urban colleges and universities in California have a special potential to tap widespread student interest in this field. For good results, we should recast all our thinking about master's training into interdisciplinary terms. The aim is not to develop generalists, who do not in fact exist except on paper, but to train people whose special talents can form bridges between isolated intellectual communities.

At the level of doctoral research, the future seems haziest to me. Some geological dissertations will prove to be vital to some phases of environmental planning, and their writers may well revolutionize some aspect of environmental geology in due course, but doctoral research on environmental problems is something else again. The outlines of such research are nearly impossible to specify. To merit the adjective en-vironmental, the research should probably be so thoroughly interdisciplinary, in relation to traditional fields, that we might not know whether to call the doctoral candidate a geologist or not. For this reason, I think we need some loose but energetic interdepartmental or supradepartmental committees or institutes in universities to foster and guide environmental research. These will be unusual entities, for they cannot restrict themselves to physical scientists alone, but must welcome social scientists and humanists as well. Nor can they fully supplant present departments, for the really tough environmental problems yield only to basic approaches grounded in the separate disciplines.

THE UNIVERSITY AND THE ENVIRONMENT

With this thought of multidisciplinary environmental research, we reach what is to me the most exciting potential of the idea of mankind living in balance with his environment. This idea has the capacity, I think, to heal the biggest rifts in our intellectual community. The present splits between physical scientists, social scientists, and humanists are not only absurd, but in the long run destructive. Intellectual divisions on issues and even on principles are to be expected and welcomed. Fierce intellectual antagonisms of a temporary kind are valuable, but problaby no culture can remain whole in the face of permanent and deep differences in the values and life styles of its intellectuals. I hope humanists and scientists alike can make common cause of the goal of harmony between man and his environment. I think geologists, through their traditional view of the world as a total system, have an important role to play in this potential fusion.

60. ENVIRONMENT: PREPARING FOR THE CRUNCH

CARROLL L. WILSON

There was a time in our history when the prevailing value system assigned an overriding priority to the primary effects of applied science and technology: the goods and services produced. We took side effects such as pollution in stride. There now seems to be a shift in values that assigns a much higher priority to the control of the side effects. But when the crunch comes and the implications of remedial action and necessary choices become clear, will we have second thoughts? Will we bog down in confusion and frustration? Or will we hold to our course, insisting that our society make a more thorough and imaginative effort to achieve a much better balance between the production we need and the side effects that we must bring under control?

Last July, a group of fifty scientists and professionals wrestled with some of these questions at Williams College in Williamstown, Massachusetts, where a month-long study was conducted to assess man's impact on the global environment. The project, called the Study of Critical Environmental Problems (SCEP), focused on the need to gather more information about pollution of the planet. Our hope was that this information would improve our understanding of the impact of man's activities on the earth's resources of air, water, and land: that is, the ecological demand of man's activities.

The study, sponsored by the Massachusetts Institute of Technology, explored the climatic effects of increasing carbon dioxide in the atmosphere and of increasing the particle load. It also investigated the atmospheric effects of contamination produced by combustion from supersonic transport aircraft (SST). DDT and other toxic insecticides were studied for their ecological effects, as were mercury and other toxic heavy metals, petroleum in the oceans, and nutrients in estuaries. In each case, we tried to estimate the background level of naturally oc-

curring products, for example carbon dioxide and particles, in order to assess the amount and effect of increments arising from man's activities. We formulated recommendations on measurement, research, and abatement action, where we considered it justified. *Man's Impact on the Global Environment,* a detailed report of the project, has been published by the MIT Press. Its major findings and recommendations can be summarized as follows:

- The concentration of carbon dioxide in the atmosphere is increasing steadily as a result of man's activities. It may be up nearly 20 per cent by the year 2000. This could lead to an increase of global temperature of a half degree centigrade, which is not alarming. But if carbon dioxide concentration doubled, it could raise the global temperature two degrees centigrade, and this could be disturbing: It takes only a two-degree change in the global temperature to initiate the kind of warming of the planet that has been predicted by those who said the icecaps were going to melt, the oceans were going to rise, and we were all going to drown. We didn't find a crisis here, but we thought the consequences of having to change our habits and not generate too much carbon dioxide were so great that we should begin measuring it carefully.

- Man puts large quantities of sulfates, nitrates, and hydrocarbons into the atmosphere that become fine particles, including such special species as urban smog. These particles change the heat balance of the earth because they both reflect and absorb radiation from the sun and earth. Large amounts of such particles enter the troposphere (the zone up to 40,000 feet) from natural sources such as sea spray, wind-blown dust, volcanoes, and from the conversion of naturally occurring gases — sulfur dioxide, nitrogen oxides, and hydrocarbons. We don't know enough about the optical properties (reflection vs. absorption) of

Reprinted with permission of the publishers from *Saturday Review,* v. 54, no. 4, p. 42,43 and 93, January 23, 1971, a special issue produced in cooperation with the Committee for Economic Development. Copyright 1971 by Saturday Review, Inc.

particles to know whether they produce warming or cooling of the earth's surface. Therefore we recommended studies to determine their characteristics, as well as their sources, transport processes, size distributions, and concentrations in the atmosphere.

- As expected, SCEP's findings concerning the SST received the most public attention. We examined the Federal Aviation Administration's estimates of the effects of 500 SSTs being operational in 1985, flying at 65,000 feet for seven hours a day. Such a fleet would consume sixty million tons of fuel a year. SCEP's meteorologists, atmospheric chemists, and other experts considered the duration that the gases and particles produced by jet exhaust remain in the stratosphere — about two years. Then we looked for a yardstick. The only one we could find was the volcanic eruption in Bali in 1963. We thought it might be possible that such a fleet of 500 SSTs could create similar effects and these might disturb the climate significantly, especially in the Northern Hemisphere, the region of highest traffic density. Hence, we recommended that uncertainties about SST contamination and its effects be resolved before large-scale operation of SSTs begins, and that a program to measure and monitor the impact of the SST on the stratosphere be made as soon as possible.

- The ecological effects of DDT were found to be globally distributed. Pest control in crops generally requires continued and increased use of different and stronger pesticides. This is the result of a complex ecological system in which a reduction of one pest and of several predators (innocuous to man) allows new pests to become dominant. DDT also can have specific effects on species other than pests. For example, the eggshells of many birds are becoming thinner, reducing hatching success, and in several species these effects now seriously threaten reproductive capabilities. In an ecological system, damage to these predators tends to create a situation in which pest outbreaks are likely to occur. SCEP recommended a drastic reduction of the use of DDT as soon as possible and urged that subsidies be furnished to developing countries to enable them to use non-persistent but more expensive pesticides and

other pest control techniques. We also proposed a greatly expanded effort in research and development of integrated pest control, combining minimum use of pesticides with maximum use of biological control, and greatly increased financial support for that effort.

- As to the amount of oil in the oceans, we guessed that it might be two to five million tons. This is a very small percentage of the amount that is carried by tanker, but in absolute amounts it is large. We don't know where it goes; we don't know what it does. But we do know that in the few cases where spills have been closely monitored the effect on bottom life has been severe. SCEP recommended a much greater study of oil spills. We also urged that the load-on-top procedure of tankers be used universally — a move recently supported by the U.S. Secretary of Transportation. An estimated 80 per cent of the tanker fleet that now practices this method dumps 30,000 tons of oil into the sea each year; the 20 per cent that doesn't dumps an estimated 500,000 tons each year.

- Many heavy metals are highly toxic to specific life stages of a variety of organisms, especially shellfish. Most are concentrated in terrestrial and marine organisms by factors ranging from a few hundred to several hundred thousand times the concentrations in the surrounding environment. The major sources of mercury are industrial processes and biocides. Although the use of mercury in biocides is relatively small, it is a direct input into the environment. There are many other possible routes, but scanty data exist about the rates of release to the environment.

SCEP recommended 1) that pesticidal and biocidal uses of mercury should continue to be drastically curtailed, particularly where safer, less persistent substitutes can be used; 2) that industrial wastes and emissions of mercury should be controlled and recovered to the greatest extent possible, using available control and recovery methods; and 3) that world production, uses, and waste products should be carefully monitored.

- Eutrophication of waters through over-fertilization (principally with nitrogen and phosphorus) produces an excess of organic

Computer Simulation of Pollution Limit
to World Growth

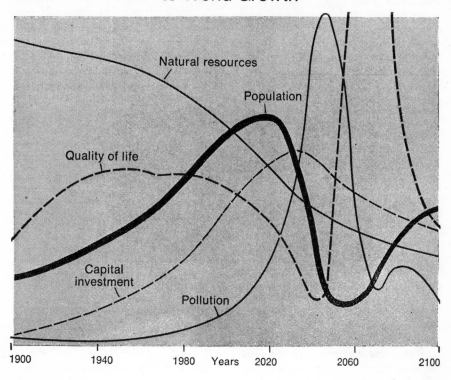

Figure 1. Modern life has become so complex that man is no longer able to forecast the long-term consequences of his policies and activities. At MIT, a program directed by Professor Jay W. Forrester is using computer simulation models to study the dynamic behavior of interacting systems and how they would react to certain policy changes. The simulation above shows what might happen if capital investment were increased now by 20 per cent in an effort to reverse a decline in the quality of life. The pollution crisis worsens when the upsurge of industrialization overtaxes the environment before a depletion of natural resources has a chance to depress industrialization. An apparently desirable change in policy has caused unexpected consequences. The quality of life continues to decline until rising pollution and other factors produce a drop in total population and an increase in the availability of goods and services.

matter that decomposes, removes oxygen, and kills fish. Estuaries increasingly are being eutrophied. Pollution of in-shore regions eliminates the nursery grounds of fish, including many commercial species that inhabit the oceans.

Most (probably between 60 per cent and 70 per cent) of the phosphorus causing over-enrichment of water bodies comes from municipal wastes. In the United States about 75 per cent of the total phosphorus in these waters comes from detergents. Urban and rural land runoff contributes the remainder (approximately 30 per cent to 40 per cent). A major contributor is runoff from feed lots, manured lands, and eroding soil.

Trends in both nutrient use and loss are rising. Fertilizer consumption is expected to increase greatly in both developed and developing countries in the next decade, increasing the nutrient runoff from agricultural lands. Concentration of animal production will continue with

the result that losses of nutrients from feed-lot runoff will quadruple by 2000. Urban waste production is expected to quadruple by 2000, which means greater potential loss of nutrients directly into coastal waters.

We should develop and apply technology to reclaim and recycle nutrients in areas of high concentrations, such as sewage treatment plants and feed lots. We also should avoid use of nutrients in products that are discharged in large quantities into air or water. For example, reformulate detergents to eliminate or reduce waste phosphates, but be certain the substitutes degrade and do not poison the ecosystem. Finally, there should be control of nutrient discharges in natural regions, such as river basins, estuaries, and coastal oceans, through appropriate institutions.

- To prevent further deterioration of the biosphere, and to repair some of the present damage, action is urgently needed. In addition to a variety of specific recommendations such as those accompanying the specific problem areas, SCEP recommends that the following activities be developed in national and international programs:

1. *Technology Assessment:* An information center that centralizes data on products of industry and agriculture, especially new products and new increases in production. Such a center should also identify potentially hazardous materials and promote research on their toxicity and persistence in nature.
2. *Environmental Assessment:* Another information facility that centralizes data on the distributions of pollutants, and on the health and pollution loads of organisms.
3. *Problem Evaluation:* A think center to evaluate problems on the basis of the above information, to determine the urgency for action, and to identify options. Developing controls presents a most complex challenge. Efforts must be carefully evaluated in terms of their impact upon such elements as population, natural resources, and capital investment. The interaction of these factors, particularly how adjustments in one alter the others, is the topic of a most important study directed by Professor Jay W. Forrester of MIT. (See Figure 1.)
4. *Public Education:* A service center to present the results in simple form and to distribute such materials to educational institutions and news media.

The existence of global pollution does not imply the need for a global solution. The activities of man that befoul his environment may often be effectively regulated wherever they occur. Most corrective action will probably have to be taken at national, regional, or local levels. At the same time, it is not enough for the United States, or any single nation, to exercise control. If other nations pollute our common resources of the air and the oceans, the perils remain. Research and development programs offer a great potential for international cooperation, and this could increase the likelihood of smooth international relations should a global pollution problem ever demand strict international regulation or control. The U.N. Conference on Man and the Environment, which will take place in Stockholm in 1972, is an ideal world forum for a serious deliberation of these issues.

61. ENVIRONMENTAL EDUCATION AND CITIZEN RESPONSIBILITY

CITIZENS' ADVISORY COMMITTEE ON ENVIRONMENTAL QUALITY

Citizen concern over the quality of our environment is not a transitory phenomenon. It was long in coming, is decidedly here to stay, and will grow stronger with the passage of time.

Only a few years ago the word "ecology" was little heard of. As it had been since the turn of the century, environmental quality was the concern of a relatively small number of individuals, and they were interested primarily in the preservation of natural resources. Much was accomplished: the preservation and management of timber, range, and water in the national forests; establishment of national parks, parkways and trails, historic sites and national wildlife refuges.

CITIZEN CONCERN

But now there is a greatly broadened interest. The total environment has become the cause, and in this more embracing concept the emphasis is increasingly on the delicate relationship between people and resources. The mass media have grasped the connection and have elevated environment to a prime human interest topic: witness the massive coverage given the proposed Alaskan pipeline, the SST, and mercury contamination in seafood.

The change in public attitudes has been dramatic. A recent poll indicates that Americans now rank pollution as the number one problem facing their local communities, and favor increasing governmental and citizen action. Indeed, during the last two years, thousands of citizen groups have emerged to lend their efforts to the battle for environmental quality.

But when it gets down to specifics, let it be noted, citizens can be inconsistent. "Popular" attitudes toward electric power and water consumption, for example, have surely complicated the energy and water pollution problems facing this country. The poor response to campaigns for recycling the "returnable" container is another

Extracted with permission from "Report to the President and to the Council on Environmental Quality" by the Citizens' Advisory Committee on Environmental Quality, 56 p., April 1971, Washington, D.C.

example; still another is the response to local anti-litter laws, that demand little and too often receive inadequate cooperation. The Committee believes that a nationwide education campaign aimed at the reduction of waste of all types would be a valuable contribution to environmental quality.

The best way to spur action by citizens is to involve them in the decision-making processes. We would urge more consumer-oriented organizations like that of The Environmental Defense Fund, and even ad hoc, single-purpose groups created to challenge public or private action posing a threat to the environment.

FEDERAL PROGRAMS

Federal environmental education programs can help greatly. To date, most of the federal activity has been under the aegis of legislation for Office of Education programs. With the enactment in 1970 of the National Environmental Education Act, a strong new impetus has been added. The Act authorizes grants and contracts to institutions of higher education, state and local educational agencies, regional educational research organizations, and nonprofit public and private agencies such as libraries and museums. Through these grants and contracts, eligible organizations can develop programs, and provide public information, technical assistance, and both pre-service and in-service training for teachers and other public service personnel. Small grants may be awarded to citizens' organizations and volunteer groups for a variety of adult education programs. To provide a coordinating agency for federal programs, the Act establishes an Office of Environmental Education in the Office of Education.

We urge full implementation of the Act as soon as feasible. We also urge increased use of Title III funds for pilot environmental education programs, including evaluation of the programs to determine which approaches are worth widespread adoption.

Other federal programs deserve commendation. The National Park Service of the Interior Department has developed two model environmental education programs, NEED and NESA, aimed at elementary and high school students. The Agriculture Department's Cooperative Extension Service and the Forest Service have initiated a number of environmental education projects. The National Science Foundation has financed several successful environmental curriculum development programs.

The newly authorized Youth Conservation Corps, to be administered by the Departments of Interior and Agriculture, will provide good training and at the same time provide vital manpower for many necessary projects.

PRIVATE EFFORTS

Many environmental education programs are being conducted by conservation groups, citizen organizations, corporations, and by business and professional groups. Time and again groups have formed around a particular environmental issue with the aim of urging the public to action. Consumer education groups, perhaps, constitute the most striking example of this.

Valuable as the private programs have been, however, there have not been enough of them, nor have they been meshed sufficiently with one another. We believe that there ought to be much stronger information campaigns via all media.

How-to information for citizens is too often scattered, overlapping, incomplete, and sometimes nonexistent. A good base for an adequate program, we believe, would be a national clearinghouse for environmental information, coupled with a well-advertised outreach mechanism to the people.

During the coming year, the Committee plans to expand its contacts with citizen groups with the dual purpose of encouraging their efforts and obtaining as broad a cross section as possible of citizen thinking.

Corporations have been enlisting in the environmental cause. Here are some of the ways:

- Participation in joint industry-governmental projects, such as the Commerce Department's advisory National Industrial Pollution Control Council, the Defense Department's Jobs for Veterans program, and the Electric Utility Industry Task Force on Environment set up by the Citizen's Advisory Committee.

- Industrial and business sponsorship of citizen education programs about the environment. A good example is the Xerox Corporation's television series, "Mission: Possible," and their publicizing of the Committee's citizen action guide.

- Industry-wide programs to develop pollution abatement technology, to deal with waste products. The efforts of the American Paper Institute and others, to spur the recycling of paper, newspapers and magazines, are an example.

- Voluntary action taken by business firms, such as programs of oil companies to reduce visual pollution at service stations.

Positive governmental incentives to encourage industrial responsibility include: channeling more funds to spur industrial housecleaning programs; offering tax incentives; underwriting research and development work in the field of pollution abatement; and eliminating certain legal barriers to large scale cooperative efforts by corporations for cleaning up the environment.

It is obvious that some of the corporate embraces of the environment have been self-serving public relations and little else. To spur a more complete conversion, governmental sanctions must be used also. Enforcement of existing regulations and enactment of new legislation or executive action designed to curb certain corporate practices would be in order, as would imposing penalty taxes or fines on and requiring full disclosure of corporate practices and products considered detrimental to the environment. User fees, licensing powers, and selective government procurement practices can also exert beneficial leverage.

ENVIRONMENTAL RESEARCH

On some environmental problems not enough is known for effective action. In too many cases, a problem has been attacked without concern for its relationship with other problems. As a consequence, one kind of pollution may unwittingly be traded off for another; a dam built to solve a water supply problem may create worse problems for the overall ecology.

A group of top level scientists who met on environmental problems reported that:

> . . . In the process of making judgments we found that critically needed data were fragmentary, contradictory, and in some cases completely unavailable. This

was true for all types of data — scientific, technical, economic, industrial, and social : . .

They proposed that an institute be set up to tackle such problems.

The President has announced the creation of such a mechanism — the Environmental Institute. It will be supported by both public and private financing, and will conduct both basic and applied research on environmental quality problems.

To supplement the work of the Institute, the Committee suggests increased federal support of university-based environmental research and demonstration programs. Such action, we feel, would allow the much needed talents of our scientific community — in the past heavily involved in aerospace and defense-related research — to turn their skills to environmental problems.

LOW COST PROGRAMS

Many of the action programs recommended can yield large benefits, yet involve little or no additional federal expenditures:

- Support of federal and state regulation, enforcement, and research, with emphasis on air and solid waste pollution.

- Strengthening of the Council on Environmental Quality review procedure under Section 102 of the National Environmental Quality Act of 1970 for federal agency activities affecting the environment. New legislation and additional funding should be sought if necessary to make the procedure more effective. Careful review of proposed projects can produce outright budget savings. Establishment by states and cities of review procedures analogous to those of Section .102 would produce comparable benefits to environmental quality.

- Encouragement of effective land-use planning at all levels of government.

- Increasing attention to the problems of population growth and distribution; and expansion of programs of family planning education, information, and action.

- Stimulation of efforts by private industry.

- Increasing use of federal government procurement policies to force compliance with environmental quality standards and programs on the part of sellers of goods and services.

- Conscientious exercise of the federal licensing power to protect and enhance environmental quality, through such agencies as the Federal Power Commission, Atomic Energy Commission, Corps of Engineers, Forest Service, and Bureau of Land Management.

- Application of the currently underutilized portion of the nation's advanced technology and manpower base — such as the capabilities of the hard hit aerospace industry and the potential of returning veterans — to the problems of air, water, and solid waste management and control.

62. ENVIRONMENTAL SCIENCE: CHALLENGE FOR THE SEVENTIES

NATIONAL SCIENCE BOARD

Modern civilization has reached the stage where, henceforth, no new use of technology, no increased demands on the environment for food, for other natural resources, for areas to be used for recreation, or for places to store the debris of civilization, can be undertaken to benefit some groups of individuals without a high risk of injury to others. No environmental involvement of man can any longer be regarded as all good or all bad. Problems can be mitigated, but absolute solutions are probably unattainable. The best that can be sought, therefore, is to optimize, to try to achieve the wisest cost-benefit decision for society for each action contemplated. Such a strategy requires a strong base of scientific knowledge and understanding of the environment, ability to predict reliably its future course, and, especially, the ability to construct models through systems analysis of the environment and of man's interaction with it on a scale never previously achieved.

It is within this perspective that the present status of Environmental Science has been examined. *Environmental Science is conceived in this report as the study of all of the systems of air, land, water, energy, and life that surround man. It includes all science directed to the system-level of understanding of the environment, drawing especially on such disciplines as meteorology, geophysics, oceanography, and ecology, and utilizing to the fullest the knowledge and techniques developed in such fields as physics, chemistry, biology, mathematics, and engineering.* Included, therefore, are such diverse matters as climate, air turbulence, the air-sea interface, estuaries, forests, epidemics, earthquakes, and groundwater. These environmental systems contain the complex processes that must be mastered in the solution of such human problems as the maintenance of renewable resources (water, timber, fish), the conservation of nonrenewable resources (fuel, metals, species),

Extracted from "Environmental Science: Challenge for the Seventies" report of the National Science Board, 50 p., 1971. U.S. Government Printing Office, Washington, D.C.

reducing the effects of natural disasters (earthquakes, tornadoes, floods), alleviating chronic damage (erosion, drought, subsidence), abating pollution by man (smoke, pesticides, sewage), and coping with natural pollution (allergens, volcanic dust, electromagnetic "noise").

Environmental Science is now exceedingly vigorous, considered in relation to its development over many centuries. Notable advances are being recorded at an accelerating rate. New tools and techniques, borrowed from all of science and technology, are being brought to bear on the problems of observation, measurement, and analysis. Across all of environmental science there is a heightened awareness of the essential nature of the environment and the directions that scientific effort should take. Nevertheless — and it is the principal conclusion of this report —

> Environmental science, today, is unable to match the needs of society for definitive information, predictive capability, and the analysis of environmental systems as systems. Because existing data and current theoretical models are inadequate, environmental science remains unable in virtually all areas of application to offer more than qualitative interpretations or suggestions of environmental change that may occur in response to specific actions.

There are two primary reasons for this state of affairs. One involves the nature of environmental science itself, the other the resources available for its advancement.

1. The natural environment is not a collection of isolated events and phenomena, but rather a vast, integral, mutually interacting system. The recent advent of new technology and technique (satellites, advanced computers, instrumentation of many types, and the methods of systems analysis) for the use of environmental science has, indeed for the first time, provided feasibility for attacking the scientific problems that this environ-

mental system presents. The tasks ahead, however, are of unprecedented magnitude and difficulty.

2. The trained scientific manpower available to meet this challenge is extremely limited in each of the essential aspects of environmental science. More serious is the fact that this manpower is spread exceedingly thin, both with respect to the manifold problems presented and to the institutions within which research is conducted, new scientists are educated, and scientific results are applied to the solution of problems of the public interest. Indeed, the institutions of environmental science, as here defined, remain in an early stage of development.

This situation constitutes a crisis for the nation. While environmental problems are so diverse and diffused that virtually every activity of civilization interacts with the environment, few persons can be aware of the full scope of challenge that lies ahead. The current mismatch between capability and need is at least comparable to any other challenge to science and technology that was encountered during this century.

To meet this situation the National Science Board offers five groups of recommendations:

1. NATIONAL PROGRAM

Several factors emphasize the urgency of establishing a national program for advancing the science of environmental systems: (a) New organizations formed at the highest level of the federal government, the Council on Environmental Quality and the Environmental Protection Agency, have been charged with responsibilities that include the assessment of the environmental impact of civilized man. These agencies must foresee secondary effects and compare quantitatively the multiple consequences of alternative courses of action. Such efforts are severely limited by the present level of understanding of the behavior of environmental systems. They would become progressively more feasible as advances in environmental science increase man's predictive power. (b) The use of energy and the processing of material by man are doubling every 14 years.* Correspondingly, the number and

severity of environmental problems will increase, while the adequacy of *ad hoc* piecemeal expedients will decrease. (c) As population grows, and with it the artifacts of civilization, the human and economic losses due to sporadic natural disasters, already great, will increase in scale. (d) At the same time, the intensification of man's needs for both renewable and nonrenewable resources requires even greater manipulation and mastery of the natural and man-made systems that constitute the environment.

It is, therefore, recommended that this urgency be recognized through the early development of a comprehensive national program to expedite the progress of environmental science.

The problems with which environmental science must deal, however, do not respect local, state, or even national boundaries. It is thus further recommended that this national program explicitly provide for the essential federal role in encouraging and supporting the work of environmental science, quite apart from the role the federal government is already exercising with respect to improving and protecting the environment (e.g., programs of soil conservation, sewage treatment, air and water pollution control, etc.). Both nationally and in matters of international cooperation the federal government must assume leadership in fostering scientific advance.

This national program should be based on three efforts:

1. Emphasis should be given to projects, manned by coordinate teams, directed to intermediate scale or "mesoscale" problems, that is, problems on the scale of lakes and estuaries, urban areas, regional weather systems, and oceanic fisheries. Advances on this scale will provide immediate benefits to man.

2. At the same time, the program must ensure continued effort on global problems, even though their solution may require the resolution of smaller scale issues. In the long run it is the global constraints that will shape and delimit the future development of civilization.

3. Finally, the program should ensure the

*Both activities have shown 5% average annual growth rates for the last 20 years, as reported in *Man's Impact on the Global Environment: Assessment and Recommendations for Action,* MIT Press, Cambridge, Mass., 1970. The total consumption of fossil fuel in the

United States also grows about 5% per year; the conversion of an increasing fraction of fossil energy to electrical energy leads to a higher annual growth rate in the utilities.

continued vigor of those aspects of disciplinary research and graduate education needed to provide the specialists and new knowledge required for environmental science.

The remaining recommendations form an important part of the total recommendation of a national program. The entire program should be established at the earliest practicable date, if progress during this decade and its culmination during the following decades are to be commensurate with the urgency now faced.

2. PRIORITIES

One of the inescapable conclusions of this report is that the number and complexity of scientific problems, both theoretical and experimental, that confront environmental science far exceed the capability of available manpower to attack all of them effectively at the same time. If these resources remain distributed as they are, scattered and fragmented, and if problems to be solved are selected largely on the basis of the perceptions of individuals or small isolated groups, progress in environmental science cannot meet the needs of expressed national goals and purposes.

Accordingly, it is recommended that early consideration be given to strengthening arrangements whereby priorities for environmental science can be set, matched to existing and required scientific and engineering manpower, and changed as circumstances warrant. In setting such priorities appropriate weight must be given to the feasibility of achieving scientific solutions in a reasonable time and to the social and economic costs and benefits that could accrue if solutions were attained.

3. ORGANIZATION FOR ENVIRONMENTAL SCIENCE

The scope encompassed by the national program, proposed above, the federal role inherent in this broad effort, and the patent need for establishing priorities raise serious questions of the adequacy of present arrangements within the federal government for planning, coordinating, managing, and reviewing programs of environmental science. As for all science, environmental science today is the responsibility of many agencies, often with conflicting interest under differing agency missions and responsive to many Congressional committees. At the same time the problems to be solved are broader, more

difficult, and more dependent upon the coordinated use of scientific resources than those faced in the earlier development of nuclear energy, radar, and space exploration.

For these reasons, it is strongly urged that the federal responsibility for environmental science, and for its promotion, organization, and support, be considered as important as the corresponding but separate responsibility for environmental quality. In particular, arrangements for federal decision-making must be especially effective for the following activities:

1. The setting of priorities affecting all research and development in environmental science supported by the federal government.

2. The determination of appropriate and feasible time schedules for the projects of the national program and ensuring that projects are managed in accordance with such schedules.

3. The provision of full coordination of the efforts of all federal agencies engaged in the support or performance of research in environmental science, quite apart from efforts in application or regulation.

4. The establishment of organizational and employment incentives suitable for the types of projects that are characteristic of environmental science through the support of national centers and specialized institutes.

5. The encouragement of state and local governments and private supporting organizations to subscribe to the national program, as it is developed, and to the pattern of priorities adopted.

With respect to the organizations where the work of environmental science is done, several considerations are of the greatest importance.

Environmental science, as defined in this report, should be viewed as a distinctive type of activity lying between the extremes of traditional, basic science, on the one hand, and the organizations established by society for the application and use of science and technology. It shares the scientific motivations of the former and the multidisciplinary and organizational complexity of the latter.

Various types of organizational structures should thus be attempted, as experiments in the management of environmental science. Two conclusions are especially important:

a. In academic institutions, which employ two-thirds of the manpower in environmental science, the need for strong departmental structures has historically hindered the development of effective interdepartmental programs. Within the last few years, however, new capability and experience in systems management, often combined with central funding for complex problems, have given a new vitality to multidisciplinary efforts. A few research institutes and national laboratories have also begun ambitious multidisciplinary studies of environmental problems. These experiments in organization should be continued, expanded, and followed closely.

b. Industry possesses great capability in systems analysis and systems management, but rarely offers the broad array of scientific competence needed in environmental science. Government has additional strengths, particularly in the application of environmental science to environmental management. A more effective use of these resources can be made by combining the talents of industry, government, and universities in new types of research organizations and by seeking new approaches to the management of environmental science.

4. FUNDING FOR ENVIRONMENTAL SCIENCE

If progress in environmental science is to be made at an acceptable rate it is essential that additional manpower be made available both through education and through transfer from other fields and activities. This will occur only if appropriate employment opportunities and incentives are provided. The character of funding is especially important to this end.

In addition to the opportunity provided by new types of organizations, as recommended above, provision should be made for continuity of funding of programs of environmental science as being one of the principal means for attracting the best talent.

It is further recommended that the funding of equipment, facilities, and logistics for environmental science be consistent with scientific needs and opportunities. The highest priority should be given to the needs of multidisciplinary teams engaged in the study of environmental systems.

5. DEVELOPMENT OF ADDITIONAL MANPOWER

While it is essential that the disciplinary strength of academic institutions be maintained and increased across all fields of science, these institutions also have a responsibility specifically with respect to the manpower of environmental science.

Although competent specialists transferring from related disciplines can constructively enter fields of environmental science through on-the-job training, the process can often be faster and more effective if retraining opportunities are available within the educational context. Hence, it is recommended that colleges and universities consider appropriate means for supplementary education in environmental science for scientific and technical personnel.

Of special importance to implementing a national program for environmental science is the existence of an informed citizenry, both as a source of future scientists and as the necessary basis for national understanding and motivation of the entire program. The colleges and universities thus have a special opportunity to contribute by the development of new curricula in which to present the perspective of environmental science, as well as of new courses and programs, especially directed to the undergraduate.

Manpower needs related to environmental science are not confined to the scientists, engineers, technicians, and others who contribute to scientific progress. As environmental science advances, there will be an increasing need for "natural resource administrators" to serve in local, state, or federal governments. The education of these public administrators involves two types of interdisciplinary training. On the one hand, scientists and engineers must gain a better understanding of the social, economic, legal, and political environment within which practical action must be sought. On the other hand, students of public administration must gain a better perception of the scientific process and a better understanding of how scientists can contribute effectively to the practical solution of environmental problems. It is recommended that substantial and adequate funding be made available for these purposes.

Even with the implementation of these recommendations only gradual progress can be anticipated. Environmental science is too diffi-cult, too broad in scope, and too near the beginning for an effective match with societal need to be achieved during this decade. But, correspondingly, the stakes are too high to miss the opportunity for making the 1970s the base on which a constructive future for mankind will be established.

APPENDIX I

THE GEOLOGIC TIME CHART

Era	Period	Epoch	Duration (Millions of years)	Millions of years before present
CENOZOIC	Quaternary	Holocene Pleistocene	2	
				— 2 —
	Tertiary	Pliocene Miocene Oligocene Eocene Paleocene	63	
				— 65 —
MESOZOIC	Cretaceous		70	
				— 135 —
	Jurassic		55	
				— 190 —
	Triassic		35	
				— 225 —
PALEOZOIC	Permian		55	
				— 280 —
	Pennsylvanian		40	
				— 320 —
	Mississippian		25	
				— 345 —
	Devonian		55	
				— 400 —
	Silurian		40	
				— 440 —
	Ordovician		60	
				— 500 —
	Cambrian		70	
				— 570 —
PRECAMBRIAN ERAS	No widely recognized period names		4130	
				— 4700 —

APPENDIX II

MATHEMATICAL INFORMATION

Prefixes For International System of Units

Multiples and Submultiples	Prefixes	Symbols
$1{,}000{,}000 = 10^6$	mega	M
$1{,}000 = 10^3$	kilo	k
$100 = 10^2$	hecto	h
$10 = 10$	deka	da
$0.1 = 10^{-1}$	deci	d
$0.01 = 10^{-2}$	centi	c
$0.001 = 10^{-3}$	milli	m
$0.000001 = 10^{-6}$	micro	μ

Units of Measure

Linear Measure

1 mile (mi)	= 5280 feet (ft)		1 kilometer (km)	= 1000 meters (m)	
1 chain (ch)	= 66 ft		1 km	= 10^3 m	
1 rod (rd)	= 16.5 ft		1 centimeter (cm)	= 0.01 m = 10^{-2} m	
1 fathom (fm)	= 6 ft		1 millimeter (mm)	= 0.001 m = 10^{-3} m	
1 nautical mile	= 6076.115 ft		1 angstrom (Å)	= 0.0000000001 m = 10^{-10} m	
			1 micron (μ)	= 0.001 mm	

Area Measure

1 square mile	=	640 acres
1 acre	=	43,560 square feet
1 acre	=	4,840 square yards
1 acre	=	160 square rods
1 mile square	=	1 section
6 miles square	=	1 township
1 square meter	=	10,000 square centimeters (cm)
100 square meters	=	1 are (a)
100 ares	=	1 hectare (ha)
100 hectares	=	1 square kilometer

Volume and Cubic Measure

1 quart	= 2 pints = 57.75 cubic inches
4 quarts	= 1 gallon = 231 cubic inches
1 cubic foot	= 1,728 cubic inches
1 cubic yard	= 27 cubic feet
1 barrel (oil)	= 42 gallons
1 barrel (proof spirits)	= 40 gallons
1 cubic foot	= 7.48 gallons
1 cubic inch	= 0.554 fluid ounce
1 gallon (U.S.)	= 128 U.S. fluid ounces = 0.833 British gallon
1 liter	= 0.001 cubic meter = 1 cubic decimeter
1 liter	= 1,000 milliliters
10 milliliters	= 1 centiliter
1 milliliter	= approximately 1 cubic centimeter (cc)
1 cubic meter (m^3)	= 1,000,000 cubic centimeters

Weights and Masses

1 short ton	= 2,000 pounds
1 long ton	= 2,240 pounds
1 pound (avoirdupois)	= 7,000 grains
1 ounce (avoirdupois)	= 437.5 grains
1 gram	= 15.432 grains
1,000 grams	= 1 kilogram
1,000 kilograms	= 1 metric ton

Force

1 dyne (d) = the force that will produce an acceleration of 1 centimeter/second^2 when applied to a 1-gram mass

1 newton (nt) = the force that will produce an acceleration of 1 meter/second^2 when applied to a 1-kilogram mass.

1 nt = 100,000 d = 1 × 10^{5}d

Energy and Power

1 erg = the work done by a force of 1 dyne when its point of application moves through a distance of 1 centimeter in the direction of the force.

1 erg = 9.48 × 10^{-11} British thermal unit (BTU)
1 erg = 7.367 × 10^{-8} foot-pounds
1 erg = 2.778 × 10^{-14} kilowatt-hours
1 kilowatt-hour = 3,413 BTU = 3.6 × 10^{13} ergs
1 BTU = 2.928 × 10^{-4} kilowatt-hours = 1.0548 × 10^{10} ergs
1 watt = 3.4129 BTU/hour
1 watt = 1.341 × 10^{-3} horsepower
1 watt = 1 joule per second
1 watt = 14.34 calories per minute
1 joule = 1 × 10^7 ergs
1 joule = 1 newton-meter

Heat

1 calorie (cal) = the amount of heat that will raise the temperature of 1 gram of water 1 degree Celsius with the water at 4 degrees Celsius.

1 calorie (gram) = 3.9685 × 10^{-3} BTU = 4.186 × 10^7 ergs

Pressure

1 millibar (mb) = 1000 dynes per cm^2

Additional Conversions

1 gallon of water = 8.3453 pounds of water
1 gallon per minute = 8.0208 cubic feet per minute
1 acre-foot = 1,233.46 m^3

Temperature

To change from Fahrenheit (F) to Celsius (C)

$$°C = \frac{(°F-32°)}{1.8}$$

To change from Celsius (C) to Fahrenheit (F)

$$°F = (°C × 1.8) + 32°$$

English-Metric Conversions

1 inch	= 25.4 millimeters
1 foot	= 0.3048 meter
1 yard	= 0.9144 meter
1 mile	= 1.609 kilometers
1 square inch	= 6.4516 square centimeters
1 square foot	= 0.0929 square meter
1 square yard	= 0.836 square meter
1 acre	= 0.4047 hectare
1 cubic inch	= 16.39 cubic centimeters
1 cubic foot	= 0.0283 cubic meter
1 cubic yard	= 0.7646 cubic meter
1 quart (liq)	= 0.946 liter
1 gallon (U.S.)	= 0.003785 cubic meter
1 ounce (avdp)	= 28.35 grams
1 pound (avdp)	= 0.4536 kilogram
1 horsepower	= 0.7457 kilowatt

Metric-English Conversions

1 millimeter	= 0.0394 inch
1 meter	= 3.281 feet
1 meter	= 1.094 yards
1 kilometer	= 0.6214 mile
1 sq centimeter	= 0.155 sq inch
1 sq meter	= 10.764 sq feet
1 sq meter	= 1.196 sq yards
1 hectare	= 2.471 acres
1 cu centimeter	= 0.061 cu inch
1 cu meter	= 35.3 cu feet
1 cu meter	= 1.308 cu yards
1 liter	= 1.057 quarts
1 cu meter	= 264.2 gallons (U.S.)
1 gram	= 0.0353 ounce (avdp)
1 kilogram	= 2.205 pounds (avdp)
1 kilowatt	= 1.341 horsepower

APPENDIX III

GLOSSARY OF SELECTED
ENVIRONMENTAL AND GEOLOGIC TERMS

ACID MINE DRAINAGE. Drainage with a low pH (2-4.5) from mines. Pyrite (FeS_2) in mines is oxidized by oxygen or ferric iron to produce ferrous sulfate and sulfuric acid. At low pH, heavy metals such as iron, magnesium, manganese, copper, zinc, and calcium are more soluble and further pollute the water.

ACTIVATED SLUDGE. A process that removes organic matter from sewage by saturating it with air and biologically active sludge.

AD VALOREM TAXES. Taxes in proportion to estimated value of goods.

AEROBIC. Pertaining to organisms which live or are active only in the presence of oxygen.

AFTERSHOCK. An earthquake which follows a larger earthquake. A series of aftershocks, which originate at or near the focus of the larger earthquake, generally follow a major earthquake and decrease in frequency with time.

AGGREGATE. Uncrushed or crushed gravel, crushed stone or rock, sand, or artificially produced inorganic materials, which form the major part of concrete.

AIRBORNE MAGNETOMETER. An instrument carried by an aircraft which is used to measure variations in the earth's magnetic field.

ALLUVIUM. A general term for all sediment deposited in land environments by streams.

ALPHA PARTICLE. A type of particle involved in radioactivity which is identical with the nucleus of an atom of helium, consisting of 2 protons and 2 neutrons and therefore having a double positive charge.

AMPLITUDE. 1) The extent of vibratory movement of oscillation. 2) The elevation of the crest of a wave above the adjacent troughs.

ANAEROBIC. Pertaining to organisms which live or are active in the absence of free oxygen.

ANHYDRITE. A mineral, $CaSO_4$, anhydrous calcium sulfate, common in evaporite beds.

ANION. A negative ion.

ANTHRACITE. Coal containing a high percentage of fixed carbon and a low percentage of volatile matter, commonly called "hard coal" and generally formed as a result of metamorphism of bituminous coal.

AQUICLUDE. A rock formation which, although porous and capable of absorbing water slowly, will not transmit it rapidly enough to furnish an appreciable supply of water for a well or spring.

AQUIFER. Permeable rock strata below the surface through which ground water moves, which is generally capable of producing water for a well.

ARTESIAN. Refers to ground water which is under sufficient pressure to rise above the aquifer containing it.

ASBESTOS. 1) Fibrous minerals used for their resistance to heat and chemical attack. 2) Fibrous variety of amphibole, usually tremolite or actinolite, or of chrysotile, the fibrous variety of serpentine.

ASH (VOLCANIC). The finest rock material derived from volcanic explosions. Less than 4 mm in grain size.

ATOMIC ENERGY (NUCLEAR ENERGY). The energy liberated by a nuclear reaction (fission or fusion) or by radioactive decay.

AVALANCHE. A large mass of snow or ice and accompanying materials moving rapidly down a steep slope.

BARREL (OIL). A volumetric unit of measurement equivalent to 42 U.S. gallons.

BARRIER BAR. An elongate ridge of sand and gravel which parallels the coast and is submerged at least at high tide.

BASALT. A fine-grained, dark-colored igneous rock which is generally of extrusive origin.

BEDDING. A term which signifies the existence of beds (strata) or laminae in rocks which are generally of sedimentary origin.

BEDROCK. Continuous solid rock that outcrops at the surface locally but generally is overlain by unconsolidated material.

BENCH. A name applied to ledges that are shaped like steps or terraces cut into the side of hills in the removal of coal.

BENCH MARK. A permanent marker which designates a point of known elevation.

BENTONITE. A clay formed from the decomposition of volcanic ash. Bentonite commonly has great ability to absorb water and to swell accordingly. It is usually white to light green in color, but light blue when fresh.

BIOCIDE. Any agent that kills organisms.

BIODEGRADABLE. An organic substance that is quickly broken down by normal environmental processes.

BIOGEOCHEMISTRY. The science dealing with the relation of earth chemicals to plant and animal life.

BIOSPHERE. The zone at and adjacent to the earth's surface where all life exists; all living organisms on the earth.

BITUMINOUS COAL. Firm soft coal that breaks into blocks and contains alternating layers with bright and dull lusters. It is mined in the Appalachian Plateau and Illinois Basin areas and is the type of coal which furnishes much of the world's heat energy.

BORAX. A mineral, $Na_2B_4O_7.10H_2O$, an ore of boron.

BRACKISH. Term which is applied to water which is intermediate in salinity between that of fresh water streams and sea water; it is slightly salty.

BRECCIA. A general term for a rock made up of coarse angular fragments as distinguished from conglomerate which is composed of rounded rock fragments. There are sedimentary as well as volcanic and other types of breccia.

BREEDER REACTOR. A reactor that produces fissionable fuel as well as consuming it, especially one that creates more than it consumes. The new fissionable material is created by capture in fertile materials (uranium-238 or thorium-232) of neutrons from fission.

BRINE. Water which is saturated or nearly saturated with salt.

CALCAREOUS. Containing calcium carbonate.

CALCINATION. A heat treatment to which many ceramic raw materials are subjected preparatory to further processing or use, for the purpose of driving off volatile chemically combined components and effecting physical changes.

CAPACITY. The ability of water or wind to transport material, as measured by the quantity that can be carried at any given time.

CAPROCK. Usually has reference to an impermeable rock layer which immediately overlies an aquifer or an oil-or-gas-bearing rock.

CARBONATE. Mineral formed by the combination of the complex ion $(CO_3)^{2-}$ with a positive ion. For example $CaCO_3$.

CATION. A positive ion.

CESIUM-137. A radioisotope recovered as a fission product from nuclear reactors, with a half-life of 33 years and a dominant characteristic radiation of 0.66 million electron volt. Suitable as a gamma-radiation source in radiography.

CHANNELIZATION. Straightening of a stream or construction of a new channel to which the stream is diverted.

CINDER (VOLCANIC). Medium-grained rock material derived from volcanic explosions.

CLAY. The term clay carries three implications. 1) Particles of very fine size, less than 1/256 mm. 2) A natural material with plastic properties. 3) A composition of minerals that are essentially hydrous aluminum silicates.

CLEAVAGE. The capacity of a mineral to break along plane surfaces as determined by the crystal structure.

COLIFORM BACTERIA. A type of bacteria whose presence in water is evidence of contamination by human or animal waste. High coliform levels indicate relatively recent pollution since their survival is short-termed.

COMPOST. A mixing of organic waste materials, i.e., garbage, grass clippings, leaves, etc., with soil in a pile to allow soil bacteria to cause decomposition and thereby return of desirable organic material to the soil.

CONNATE WATER. Water entrapped in the pore spaces of a sedimentary rock at the time the sediment was deposited.

CONTINENTAL SHELF. The gently sloping submerged margins of the continents extending from the shoreline to the first prominent break in slope. The depth of this break in slope on most shelves is less than 600 feet.

CONTOUR STRIPPING. A type of stripping in rolling to steep terrain. Removal of the overburden from the mineral seam starting at the outcrop and proceeding around the hillside. Overburden is deposited on the outer edge of the bench. Successive cuts are made until the depth of overburden becomes too great for economical retrieval of the ore.

CREEP. The imperceptibly slow, more or less continuous downslope movement of regolith.

CRITICAL MASS. The smallest mass of fissionable material that will support a self-sustaining chain reaction under stated conditions.

CRUDE OIL. Natural mixture composed mainly of liquid hydrocarbons. It is the petroleum as it comes from the reservoir rocks, prior to refining.

CRYOGENICS. That part of physics relating to the production and effects of very low temperatures.

CRYSTAL LATTICE. The regular and repeated three-dimensional arrangement of atoms or ions within a crystal.

CRYSTALLINE BASEMENT. The older, generally igneous and metamorphic foundation rocks of a continental mass.

CRYSTALLINE ROCKS. Usually refers to igneous and metamorphic rocks as opposed to sedimentary rocks, but it may also refer to any rock consisting of minerals in an obvious crystalline state.

DDT. A widely used colorless contact insecticide, discovered in 1939 and first used commercially in 1945. DDT remains active in the environment for years, passing from the air and water to plants, animals, and humans.

DARCY'S LAW. The equation for the velocity of flow of ground water which states that in material of given permeability, velocity of flow increases as the slope of the ground water table increases.

DEBRIS FLOW. The rapid downslope plastic flow of a mass of debris.

DEGRADATION. 1) The general lowering of the surface of the land by erosion processes. 2) The excessive crushing of coal during cutting, loading, and transportation.

DELTA PLAIN. Plains formed by the accumulation of fine sediment at the mouth of a stream or by overflow along the lower course of a stream.

DESALINATION (DESALINIZATION). Any process for making potable water from sea water or other saline waters. Includes distillation, electrodialysis, freezing, foam separation, liquid-liquid extraction, ion exchange, and various nonelectric membrane processes.

DESIGN FLOOD. The flood against which a given area is to be protected.

DIATOMACEOUS. Pertaining to, or composed largely of, the remains of microscopic plants called diatoms. These remains are made up of nearly pure silica.

DIFFERENTIAL EROSION. The more rapid erosion of one portion of the earth's surface, or of a rock mass, as compared to another.

DISCHARGE. The amount of water passing a given point in a given unit of time.

DISSOLVED OXYGEN (DO). The extent to which oxygen occurs dissolved in water or wastewater, usually expressed in parts per million or per cent of saturation.

DISSOLVED SOLIDS. Solids which are present in solution.

DISTRIBUTARY. A branch of a stream which is flowing away from the main stream as frequently occurs on a delta. Contrasted with a tributary.

EARTHQUAKE. 1) A local trembling, shaking, undulating, or sudden shock of the surface of the earth, sometimes accompanied by fissuring or by permanent change of level. 2) Groups of elastic waves propagating in the earth, set up by a transient disturbance of the elastic equilibrium of a portion of the earth.

ECOLOGY. Science of the relationship between organisms and their environment.

ECOSYSTEM. An integrated system in nature, sufficient unto itself, to be studied as a separate entity. The system may be a rotting log in the forest, a coral atoll, a continent, or the entire earth with all its biota.

EFFLUENT. The discharge from a relatively self-contained passage, such as from a sewage treatment plant or an industrial smokestack, or a nuclear power plant thermal discharge, generally carrying pollutants.

ELASTIC STRAIN. Deformation per unit of length produced by load on a material, which vanishes with removal of the load.

ENTRENCHED MEANDER. Streams which have reached the advanced stage of one cycle hold their courses in the second cycle and cut down in the old meanders; the result is a meandering stream in a young valley.

ENTROPY. 1) A measure of the unavailable energy in a system, i.e., energy that cannot be converted into another form of energy. 2) A measure of the mixing of different kinds of sediment; high entropy is approach to unmixed sediment of one kind.

ENVIRONMENT. 1) The aggregate of external conditions that influence the life of an individual or population. 2) The aggregate of all the surrounding conditions, influences, or forces affecting a locus of sedimentation.

EPHEMERAL. Short-lived; generally referring to a stream which does not flow continuously, perhaps flowing only in direct response to precipitation.

EPICENTER. The point on the earth's surface directly above an earthquake focus.

EPIDEMIOLOGICAL. Refers to the unarrested spread of something epidemic, as a disease.

EPITHERMAL ORE DEPOSITS. Ore deposits formed in and along fissures or other openings in rocks by deposition at shallow depths from ascending hot solutions.

ESTUARIES. Drainage channels adjacent to the sea, frequently the lower courses of streams, which are subject to the periodic rise and fall of tides.

EUTROPHICATION. An aging process that takes place naturally over a long period of time in lakes. Nutrients entering the water support an increasingly dense growth of aquatic life, which depletes the oxygen supply. The body of water progresses from lake to swamp, to marsh, and may eventually become filled. The process may be greatly accelerated by excessive nutrient enrichment resulting from the activities of man.

EVAPORITE. A sedimentary rock whose constituent minderals were precipitated from aqueous solution as a result of evaporation.

EXCHANGE CAPACITY. The capacity to exchange ions as measured by the quantity of exchangeable ions in a soil.

EXTENSOMETER. 1) Instrument used for measuring small deformations, deflections, or displacements. 2) Instrument used for measuring changes caused by stress in a linear dimension of a body.

FAULT. A fracture or fracture zone along which the opposite sides have been relatively displaced.

FAULT ZONE. A fault zone consists of numerous interlacing small faults instead of a single clean fracture.

FISSION. The splitting of atomic nuclei into smaller nuclei, accompanied by the release of great quantities of energy.

FLINT. A dense fine-grained form of silica which breaks with a conchoidal fracture and sharp edges.

FLOOD PLAIN. That portion of a stream valley which is adjacent to the stream and is built of stream-deposited sediments and which is covered with water when the stream overflows its banks at flood stage.

FLUOROSIS. An abnormal condition, such as mottled enamel on human teeth, caused by fluorine or its compounds.

FOCUS. The true center of an earthquake; the point from which the energy of an earthquake is released.

FORESHORE. The lower shore zone, between normal low and high water levels.

FORMATION. 1) A lithologically distinctive product of essentially continuous sedimentation selected from a local succession of strata as a convenient unit for mapping, description, and reference. 2) Something naturally formed, commonly differing conspicuously from adjacent objects or material, or being noteworthy for some other reason.

FOSSIL FUELS. A fuel that contains energy locked up in chemical compounds by the plants and animals of former ages. Coal, petroleum, and natural gas.

FRACTIONATION. Separation of a substance from a mixture.

FUSION. Union or blending of things as if melted together. Atomic fusion refers to the fusing of small atomic nuclei into larger nuclei, accompanied by the release of tremendous quantities of energy.

GABION. A bottomless wicker cylinder or basket, from 20 to 70 inches in diameter and from 33 to 72 inches high; used in engineering, when filled with stones, to form the foundation of a jetty.

GAGING STATION. Section in a stream channel equipped with a gage and facilities for measuring the flow of water.

GEOCHEMISTRY. Geochemistry, in the broad sense, includes all parts of geology that involve chemical changes; it may focus on the distribution of the elements.

GEOCHRONOLOGY. The study of time in relation to the history of the earth; literally the science of earth time.

GEODETIC. Refers to investigation of any scientific questions relating to the shape and dimensions of the earth.

GEOLOGIC HAZARDS. Geologic features or processes that are dangerous or objectionable to man and his works; they may be natural phenomena or man-induced phenomena.

GEOLOGIC MAP. Map showing distribution of formations, folds, faults, and mineral deposits by appropriate symbols.

GEOLOGIC SECTION. A graphic representation of geologic conditions along a given line or plane of the earth's crust.

GEOLOGY. Science dealing with the origin, history, material, and structure of the earth, together with the forces and processes now operating to produce changes on the earth's surface and within it.

GEOMORPHOLOGY. The branch of geology which deals with the form of the earth, the general configuration of its surface, and the changes that take place in the evolution of land forms.

GEOPHYSICS. The science of the physics of the earth. Deals with the structure, composition, and development of the earth and makes use of geodesy, seismology, meteorology, oceanography, magnetism, and other earth sciences. Applied geophysics deals mainly with geologic exploration or prospecting using the instruments and applying the methods of physics and engineering.

GEOSTATIC. Capable of sustaining the pressure of the weight of overlying earth materials.

GEOTHERMAL. Of or pertaining to the heat of the interior of the earth.

GEOTHERMAL GRADIENT. The rate of increase of temperature of the earth with depth. The geothermal gradient away from active volcanic areas averages $30^{\circ}C$ per km. The average heat flow at the surface of the earth is 1.25×10^{-6} calories per cm^2 per sec.

GEYSER. An orifice that erupts boiling water and steam intermittently.

GLACIER BURST. A sudden release of a reservoir of water that has been impounded within or by a glacier.

GLACIAL DRIFT. Sediment in transport in glaciers or deposited by glaciers.

GOITER. An enlargment of the thyroid gland, seen as a swelling on the anterior part of the neck, or disease of the thyroid which results in swelling and other symptoms.

GRADIENT. 1) Applied to a stream, it is the slope measured along the course of the stream. 2) Change in value of one variable with respect to another variable, i.e., geothermal gradient, change in temperature with depth.

GRAVEL. 1) Small stones and pebbles or a mixture of sand and small stones. 2) Loose, rounded fragments of rock or mineral pieces larger than 2 mm in diameter.

GROUND WATER. Water beneath the surface of the ground in a saturated zone.

GROUND-WATER RECHARGE. Addition of surface water to ground water by injection through wells or by infiltration from pits or streams.

GROUT. A pumpable slurry of cement or a mixture of cement and fine sand, commonly forced into a borehole to seal crevices in a rock.

GUN-PERFORATING. The process of perforating casing and cement in a well by shooting steel bullets or shaped charges through them.

GYPSUM. A natural hydrated calcium sulfate, $CaSO_4 \cdot 2H_2O$.

HALF-LIFE. The length of time required for the disintegration of half of the atoms in a sample of some specific radioactive substance.

HARDNESS. 1) The resistance of a mineral to scratching. 2) A relative term that describes the reaction between soap and water. Carbonate hardness refers to the hardness caused by calcium and magnesium bicarbonate; non-carbonate hardness is hardness caused by calcium sulfate, calcium chloride, magnesium sulfate, and magnesium chloride in water. Hardness is usually reported in mg/1 of $CaCO_3$: 0-60 mg/1 is soft, 61-120 mg/1 is moderately hard, 121-180 mg/1 is hard, and more than 180 mg/1 is very hard water.

HECTARE. A metric unit of area equal to 10,000 square meters or 2.471 acres.

HERBICIDE. An agent, usually a chemical, used to kill plants.

HIGHWALL. The unexcavated face of exposed overburden and coal or ore in an area mine or the face or bank on the uphill side of a contour strip-mine excavation.

HOLOCENE. The time period from the close of the Pleistocene or glacial epoch through the present; synonymous with Recent.

HOT SPRING. A thermal spring whose water temperature is higher than 98°F.

HYDROCARBON. An organic compound consisting of hydrogen and carbon. Petroleum and natural gas are natural hydrocarbons.

HYDRODYNAMICS. 1) The branch of science that deals with the cause and effect of regional subsurface fluid migration. 2) The branch of hydraulics that relates to flow of liquids through pipes and openings.

HYDROFRACTURING. Process of increasing the permeability of strata near a well by pumping in water and sand under high pressure. Hydraulic pressure opens cracks, and sand introduced into the cracks keeps them open when the pressure is reduced.

HYDROGENATION. Form of reduction in which hydrogen, in gaseous form, is caused to react with a substance in the presence of a catalyst at high pressure.

HYDROGRAPH. A graph to show the level, flow, or velocity of water in a river at all seasons of the year.

HYDROLOGIC CYCLE. The complete cycle of phenomena through which water passes from the atmosphere to the earth and back to the atmosphere.

HYDROLOGY. The science dealing with water standing or flowing on or beneath the surface of the earth.

HYDROSTATIC. Relating to pressure or equilibrium of fluids.

HYDROSTATIC PRESSURE. The pressure of, or corresponding to, the weight of a column of water at rest.

HYDROSPHERE. The aqueous envelope of the earth, including the ocean, all lakes, streams, and underground waters, and the water vapor in the atmosphere.

HYDROTHERMAL. Pertaining to or resulting from magmatic emanations high in water content.

HYPOTHERMAL ORE DEPOSIT. A mineral deposit that originated from hot, ascending solutions derived from a magma.

ICEWEDGE. A form of clear ice in perennially frozen regolith in the continuous zone of permafrost. Size ranges from 1 mm wide dikelets to wedges more than 10 m wide and 10 m deep.

IMPERMEABLE. Having a texture that does not permit water to move through it perceptibly under the head differences ordinarily found in subsurface water.

INJECT. To introduce, under pressure, a liquid

or plastic material into cracks or pores in a rock formation.

INSECTICIDE. An agent, usually a chemical, used to kill insects.

INTENSITY (EARTHQUAKE). A number related to the effects of earthquake waves on man, structures, and the earth's surface at a particular place.

ION. A charged particle formed from an atom by the addition or subtraction of one or more electrons.

ISOPACH. Of equal thickness; refers to maps in which the shape of a body is indicated by lines drawn through points of equal thickness as projected onto any particular plane.

ISOTOPE. Alternate form of an element. Elements having same number of protons but different numbers of neutrons in their nuclei. Isotopes have the same atomic number but differing atomic weights.

ISOTROPIC. Having the same properties in all directions.

JOINT. A surface that divides a rock and along which there has been no visible movement parallel to the surface.

KAOLINITE. A common clay mineral. A two-layer hydrous aluminum silicate, $Al_4(Si_4O_{10})(OH)_8$.

LAGOON. A marsh, shallow pond, or lake, especially one into which the sea flows.

LAMINATED. In thin parallel layers.

LANDFILL. A place where solid waste or earth is dumped, usually to dispose of garbage or to create new land for development.

LANDSLIDE. The downward sliding or falling of a mass of soil, regolith, rock, or a mixture of these.

LAVA. The general name for the molten outpourings of volcanoes and fissures; the same material when solidified.

LEACH. To wash or to drain by percolation. To dissolve minerals by percolating solutions.

LEACHATE. A solution obtained by leaching.

LEVEE. An embankment beside a river to prevent overflow.

LEVELING. Measurement of rises and falls, heights, and contour lines in map making.

LITHOLOGY. The character of a rock described in terms of its structure, color, mineral composition, grain-size, and arrangement of its component parts.

LITTORAL. Of or pertaining to a shore.

LOAM. A mixture of sand, silt, or clay or a combination of any of these with organic matter.

LOESS. A wind-blown silt or silty clay having little or no stratification.

LOG. The record of, or the act or process of recording, events or the type and characteristics of the rock penetrated in drilling a borehole as evidenced by the cuttings, core recovered, or information obtained from electronic devices.

MAGMA. Molten fluids generated within the earth from which igneous rocks are derived by crystallization or by other processes of consolidation.

MAGNITUDE. A number related to the total energy released by an earthquake. (See Richter Scale.)

MANGANESE NODULES. Concretions, primarily of manganese salts, covering extensive areas of the ocean floor.

MANTLE. 1) The layer of the earth between the crust and the core. 2) The soil or other unconsolidated rock material more commonly referred to as overburden.

MASS MOVEMENT. Unit movement of a portion of the land surface as in creep, landslide, or slip.

MASS-WASTING. A variety of processes by which large masses of earth materials are moved by gravity either slowly or quickly from one place to another.

MATRIX. 1) The rock containing a mineral or metallic ore. 2) The principal phase or aggregate in which another constituent is embedded.

MEANDER BELT. That part of a flood plain between two lines tangent to the outer bends of all meanders.

MEANDERS. A series of regular and looplike bends in the course of a stream.

MERCALLI SCALE. A scale of earthquake intensity ranging from I for an earthquake detected only by seismographs to XII for one causing total destruction of all buildings.

MESOTHERMAL. Applied to hydrothermal deposits formed at intermediate temperature and intermediate pressure.

METALLURGY. The science and technology of metals.

METEORIC WATER. Water derived from rain, water courses, and other bodies of water. Water in or derived from the atmosphere.

METEOROLOGY. The study of atmospheric phenomena.

METHANE. CH_4, an odorless, flammable gas that is the major constituent of natural gas; the simplest member of the paraffin series.

MICROFOSSILS. Any fossil too small to be studied without magnification.

MILLS/KWHR. The cost of energy. One mill is 1/1000 U.S. dollar. A kilowatt-hour is the energy expended in one hour at a steady rate of one kilowatt (1 kw is about 1.34 horsepower).

MINERAL. An inorganic substance occurring in

nature, which has a definite or characteristic chemical composition and molecular structure and distinctive physical properties.

MINERAL FUELS. Coal and petroleum, including natural gas.

MINERALOGY. The science and study of minerals.

MOBILE BELTS. An elongated zone of the earth's crust subjected to relatively great structural deformation.

MODULUS OF ELASTICITY. Ratio of stress, within proportional limit, to corresponding strain.

MONOCLINAL. Dipping only in one direction, or composed of strata so dipping.

MONTMORILLONITE. Clay minerals which have a theoretical composition of essentially $Al_4Si_8O_{20}(OH)_4 \cdot nH_2O$.

MUDFLOW. A rapidly moving stream of mixed soil or rock and water having the consistency and composition of mud.

MUD VOLCANO. A conical hill of mud, from which material is ejected, generally cold, by and with various gases.

NATURAL GAS. A mixture of gaseous hydrocarbons, predominantly methane, found in nature.

NEUTRONS. An uncharged elementary particle with a mass slightly greater than that of the proton, found in the nucleus of every atom heavier than hydrogen. A free neutron is unstable and decays with a half-life of about 13 minutes into an electron, proton, and neutrino. Neutrons sustain the fission reaction in a nuclear reactor.

NUCLEAR POWER PLANT. Any device that converts nuclear energy into some form of useful power such as mechanical or electrical power. In a nuclear electric power plant, heat produced by a reactor is generally used to make steam to drive a turbine that in turn drives an electric generator.

NUCLEAR REACTOR. A device in which a fission chain reaction can be initiated, maintained, and controlled. Its essential component is a core with fissionable fuel. It usually has a moderator, a reflector, shielding, coolant, and control mechanisms. Sometimes called an atomic "furnace," it is the basic machine of nuclear energy.

NUCLIDE. A general term applicable to all atomic forms of the elements. The term is often erroneously used as a synonym for "isotope," which properly has a more limited definition. Whereas isotopes are the various forms of a single element (hence are a family of nuclides) and all have the same atomic number and number of protons, nuclides comprise all the isotopic forms of all the elements. Nuclides are distinguished by their atomic number, atomic mass, and energy state.

OCEANOGRAPHY. Embraces all studies relating to the sea.

OIL SHALE. Shale impregnated with hydrocarbons from which petroleum may be produced on slow distillation.

OPEN-PIT MINING. A form of operation designed to extract minerals that lie near the surface by removal of overburden and then removal of the minerals.

ORE. A mineral or aggregate of minerals from which a constituent of value can be profitably extracted.

ORGANIC. Being, containing, or relating to carbon compounds in which hydrogen is attached to carbon. Pertaining to, or derived from, living organisms.

ORGANIC EVOLUTION. The theory that the various types of animals and plants have their origin in earlier types with the differences being due to modifications in successive generations.

OSMOSIS. The passage of a solvent through a membrane from a dilute solution into a more concentrated one.

OSTEOMALACIA. A softening of the bones caused by a deficiency of minerals, such as calcium and phosphorous, and of vitamin D.

OUTCROP. That part of the mineral formation that appears at the surface of the ground. It does not necessarily imply visible presentation of the mineral on the surface of the earth, but includes those deposits that are near to the surface.

OUTSLOPE. The outer (away from the highwall) edge or face of a bench.

OVERBURDEN. Material that overlies a deposit of useful material, especially those deposits that are mined by surface mining techniques.

OXIDATION. The process of combining with oxygen.

OZONE. A faintly blue, irritating gas (O_3) occurring in minute quantities near the earth's surface and in larger quantities in the stratosphere as a product of the action of ultraviolet light of short wavelengths on ordinary oxygen. Ozone, concentrated in a layer about 15 miles above the earth, shields the earth from UV radiation in the range of 2,400-3,000 Å by absorption.

PALEONTOLOGY. The science that deals with the life of past geological ages, as based on the study of the fossil remains of organisms.

PATHOGENS. Agents, such as fungi, bacteria, viruses, nematodes, and certain insects, which cause infectious diseases.

PEAT. A brownish, lightweight mixture of partly

decomposed plant remains in which parts of plants are still recognizable.

PERMAFROST. Permanently frozen ground.

PERMEABILITY. The permeability of rock or unconsolidated material is its capacity for transmitting a fluid.

PESTICIDES. Agents, usually chemicals, including herbicides and pesticides, used to kill nonhuman organisms considered by man to be pests.

PETROCHEMICALS. Chemical compounds made with a petroleum hydrocarbon as one of their basic components.

PETROLEUM. Gaseous, liquid, or solid substances, occurring naturally and consisting chiefly of chemical compounds of carbon and hydrogen.

pH. A measure of acidity or alkalinity. It is the negative logarithm of the hydrogen ion activity; pH_7 indicates an H+ concentration (activity) of 10^{-7} mole/litre.

PHENOL. A soluble, crystalline acidic compound, C_6H_5OH, present in coal tar and urine. Used in making resins, plastics, dyes, and pharmaceuticals.

PHOSPHATES. 1) A salt or ester of phosphoric acid. 2) An ore of any metal or metals with which phosphorus and oxygen are chemically united.

PHOSPHORITE. A sedimentary rock composed chiefly of phosphate.

PHOTOGRAMMETRY. The art and science of obtaining reliable measurements from photographs.

PHREATIC EXPLOSION. A volcanic explosion caused by the conversion of ground water to steam.

PHYSIOGRAPHY. Physical geography. A description of the natural features of the surface of the earth.

PICKLING ACID. Acid used to remove scale or oxide from metal objects to obtain a chemically clean surface prior to galvanizing or painting. For steel, sulfuric acid and hydrochloric acid are used.

PICRIC ACID. A yellow crystalline compound, $C_6H_3N_3O_7$, used in dyeing and as an ingredient in certain explosives.

PIEZOMETRIC. Refers to the surface to which the water from a given aquifer will rise under its full head.

PLASTIC FLOW. A continuous and permanent change of shape in any direction without breakage.

PLATEAU BASALTS. A term applied to widespread nearly horizontal layers of extrusive basalt.

PLAYA. A dry bed of an ephemeral shallow lake in a nearly level area on the floor of a desert basin.

PLUTONIUM-239. A radioactive metallic element of the actinide series, similar chemically to uranium, and usually produced in nuclear reactors as the long-lived isotope of mass number 239 (half-life is 24,360 years).

PODSOLIZATION. Process by which soils are depleted of bases, becoming acid, and develop eluvial A-horizons and illuvial B-horizons. A podsol develops with more rapid removal of iron and alumina than of silica.

POLLUTION. The process of contaminating air, water, and land with impurities to a level that is undesirable and results in a decrease in usefulness of environment for beneficial purposes; adverse effects on the environment that are definitely man-produced.

POLYGONAL. Having straight sides, usually more than four.

POROSITY. The proportion, usually stated as a percentage, of the total volume of a rock material or regolith that consists of pore space or voids.

POROUS. Containing pores, voids, or other openings which may or may not be interconnected.

POTABLE. Refers to water which is drinkable.

PRECIPITATION. 1) The discharge of water, in liquid or solid state, from the atmosphere onto the earth's surface. 2) The process by which mineral constituents are separated from a solution by evaporation.

PROTON. An elementary particle with a single positive electrical charge and a mass approximately 1,847 times that of the electron. The atomic number of an atom equals the number of protons in its nucleus.

PUTRESCENT. Characteristic of or relating to the decomposition of organic matter.

PYRITE. A mineral, FeS_2, commonly called fool's gold because of its brassy yellow color. The iron sulfide minerals, mainly pyrite and marcasite, are the minerals which break down chemically and form mine acids.

QUICKSAND. Sand which becomes semiliquid or easily moveable when it is soaked with an excess of water.

RADIOACTIVE WASTE. Equipment and materials (from nuclear operations) which are radioactive and for which there is no further use. Wastes are generally classified as high-level (having radioactivity concentrations of hundreds to thousands of curies per gallon or cubic foot), low-level (on the order of 1 microcurie per gallon or cubic foot), or intermediate (between these ranges).

RADIOACTIVITY. The property of certain isotopes of spontaneously emitting radiation to form new isotopes.

RADIOCARBON (CARBON-24). A radioactive isotope of carbon with an atomic weight of 14, which is produced by collisions between neutrons and atmospheric nitrogen. It is useful in radiometric age determinations of carbonaceous material up to a maximum age of about 50,000 years.

RECLAMATION. 1) The act or process of restoring to cultivation or other use land that has been mined. 2) The recovery of coal or ore from a mine, or part of a mine, that has been abandoned because of fire, water, or other cause.

RECOVERY. The proportion of a desired metal or mineral obtained in the treatment of an ore.

REGOLITH. The layer or mantle of loose, incoherent rock material, of whatever origin, that nearly everywhere forms the surface of the land and rests on the bedrock.

REPRESSURING. The injection of water, natural gas, or compressed air to increase the reservoir oil pressure.

RESERVOIRS. A natural underground container of liquids, such as oil or water, and gases.

RESISTIVITY. The opposite of conductivity of an electrical current passing through fluid-bearing rock formations.

REVERSE FAULT. A fault along which the hanging wall has moved up relative to the foot wall.

RICHTER SCALE. A scale of earthquake magnitude based on the logarithm (base 10) of the amplitudes of the deflections created by earthquake waves and recorded by a seismograph.

ROCKBOLT. A steel bar inserted into drill-holes in rock and secured for the purpose of ground control.

RUNOFF. Water that runs off or flows over the land surface.

SALINE. Salty. Possessing a high degree of dissolved mineral matter, i.e., common salts, in water.

SAND. 1) Particles of sediment having a size range of 1/16 mm – 2 mm. 2) Commonly refers to siliceous detrital material composed mainly of quartz particles of sand size.

SANITARY LANDFILL. A disposal area for solid wastes where the wastes are compacted and covered by a layer of impermeable material, such as clay, daily.

SCARP. A cliff, escarpment, or steep slope of some extent formed by a fault or a cliff or steep slope along the margin of a plateau, mesa, or terrace.

SEDIMENT. Solid material, both mineral and organic, that is in suspension, is being transported, or has been moved from its place of origin and deposited by air, water, or ice.

SEDIMENTARY ROCKS. Rocks formed by the accumulation of sediment in water (aqueous deposits) or from air (eolian deposits). A characteristic feature of sedimentary deposits is a layered structure known as stratification or bedding.

SEICHE. An apparent tide in a lake due to pendulous motion of the water when excited by wind.

SEISMIC. Pertaining to shock waves within the earth produced by earthquakes, or in some cases artificially produced shockwaves.

SEISMOGRAPH. An instrument for recording earthquake or seismic waves. The record made by a seismograph is called a seismogram.

SEISMOLOGY. The science of earthquakes and the study of seismic waves.

SEPTIC TANK. A tank in which bacterial action is encouraged to break down sewage to harmless constituents.

SERPENTINE. A hydrous magnesium silicate, Mg_6 (Si_4O_{10}) $(OH)_8$, of secondary origin. The name includes two minerals, antigorite and chrysotile, the latter being the most common form of asbestos.

SERPULID REEFS. Calcareous reefs made up of tubes built by tubiculous annelids (worms) such as *Serpula*.

SHEAR STRENGTH. The stress or load at which a material fails in shear.

SHORT-WAVE SOLAR RADIATION. Most of the radiation from the sun is in the short wavelengths to which the atmosphere and window glass are fairly transparent. Bodies at lower temperatures, such as the earth's surface, emit long-wave radiation to which glass and the atmosphere are not transparent.

SILICATE. A compound whose crystal lattice contains SiO_4 tetrahedra, either isolated or joined through one or more of the oxygen atoms to form groups, chains, sheets, or three-dimensional structures.

SILICOSIS. A disease of the lungs caused by the inhalation of quartz or silicate dust.

SILT. A fine-grained sediment having a particle size intermediate between that of fine sand and clay, between 1/16 and 1/256 mm in diameter.

SINKHOLE. A closed depression resulting from solution or collapse in areas of limestone bedrock. Synonym for sink.

SLIDE. The descent of a mass such as earth, rock, or snow, down a hill or mountainside. A landslide.

SLUMP. The downward slipping of a mass of rock or unconsolidated material, moving as a unit or as several subsidiary units, usually with backward rotation; or the material that has slid downslope.

SLURRY. A mixture of cement and water pumped into a borehole or oil well to support the casing and prevent movement of underground fluids.

SOIL. 1) The unconsolidated material above the bedrock that forms as a result of weathering by organic and inorganic processes. 2) In pedology, the weathered material that will support rooted plants. 3) In engineering geology, soil is equivalent to regolith.

SOIL HORIZON. A layer of soil approximately parallel to the surface, which differs from adjacent layers in chemical and physical properties.

SORPTION. Any type of retention of a material at a surface, especially when the mechanism is not specified.

SPILLWAY. Release overflow for water impounded by a dam.

SPOIL. Debris or waste from a coal mine.

SPOIL BANK. The accumulation of overburden or non-ore material removed in gaining access to the ore or mineral material in surface mining.

SPONTANEOUS POTENTIAL METHOD. An electrical method in which a potential field caused by spontaneous electrochemical phenomena is measured.

STABLE ISOTOPE. A nuclide that does not undergo radioactive decay.

STRAIN. Deformation resulting from applied force; within elastic limits strain is proportional to stress.

STRATA. Sedimentary rock layers.

STRATOSPHERE. The second lowest layer of the atmosphere; characterized by more or less isothermal conditions and a highly stable stratification. The stratosphere extends from about 7 to 20 miles above the earth's surface and contains little moisture or dust but most of the ozone.

STRIP MINING. The mining of coal by surface mining methods as distinguished from the mining of metalliferous ores by surface mining methods, known as open-pit mining.

STRONTIUM. One of the alkaline-earth metals. It is always combined in nature, chiefly in the minerals celestite ($SrSO_4$) and strontianite ($SrCO_3$). It also occurs in mineral springs. Strontium-90 is the most important of the 16 known isotopes (strontium-80 to strontium-95). Strontium-90 has a half-life of 28 years; is one of the best long-lived, high-energy beta particle emitters known; is a product of nuclear fallout; and as such constitutes a serious health problem.

STRUCTURAL. Pertaining to, part of, or consequent upon the geologic structure; as, a structural valley.

SUBMERGENCE. A term which implies that part of the land has become inundated by the sea.

SUBSIDENCE. Sinking or lowering of a part of the earth's crust.

SULFUR DIOXIDE. Colorless gas or liquid (SO_2) with suffocating odor, soluble in water and forms sulfurous acid (H_2SO_3).

SUPERCONDUCTIVITY. The abrupt and large increase in electrical conductivity exhibited by some materials as the temperature approaches absolute zero.

SYNCLINAL. Characteristic of, pertaining to, situated in, or forming a syncline; consisting of down-folded strata.

TACONITE. Any grade of extremely hard, lean iron ore that has its iron either in banded or well-disseminated form and which may be hematite or magnetite, or a combination of the two in the same ore body.

TALUS. The heap of coarse rock waste at the foot of a cliff or a sheet of waste covering a slope below a cliff.

TAR SANDS. Sands or sandstone naturally impregnated with petroleum from which the lighter portions have escaped.

TECTONIC. Pertaining to rock structures and topographic features resulting from deformation of the earth's crust.

TEXTURE. The physical appearance of a rock, as shown by size, shape, and arrangement of the particles in the rock.

THERMAL SPRING. A spring that brings warm or hot water to the surface. Water temperature is usually $15^{\circ}F$ or more above mean air temperature.

TILL. Nonsorted, nonstratified sediment carried or deposited by a glacier.

TILTMETER. A device for observing surface disturbances on a bowl of mercury; employed in an attempt to predict earthquakes.

TOPOGRAPHY. The configuration of a surface, including its relief.

TOXIC. Having poisonous effects.

TRACE ELEMENTS. Elements present in minor amount in the earth's crust; all elements except the eight abundant rock-forming elements, O, Si, Al, Fe, Ca, Na, K, and Mg. Also known as minor elements and accessory elements.

TRIBUTARY. An affluent flowing into a larger stream; any stream feeding a larger stream or lake.

TROPOSPHERE. The lowest main layer of the atmosphere; characterized by a steep lapse rate, a low degree of hydrostatic stability, with frequent overturnings. The average thickness of the layer is 7 miles; it makes up 75 percent of all the weight of the atmosphere and contains almost all the moisture and dust.

TSUNAMIS. A very long water wave caused by a submarine earthquake or volcanic eruption; mistakenly used as a synonym for tidal wave.

TURBIDITY CURRENT. A large-volume, rapid, downslope underwater current, usually generated by a seismic disturbance, which causes a slumping of sediment on the slope and starts a flow of sediment and water.

ULTRA-VIOLET. Radiation beyond the visible spectrum at its violet end; having a wavelength shorter than those of visible light and longer than those of x-rays.

URBAN GEOLOGY. The application of geology to problems in the urban environment.

UNCONSOLIDATED STRATA. Rocks consisting of loosely coherent or uncemented particles, whether occurring at the surface or at depth.

UNIFORMITARIANISM. The concept that the present is the key to the past.

VIRUS. Any of a group of submicroscopic infective agents causing important diseases in plants and animals. They may be living organisms or complex protein molecules capable of growth and multiplication only in living cells.

VISCOSITY. 1) Any resistance to deformation that involves dissipation of energy by internal friction. 2) The resistance of liquids, semisolids, and gases to movement.

VOID. A general term for pore space or other openings in rock.

WATERSHED. The area contained within a drainage divide above a specified point on a stream. Also drainage area or drainage basin.

WATER TABLE. The upper limit or surface of the zone of saturation of groundwater. It approximates the profile of the land surface.

WEATHERING. Response of materials that were once in equilibrium within the earth's crust to new conditions at or near contact with water, air, and living matter. With time the materials change in character and decay to form soil.